REFERENCE GUIDES IN LITERATURE
NUMBER 7
Joseph Katz, *Consulting Editor*

William Faulkner:
A Reference Guide

Thomas L. McHaney

G. K. HALL & CO., 70 LINCOLN STREET, BOSTON, MASS.

Copyright © 1976 by Thomas L. McHaney

Library of Congress Cataloging in Publication Data

McHaney, Thomas L
    William Faulkner.

    (Reference guides in literature ; no. 7)
    Bibliography: p.
    Includes index.
    1. Faulkner, William, 1897-1962--Bibliography.
Z8288.M22 [PS3511.A86]   016.813'5'2   76-2490
ISBN 0-8161-1132-4

This publication is printed on permanent/durable acid free paper
MANUFACTURED IN THE UNITED STATES OF AMERICA

Contents

Preface

This is a chronological survey, with annotations, of what I believe to be all the serious and substantial writing about the life,
fiction, poetry, non-fiction prose, and thought of William Faulkner
from 1924 through 1973, nearly fifty years of reaction to a remarkable literary career; the geographical range is worldwide, although
entries for foreign criticism are not as thorough as for American
and English criticism. The majority of the entries report on book-
length studies in all languages devoted exclusively to Faulkner,
English-language critical essays in scholarly journals, little magazines, and popular periodicals, and portions of books and articles
which refer to Faulkner or his work. Regarding these I have sought
to be comprehensive. I have limited the inclusion of contemporary
book reviews to those in major American and English popular periodicals, selected foreign papers and journals, and three important Southern regional newspapers--the Atlanta Journal-Constitution, Memphis
Commercial Appeal, and New Orleans Times-Picayune. To keep the book
within manageable and useful proportions and to allow fuller annotations for the entries selected, I have not surveyed the national daily press nor included all "brief mention" notices in magazines.
Foreign criticism is listed and annotated to a representative measure;
the aim was to set down important and useful work in French, German,
Italian, and Spanish and to point out something of what has been done
in Scandinavian, Slavic, Japanese, Indian, African, and Middle-East-
ern criticism, whether in English or native tongues. Where first-
hand reporting was not possible, I have relied upon translations or
English-language summaries and upon articles which survey Faulkner's
critical reception in a linguistic or geographical area. Except
where an asterisk appears in the left margin, I have read in its en-
tirety each item entered in this book. I have given a bibliographical source in a standard union list, check-list, or bibliography for
the asterisked items and, in many cases, have reported on the con-
tents of the article or book from secondary sources. The index lists
authors, titles, and a broad range of subjects which include members
of Faulkner's family, important associates of his over the years,
places relevant to his career, and the titles, principal characters,
and themes of his work, as well as a variety of critical approaches
(as, for instance, myth criticism, psychological criticism, character

study, etc.). Where appropriate, the main entries are cross-refe-
renced to related entries or to forms of re-publication, including
reprints and inclusion in anthologies or larger studies. Recurring
critical issues and arguments, queries and replies, and rejoinders
in debate are identified in the cross-references and, if relevant,
in the index.

The chronological arrangement of this reference guide makes it
possible to survey Faulkner's reception as a writer and to study the
shifting and sometimes developing criticism of his work. Happily, we
are beginning to achieve some valid unanimity about aspects of Faulkner's life and fiction, though it has been slow in evolving. Since
the entries in this reference guide are descriptive rather than evaluative, and since no compilation is going to help the unwary or uncritical reader, I offer several suggestions. A compilation of this
scale, while it contains all that is good and useful about an author,
also contains much that, by any standard, must be reckoned harmless-
ly bland, specious, acutely wrong-headed, or simply malevolent.
There is no substitute for knowing the work of your author well before you consult the critics, but the inexperienced student should
remember to prefer the critic who demonstrates honesty and documents
his evidence, who proves that he has read the author's work and the
relevant criticism about it, and who uses reliable and authoritative
texts of the author's works and quotes them accurately. The index
to this reference guide will be helpful in determining which authors
of criticism meet these standards, though a long bibliography, for
instance, does not make a scholar, and some critics have published
extensively but unhelpfully on a narrow range of Faulkner's work or
even published the same article in more than one periodical at the
same time! There are a large number of articles on Faulkner (as on
other authors) which give the impression of doing no harm, if they do
no good. Analysis proves them to be chiefly bland and reasonably accurate plot summaries; they should not be allowed to clutter the
notes of subsequent criticism. There are also books and articles on
Faulkner which repeat demonstrably incorrect biographical and critical opinions which had their origins, chiefly, though not exclusively,
in the 1950's. Do not be deceived when a recent critic cites five or
six of these "authorities" as evidence of a biographical or critical
point, for they are usually genetic, having spawned one another; to
cite six of them is to compound error or give credence to rumor merely
because it was repeated. Be sure to consult the evaluative surveys
of Faulkner criticism in Sixteen Modern American Authors: A Survey of
Research and Criticism and in American Literary Scholarship: An Annual.
Finally, though I have not sought to judge the merits of individual
entries, the alert reader will note that bad essays and books, over
the long run, more or less identify or damn themselves in their own
words or viewpoints or become identified by the corrections and rejoinders of better critics.

The amount of Faulkner criticism makes it impractical if not impossible to write a narrative overview of the reception and interpretation of Faulkner's work. (I searched out and read around 3000

items.) Worth mention here, however, is that Faulkner was more fortunate in his early critics than has generally been stated, chiefly
because his work always attracted the attention of other artists--
poets and novelists--who responded to him in print with intelligence,
understanding, and praise. Against their work, the reviews done by
"professional" critics in major reviewing media look rather shameful.
These writers include Richard Hughes, L. A. G. Strong, Arnold Bennett,
and others in England; Malraux, Sartre, Camus and others in France;
a few in Italy and Latin America (as, for example, Borges); and too
many to mention in America, from Conrad Aiken and Warren Beck to
Robert Penn Warren and Eudora Welty. Faulkner has been the novelist's
novelist, a fact plainly revealed in contemporary reviews of his work
from the late 1920's onward. By itself, the receptivity of other
writers to Faulkner's work should have dispelled the myth that he was
a provincial, primitive genius. Now that we have a full-scale biography from Joseph Blotner (which appeared in 1974 and thus is not
listed in this reference guide), we possess some detailed information
about the professional Faulkner whom his peers discerned and admired
on both sides of the Atlantic. The partial story--as revealed both
in this survey of criticism and in Blotner's biography--is that major reviewers in national media seldom appreciated Faulkner, misin-
terpreted his work and distorted his life, and labeled him in a way
that probably helped keep his sales disappointing, while, for his
part, Faulkner seems to have paid little or no attention to his critics and certainly never lost confidence in the conduct of his artistic life; he continued the innovations and complexities which were--
to quote the complaint of a reviewer of A Fable--the "bane of the
weekly reviewer" with a stack of books to hurry through. It is ironic that weekly reviewers, unable to put a legitimate handle on Faulkner, first typified him as the apostle of violence, madness, and decadence and found his pre-Nobel Prize work sensational and inartistic;
then they criticized the post-Nobel Prize fiction for failing to
attain the high standards of his early work.

Typical problems in Faulkner scholarship are laid out and discussed cogently in James B. Meriwether's Faulkner essay in Sixteen
Modern American Authors. Biographical, textual, and critical cruxes
in the study of Faulkner's literary career persist, and problems in
each area have had repercussions in other areas, so that false biography and corrupt texts have led to critical mistakes and misappre-
hensions while certain mistaken critical viewpoints have created
false biographical and textual generalizations. From the beginning,
however, good results were obtained by critics who read Faulkner
carefully, granted him intelligence and seriousness of purpose, and
did not worry too much about where he lived or how he spent his time
when he was not writing. Faulkner's international reputation was in
its inception the result of this kind of serious, objective reading.
Writers and intellectuals in Europe responded directly to Faulkner's
work and spoke their admiration in influential essays and introductions to translations. These critics were not alone in the world, as
I have noted, but were really characteristic of a phenomenon that one

observes in England and America, too. There are more differences
which I cannot hope to spell out here, but one, at least, seems to be
the difference between the audience for, say, the Nouvelle Revue
Française and that for the hard-pressed American little magazine;
American writers who championed Faulkner did not reach as wide a
readership as their European counterparts and moreover had to compete
with a basically hostile press of large and loud proportions. I mention this only to put into context the apparently expanding European
claims to having discovered Faulkner, a view that needs some modifi-
cation; we can agree that certain Europeans were more successful in
advertising Faulkner's good qualities than certain Americans and
Englishmen. As academic criticism in Europe has adopted Faulkner,
however, a number of scholars there have repeated the worst qualities
of American popular and academic criticism, unwittingly or through
mistaken applications of thoroughness, with the result that our old
critical horrors occasionally come back from foreign shores to haunt
again.

In "Faulkner's Point of View" (1941.B2), Warren Beck, himself a
novelist, hoped for a "virile" criticism of Faulkner's work which
would recognize his humanism and his rational intellectuality and
then go on to explore the sources of his work and the brilliant technical adumbration of his themes, characters, and ideas. There is
still need for that kind of criticism. The poetry, the early
sketches, and especially the majority of the short stories, are relatively unexplored; Faulkner's first two novels still require full
and sympathetic study, as, in fact, do most of the novels, including
The Unvanquished and Go Down, Moses. Much biographical work can
still be done, despite Blotner's massive life and pending the appearance of Carvel Collins' announced biography. Splendid opportunities exist for serious and reliable work on pre-publication forms
of Faulkner's stories, novels, poems, and non-fiction, on the incomplete and unpublished materials, and on the reliability of the published texts themselves. It is time for these opportunities to be
taken so that the Faulkner field ceases to suffer so much from what
Michael Millgate, in American Literary Scholarship 1972, called the
"depressing sameness" of articles and books (and the dissertations
from which many of them come).

My chief hopes for this reference guide are that writers of criticism use it fully and regularly and that referees and editors of
learned journals and little magazines apply it to the task of rig-
orously limiting acceptance in their pages to new and reliable criticism. Those who find errors of omission or commission are urged to
communicate them to me.

Georgia State University provided released time from teaching
and travel funds which aided in the preparation of this book. Kathy
Cripe, Cara Marris, Pam Thomas and Kent Murphy helped with proofreading. My wife, Karen, helped with proofreading and indexing.

List of Periodical Abbreviations

Aegis
AES   Abstracts of English Studies
AH   American Heritage
AI   American Imago
AL   American Literature
ALitASH   Acta Litteraria Academiae Scientiarum Hungaricae
                       (Budapest)
AMerc   American Mercury
AmPref   American Prefaces
AmRev   American Review
AmRs   Amerikanische Rundschau
AN&Q   American Notes and Queries (New Haven, Conn.)
AntB   Antiquarian Bookman
AQ   American Quarterly
AR   Antioch Review
Archiv   Archiv für das Studium der Neueren Sprachen und
                       Literaturen
ArielE   Ariel: A Review of International English
                       Literature
ArlQ   Arlington Quarterly
ArQ   Arizona Quarterly
AS   American Speech
ASch   American Scholar
AtlM   Atlantic Monthly
BA   Books Abroad
BAASBull   British Association of American Studies Bulletin
BB   Bulletin of Bibliography
BBr   Books at Brown
BC   Book Collector
BFLS   Bulletin de la Faculté des Lettres de Strasbourg
BRD   Book Review Digest
BRMMLA   Bulletin of the Rocky Mountain Modern Language
                       Association
BSTCF   Ball State Teachers College Forum
BSUF   Ball State University Forum
BuR   Bucknell Review
BUSE   Boston University Studies in English
BYUS   Brigham Young University Studies

List of Periodical Abbreviations

Cahiers LM	Cahiers des Langues Modernes
CanF	Canadian Forum
CarQ	Carolina Quarterly
CaSE	Carnegie Series in English
CathW	Catholic World [Now New Catholic World]
Catholic Worker	
CCC	College Composition and Communication
CE	College English
CEA	CEA Critic
CentR	The Centennial Review (Michigan State University)
ChiR	Chicago Review
ChrCent	Christian Century
ChrOk	Chronicles of Oklahoma
ChrSch	Christian Scholar
CimR	Cimarron Review (Oklahoma State University)
CL	Comparative Literature
CLAJ	College Language Association Journal (Morgan State College, Baltimore)
CLS	Comparative Literature Studies (University of Illinois)
ColQ	Colorado Quarterly
ConL	Contemporary Literature (Supersedes WSCL)
ConnR	Connecticut Review
Costerus: Essays in English and American Languages and Literature	
CR	The Critical Review (Melbourne; Sydney)
CrCur	Cross Currents
CRevAS	Canadian Review of American Studies
Crit	Critique: Studies in Modern Fiction
Criticism (Wayne State)	
CritQ	Critical Quarterly
CWHi	Civil War History
DenvQ	Denver Quarterly
DeuRs	Deutsche Rundschau
DQR	Dutch Quarterly Review of Anglo-American Letters
DR	Dalhousie Review
DUJ	Durham University Journal
EA	Études Anglaises
EdLr	Educational Leader
EIE 1952	English Institute Essays, 1952, ed. Alex P. Parker
EigoS	Eigo Seinen
EJ	English Journal
ELLS	English Literature and Language (Tokyo)
ELN	English Language Notes (University of Colorado)
EmUQ	Emory University Quarterly
EngR	English Record
ES	English Studies
ESA	English Studies in Africa (Johannesburg)
ESQ	Emerson Society Quarterly
Esquire	
ESRS	Emporia State Research Studies

List of Periodical Abbreviations

EWR	East-West Review (Doshisha University, Kyoto, Japan)
Expl	Explicator
FauSt	Faulkner Studies
FigLit	Figaro Littéraire
FMLS	Forum for Modern Language Studies (University of St. Andrews, Scotland)
FMod	Filología Moderna (Madrid)
FQ	Florida Quarterly
'48, The Magazine of the Year	
Frontiers (Lutheran Student Association of America)	
FSUSt	Florida State University Studies
FurmMag	Furman Magazine
FurmS	Furman Studies
Genre (University of Illinois at Chicago Circle)	
GHQ	Georgia Historical Quarterly
GLet	Gazette des Lettres
GR	Germanic Review
HAB	Humanities Association Bulletin (Canada)
Harper's	Harper's Magazine
HarvAv	Harvard Advocate
Hasifrut: Quarterly for the Study of Literature	
HemN	Hemingway Notes
HistIdN	History of Ideas Newsletter
HitJA&S	Hitotsubashi Journal of Arts and Sciences
HLQ	Huntington Library Quarterly
HopR	Hopkins Review
HPCS	High Point College Studies
HSL	Hartford Studies in Literature
HudR	Hudson Review
IEY	Iowa English Bulletin: Yearbook
IJAS	Indian Journal of American Studies
IQ	Italian Quarterly
JA	Jahrbuch für Amerikastudien
JAF	Journal of American Folklore
JAmS	Journal of American Studies
JFI	Journal of the Folklore Institute (Indiana University)
JHS	Journal of Historical Studies
JIAS	Journal of Inter-American Studies
JMH	Journal of Mississippi History
JOFS	Journal of the Ohio Folklore Society
Johns Hopkins Magazine	
JPC	Journal of Popular Culture (Bowling Green, Kentucky)
JSoH	Journal of Southern History
KanQ	Kansas Quarterly (Formerly KM)
Katallagete Be Reconciled (Journal of the Committee of Southern Churchmen)	
KBAA	Kieler Beiträge zur Anglistik und Amerikanistik
KFR	Kentucky Folklore Record

KM	Kansas Magazine
KN	Kwartalnik Neofilologiczny (Warsaw)
KR	Kenyon Review
KRQ	Kentucky Romance Quarterly (Formerly KFLQ)
KuL	Kunst und Literatur
L&I	Literature and Ideology (Montreal)
L&P	Literature and Psychology (University of Hartford)
LaHist	Louisiana History
LaS	Louisiana Studies
LauR	Laurel Review (West Virginia Wesleyan College) [Superseded by NLauR]
LC	Library Chronicle (University of Pennsylvania)
LCUT	Library Chronicle of the University of Texas
L/FQ	Literature/Film Quarterly
LJ	Library Journal
LonMag	London Magazine
LonMerc	London Mercury
LWU	Literatur in Wissenschaft und Unterricht (Kiel)
M&M	Masses and Mainstream
MASJ	Midcontinent American Studies Journal
MercdeFr	Mercure de France
MFS	Modern Fiction Studies
MidR	Midwest Review
MinnR	Minnesota Review
MissFR	Mississippi Folklore Review
MissQ	Mississippi Quarterly
MLN	Modern Language Notes
ModA	Modern Age (Chicago)
Moderna Sprak	
Mosaic:	A Journal for the Comparative Study of Literature and Ideas
MQ	Midwest Quarterly
MQR	Michigan Quarterly Review
MR	Massachusetts Review (University of Massachusetts)
MSE	Massachusetts Studies in English
MTJ	Mark Twain Journal
Names	
N&Q	Notes and Queries
NAR	North American Review
NassauR	Nassau Review
NatRev	National Review
NConL	Notes on Contemporary Literature
NDEJ	Notre Dame English Journal
NEGalaxy	New England Galaxy
NEQ	New England Quarterly
NewL	New Leader
NewSt	New Statesman and Nation/New Statesman
NL	Nouvelles Littéraires
NM	Neuphilologische Mitteilungen
NMQ	New Mexico Quarterly

NouCrit   Nouvelle Critique
Novel: A Forum on Fiction (Brown University)
NRep   New Republic
NRF   Nouvelle Revue Française
NRs   Neue Rundschau
NS   Die Neueren Sprachen
NwRev   Northwest Review
NWW   New World Writing
NY   New Yorker
NYHTB   New York Herald-Tribune Book Review
NYT   New York Times (daily)
NYTBR   New York Times Book Review
O&I   Outlook and Independent (New York)
OhioUR   Ohio University Review
Opportunity, Journal of Negro Life
PBSA   Publications of the Bibliographical Society of
                     America
Person   The Personalist
Perspective (Washington University)
PLL   Papers on Languages and Literature
PMASAL   Papers of the Michigan Academy of Science, Arts
                     and Letters
PMLA: Publications of the Modern Language Association of America
PN   Poe Newsletter
PQ   Philological Quarterly (Iowa City)
PR   Partisan Review
Proof: Yearbook of American Bibliographical and Textual Studies
PrS   Prairie Schooner
PURBA   Punjab University Research Bulletin (Arts)
QQ   Queen's Quarterly
RALS   Resources for American Literary Studies
RANAM   Recherches Anglaises et Américaines
RDM   Revue des Deux Mondes
REngLit   Review of English Literature (London)
RJN   Robinson Jeffers Newsletter
RLM   La Revue des Lettres Modernes
RLMC   Rivista di Letterature Moderne e Comparate
                     (Firenze)
RLV   Revue des Langues Vivantes (Bruxelles)
RMR   Rocky Mountain Review
RN   Revue Nouvelle
RoR   Romanian Review
RS   Research Studies (Washington State University)
SA   Studi Americani (Roma)
SAB   South Atlantic Bulletin
SAF   Studies in American Fiction
SALit   Studies in American Literature
SAQ   South Atlantic Quarterly
SatR   Saturday Review
SB   Studies in Bibliography: Papers of the Biblio-
                     graphical Society of the University of
                     Virginia

SCB	South Central Bulletin
SCR	South Carolina Review
SDR	South Dakota Review
Semiotica:	Revue Publiée par l'Association Internationale de Sémiotique
Serif	The Serif (Kent, Ohio)
SFR	Southern Folklore Quarterly
Shenandoah	
SHR	Southern Humanities Review
Signal:	Approaches to Children's Books
SLJ	Southern Literary Journal
SoLiv	Southern Living
SoQ	The Southern Quarterly (University of Southern Mississippi)
SoR	Southern Review (Louisiana State University)
SoRA	Southern Review: An Australian Journal of Literary Studies (University of Adelaide)
SovL	Soviet Literature
SR	Sewanee Review
SS	Scandinavian Studies
SSL	Studies in Scottish Literature (University of South Carolina)
StH	Studies in the Humanities (Indiana University of Pa.)
StN	Steinbeck Newsletter
StTwC	Studies in the Twentieth Century
Style (University of Arkansas)	
Sur	Buenos Aires
SUS	Susquehanna University Studies (Selingsgrove, Pennsylvania)
SWR	Southwest Review
TaR	La Table Ronde
TC	Twentieth Century
TCL	Twentieth Century Literature
TFSB	Tennessee Folklore Society Bulletin
The Tablet	
Theoria	A Journal of Studies in the Arts, Humanities, and Social Sciences
Thoth (Department of English, Syracuse University)	
THQ	Tennessee Historical Quarterly
TLS	[London] Times Literary Supplement
TM	Temps Modernes
Torre, Revista General de la Universidad de Puerto Rico	
TQ	Texas Quarterly (University of Texas)
TSL	Tennessee Studies in Literature
TSLL	Texas Studies in Literature and Language
UChiMag	Univesity of Chicago Magazine
UKCR	University of Kansas City Review
UMSE	University of Mississippi Studies in English
UR	University Review (Kansas City, Missouri)
UTQ	University of Toronto Quarterly

List of Periodical Abbreivations

UWR	University of Windsor Review (Windsor, Ontario)
VLit	Voprosy Literatury
VQR	Virginia Quarterly Review
WGCR	West Georgia College Review
WHR	Western Humanities Review
WR	Western Review: A Journal of the Humanities
WrD	Writer's Digest
WSCL	Wisconsin Studies in Contemporary Literature (superseded by ConL - Contemporary Literature)
WVUPP	West Virginia University Philological Papers
XUS	Xavier University Studies
YFS	Yale French Studies
YR	Yale Review
YULG	Yale University Library Gazette
ZAA	Zeitschrift für Anglistik und Amerikanistik (East Berlin)

List of Writings

LIST OF WRITINGS

1967   The Wishing Tree
1973   Flags in the Dust, edited by Day

       Interviews

1959   Faulkner in the University, edited by Gwynn & Blotner (rev. ed. 1965)
1964   Faulkner at West Point, edited by Fant and Ashley
1968   Lion in the Garden, edited by Meriwether and Millgate

Writings About William Faulkner, 1924 - 1973

1924 A BOOKS – NONE

1924 B SHORTER WRITINGS

1   STONE, PHIL. "Preface" to The Marble Faun. Boston: Four
     Seas Company, pp. 6–8.
       These "poems of youth and a simple heart" react directly
     to the experience of nature. The promise they show ap-
     pears in the love of language, "an instinct for color and
     rhythm." The author is a well-read, humorous, rigidly
     honest Mississippian. Reprinted in The Marble Faun and A
     Green Bough (New York: Random House, 1965).

1925 A BOOKS – NONE

1925 B SHORTER WRITINGS

1   ANON. Review of The Marble Faun, SatR (7 March), p. 587.
       Faulkner's verse is fluent and meditative; he does not
     strain for effects, but his sensitivity to language is not
     fully developed.

2   COOPER, MONTE. Review of The Marble Faun, Memphis (Tenn.)
     Commercial Appeal (5 April), Section III, p. 10.
       Using Faulkner's "Verse Old and Nascent: A Pilgrimage,"
     from the April 1925 New Orleans Double Dealer as Faulk-
     ner's credo, the reviewer notes the over-reliance upon
     Swinburne. At his best, Faulkner achieves a "sweet and
     rather plaintive resignation." More often, his verse is
     "silvery" but monotonous or, at worst, marred by unhappy
     metaphor, disregard for meaning of words, and crude lines.
     The "localism" of his pronunciation, rhyming "dim" and
     "rim" with "them," is deplorable. His essay "On Criticism"
     in the January-February Double Dealer suggests that he is
     anti-feminist.

1925

3   McCLURE, JOHN. "Literature and Less," New Orleans Times-
     Picayune (25 January), Magazine Section, p. 6.
        The odds against a young poet writing a successful long
     poem have defeated Faulkner in The Marble Faun, but he has
     failed with honor. He is a "born poet," merely unprac-
     ticed in this volume, which was written during his late
     teens and early twenties; a more mature volume is in prepa-
     ration. Faulkner has led a varied life up to his twenty-
     seventh year. A number of lines are quoted from the poem.

1926 A   BOOKS - NONE

1926 B   SHORTER WRITINGS

1   *ANON. Interview with Faulkner, New Orleans Item.
        In New Orleans, Faulkner announces Mosquitoes, tells of
     working on a Pascagoula, Miss., fishing schooner and in a
     lumber mill, and announces that he made a hole-in-one at
     the Oxford, Miss., golf course. Reprinted in Lion in the
     Garden (1968.A6) from Carvel Collins' introduction to New
     Orleans Sketches (1958.B18), where it is excerpted and at-
     tributed to the Item. Bassett (1972.A2) erroneously cites
     a 1951 interview in place of this one as his item DD3.

2   ANON. "War's Aftermath," NYTBR (11 April), p. 8.
        Soldiers' Pay is a re-creation of the lives of the dis-
     illusioned and out-of-place who returned from the war. It
     "rings true," and though not grandly tragic, the book
     still touches us. It has a Hellenic regard for sensory
     experience and a leavening humor.

3   *BARRETTO, LARRY. "Men Without Faces," NYHTB (6 June), p. 6.
        Soldiers' Pay, which is almost a great book, has more
     irony than pity. (BRD 1926, p. 227.)

4   BOYD, THOMAS. "Honest But Slap-Dash," SatR (24 April),
     p. 736.
        Soldiers' Pay is an esoteric, high-pitched story of
     strange humans in the period after the Armistice. The
     book is impressionistic; the style suspiciously Joycean.
     It has "fervor and strength" but lacks control.

5   *DAVIDSON, DONALD. "William Faulkner," Nashville Tennessean
     (11 April).
        Faulkner is a poet in prose; Soldiers' Pay is superior
     to the work of the widely acclaimed John Dos Passos.
     Faulkner uses his modernism judiciously, although he is

2

(DAVIDSON, DONALD)
occasionally shocking or too arty. The novel depicts the
grimness of coming to terms with post-war life in a typical
Southern town where the war, so powerful an effect on the
soldier, has remained very remote.
Reprinted 1966.B42.

6 *DOUNCE, HARRY ESTY. Review of Soldiers' Pay, NY (3 April),
p. 54.
R. O. Johnson, Index to Literature in The New Yorker,
Volumes I-XV, 1925-1940. Metuchen, N. J.: Scarecrow
Press, 1969, Item 16769.

7 KRONENBERGER, LOUIS. "Soldiers' Pay," Literary Digest, IV
(26 July), 518-19.
Soldiers' Pay might be called "What Price Victory?"
Concentrating on effects rather than causes, it is richly
imagined, complexly arranged.

8 McCLURE, JOHN. "Literature and Less," New Orleans Times-
Picayune (11 April), Magazine Section, p. 4.
A "corking first novel" on the theme of the returned war
hero, Soldiers' Pay suffers only from its rambling struc-
ture and somewhat implausible gathering of characters.
Januarius Jones appears to have "dropped from the moon."
The style, however, is admirable.

9 MORRIS, LAWRENCE S. "Flame and Ash," NRep (23 June),
pp. 147-48.
Soldiers' Pay reveals a "nervous, swift talent," but it
is generally too arty.

1927 A BOOKS - NONE

1927 B SHORTER WRITINGS

1 AIKEN, CONRAD. Review of Mosquitoes, New York Evening Post
(11 June), p. 7.
Character, humor, style, dialogue, and setting in Mosquitoes demonstrate Faulkner's talents. When he has out-
grown his mannerisms--self-indulgent "preciosity" and "romantic fantasy"--he will produce "a really first-rate·
piece of fiction."
Reprinted in A Reviewer's ABC (1958.B2).

2 ANON. Review of Mosquitoes, SatR (25 June), p. 933.
Despite detestable characters, Mosquitoes has remarkable

1927

(ANON.)
passages. Wistful and poetic as well as cynical, it is a
"cut above the average novel."

3   BENÉT, WILLIAM ROSE. "Phoenix Nest," SatR (18 June), p. 920.
The young author of Mosquitoes can write, but his effects
are ugly and boring. Joyce is an obvious influence.

4   *DAVIDSON, DONALD. Review of Mosquitoes, Nashville Tennessean
(3 July).
A languorous Mississippi Joycean, Faulkner lays about
satirically and manages to leave us more aware of the author than his subjects. Still, Mosquitoes is well and happily done.
Reprinted 1966.B42.

5   *HELLMAN, LILIAN F. "Futile Souls Adrift on a Yacht," NYHTB
(19 June), p. 9.
Cited in Bassett (1972.A2), item C7.

6   McCLURE, JOHN. "Literature and Less," New Orleans Times-
Picayune (3 July), Magazine Section, p. 4.
A "clever interlude" not up to the standard of Soldiers'
Pay, Mosquitoes seems too much the tour de force. Cruel
or joking by turns, it will be disconcerting to "Puritan"
readers.

7   W[YLIE], E[LINOR] H[OYT]. "Mosquitoes," NRep (20 July),
p. 236.
"The author has wit, and an ear neatly attuned to the
idiom of professional conversationalists," but Mosquitoes
is no South Wind [by Norman Douglas]. The story becomes
boring because of the tedious characters; the style is
marred by Joycean prose and "purple lyricism." It is,
nevertheless, promising.

1929 A BOOKS - NONE

1929 B SHORTER WRITINGS

1   BENÉT, WILLIAM ROSE. "Phoenix Nest," SatR (5 October), p.
222.
Cape and Smith "set much store by" Faulkner, whose The
Sound and the Fury "involved several studies of madness."

2   DAVENPORT, BASIL. "Tragic Frustration," SatR (28 December),
pp. 601-02.
The "tragedy constantly deepens" in The Sound and the

(DAVENPORT, BASIL)

Fury as the four-part narrative moves from fantasy to fact. It consists not in the single events of the novel, but in the wretched life that remains once tragedies have occurred. "This is a man to watch."

3　*DAVIDSON, DONALD.　Review of Sartoris, Nashville Tennessean (14 April).

As "stylist and as acute observer of human behavior," Faulkner has few betters. The veteran Bayard of Sartoris must do himself in with machines, a perhaps symbolic comment on the age. Those who suffer his folly and grief in the novel are a more normal cross-section of the Southern community; the women are well-drawn. Reprinted 1966.B42.

4　EVANS, MEDFORD.　"Oxford, Mississippi," SWR, XV (Autumn), 46-63.

A page and a half on Faulkner notes that he is temperamental, even with friends.

5　MARTIN, ABBOTT.　"Faulkner's Difficult Novel Has Sin and Decay as Theme," Memphis (Tenn.) Commercial Appeal (17 November), Section VI, p. 8.

Faulkner's stream-of-consciousness is more concentrated, organic, and understandable than Joyce's. The Sound and the Fury has the beauty of "pathos and tragedy." Faulkner loves and writes well of the South; he is not the "exotic" he is often branded, although his work does have universal appeal. Condensed in 1930.B11.

6　MORRIS, LAWRENCE S.　Review of Sartoris, Bookman, LXIX (May), 310.

Sartoris is melodramatic and immature.

7　SAXON, LYLE.　"A Family Breaks Up," NYHTB (13 October), p. 3.

The Sound and the Fury is "as merciless as anything that I know which has come out of Russia," yet the author is so American he should not be compared to the Europeans; it mirrors a world "insane and monstrous."

8　SCOTT, EVELYN.　On William Faulkner's The Sound and the Fury. New York: Jonathan Cape and Harrison Smith.

The Sound and the Fury is proof that the modern age can still produce significant tragedy. Faulkner's characters symbolize the despair that is the human condition. Each

1929

(SCOTT, EVELYN)
section of this story of the "fall of a house" depicts the
circumstances in different terms, until Dilsey, in the
final section, "without so much as a theory to controvert"
Jason's mechanism, "doing the best she can," recovers human dignity and grandeur for us.
Reprinted, condensed, 1968.A3.

9   SMITH, AGNES W. Review of The Sound and the Fury, NY (16 November), pp. 111-12.
A Southern family goes "to pieces before your very eyes"
in The Sound and the Fury, which is difficult reading and
sometimes horrible in its implications.

10   *SMITH, HENRY NASH. "Three Southern Novels," SWR, XV (Autumn),
iii-iv.
Review of The Sound and the Fury. Bassett (1972.A2),
Item E16.

11   TASKER, J. DANA. "This Week's Reading," O&I (20 February),
pp. 311, 314.
Sartoris is "a story of woman's adjustment to man's
point of view," and it ends most tragically. The tragedy
is offset by moonlight and magnolia romanticism. The
Snopes episodes seem superfluous.

1930 A BOOKS - NONE

1930 B SHORTER WRITINGS

1   ANON. "William Faulkner," Wilson Bulletin, IV (February),
252.
Faulkner's life is sketched briefly.

2   ANON. "New Novels: Soldiers' Pay," TLS (3 July), p. 552.
Soldiers' Pay shows "fertile invention," good characterization, and a flair for both comic and tragic, but it is
overburdened with sex and death.

3   ANDERSON, SHERWOOD. "They Come Bearing Gifts," AMerc, XXI
(October), 129-37.
Anderson's essay about young writers includes his brief
anecdotal reminiscence of early encounters with Ernest
Hemingway and Faulkner, including a brief account of quar-
rels with both.

4   B[AKER], J[ULIA] K. W. "Literature and Less," New Orleans
     Times-Picayune (29 June), p. 23.
         Fulfilling the promise of Soldiers' Pay, Faulkner has
     written a true tragedy, rivaling Joyce in his technique.
     The method of The Sound and the Fury is not always success-
     ful, and the book will require more than one careful read-
     ing to be appreciated, but the achievement is real and
     doubtless germinal for the novel as a form.

5   _____. "Literature and Less," New Orleans Times-Picayune
     (26 October), p. 32.
         Unlike Hemingway and most of his contemporaries, Faulkner
     continues to experiment and grow as a writer. As I Lay
     Dying, though less rich and complex than The Sound and the
     Fury, is a clear move toward consolidation of Faulkner's
     gains; it is simple and powerful. The "horror" of the
     novel, which may bother the squeamish, is mitigated by the
     point of view--the Bundrens do not perceive their own in-
     decency.

6   COATES, ROBERT M. Review of As I Lay Dying, NY (25 October),
     p. 94.
         As I Lay Dying is based on a "gruesome idea," but it is
     rarely horrible. The style and dialogue are good, and it
     is recommended to readers who are interested in the chang-
     ing form of the movern novel.

7   DAVENPORT, BASIL. "In the Mire," SatR (22 November), p. 362.
         Much like, but not a repetition of The Sound and the
     Fury, As I Lay Dying uses insanity like "lightning in the
     night" to brighten the events of the novel. It is bleak,
     but it establishes Faulkner as one of the most original
     and powerful newer writers.

8   DAWSON, MARGARET CHENEY. "Beside Addie's Coffin," NYHTB
     (5 October), p. 6.
         A modified version of the structure and style of The
     Sound and the Fury, As I Lay Dying is clearer. There is
     still obscurity; Faulkner's evocations of the "half-
     formed images that floated through young Vardaman's brain"
     do not always work, but the imaginative style also fre-
     quently gives the work "hot, subterranean power." The
     reviewer wonders what Faulkner would accomplish if he ex-
     perimented with more traditional forms.

9   FADIMAN, CLIFTON. "Hardly Worth While," Nation (15 January),
     pp. 74-75.
         Theme and characters in The Sound and the Fury are not

1930

(FADIMAN, CLIFTON)
worthy of the technique expended upon them. Imbecility,
incest, paranoia, and sadism are Faulkner's material; a
banal plot from Poe is beneath his complexity.

10   HUGHES, RICHARD. "Preface" to Soldiers' Pay. London: Chatto
and Windus, pp. ix-xi.
Faulkner, who avoids literary people, has written three
first class books. Soldiers' Pay is about the peacetime
aftermath of the war--a "tragic, fascinating, and beautiful story...by a man who is a novelist to his finger-
tips." Invention, a good sense of form, a "highly and
widely educated" mind, and a true humanity are Faulkner's
characteristics.

11   MARTIN, ABBOTT. "Signifying Nothing," SR, XXXVIII (January),
115-16.
The style of The Sound and the Fury is praiseworthy; the
method is comparable to Joyce's. Condensation of 1926.B5.

12   MYERS, WALTER L. "Make-Beliefs," VQR, VI (January), 139-48.
The technique of The Sound and the Fury, discussed on
pp. 140-41, is difficult and not all that it might be,
but the book is impressive and significant.

13   PRIESTLEY, J. B. "A Letter from London," SatR (9 August),
p. 41.
Soldiers' Pay and Thomas Wolfe's Look Homeward, Angel
have been getting good reviews in England; both are difficult books and the Faulkner book has been praised "beyond
its deserts."

14   WHITE, KENNETH. "As I Lay Dying, by William Faulkner," NRep
(19 November), p. 27.
Faulkner has added little in matter or scope to the
literature of the poor white in As I Lay Dying, which is
not an inspiring view of humanity but a powerful book.

1931 A   BOOKS - NONE

1931 B   SHORTER WRITINGS

1   ANON. "The Sound and the Fury," TLS (14 May), p. 386.
Richard Hughes' introduction to The Sound and the Fury
(English edition; See 1931.B22) attempts to "reconcile"
the reader to the difficulties of the novel. Hughes'
three readings and his interest as a creative writer in

1931

(ANON.)
Faulkner's experiments may explain his high regard for the
"jigsaw puzzle in four parts," but unless the general
reader prefers to see the decent elements of young minds
brought low, he may not like the novel.

2   ANON. "Sanctuary," TLS (24 September), p. 732.
Unfortunately, Faulkner seems at his best only when dealing with the brutal, violent, and sordid. Sanctuary is of
interest only to the "neurologist and the criminologist."

3   ANON. "Les romans horribles de M. William Faulkner," Le Mois
(November), pp. 165-69.
The germ of Faulkner's work is in Soldiers' Pay. His
subjects are all equally horrible, as an excerpt from
Sanctuary (Red's funeral) demonstrates. The critical debate over Faulkner's work is reviewed and his novels summarized.

4   *ANON. "Slavery Better for the Negro, Says Faulkner," NYHTB
(14 November).
Faulkner is a "Southern sage who reads scarcely at all,
thinks the Negroes were better off under slavery, and
votes Democratic to protect his property."
Reprinted 1968.A6.

5   ANON. "Oxford Man," NY (28 November), pp. 12-13.
Paraphrase and one quote from an interview with Faulkner
in New York, where he was working on Light in August: he
talks about his education, his war experience, and his
"plantation."
Reprinted 1968.A6.

6   BENÉT, WILLIAM ROSE. "Phoenix Nest," SatR (18 April), p. 766.
Halfway through Sanctuary, the reader finds it terrify-
ing, but "the sheer writing is such that one must acknowl-
edge the literary mastery of the author."

7   _____. "Phoenix Nest," SatR (3 October), p. 178.
These 13 is one of the new books which must be read.
Faulkner is a "genius" who pushes the "intensely sinister
to the point that is hardly bearable."

8   _____. "Phoenix Nest," SatR (26 December), p. 420.
Random House is issuing a limited edition of Idyll in
the Desert, a new Faulkner story written while he was

9

1931

(BENÉT, WILLIAM ROSE)
visiting New York. His publishers say that Publishers'
Weekly recently carried 19 separate inquiries for first
editions of Soldiers' Pay.

9   B[AKER], J[ULIA] K. W. "Literature and Less," New Orleans
Times-Picayune (26 April), p. 26.
"The terrific irony of life," not the Bonnie Blue Flag,
is Faulkner's motivation as a writer. He writes high
tragedy that many of his Southern brothers do not understand. Only an opportunist would claim that Sanctuary approaches The Sound and the Fury and As I Lay Dying, but it
is an effective novel of American life during the prohibi-
tion era.

10   BROWN, STERLING. "The Point of View," Opportunity, IX (November), 347, 350.
"That Evening Sun Go Down" in These 13 is an example of
deep insight into the real world inhabited by certain
small-town blacks.

11   BURNHAM, JAMES. "Trying to Say," Symposium, II (January),
51-59.
Faulkner, as opposed to most other modern novelists, is
never dull. His "excitement...depends on gradual
dramatic disclosures of relations between persons." He is
constructing his own world. His "central intuition" is
human inarticulateness, as Soldiers' Pay, The Sound and
the Fury, and As I Lay Dying show. Darl is the "author"
of As I Lay Dying.

12   CANBY, HENRY SEIDEL. "The School of Cruelty," SatR
(21 March), pp. 673-74.
A calm hatred and a cool cruelty characterize Faulkner's
Sanctuary, a book without a moral. Temple and Gowan are
worse than the underworld figures to whom they descend.
Benbow, a kind-hearted liberal, merely succeeds in stoking
the lynchers' fire. The novel is the peak of current
sadism, and now Faulkner must put aside hysteria in order
to discover America.

13   CANTWELL, ROBERT. "Faulkner's Thirteen Stories," NRep
(21 October), p. 271.
The stories of These 13 should be read as adjuncts to
the novels. The characters are under strains which precede the action of the stories. Violence and half-hearted
protest are the conflict in Faulkner's work.

14   CHAMBERLAIN, JOHN. "Dostoefsky's Shadow in the Deep South,"
      NYTBR (15 February), p. 9.
          Powerful, but not as significant as The Brothers
      Karamazov, Faulkner's Sanctuary is a frightening tale of
      human evil and its effects. Living in the "backward
      South," Faulkner cannot know the values and ideas that
      make a great writer.

15   C[OATES], R[OBERT] M. Review of Sanctuary, NY (7 March),
      p. 84.
          On the occasion of Sanctuary's publication, the reviewer
      recommends As I Lay Dying instead. Both are a little melo-
      dramatic at times, but Faulkner's sincerity is obvious.
      Sanctuary tells two tales, either of them quite enough for
      one book; it has scenes and characters that are unforget-
      table.

16   COINDREAU, MAURICE EDGAR. "Lettres Étrangères: William
      Faulkner," NRF, XXXVI (June), 926-30.
          Faulkner's career proves him to be one of the most inter-
      esting figures in American literature. The Sound and the
      Fury revealed him; As I Lay Dying and Sanctuary mark his
      mastery of control. His men want to become angels, but
      since they cannot, they become beasts. He uses images in
      place of words, symbols instead of facts; style and matter
      are in perfect accord.
      Reprinted, translated 1971.B18.

17   CUSHING, EDWARD. "A Collection of Studies," SatR (17 Octo-
      ber), p. 201.
          Faulkner is "first of all" concerned with method; These
      13 is a "collection of études," studies in technique.
      His best work is in the war stories and pieces akin to
      The Sound and the Fury. He must overcome his interest in
      method if he is to live up to his promise.

18   DANIEL, FRANK. "Sanctuary," Atlanta Journal (1 March), Maga-
      zine Section, p. 22.
          Representative of the "literature of despair" and too
      violent and horrible to be summarized in a family news-
      paper, Sanctuary is a powerful, bleakly pessimistic work
      of fiction. Reviews in NYTBR (1931.B14) and NYHTB
      (1931.B4) are quoted.

19   ENOS, BERTRAM. "William Faulkner," SatR (19 December),
      p. 398.
          Replying by letter to the review of These 13 (1931.B17),
      the writer chides the critic for comments about Faulkner's

1931

(ENOS, BERTRAM)
   writing. Faulkner is clear, classic; he never wastes a
   word. The brilliance of his characters blinds us. Critics should stop trying to label him.

20   FADIMAN, CLIFTON. "The World of William Faulkner," Nation
      (15 April), pp. 422-23.
         After listing the perversion and violence he finds in
      Sanctuary, the reviewer notes that Faulkner "has an almost
      Joycean power of exteriorizing his horror-obsession."
      Sanctuary is better than the two novels which preceded it,
      and Faulkner is "among the most interesting" of young
      American writers.

21   HICKS, GRANVILLE. "The Past and Future of William Faulkner,"
      Bookman, LXXIV (September), 17-24.
         Faulkner's work is dominated by the tone which horror
      and violence lend. His technical virtuosity is original
      but seems less organic than Dos Passos' methods. His
      tragic vision does not measure up to Robinson Jeffers'.
      Like Poe and Bierce, he is quirky and thin; he has too
      much talent.

22   HUGHES, RICHARD. "Introduction" to The Sound and the Fury,
      London: Chatto and Windus, pp. vii-ix.
         There is no need to untangle the confusion of Benjy's
      undifferentiated past and present; the meaning is revealed
      as the reader goes along. Faulkner's difficulties are ar-
      tistic necessities. With each succeeding section, the
      story, including Benjy's portion, grows more clear. See
      also 1963.B46.

23   *[LANGFORD, GERALD]. Interview with Faulkner, College Topics
      (2 November).
         A midnight interview with Faulkner during the 1931
      Southern Writers' Conference at Charlottesville, Va.: he
      talks to a representative of the undergraduate college
      weekly about his favorite books--Moby Dick and The Nigger
      of the Narcissus--and about his writing (the story is the
      thing). The interviewer notes "one of Dumas' less impor-
      tant works," in paperback, on Faulkner's bureau.
      Reprinted 1968.A6; Langford's authorship revealed in
      1973.B61.

24   MUNSON, GORHAM BERT. "Our Post-War Novel," Bookman, LXXIV
      (October), 141-44.
         Faulkner's style is better than Hemingway's and his sub-
      ject matter better than Fitzgerald's. He struggles with

(MUNSON, GORHAM BERT)
form and is attracted to pathological subjects, a "Grand
Guignol naturalist."
Reprinted, translated into French, 1932.B16.

25   *PRAZ, MARIO. "William Faulkner," La Stampa (4 December).
According to Materassi (1971.B60), Praz says that Faulk-
ner, for all his interest in the pathological, still cen-
ters his novels on normal characters, like Mrs. Powers of
Soldiers' Pay and Benbow of Sanctuary. He is a novelist
in the old protestant tradition. His achievement in the
novel justifies his complicated style in The Sound and the
Fury.
Reprint edition Cronache letterarie anglosassoni, Roma:
Edizione di Storia e Letteratura, 1951, pp. 246-56.

26   ROBBINS, FRANCES LAMONT. Review of Sanctuary, O&I, CLVII
(11 March), 375.
Sanctuary is a "horrifying morality play on the theme of
Don't Monkey With the Buzz-Saw." The style is clearer
than usual for Faulkner. Set in the "Tennessee woods," it
is a powerful novel.

27   SHERWOOD, ROBERT E. Review of Sanctuary, Scribner's (April)
p. 13.
Frantically paced, nightmare-like, Sanctuary is a great
novel which addresses itself directly to the senses.

28   SHIPMAN, EVAN. "Violent People," NRep (4 March), pp. 78-79.
Caught in inexplicable complexities, Faulkner's characters are shown at the breaking point. Temple and Gowan,
who think they are invulnerable, put themselves into the
hands of dangerous people. The second half of Sanctuary
falls down, but it is a successful experiment with style.

29   *SMITH, MARSHALL J. Interview with Faulkner, Memphis Press-
Scimitar (10 July).
The author of Sanctuary is "dirt farming with a hoe and
a plow," working on a book of stories, and talks of "men,
of the fishing in the Tallahatchie, of the corn in the
bottoms." As I Lay Dying, he says, is his best novel, and
he tells how and where he wrote it. Reprinted, expanded
and with photographs, in 1931.B30. Both versions
in 1968.A6.

30   _____. "Faulkner of Mississippi," Bookman, LXXIV
(December), 411-17.
Expanded version of 1931.B29, with eight photos of

1931

(SMITH, MARSHALL J.)
Faulkner's home, Oxford and environs. Faulkner claims
that he hasn't written a real novel yet.
Reprinted 1968.A6.

31 *____. Interview with Mrs. William Faulkner, Memphis Press-
Scimitar (1 December).
The wife of the "sad-eyed" and "solemn-faced" Mississippi
novelist talks about him and his work, reporting that he
gave her Joyce's Ulysses to read on their honeymoon and
that it helped her understand Sanctuary.
Reprinted 1968.A6.

32 STRONG, L. A. G. "Children--and Adults," Spectator (19 September), pp. 362, 364.
Sanctuary strengthens the evidence that Faulkner is a
writer of the first importance, though the subject matter
does not allow it to be generally recommended. Technically
astonishing, it is nevertheless more than mere technique.

33 ____. "Mr. Faulkner Again," Spectator, (25 April),
p. 674.
The Sound and the Fury is a magnificent experiment with
language and form; it works so well one cannot imagine
how it could have been done differently. It repays one's
difficulties in reading it. Richard Hughes' introduction
(to the English edition; 1931.B22) is helpful.

34 SWINNERTON, FRANK. "Writers Who Know Life," London Evening
News (15 May), p. 8.
Faulkner is the "most powerful and the most enigmatic"
of the new American literary figures. The Sound and the
Fury is, however, unintelligible and unjustifiably complex, though, like great music, it may become clearer
with greater familiarity. "One is conscious of immense
power, a terrific drive of creative invention," for all
that the meaning of the counterpointed sections does not
come through.

35 THOMPSON, ALAN REYNOLDS. "Sanctuary, by William Faulkner,"
Bookman, LXXIII (April), 188-89.
"Tennessee folkways" are depicted with violence in
Sanctuary; though one has to admire Faulkner's ability
and his formal skills, the novel is unjustifiably ugly.

36 TRILLING, LIONEL. "Mr. Faulkner's World," Nation, CXXXIII
(4 November), 491-92.
Despite the "tone and emotional impact of a major

14

(TRILLING, LIONEL)
writer," Faulkner's work has trivial implications. "A
Rose for Emily" is an example. Soldiers' Pay and Sartoris
are idyllic or confectionary. Even The Sound and the Fury
and As I Lay Dying, though more richly symbolic, are paro-
chial. "Dry September" and "Victory" in These 13 are pre-
ferred.

37   WADE, JOHN DONALD. "The South in Its Fiction," VQR, VII
(January), 125-26.
The reviewer recites a few of the "horrors" in As I Lay
Dying but grants that it is "Art."

38   WHEELRIGHT, PHILIP ELLIS. "Sanctuary, by William Faulkner,"
Symposium, II (April), 276-80.
Faulkner is an example of what American novelists must
be. Sanctuary, like his previous work, uses symbols to
gradually clarify the main events of the narrative. Irony
is the prevailing mode.

1932 A   BOOKS - NONE

1932 B   SHORTER WRITINGS

1   ANON. Review of Sartoris, NewSt (2 April), pp. 428, 430.
Dizzying in its violence and pace, Sartoris yet leaves
us strangely sympathetic toward all life and its mysteries.
His pictures of women are admirable. His style is varied
and rich.

2   ANON. "A 'Prentice Faulkner," NYTBR (29 May), p. 20.
Selections of Faulkner's early work printed in Sal-
magundi--all but one from the Double Dealer--have "curiosity value," but they also show Faulkner's love of words.

3   ANON. "A Faulkner Item in a Limited Edition," NYTBR
(17 July), p. 9.
Henry Nash Smith's introduction to Miss Zilphia Gant illuminates the motivation of Faulkner's characters. The
story displays a "bare horror, achieved by Faulkner's un-
erring use of the right words."

4   ADAMS, J. DONALD. "Mr. Faulkner's Astonishing Novel," NYTBR
(9 October), pp. 6, 24.
Light in August, which has crude and brutal power but
also discipline, represents a step forward for Faulkner.
Despite his apparent "furious contempt" for humankind,
Faulkner has allowed compassion a place in this novel.

1932

(ADAMS, J. DONALD)
After writing like a man wounded by life, he seems to have
regained his balance.

5   BEACH, JOSEPH WARREN. The Twentieth Century Novel: Studies
in Technique. New York: Century Co., pp. 516, 520-22.
The Sound and the Fury ("highly original and decidedly
bewildering") and As I Lay Dying are summarized with particular attention to the way they use stream-of-consciousness technique. Faulkner's moving away from this technique, as in Sanctuary and These 13, may be a sign of the
times. He is one of the great talents of the age.

6   BRICKELL, HERSCHEL. "The Literary Landscape," NAR, CCXXXIII
(April), 376-77.
Mississippians are disapproving of Sanctuary, but they
will end by acknowledging Faulkner's greatness. His biography is sketched.

7   _____. "The Literary Landscape," NAR, CCXXXIV
(December), 571.
There is genius in Faulkner, as Light in August proves
even more than his previous work. It is lightened by humor. Readers who condemn Faulkner without reading him
deserve chiding.

8   CANBY, HENRY SEIDEL. "The Grain of Life," SatR (8 October),
pp. 153, 156.
Extraordinarily rich and forceful, Light in August is
unified by the theme of the opposition between those whom
life rejects and those whom it accepts. The events of
the novel are clustered "along the road of Lena's story."
Faulkner must have attended a fundamentalist church in
his youth, for it is this spirit which overinforms his
fiction and creates dark and morbid fantasies.
Reprinted 1971.A3.

9   COATES, ROBERT M. Review of Light in August, NY (15 October), p. 69.
Faulkner is not writing about familiar Southerners.
The story of "Lee Christmas" is almost too complicated to
unravel. Faulkner's "grasp of the scene and his peculiar
predilection for the ominous and foreboding lift the narrative to a level of high intensity."

10   COCHRAN, LOUIS. "William Faulkner, Literary Tyro of Mississippi, Overwhelmed by Fame of His Astounding Novels,"
Memphis Commercial Appeal (6 November), Magazine Section,
p. 4.

16

(COCHRAN, LOUIS)
A man who had known Faulkner at the University of Mississippi gives an account of Faulkner's college years and of his early success. Faulkner "lives a sane, well balanced life, writes every day...as though he were still a carpenter," and may yet become, as his friend Phil Stone thinks, the "great American humorist" who can fill Mark Twain's shoes.

11 DAWSON, MARGARET CHENEY. "A Rich, Sinister and Furious Novel," NYHTB (9 October), p. 3.
Faulkner's name evokes images of the subhuman created in "furious" terms by a "highly civilized art." Light in August is broader and stouter than anything he has done before; the Lena Grove material is a "full and marching epic" which surrounds the violence of the "more to be expected" story of Joe Christmas.
Reprinted 1971.A3.

12 GREEN, A. WIGFALL. "William Faulkner at Home," SR, XL (Summer), 294-306.
Oxford, Mississippi, and environs are the source of Faulkner's material, along with his adventurous life. His work is summarized sympathetically.
Reprinted 1951.A2.

13 HEMINGWAY, ERNEST. Letter to Robert Coates, NY (5 November), pp. 74-75.
"There weren't any cracks against Faulkner" in Death in the Afternoon. "There was...a pretty damned friendly mention." "I have plenty of respect for Faulkner and wish him all luck."

14 HICKS, GRANVILLE. "John Dos Passos," Bookman, LXXV (April), 32-42.
Hemingway and Faulkner, like other writers of their generation, do not measure up to Dos Passos; they write escape fiction.

15 LEWISOHN, LUDWIG. The Story of American Literature. New York: Harper, pp. 520-22.
Neonaturalists like Faulkner describe man as vile and loathsome; Faulkner specifically lashes out at all he hates, a neurotic circle.

16 MUNSON, GORHAM. "Le roman d'après guerre aux états-unis," translated by Louis and Renée Guilloux, Europe, XXXIX (15 August), 617-23.

1932

(MUNSON, GORHAM)
Faulkner is a rising star; his style is better than
Hemingway's and his power and subject matter exceed Fitz-
gerald's. He still struggles with form and is attracted
by violent and pathological subjects.
Reprint of 1931.B24.

17   O'DONNELL, GEORGE MARION. "A Mellower Light," Memphis Commercial Appeal (9 October), p. 4-E.
More humane and less morbid than Sanctuary, Light in
August remains tragic and unconventional. The flashback
technique makes the structure too loose, but Faulkner
comes close to achieving the synchronization he apparently
desires. It is his most mature work to date.
Reprinted 1971.A3.

18   RATLIFF, WALTER. "Light in August by William Faulkner,"
Atlanta Journal (23 October), Magazine Section, p. 18.
Light in August is a "parade of powerful vignettes."
The reviewer quotes from NYTBR (1932.B1) and NYHTB
(1932.B11).

19   SMITH, HENRY [NASH]. "Preface" to Miss Zilphia Gant.
Dallas, Texas: Book Club of Texas, pp. vii-xi.
Faulkner's characters live subconsciously, their struggles symbols of the author's inner conflicts. His novels
evoke strange moods. Nature--"cruel, beautiful, and un-
ambiguous"--is all he puts faith in.
Reprinted 1953.B38.

20   _____. "Writing Right Smart Fun, Says Faulkner," Dallas
Morning News (14 February), Section IV, p. 2.
In an interview Faulkner talks about his writing habits
and claims never to have read Ulysses, although there is
a 1924 edition within reach of his writing table.
Reprinted 1968.A6.

21   STONE, GEOFFREY. Review of Light in August, Bookman, LXXV
(November), 736-38.
Faulkner is a Romantic; Light in August is full-blown
Gothic. The novel is filled with violence of action and
feeling. Faulkner's structural and stylistic peculiari-
ties are, like his characters and incidents, overdone.

22   STRONG, L. A. G. Review of Sartoris, Spectator (27 Febru-
ary), pp. 296, 298.
One must accept a man of genius whole or not at all.
Faulkner is such a genius and the reviewer is prepared to

(STRONG, L. A. G.)
"swallow him whole." Sartoris shows a new simplicity with
the old muscle.

23 THOMPSON, ALAN REYNOLDS. "The Cult of Cruelty," Bookman,
LXXIV (January-February), 477-87.
Faulkner and Jeffers are identified with the new breed
of violent writers. The title is "the only amiable
thing" about Sanctuary, which is needlessly shocking.

24 THOMPSON, FREDERIC. "American Decadence," Commonweal (30 November), p. 139.
Faulkner's art is "in its very extremity supreme" among
the works of modern writers. Light in August shows how
"diabolism triumphs among people who have no true religion." All the "simple qualities of the beatitudes" are
lacking--it is a story of the "savage tyrannies of evil."

25 THORP, WILLARD. "Four Times and Out?" Scrutiny, I (September), 172-73.
Faulkner has succumbed to mediocrity, writing the kind
of fiction that sells mouthwash to 50 million Americans
in Saturday Evening Post. Sartoris puts modernist technique to new use by achieving simultaneity for events
widely separated in time, but Bayard is not a sympathetic
character. Faulkner has not been able to understand why
the Sartoris men throw their lives away so recklessly.

26 VAN DOREN, DOROTHY. "More Light Needed," Nation (26 Octo-
ber), pp. 402-03.
The Sound and the Fury remains Faulkner's best novel;
Light in August is a matter of his repeating himself.
The novel leaves too many unanswered questions.
Reprinted 1971.A3.

27 VERNON, GRANVILLE. "Fallen Angel?" Commonweal (20 January),
pp. 332-33.
The stories of These 13 are powerful but generally concerned with the "loathsome and degenerate." Faulkner's
advent is what one should expect in an age without belief.

28 WARREN, ROBERT PENN. "Not Local Color," VQR, VIII (January),
160.
The sense of place is "the most triumphant aspect" of
the stories in These 13.

1933

1933 A   BOOKS - NONE

1933 B   SHORTER WRITINGS

1   ANON. "Light in August," TLS (16 February), p. 106.
    A compound of "horror, hatred, lust, brutality, and ob-
    session," Light in August still displays life with a
    "thunderous threatening beauty." Lena's story does not
    quite compensate for Joe Christmas's or Gail Hightower's.
    They are volitionless slaves to their past lives.

2   ANON. "These Thirteen," TLS (28 September), p. 648.
    The theme of "All the Dead Pilots" and the words of the
    subadar in "Ad Astra" characterize everything that Faulk-
    ner writes about the war. "Carcassonne" reveals a "poet's
    mind, tugging at the chain of the body like an angry
    watchdog," and explains the source of Faulkner's earthy
    brilliance in work like the stories of These 13.

3   BENÉT, WILLIAM ROSE. "Round About Parnassus: Faulkner as
    Poet," SatR (29 April), p. 565.
    A Green Bough reveals obvious borrowing from Eliot,
    Housman, Cummings, and others. As poet, Faulkner seems no
    more than a gifted amateur.

4   BRICKELL, HERSCHEL. "The Fruits of Diversity," VQR, IX (Jan-
    uary), 114-19.
    Faulkner's Light in August demonstrates a surer touch
    than his previous work; he has "amazing talent."

5   CESTRE, CHARLES. "William Faulkner: Light in August," Revue
    anglo-américaine, No. 5 (June), 466-67.
    Faulkner's power is apparent in Light in August; his art
    needs refinement.

6   EDGAR, PELHAM. "Four American Writers: Anderson, Hemingway,
    Dos Passos, Faulkner," The Art of the Novel from 1700 to
    the Present Time. New York: Macmillan, pp. 338-51.
    Faulkner's mastery of conventional writing methods is so
    complete, where exhibited, one wonders why he indulges in
    willful experimentation that obscures his meaning.

7   FIELD, LOUISE MAUNSELL. "The Modest Novelists," NAR, CCXXXV
    (January), 66-67.
    The general impression of Light in August is one of
    "foulness and corruption," despite Byron Bunch and "High
    Tower's" final vision.

8   GARNETT, DAVID. "Current Literature," NewSt (30 September),
        p. 387.
            Like Wordsworth and Dickens, Faulkner is one of those
        uneven writers whose work is apt to plunge on unexpectedly
        "into an abyss of silliness or of bad taste," as the sto-
        ries in These 13 occasionally prove, especially "All the
        Dead Pilots." "Victory" is the only complete failure;
        "Red Leaves" is mysterious and wonderful.

9   HICKS, GRANVILLE. "William Faulkner," The Great Tradition:
        An Interpretation of American Literature Since the War.
        New York: Macmillan, pp. 265-68.
            Like Jeffers, Faulkner is a searcher-out of despair and
        suffering, in which he finds no meaning; his characters
        are out of the pathology textbook; he hates humanity.

10   JOSEPHSON, MATTHEW. "The Younger Generation: Its Young Nov-
        elists," VQR, IX (April), 243-61.
            Faulkner is an "expressionistic poet"; his work is dis-
        cussed in one paragraph along with Fitzgerald, Caldwell,
        Robert Cantwell, Katherine Anne Porter, Kay Boyle, and
        Kenneth Burke.

11   LEAVIS, F. R. "Dostoevsky or Dickens?" Scrutiny, II (June),
        91-93.
            Faulkner is more like Dickens in Light in August, though
        he is still too much concerned with technique and uncer-
        tain of method. Faulkner pumps in the significance during
        Joe's death scene. Lena and Byron are the surest parts of
        his creation. "The Old South is the strength of his
        book."
        Reprinted 1971.A3.

12   LINN, ROBERT. "Robinson Jeffers and William Faulkner," Amer-
        ican Spectator (November), p. 1.
            Faulkner and Robinson Jeffers are artists solely for the
        "intelligentsia." Faulkner is a combination "Gertrude
        Stein and humorless Aristophanes." His Light in August is
        monstrous, omitting all virtue. His art is just what a
        dead America deserves.

13   MALRAUX, ANDRÉ. "Préface à 'Sanctuaire' de W. Faulkner," NRF,
        XLI (November), 744-47.
            Sanctuary is a detective novel without detectives and
        with elements of Greek tragedy. Faulkner has the same
        images, hatreds and obsessions as Poe and E. T. A. Hoff-
        mann. His chief subject is man's confrontation with the
        "irréparable." Reprinted with Sanctuaire (Paris: Galli-
        mard, 1933); translated 1952.B31; portions in 1966.A8.

21

1933

14   MARICHALAR, ANTONIO. "William Faulkner," Revista de occi-
     dente, XLII (October), 78-86.
         A translation of "All the Dead Pilots" follows a Spanish-
     language account of Faulkner's reception in France and
     America and of his career. Faulkner's work is "tenebroso,
     siniestro, terrorífico," and the critic prefers Light in
     August. Reprinted as Preface to Santuario (Madrid:
     Espasa-Calpe, 1934), the essay argues for the social con-
     tent, though not the realism, of Sanctuary.

15   P. E. GEMINI QUERCUS [pseud. Morley, Christopher]. "Trade
     Winds," SatR (22 July), p. 12.
         Morley reports that Sanctuary was retitled "The Story of
     Temple Drake" for the movies at the insistence of censor
     Will Hays and that Random House will issue Sanctuary "this
     fall with the text printed in three colors--one color for
     the narrative, a second for the character's conscious
     thoughts, a third for his unconscious thoughts." [An ap-
     parent confusion with plans for The Sound and the Fury;
     See Meriwether, "The Textual History of The Sound and the
     Fury," 1962.B85 and 1970.A6.]

16   NOVAS CALVO, LINO. "El demonio de Faulkner," Revista de
     occidente, XXXIX (January), 98-103.
         The first article in the Spanish-speaking world on
     Faulkner, according to Chapman (1966.B11), it chided Span-
     ish critics for failing to notice Faulkner's work. The
     influence of Anderson and of Puritanism, the thematic em-
     phasis upon the death-struggle of the old order, and a
     native dramatic ability are Faulkner's characteristic
     sources.

17   PATTEN, MERCURY. "Books in General," NewSt (11 February),
     p. 163.
         After struggling with Sanctuary, The Sound and the Fury,
     and Light in August during an eight-day Atlantic crossing,
     the reviewer reports on Faulkner's obscurity, his power,
     and the difficulty of reading him. Light in August is
     quite different from the earlier work; it recalls Conrad
     and Stephen Crane; it plasters Gertrude Stein on the old
     plantation house. Faulkner is unfortunately reckless and
     uncritical, so the novel, though "finely conceived," is
     badly planned.

18   SCHAPPES, MORRIS U. "Faulkner as a Poet," Poetry, XLIII
     (October), 48-52.
         Faulkner in his fiction is apparently unaware of the
     social background of the lives he depicts, but at least

(SCHAPPES, MORRIS U.)
his fiction has some concreteness, while his poetry has
"neither background nor foreground." A Green Bough is
full of emotional poses, and it is unrelated to the Southern scene.

19   STRONG, L. A. G. "Fiction," Spectator (17 February), p. 226.
Light in August is "a fine, significant and important
piece of work," but one which every reader may not enjoy.
Faulkner approaches his diverse story from many directions;
his book "burns throughout with a fierce indignation
against cruelty, stupidity and prejudice."

20   TROY, WILLIAM. "Faulkner in Hollywood," Nation (24 May),
pp. 594-95.
The film version of Sanctuary ("The Story of Temple
Drake") conveys the fascination of evil and sustains the
moral horror of the novel.

21   WALDMAN, MILTON. "Tendencies of the Modern Novel III. America," Fortnightly Review, N. S. No. 134 (December),
717-25.
Faulkner's small-town nightmare and horror, by Sinclair
Lewis out of James Joyce, is convincing and powerful. In
Light in August, most recently, he irons out his stylistic
crudities.

22   WEEKS, EDWARD. "Atlantic Bookshelf," AtlM, CLI (January), 10.
Light in August depicts "the futility and superficiality
of civilization"; characterization and writing are both
praiseworthy.

1934 A   BOOKS - NONE

1934 B   SHORTER WRITINGS

1   ANON. "Doctor Martino," TLS (13 September), p. 618.
"Battle, murder and sudden death" are a major part of
the remarkable and imaginative stories in Doctor Martino.
The title story and "Leg" are Gothic in their effects.

2   BENÉT, STEPHEN VINCENT. "Fourteen Faulkner Stories," SatR
(21 April), p. 645.
Doctor Martino shows a range enlarged from These 13; it
is "above the average." "Elly" and "Mountain Victory" are
praiseworthy; "Black Music" is a good piece of humor.

1934

3   BROOKS, VAN WYCK. "From a Critic and Biographer," SatR
     (10 November), p. 272.
        The writer questions Lawrence Kubie's assertion (See
     1934.B15) that neurosis and defeat are "closer to Truth"
     than mental health and victory.

4   *CAMERINO, ALDO. "Novila de William Faulkner."
        According to Materassi (1971.B60, p. 79), who gives no
     publishing information, Camerino's article found Faulk-
     ner's work overdone, especially on the level of the emo-
     tions and violence. But Faulkner is not a naturalist;
     there is an inherent moral view behind his work. His imag-
     inative range is limited.
     Reprinted 1968.B19.

5   CANBY, HENRY SEIDEL. "The Literature of Horror... Intro-
     ductory Essay," SatR (20 October), pp. 217-18.
        Introducing three psychological analyses of modern fic-
     tion, Canby writes that the work of writers like Hemingway
     and Faulkner manifests "defeatism" and reads like case
     histories about which the authors have no personal convic-
     tions. The essays to come (See 1934.B15) seek to diagnose
     the malady which produces this kind of writing.

6   *CECCHI, EMILIO. "William Faulkner," Pan, II (May), 64-70.
        Materassi (See 1971.B60, pp. 52-53) calls it the best of
     the early Italian criticism of Faulkner. The physical soli-
     tude of Faulkner's characters mirrors their moral isola-
     tion; his "representation is...humanly saturated"
     with compassion. Reprinted, revised, in "Note su William
     Faulkner" in William Faulkner: Venti anni di critica,
     edited by F. J. Hoffman and O. W. Vickery (Parma: Guanda,
     1957), pp. 102-10, 1957.A1; an expanded version of
     1951.A2

7   DABIT, EUGÈNE. Review of Sanctuaire, Europe (15 April),
     pp. 599-600.
        The problems of the novel's technique are overruled by
     the novel's power. We are exposed directly to a horrible,
     senseless world, a drama of high tragic intensity.

8   _____. Review of Tandis que j'agonise, Europe (15 October),
     pp. 294-96.
        The reviewer, himself a novelist, envies the American
     writers their subject matter and style. Faulkner's char-
     acters seem to operate only in a tragic mode.

9   FADIMAN, CLIFTON. Review of Doctor Martino, NY (21 April),
     pp. 85-86.

(FADIMAN, CLIFTON)
Finishing a Faulkner book is a pleasant relief. The reviewer, laying stress on the horror he finds in the stories of Doctor Martino, complains of his inability to understand the work, except for "Smoke" and "Turnabout,"
which he likes and admires.

10 *FINGERIT, JULIO. "Los 'Frankenstein' de William Faulkner,"
La Nación (24 June), section two, p. 2.
According to Chapman (1966.B11, p. 217), the reviewer
believes Sanctuary is a fraud--unmotivated characters are
the primary fault, but the Grand Guignol horror still
grips the reader and frays his nerves.

11 GARNETT, DAVID. Review of Doctor Martino, NewSt (29 September), p. 396.
Faulkner's work is characterized by "violence of subject
and of expression"; we look at the events of his stories
through "strange minds" and hear them told in odd dialogue. Although pieces like "Death Drag" and "Turn About"
are the staple of vigorous magazine fiction, Faulkner has
made them nearly unique. Nothing equals "Red Leaves" out
of These 13, but "The Hound" and "Wash" are very good.
"Black Music" may be compared, unfavorably, with E. M.
Forster's The Celestial Omnibus.

12 GENÊT [pseud. Janet Flanner]. Review of Sanctuaire, NY (20
January), p. 27.
The columnist recounts the impact of the French translation of Sanctuary in Paris, including long quotes from a
review by "Maxence" in Gringoire who welcomes the novel
as a revelation of heretofore unknown Franco-American affinities. In a tragic epoch, the French instinctively
turn to profound, original work.

13 HARTWICK, HARRY. "The Cult of Cruelty," Foreground of American Fiction. New York: American Book Co., pp. 160-66.
Faulkner has given over to his anarchic world, producing
extremely naturalistic fiction marked by pessimism and
horror, limited to recording sensation, lacking depth.

14 HATCHER, HARLAN. "The Torches of Violence," EJ, XXIII (February), 91-99.
Faulkner and Jeffers are in the ranks of a host of contemporary writers who exploit the horrible and sensational. It is realism gone to excess because of World
War I and Freudianism. The indestructible human spirit
will survive this phenomenon.

1934

15   KUBIE, LAWRENCE S., M. D. "William Faulkner's Sanctuary: An
      Analysis," SatR (20 October), pp. 218, 224-26.
         Up to Temple's rape, Sanctuary is a nightmare of ironic
      dimensions; from this point, she behaves as if dead and
      she harms those who have helped, not harmed, her, as if
      avenging herself on the male principle, including a father
      and four brothers whom she hates. The psychological con-
      flict between instinctual evil and the evils of a savage
      conscience dramatizes an Id-Superego conflict, with Horace
      Benbow as Ego caught between the two. Only Ruby and Lee
      have a healthy attitude toward bodily functions. The
      novel seems to work out in fantasy the problems of male
      impotence.
      Reprinted 1966.A8.

16   *LARBAUD, VALÉRY. "Préface," Tandis que j'agonise, translated
      by M. E. Coindreau. Paris: Gallimard.
         As I Lay Dying can be regarded seriously as epical--
      "l'épisode des obsèques de la reine (homérique) Addie
      Bundren"--with a full mythological cast.
      Reprinted 1936.B11.

17   LENORMAND, H. R. "American Literature in France," SatR
      (27 October), p. 244.
         Faulkner was immediately recognized in France as in the
      tradition of Poe because of the power and innovative na-
      ture of his writing.

18   LEWIS, WYNDHAM. "A Moralist With a Corn-Cob: A Study of
      William Faulkner," Life and Letters, X (June), 312-28.
         As a literary artist, Faulkner, in his ardent Puritan
      morality, has no sense of the mot juste, sounding like the
      Sherwood Anderson whom Hemingway parodied in Torrents of
      Spring, but his work is passionate and filled with unfor-
      gettable characters. His simplistic conception of fatal-
      ity ensures violent death to his heroes. He reveals only
      superficial acquaintance with Joyce, none with Stein; he
      is closest to Conrad, though kin to Dickens. Sanctuary is
      his best book, a mordant moral satire.
      Reprinted 1934.B19.

19   _____. "William Faulkner: Moralist with a Corn-Cob," Men
      Without Art. New York: Harcourt, Brace; Edinburgh:
      Cassell & Co., pp. 42-64.
      Reprint of 1934.B18.

20   LOVEMAN, AMY. "The Clearing House," SatR (8 December),
      p. 359.
         Presenting a list of Southern writers, the reviewer

(LOVEMAN, AMY)
notes that Faulkner's setting is "the appalling world of
perverts, degenerates, and men of savage primitive passions." To read him is to be in a nightmare. He is not
representative of Southern life.

21 *PAVESE, CESARE. "Faulkner, cattivo allievo di Anderson," La
Cultura (April).
Sanctuary, in the French translation and as a film [en-
titled Perdizione], is becoming fashionable in Italy. The
plot is summarized with emphasis on the horrific elements.
Faulkner remains high above the action. Benbow, who shows
Anderson's influence--the "slow motion" revelation of
character through self-questioning--has nothing to say,
hence Faulkner's description as a "bad" pupil. The novel
is an overly-ambitious thriller.
Reprinted, translated, 1970.B59.

22 RICE, PHILIP BLAIR. "The Art of William Faulkner," Nation
(25 April), p. 479.
One of America's greatest novelists, whose work ranks
with Joyce, Woolf, and Mann, Faulkner is "in the main tradition" of the short story; style and subject matter both
fit the compressed form, as the pieces in Doctor Martino
show. But the ending of "Turn About" indicates that
Faulkner had best leave "ideas" out of his fiction.

23 SAINT JEAN, ROBERT de. "La vie littéraire:--Sanctuaire,"
Revue hebdomadaire (21 April), pp. 488-91.
The horror of the world of Sanctuary makes man conscious
of his smallness and the beauty of a sort of tragedy of
life.

24 SCOTT, EVELYN. "From a Novelist," SatR (10 November),
pp. 272, 280.
The writer replies to Kubie's psychoanalytic study of
Sanctuary (1934.B15) on several theoretical points and
specifically by asking how Popeye, the least convincing
character in the novel, obviously not a sympathetic character, can come to have so much significance. She doubts
the interpretation Kubie assigns him. Writers are not out
to shock their readers.

25 STARKE, AUBREY. "An American Comedy: An Introduction to a
Bibliography of William Faulkner," Colophon, V, part 19,
no page numbers [12 pp.].
Faulkner's "comedy" is modeled after the work of his
favorite author, Balzac, forged chiefly out of the novels,

1934

(STARKE, AUBREY)
with the stories as chains which bind. A bibliography of
Faulkner is a reader's guide because of the interrelatedness of his work. The Sartoris/Snopes conflict is central.

26   STONE, PHIL. "William Faulkner: The Man and His Work," Oxford Magazine, I (April), 13-14; II (June), 11-15; III
(November), 3-10.
In three parts of an uncompleted essay in an abortive
local magazine, Stone, on the basis of "twenty years of
personal association," gives Faulkner's literary history.
Faulkner is the "sanest and most wholesome person I have
ever known." The writer sketches Faulkner's family background, including much about Col. W. C. Falkner, and describes Oxford as the ideal place for a talent like Faulkner's to be nourished. Reprinted in "Early Notices of
Faulkner," 1964.B51, and, shortened and entitled "The Man
and the Land," in 1965.A5.

27   THIEBAUT, MARCEL. "Parmi les livres," Revue de Paris (15
July), pp. 74-76.
As I Lay Dying is worth the difficulty of reading it.

28   WARREN, ROBERT PENN. "T. S. Stribling: A Paragraph in the
History of Critical Realism," AmRev, II (November 1933-
March 1934), 463-86.
Comparing Stribling's work with Faulkner's, especially
As I Lay Dying and Light in August, one must conclude that
Faulkner is concerned with deeper issues and meanings,
that he is poetic and contemplative while Stribling works
only the surface.

1935 A BOOKS - NONE

1935 B SHORTER WRITINGS

1   ANON. "Pylon," TLS (11 April), p. 242.
Strange, exciting, and difficult, well-written despite
its eccentricities, Pylon captures the glitter and tawdri-
ness of American contemporaneity, which Faulkner loathes.

2   ANON. "Literature and Less," New Orleans Times-Picayune
(21 April), Section II, p. 5.
Pylon has more sunlight than some of Faulkner's previous
books, but only one of his admirers will find much pleasure in it. The Joycean wordplay is obvious; the course
of the plot is "muddy."

3 ANON. "As I Lay Dying," TLS (26 September), p. 594.
   As I Lay Dying, just published in England, is an "Odyssey
   of human misery, courage and cowardice which Mr. Faulkner
   has set down with all his painful skill."

4 BASSO, HAMILTON. "Letters in the South," NRep (19 June),
   pp. 161-63.
   Faulkner has made his own adjustment to the South as he
   sees it. He is not one with the Agrarian realists like
   Glasgow.

5 BENÉT, WILLIAM ROSE. "Phoenix Nest," SatR (27 July), p. 19.
   The critic devotes two paragraphs to The Marble Faun,
   with a long quote from Phil Stone's introduction (See
   1924.B1) and remarks that Faulkner will not be remembered
   for his poetry.

6 CANBY, HENRY SEIDEL. "Fiction Tells All," Harper's, CLXXI
   (August), 308-15.
   Kubie (1934.B15) documents that Faulkner and others are
   writing literature from the underworld of the mind.
   Faulkner's Mississippi is a "madhouse for the mildly insane." Having seen the results of poverty and frustration, Faulkner has rushed his visions into print without
   waiting to present the other side of humankind. For all
   its truth, let there be an end to sick literature.

7 CHAPMAN, MARISTAN. "Is Our Ink Well?...Decadence and the
   Neo-Naturalists," Westminster, XXIII (January-March),
   267-69.
   Faulkner is no freak but a serious, powerful writer with
   something to say.

8 COINDREAU, MAURICE E. "A propósito de la última novela publicada por William Faulkner," La Nación (3 March), section
   two, p. 2.
   The most vigorous and most profound of Faulkner's novels, Light in August--which Coindreau was translating into
   French--is not deliberately shocking or obscure. The main
   elements of Faulkner's art are Puritanism, the manipula-
   tion of time, and symbolic language and character.

9 COINDREAU, MAURICE E. "Préface," Lumière d'août. Paris:
   Gallimard, pp. vii-xv.
   The "horror" in Faulkner's work is inevitable, not gra-
   tuitous, for he depicts a world with puritanical obsessions where life is a tragic involvement with sex and
   death. Light in August provides a perfect demonstration

1935

(COINDREAU, MAURICE E.)
of Faulkner's characteristics in the psychological analysis of the doomed Christmas. Published as "Le Puritanisme de William Faulkner," 1935.B10.
Reprinted, translated, 1971.B18.

10 _____. "Le Puritanisme de William Faulkner," Cahiers du Sud (April), pp. 259-67.
Reprinted 1935.B9. Translated 1971.B18.

11 CONNOLLY, CYRIL. "New Novels," NewSt (13 April), pp. 525-26.
Hemingway is the only great American writer; Faulkner fails, by comparison, because he lacks purity of emotion and purity of form. He ruins good work by his prolixity. Pylon is careless and overdone.

12 C[OOPER], M[ONTE]. Review of Pylon, Memphis Commercial Appeal (24 March), Section V, p. 3.
Pylon has "nervous vitality," and, only if because we are now used to Faulkner, is less shocking than his earlier work. There are excessive stylistic mannerisms, but the phantasmal nightmarish quality is well achieved.

13 COWLEY, MALCOLM. "Voodoo Dance," NRep (10 April), pp. 254-55.
Human passions dance to the rhythms of Faulkner's poetic prose in Pylon, a story with symbolic meaning, a "legend of contemporary life." The novel does not mean as much to the reader, however, as it must to the author.
Reprinted 1967.B23.

14 FADIMAN, CLIFTON. "Books--Medley," NY (30 March), pp. 73-74.
The reviewer gives six reasons for his disliking Pylon, among them the presence of excessive violence and too much Joycean wordplay.

15 FREDERICK, JOHN T. "New Techniques in the Novel," EJ, XXIV (May), 355-63.
Multiple point of view in As I Lay Dying and The Sound and the Fury is not to be blamed as a technique merely because these novels leave a poor impression; the style lacks variety.

16 HARNACK-FISCH, MILDRED. "William Faulkner: Ein Amerikanischer Dichter aus grosser Tradition," Die Literatur, XXXVIII, 64-67.
Faulkner's work is summarized in view of his place as one of the new American talents.

17   HATCHER, HARLAN. "Ultimate Extensions," Creating the Modern
      American Novel. New York: Farrar and Rinehart,
      pp. 234-43.
         Like other postwar writers, Faulkner applied the torch
      of violence to civil life; he is the "most brilliant" of
      the young writers of this generation. Faulkner's novels,
      through Pylon, receive an appreciative summary.

18   HUXLEY, JULIAN SORELL. "The Analysis of Fame: A Revelation
      of the Human Documents in Who's Who," SatR (11 May),
      pp. 12-13.
         Hemingway is in Who's Who 1935 but not Faulkner.

19   JOHNSON, GERALD W. "The Horrible South," VQR, XI (April),
      201-17.
         Since the mid-Twenties there has been a trend toward
      violence and depravity in Southern fiction. Faulkner's
      Sanctuary and As I Lay Dying, part of the phenomenon, are
      "tricks," but one still must admire the artfulness and
      shock value of Sanctuary.

20   JONES, HOWARD MUMFORD. "Social Notes on the South," VQR, XI
      (July), 452-57.
         Pylon is Faulkner imitating himself.

21   LINN, JAMES WEBER, and HOUGHTON WELLS TAYLOR, "Counterpoint:
      Light in August," A Foreword to Fiction. New York: Apple-
      ton-Century, pp. 144-57.
         Faulkner manipulates dramatic scenes, stream-of-con-
      sciousness passages, summary narrative, and monologue to
      achieve a constantly shifting point of view that moves the
      reader around the central objects of Light in August.
      Lena's story is in strong contrast to Joe's tragic flight,
      and the separate treatment of other characters creates a
      design which, like musical form, is a "meaning in itself."

22   McCOLE, CAMILLE. "The Nightmare Literature of William Faulk-
      ner," CathW, CXLI (August), 576-83.
         Faulkner's subject matter is obnoxious, his formal sense
      is weak, and his "dribbling stream-of-consciousness" is
      ineffective. He is part of a deplorable trend toward vio-
      lence and horror. Sartoris is his best work; The Sound
      and the Fury follows the "literary imposter" Joyce; the
      rest is gibberish and Faulkner a charlatan.
      Included in 1937.B13.

23   McGILL, RALPH. Review of Pylon, Atlanta Constitution
      (7 April), p. 8-B.
         Pylon is a horrible story, on a par with Faulkner's

1935

(McGILL, RALPH)
other violent, horrible books. The writing, however, is
exciting.

24   MADGE, CHARLES. "Time and Space in America," LonMerc, XXXII
(May), 83.
Faulkner is "impersonated" in Pylon by the "drunken
journalist." The book is a modern "tragedy of the Coper-
nican universe."

25   MASON, H. A. "American and English Earth," Scrutiny, IV
(June), 74-79.
Faulkner's aviators in Pylon have become superior beings
by virtue of the association with machines. The characters are not worth the author's attention.

26   O'BRIEN, EDWARD J. The Short Story Case Book. New York:
Farrar and Rinehart, pp. 324-61.
In a paragraph-by-paragraph commentary on "That Evening
Sun Go Down," the critic discusses the ironies, the por-
trait of the community, and the effectiveness of the nar-
rative point-of-view of the children.

27   O'FAOLAIN, SEAN. Review of Pylon, Spectator (19 April),
p. 668.
Faulkner's novels display a "misanthropic spirit and a
masochistic joy." Pylon shows him excited "beyond co-
herence," a "great talent driven to frenzy." Though one
of America's great writers, Faulkner has not learned to
control his powers.

28   QUENNELL, PETER. Review of As I Lay Dying, NewSt (5 October), pp. 453-54.
The critic laments his inability to appreciate an author
who is all the rage. He sees Faulkner as a "masochist in
prose," with an undisciplined mind. "As I Lay Dying is a
portentous and difficult volume."

29   RANSOM, JOHN CROWE. "Modern with the Southern Accent," VQR,
XI (April), 184-200.
In an overview of Southern writing, the reviewer contrasts Faulkner and Stark Young in a few paragraphs.
Faulkner is "the most exciting figure in our contemporary
literature just now," with a great breadth of subject and
theme. As I Lay Dying is quoted by way of illustration.

30   REDMAN, BEN RAY. "Flights of Fancy," SatR (30 March),
pp. 577, 581.

(REDMAN, BEN RAY)
Pylon demonstrates that Faulkner is "mannered, tricky, extremely clever," and a "talented sensationalist."

31   STALLINGS, LAWRENCE. "Gentleman from Mississippi," AMerc, XXXIV (April), 499-501.
There are three Faulkners: the comic genius of such pieces as "A Rose for Emily": the nostalgic local colorist, affectionate for the "gallantries of Thomas Nelson Page," of the Saturday Evening Post stories; and the overheated prose technician of Pylon, who still fascinates and beguiles.

32   TROY, WILLIAM. "And Tomorrow," Nation (3 April), p. 393.
The narrator of Pylon is like a caricature of the postwar generation's typical hero. Much the best Faulkner has written, the novel depicts the modern flight into action in appropriate terms and in a style compatible with the material.

33   *VAN DOREN, MARK. "A Story Written With Ether, Not Ink," NYHTB (24 March), p. 3.
A review of Pylon. Cited in Bassett 1972.A2, Item I64.

34   WARWICK, RAY. Review of Pylon, Atlanta Journal (14 April), Magazine Section, p. 12.
Lacking the depth and breadth of Light in August, Pylon is still a fast-moving yarn and brilliantly executed. The style renders the action as a dreamlike state, making it more vivid. Humor and illuminating minor incidents are used to good effect.

35   WEEKS, EDWARD. "Atlantic Bookshelf," AtlM, CLV (June), 16, 18.
The reviewer praises the "tough good humor" and realism of Pylon, but does not like the Joycean wordplay or the sexual episodes.

1936 A   BOOKS - NONE

1936 B   SHORTER WRITINGS

1   ANON. "Reviewing Reviews," SatR (5 December), p. 58.
The contrary opinions elicited by Faulkner's Absalom, Absalom! in the New York media are surveyed.

1936

2   BOYNTON, PERCY H.   Literature and American Life.   Boston:
        Ginn & Co., pp. 862–63.
            Faulkner has felt the influence of Anderson and Stein.
        As I Lay Dying and The Sound and the Fury "reach the
        abysses frequented by Jeffers." Sanctuary is "cynicism
        raised to a high power" and means nothing.

3   BREUIL, ROGER. "William Faulkner: Lumière d'août," Esprit,
        I (January), 612–14.
            Faulkner depicts man as violent, moved by forces he does
        not understand, confronted with destruction and yet able
        to remain man. He can bear anything. Light in August is
        an illustration.

4   CAMERON, MAY. "An Interview with Thomas Wolfe," Press Time--
        A Book of Post Classics. New York: Books, Inc.,
        pp. 247–52.
            Thomas Wolfe says, "I have met both Hemingway and Faulk-
        ner and my own deep feeling is that neither has begun to
        reach full maturity." Faulkner has not begun to use his
        knowledge; he deals too much with "the horrible and the
        demented." The Sound and the Fury and As I Lay Dying are
        discussed.

5   CANBY, HENRY SEIDEL. "The School of Cruelty," Seven Years'
        Harvest. New York: Farrar and Rinehart, pp. 77–83.
        Reprints 1931.B12.

6   *COINDREAU, MAURICE E. "William Faulkner y su último gran
        libro," La Nación (13 December), section two, p. 1.
            According to Chapman (1966.B11, p. 136) Coindreau calls
        Absalom, Absalom! Faulkner's most difficult book: "es un
        vasto poema bárbaro."

7   COWLEY, MALCOLM. "Poe in Mississippi," NRep (4 November),
        p. 22.
            Faulkner may be ranked with the novelists and writers
        of effect, from Byron to Baudelaire and including "Monk"
        Lewis, E. T. A. Hoffman, and Poe. In this vein, Absalom,
        Absalom! is one of Faulkner's most unified books. It is
        Poe modified by Joyce and Freud. The reviewer interprets
        the novel symbolically and finds that it falls short of
        its potential; he deprecates the excessive style.

8   DeVOTO, BERNARD. "Witchcraft in Mississippi," SatR (31 Octo-
        ber), p. 3.
            Faulkner's style in Absalom, Absalom!, based on "approx-
        imations," is "the most expert in contemporary American

(DeVOTO, BERNARD)
fiction," yet his characterization and motivation remain
mysterious. Faulkner is apparently a mystic, practicing
fictional witchcraft rather than writing conventional novels. His novels have no meaning.
Reprinted 1940.B6.

9   FADIMAN, CLIFTON. "Faulkner: Extra-Special, Double-Dis-
tilled," NY (31 October), pp. 62-64.
The reviewer gives a parodic summary of the plot of
Absalom, Absalom!

10 HENDERSON, PHILIP. "William Faulkner," The Novel Today.
London: John Lane, pp. 147-50.
Death is Faulkner's central theme, depravity his obses-
sion, cheap cleverness his forte.

11 LARBAUD, VALÉRY. "Un roman de William Faulkner. Tandis que
j'agonise," Ce vice impuni, la lecture. Domaine anglais.
Paris: Gallimard, pp. 218-22.
Reprints 1934.B16.

12 LAWTON, MARY. "Different," Atlanta Constitution (23 November), Magazine Section, p. 9.
In Absalom, Absalom! Faulkner's "usual themes" are done
up in a confusing structure and style. It is about incest
and miscegenation. Perhaps he is forcing himself to be
different. The story remains compelling.

13 [LOVATI, GEORGIO]. "Faulkner, Soldati, and America," Living
Age, CLI (September), 71-72.
A reprint of the Lovati piece, source undisclosed. Not
a pure realist, Faulkner still captures the "spirit and
flavor" of American life, as in Sanctuary and Light in
August--the puritanical, money-grubbing obsessions and the
abolition of all but money values. America has deformed
him. A truer picture of the country is in Mario Soldati's
America, My First Love.

14 PASCHAL, WALTER. Review of Absalom, Absalom!, Atlanta Journal
(8 November), Magazine Section, p. 12.
Absalom, Absalom! is a vindictive moral allegory about
the South, blind to its own evil, breeding its own destruction. Hewing to the line--unlike Joyce's tangential devel-
opment--Faulkner has made the first advance in the stream
of the novel since Proust.

1936

15   PATERSON, ISABEL. "An Unquiet Ghost Out of the Old South,"
      NYHTB (25 October), p. 3.
          Faulkner's nightmare world is again evoked in Absalom,
      Absalom!, and here the ghost emerges to tell her tale.
      Sutpen is doomed, if for no other reason than that "two of
      his sons" are offspring of mulatto women. Faulkner is a
      "manichaean" for whom evil exists.

16   ROUECHÉ, BERTON. Review of Absalom, Absalom!, UKCR, III
      (Winter), 137-38.
          It is doubtful that Absalom, Absalom! will win many
      readers for Faulkner; it is filled with "repetition, mod-
      ification, verbosity and a shambling sense of time," with
      all the perversion and brutality he can imagine.

17   STRAUSS, HAROLD. "Mr. Faulkner is Ambushed in Words," NYTBR
      (1 November), p. 7.
          Faulkner's "tenebrous mind" has created an amazingly in-
      direct narrative, touching once again on the "psycho-
      pathology of sex." Quentin and his roommate weave unwea-
      rily to veil the story in obscurity. It is a puzzle.

18   TROY, WILLIAM. "The Poetry of Doom," Nation (31 October),
      pp. 524-25.
          Absalom, Absalom! must be read like the most subjective
      lyric poetry. The story, told through at least a "half-
      dozen voices," is always in Faulkner's later prose style.
      It is ambitiously conceived and executed, and it is uni-
      versal rather than simply Southern, but it suffers from
      the limitations of Faulkner's vision of the complexity of
      the human soul.

1937 A   BOOKS - NONE

1937 B   SHORTER WRITINGS

1   ANON. "Doom in Mississippi," TLS (20 February), p. 128.
          Faulkner presents "life as frustration, as decay, as
      evil," and does so in a special uncompromising way, re-
      fracting his narrative through several points of view,
      each of them a little dream-haunted. For all its crudi-
      ties and difficulties, however, the story in Absalom, Ab-
      salom! lives, often beautifully.

2   ANON. "Best Novel Still Unwritten, Faulkner Admits at Ox-
      ford," Memphis Commercial Appeal (18 November), p. 13.
          Faulkner gives his impressions of Hollywood and popular

(ANON.)
novels like Gone With the Wind and Anthony Adverse, which
he has not read; he announces The Unvanquished.
Reprinted 1968.A6.

3   BROWN, STERLING. "William Faulkner," The Negro in American
Fiction. Washington, D. C.: Associates in Negro Folk
Education, pp. 177-79.
Faulkner's Negro characters in Sartoris and The Sound
and the Fury are convincing and "miles away from the plantation tradition menials." Joe Christmas is a memorable
creation. As a naturalist, Faulkner presents black and
white in a harsh light. His Negro characters have a
"surly understanding" of their bitter lives in a hostile
South.

4   COINDREAU, MAURICE E. "Absalon, Absalon! par William Faulkner," NRF, XLVIII (January), 123-26.
Absalom, Absalom! is not one with So Red the Rose and
Gone With the Wind; it is the agony of a civilization symbolized by the slow failure of the house of Sutpen and the
frightful legacy which it leaves. Three narrators question Quentin Compson in order to reveal the story. Inspired by his father's letter, Miss Rosa's death, and his
roommate's speculations, Quentin launches a "divination
du temps perdu" in order to explain Sutpen, his family,
and the South.

5   _____. "France and the Contemporary Novel," UKCR, III
(No. 4), 273-79.
In an unpublished French text, translated here by
Madeline Ashton, Coindreau says that the French have found
Faulkner interesting--and he has translated him--because
he depicts a complete and real world, a requisite for the
French reader, and because of his equally admirable psycho-
logical acuteness.
Reprinted 1971.B18.

6   _____. "Panorama de la actual literatura joven norte-
americana," Sur, VII (March), 49-65.
Faulkner is the chief writer of his generation. He is
a disciple of Anderson, and he is noted chiefly for his
psychological insight and technical mastery. A puritan,
he fills his work with the horrors, fears, and consequences of sin. His technique depends on musical form and
the puzzle.

1937

7   COLUM, MAY M. "Life and Literature...Faulkner's Struggle
with Technique," Forum and Century, XCVII (January), 35-36.
    Faulkner's skill with language is evident, but the form
is "incoherent." His novels are disturbing "because they
give us the sense that human beings will never be satis-
fied with anything that society can give them." If Faulkner had a café table where he could thrash out his ideas,
he would be a better writer. Southern novels seem to have
a greater sense of complex, tragic inner life than others
from America. The reviewer points out some biblical parallels in Absalom, Absalom!

8   FAŸ, BERNARD. "L'école de l'infortune," Revue de Paris, XXIV
[Massey 1968.A4, item 1453.], 654-61.
    Quoting "A Rose for Emily" at length, the critic empha-
sizes the way Faulkner's work assaults the senses and argues that Faulkner's obscurities are deliberate.

9   GREENE, GRAHAM. "The Furies in Mississippi," LonMerc, XXXV
(March), 517-18.
    Faulkner's historical novels are full of "bogus romance."
Absalom, Absalom! specifically has no real characters,
though it does impart a "new sense of spiritual evil."
The excessive style obscures the absence of theme. It is,
nevertheless, a welcome change from popular fiction.

10   LAWS, FREDERICK. Review of Absalom, Absalom!, NewSt, XIII
(6 March), 380.
    Unlike Joyce, whose method Faulkner does not use, Faulk-
ner does not justify his all-inclusiveness by either the
quality of his writing or the quality of his intelligence.
Absalom, Absalom! is very obscure.

11   Le BRETON, MAURICE. "Technique et psychologie chez William
Faulkner," EA, I (September), 418-38.
    Faulkner involves us in his fiction by his technique;
Absalom, Absalom! is an example of his practice.

12   LOGGINS, VERNON. "William Faulkner," I Hear America...
Literature in the United States Since 1900. New York:
Crowell, pp. 109-12.
    Faulkner is an entertainer, an "artist of escape," whose
psychology cannot be taken seriously. He has one-upped
Poe because "he fought in the most brutal war known to history." A master story-teller, he writes not like an angel
but like a demon.

13   McCOLE, CAMILLE. "William Faulkner: Cretins, Coffin-Worms,
        and Cruelty," <u>Lucifer at Large</u>. New York: Longmans,
        pp. 203-28.
            Perversion, violence and pathology dominate Faulkner's
        work; his style is often obscure. A list of his abnormal
        characters proves the degree of his obsession, but he can
        create and he often writes with humor. Includes material
        from 1935.B22.

14   MULLER, HERBERT JOSEPH. <u>Modern Fiction: A Study of Values</u>.
        New York: Funk and Wagnalls, pp. 405-07.
            Faulkner may be ranked among the "curiosities" of liter-
        ature, despite his brilliance, because recent work (<u>Pylon</u>
        and <u>Absalom, Absalom!</u>) is merely exploitng Grand Guignol
        horrors.

15   PARKS, EDD WINFIELD. "Six Southern Novels," <u>VQR</u>, XIII (Win-
        ter), 154-60.
            Sutpen, in <u>Absalom, Absalom!</u>, is presented convincingly
        and in great complexity. Faulkner may never be popular,
        but his excellence is evident.
            Reprinted <u>Segments of Southern Thought</u> (Baltimore:
        Waverly Press, 1938), pp. 129-30.

16   PLOMER, WILLIAM. "Fiction," <u>Spectator</u> (26 February), p. 376.
            Faulkner is a fictional Jeremiah, thriving on the woes
        of his miasmal South. The plot of <u>Absalom, Absalom!</u> is
        not clear, but apparently the House of Sutpen falls be-
        cause of some dark involvement with miscegenation.

17   SMITH, HENRY NASH. "Notes on Recent Novels," <u>SoR</u>, II (Win-
        ter), 577-93.
            Devoting three paragraphs of a compendium review to <u>Ab-
        salom, Absalom!</u>, the reviewer finds Faulkner's world to be
        a vacuum inhabited by distorted characters, but his South
        remains real and mysterious, a place that can be both
        loved and hated.

<u>1938 A   BOOKS - NONE</u>

<u>1938 B   SHORTER WRITINGS</u>

1   ANON. "War in Tennessee," <u>TLS</u> (14 May), p. 333.
            First choice as fiction of the week, <u>The Unvanquished</u> is
        seen as a simpler, more episodic novel than Faulkner's
        previous work. It portrays the consequences of violence,
        often using the "oracular" language Faulkner found neces-
        sary.

1938

2   BIRNEY, EARLE. "The Two William Faulkners," <u>Canadian Forum</u>,
       XVIII (June), 84–85.
       A "stylized and morbid mystic" and a "sharp and bril-
       liant narrator of short stories" struggle within Faulkner.
       His novels do not stand alone, but must be read in connec-
       tion. He handles action as in the short story and employs
       theme only in the context of the larger Yoknapatawpha
       epic. <u>The Unvanquished</u> falls between two stools, since it
       is made of stories revised out of shape to make the larger
       book.

3   BOYLE, KAY. "Tattered Banners," <u>NRep</u> (19 March), pp. 136–37.
       There are two Faulkners--the Southerner and the man with
       European experience--and between them they "possess the
       strength and the vulnerability which belong only to the
       greatest artists." He is best seen whole, in terms of the
       total canon. He ranks with the most ambitious, hard-work-
       ing, and enduring artists. <u>The Unvanquished</u> is reviewed.

4   BUTTITA, ANTHONY. "William Faulkner: That Writin' Man of
       Oxford," <u>SatR</u> (21 May), pp. 6–8.
       The writer recounts a visit to Oxford, mixing biography
       and such misinformation as a reference to Faulkner's
       "four-year-old boy, Joe" and to <u>Mississippi: A Guide to
       the Nutmeg State</u>.

5   CALVERTON, V. F. "William Faulkner: Southerner at Large,"
       <u>Modern Monthly</u>, X (March), 11–12.
       "William J. Faulkner" interests the English because he
       is so completely American. He is Hardyesque in his atten-
       tion to detail.

6   COINDREAU, MAURICE E. "La guerra civil y la novela norte-
       americana," <u>La Nación</u> (20 November), section two, p. 1.
       The Faulkner novel most suitable for a general reader-
       ship, <u>The Unvanquished</u> is also a very artistic piece of
       work.

7   _____. "Préface pour <u>Le Bruit et la fureur</u>," <u>La vie réelle</u>,
       IV, 83–87.
       The novel is discussed in musical terms, by "movements."
       Coindreau also draws on conversations with Faulkner about
       the composition of the book. Printed with the translation
       (Paris: Gallimard, 1938); reprinted, translated, 1966.B12
       and 1971.B18.

8   DeVOTO, BERNARD. "Faulkner's South," <u>SatR</u> (19 February),
       p. 5.
       The stories of <u>The Unvanquished</u> are good magazine

1938

(DeVOTO, BERNARD)
fiction but nothing more. The reviewer somewhat face-
tiously notes that these stories clear up obscurities or
ambiguities in earlier novels.

9   FADIMAN, CLIFTON. "An Old Hand and Two New Ones," NY
     (19 February), pp. 60-61.
     Is Faulkner the "Rube Goldberg of the American novel"?
     The Unvanquished is his "most Confederate book." It takes
     an act of the will to read him.

10   HOWARD, BRIAN. Review of The Unvanquished, NewSt, XV
     (14 May), 844, 846.
     There "is no better writer in America," though The Un-
     vanquished is "one of those small, violent" novels which
     one reads easily. Faulkner has not altogether resisted
     the temptation of the purple patch.

11   KORN, KARL. "Moira und Schuld," NRs, No. 49 (December), 603-09.
     The reviewer summarizes the plot of Absalom, Absalom!

12   KRONENBERGER, LOUIS. "Faulkner's Dismal Swamp," Nation
     (19 February), pp. 213-14.
     Bayard's "substitution of moral for physical bravura"
     does not answer the questions which The Unvanquished
     raises. The book seems as "willful, cluttered, sunless"
     as any of Faulkner's books, though superficially simpler.
     The South is a swamp which is swallowing Faulkner's un-
     doubted talent.

13   LOCKHART, JACK. Review of The Unvanquished, Memphis Commer-
     cial Appeal (27 February), Section IV, p. 9.
     The Unvanquished is a conventionally told story of
     Southern chivalry with a sympathy and humor new in Faulk-
     ner.

14   SARTRE, JEAN-PAUL. "Sartoris, par W. Faulkner," NRF, L (Feb-
     ruary), 323-28.
     Faulkner's machinations are visible in Sartoris, as
     they are not in Light in August, which is so organic it
     is critically impenetrable. Faulkner's chief character-
     istic is "disloyalty"--withholding, deceiving, playing
     upon the effect he achieves thereby.
     Reprinted 1947.B8; reprinted, translated, 1952.B47 and
     1955.B51.

15   SCHNEIDER-SCHELDE, RUDOLF. Review of Absalom, Absalom!,
     Literatur, XL (July), 693-94.
     Faulkner has three books--Light in August, Pylon, and

1938

(SCHNEIDER-SCHELDE, RUDOLF)
Absalom, Absalom!--now in German; each is more difficult
than the one before. Perhaps he is wrong to write so ob-
scurely.

16   YOUNG, STARK. "New Year's Craw," NRep (12 January),
pp. 283-84.
Young seeks to correct an earlier NRep article, which he
mistakenly attributes to Hamilton Basso [it was R. M.
Lovett, "Sherwood Anderson," NRep (25 November 1936), pp.
103-05], by reporting that credit for "discovering" Faulkner should go to Phil Stone of Oxford, not Anderson, and
he explains how Stone brought Faulkner to Young's attention, how Faulkner met Elizabeth Prall, who married Anderson, and the results.

1939 A BOOKS - NONE

1939 B SHORTER WRITINGS

1   ANON. "When the Dam Breaks," Time (23 January), pp. 45-46,
48.
A cover story on Faulkner and The Wild Palms sees parallels or contrasts between the two elements of the novel
(although the author believes that "Old Man" comes first),
sets down biographical information on Faulkner, including
his war service in France, and refers to his stories of
the "Swopes" family.

2   ANON. "Mississippi Tragedy," TLS (18 March), p. 161.
First choice as novel of the week, The Wild Palms is in
Faulkner's characteristically intoxicating style, which
for all its difficulty has the value of evoking what it
describes. The power and excitement of the book is unde-
niable, though the morals are deplorable. The parallel
stories run in opposite directions. Harry "gratefully
accepts" cyanide at the end.

3   AIKEN, CONRAD. "William Faulkner: The Novel as Form," AtlM,
CLXIV (November), 650-54.
After remarking on some of Faulkner's excesses and the
difficulties of his prose style, Aiken discusses briefly
the effectiveness of that style, its ability to immerse
one in the novel, its functionalism and beauty. Faulkner
seeks an uninterrupted flow of the moving present moment.
The Wild Palms ranks with Faulkner's best work. Faulkner
is distinguished by his concern with form, which may be
discussed by analogy to music--the symphony, the fugue.
Reprinted 1951.A2, 1951.B2, 1958.B2, 1960.A1, 1966.A8,
1973.A9.

4   *A[MRINE], M[IKE]. "William Faulkner Here Has Good Word for
        His Homeland," New Orleans Item (5 April), Section I, p.
        1. Cited in Bassett (1972.A2), Item DD8.
            Paraphrasing remarks by Faulkner, the reporter hears
        Faulkner saying that the South is more artistic than the
        North and that The Wild Palms was written as two novels
        and then shuffled together (compare Faulkner's quoted re-
        marks on the same subject in 1956.B44).
        Reprinted 1968.A6.

5   BANNING, MARGARET CULKIN. "Changing Moral Standards in Fic-
        tion," SatR (1 July), pp. 3-4, 14.
            The Wild Palms has opened formerly forbidden areas in
        its frank treatment of sexuality. Its lack of popular
        success cannot be attributed to subject matter, which is
        the kind of shocking thing that ought to sell; perhaps it
        is due to Faulkner's philosophy or to the difficulty of
        the book.

6   BENTLEY, PHYLLIS. "I Look At American Fiction," SatR
        (13 May), pp. 3-4, 14-15.
            Faulkner's prose is "fire and smoke," and, to an English-
        woman, his world is lurid. His work fails of greatness
        because it lacks universality.

7   BISHOP, JOHN PEALE. "Myth and Modern Literature," SatR (22
        July), pp. 3-4, 14.
            Comparing the flourishing of writing in the South to the
        Irish Renaissance, the author points out the role played
        by consciousness of a heroic age and the contradictory
        concentration upon the essential cruelty of life in Cald-
        well and Faulkner, who engage in anti-Romanticism and ex-
        plode the myth of the Old South. If Faulkner damns the
        South, he damns man's inhumanity; if he praises it, he
        praises the humane tradition.

8   CALVERTON, V. F. "Steinbeck, Hemingway, and Faulkner," Mod-
        ern Quarterly, X (March), 36-44.
            Faulkner is a realist without profundity. His recent
        work, The Unvanquished and The Wild Palms, is not marred
        by phoney tricks.

9   CHAMBERLAIN, JOHN. "The New Books," Harper's, CLXXVIII (Feb-
        ruary), unnumbered advertising pages.
            The Wild Palms is two novels "put together in an arbi-
        trarily contrived jumble." It exhibits all Faulkner's
        "merits and defects." "Old Man" may be an unintentional
        political allegory.

1939

10   COWLEY, MALCOLM. "Sanctuary," NRep (25 January), p. 349.
        The two plots of The Wild Palms are related allegorical-
      ly, by contrast: some people will fight and die to create
      their own world, while others will perform prodigies to
      escape freedom itself. The convict is a fascist. When
      Faulkner tries to explain emotion, his prose is too rich;
      these passages would be better in verse.

11   DUESBERG, JACQUES. "'Le bruit et le tumulte' de William
      Faulkner," Revue générale (15 December), pp. 834-41.
        Quoting and summarizing extensively, the reviewer com-
      plains of the contrast between the "poetry of the first
      two sections and the prosaic character of the last two
      sections of The Sound and the Fury.

12   FADIMAN, CLIFTON. "Mississippi Frankenstein," NY (21 Janu-
      ary), pp. 60-61.
        The net effect of The Wild Palms is not memorable; it is
      a case of excessive imagination. The reviewer prefers the
      love story.

13   GARDNER, JENNIE B. Review of The Wild Palms, Memphis Commer-
      cial Appeal (22 January), Section IV, p. 9.
        Though his money may come from Hollywood and the New
      York market, Faulkner's talent and his standards do not.
      His books are all interesting and independent. The Wild
      Palms dramatizes the fate which dogs a couple who violate
      the creative life, a tragic love story which is alternated
      with "the most amazing original odyssey of our recent lit-
      erature." The reviewer would still prefer each story un-
      der separate covers.

14   JACK, PETER MUNRO. "Mr. Faulkner's Clearest Novel," NYTBR
      (22 January), p. 2.
        Though the reviewer discerns that Faulkner means "Wild
      Palms" to be the main story, he treats "Old Man," in The
      Wild Palms, as if it were predominant.

15   HERRON, IMA HONAKER. "William Faulkner," The Small Town in
      American Literature. Durham, N. C.: Duke University
      Press, pp. 416-22.
        Among the "crusaders and skeptics" who have treated the
      small town fictionally, Faulkner has a morbid outlook but
      a lively sensibility of all the dimensions of his subject.
      Reprinted New York: Pageant Books, 1959.

16   KAZIN, ALFRED. "A Study in Conscience," NYHTB (22 January),
      p. 2.
        The "ghost" that haunts Faulkner does not wear a

1939

(KAZIN, ALFRED)
Confederate uniform; it haunted Thomas Wolfe in Brooklyn and Kay Boyle in Paris. Faulkner's interest in life "begins past the last stage of normal disillusionment." The two stories of The Wild Palms are parts of a single narrative on the theme of flight. Despite "soggy writing," the book "crackles with life." The ending, with both men in prison, seems appropriate as a metaphor for all Faulkner's characters.

17 Le BRETON, MAURICE. Review of The Wild Palms, EA, III (July-September), 313-14.
The Wild Palms depicts "l'éternelle énigme de l'homme en présence de la femme" in two series of alternating and contrasted images. Both Harry and the convict are driven by the need for expiation. Faulkner's puritanism is plain.

18 LIND, LEVI ROBERT. "The Crisis in Literature," SR, XLVII (January-March), 35-62.
Writing on the "decline" of literature, the author finds Faulkner the "least constructive" of "cult of cruelty" writers like Hemingway and Jeffers. His art is warped, sterile.

19 LOVETT, ROBERT MORSS. "Ferocious Faulkner," Nation (4 February), p. 153.
The reviewer notes comparison and contrast between the two plots of The Wild Palms, granting the symmetry of the arrangement, but suggesting that the book is, in essence, nihilistic, a picture of the "grim cosmic ferocity of nature against which the pitiful melodrama of human life" is acted out.

20 McILWAINE, SHIELDS. "Naturalistic Modes: The Gothic, the Ribald, and the Tragic--William Faulkner and Erskine Caldwell," The Southern Poor-White from Lubberland to Tobacco Road. Norman, Okla.: University of Oklahoma Press, pp. 217-40.
Faulkner and Caldwell have brought attention to the poor-white character by focusing coldly on his violence, sexuality, low intelligence. As I Lay Dying, perhaps an example of "modernistic trickery," is the chief source.

21 MAIR, JOHN. Review of The Wild Palms, NewSt, XVII (18 March), p. 427.
Faulkner is a classicist in tragedy, but The Wild Palms is a "trick" novel where the alternating plots do not achieve any valuable effects. The love story is unbeliev-

1939

(MAIR, JOHN)
able. The river story contains some of Faulkner's best
writing.

22   MAXWELL, ALLEN. "The Wild Palms," SWR, XXIV (April), 357-60.
The Wild Palms succeeds despite the difficult style.
The parts of the book are the stuff of two novels sliced
into alternate chapters. It is the best Faulkner has done
in years.

23   MELLERS, W. H. "Hollywooden Hero," Scrutiny, VIII (December),
335-44.
In a review of Hemingway's work, the critic devotes half
a page to Faulkner as more mannered and artificial, though
representing a view of life no less "banal" than Hemingway.
Faulkner's experiments are "factitious" and his imagination chaotic.

24   *MOK, MICHEL. "The Squire of Oxford," New York Post (17 Octo-
ber), p. 9.
The "beardless Dostoievsky of the cane-brakes" talks
about Snopeses, includes anecdotes that would appear in
The Town, and tells a tale about his Hollywood experience.
Reprinted 1968.A6.

25   O'BRIEN, KATE. "Fiction," Spectator (14 April), pp. 645-46.
The "heat and turgid violence" of The Wild Palms is only
worsened by the echo arrangement of the two plots. "Old
Man" is the better. It is a stormy book choked with words.

26   O'DONNELL, GEORGE MARION. "Faulkner's Mythology," KR, I (Summer), 285-99.
The "Southern social-economic-ethical tradition" is the
principle of unity in Faulkner's books, which are mythic
renderings of the conflict between that tradition and the
forces of modernity. The critic introduces the Sartoris/
Snopes dichotomy and discusses its presence in selected
novels through The Wild Palms. He allegorizes Sanctuary
as the rape of Southern womanhood by amoral Modernism.
Reprinted 1951.A2, 1960.A1, 1966.A8, 1973.A9.

27   REDMAN, BEN RAY. "Faulkner's Double Novel," SatR (21 January), p. 5.
The stories of The Wild Palms are related only by being
printed between the same covers. The love story and its
characters are high-pitched but believable; the story of
the convict is a "strangely monochordic" tall tale. Neither story gains by the juxtaposition. Though the style

(REDMAN, BEN RAY)
    generally serves Faulkner well, there are deplorable
    lapses and duffel-bag sentences.

28   SARTRE, JEAN-PAUL. "A propos de 'Le Bruit et la Fureur': la
       temporalité chez Faulkner," NRF, LII (June), 1057-61; LIII
       (July), 147-51.
       Faulkner's metaphysic conceives Time as man's misfortune
    and the present as a creeping catastrophe. Man views
    events like one looking backward from a moving vehicle--
    his life is a fatality he cannot and will not look at.
    For Faulkner, there is no future, a serious flaw in his
    philosophy which leaves man no prospect.
    Reprinted 1947.B7; translated 1951.A2, 1955.B52, 1960.A1,
    and 1966.A8.

29   SPENCER, BENJAMIN T. "Wherefore This Southern Fiction?" SR,
       XLVII (October-December), 500-13.
       Faulkner "most brilliantly" expresses violence and con-
    fusion in modern Southern life. Though not appreciated by
    the Agrarians, he is an ally of theirs.

30   STEGNER, WALLACE. "Conductivity in Fiction," VQR, XV (Sum-
       mer), 443-47.
       No one writing can evoke a violent scene like Faulkner.
    The orchestration of the two stories of The Wild Palms is
    justifiable. Reading Faulkner is "like taking hold of an
    electrified fence."

31   STEVENS, GEORGE. "Wild Palms and Ripe Olives," SatR (11 Feb-
       ruary), p. 8.
       An editorial on the vagaries of book reviewing uses The
    Wild Palms as an example of a book about which there are
    radically opposite opinions. Current reviews are quoted.

1940 A BOOKS - NONE

1940 B SHORTER WRITINGS

1   ANON. "Village Napoleon," TLS (21 September), p. 481.
       Faulkner is "more nearly unreadable" in The Hamlet than
    ever before, obscure when not merely "silly."

2   BENÉT, STEPHEN VINCENT. "Flem Snopes and His Kin," SatR
       (6 April), p. 7.
       Reading The Hamlet is like listening to backwoods gossip,
    tall tales, and commentary on human motives. The style is
    frequently superb, the form well orchestrated.

1940

3   BOYNTON, PERCY. <u>America in Contemporary Fiction</u>. Chicago:
     University of Chicago Press, pp. 103-12.
        In his chapter on "The Retrospective South," the author
     sees Faulkner as a variant Agrarian, writing of the gen-
     try's defeat by the hateful poor whites. The emphasis on
     the poor white has led, in turn, to a general concern with
     degeneracy and "ultimate forms of decadence" in the other
     novels. He admits Faulkner's technical skill but wonders
     whether there is any lasting substance to his content.

4   CASH, WILBUR J. "Literature and the South," <u>SatR</u> (28 Decem-
     ber), pp. 3-4, 18-19.
        An excerpt from <u>The Mind of the South</u> (1941.B7) on the
     growth of Southern literature considers Faulkner, with
     Wolfe and Caldwell, to be reacting against his region.
     Though he has been "to school to the Middle Westerners and
     the Russians and to Joyce," Faulkner still has in his
     style something distinctly Southern.

5   COWLEY, MALCOLM. "Faulkner by Daylight," <u>NRep</u> (15 April),
     p. 510.
        A "new sort of novel," <u>The Hamlet</u> is discursive and easy
     to read, not, like Faulkner's earlier work, based on the
     plantation legend of aristocratic guilt and defeat. He has
     come from the Gothic gloom into daylight--his book has
     "friendliness."
     Reprinted 1967.B23.

6   DeVOTO, BERNARD. "Witchcraft in Mississippi," <u>Minority Re-
     port</u>. Boston: Little, Brown, pp. 209-18.
     Reprinted from 1936.B8.

7   FADIMAN, CLIFTON. "Horrors, Charm, Fun," <u>NY</u> (6 April), p. 73.
        <u>The Hamlet</u> is "Grade B Faulkner," in a style that is
     overdone.

8   HAWKINS, DESMOND. "New Novels," <u>NewSt</u> (28 September),
     pp. 312-14.
        Of the Big Name novelists, only Faulkner has remained
     fully committed to his form. <u>The Hamlet</u> is characteristic
     of his gifts and his faults. Its structure is weak--parts
     having been previously published--and he exhausts his
     characters in overwriting. The novel remains a piece of
     virtuosity against which the usual run of novels seems
     pale.

9   KRONENBERGER, LOUIS. "The World of William Faulkner," <u>Na-
     tion</u>, CL (13 April), pp. 481-82.
        <u>The Hamlet</u> is magnificent poetry, but of the senses

1940

(KRONENBERGER, LOUIS)
only, not the emotions; its humor robs events of their horror. "Mr. Faulkner's forte, like that of the South he inhabits, is decay." The Snopeses are too bad to be believable; there is no pity in the book.

10   McILWAINE, SHIELDS. Review of The Hamlet, Memphis Commercial
      Appeal (14 April), Section IV, p. 10.
        Humorous and in a more even style than Faulkner's usual
      one, The Hamlet presents a deeper view than his earlier
      work of the poor white and introduces a new settlement,
      Frenchman's Bend. There is still an episode too rough for
      most readers, but Faulkner's achievement--after 16 books
      in 16 years--is undoubted.

11   MILLETT, FRED B. Contemporary American Authors. New York:
      Harcourt Brace, pp. 34, 96, 346-48.
        Among other biographical revelations, the author says
      that Faulkner read Elizabethan poetry at Oxford University.

12   PARKES, H. B. "The American Cultural Scene: (IV) The Novel,"
      Scrutiny, IX (June), 2-8.
        Faulkner has an original talent but no point of view.
      His stylistic tricks and preoccupation with violence are
      exaggerated to absurdity in recent books.

13   PICON, GAËTAN. "Treize histoires, par William Faulkner,"
      Cahiers du Sud, XVII (Winter), 133-36.
        The stories of These 13 are authentically Faulkner;
      everything is irremediable (See 1933.B13).

14   RASCOE, BURTON. "Faulkner's New York Critics," AMerc,
      L (June), 243-47.
        Rascoe satirizes Milton Rugoff's review of The Hamlet
      (1940.B15) for its overdone prose--what Rascoe calls
      "Adamic verse"--and "quasi-intellectual" viewpoint of the
      typical New York critic toward both Faulkner and the
      South. The trouble with these critics is that they take
      Ratliff's tall tales in The Hamlet literally--believing,
      for example, that one can really blow up a horse with a
      bicycle pump.

15   RUGOFF, MILTON. "Out of Faulkner's Bag," NYHTB (31 March),
      p. 4.
        Faulkner's Southern "Jukes and Kallikaks," the Snopeses,
      are repulsively reptilian. The Hamlet is typically Faulk-
      ner, with humor added. The prose is obscure, but the
      style and vision are compelling. See reply, 1940.B14.

1940

16   SMITH, JANET ADA. "New Novels," Spectator (27 September),
        pp. 323-24.
            Faulkner has "an unusual gift for presenting an idiot's
        view of the world." The Hamlet depicts loosely connected
        scenes in a "Kentucky village" at the end of the century.
        The Snopeses have a "terrifying Puritan individualism."
        The book is boring.

17   STEGNER, WALLACE. "The New Novels," VQR, XVI (Summer), 459-
        65.
            Despite structural disjointedness. The Hamlet is Faulk-
        ner at his best.

18   STRAUSS, HAROLD. "Mr. Faulkner's Family of Poor Whites,"
        NYTBR (7 April), p. 2.
            "The Hamlet is meant to describe the long, slow, wary,
        losing fight" of Frenchman's Bend against the Snopeses.
        As a whole unconnected, the novel has rich moments and
        raw humor.

1941 A BOOKS - NONE

1941 B SHORTER WRITINGS

1   BEACH, JOSEPH WARREN. "American Letters Between Wars," CE,
        III (October), 1-12.
            Faulkner and Thomas Wolfe are "exceptions" to much of
        the "interbellum" literature Beach discusses. Both ex-
        hibit "a kind of fierce paganism," along with a fierce and
        pitiless realism, that makes them contemporary with the
        less rhetorical authors of their time.

2   BECK, WARREN. "Faulkner's Point of View," CE, II (May),
        736-49.
            Much Faulkner criticism is misguided, naive, erroneous,
        or otherwise inadequate to perceive and appreciate Faulk-
        ner's moral vision of the human potential for good and
        evil. Faulkner's best characters struggle against the
        folly and vice of this world, including the acts which
        they themselves often commit. His worst characters drama-
        tize an "apocalyptic vision of sin and its complex conse-
        quences." A "virile" criticism will recognize Faulkner's
        humanity and rationality and go on to explicate his
        sources and their brilliant technical adumbration.
        Reprinted CE, XXII (November 1960), 86-93.

3   _____. "Faulkner and the South," AR, I (March), 82-94.

(BECK, WARREN)
Beck summarizes and estimates the extent and manner of
Faulkner's treatment of Southern materials in the novels.
He sees no easy symbolism and discerns no uncritical nos-
talgia in Faulkner's work. Translated into French,
1959.B11.

4 _____. "William Faulkner's Style," AmPref, VI (Spring),
195-211.
Using examples from "Spotted Horses" and The Hamlet; The
Wild Palms; Pylon; Sanctuary; Absalom, Absalom!; The Unvanquished and other works, Beck demonstrates the diversity, adaptability, richness, and accuracy of Faulkner's
prose style. Style and point of view are closely related
in Faulkner's work; the style thus also reflects the mysteries and obscurities which Faulkner depicts in his fiction.
Reprinted 1951.A2, 1960.A1, 1966.A8, 1973.A9; translated
into French in 1959.B12.

5 BROOKS, VAN WYCK. "Fashions in Defeatism," SatR (22 March),
pp. 3-4, 14.
Faulkner, along with Hemingway, Dos Passos, and Farrell,
is an example of the pessimistic writer who dramatizes the
age's despair. The essay is excerpted from On American
Literature (New York: Dutton, 1941).

6 CARGILL, OSCAR. Intellectual America: Ideas on the March.
New York: Macmillan, pp. 370-86.
Faulkner has written too much, none of it masterly, and
is too dominated by "Primitivism," which causes him to
approve of characters like young Bayard Sartoris. Even
his great experimental work, The Sound and the Fury,
fails; it is no one's tragedy. Up to The Hamlet, Faulkner's work is faulty in the extreme, but The Hamlet is
second only to the novel of the Compson family.

7 CASH, WILBUR J. The Mind of the South. New York: Knopf,
pp. 376-79.
Same as 1940.B4.

8 LUCCOCK, HALFORD. American Mirror. New York: Macmillan,
pp. 69-71.
Faulkner's work specializes in horror, contains no humor, and is for the intelligentsia.

9 McCULLERS, CARSON. "The Russian Realists and Southern Literature," Decision, II (July), 15-19.
The tag "Southern Gothic" is unfortunate; it does not

1941

(McCULLERS, CARSON)
refer to style but effect. The Southern writers are
closer to the Russian realists, like Dostoevsky, than to
the "Gothic" writers, as Faulkner's As I Lay Dying may be
used to show. Faulkner fuses farce and tragedy as Dostoevsky does because in the South, as in nineteenth-century
Russia, life is cheap. Southern writers are not as good
as the Russians, however, and will not be until their work
takes on a philosophical depth of its own.
Reprinted 1971.B56.

10   SCHWARTZ, DELMORE. "The Fiction of William Faulkner," SoR,
VII (Summer), 145-60.
The reviewer lists a "constellation" of Faulkner's
themes. He prefers the primitives, dislikes the obsessed
lovers, claims there are "more novels which contain idiots
than novels without them." Faulkner's failed intellectuals
represent Faulkner's own failure to adequately present the
"intellectual in himself." Horror and the irrationality
of life are the unifying principles of Faulkner's work.
His style uses deliberate mystification; it is faulty and
careless. None of his work is completely successful.
Reprinted 1970.B70.

11   STANFORD, DON. "The Beloved Returns and Other Recent Fiction," SoR, VI (Winter), 610-28.
The Hamlet is Faulkner's "latest explosion in a cess-
pool." The episode of Ike and the cow is the "climax of
Faulkner's literary career."

12   WARREN, ROBERT PENN. "The Snopes World," KR, III (Spring),
253-57.
Pride motivates Mink and Ab Snopes, not greed; Frenchman's Bend, which falls prey to Flem's self-interest and
aggrandizement, is not aristocratic. Thus the Sartoris/
Snopes dichotomy is an oversimplification of Faulkner.
The structure of The Hamlet depends on an intricate pattern of contrasts in the novel.

1942 A   BOOKS

1   DANIEL, ROBERT W. A Catalogue of the Writings of William
Faulkner. New Haven: Yale University Press.
Early editions of Faulkner's books are described for
the collector.

1942

1942 B   SHORTER WRITINGS

1   ANON. "Faulkneresque," TLS (10 October), p. 497.
     Go Down, Moses, first choice fiction of the week, "may
     be recommended for a degree of seriousness, an integrity
     of sentiment, and a power of visual concentration." It
     displays Faulkner's "slightly Rousseau-ish primitivism"
     regarding the South and his deep "fraternal sentiment" for
     the "Mississippi Negro as he was and is." Faulkner's ver-
     bosity is deplorable, but more often than not his style
     catches fire. "Pantaloon in Black" is perhaps the most
     impressive portion of the book.

2   BEACH, JOSEPH WARREN. "William Faulkner: Virtuoso," Amer-
     ican Fiction 1920-40. New York: Macmillan, pp. 145-69.
     Faulkner is a prodigy of imagination, clever structural
     arrangements, and profound style, though there are excesses
     in all these areas of his work. He most resembles Conrad.
     Many things in his work are puzzling.

3   BECK, WARREN. "A Note on Faulkner's Style," RMR, VI (Spring-
     Summer), 5-6, 14.
     Faulkner's style is unfairly criticized when a single
     sentence is extracted from context and called obscure.
     Style depends on variety, tensions between different ele-
     ments of long passages, the inspired synthesis of diverse
     elements. Faulkner, the most brilliant writer in America,
     gives us this diversity in plenty. Critics apparently
     cannot read.

4   BROOKS, CLEANTH. "What Deep South Literature Needs," SatR
     (19 September), pp. 8-9, 29-30.
     In a contribution to a special issue on "Deep South Lit-
     erature," Brooks notes that the Southern writer who "es-
     says the fantastic" may find himself described as a merci-
     less realist. Faulkner is a tragedian frequently misunder-
     stood. He is neither cynic nor propagandist. His style,
     though occasionally out of control, is at its best an ad-
     junct to form. Southern literature needs more intelligent
     readers.

5   COWLEY, MALCOLM. "Go Down to Faulkner's Land," NRep (29
     June), p. 900.
     Go Down, Moses is a "loosely jointed" collection "mas-
     querading" as a novel. As a whole, the episodes are too
     independent, the book too formless to stand as a novel.
     The stories were written for magazines and revised by the
     addition of Faulkner's "curious idiom." It is a part of
     Faulkner's "Mississippi legend."

1942

6   *DICKMAN, MAX. "William Faulkner, escritor diabolico," Revista
     de las Indias, XIII, No. 39 (March), 107-16.
        After a sketch of Faulkner's region and his life, Dickman
     outlines Faulkner's fiction to date, discusses his symbol-
     ic, subtly related language in the sections of As I Lay
     Dying, and concludes by seeing two trails in Faulkner's
     work: "exoticism" of theme and "singularity" of technique.
     (Summarized in Chapman, 1966.B11, and abstracted in Faulk-
     ner Studies I [1952], p. 63.)
        Reprinted Preface, Mientras yo agonizo (Buenos Aires:
     Santiago Rueda, 1942).

7   GEISMAR, MAXWELL. "William Faulkner: The Negro and the Fe-
     male," Writers in Crisis. Boston: Houghton Mifflin, pp.
     143-83.
        At the center of Faulkner's work, where violence is
     coupled with rape, incest, misogyny and miscegenation,
     there is a deep scorn of the modern female and the emanci-
     pated Negro as the twin causes of the South's fall and
     present condition. Faulkner is a fascist.

8   GRAVES, JOHN TEMPLE, II. "Faulkner...," SatR (2 May),
     p. 16.
        The style and structural arrangement of Go Down, Moses
     can only be complained of, although the conception is
     timely and powerful. Faulkner's "usual" subjects are pre-
     sented: "miscegenation, rot, murder, and ruin."

9   KAZIN, ALFRED. "Faulkner: The Rhetoric and the Agony," VQR,
     XVIII (Summer), 389-402.
        Soldiers' Pay, a "weary epilogue" to the "autobiography
     of war," did not predict the Gothic revival Faulkner's
     work was to represent. Faulkner is bitter at being a
     "Sartoris . . . in a Snopes world." His fiction lacks a
     center; his characters are abstractions acting roles in
     "the general myth" of the "jungle South," everything they
     do unnecessarily raised to the "tenth power." Faulkner's
     work is not representatively American, but personal and
     tormented. His difficulties substitute for lack of sub-
     stance.
        Reprinted On Native Grounds (New York: Reynal and Hitch-
     cock, 1942).

10   O'BRIEN, KATE. Review of Go Down, Moses, Spectator (30 Octo-
     ber), p. 418.
        The reviewer is "out of sympathy with the thickening
     self-consciousness and sentimentality" of Faulkner's re-
     cent style. The atmosphere of Go Down, Moses is good, but
     the characters are exaggerated.

11   PEEPLES, EDWIN. Review of Go Down, Moses, Atlanta Constitu-
      tion (14 July), Section D, p. 6.
         Faulkner's unusual style allows him to create tension by
      piling fact on fact. The self-admitted "young reviewer"
      can only say that Go Down, Moses is Faulkner at his finest.

12   PEERY, JAMES R. Review of Go Down, Moses, Memphis Commercial
      Appeal (10 May), Section IV, p. 10.
         A parody of Faulkner's marathon sentence, this one-para-
      graph review implies that Faulkner desires the same devo-
      tion from his readers as he feels toward his material him-
      self. The attitude, manifest in Go Down, Moses, will not
      help Faulkner win an audience or sell a book.

13   RUGOFF, MILTON. "The Magic of William Faulkner," NYHTB
      (17 May), p. 1.
         Go Down, Moses presents independent but related narra-
      tives of black/white relationships from slavery days
      through the coming of the New South. "The Bear" is a
      story of "the mysterious teleology of nature such as was
      Moby Dick." Both Faulkner's "magic" and his perverse ob-
      scurity appear in the collection. His humor is the
      "warped descendent ... of frontier tall tales."

14   SANCHEZ-RIVA, ARTURO. "William Faulkner, Luz de Agosto,"
      Sur, XII (November), 75-77.
         Faulkner must be horrified by his own compelling, will-
      less creatures as they move like "zombies" to their fates.

15   SHATTUCK, CHARLES. Review of Go Down, Moses, Accent, II
      (Summer), 236-37.
         The "theme is, as ever, the land-bound, tradition-bound
      culture of the South." Half-breeds who are "mystically
      intimate" with the land are Faulkner's characteristic
      heroes. His style in Go Down, Moses is difficult, but his
      fictional manner is generous.

16   STONE, PHIL. "William Faulkner and his Neighbors," SatR
      (19 September), p. 12.
         Faulkner's early friend gives a personal view of Faulk-
      ner and his relationship with his home town: the better
      families scoffed, but the poorer people, generally igno-
      rant of his books, liked him because he "is a square,
      honorable, decent person."
      Reprinted Saturday Review Treasury (New York: Simon and
      Schuster, 1957), pp. 230-32.

17   TOYNBEE, PHILIP. Review of Go Down, Moses, NewSt, XXIV
      (31 October), 293.

1942

(TOYNBEE, PHILIP)
Style and structure combine to overwhelm the reader of
Go Down, Moses, a book that apparently reflects Faulkner's
artistic exhaustion.

18   TRILLING, LIONEL. "The McCaslins of Mississippi," Nation
(30 May), pp. 632-33.
Six of the seven stories of Go Down, Moses are united by
theme and character; "Pantaloon in Black" is inferior and
an anomaly. Ike's experience sets a premium on the "dignity of freedom" in contrast to the other members of his
family, who think in terms of possession. The book offers
no "solution" to Southern racial problems, but it does
dramatize their iniquity.

1943 A   BOOKS - NONE

1943 B   SHORTER WRITINGS

1   *BAIWIR, ALBERT. "William Faulkner," Le déclin de l'indi-
vidualisme chez les romanciers américains contemporains.
Paris: Société d'Editions les Belles Lettres, pp. 313-32.
Massey (1968.A4), Item 1082.

2   BROOKS, CLEANTH, JR., and ROBERT PENN WARREN. Understanding
Fiction. New York: F. S. Crofts, pp. 409-14.
The authors comment upon "A Rose for Emily," compare it
with Poe's "The Fall of the House of Usher," and list
questions for discussion. Revised in the second edition:
See Brooks (1959.B14).

3   CAMPBELL, HARRY M. "Experiment and Achievement: As I Lay
Dying and The Sound and the Fury," SR, LI (April), 305-20.
As I Lay Dying wanders into anticlimax, its technique
unjustified. The first section of The Sound and the Fury
would be skillful except for the clarity of Benjy's reports of the speech of others. The author suggests that
Quentin contemplates Caddy's murder by drowning with flat-
irons. He argues against O'Donnell (1939.B26), that a
clear Sartoris/Snopes division in Faulkner's work does not
exist. See O'Donnell's reply, 1943.B6.

4   MALHERBE, HENRI. "L'avenir du roman," Confluences, No. 21-24,
392-97.
In a special issue devoted to problems in the novel, the
author includes a paragraph on Faulkner and music in his
essay on the future of the contemporary novel.

1945

5   NICHOLSON, NORMAN. "William Faulkner," Man and Literature.
     London: S. C. M. Press, pp. 122-38.
          Puritan, romantic, and dualist, Faulkner, stylistically
     an inheritor of Gertrude Stein, cannot write of man simply
     as a "creature of impulses." He is classed with writers
     who present "natural man." His work through 1942 is dis-
     cussed briefly.

6   O'DONNELL, GEORGE MARION. "Correspondence," SR, LI (Summer),
     446-47.
          Replying to Campbell (1943.B3), O'Donnell claims never
     to have equated Faulkner and Dante and explains that he
     had said that the Compsons should act like Sartorises but
     do not.

7   WILSON, JAMES SOUTHALL. "The Novel in the South," SatR
     (23 January), pp. 11-12.
          In a special issue on "The Old South," the author sur-
     veys the Southern literary scene, noting that the old ta-
     boos are no longer red lights but green ones. Faulkner is
     mentioned.

1944 A   BOOKS - NONE

1944 B   SHORTER WRITINGS

1   ADAMS, J. DONALD. The Shape of Books to Come. New York:
     Viking Press, pp. 91-95.
          In a discussion of modern novelists, Adams couples Faulk-
     ner with Anderson and Thomas Wolfe as writers who produced
     one or two good books then floundered in the "morass of
     their own confusion." Faulkner is helplessly mired in
     technical experiment, blocked by his preoccupation with
     pathology. His work is meaningless because it does not
     show the conflict of good and evil or the "mystery of
     life."

2   COWLEY, MALCOLM. "William Faulkner's Human Comedy," NYTBR
     (29 October), p. 4.
          Faulkner is writing a Balzacian saga, but not dividing
     it into parts. He writes Gothic psychological horror and
     frontier humor.

1945 A   BOOKS - NONE

1945

1945 B   SHORTER WRITINGS

1   COWLEY, MALCOLM. "William Faulkner Revisited," SatR
           (14 April), pp. 13-16.
              Prelude to the Viking Portable Faulkner introduction,
           this essay advances Cowley's theory about Faulkner's con-
           cern to create a mythical domain and a Southern legend.
           Faulkner is at his best writing long stories "in a single
           burst of creative energy" rather than in writing novels.
           He is a "bardic poet in prose" who may be compared to
           Hawthorne.

2   _____. "William Faulkner's Legend of the South," SR, LIII
           (Summer), 343-61.
              Cowley further ventilates his theory that Faulkner is
           writing a myth of the changing South, the Yoknapatawpha
           Saga, in a series of interconnected novels. Absalom, Ab-
           salom! is a general metaphor for the decline of the Old
           South order, though such a simplification does not reveal
           the author's chief intention. Faulkner is both fatalist
           and idealist. See also 1946.B2, 1951.A2, 1952.B14,
           1960.A1, 1966.A8.

3   *FAUCHERY, PIERRE. "La mythologie faulknerienne dans Pylon,"
           Espace (June), pp. 106-12.
              Transatlantic Migration (1955.B54), Item 438.

4   MACLACHLAN, JOHN M. "William Faulkner and the Southern
           Folk," SFQ, IX (September), 153-67.
              Faulkner's fiction, viewed sociologically, differen-
           tiates clearly in its attitudes toward poor whites and the
           aristocrats, for whom he reserves his most lofty and mel-
           ancholy tones. He favors the pure black servant; and he
           portrays the mulatto, a living symbol of society's break-
           down, as tragic or doomed. In the interest of naturalism,
           Faulkner ignores the folk culture and its values.

5   WRIGHT, LOUIS B. "Myth-Makers and the South's Dilemma," SR,
           LIII (Autumn), 544-58.
              Faulkner is identified with the Gothic romance. The au-
           thor imagines that Faulkner must be surprised by his se-
           rious reception.

1946 A   BOOKS - NONE

1946 B   SHORTER WRITINGS

1   CAMPBELL, HARRY M., and J. P. PILKINGTON. "William Faulk-
       ner's Sanctuary," Expl, IV (June), Item 61.
            Temple is afraid of Popeye, so she perjures herself.
       The title of Sanctuary is ironic. A reply to 1946.B3.

2   COWLEY, MALCOLM. "Introduction," The Viking Portable Faulk-
       ner. New York: Viking Press, pp. i-xxiv. Revised edi-
       tion 1967.
            Faulkner is a self-taught, deliberately provincial
       writer of great unrefined power, a "solitary worker" who
       would have benefited from dialogues with literary people
       in the art capitals of America and Europe. His greatest
       success is the whole of the Yoknapatawpha cycle, not the
       individual novels or stories. Possessed himself by the
       urge to write, Faulkner writes about characters who are
       equally under compulsions--of their past, their dreams,
       their very natures.
       Reprinted 1951.A2, 1960.A1, 1966.A8.

3   ESCHELMAN, WILLIAM R. "Faulkner, Sanctuary," Expl, IV (June),
       Query 8.
            Why does Temple bear false witness in Sanctuary? See
       replies at 1946.B1 and 1947.B1.

4   GORDON, CAROLINE. "Mr. Faulkner's Southern Saga," NYTBR
       (5 May), pp. 1, 45.
            Reviewing the Viking Portable, Gordon validates Cowley's
       conception of Faulkner's legend of the South but argues
       that the limited selection of the anthology is inadequate
       to give a true picture of Faulkner's "brooding intensity,"
       his elaborate manipulation of time and point of view, or
       his "worst faults"--obscurity of style and occasional
       structural weakness. Faulkner's greatness lies in his
       ability to create character, his compassion, his eye for
       detail. She agrees with Cowley that he most resembles
       Hawthorne.

5   JACKSON, JAMES TURNER. "Delta Cycle: A Study of William
       Faulkner," Chimera, V (Autumn), 3-14.
            The author provides a poetic summary of the main ele-
       ments of Faulkner's fiction through Go Down, Moses, center-
       ing attention on the class of Sutpen and Sartoris and
       their progeny--for example, Ike McCaslin--as the 100 years
       of Faulkner's "delta cycle" unfolds.

6   JARLOT, GERARD. "Pylone, par William Faulkner," Fontaine,
       X (November), 653-57.

1946

(JARLOT, GERARD)
Pylon seems like self-parody; it is as if Faulkner were paralyzed in hesitation between the conventional novel and his own best instincts for innovation.

7   KENT, MICHAEL. "Realism and Reality: A Plea for Truth in Fiction," CathW, CLXIII (June), 224-29.
Faulkner and other contemporary writers are making America look like hell to Europeans, suppressing man's rationality and morals and heroism.

8   *NICHOLSON, NORMAN. "William Faulkner," The New Spirit, ed. Ernest W. L. Martin. London: Dennis Dobson, pp. 32-41.
Massey (1968.A4), Item 2004.

9   POUILLON, JEAN. "Temps et destinée chez Faulkner," Temps et roman. Paris: Gallimard, pp. 238-60.
For Faulkner's characters the past alone is real--it is not merely a matter of technique that makes Faulkner's novels, whatever their form, explore the ramifications and reality of former events. Gobbling up the present as it comes, the past is the unrolling of fate. Faulkner differs from Proust in generalizing the power and effect of past time; it is not the single individual recalling his past but everyone in Faulkner's novels who lives the sum of a past life. For Proust the past is separate; for Faulkner it is not. As a consequence, his technique deals with consciousness and the past tense, not knowledge and the present. He is, however, not deterministic; the fates of his characters come from within, not without.
Reprinted, translated as "Time and Destiny in Faulkner," in 1966.A8.

10   _____. "William Faulkner, un témoin (à propos de Pylône)," TM, I (October), 172-78.
Pylon makes us more aware of Faulkner than of his characters.

11   RAIMBAULT, R-N. "Faulkner au naturel," GLet (14 September), p. 15.
Faulkner tells us not to hope, not even to wait, just to suffer, but also that God is a gentleman. Faulkner is a realist, an idealist, a puritan, a Freudian, a fatalist, and more.

12   RIVALLAN, JEAN. "Pylône," Paru, No. 23 (October), 48-49.
American critics did not like the subject matter or method of Pylon, but French critics prefer it to many of Faulkner's earlier works.

13   SARTRE, JEAN-PAUL. "American Novelists in French Eyes,"
       AtlM, CLXXVIII (August), 114-18.
           Faulkner, Dos Passos, Hemingway and Steinbeck were major
       influences on Sartre's generation. Sartre discusses Faulk-
       ner's impact in France and compares French admiration for
       Faulkner with American intellectuals' dislike of him, sug-
       gesting that the French novels which Faulkner influenced
       will help America "discover" him.

14   SNELL, GEORGE. "The Fury of William Faulkner," WR, XI (Au-
       tumn), 29-40.
           Faulkner's narrative methods, his nihilism, and his in-
       volved prose combine to alienate the ordinary reader.
       These elements of Faulkner's art are bearable in the sto-
       ries, but seldom so in the novels, which never "add up to
       the excellence" of their parts. Faulkner's reputation,
       for all the good qualities of The Sound and the Fury, will
       "rest largely" on These 13, Doctor Martino, The Unvan-
       quished, Go Down, Moses, and hitherto uncollected tales.
       Reprinted 1947.B9.

15   SPEARS, MONROE K. "Les romanciers américains devant le
       public et la critique des Etats-Unis," translated by R.
       Grandbois, CahiersLM (December), pp. 287-313.
           Relying on Cowley's "Legend of the South" essay
       1945.B2), the author discusses aspects of Faulkner's Amer-
       ican reputation.

16   WARREN, ROBERT PENN. "Cowley's Faulkner," NRep (12 August),
       pp. 176-80; (26 August), pp. 234-37.
           For all its insight and open-eyed lack of prejudice,
       Cowley's Introduction to the Viking Portable (1946.B2)
       might be modified to lay stress on Faulkner's universality
       rather than his so-called Southern typicality. Faulkner
       takes up issues common to all mankind. He does not look
       backward; he glorifies human effort and endurance, which
       are timeless truths. Warren suggests several subjects in
       Faulkner's work that might be profitably studied, includ-
       ing Nature, which provides the rich background of much of
       his fiction; the Negro and the poor white; humor; techni-
       cal experimentation; and symbolism.
       Reprinted 1951.A2.

17   WILSON, EDMUND. Review of the Viking Portable Faulkner, NY
       (27 July), p. 58.
           Because of Cowley's introduction, his arrangement of the
       selections, and Faulkner's "genealogy" of the Compsons,
       the anthology is a "real contribution to the study of
       Faulkner's work."

1947

1947 A   BOOKS - NONE

1947 B   SHORTER WRITINGS

1   BERGEL, LIENHARD. "Faulkner's Sanctuary," Expl, VI (Decem-
    ber), Item 20.
       The title of the novel means "consecrated place" and re-
    fers to Temple Drake as an ironic revelation of hypocrisy
    in those in modern society who enjoy both respectability
    and the demimondaine. Replies to 1946.B3.

2   BURGUM, EDWIN BERRY. "William Faulkner's Patterns of Amer-
    ican Decadence," The Novel and the World's Dilemma. New
    York: Oxford University Press, pp. 205-22.
       The progression of the four narrative sections of The
    Sound and the Fury clarifies and enlarges the meanings
    found in the novel. The peace at the end is an idiot's
    peace, and Faulkner probably did not have a philosophical
    grasp of how he had revealed the chaos of existence by his
    own imposed order. As I Lay Dying is a failure, lacking
    seriousness; the ending is almost vaudeville. Sanctuary
    illustrates the problem in Faulkner's fiction: stream-of-
    consciousness technique keeps his style in check, and
    without it he becomes melodramatic. Faulkner's other nov-
    els illustrate that he sees decadence everywhere as a re-
    sult of universal greed.

3   COWLEY, MALCOLM. "William Faulkner," AmRs, No. 3 (July),
    31-40.
       German translation of 1946.B2.

4   HOPPER, VINCENT. "Faulkner's Paradise Lost," VQR, XXIII
    (Summer), 405-20.
       A romanticist in an unspiritual age, Faulkner cries out
    against the forces that have produced such a state of af-
    fairs. Bondage of spirit to sexual demands is the theme
    of The Wild Palms. Throughout Faulkner's work there are
    dualities of spirit/flesh and white aristocrat/black and
    poor white. Faulkner's chief subject is mankind.

5   McLUHAN, HERBERT MARSHALL. "The Southern Quality," SR, XLV
    (September), 357-83.
       Joe Christmas is a genuine symbol of the modern human
    condition. "By a rigorous contemplation of his own local
    experience, Faulkner has moved steadily toward universal
    statements." The "Southern temper" which Faulkner's work
    reflects is the result of history, tradition, a cult of
    beauty, and other qualities found in the work of Southern
    poets and novelists.

6   PEYRE, HENRI. "American Literature Through French Eyes,"
     VQR, XXIII (Summer), 421-38.
        Along with other American writers, Faulkner has been in-
     fluential in France.

7   SARTRE, JEAN-PAUL. "A propos de Le Bruit et la Fureur--La
     temporalité chez Faulkner," Situations I. Paris: Galli-
     mard, pp. 70-81.
        Translated as "Time in Faulkner: The Sound and the
     Fury" in 1951.A2 and 1960.A1; as "On The Sound and the
     Fury: Time in the Work of William Faulkner, 1955.B52.
     Reprint of 1939.B28.

8   _____. "Sartoris par W. Faulkner," Situations I. Paris:
     Gallimard, pp. 7-13.
        Reprinted from 1938.B14. Reprinted as "William Faulk-
     ner's Sartoris," 1952.B47; reprinted 1955.B51.

9   SNELL, GEORGE DIXON. "The Fury of William Faulkner," The
     Shapers of American Fiction 1798-1947. New York: Dutton,
     pp. 87-104.
        Faulkner is "building a vast, savage, demonic Tragédie
     Humaine." Each novel has brillian sections, but, except
     for The Sound and the Fury, none "adds up to the excel-
     lence of its parts." He may be best remembered for his
     stories, for example "A Rose for Emily" and "That Evening
     Sun." The prose of Absalom, Absalom! and "The Bear" is
     unfortunately perfervid.
     Reprinted from 1946.B14.

10   WHITTEMORE, REED. "Notes on Mr. Faulkner," Furioso, II (Sum-
     mer), 18-25.
        Considering Faulkner's philosophy seriously in conjunc-
     tion with the reprinting of Faulkner's self-parody "After-
     noon of a Cow," the author sees Faulkner's characters as
     beyond (or beneath) good and evil by virtue of a strong
     Necessity that operates in the world. Faulkner's charac-
     ters do have certain freedoms in the manner they conduct
     themselves.

1948 A BOOKS - NONE

1948 B SHORTER WRITINGS

1   ARTHOS, JOHN. "Ritual and Humor in the Writing of William
     Faulkner," Accent, IX (Autumn), 17-30.
        Beginning with the assumption that Faulkner often speaks

1948

(ARTHOS, JOHN)
directly through his characters, Arthos asserts that Faulkner is always a character in his own stories and that he
supplies commentary to explain the ritual enacted there.
Even while seeking a meaning to the violence of history,
however, Faulkner has displayed a rich humor. Most of the
fiction is mentioned briefly. The author concludes that
Faulkner has seldom achieved a proper balance between violence and humor which might diminish the "outrage" in his
work.
Reprinted 1951.A2.

2   B., E. Review of Intruder in the Dust, New Orleans Times-
Picayune (17 October), Section II, p. 17.
Though slightly ponderous at times, Intruder in the Dust
creates and sustains a mood. In the hands of anyone else
it would be only a detective story; Faulkner uses it to
depict the Negro problem in the South, showing great understanding.

3   BOWLING, LAWRENCE EDWARD. "The Technique of The Sound and
the Fury," KR, X (Autumn), 552-66.
The author guides the reader first through the Benjy section of The Sound and the Fury, pointing out how one discovers the nature, content, and meaning of the time-shift-
ing stream-of-consciousness. Faulkner has simplified the
mental processes of his characters so that there is no material extraneous to the themes and events of the novel.
The current order of the parts is deliberate, more effective than any other order, and sufficiently understandable
to the attentive reader. The first and last sections are
comprehensive; the two middle sections are specific, providing the book with a neat formal balance.
Reprinted 1951.A2.

4   BRADFORD, ROARK. "The Private World of William Faulkner,"
'48, The Magazine of the Year (May), pp. 83-84, 90-94.
The author gives an anecdotal account of Faulkner the
man, of his home and home town, of the legends surrounding
him, including Hollywood stories, and mentions work on A
Fable.

5   BREIT, HARVEY. "Faulkner After Eight Years: A Novel of Murder and Morality," NYTBR (26 September), p. 4.
Faulkner is a poet who makes solitary and often bewildering solutions to aesthetic problems. His talent is sure;
he is a virtuoso. Intruder in the Dust, however, represents a new development in his writing--and not an aesthetic one. Not so good as the early fiction, it does

(BREIT, HARVEY)
show an altered "political-social" content. The fast-paced
tale, which has the attributes of a good movie script, may
be a reflection also of what Faulkner has learned in Hollywood.

6   CAMPBELL, HARRY M.   "Faulkner's Absalom, Absalom!," Expl, VII
(December), Item 24.
Interprets and justifies the complicated syntax of a
sentence from Absalom, Absalom! which Joseph Warren Beach
had singled out as meaningless in American Fiction 1920-
1940.

7   CHASE, RICHARD.   "The Stone and the Crucifixion: Faulkner's
Light in August," KR, X (Autumn), 539-51.
Flight and pursuit and images of line and curve create
a central pattern in Light in August. Faulkner does not
know how to handle a Christ theme, and he does not live up
to the expectations he creates, though he has his merits.
There is an "uncomfortable hiatus" between Faulkner's "portrayal" of manners and his "consciousness" of their meaning.
Reprinted 1951.A2, 1951.B14, 1952.B10, 1971.A3.

8   COWLEY, MALCOLM.   "William Faulkner's Nation," NRep (18 October), pp. 21-22.
Intruder in the Dust proves Faulkner's love for his
people and place. It takes its place in the "Saga" as a
book about Southern nationalism and the Southern desire to
set its own house in order without interference.

9   DANIEL, FRANK.   "Yoknapatawpha County Law," Atlanta Journal
(13 October), p. 35.
Intruder in the Dust is "wholly detached" from Faulkner's earlier work. It is about the old relationships between white and black which create loyalty and understanding.

10   EVANS, WALKER.   "Faulkner's Mississippi," Vogue, CXII (October), 144-49.
Photographs of scenes in Faulkner's region that reflect
passages in the fiction.

11   F[LOWERS], P[AUL].   Review of Intruder in the Dust, Memphis
Commercial Appeal (26 September), Section IV, p. 16.
In Intruder in the Dust Faulkner has struck a balance
that should please readers in both North and South. It
is a book which will make the reader think. Lucas Beauchamp is presented simply as a proud man. Lawyer Stevens'

1948

(F[LOWERS], P[AUL])
words are wise and appropriate to current discussions of
"minority questions."

12   GEISMAR, MAXWELL. "Ex-aristocrat's Emotional Education,"
       SatR (25 September), p. 8.
          Intruder in the Dust is inferior to other Faulkner work,
       though he is a great writer. An editorial introduction to
       the review mentions Faulkner's European reputation; on the
       same page is a biographical sketch.
       Reprinted 1958.B26.

13   GILES, BARBARA. "Unreconstructed Faulkner," M&M, I (Novem-
       ber), 78-81.
          In Intruder in the Dust Faulkner's spokesman threatens
       Civil War if the South is not left to its racism.

14   *GLOSTER, HUGH M. Negro Voices in American Fiction. Chapel
       Hill, N. C.: University of North Carolina Press, pp. 202-
       03.
          Massey (1968.A4), Item 1520.

15   GORDON, CAROLINE. "Notes on Faulkner and Flaubert," HudR, I
       (Summer), 222-31.
          Faulkner's method of rendering scene and character is
       akin to Flaubert's; Faulkner unites "historical detail
       with lyricism." "Spotted Horses" is compared with "Un
       Coeur Simple."
       Reprinted, revised, in Caroline Gordon and Allen Tate, The
       House of Fiction (New York: Scribner's, 1950), pp. 531-34.

16   HARDWICK, ELIZABETH. "Faulkner and the South Today," PR, XV
       (October), 1130-35.
          A paean to Faulkner's "mad" genius and a poke at Clifton
       Fadiman and Maxwell Geismar for their negative criticism
       precede a review of Intruder in the Dust. Lucas seeks
       lynching by refusing to defend himself, and he thereby be-
       comes the conscience of the South. Not content with dram-
       atization, Faulkner gives a states' rights diatribe to
       Gavin Stevens to overplead his case. The problem is that
       Faulkner's South has changed; there are no more Dilseys
       and Lucases, and his new material is so intractable that
       he must force it to say what he still believes.
       Reprinted 1951.A2, 1966.A6.

17   HOWE, IRVING. "The South and Current Literature," AMerc,
       LXVII (October), 494-503.
          Intruder in the Dust explores the "terror of Southern

(HOWE, IRVING)
life," which is the possibility, rather than the accomplishment, of such acts as Lucas's near lynching. Lucas is a symbol of the black man's greatest qualities as Faulkner sees them. Gavin's rhetoric is Faulkner's own voice; the speeches prove that Faulkner's imagination is more powerful than his intellect.

18   HUTCHENS, JOHN K. "On the Books," NYHTB (31 October), p. 6.
      Faulkner the farmer, in New York after "ten years," talks about reading Don Quixote, Moby Dick, The Nigger of the Narcissus, Shakespeare and Dickens.
      Reprinted 1968.A6.

19   JOHNSON, C. W. M. "Faulkner's 'A Rose for Emily,'" Expl, VI (May), Item 45.
      The author challenges the reading in Understanding Fiction (1943.B2) which characterizes Emily as one who refuses external order. Emily learns to act furtively and succeeds in denying change. The theme is "If one resists change, he must love and live with death." See reply 1948.B28.

20   MAGNY, CLAUDE-EDMONDE. "Faulkner ou l'inversion théologique," L'Age du roman américain. Paris: Editions du Seuil, pp. 196-243.
      Faulkner inverts the order of his stories and uses two plots at once, either juxtaposed or contrasted, and delights in fictional "puzzles" such as withholding or confusing characters' names. The absurdities produced by these techniques are augmented by a difficult style. Faulkner's meaning is complicated by his structural and stylistic postures, which are functions of his concept of time. Puritan repugnance toward sex and misogyny in Faulkner's work are related. We see that he lives in a world without redemption. His devices involve us directly in his fiction. He is comparable to Balzac.
      Reprinted, translated, 1954.B53, 1966.A8, 1972.B69.

21   *MAYOUX, JEAN JACQUES. "Le temps et la destinée chez William Faulkner" (Cahiers du College Philosophique). La Profondeur et le rythme. Paris: B. Arthaud, pp. 303-31.
      Woodworth, "Selection Bibliographique" (1957.B72), p. 194.

22   MILANO, PAOLO. "Faulkner in Crisis," Nation (30 October), pp. 496-97.
      There are two Faulkners—the American regionalist and

1948

(MILANO, PAOLO)
the "European writer"--reflected in the contrast between
Sartre's view of him (1939.B28) and Cowley's (1946.B2).
Sartre's interpretation of Faulkner as a man writing about
heroes in a moral and historical limbo is, however, con-
tradicted by Intruder in the Dust, where Faulkner contrives
to choose between good and evil. Chick and Gavin are both
mouthpieces for Faulkner's philosophy, "the manifesto of a
lyrical Dixiecrat."

23 MOOSE, ROY C. "Intruder in the Dust, by William Faulkner,"
CarQ, I (Fall), 65-67.
Intruder in the Dust is an important novel, not only for
its fictional qualities but for its social content as well.

24 PRESCOTT, ORVILLE. "Books of the Times," NYT (27 September),
p. 21.
Faulkner is naturally gifted but he has never made himself a craftsman, as Intruder in the Dust reveals. The
reviewer is puzzled that such "unsuccessful" books can be
so powerful, and he summarizes what he believes are Faulkner's personal opinions. "A miasma of hate lies low over
Yoknapatawpha County." Faulkner has rendered his work in-
effective by experimentation and concentration on "sexual
degeneracy." Intruder is a typical failure, killed by
style.

25 SMITH, BRADLEY J. "The Faulkner Country," '48, The Magazine
of the Year (May), pp. 85-89.
Photographs of Oxford, Sardis, and environs accompany
Bradford's article (1948.B4).

26 THOMPSON, RALPH. "In and Out of Books," NYTBR (7 November),
p. 8.
Responding to an interviewer, Faulkner answers questions
about "linear discreteness" in his work with the carpenter
metaphor, saying he writes about what he knows. He is indifferent to criticism. A further note reveals that The
Wild Palms and Sanctuary have been seized in Philadelphia
along with other "obscene" novels.
Interview reprinted 1968.A6.

27 WEST, RAY B., JR. "Faulkner's 'A Rose for Emily,'" Expl, VII
(October), Item 8.
Replying to 1948.B19, the author argues that Emily does
not always resist change, that she had been "normal" until
betrayals by her father and lover. The story is about the
tragic consequences of man's resistance of time, a "di-

(WEST, RAY B., JR.)
lemma of our age" not confined to the American South.
Emily lives with death without really knowing it.

28   WILSON, EDMUND. "William Faulkner's Reply to the Civil-Rights
      Program," NY (23 October), pp. 120-28.
         From Pylon, Faulkner's work has shown a clear romantic
      morality that is the result of his Southern heritage and
      his immersion in the mentality of the "community where he
      was born." For all its humanity, Intruder in the Dust may
      paint too rosy a picture of the Negro's hopes for justice
      in the South. The style is the result of Faulkner's "in-
      dolent taste" and negligence; the structure is slipshod
      because Faulkner is practicing his art so far from such
      cities as produced writers like Flaubert and Joyce. Wil-
      son attempts to summarize Faulkner's social and political
      opinions by quoting and paraphrasing Gavin Stevens, but he
      concludes with praise for the book and for Lucas as a char-
      acter. See reply by Eudora Welty (1949.B35).
      Reprinted in Classics and Commercials (New York: Farrar,
      Straus and Young, 1950), and in 1966.A8.

1949 A   BOOKS - NONE

1949 B   SHORTER WRITINGS

1   ANON. "Une discussion sur Faulkner chez les étudiants com-
     munistes américains," NouCrit (July-August), pp. 87-96.
        The article reprints a discussion from the Autumn 1948
     New Foundations on Faulkner as a fascist writer. A letter
     to NouCrit (October 1949), pp. 120-21, by Al Greenburg
     says that New Foundations is not communist but open to all.

2   ANON. Review of Intruder in the Dust, TLS (7 October),
     p. 645.
        Intruder in the Dust, with its slight plot weighed down
     under a heavy style, might better have been a long short
     story instead of a novel.

3   ALLEN, WALTER ERNEST. "Mr. Faulkner's Humanity," NewSt
     (15 October), pp. 428-30.
        Faulkner's clearest and best-disciplined book since Sol-
     diers' Pay, Intruder in the Dust may make its meaning too
     plain. Faulkner lives in the old Southern past and sees
     white and black as part of one family; his novel is "posi-
     tively inspiriting" as a study of a community's sudden
     discovery of guilt in its own midst.

1949

4   BOUTANG, PIERRE. "Sur Faulkner méconnu," Aspects de la
       France (21 July), p. 3.
          The avant-gardists and existentialists have misappre-
       hended Faulkner in their own image, oblivious to his com-
       passion, his breadth of character. If America had given
       France only Faulkner and Poe, she had done more than the
       Marshall Plan. The critic writes an appreciation of The
       Unvanquished and says that one needs the Viking Portable
       Faulkner to understand Faulkner.

5   BUNKER, ROBERT. "Faulkner: A Case for Regionalism," NMQ,
       XIX (Spring), 108-15.
          Intruder in the Dust does not say that the South is any
       nearer to solving its racial problems than before, but it
       does say that a boy can discover the meaning of "what a
       world must be" and save a Negro whom he misunderstands and
       dislikes. The value of regionalism is that it preserves
       values and strengths which can meet some of the tests of
       existence.

6   CAPOTE, TRUMAN. "Faulkner Dances," ThA, XXXIII (April), 49.
          Valerie Bettis's adaptation of Faulkner's As I Lay Dying
       into dance does not succeed, perhaps due to the relative
       impossibility of translating from one medium to another, a
       metamorphosis of which Capote disapproves.

7   F[LOWERS], P[AUL]. Review of Knight's Gambit, Memphis Com-
       mercial Appeal (4 December), Section IV, p. 12.
          Faulkner's insights into the human comedy are too mor-
       bid, even in these short pieces with the Phi Beta Kappa
       hero.

8   FOSTER, RUEL E. "Dream as Symbolic Act in Faulkner," Per-
       spective, II (Summer), 179-94.
          Faulkner's preoccupation with psychopathology takes in
       one form the repeated use of dream images and states based
       on the Freudian interpretation of sexual stimuli as causal.
       Sex aberration is Faulkner's chief "sigil" of evil modern-
       ism. He also employs the death urge defined by Freud.
       The Sound and the Fury is explicated in terms of such
       images.

9   FROHOCK, W. M. "William Faulkner: The Private versus the
       Public Vision," SWR, XXXIV (Summer), 281-94.
          Faulkner's most consistent and striking characteristic
       is his use of narrative point of view, purposely violating
       the reader's normal expectations of consciousness and vo-
       cabulary in order to achieve impressionistic effects and

(FROHOCK, W. M.)
     to deal with mutations of time and time-consciousness. He
     is a writer of dark and irrational tragedy, withholding
     information in order to heighten the effect of the inevi-
     table recognition. He is the "finest novelist writing in
     English today."

10   GLICKSBERG, CHARLES I.   Review of Intruder in the Dust, ArQ,
     V (Spring), 85-88.
         Intruder in the Dust is so full of faults it would have
     been rejected by a publisher who received it from an un-
     known novelist, but it demonstrates that Faulkner's natu-
     ralism was only a mask. His reactionary and violent views
     are laid bare; the novel is propaganda.

11   _____. "The World of William Faulkner," ArQ, V (Spring),
     46-58.
         Though Faulkner is no moralist, his choices of situation
     and character betray a philosophy: a "ne plus ultra of
     naturalistic pessimism." Mr. Compson of The Sound and the
     Fury seems to sum up Faulkner's philosophy. From this
     point of view, and assuming that Faulkner is giving an ac-
     curate picture of a decadent South, the author summarizes
     the plots of Faulkner's novels.

12   _____. "William Faulkner and the Negro Problem," Phylon,
     X (No. 2), 153-60.
         Summarizing the presentation of Negro characters in The
     Unvanquished, Absalom, Absalom!, The Sound and the Fury,
     and Light in August as from simplest to most complex treat-
     ment, the author finds Faulkner's depiction "fairly faith-
     ful," deliberately mirroring the South's obsessions with-
     out preaching. Faulkner wastes no pity on the Negro, but
     describes his plight with unrelieved realism.

13   GLOSTER, HUGH M.   "Southern Justice," Phylon, X (No. 1),
     93-95.
         Intruder in the Dust "repeats the mildewed doctrine"
     that the South must be left alone to settle its racial
     problems. Faulkner struggles to reconcile his personal
     prejudices with his astute analysis of the South. It is
     a shame that Faulkner is a Dixiecrat.

14   HIRSHLEIFER, PHYLLIS.   "As Whirlwinds in the South: An Analy-
     sis of Light in August," Perspective, II (Summer), 225-38.
         The central theme of Light in August is man's inhumanity,
     and it is underscored by images of violence, disorder, and
     flight. The imagery and pointedly related situations hold

1949

(HIRSHLEIFER, PHYLLIS)
the novel together.
Reprinted 1973.A9.

15   HOWE, IRVING. "Minor Faulkner," Nation (12 November),
      pp. 473-74.
           Even in the potboilers of Knight's Gambit one finds the
      serious themes and occasional flashes of technique which
      mark Faulkner's best work, yet the detective story, which
      Faulkner does not do with great skill, and the Faulkner
      style are not happily married. In effect, we may blame
      the Saturday Evening Post for the inadequacies of this one.

16   _____. "William Faulkner and the Quest for Freedom,"
      Tomorrow, IX (December), 54-56.
           In "Wild Palms," Harry and Charlotte battle against
      reality, carry the fight to "the level of a life prin-
      ciple," and inevitably fail. The very techniques of the
      civilization they flee from doom them. In "Old Man,"
      Faulkner's primitive hero has been reduced by civilization
      and its institutions to the point that he cannot accept
      freedom. The two stories of The Wild Palms form a counter-
      point that should not be overlooked.

17   JONES, HOWARD MUMFORD. "Loyalty and Tiresias of Yoknapataw-
      pha," SatR (5 November), p. 17.
           Faulkner's narrative power, the theme of loyalty, and
      "atmosphere created by style" provide unity in the collec-
      tion Knight's Gambit.

18   KOHLER, DAYTON. "William Faulkner and the Social Con-
      science," CE, XI (December), 119-27.
           Faulkner, "who had seen the violence of war at close
      range," found a counterpart in his South. Yet he also
      writes about the "disorders of our time" in a general way.
      Yoknapatawpha County is a "compass point in the geography
      of man's fate." Intruder in the Dust calls up a survey of
      the social responsibility of Faulkner's best work. He has
      created a human rather than an abstract world. Absalom,
      Absalom! is the key novel.

19   _____. "William Faulkner and the Social Conscience,"
      EJ, XXXVIII (December), 545-53.
           The same essay as 1949.B18.

20   LYTLE, ANDREW. "Regeneration for the Man," SR, LVII (Win-
      ter), 120-27.
           Intruder in the Dust is about Chick's education in good

(LYTLE, ANDREW)
and evil; it is dramatic, not polemical. The relationship
between Chick and Gavin creates a moral dialogue in which
Faulkner plays out the "flow of reverie and comment" which
establishes the story's meaning. Incidentally the story
might be read as a myth of regeneration.
Reprinted 1951.A2, 1968.A8, 1966.B48.

21   MILES, GEORGE. Review of Knight's Gambit, Commonweal (9 December), pp. 275-76.
These detective stories are not up to Faulkner's standard; they lack distinction. Given the faults of Sanctuary, The Sound and the Fury, and As I Lay Dying, one attributes Faulkner's success to the "urgent persuasive
rhythm" of his books.

22   MORRIS, LLOYD. "Heritage of a Generation of Novelists: Anderson and Dreiser, Hemingway, Faulkner, Farrell and Steinbeck," NYHTB (25 September), pp. 12-13, 74.
Faulkner "wished to account for the retarded state of
civilization in the South." His "saga" shows the present
as a "time of moral confusion and social decay" brought on
by the devastation of the Civil War and the rise of ma-
chine civilization.

23   NORTON, DAN S. "This Man's Art and That Man's Scope," VQR,
XXV (Winter), 128-35.
The reviewer assumes that Gavin Stevens in Intruder in
the Dust is Faulkner's spokesman.

24   P., J. Review of Knight's Gambit, New Orleans Times-Picayune
(11 December), Section II, p. 7.
The collected tales in Knight's Gambit, which differentiate justice from mere truth, are typical of Faulkner's
work.

25   PICK, ROBERT. "Old World Views on New World Writing," SatR
(20 August), pp. 7-9, 35-38.
A look at European interest in American writing reveals
a startling disparity between Faulkner's reputation at
home and his fame abroad. The writer quotes several foreign critics on Faulkner and his work.

26   POWELL, SUMNER C. "William Faulkner Celebrates Easter,
1928," Perspective, II (Summer), 195-219.
Among the many levels of symbolism in The Sound and the
Fury, Faulkner emphasizes that Benjy is a Christ symbol
and plays repeatedly on the Wasteland aspect of April

1949

(POWELL, SUMNER C.)
1928 in Jefferson. Quentin's section uses water symbolism and time; it is a bit too rich for easy comprehension. Jason, a devil operating on Good Friday, satirizes social behavior. Dilsey draws the disparate threads together-- order and history, peace and belief, love, "singing 'Shantih Shantih Shantih.'" Includes a chronology of the Compson family.

27 ROBERTS, KENNETH LEWIS. I Wanted to Write. Garden City, N. Y.: Doubleday, pp. 236-37.
The author recounts Booth Tarkington's animadversions on Faulkner's Sanctuary and his appearance in Scribner's.

28 ROTH, RUSSELL. "The Brennan Papers: Faulkner in Manuscript," Perspective, II (Summer), 219-24.
Faulkner is a craftsman who revises, polishes, shapes the form of his books carefully, contrary to popular notions about him. Evidence of this is in some rejected sheets of Go Down, Moses which Faulkner gave to a young writer who visited him in 1940 (See 1955.B7).

29 _____. "William Faulkner: The Pattern of Pilgrimage," Perspective, II (Summer), 246-54.
O'Donnell (1939.B26) is wrong to suppose that Faulkner has a static Sartoris/Snopes center in his fiction; his criticism fails altogether when Faulkner's novels are about something else. Faulkner's thought is evolutionary, as seen best in Go Down, Moses. Light in August and Pylon are pivotal; Absalom, Absalom! is transitional. Faulkner's new view is a "transcendental religious" one. Ike McCaslin's repudiation of his heritage is a positive act which seeks to change his culture; he represents the positive Sartoris values. The Negro equals "the hope of all that is human."

30 ROUSSEAUX, ANDRÉ. "Mystique et tragique de Faulkner," Littérature du vingtième siècle, 3rd series. Paris: Editions Albin Michel, pp. 238-46.
All Faulkner's characters are puppets of destiny, including Jiggs and the reporter who serves as "observer" in Pylon. Faulkner writes of man's hopeless struggles against fate; he is the greatest tragic writer of our time.

31 SIGAUX, GILBERT. "Sur Faulkner," La Nef, VI (February), 117-20.
The author discusses Magny's essay (1948.B20), praising its insights.

32   SIMKINS, FRANCIS BUTLER. The South Old and New. New York:
      Knopf, pp. 347-48.
          Faulkner created a lightless land which looked only to
      the past.

33   TRILLING, LIONEL. "Contemporary American Literature in Its
      Relation to Ideas," AQ, I (Fall), 195-208.
          Piety--both cultural and religious--has a lot to do with
      the energies and commitment an artist can bring to his
      work. As a Southerner, Faulkner brings the cogency of his
      beliefs to fiction. Why hasn't the liberal democratic
      ideal produced a literature by means of its pieties?

34   WARREN, ROBERT PENN. "Thèmes de William Faulkner," Revue
      Internationale (February), pp. 140-48.
          A translation of 1946.B16.

35   WELTY, EUDORA. "Department of Amplification," NY (1 Jan-
      uary), pp. 50-51.
          The Mississippi author challenges Edmund Wilson's state-
      ments about Faulkner's expertise in the novel (1948.B28)
      and doubts that it has anything to do with Faulkner's home
      address. Faulkner's superiority is related to his intel-
      ligence and imagination. Wilson's remarks about the opac-
      ity of Faulkner's style are curious; Faulkner's pages "are
      clear to me."

36   _____. "In Yoknapatawpha," HudR, I (Winter), 596-98.
          Intruder in the Dust concerns the maddening physical la-
      bor and riddling which accompany the proving of innocence.
      Welty praises the humor which grows out of the terrible
      situations of the novel; Faulkner's clear communication of
      his vision of a world; and his "intolerantly and intoler-
      ably unanalyzable" style.

37   _____. Short Stories. New York: Harcourt, Brace,
      pp. 39-47.
          Welty quotes "The Bear" extensively and compares it to
      D. H. Lawrence's "The Fox," noting that the fox is of the
      inner world, the bear purely of the outer, and both are
      vanquished "by acts of the destructive will of man's ag-
      gression." Faulkner is a "divining writer," one who
      writes speedily yet with control and musical organization.

38   WEST, RAY B., JR. "Atmosphere and Theme in Faulkner's 'A
      Rose for Emily,'" Perspective, II (Summer), 239-45.
          Characters, images, and situation in "A Rose for Emily"
      set up a contrast between past and present. Though

1949

(WEST, RAY B., JR.)
heroic, Emily's attempt to resist time and change is also
tragic, because Homer is not retained, he is dead.
Reprinted 1951.A2, 1973.A9.

39 WILSON, EDMUND. "Books," NY (24 December), pp. 58-59.
In view of his recently arrived at opinion that Faulkner
is probably the greatest living novelist, the reviewer
judges Knight's Gambit below the mark. It has the flavor
of magazine fiction and a reckless style.

40 WILSON, JOHN W. "Delta Revival," EJ, XXXVIII (March), 117-24.
Faulkner's influence on all the writers of the Mississippi Delta is evident, though he is properly viewed as a
hill-country resident and writer. Eudora Welty is the
chief writer of the specifically "Delta" renaissance.

41 YGLESIAS, JOSÉ. "Neurotic Visions," M&M, II (December), 74-
76.
"A Courtship" (appearing in Prize Stories of 1949: The
O. Henry Awards, which is reviewed) is a dream of racial purity which tells "the story of an unrealized homosexual
passion."

1950 A BOOKS - NONE

1950 B SHORTER WRITINGS

1 AYMÉ, MARCEL. "What French Readers Find in William Faulkner's Fiction," NYTBR (17 December), p. 4.
To the French, Faulkner seems rooted in his native soil,
the most American of American writers. A violent God is
present in Faulkner's work, a Puritanism that is alive to
the Frenchman. Faulkner's obscurities and other fictional
devices seem unnecessary and extreme. The French admire
his characters because they like the Southerner and they
understand Faulkner's compassion for the "misfortunes of
his own part of his country."
Reprinted 1954.B7.

2 BRUMM, URSULA. "William Faulkner Im Alten Süden," Welt-
Stimmen (Stuttgart), XIX (May), 374-80.
The author gives a general introduction to Faulkner's
world and work with emphasis upon his violence and pessimism and an account of Light in August and Absalom, Absalom!

3   CAMPBELL, HARRY MODEAN. "Structural Devices in the Works of
      Faulkner," Perspective. III (Autumn), 209-26.
           Faulkner's intensity derives from the subtle heightening
      of his realism; despite meticulous detail in scene, dia-
      lect, and character presentation, Faulkner manages to ele-
      vate and distort his fiction for effect, carrying it to
      symbolic levels which, in turn, work to unify theme, tone
      and plot in the novels. The unity of Light in August, Ab-
      salom, Absalom!, "The Bear" and Go Down, Moses, The Hamlet
      and other works can be demonstrated by paying attention to
      counterpoint, shifting point of view, the reiteration of
      image, symbol, plot, and theme, proving Malcolm Cowley's
      assertion about the disunity of individual novels to be
      wrong. Incorporated into 1951.A1.

4   COINDREAU, MAURICE E. "L'Art de William Faulkner," France-
      Amérique, No. 237 (3 December), 9-10.
           Inspired by the relative indifference of the American
      press to Faulkner's Nobel award, Coindreau discusses Faulk-
      ner's difficulties: his grim subjects, his modern tech-
      niques. But Faulkner, a "moral psychologist," is directly
      in the line of Western literary tradition, from the Old
      Testament to the Greek drama. He quotes Sartre and com-
      pares Faulkner to Proust.
      Reprinted, translated, 1971.B18.

5   _____. "William Faulkner: Prix Nobel de littérature,"
      France-Amérique, No. 236 (26 November), p. 9.
           Coindreau recounts his personal discovery of Faulkner
      and his early efforts to popularize his work in France.
      Faulkner's adopted "parents" in France, knowing his enor-
      mous reputation in their country, are proud that he has
      received the Nobel award.
      Reprinted, translated, 1971.B18.

6   DANIEL, ROBERT W., and JOHN L. LONGLEY, JR. "Faulkner's
      Critics: A Selective Bibliography."
      See 1950.B15.

7   DOWNING, FRANCIS. "An Eloquent Man," Commonweal (15 Decem-
      ber), pp. 255-58.
           Faulkner has triumphed over the Yankee Protestant "sense
      of shame of words." He has created a true world--"as hate
      is true or violence"--and he has done it consciously, de-
      liberately, and with artistry.

8   FIEDLER, LESLIE. "William Faulkner: An American Dickens,"
      Commentary, X (October), 384-87.
           Faulkner is "essentially a short story writer," despite

1950

(FIEDLER, LESLIE)
one's admiration for The Sound and the Fury and Light in
August. Faulkner writes in gasps and has no talent for
sustained narration. The detective story--featuring the
"poor man's intellectual," Gavin Stevens--is the crown of
Faulkner's work: Knight's Gambit and Intruder in the Dust.
Faulkner is capable of giving the great public better than
they deserve or understand.
Reprinted 1960.B27.

9   GILES, BARBARA. "The South of William Faulkner," M&M, III
(February), 26-40.
The violence of Faulkner's novels is purgative. For example, the motives of the Bundrens for going to town are
base, but the moving spirit, the dead Addie, sends them
through fire and flood, providing a nobility the family
lacks. Quentin in The Sound and the Fury is not in love
with death but despairing of life. Ike McCaslin is Faulkner's spokesman. The enemies of man are the Negro, the
female, and the flesh--a life-denying view. The end of
Absalom, Absalom! represents the white supremacist's
nightmare: Jim Bond. Faulkner, like his characters, is
lost in the past.

10   GREET, TOM Y. "Toward the Light: The Thematic Unity of
Faulkner's 'Cycle,'" CarQ, III (Fall), 38-44.
Quentin Compson's disillusion with Caddy parallels Faulkner's disillusion with the South. Quentin and Faulkner
both turn to the past for an answer in Absalom, Absalom!,
which, with The Unvanquished, "convinced Faulkner of the
unworthiness of his ideal." Go Down, Moses is the result,
and Ike's failure to set himself free is Faulkner's.
Yoknapatawpha County is a quest. Intruder in the Dust
shows a willingness to accept modern reality. The author
taxes Kazin, Geismar, and Beach for their preconceptions
and limited insight.

11   GREGORY, HORACE. "In the Haunted, Heroic Land of Faulkner's
Imagination," NYHTB (20 August), pp. 1, 12.
Far from being a writer of "perfect" stories, Faulkner
nevertheless is one of the most compelling and influential
modern workers in the medium. Like Melville, Dostoevsky,
Kafka, D. H. Lawrence, and Joyce, Faulkner evokes the mystery of existence. The Collected Stories is an omnibus
with "Elizabethan richness."

12   HUDSON, TOMMY. "William Faulkner: Mystic and Traditionalist," Perspective, III (Autumn), 227-35.
Faulkner's work reaffirms a "mystical outlook," posits a

78

(HUDSON, TOMMY)
　　spiritual relation between man and nature, and contains
　　many characters who have extrasensory perception. Faulk-
　　ner's message is that the spiritual values, including
　　trust and charity, are dead.

13　LaBUDDE, KENNETH. "Cultural Primitivism in Faulkner's 'The
　　　　Bear,'" AQ, II (Winter), 322-28.
　　　　Primitive ritual and primitive attitudes toward the bear
　　　find parallels in Faulkner's story. Ike is transcendental;
　　　"learning of the wilderness, [Ike] had learned of God,"
　　　carrying his knowledge into the act of repudiation.
　　　Reprinted 1964.A9.

14　LARBAUD, VALÉRY. "Un Roman de William Faulkner," Ce vice im-
　　　　puni, la lecture. Paris: Gallimard, pp. 300-06.
　　　　Reprinted from 1934.B16 and 1936.B11.

15　LONGLEY, JOHN L., JR. and ROBERT W. DANIEL. "Faulkner's
　　　　Critics: A Selective Bibliography," Perspective, III (Win-
　　　　ter), 202-08.
　　　　A brief list of criticism divided into hostile and sym-
　　　pathetic camps.

16　OLSON, LAWRENCE. "Knight's Gambit," Furioso, V (Spring), 86-
　　　　88.
　　　　Not up to Faulkner's best, the stories of Knight's Gam-
　　　bit are dominated by the puzzling figure of Gavin Stevens,
　　　who, like Faulkner, is hard to estimate.

17　PEDEN, WILLIAM. "Sartoris, Snopes and Everyman," SatR
　　　　(26 August), p. 12.
　　　　Collected Stories is hardly representative of Faulkner's
　　　total production as a story writer. Some of his best work
　　　is not included. The variety of subjects, themes, and
　　　moods proves, however, that Faulkner is not obsessed by
　　　violence.

18　ROVERE, RICHARD. "Introduction," Light in August. New York:
　　　　Modern Library, pp. v-xiv.
　　　　For all the magnificence of his prose, the memorableness
　　　of his characters, and the significance of the legend of
　　　the South, Faulkner is often careless or unsure of his own
　　　effects. Light in August is a deeply flawed and at the
　　　same time deeply moving drama, the last book of Faulkner's
　　　great creative period. The theme is innocence.

1950

19   RUBIN, LOUIS D., JR. "Five Southerners ... Knight's Gambit,
      by William Faulkner," HopRev, III (Spring), 42–45.
      Knight's Gambit is strictly "whodunit" material.

20   SIMON, JEAN. "William Faulkner," Le roman américain au XXe
      siècle. Paris: Boivin & Cie, pp. 119–31.
          Faulkner's French reputation, which grew much faster
      than his American one, obliges one to read him despite the
      difficulties. As a disaffected war aviator, Faulkner be-
      gan a fictional career with the characteristic war novel.
      Surveying Faulkner's books, one notes the horror, the af-
      finities with Sherwood Anderson and Melville.

21   SMITH, HARRISON. "The Nobel Winners," SatR (25 November),
      pp. 20–21.
          Faulkner's "region of Mississippi is an allegory in his
      mind . . . of the whole South." Critics have failed to
      note his simplicity, his humanity, or to appreciate his
      intensity and insight. He is writing a "Tragédie Humaine."

22   STONE, PHIL. "Faulkner Classified," Memphis Commercial Ap-
      peal (19 November), Section V, p. 3.
          In a four-sentence note, Stone disputes an editorial
      which called Faulkner a "photographic realist." According
      to Stone, Faulkner is a "romanticist, sometimes almost
      Gothic. It is a civilization that is gone for which he
      mourns."

23   STONE, PHIL. Letter to the editor, Oxford (Miss.) Eagle
      (16 November), pp. 1, 3.
          Stone recalls his first acquaintance with Faulkner and
      their literary friendship, which included Stone's provi-
      sion of books to read, criticism, secretarial help, and
      financial patronage. Faulkner "is even greater as a man
      than he is as a writer"; he "lives" decency, honor, loyalty
      and gratitude.

24   TRÉDANT, PAUL. "Faulkner à Paris," NouLit (14 December),
      p. 1.
          Faulkner, interviewed in New York on his way to Stock-
      holm by a French correspondent, reiterates his identity as
      a farmer and horseman and says he is going to take Jill,
      his daughter, to Paris.

25   TRILLING, LIONEL. "Contemporary American Literature in Its
      Relation to Ideas," The American Writer and the European
      Tradition, edited by Margaret Denny and William H. Gilman.

1951

(TRILLING, LIONEL)
Minneapolis: University of Minnesota Press, for the University of Rochester, pp. 132-53.
Reprints 1949.B33.

26   [VICKERY], OLGA WESTLAND. "As I Lay Dying," Perspective, III (Autumn), 179-91.
The method of As I Lay Dying is an extension of that in The Sound and the Fury, both adaptations of Henry James's technique of "lamps" around a central object illuminating and taking illumination from that center. Addie is the central figure; the other Bundrens take meaning from her. The outsiders make up a multifold disinterested spectator to give scope; and they provide the humor.
Reprinted 1951A.2; incorporated into 1959.A4.

27   WHAN, EDGAR W. "Absalom, Absalom! as Gothic Myth," Perspective, III (Autumn), 192-201.
In Absalom, Absalom! Faulkner is both creating myth and elaborating on it, combining the technique of books like Moby Dick with that of ones like Ulysses. Symbolically it is both the drama of the South as a doomed civilization and a Gothic tale of man's lostness in a world without order. The novel is comparable to the classic Gothic novels of the late eighteenth and early nineteenth centuries.

28   WILSON, EDMUND. Review of Collected Stories, NY (9 December), pp. 145-46.
Less a short story writer than a chronicler, Faulkner is best in his comprehensive view of the South, the Yoknapatawpha material. Stories in which familiar characters appear depend on one's knowing these characters for their best effect, while the non-Yoknapatawpha pieces are mediocre. Faulkner is careless with words and names.

1951 A   BOOKS

1   CAMPBELL, HARRY M., and RUEL FOSTER. William Faulkner: A Critical Appraisal. Norman, Okla.: University of Oklahoma Press.
A New Critic approach to Faulkner's work, the study is philosophically informed by Donald Davidson's idea that Nature is the norm in Faulkner's fiction. There are chapters on imagery, on depth-psychology and symbolism and other structural and thematic devices, on humor, and on Faulkner's "cosmic pessimism," which is his sometimes contradictory presentation of a world without meaning (an outlook modified in his later work). Faulkner prefers the

1951

    (CAMPBELL, HARRY M., and RUEL FOSTER)
        natural and the primitive to the sophisticated and modern.
        Faulkner's greatest concern and achievement is in the care-
        ful manipulation of structure.

2   HOFFMAN, FREDERICK J., and OLGA VICKERY, eds., William Faulk-
        ner: Two Decades of Criticism. East Lansing, Mich.:
        Michigan State College Press.
        An anthology of essays on Faulkner's life and work, this
        collection features an introduction by Hoffman which sur-
        veys Faulkner's career and reception and a selective bib-
        liography of criticism compiled by Vickery.
        Reprints 1932.B12, 1939.B3, 1939.B26, 1939.B28, 1941.B4,
        1946.B2, 1946.B16, 1948.B1, 1948.B3, 1948.B7, 1948.B16,
        1949.B20, 1949.B38, 1950.B26, and 1951.B50. See also
        Poirier, 1951.B46.

1951 B SHORTER WRITINGS

1   ANON. Review of Notes on a Horsethief, NY (14 April),
        pp. 121-22.
        Though similar in theme and manner to Intruder in the
        Dust, Notes on a Horsethief does not come off so well.

2   ANON. Review of Requiem for a Nun, New Orleans Times-Pica-
        yune (23 September), Section II, p. 8.
        Requiem for a Nun is tragic, "soaring and dense," enig-
        matically titled. It strips the layers of good and bad
        from Faulkner's characters. Unorthodox in form, the novel
        alternates narrative and dramatic material. The play por-
        tion is destined for Broadway "later this year."

3   AIKEN, CONRAD. "William Faulkner: The Novel as Form," HarAv,
        CXXXV (November), 13, 24-26.
        Reprinted from 1939.B3.

4   ALEXANDER, SIDNEY. "The Nobel Prize Comes to Mississippi:
        How Yoknapatawpha County Sees Its Author," Commentary, XII
        (Summer), 176-80.
        The author recounts a trip to Oxford and interviews with
        townspeople, including John Faulkner, Phil Stone, Mack
        Reed and others, on the subject of Faulkner.

5   ALLEN, R. M. Mimeographed notes of a classroom interview
        with Faulkner in spring 1947 at the University of Missis-
        sippi.
        A correction to Lavon Rascoe's account of these Faulkner
        interviews which had been published in WR (1951.B53); the

(ALLEN, R. M.)
compiler was also a student in the classes. See explana-
tory note in Lion in the Garden (1968.A6), pp. 52-53.
Faulkner ranks himself and his contemporaries and talks
about his books. Reprinted 1968.A6.

6   ASTRE, GEORGES ALBERT. "L'apport Américain au roman contempo-
rain," Age nouveau, No. 68 (December), 29-32.
Faulkner is discussed briefly in a survey of the American novel.

7   BREIT, HARVEY. "Introduction," Absalom, Absalom! New York:
Modern Library, pp. v-xii.
The father-son story seems to be Faulkner's "objective
correlative of a vision of the South." Absalom, Absalom!
is the "most structurally perfect" of Faulkner's novels;
its high-pitched style is in accord with the pitch of
events. The complex unraveling of the secret story illuminates the tragic humanity of both the narrators and the
subject.

8   _____. "A Sense of Faulkner," PR, XVIII (January-February),
88-94.
Faulkner is in the main line of the "American creative
impulse," and he reflects its characteristic features:
"isolation, introspection, moralism, and an obsessive"
need to work things out in singular terms both philosophically and syntactically. The author seeks to dispel
myths of Faulkner's violence, illiteracy, or simple rus-
ticity.

9   _____. "William Faulkner," AtlM, CLXXXVIII (October),
53-56.
American criticism failed to appreciate Faulkner and did
not create an audience for him. Faulkner's difficulties
are justifiable; he is the greatest prose virtuoso since
Melville and James. His education is extensive and per-
sonal--without superfluity. Light in August is a good
starting point for the new reader.

10   BROOKS, CLEANTH. "Absalom, Absalom!, The Definition of Innocence," SR, LIX (Autumn), 543-58.
Sutpen's innocence regarding what it means to be human--
about the nature of reality--lies at the root of his tragedy. His plan is paramount; in most respects he is outside the community where he settles, and his attitudes
correspond to community values only by accident or necessity. He neither hates nor loves. Judith, accepting

1951

(BROOKS, CLEANTH)
Bon's son and dying of the same yellow fever, repudiates
Sutpen's design fully. She and Henry suffer and learn.
Sutpen never learns anything.

11 _____. "Notes on Faulkner's 'Light in August,'" HarAv,
CXXXV (November), 10-11, 27.
The furniture dealer whose tale of Lena and Byron closes
Light in August is one of the voices of the community, a
reminder of the power of community and its importance in
the novel. The main actors are defined by their positions
outside the community. Byron's quandary in the closing
scene is a thematic reflection of the tragic stories that
have preceded. Like Joe, Joanna, and Hightower, Byron is
still "unable to fathom or perform his nature."

12 BYAM, MILTON S. "Requiem for a Nun," LJ, LXXVI (August),
1220.
The novel is a six-part requiem composed of "dirge-like"
choruses and solos in Faulkner's best style.

13 CAMUS, ALBERT. [Letter], HarAv, CXXXV (November), 21.
Camus regrets being unable to contribute to the Faulkner
issue of HarAv but acknowledges his admiration for Faulkner, who is the greatest of contemporary writers, the only
one who writes in the tradition of the nineteenth-century
giants like Melville, Dostoevsky, and Proust. Sanctuary
and Pylon are Faulkner's "chefs-d'oeuvre."

14 CHASE, RICHARD. "The Stone and the Crucifixion: Faulkner's
Light in August," The Kenyon Critics, edited by John Crowe
Ransom. Cleveland: World Publishing Co., pp. 115-26.
Reprints 1948.B7.

15 CHATELET, JEAN-MARIE. "William Faulkner et la théologie de
Satan," Consciences Algériennes (February-March),
pp. 77-82.
Faulkner offers no excuses, panaceas, or palliatives for
the human condition. His Creation is Absurd, but his sympathy for man is so great that the picture of the human
condition is still ennobled.

16 COLLINS, CARVEL. "A Note on 'Sanctuary,' HarAv, CXXXV (November), 16.
Faulkner based Sanctuary on a story he heard in a night-
club in the mid-1920s. He did not invent a horrific tale;
he brooded over a real story and tried to capture its horror and meaning in fiction.

17   COOKE, ALISTAIR. "William Faulkner's Road to Stockholm,"
      Manchester Guardian Weekly (5 April), p. 13.
         Faulkner is hard to take, but there he is, demanding our
      attention.

18   COWLEY, MALCOLM. "Twenty-Five Years After: The Lost Genera-
      tion Today," SatR (2 June), 6-7, 33-34.
         Faulkner's supposed activities during and after World
      War I are mentioned in a piece drawn from the "revised edi-
      tion" of Cowley's Exile's Return (New York: Viking, 1951).

19   DENOREAZ, MICHEL. "William Faulkner, ou le parti pris de la
      fausse réalité," NouCrit, III (January), 74-84.
         Faulkner won the Nobel Prize because his work perfectly
      reflects the bourgeois world; his selection was a fitting
      succession to that of André Gide, the apologist of peder-
      asty. Faulkner celebrates fascism.

20   DORAN, LEONARD. "Form and the Story Teller," HarAv, CXXXV
      (November), 12, 38-41.
         Faulkner's ease with his material, his moving back and
      forth in the chronology of his people, indicates that he
      possesses a store of material to draw from at will. His
      non-Yoknapatawpha novels indicate he is best with the Jef-
      ferson locale. Far from obscure, Faulkner uses the clas-
      sical pyramid form--exposition, climax, denouement--the
      unities, and the choric commentary in much of his work.
      His formal devices are less calculated than natural, how-
      ever; he creates appetite in the reader and then satisfies
      it.

21   DUESBERG, JACQUES. "Monnaie de singe," Monde nouveau
      (9 July), pp. 58-59.
         Soldiers' Pay is a young man's book.

22   EMMANUEL, PIERRE. "Faulkner and the Sense of Sin," HarAv,
      CXXXV (November), 20.
         Faulkner's characters are related to the world but not
      fully aware of it, and that is the way he dramatizes what
      theologians call the sense of sin--original sin, the human
      condition itself.

23   FLOWERS, PAUL. "Nobility Out of Depravity," Memphis Commer-
      cial Appeal (14 October), Section V, p. 12.
         In the context of the Nobel address, Faulkner, in Req-
      uiem for a Nun, has contrived to endow a prostitute and
      dope addict with a nobility many will find it difficult to
      understand. Most critics, raving over avant-garde devices,
      will miss the morality of the novel.

1951

24   GAVIN, JEROME. "Light in August: The Act of Involvement,"
      HarAv, CXXXV (November), 14-15, 34-37.
          "Both of Christmas's murders [i.e., McEachern and
      Joanna] occur when the sexual adjustment he has made is
      threatened...by a religious fanatic." Food, sex, and
      negritude are repeatedly linked in Joe's mind, from the
      toothpaste episode to his encounter with Joanna. His dual
      nature, human and divine, is represented by his mixed
      blood; the failure to fuse the two is his tragedy.

25   GROSECLOSE, FRANK. Review of Requiem for a Nun, CarQ, IV
      (December), 59-62.
          Requiem for a Nun seems hurried and carelessly produced
      by Faulkner's publisher. The narrative and dramatic parts
      do not seem well integrated, though the drama itself is
      admirable.

26   GUÉRARD, ALBERT, JR. "'Requiem for a Nun': An Examination,"
      HarAv, CXXXV (November), 19, 41-42.
          Not a major achievement, Requiem for a Nun remains a
      powerful work, slightly weakened by anticlimax, but, never-
      theless, like so much of Faulkner's fiction it forces us
      to redefine what a novel may be.

27   _____. "William Faulkner, chroniqueur de l'apocalypse,"
      RN (January), 81-90.
          It is appropriate that Faulkner has received an award
      created by the fabricator of dynamite. His universe is
      dominated by the punishment inflicted by a vengeful God
      and by the internal logic of our own acts.

28   GUYARD, MARIUS FRANÇOISE. "Faulkner le tragique," Études,
      CCLXVIII (February), 172-83.
          Faulkner is a puritan or at least reflects Puritan
      stringency in his novels. He gets historic, moral, and
      religious significance out of his heritage. His work de-
      picts the plight of modern man for whom there is no re-
      demption.

29   HICKS, GRANVILLE. "Faulkner's South: A Northern Interpreta-
      tion," GaR, V (Fall), 269-84.
          Attempting a path between the views that Faulkner either
      hates or loves the South, Hicks finds that The Sound and
      the Fury is not particularly Southern nor about aristo-
      cratic decay, since the later Compson Appendix indicates
      that even the earliest members of the family were fail-
      ures; it is about the absence of love in a human family.
      Faulkner's novels on the black-white theme are novels

(HICKS, GRANVILLE)
about a problem, not "problem novels." Ike is Faulkner's
hero; Gavin Stevens, at least partially, is his spokesman.

30   ____. "Our Novelists' Shifting Reputations," CE, XII
(January), 187-93.
Faulkner's growing reputation results not only from re-
evaluations like Cowley's (1946.B2) but even more from the
opinions of other novelists about his work.

31   HOFFMAN, FREDERICK J. "William Faulkner," The Modern Novel
in America. Chicago: Henry Regnery, pp. 26-27, 154-64,
201-02.
Accepting Roth's schematization of Faulkner's heroes
(1949.B29), Hoffman discusses the novels, taking special
note of Faulkner's preoccupation with formal experiments,
his conception of time, and his comedy.

32   HOFFMANN, A. C. "Faulkner's Absalom, Absalom!," Expl, X (November), Item 12.
Events and techniques used in the later Absalom, Absalom!
underlie and inform The Sound and the Fury; the two novels
are opposite sides of one coin: Quentin's defeat by time
is echoed in Benjy, and Sutpen's grand design becomes
Jason's petty plans. The chaotic time sequences of Absalom leads to the controlled panels of The Sound and the
Fury.

33   HOWE, IRVING. "Faulkner: An Experiment in Drama," Nation
(29 September), pp. 263-64.
Requiem for a Nun does not equal Faulkner's best work;
it is a "sequel to one of his weakest novels." Essentially undramatized, the story is told in good part by
Temple; the narrative interludes which introduce the acts
are "major Faulkner." Time has caught up with the South
and with Yoknapatawpha.

34   ____. "The Southern Myth and William Faulkner," AQ, III
(Winter), 357-62.
Southern writing originates in the post-World War I decay of regional consciousness. It is not true that Faulkner draws on the Southern myth. As often as not he writes
against his tradition, testing the myth against the realities he sees or intuits with his "growing vision as an
artist."

35   ____. "William Faulkner and the Negroes," Commentary,
XII (October), 359-68.
Faulkner's work contains every conceivable attitude

1951

(HOWE, IRVING)
    toward the South. Dilsey, Joe Christmas, and Lucas Beau-
champ of Intruder in the Dust represent a progression in
Faulkner's use of racial material. Dilsey "belongs" to a
crumbling world; Joe is the outsider suffering because of
society's injustice. Lucas transcends them both; he is
fully a man.

36   KAZIN, ALFRED. "Faulkner's Vision of Human Integrity," HarAv,
    CXXXV (November), 8-9, 28-33.
        The voice, if not the explicitness of the Nobel address,
and the premium put on love and courage in the speech are
what holds Faulkner's novels together. A "false professionalism" among critics has caused them to misunderstand
Faulkner's style. His vocabulary is necessary and meaningful; style and content exemplify the human continuum reveal our common bond in the human condition, and yet show
us to be individual.

37   *KIMBROUGH, EDWARD. "Novelist Gives Forth on Work, Food, Foot-
    ball," New Orleans Item (29 October).
        Bassett (1972.A2), DD2, erroneously puts this interview
in 1931 and lists it as 30 October. During a trip to New
Orleans to accept the French Legion of Honor, Faulkner
talks about his pleasure in his work, silence, horses, and
trees, and deplores the regimentation of modern football.
Reprinted 1968.A6.

38   KRIM, SEYMOUR. "Short Stories by Six," HudR, III (Winter),
    626-33.
        One of Faulkner's main effects is to throw the reader
into an on-going experience and allow him to pick up the
background, which already exists, as he reads. Faulkner's
stories are "invented in the typewriter." More than half
are tours de force. Review of Collected Stories.

39   *LeBRETON, MAURICE. "Temps et personne chez William Faulkner,"
    Journal de psychologie normale et pathologique, XLIV (Jan-
    uary-June), 344-54.
        Transatlantic Migration (1955.B54), Item 453.

40   LEWIS, R. W. B. "The Hero in the New World: William Faulk-
    ner's 'The Bear,'" KR, XIII (Autumn), 641-60.
        Ike McCaslin is Faulkner's "first full-fledged hero,"
and in "The Bear" the balance is tipped in favor of an affirmation of life. The fourth section of the story duplicates the structure of the first three combined. Ike's
age at various levels is emphasized by repeated movement

(LEWIS, R. W. B.)
in time, particularly in the form of returns across the
years he is 16 and 21. Ike is born into virtue and sees a
vision of evil. He is a transcendental hero rising above
the lost wilderness of the American dream.

41   McLAUGHLIN, RICHARD. "Requiem for Temple Drake--A Nobel
      Prize Winner Comes to Broadway," ThA, XXXV (October), 50,
      77.
         Based on a review of the dramatic portions of Requiem
      for a Nun, prior to its pending adaptation for the stage,
      the essay pronounces Faulkner the "unmistakable soothsayer
      of doom." The reviewer is impressed by the poetic language
      but not by the philosophical content.

42   MacLEISH, ARCHIBALD. "Faulkner and the Responsibility of the
      Artist," HarAv, CXXXV (November), 18, 43.
         Faulkner's Nobel address was well received not merely
      because of his stature or his diagnosis of modern ills,
      but also because it is artistically correct--the artist's
      duty is "to take the side of man."
         Reprinted A Continuing Journey (Boston: Houghton Mifflin,
      1967).

43   MANN, THOMAS. [Letter], HarAv, CXXXV (November), 21.
         Mann regrets being unable to contribute to the Faulkner
      issue of HarAv and expresses his admiration for Faulkner.

44   MATCH, RICHARD. "The 'New' Faulkner," NRep (5 November),
      pp. 19-20.
         Requiem for a Nun is implausible but attracts interest
      because of the dramatic form and its recapitulation of
      Yoknapatawpha "history." It represents a "new" Faulkner,
      tamed to a softer view of humankind.

44.5 PERRY, BRADLEY T. "A Selective Bibliography of Critical
      Works on William Faulkner," UKCR, XVIII (Winter), 159-64.
         The bibliography, divided into two parts, lists articles
      and sections from books; some entries are annotated
      briefly.

45   PFAFF, WILLIAM. "The Future That is Already Here," Common-
      weal (28 September), p. 601.
         The dramatic part of Requiem for a Nun is "concerned
      with how yesterday is a part of today," and the historical
      introductions to each act are a vertical history of the
      place. The whole theme of the Yoknapatawpha novels is
      that man can bear anything. The characters of the book do
      all talk like Faulkner, but that is all right for them.

1951

46   POIRIER, WILLIAM. "'Strange Gods' in Jefferson, Mississippi:
      Analysis of Absalom, Absalom!," William Faulkner: Two
      Decades of Criticism, edited by Hoffman and Vickery
      (1951.A2), pp. 217-43.
         Original publication unlocatable; Hoffman and Vickery,
      above, incorrectly cite SR, LIII (Summer 1945). Attempts
      to create history and to derive meaning from it are at the
      thematic center of Absalom, Absalom! Though Quentin,
      like Rosa, has a personal stake in the Sutpen story, his
      interest is broader than hers, because he seeks to under-
      stand a whole society. Sutpen is atypical and his design
      reflects his own psyche, not a Southern myth. The non-
      chronological order of events allows Faulkner to do the
      best dramatization of his central themes. Quentin, at the
      end, refuses to accept the meaninglessness of existence;
      his anguished cry is for humanity: man can learn from,
      not merely react blindly to his history.
      Reprinted 1971.A2.

47   POSTER, HERBERT. "Faulkner's Folly," AMerc, LXXIII (Decem-
      ber), 106-12.
         Faulkner, a self-styled seer and prophet like most Amer-
      ican writers, struggles for more acute insights and more
      recondite symbols, coupling them with popular subject mat-
      ter, to lead man out of his perplexity. In Requiem for a
      Nun he plays the popular against the sublime, but the
      novel does not carry the conviction or dramatic power of
      earlier work. Faulkner, whose personal views are "dixie-
      crat" and "states' rights," has pushed the mystique of the
      Negro beyond the poetic and philosophical beauty found in
      his previous fiction. The narrative introductions contain
      the kind of language and folk humor he does best.

48   PRITCHETT, V. S. "Vogue of Faulkner," NewSt, XLI (2 June),
      624, 626.
         Working in what is America's richest fictional soil--be-
      cause of the Negro and the Civil War--Faulkner has docu-
      mented a culture; his prose and structures are fiendishly
      difficult and willful, his best characters are thin occa-
      sionally, but he gets to the human heart of things, merci-
      lessly. Revised as "The Hill-Billies," Books in General
      (New York: Harcourt, Brace, 1953), pp. 242-47.

49   QUEEN, ELLERY. "Knight's Gambit," Queen's Quorum: A History
      of the Detective-Crime Short Story. Boston: Little
      Brown, pp. 107-10.
         Uncle Gavin and Chick of Knight's Gambit remind the au-
      thor of Melville Davison Post's Uncle Abner stories,

(QUEEN, ELLERY)
especially "The God of the Hills." Faulkner's publisher
is criticized for low-rating the detective genre.

50   RABI. "Faulkner et la génération de l'éxil," Esprit, XIX
(January), 47-65.
Faulkner does not convey solidity or permanence but an
approximate sense of the world's complexity. His work re-
minds one of Greek tragedy. He regrets a lost past.
Reprinted 1951.A2.

51   RANDALL, JULIA. "Some Notes on As I Lay Dying," HopR, IV
(Summer), 47-51.
As I Lay Dying is a sequential array of clear visual
images. The events of the novel are functions of the mind;
events do not take place until conceptualized. Darl's observations provide a metaphor of the method, but Addie's
fading consciousness is what holds it all together. She
looks on from beyond time as she dies in the minds of the
bereaved.

52   RANSOM, JOHN CROWE. "William Faulkner: An Impression,"
HarAv, CXXXV (November), 17.
The Sound and the Fury, As I Lay Dying, and Light in
August are Faulkner's greatest works and sufficient proof
of his genius and power. Faulkner is not, however, "a man
of great learning."

53   RASCOE, LAVON. "An Interview with William Faulkner," WR, XV
(Summer), 300-04.
An unauthorized and apparently inaccurate account of an
interview Faulkner gave to English classes at the University of Mississippi in 1947; See 1951.B3 and 1968.A6,
pp. 52-53.

54   ROGERS, W. G. Review of Requiem for a Nun, Atlanta Journal-
Constitution (23 September), Section B, p. 12.
Requiem for a Nun is perhaps Faulkner's confession as
well as Temple Drake's, an affirmation that God gives us
the best life He can, including the chance to suffer. The
dramatic portions are far superior to the willful narratives.

55   ROSENFELD, ISAAC. "Faulkner and Contemporaries," PR, XVIII
(January), 106-09.
Faulkner's work always comes back to "the basic themes
of blood, land, and the fusion of the two in human character." Collected Stories displays a range of Faulkner's

1951

(ROSENFELD, ISAAC)
work but does not give a full impression of his "legend of
the South." Faulkner writes "poorly" of the "legend," his
style excessive (except in Absalom, Absalom! where it
seems to fit the material), because there is no legend:
the South is no longer different from the rest of the
world. Faulkner believes only in death.

56 SMITH, HARRISON. "The Duty of the Writer," SatR (3 February),
p. 18.
The editor praises Faulkner's Nobel address and his
ideas about the "old verities and truths of the heart."

57 _____. "More Gold Medals," SatR (17 March), pp. 22-23.
Faulkner wins the National Book Award for Collected
Stories.

58 _____. "Purification by Sacrifice," SatR (29 September),
p. 12.
The narrative introductions of Requiem for a Nun are
Faulkner at his best; the dramatic portions, as read, do
not illuminate the characters as well as Faulkner could
have done using novelistic technique, but perhaps dramatization will give them more life. It "might become one of
the most remarkable dramas of our times."

59 STRAUMANN, HEINRICH. "William Faulkner," American Literature
in the Twentieth Century. London: Hutchinson House, pp.
86-89.
Faulkner is both a modernist and a searcher after tradition; his love-hate relationship with the South and his
willful, personal technique are obvious traits. In The
Sound and the Fury, Quentin and Caddy commit incest; that
and other events make it a nihilistic novel. Faulkner's
work repeats the moral condemnation of evil.

60 STYLITES, SIMEON [pseud.]. "In the Name of Allah, Figs!,"
ChrCent (10 January), p. 41.
Referring to a "letter" from Faulkner to The New Yorker
[actually a reprinting of the "Beer Broadside"], the author takes issue with Faulkner's "New Testament exegesis,"
saying that ministers do have a duty to be involved in temporal politics. (See NY [25 November], p. 29, where it is
noted that the most interesting thing about Faulkner's
handbill is the clarity of its prose; "To the Voters of Oxford," the broadside, is reprinted in Essays, Speeches,
and Public Letters [1965.B52].)

61   SULLIVAN, WALTER. "The Tragic Design of Absalom, Absalom!,"
      SAQ, L (October), 552-66.
         Man's failure to choose properly between good and evil
      is the overriding theme which unites all Faulkner's con-
      cerns in the Yoknapatawpha novels. Absalom, Absalom! is
      the key novel in the saga and a genuine tragedy. Sutpen
      is more properly "aristocratic" than Cowley (1946.B2) has
      said.

62   WARREN, ROBERT PENN. "William Faulkner and His South,"
      First Peters Rushton Seminar in Contemporary Prose and
      Poetry, University of Virginia, 13 March. Mimeograph copy,
      15 pp.
         An item in the Massey Collection at the University of
      Virginia, this is a revised version of 1946.B16; reviewed
      further in Warren's Selected Essays (1958.B64); it con-
      tains on p. 15 an anecdote, omitted from published ver-
      sions, about a young Italian who accosted Warren at a
      cocktail party in Rome to say that Faulkner is a "great
      writer . . . a barbarian . . . because he believes in good
      and evil."

63   WEST, ANTHONY. "Requiem for a Dramatist," NY (22 September),
      pp. 109-14.
         The dramatic portions of Requiem for a Nun tell more
      than one can bear about Temple Drake; the overblown narra-
      tives are there for the "higher symbolism." The novel is
      way off Faulkner's best pace.

64   WORSLEY-GOUGH, BARBARA. Review of Knight's Gambit, Spec-
      tator (27 April), p. 566.
         Faulkner's story-telling can turn the old chestnuts of
      the murder mysteries into compassionate, vivid portraits
      of character, as Knight's Gambit demonstrates.

1952 A BOOKS

1   HOWE, IRVING. William Faulkner: A Critical Study. New
     York: Random House.
        Faulkner writes moral fable, a chronicle universal in
     implication that uses the clans and history of the South
     as material. A provincial, he made his great leap in fic-
     tion writing by discovering, in The Sound and the Fury,
     the full force of "the Southern memory, the Southern myth,
     the Southern reality," and writing in opposition to the
     myth as well as under its charm. As his world becomes
     more middle class it becomes more intractable. In his

1952

(HOWE, IRVING)
   treatment of race, Faulkner transcends all stereotypes
   and frees himself from his Southern phobia, especially in
   Intruder in the Dust. Faulkner's moral vision puts emphasis upon the ways man has cursed his own existence and the
   gestures he can make to reaffirm his humanity--his ability
   to survive his own folly. Separate discussions of the major novels--Soldiers' Pay, Sartoris, Knight's Gambit, and
   The Unvanquished excluded--follow general remarks. Revised edition, New York: Vintage, 1962. See 1972.B59 for
   a correction.

2   MINER, WARD L. The World of William Faulkner. Durham, N. C.:
    Duke University Press.
       Oxford, Mississippi does not compare very well with the
    author's own home town in Iowa where the transplanted "New
    England tradition" nourished him in a way it did not nour-
    ish Faulkner. "The children of Oxford would not have
    the thrill I had." He praises Faulkner for coming at last
    to an affirmative view of life.
    Reprinted New York: Grove Press, 1959.

1952 B   SHORTER WRITINGS

1   ARCHER, H. RICHARD. "Ups and Downs of a Faulkner Collector,"
    AntB, IX (5 January), 13-14.
       An account of the vagaries of collecting Faulkner which
    mentions a few letters and the uncorrected proof of The
    Hamlet and says that a "watered-down radio version" of The
    Wild Palms was broadcast, apparently in the 1940s. See
    also 1952.B2.

2   _____. "Collecting Faulkner Today," FauSt, I (Fall),
    42-43.
       An account of acquiring foreign editions of Faulkner's
    works. See also 1952.B1.

3   BAKER, JAMES R. "Notes and Queries," FauSt, I (Spring), 4-7.
       The building of the courthouse in the narrative section
    of Requiem for a Nun dramatizes the relinquishment of in-
    dividual responsibility and ethical judgment in favor of
    law. History is a struggle between "Progress"--typified
    by mass-law--and the individual conscience. The dramatic
    chapters show this theme as it works in contemporary human
    terms.

4   _____. "The Symbolic Extension of Yoknapatawpha County,"
    ArQ, VIII (Autumn), 223-28.
       The Southern dream of success, built on the need for

(BAKER, JAMES R.)
    slavery, was doomed from the start. This theme of Faulk-
    ner's Yoknapatawpha stories may be extended to comment
    upon the dialectic of disparity between Was and Is in mod-
    ern culture. The Wild Palms and Pylon demonstrate the ap-
    plicability to more general and not just specifically
    Southern culture. Man's hope is his continual ability to
    modify his approach to life.

5   BRASPORT, MICHEL. "Autant n'en emportera pas le vent,"
    Réforme (16 February), p. 7.
        The title phrase, which translates "all that is not idle
    talk," applies to all of Faulkner's books. He enthralls
    one.

6   BROOKS, CLEANTH. "Primitivism in The Sound and the Fury, EIE
    1952.
        See 1954.B16.

7   CAMPBELL, HARRY M. "Mr. Roth's Centaur and Faulkner's Symbol-
    ism," WR, XVI (Summer), 320-21.
        The author questions the accuracy and meaningfulness of
    Roth's observations (1952.B44) about Faulkner's symbolism.

8   CANTWELL, ROBERT. "The Faulkners: Recollections of a Gifted
    Family," NWW #2. New York: New American Library,
    pp. 300-15.
        Cantwell recounts his meeting with Faulkner in 1938 when
    doing a Time cover story. What Faulkner told him about
    the family is supplemented by what he was able to learn
    later, including a contemporaneous newspaper account of
    Col. W. C. Falkner's murder.
    Reprinted 1960.A1. See also 1953.B8 and 1953.B9.

9   CARTER, EVERETT. "The Meaning of, and in, Realism," AR, XII
    (Spring), 78-94.
        Discussing the qualities and usefulness of realism, with
    examples from American writing, the author concludes that
    it is still a valid literary approach, using Intruder in
    the Dust as an example of the fictional illusion by which
    an "improbable story" and a "primitive myth" are made con-
    vincing. The realist's framework, with Chick as point of
    view, negates the "illusion" and makes the book honest.

10   CHASE, RICHARD. "The Stone and the Crucifixion: Faulkner's
    Light in August," Critiques and Essays on Modern Fiction,
    1920-1951, edited by John W. Aldridge. New York: Ronald
    Press, pp. 190-99.
        Reprinted from 1948.B7.

11   COINDREAU, MAURICE E. "Préface aux Palmiers sauvages," TM,
      VII (January), 1187-96.
         The alternated plots of The Wild Palms are carefully in-
      woven through theme and plot. Tragic and heroic modes of
      a similar story, the stories use the eternal myths, the
      primal elements to underscore the single meaning of the
      book. Coindreau draws upon the psychological animism of
      Gaston Bachelard to discuss Faulkner's use of the elements.
      Reprinted with Les palmiers sauvages (Paris: Gallimard,
      1952), pp. i-xiv. Translated 1971.B18.

12   ____. "William Faulkner in France," YFS, No. 10 (Fall),
      85-91.
         Coindreau surveys French interest in Faulkner and his
      work as indicated by reviews, translations and prefaces,
      and personal letters. Faulkner's themes, announced in the
      Nobel address, have been the "essence" of French novels
      for a long time, a fact which explains French interest in
      Faulkner. Faulkner's influence on Eugene Dabit and Sartre
      is cited and criticism by Pouillon and Magny recognized.
      Reprinted 1971.B18.

13   COLLINS, CARVEL. "The Interior Monologues of The Sound and
      the Fury," EIE 1952.
         See 1954.B25.

14   COWLEY, MALCOLM. "William Faulkner: An Introduction," Cri-
      tiques and Essays on Modern Fiction, 1920-1951, edited by
      John W. Aldridge. New York: Ronald Press, pp. 427-46.
         Said to be in complete form "for the first time," this
      combines 1945.B2 and 1946.B2.

15   ELSEN, CLAUDE. "Faulkner et le roman noir," Réforme (16 Feb-
      ruary), p. 7.
         Faulkner is the father of the roman noir, but not re-
      sponsible for the excesses of his followers. Sanctuary is
      the foundation stone.

16   ENGLISH, H. M., Jr. Review of Requiem for a Nun and Two Dec-
      ades of Criticism (1951.A2), Furioso, VII (Winter), 60-63.
         Faulkner's novels are like parlor games in which the au-
      thor imposes motivations on a set of given facts. In Re-
      quiem for a Nun the rhetoric which sustains the illusion
      and covers up the improbability is separated from the ac-
      tion. The "requiem" is for Nancy, dead in the eyes of the
      law from the first, and for the "old" Temple Drake.

1952

17 GEISMAR, MAXWELL. "A Rapt and Tumid Power," SatR (12 July),
    pp. 10-11.
        Reviewing Howe's book (1952.A1), Geismar agrees with
    Edith Hamilton's evaluation of Faulkner (1952.B19) and
    says that Howe minimizes the weaknesses of style Hamilton
    points out. Faulkner is the supreme literary voice of
    Southern phobias and haunting fears.
    Reprinted 1958.B26.

18 GUÉRARD, ALBERT J. "Some Recent Novels," Perspective U.S.A.,
    No. 1 (Fall), 171-72.
        At first glance, Requiem for a Nun seems repetitive,
    self-derivative, but a close look reveals the drama as a
    morality play in which Temple and the "Golden Dome" of the
    state capitol were "doomed" to degradation and an attempt
    to salvage decency and honor.

19 HAMILTON, EDITH. "Faulkner: Sorcerer or Slave?," SatR
    (12 July), pp. 8-10, 39-41.
        Our "leading romanticist," Faulkner is the most bril-
    liant of a class of writers who abhor nature and write
    about "ugly people in an ugly land." His attitude is the
    result of a strict Calvinist upbringing. His style is ex-
    cessive, but he makes his books live. Requiem for a Nun,
    with its perversity and sentimentality, indicates that
    Faulkner's point of view has overwhelmed him.
    Reprinted 1959.B29.

20 HARRINGTON, EVANS B. "Technical Aspects of William Faulk-
    ner's 'That Evening Sun,'" FauSt, I (Winter), 54-59.
        There are disadvantages, as well as advantages to Faulk-
    ner's use of Quentin as narrator of "That Evening Sun,"
    the events of which occurred when he was only nine. Negri-
    tude is characterized as an ironic anonymity which protects
    the individual from "problems," a result of Faulkner's
    dramatization of the way life in the South dehumanizes the
    black person.

21 HEILMAN, ROBERT B. "School for Girls," SR, LX (Spring), 299-
    309.
        The introductory historical narratives in Requiem for a
    Nun are, by style and content, made germane to a full ap-
    preciation of the dramatic scenes. They provide continu-
    ity, rhythm. The dramatic passages are appropriately used
    to depict the public confession of the knowledge of good
    and evil which comes from Temple.

1952

22   HEILMAN, ROBERT B. "The Southern Temper," HopR, VI (Fall)
5-15.
Faulkner has all the "Southern senses"--his work picks
up the concrete, elemental, ornamental, and representative.

23   HUMPHREY, ROBERT. "The Form and Function of Stream of Consciousness in William Faulkner's The Sound and the Fury,"
UKCR, XIX (Autumn), 34-40.
Plot, time-unity, scenic arrangement, and symbolic framework provide the functional form of The Sound and the Fury.
The psychic drama in the stream-of-consciousness is used
to illustrate "the collapse of humanism" in a Sartoris
world. Quentin is the novel's central figure.

24   *HUNT, WALLACE. "The Stratagems of William Faulkner," Gambit,
I (Spring), 8-12.
Massey (1968.A4), Item 1703.

25   KIRBY, JOHN PENDY. "Fashions in Sinning," VQR, XXVIII (Winter), 126-30.
The terror and violence of Nancy's act in Requiem for a
Nun forces Temple to seek salvation. The historical narration makes it plain that Yoknapatawpha is a "universal
symbolic setting for the drama of mankind." The form of
the book gives evidence that Faulkner wants to be understood.

26   LITZ, WALTON. "Genealogy as Symbol in Go Down, Moses," FauSt,
I (Winter), 49-53.
The McCaslin genealogy is a comment on Southern history,
and the mixed McCaslin-Beauchamp blood is a symbol of the
South's "original sin." Lucas, in whom the two bloods are
at war, triumphs in "The Fire and the Hearth" when his
Negro heritage dominates. Ike's gift of the hunting-horn
to Roth's mulatto paramour in "Delta Autumn" is a positive
act, "emblem of the lost paradise of love which must be
regained.

27   _____. "William Faulkner's Moral Vision," SWR, XXXVII
(Summer), 200-09.
Go Down, Moses is an especially good source for showing
the consistent moral vision--taken from Biblical themes--
which runs through Faulkner's fiction. History is a burden; man is saddled with the sins of the past. But the
individual has the inner resources to outlast and transcend his heritage, however bad it may be, a gift from
nature. Faulkner's work dramatizes the biblical scheme of
man's broken covenant with God, his attempt to exploit

(LITZ, WALTON)
nature, and the heavy emotional and spiritual price he pays
for his sin. Ike is the emblem of Faulkner's own views
about how the South can expiate its sins; his hail to the
snake indicates his harmony with the natural order.

28   LOWREY, PERRIN. "Concepts of Time in The Sound and the Fury,"
EIE 1952.
See 1954.B49.

29   LYDENBERG, JOHN. "Nature Myth in Faulkner's 'The Bear,'" AL,
XXIV (March), 62-72.
Faulkner sees man as "natural, unthinking (but always
moral) animal"; this is Faulkner's primitive nature myth.
His other myth is the myth of the South. The two appear
together in "The Bear," where the primitive value of the
ritual is undercut by the hunters' heritage of association
with owning land and slaves; the chase of "Old Ben" becomes
a rape.
Partially reprinted 1964.A9; reprinted 1966.B47.

30   McCAMY, EDWARD. "Byron Bunch," Shenandoah, III (Spring), 8-
12.
Light in August dramatizes the conflict between the "representatives" of Lena Grove, who stand for peace, love, the
acceptance of life, and the representatives of Joe Christmas, who stand for violence and self-destruction and the
rejection of love. They meet, appropriately, at Hightower,
in whom the conflict is raging. Byron Bunch represents the
convert--moved from Hightower's orbit to Lena's; he can
change because he is not tyrannized by the past.

31   MALRAUX, ANDRÉ. "A Preface for Faulkner's Sanctuary," YFS,
No. 10 (Fall), 92-94.
Translation of 1933.B13.

32   MARVIN, JOHN R. "Pylon: The Definition of Sacrifice," FauSt,
I (Summer), 20-23.
Schumann's death in Pylon is a sacrificial one which af-
fects the lives of Jack, Laverne, and their unborn child.
It is not tragic, however, but a symbol of total conscious-
ness.

33   *MAYOUX, JEAN JACQUES. "La création du réel chez William
Faulkner," EA, V (February) 25-39.
Faulkner's style, as in the striking opening scene of
Sanctuary, recalls Conrad. Vivid physical signs create
immediacy and reality, a sharp sense of "a complex and

1952

(MAYOUX, JEAN JACQUES)
sorrowful human reality." His stories are full of evil
apparitions like Popeye--the destructive and the antihuman.
Faulkner is, philosophically, an idealist for whom reality
is only a manifestation of consciousness. Translated as
"The Creation of the Real in Faulkner," in 1960.Al,
pp. 156-73.

34 _____. "Faulkner, ou le sens tragique," Combat (6 March),
pp. 12-13.
Taking issue with Coindreau's preface to Les palmiers
sauvages (1952.B11), Mayoux denies Faulkner's glorification
of the primitive at the expense of the bourgeois: the convict turns his back on peril and suffering and denies the
human condition. The novel is about Time and the impossible attempt to transcend the limitations of existence.
Pylon is also discussed.

35 MOHRT, MICHEL. "Les lettres américaines: Les prisonniers du
temps," TaR, No.59 (November), p. 1.
Never previously having read the two parts of The Wild
Palms as they were written and first published but only as
separate texts, the reviewer had not seen what force they
gain by being properly reunited. Mohrt prefers "Wild
Palms" and feels it loses some drama, while gaining eso-
teric significance, by being paired. He praises Coindreau's preface (1952.B11). Harry and the convict choose
prison for the same reasons--the memory of a woman.

36 MORGAN, FREDERICK. "Seven Novels," HudR, V (Spring), 154-60.
Requiem for a Nun is not clearly a novel. The introductory narratives, especially "The Courthouse," have Faulkner's "imaginative sweep," sense of place, and balanced
rhetoric, but the dramatic sections do not come alive and
the whole book is morally obtuse.

37 MORRIS, WRIGHT. "The Violent Land: Some Observations on the
Faulkner Country," Magazine of Art, XLV (March), 99-103.
The novelist reflects on similarities between Faulkner's
fiction and the work of expressionist painters--Soutine,
Van Gogh, Kokoscha, Munch, Rouault. At the heart of
Faulkner's violent landscapes is a "flowering wilderness."

38 O'CONNOR, WILLIAM VAN. "A Short View of Faulkner's Sanctuary," FauSt, I (Fall), 33-39.
The two kinds of evil in Sanctuary are that inherent in
man and that spawned by modern materialism and disharmony
with nature. Faulkner's imagery is used to reveal this
theme.

39   O'CONNOR, WILLIAM VAN. "The State of Faulkner Criticism," SR,
      LX (Winter), 180-86.
         Faulkner's work divides into three periods: up to and
      partly through Sartoris it is influenced by fin de siècle
      atmosphere; through The Wild Palms it is experimental in
      form and focused on violence. From The Hamlet it offers
      "some hope for the human condition." The reviewer surveys
      the critical views represented in Two Decades of Criticism
      (1951.A2) and suggests that Faulkner's themes and style
      are new areas for critics.

40   PEARSON, NORMAN HOLMES. "Lena Grove," Shenandoah, III
      (Spring), 3-7.
         Lena Grove is the focal point of Light in August, symbol
      of the "still unravished bride of quietness" around whom
      there revolves the mad pursuit and the attempts to escape
      the constant circle of life. The novel is Faulkner's hom-
      age to Keats.

41   *POUILLON, JEAN. "Le gambit du cavalier," TM, VII (February),
      1490-96.
         Transatlantic Migration (1955.B54), Item 460.

42   PRESCOTT, ORVILLE. "The Eminently Obscure: Mann, Faulkner,"
      In My Opinion. New York: Bobbs-Merrill, pp. 75-91.
         Hate, cruelty, and violence predominate in the fiction
      of Faulkner, who has never bothered to learn the craft of
      writing.

43   RIDGELY, JOSEPH V. "A Moral Play," HopR, V (Spring), 81-83.
         The dramatic segments of Requiem for a Nun detail
      Nancy's attempt to save Temple, not the reverse. The
      prose narratives are a panorama of "collectivism and em-
      bodied law gradually triumphing over individualism and
      justice." The moral is plain, but no less hard to act
      upon.

44   ROTH, RUSSELL. "The Centaur and the Pear Tree," WR, XVI
      (Spring), 199-205.
         Faulkner's style--and specifically his "not that, but
      this" constructions--force the reader to accept both il-
      lusion and reality, intuiting qualities about things which
      we cannot know directly. A passage in "Spotted Horses"
      illustrates the purpose and meaning of Faulkner's habitual
      style. Images of violence and death, movement and fixa-
      tion are juxtaposed to say that the spring of the spotted
      horses is a time without meaning. See Campbell's reply,
      1952.B7.

1952

45   ROTH, RUSSELL. "Ideas and Queries," FauSt, I (Summer), 23-26.
      Academic criticism of Faulkner fears to see what he has
      been "getting at" because he "flatly denies"--or takes se-
      rious issue with--most of our cherished assumptions about
      our individual relationship with the world. Is there
      "medievalism" in Faulkner's work--i.e., a pre-Enlighten-
      ment point of view?

46   SANDEEN, ERNEST. "William Faulkner: Tragedian of Yoknapataw-
      pha," Fifty Years of the American Novel: A Christian Ap-
      praisal, edited by Harold C. Gardiner. New York: Scrib-
      ner's, pp. 165-82.
      The function of Faulkner's fiction is to bring his re-
      gion face to face with itself. The old South ideal of
      honor--in excess or in defect--is repeatedly challenged:
      it is the basis of Faulkner's tragic vision. Faulkner's
      so-called naturalism and gothicism are merely a passion
      and a penchant for documenting the society he writes about
      and a means to create a proper moral outrage. His violence
      is ethically conceived. His ability to create character
      and tell a story is not harmed by his technical innovation.

47   SARTRE, JEAN PAUL. "William Faulkner's Sartoris," translated
      by Melvin Friedman, YFS, No. 10 (Fall), 95-99.
      Reprints 1938.B14 and 1947.B8.

48   SCHERMAN, DAVID E., and ROSEMARIE REDLICH. Literary America.
      New York: Dodd, Mead, pp. 148-51.
      A photo-essay, this piece has five scenes in and around
      Oxford with quotes from Faulkner's fiction; a brief life
      is included, and Faulkner is taxed for finding the "eman-
      cipated Negro and the modern Southern woman" as chief per-
      petrators of the South's desecration.

49   SCHMIDT, ALBERT-MARIE. "L'esprit et les lettres: Honnêteté
      américaine," Réforme (16 February), p. 7.
      According to Faulkner, crimes are committed by persons
      who seek to free themselves from the constraints of birth,
      environment, and history. Review of Knight's Gambit.

50   STALLMAN, ROBERT WOOSTER, compiler. "Selected Bibliography
      of Faulkner Criticism," Critiques and Essays on Modern
      Fiction, 1920-1951, edited by John W. Aldridge. New
      York: Ronald Press, pp. 582-86.
      A bibliography of criticism which draws on 1951.B44.A.

51   SUTHERLAND, DONALD. "Time on Our Hands," YFS, No. 10 (Fall),
      5-13.

1952

(SUTHERLAND, DONALD)
    The author's discussion of time in the novel accepts as
    valid Sartre's interpretation of Faulkner (1939.B28).

52   THOMPSON, LAWRANCE. "Faulkner's The Sound and the Fury: In-
          troduction," EIE 1952.
          See 1954.B74.

53   _____. "Mirror Analogues in The Sound and the Fury,"
          EIE 1952.
          See 1954.B75.

54   WAGENKNECHT, EDWARD. Cavalcade of the American Novel. New
          York: Holt, pp. 417-25.
          Faulkner's stories and novels are "elaborately interre-
          lated" in a legend or myth of the South. He is a moral
          writer who dramatizes the results of human exploitation of
          both land and men. Some of his technical devices are
          self-defeating.

55   *WAGNER, GEOFFREY. "American Fiction in England," The Adelphi,
          XXVIII (August), 663-72.
          Bassett (1972.A2), Item GG25.

56   WEST, RAY B., JR. "Hemingway and Faulkner: Two Masters of
          the Modern Short Story," The Short Story in America 1900-
          1950. Chicago: Henry Regnery, pp. 85-106.
          Faulkner's stories fill gaps in the Yoknapatawpha chron-
          icle, though they are not dependent upon it. Faulkner and
          Hemingway both seem concerned with the changing valuation
          of the past and its social and moral conceptions. Stylis-
          tically Faulkner's work is more varied. Both write stories
          of initiation.

57   _____. "William Faulkner: Artist and Moralist," WR, XVI
          (Winter), 162-67.
          The jail is a constant reminder of man's limitations,
          failures, and, hence, his humanity, and Requiem for a Nun
          is a continuation of the Yoknapatawpha saga which must be
          read in context with all Faulkner's work. Gavin's wisdom
          seems hubris; Temple and Nancy are not given enough depth.
          The book represents amateur moralism, not the genuine art
          of Faulkner's earlier periods.

58   WILLIAMS, CECIL B. "William Faulkner and the Nobel Prize
          Awards," FauSt, I (Summer), 17-19.
          Faulkner is the first American to win the Nobel Prize
          for literature whose honor met almost no opposition in the
          public press or literary journals.

1953

1953 A BOOKS

1   YNDURÁIN, FRANCISCO. La Obra de William Faulkner. Madrid:
    Anteneo.
       A brief six-part study of Faulkner and his work empha-
    sizes his despair, his pessimism, his difficult style, and
    his treatment of the "problema negro."

1953 B SHORTER WRITINGS

1   ANON. "Doom," NY (28 February), pp. 18-20.
       A reporter visits the office of Saxe Commins, Faulkner's
    editor at Random House, and records Faulkner's behavior
    and remarks while working on A Fable. Faulkner tells
    about the horse he acquired for his daughter in Califor-
    nia in 1944.
    Reprinted in 1968.A6.

2   ADAMS, ROBERT M. "Poetry in the Novel: or Faulkner Esem-
    plastic," VQR, XXIX (Spring), 419-34.
       A preliminary discussion of Coleridge's definition of
    poetry and his refusal to acknowledge prose fiction as im-
    portant precedes an argument for the novel which claims
    that many novelists fit Coleridge's requirements. Faulk-
    ner, with The Sound and the Fury, is the prime example:
    Benjy is a fitting consciousness to demonstrate the living
    consequence of past events. Faulkner is a "composer of
    human natures." The sections of the novel progress from
    the pit of human nature to a meagre "normalcy."

3   ALLEN, WALTER. Review of Requiem for a Nun, NewSt, XLV (21
    February), 214.
       Faulkner is "the greatest living novelist in English,"
    and though Requiem may not be up to his best, it may be a
    key to all his work because of the "religious note" of the
    ending. He has not achieved the poetry of tragedy.

4   ARNAVON, CYRILLE. Histoire littéraire des États-Unis. Paris:
    Librairie Hachette, pp. 311-12, 340-43.
       Faulkner's documentation of a society is not his chief
    value; he is in the tradition of Bierce and Poe as a vi-
    sionary and a skilled technician, and obviously he is in-
    fluenced by Joyce; but his imagination is his own and it
    creates a unique poetic language to go with his intense
    characterizations.

5   AURY, DOMINIQUE. "Le péché des origines," NRF, N. S. I (No-
    vember), 886-93.
       Absalom, Absalom! in the translation by Raimbault and
    Vorce is one of the best French versions of Faulkner's nov-

1953

(AURY, DOMINIQUE)
els, and of Faulkner's novels it is perhaps itself the most significant. Faulkner seeks a truth that can never be surely apprehended by systematic analysis. The primary narrator, Quentin Compson, speaks, despite the fact that his biography in The Sound and the Fury is ignored, from beyond the grave.

6 *BARJON, LOUIS. "Retour aux enfers de Faulkner: Absalon, Absalon!," Études, CCLXXIX (November), 225-36.
Massey (1968.A4), Item 1094.

7 BROOKS, VAN WYCK. The Writer in America. New York: Dutton.
Scattered references to Faulkner stress his importance as a model for young Southern writers, his remarks on the "loss of nerve" in modern authorship, and his defense of the South. The "Negro" hero of "Old Man" is a good example of Faulkner's belief in man's ability to endure, but the sentiments of the Nobel address are not frequently borne out in his fiction.

8 CANTWELL, ROBERT. "Introduction," Sartoris. New York: Signet, pp. vii-xxv.
Sartoris is the "key volume" in Faulkner's works, introducing the two families in his "cycle"--Sartoris and Snopes--whose conflict provides Faulkner's major theme. Also includes material from 1952.B8. Revised and shortened version published with Sartoris (New York: New American Library, 1964), pp. vii-xviii (1964.B13).

9 _____. "Introduction," The White Rose of Memphis, by Col. William C. Falkner. New York: Coley Taylor, pp. v-xxvii.
The White Rose of Memphis, a romantic novel, was written by Faulkner's great-grandfather. The Introduction gives the circumstances of its publication, summarizes the plot, and includes a brief account of Col. Falkner's life. See also 1952.B8.

10 CARTER, HODDING. "Faulkner, Fish, Fowl and Financiers," Where Main Street Meets the River. New York: Rinehart, pp. 199-213.
The Greenville, Miss., editor gives a brief account of the Levee Press and of Faulkner signing copies of Notes on a Horsethief in Greenville.

11 COLLINS, CARVEL. "Are These Mandalas?," L&P, III (November), 3-6.
Jung's theory of the mandala as the symbol of synthesis and peace in the individual may be reflected in the con-

1953

(COLLINS, CARVEL)
cluding pages of "The Bear." Ike is a "psychologically autobiographical" character who survives the conflict of heritages in himself. A similar use of the image may be in Sartoris. Expanded in 1954.B26.

12   _____. "A Conscious Literary Use of Freud?," L&P,
III (June), 2-4.
The monologues of The Sound and the Fury are based on identification of the characters with id, ego, and super-ego. Caddy represents che libido. Each aspect of the psyche has been warped or otherwise harmed by the "poison" in the Compson family--the failure of love.

13   _____. "Nathanael West's The Day of the Locust and
Sanctuary," FauSt, II (Summer), 23-24.
West seems to borrow from Faulkner.

14   COUGHLAN, ROBERT. "The Private World of William Faulkner,"
Life (28 September), pp. 118-36; "The Man Behind the Faulk-ner Myth," Life (5 October), pp. 55-68.
Anecdotes and pictures from Faulkner's family and neigh-bors make up a kind of treatment of his life. Published as 1954.A1.

15   EDMONDS, IRENE C. "Faulkner and the Black Shadow," Southern
Renascence: The Literature of the Modern South, edited by Louis D. Rubin, Jr. and Robert D. Jacobs. Baltimore, Md.: Johns Hopkins University Press, pp. 192-206.
For Faulkner "the collapse of Southern morality and tra-dition" is a result of the conflict between Christian val-ues and unchristian behavior; it creates the Southern bad conscience which is portrayed graphically by the black shadow of the Negro across the pages of Southern history. Faulkner himself is ambivalent about Negroes, showing some abhorrence--especially regarding miscegenation--as in his unwillingness to make a black Joe Christmas unequivocally a Christ figure. Gavin Stevens is his mouthpiece. Faulk-ner's liberalism has expanded over the years, but he is still ambivalent.

16   *ELLISON, RALPH. "Twentieth Century Fiction and the Black Mask
of Humanity," Confluences (December).
Though often using stereotypes, Faulkner has explored the possibility of black humanity better than any other writer. Like the great nineteenth-century novelists, he has seen the Negro as a symbol of man, of the human condition. He has gone beneath stereotypes to see why they exist.

(*ELLISON, RALPH)
    Reprinted in Shadow & Act. New York: Random House, 1964,
    pp. 24-44 (1964.B22). Cited in Massey 1968.B4, Item 1423.

17   ERVAL, FRANÇOIS. "Faulkner après le Prix Nobel," TM, VIII
      (June), 2024-30.
      Faulkner's work, including the recent Requiem for a Nun,
    has never had a large audience even in France. He has not
    been lucky in his translations, either; Absalom, Absalom!,
    the "pièce maîtresse" of his fiction, is not yet available.
    Cowley's Portable gives a wide view of Faulkner's chrono-
    logical development. Despite much critical comparison to
    Balzac, Faulkner is different; his goals are with the in-
    dividual novel, not in a chronologically related series.
    Faulkner does not offer solutions to the Negro problem or
    to any other problem; he believes in the individual's abil-
    ity to resolve his own problems. As his message becomes
    more plain, his fictional powers weaken.

18   FREY, LEONARD H. "Irony and Point of View in 'That Evening
      Sun,'" FauSt, II (Autumn), 33-40.
      Faulkner's use of the adult Quentin to give a child's
    viewpoint in the narration of "That Evening Sun" creates,
    in its disparity, an ironic twist that blends into the
    story's structure. Quentin gives all the elements of the
    tragedy except the murder without ever actually realizing
    that Nancy is knowingly under a sentence of death. Her
    figure dominates the story.

19   GWYNN, FREDERICK L. "Faulkner's Prufrock--and Other Observa-
      tions," JEGP, LII (January), 63-70.
      There are numerous echoes of T. S. Eliot's work in Mos-
    quitoes and Pylon, weakening Faulkner's work. Talliaferro
    in Mosquitoes is a Prufrock figure, weak and frustrated.

20   HOFFMANN, A. C. "Point of View in Absalom, Absalom!," UKCR,
      XIX (Summer), 233-39.
      The past is the thing of great importance in Absalom,
    Absalom!, with Quentin as the link between past and pres-
    ent. Faulkner uses his different narrative points of view
    --Compson and non-Compson--in stark contrast. Quentin is
    the only character who does not escape the past.

21   HORNBERGER, THEODORE. "Faulkner's Reputation in Brazil,"
      FauSt, II (Spring), 9-10.
      Faulkner is somewhat neglected in Brazil in terms of
    translations, criticism, and general awareness.

1953

22   JACOBS, ROBERT D. "Faulkner and the Tragedy of Isolation,"
        HopR, VI (Spring-Summer), 162-83.
            Quentin Compson, Joe Christmas and Thomas Sutpen, "the
        chief protagonists of William Faulkner's tragic drama,"
        all have in common their attempts to master time, and all
        fail because they lack understanding of man's obligations
        to "love and honor and pity and sacrifice." Each causes
        his own defeat. Light in August and Absalom, Absalom! are
        discussed at length. The alternative to tragic isolation
        is Chick Mallison of Intruder in the Dust who does not al-
        low the "doom of blood" to excuse him from moral responsi-
        bility. Sutpen's pride should reveal to Quentin the
        brigandage that has created the pride--and Fate--of his
        own family.
        Reprinted as "Faulkner's Tragedy of Isolation," in South-
        ern Renascence, edited by Rubin and Jacobs (Baltimore:
        Johns Hopkins University Press, 1953), pp. 170-90.

23   JAFFARD, PAUL. "Le double aspect de l'oeuvre de Faulkner,"
        Crit, IX (June), 496-507.
            Faulkner's metaphysical "désespoir" makes him congenial
        to the young French writers. His South is truer than na-
        ture; it is universal.

24   LISCA, PETER. "Some New Light on Faulkner's Sanctuary,"
        FauSt, II (Spring), 5-9.
            The trial is the key to Sanctuary's meaning. Temple per-
        jures herself under pressure from her family, who know
        everything, somewhat against her wishes. The Drakes barter
        "honor for its name in the world." There is a Sartoris/
        Snopes conflict in the background.

25   MACLACHLAN, JOHN M. "No Faulkner in Metropolis," Southern
        Renascence: The Literature of the Modern South," edited
        by Louis D. Rubin, Jr. and Robert D. Jacobs. Baltimore:
        Johns Hopkins University Press, pp. 101-11.
            In Europe artists congregate in the cities; but American
        cities have produced no writer of Faulkner's genius. The
        author discusses differences between the American city and
        Faulkner's Jefferson. Faulkner's county and town "wring
        out the inner realities" of a broad Southern culture con-
        tained in many places. The isolation and disapproval
        faced by the artist in a small town leave only the giants
        alive to create.

26   MOSES, W. R. "Where History Crosses Myth: Another Reading
        of 'The Bear,'" Accent, XIII (Winter), 21-33.
            Ike remains a child, an inhabitant of the myth-world of

(MOSES, W. R.)
the lost past; he examines history and finds it evil,
whereupon he rejects it along with material necessity and
worldly responsibility. The fyce dog has a figuratively
proper attitude, showing courage, unselfconsciousness,
ridiculousness but no shame. Ike is seen as "comfortable
enough" in his old age.

27   O'CONNOR, WILLIAM VAN. "Faulkner's Legend of the Old South,"
WHR, VII (Autumn), 293-301.
Strict allegorical interpretation of Faulkner's work is
too simplistic; Faulkner attributes virtues to many
classes, though his early work glorifies the antebellum
South. Absalom, Absalom! and The Unvanquished demonstrate
Faulkner's ability to go beneath the romantic stereotype
of the old South, as in "An Odor of Verbena."

28   _____. "William Faulkner's Apprenticeship," SWR, XXXVIII
(Winter), 1-14.
The author recounts Faulkner's early life, derived from
published interviews and accounts, and discusses his early
work, including the pieces from the New Orleans Times-
Picayune and the first three novels.

29   _____. "Protestantism in Yoknapatawpha County," Southern
Renascence: The Literature of the Modern South,
edited by Louis D. Rubin, Jr. and Robert D. Jacobs.
Baltimore: Johns Hopkins University Press, pp. 153-
69.
Faulkner's interest in Protestantism springs from his
observations of Southern society, where rigidity, the desire for punishment for real or imagined sins, and a sharp
contrast with Latin ability to be at ease in the world are
the puritan qualities. Light in August can be understood
perfectly only when one sees that the spirit of Puritanism
broods over the story and holds the separate plots together. The novel's ending shows that the discipline of the
Southern religion has its consolations.

30 * _____. "The Sound and the Fury and the Impressionist Novel,"
Northern Review, VI (June-July), 17-22.
Bassett (1972.A2), Item E46. Included in 1954.A2.

31   _____. "The Wilderness Theme in Faulkner's 'The Bear,'"
Accent, XIII (Winter), 12-20.
The wilderness is no panacea for present ills such as
racial injustice, but a lost world, a "neurotic dream" of
escape. Ike McCaslin's indoctrination into the mysteries

1953

(O'CONNOR, WILLIAM VAN)
of the wilderness does not fit him for successful life in the real present world.

32   ODUM, HOWARD W. "On Southern Literature and Southern Cul-
      ture," Southern Renascence: The Literature of the Modern
      South, edited by Louis D. Rubin, Jr. and Robert D. Jacobs.
      Baltimore: Johns Hopkins University Press, pp. 84-100.
         The sociologist Odum replies to Donald Davidson's "Why
      the Modern South has a Great Literature" (See 1957.B15),
      adding to Cowley's list of Faulkner's themes (1946.B2):
      the power of the historic evolutionary past; the deep sub-
      conscious struggle for survival and mastery of life; and
      the theme of the Negro, his background and on-going history.

33   PAVESE, CESARE. "Un angelo senza cura d'anima," La lettera-
      tura americana e altri saggi, 2nd ed. Torino: Einaudi,
      pp. 167-70.
         Sanctuary is a pretentious thriller, with nothing by way
      of content. Faulkner's style is too slow-paced; his tone
      too anguished. Faulkner is "an angel . . . with no care
      of souls."
      Reprints 1934.B21.

34   PERRY, BRADLEY T. "Faulkner Critics: A Bibliography Break-
      down," FauSt, II (Spring-Winter), 11-13, 30-32, 60-64.
         The compiler lists reviews and essays about specific
      Faulkner works, alphabetically by book; citing number of
      words in reviews.

35   POUILLON, JEAN. "À propos d'Absalon, Absalon!," TM, IX (Oc-
      tober), 742-52.
         Faulkner's so-called obscurities have faded with the pas-
      sage of time, so the 1953 French translation of Absalom,
      Absalom! is less difficult than it would have been in 1936,
      the year of its American publication. But it is not just
      time that has made the difference: we have come to under-
      stand Faulkner's world. Faulkner does not create puzzles.
      Absalom, Absalom! is about noncommunication. And the South
      is dead because of the way black people have been treated.

36   RYAN, MARJORIE. "The Shakespearean Symbolism in The Sound
      and the Fury," FauSt, II (Autumn), 40-44.
         Quentin Compson in The Sound and the Fury, who was never
      intended as the "hero" of the book, is appropriately char-
      acterized by imagery out of Shakespeare: he is no Prince
      Hamlet, nor was meant to be, but identified with Macbeth

(RYAN, MARJORIE)
of the speech which is the source of the title. Time symbolism and the motif of the walking shadow make it seem
that, like Macbeth, Quentin sees life as "empty, meaningless, futile." He is not merely a neurotic obsessed with
chastity, but the "shadow of a tragic hero" in a world
empty of love.

37   SCOTT, ARTHUR L. "The Faulknerian Sentence," PrS, XXVII
(Spring), 91-98.
The author complains of Faulkner's obscurity of style
and difficult structure. The second sentence of Absalom,
Absalom! is an example which reveals Faulkner's faults and
virtues, as well as his "pet" words. A new generation of
readers seems to find intuitively new and better ways to
read Faulkner.

38   SMITH, HENRY NASH. "Faulkner and Reality," FauSt, II (Summer), 17-19.
Reprints 1932.B19, under a new title.

39   STANZEL, FRANZ. "Die Zeitgestaltung in William Faulkners
'The Bear,'" NS, III, 114-21.
Faulkner skillfully manipulates several planes of time
in "The Bear," and uses time-consciousness and tensions
between time-"terrasse" as structure.

40   SULLIVAN, WALTER. "Southern Novelists and the Civil War,"
Southern Renascence: The Literature of the Modern South,
edited by Louis D. Rubin, Jr. and Robert D. Jacobs. Baltimore: Johns Hopkins University Press, pp. 112-25.
The Civil War is a period in which the truths of the
human heart which Faulkner liked to write about were mani-
fest. The Unvanquished provides an example: Bayard modifies traditional morality with Christian principles.

41   SWIGGART, PETER. "Moral and Temporal Order in The Sound and
the Fury," SR, LXI (Spring), 221-37.
Quentin and his father foresee no future, find the present illusory, and lose themselves in an absorption with
the past in The Sound and the Fury. If the past then becomes intolerable, one can no longer live. Quentin's
chief fault is that he is lost in egotism; thus he cor-
rupts his idealism. By contrast, the innocent Benjy, unaware of self and ignorant of time's passage, sees things
whole. Dilsey, another primitive, is likewise contrasted:
in her, love projects outward.

1953

42   THOMAS, DOUGLAS M. "Memory-Narrative in Absalom, Absalom!,"
        FauSt, II (Summer), 19-22.
          Absalom, Absalom! gets its form and power from "memory-
        narrative"--a device whereby events just reappear in the
        mind as impressions dominated by emotion, then only grad-
        ually are reconstructed by a full recollection of all that
        preceded and constituted them. The final effect comes
        when all visual-emotional events suddenly form into a
        whole--the denouement of the reader's long struggle with
        the novel.

43   VICKERY, OLGA. "Gavin Stevens: From Rhetoric to Dialectic,"
        FauSt, II (Spring), 1-4.
          Gavin Stevens shows growth from book to book. Ironic
        and ineffective in Intruder in the Dust, he becomes in-
        creasingly active until in Requiem for a Nun he is a power-
        ful moral force.

1954 A BOOKS

1   COUGHLAN, ROBERT. The Private World of William Faulkner.
        New York: Harper & Brothers.
          This impression of Faulkner's life and art is expanded
        from the Life pieces (1953.B14); it includes photographs
        of related people and places. The land lies at the center
        of Faulkner's philosophy and his fiction.
        Reprinted New York: Cooper Square, 1972.

2   O'CONNOR, WILLIAM VAN. The Tangled Fire of William Faulkner.
        Minneapolis: University of Minnesota Press.
          O'Connor offers his antidote to Faulkner criticism which
        relies on the Sartoris/Snopes formula and the view of
        Faulkner as traditionalist mourning bygone values and de-
        crying the amoral present. Summarizing the fiction and
        interspersing anecdotal biography, the author offers a
        broader, more universal, humanistic Faulkner. Faulkner's
        work is in three periods: fin de siècle decadence in the
        first three novels; great, grim, dignified novels up
        through The Wild Palms; and a late, hopeful period. The
        style and structure are often weak in Faulkner's novels.
        Portions previously published: 1952.B38, 1952.B39,
        1953.B28, 1953.B29, 1953.B30, 1953.B31.
        Reprinted 1968.A8.

1954 B SHORTER WRITINGS

1   ANON. Review of Mirrors of Chartres Street, NY (30 January),
        pp. 91-92.

1954

(ANON.)
A "heartless, not to say morbid disinterment" of juvenile work better left alone is the reviewer's judgment upon the collection of New Orleans sketches.

2   ANON. "William Faulkner: After Ten Years, A Fable," Newsweek (2 August), 48-50, 52.
    Newsmagazine journalism takes a look at A Fable and its author in a cover story.

3   ANON. "Faulkner Wall Plot," Life, XXXVII (9 August), 77-78.
    A brief account of the outline of A Fable which Faulkner wrote on the wall of his study at Rowanoak, with photographic reproductions of Monday through Sunday, omitting the "Tomorrow" section (which is behind a door). All the passages are transcribed in 1966.B76.

4   ANON. "Faulkner Speaking," Time (23 August), p. 76.
    The interviewer records random remarks from Faulkner on writing and literature: "Capote...makes me nervous."
    He prefers Flaubert, Balzac, Don Quixote, and the Bible.

5   ANON. "Place and Time: The Southern Writer's Inheritance," TLS (17 September), p. xlviii.
    In the context of a discussion of Southern writing, it is noted that place is very important in the Yoknapatawpha saga.

6   ANDERSON, CHARLES R. "Faulkner's Moral Center," EA, VII (January), 48-58.
    Seneca and Cicero, not Calvin, seem to be the basis of Faulkner's morality. He is a humanist. No single character in his fiction speaks for him.

7   AYMÉ, MARCEL. "What French Readers Find in William Faulkner's Fiction," Highlights of Modern Literature, edited by Francis Brown. New York: New American Library, pp. 103-06. Reprinted from 1950.B1.

8   BACHE, WILLIAM B. "Moral Awareness in 'Dry September,'" FauSt, III (Winter), 53-57.
    "Dry September" is, in one sense, a parody of the Hollywood movie in which the hero rescues the pretty girl. The setting is hellish. Minnie and McLendon, who cause the murder, exchange miseries, hysteria, and loneliness at the end. There is a homonymous association between Will Mayes and "maize" and "maze" that invites interpretation. See rejoinder 1956.B20.

113

1954

9 BACKMAN, MELVIN. "Sickness and Primitivism: A Dominant Pattern in William Faulkner's Work," Accent, XIV (Winter),
   61-73.
      Faulkner's work is based on a contrast between "sick"
   characters--driven, divided, isolated figures--and spiri-
   tually whole primitives who are insulated from the violent
   forces which drive the sick heroes and who, though seldom
   triumphing, offer a reminder of the hope for man. The author discusses six novels, from Sartoris to The Wild Palms,
   in terms of his hypothesis.

10 BAKER, CARLOS. "Cry Enough," Nation (7 August), pp. 115-18.
      In A Fable Faulkner projects his story through an ironic
   reversal of the gospel story, something to be expected
   from the author of The Sound and the Fury, Light in August,
   and Absalom, Absalom! The pace is snail-like through the
   middle of the novel. The theme is the antagonism between
   the powers of the world and the simple man's "cry Enough."
   The novel is summarized at length.

11 BARTH, J. ROBERT. "A Rereading of Faulkner's Fable," America,
   XCII (9 October), 44-46.
      In a "demurrer" to the review in America by H. C. G.
   (1954.B37), Fr. Barth says that despite its difficulties,
   A Fable is intelligible. Its theme is more important than
   the symbols used to convey it. The General and the Corporal in their changing roles represent the qualities of
   Everyman--the duality of earthbound man who has spiritual
   aspirations. It is a positive "critique" of the world.

12 *BEALE, BETTY. "William Faulkner and Senator Mundt Attend A.
   Burks Summers' Big Party," Washington Evening Star
   (14 June), p. 3-B.
      Bassett (1972.A2), Item DD14. Reprinted Lion in the
   Garden (1968.A6). Faulkner expresses his low opinion of
   the McCarthy hearings to a society gossip columnist cover-
   ing an engagement party for his daughter and future son-in-
   law.

13 BENSON, CARL. "Thematic Design in Light in August," SAQ, LIII
   (October), 540-55.
      Hightower is the central character in Light in August,
   an ethical "slide rule" to measure other characters. He
   moves from isolation to involvement in the lives of Lena
   and Joe. Joe, though blameless for it, is at the opposite
   pole. Community is not an unqualified good. Hightower
   dies at the end.
   Reprinted 1973.A9.

14   *BOUVARD, LOÏC. "Entretien avec William Faulkner," France-
Amérique (January).
      Reprinted, translated, in 1960.B11 and in 1968.A6.
Faulkner discusses his use of Bergson and his love for the
French in a 1951 interview by a French graduate student at
Princeton. He answers questions on his work and beliefs.

15   BREIT, HARVEY. "In and Out of Books--Word's Worth," NYTBR
(19 September), p. 8.
      Corrects the NY reviewer of A Fable (1954.B40) who had
not been able to understand Faulkner's use of the word
"prevail." It means that man will prevail over the disas-
ters of his own creation.

16   BROOKS, CLEANTH. "Primitivism in The Sound and the Fury,"
EIE 1952. New York: Columbia University Press, pp. 5-28.
      Faulkner is not a primitivist putting a premium on the
natural instincts of the young, simple, or natural character, as The Sound and the Fury repeatedly shows. Faulkner
demands of his best people discipline, moral responsibility, and an initiated understanding of life's complexities.
The novel is about the break-up of the institution of the
family in the modern community. See rejoinder by Campbell
and Foster, 1954.B18.

17   *CAMBON, GLAUCO. "Prefazione," Assalonne, Assalonne!, translated by Glauco Cambon. Milan: Mondadori, pp. 7-17.
      Faulkner forces the reader to make contact with the
lives of the characters and with the story of Absalom,
Absalom! The drama reveals both Sutpen and the modern
narrators who confront him across the abyss of time. It
is a psychological story of Quentin's discovery of his own
tortured self in the past with which he identifies. Sutpen is the heroic and tragic South doomed by its failure
to solve racial, economic, and ethical problems, but,
larger than allegory, he is a typical culture hero, too,
like Theseus or Aeneas or Oedipus, brought low by Time.
Reprinted in part, translated into English by Cambon, in
1973.B22.

18   CAMPBELL, HARRY M., and RUEL E. FOSTER. "An Answer to
Cleanth Brooks' Attack," FauSt, III (Summer-Autumn), 40-42.
      The authors (1951.A1) cite Lovejoy and Boas's Documentary
History of Primitivism to argue, contra Brooks (1954.B16),
that their definition of primitivism is applicable to
Faulkner.

19   CARROUGES, MICHEL. "Faulkner le voyant," Monde nouveau-paru,
No. 75 (January), 74-79.
      Faulkner cannot be illuminated by a list of his themes

1954

(CARROUGES, MICHEL)
and devices; he illuminates, as Absalom, Absalom! can be
used to demonstrate. At any moment, Faulkner can capture
the presence of the past. His manipulations are not technique but magic.

20 CHAMETZKY, JULES. "Some Remarks on A Fable," FauSt, III (Summer-Autumn), 39-40.
Modified from a piece in Folio (University of Indiana),
the review asserts that A Fable fails by going into a
place and time with which Faulkner is uncomfortable and
unfamiliar.

21 CHENEY, FRANCES NEEL. "Faulkner's Fable," VQR, XXX (Autumn),
623-26.
A Fable must not be interpreted as too literal a parallel with Passion Week or the life of Christ. It is an
imitation of Christ--a human act. Cowley's review
(1954.B28) failed to appreciate that the correspondences
were not literal.

22 *COINDREAU, MAURICE E. "William Faulkner et Ernest Hemingway,"
Journal de Genève (11 and 12 December), p. 4.
On the occasion of Hemingway's Nobel Prize award,
Coindreau reflects briefly on Faulkner's comparative ob-
scurity and greater achievement.
Reprinted, translated, 1971.B18.

23 COLLINS, CARVEL. "Faulkner and Certain Earlier Southern Fiction," CE, XVI (November), 92-97.
The author summarizes critical speculations on Faulkner's relation to genteel or realistic antebellum writing,
discusses his use of the flamboyant humor, violence and
folklore of the old southwestern writers, and argues for
the serious intent, as well as the traditional literary
sources of Faulkner's use of these elements. Ike McCaslin
is one of the characters Faulkner "admires without reser-
vation." Collins reveals his discovery of Faulkner juvenilia "at the site of a house which had burned ten years
previously" [not identified as the Phil Stone home in
Oxford].

24 *____. "Faulkner's Reputation and the Contemporary Novel,"
Literature in the Modern World, edited by William J.
Griffin. Nashville, Tenn.: George Peabody College for
Teachers, pp. 65-71.
Massey (1968.A4), Item 1320.

116

25   ____. "The Interior Monologues of The Sound and the Fury,"
        EIE 1952. New York: Columbia University Press,
        pp. 29-56.
            Benjy, Quentin and Jason draw respectively on Freud's
        concepts of Id, Ego, and Super-Ego, which Faulkner might
        easily have known before composing The Sound and the Fury,
        and there is further general use of Freudian theories of
        behavior in the book.
        Reprinted in 1970.A6, revised.

26   ____. "A Note on the Conclusion of 'The Bear,'" FauSt, II
        (Winter), 58-60.
            Using C. G. Jung's definition of the mandala as a symbol
        of the unity of life, the synthesis of or reconciliation
        of warring elements of personality, Collins speculates
        about the closing scenes of "The Bear," suggesting the
        presence of the mandala in Ike's visit to the grave of
        Lion and the squirrel clearing, symbolic representations
        of Ike's reconciliation.

27   ____. "War and Peace and Mr. Faulkner," NYTBR (1 August),
        pp. 1, 13.
            Structurally firm, A Fable makes use of characteristic
        Faulkner devices such as the passion of Christ, the de-
        layed revelations, and his demanding style.

28   COWLEY, MALCOLM. "Faulkner's Powerful New Novel: Biblical
        Overtones, Daring Symbols," NYHTB (1 August), pp. 1, 8.
            A basic contradiction appears in all the great scenes of
        A Fable: Faulkner's idealism--which opposes war--and his
        logic--which recognizes war's occasional necessity--are at
        war in this complex "novel, golden legend, and . . . pas-
        sion play." Puzzling and unsatisfying, the novel is still
        better than most modern novels.

29   CUNLIFFE, MARCUS. "William Faulkner," The Literature of the
        United States. London: Penguin, pp. 284-89.
            Faulkner's view of the South is complex, sometimes inco-
        herent, but his depiction of fatality is balanced by a
        dramatization of the human ability to endure. Reprinted
        in new editions 1959, 1961, and 1964, revising the author's
        opinion about Faulkner's later work, which he sees as com-
        ing to show a "warmer interest" in decent characters.

30   DOMINICIS, A. M. "An Interview with Faulkner," translated by
        Elizabeth Nissen, FauSt, III (Summer-Autumn), 33-37.
            Original in La Fiera Letteraria (14 February 1954).
        Faulkner talks about A Fable and the reasons a man writes.

1954

31   ELIAS, ROBERT H.   "Gavin Stevens: Intruder?," FauSt, III
          (Spring), 1-4.
          Critics misinterpret Gavin Stevens as Faulkner's mouth-
       piece.   Intruder in the Dust is Chick Mallison's story.
       The scale and importance of other characters is a reflec-
       tion of his point of view.   What Chick learns—and his
       uncle's voice is one of his teachers—is the lesson of hu-
       man consciousness, responsibility, and individuality.

32   ERVAL, FRANÇOIS.   "Faulkner deuxième manière," TM, X (Novem-
          ber), 750-54.
          Before the Nobel Prize, from The Sound and the Fury to
       The Wild Palms, Faulkner's work concentrated on characters,
       not ideas; since the war, and especially since the prize,
       Faulkner has increasingly allowed his moral concerns to
       dominate his fiction.   A Fable is the most blatant example
       yet: the novel, as such, has disappeared.   Everything
       stands for something, as it did not in the earlier work.
       Faulkner has given up the novel's great subjects in favor
       of depicting goodness, which is boring.

33   FIEDLER, LESLIE.   "Stone Grotesques," NRep (23 August),
          pp. 18-19.
          Faulkner's stylistic flaws stand out grotesquely in A
       Fable because the matter of the book is itself static.
       The novel tries to make explicit the sentimental Protes-
       tant ethos that has always informed Faulkner's writing.
       The reviewer praises the figure of the Supreme Commander
       and the section on the horsethief.

34   FLINT, R. W.   "Faulkner as Elegist," HudR, VII (Summer), 246-
          57.
          Contrary to Howe (1952.A1), Light in August is meaning-
       ful as is, unified by Joe Christmas's suffering, which is
       comparable to Hightower's but which brings Hightower back
       to the world.   Faulkner's best work is neither too much in
       the past nor too much in the present.   Passages from Light
       in August, Absalom, Absalom! and Go Down, Moses are used
       to demonstrate Faulkner's firm, controlled purposeful
       style.   Faulkner writes "plain novelistic fiction with a
       poetic dimension."

35   FLOWERS, PAUL.   Review of A Fable, Memphis Commercial Appeal
          (1 August), Section V, p. 12.
          Too detailed, too symbolic, too obscure, A Fable will
       puzzle or irritate most readers.   It is symptomatic of a
       general trend toward evangelism in the work of major mod-
       ern authors.

36   FOSTER, RUEL E. "A Further Note on the Conclusion of 'The
         Bear,'" FauSt, III (Spring), 4-5.
            Boon Hogganbeck hammers the squirrel tree in the last
         scene of "The Bear" to keep the squirrels from escaping.
         The scene contrasts with his killing of the bear. What
         Ike sees in the woods, then, is an objective correlative
         for the Götterdämmerung ending the wilderness and its
         heroic age.

37   G., H. C. "William Faulkner's A Fable," America, XCI
         (21 August), 502.
            A symbolical novel, A Fable is also an enigma without
         key. Even if the key is found, however, the reviewer
         doubts "that a treasure will be found inside." See reply
         1954.B11.

38   GEISMAR, MAXWELL. "Latter-Day Christ Story," SatR (31 July),
         pp. 11-12.
            A Fable is the best Faulkner novel of the past decade,
         but it fails as a Christ allegory. Faulkner cannot accept
         the conditions of modern life; his book is a sermon on his
         own need to believe.
         Reprinted 1958.B26.

39   GÉRARD, ALBERT. "Justice in Yoknapatawpha County: Some Sym-
         bolic Motifs in Faulkner's Later Writing," FauSt, II
         (Winter), 49-57.
            Faulkner is not all apocalypse, even in his early work,
         but the point is best illustrated by "Monk" in Knight's
         Gambit, where the idiot, Faulkner's most marginal Southern
         man, has a sense of the past and an attachment to the soil.
         One must conclude from the stories in Knight's Gambit that
         "the tragedy is over," Faulkner has a hero in Gavin
         Stevens, and hope is available.

40   GILL, BRENDAN. "Fifth Gospel," NY (28 August), pp. 78-80.
            A Fable is a "calamity," a bad small novel needlessly
         padded. See Breit's rejoinder, 1954.B15.

41   GOELLNER, JACK GORDON. "A Closer Look at As I Lay Dying,"
         Perspective, VII (Spring), 42-54.
            Despite surface similarities, As I Lay Dying is quite
         different from The Sound and the Fury. The novel's mean-
         ing is found in the psychology of the Bundrens and their
         complex interrelationships; each member of the family has
         a differentiated tone, point of view, and character.
         "Cash is the finest character in the novel." The ending
         is not a farce.

1954

42   HASTINGS, JOHN. "Faulkner's Prose," SatR (18 September),
      p. 23.
           In a letter to the editor, the reader complains about
      the deliberately obscure style of A Fable, which he feels
      is a result of Faulkner's unwillingness to polish.

43   HIGHET, GILBERT. "The New Books," Harper's, CCIX (September),
      98-103.
           Reviewing A Fable, O'Connor (1954.A2) and Miner
      (1952.A2), the writer observes that as a tragic novelist,
      Faulkner understands that there must be lofty language;
      hence his style, which often falls into excess. The novel
      is a powerful, nightmarish fantasy with an incredible plot.

44   HOWE, IRVING. "Thirteen Who Mutinied, Faulkner's First World
      War," Reporter (14 September), pp. 43-45.
           A Fable is a mixture of Faulkner's strengths and weak-
      nesses; there is no strong evidence of coherence and an
      unjustifiably mannered style.

45   _____. "William Faulkner's Enduring Power," NYTBR (4 April),
      pp. 1, 22.
           The Faulkner Reader is not as useful as Cowley's Portable
      Faulkner, but it does not do as much violence to Faulkner's
      novels. Faulkner's introduction is "undistinguished and
      rather frenetic." The Sound and the Fury, printed whole,
      convinces one of Faulkner's power and universality. "The
      Bear" shows how deeply he has absorbed major American
      themes and images. His vision is comprehensive.

46   HUMPHREY, ROBERT. Stream of Consciousness in the Modern Nov-
      el. Berkeley: University of California Press, pp. 17-21,
      57-58, 64-70, 73-74, 106-111.
           The Sound and the Fury is about the collapse of humanism
      among Faulkner's aristocrats; it centers on Quentin, so
      Faulkner uses stream-of-consciousness to put the struggle
      "in terms of Quentin's psychic conflict." As I Lay Dying
      and The Sound and the Fury are used to demonstrate what
      stream-of-consciousness can do: depict multiple levels of
      meaning, achieve suspension of mental content, discontinu-
      ity or compression.

47   LEE, EDWY B. "A Note on the Ordonnance of The Sound and the
      Fury," FauSt, III (Summer-Autumn), 37-39.
           One principle behind the order of the sections of The
      Sound and the Fury may be a progression of increasing nar-
      rative action with decreasing "dream structure," keyed to
      either the use or abandonment of flashback.

48   LISCA, PETER. "The Hamlet: Genesis and Revisions," FauSt,
      III (Spring), 5-13.
         Without using MSS or TSS, Lisca argues from publication
      dates and other evidence that Snopes stories in magazines
      were taken from Faulkner work-in-progress conceived in the
      1920s; The Hamlet is a unified novel, not a collection of
      stories. The Snopeses are also more varied than critics
      of Faulkner's "mythology" have noted. Love, fertility,
      and the capture of Frenchman's Bend by Flem provide the-
      matic unity.

49   LOWREY, PERRIN. "Concepts of Time in The Sound and the Fury,"
      EIE 1952. New York: Columbia University Press, pp. 57-82.
         Each character's conception of time is appropriate to
      Faulkner's thematic and structural concerns in the novel,
      which is "not a philosophical presentation of time con-
      cepts," but a work of fiction where time concepts and de-
      vices give form to the material. Benjy has no time sense;
      Quentin and Jason are each differently obsessed with time;
      Dilsey understands and appreciates the meaning of time.

50   LUCCHESE, SAM F. Review of A Fable, Atlanta Journal-Constitu-
      tion (1 August), Section F, p. 6.
         In the "gripe department," the reviewer lists length,
      vocabulary, sentence style, certain anglicisms, and omis-
      sion of apostrophes in one-word contradictions. The
      "fable theme" is stressed at the expense of the kind of
      great "stuff" Faulkner used to write about Mississippi.

51   McGILL, RALPH. "Faulkner's Cry for Compassion," Atlanta
      Journal-Constitution (10 August), p. 1.
         The editor finds that A Fable is a powerful allegory far
      greater than the other novels of the season. Its theme is
      the corporal's effort to make men love God and their neigh-
      bors as themselves. Confusing the runner in the final
      scene with the corporal, McGill notes that A Fable is
      not supposed to be easy to read.

52   MACLEAN, HUGH N. "Conservatism in Modern American Fiction,"
      CE, XV (March), 322-25.
         Conservatism is adherence to such beliefs as "order"
      versus "natural rights," some form of human proclivity
      toward violence and error versus natural goodness, and
      doubt of human perfectibility. "The Bear," discussed in-
      dependently of the novel Go Down, Moses, is "centrally im-
      portant" to Faulkner's work, revealing the divine scheme
      for man's life and the "right reason" which will lead to
      reunion with God and Nature through relinquishment of
      selfishly motivated desires.

1954

53   MAGNY, CLAUDE-EDMONDE. "Faulkner's Inverse Theology," trans-
        lated by Elizabeth Stambler, CrCur, IV (Spring-Summer),
        204-22.
            Reprinted, translated, from 1948.B20; See also 1966.A8
        and 1972.B69.

54   MERCIER, VIVIAN. "A Search for Universality That Led Too Far
        From Home," Commonweal (6 August), pp. 443-44.
            Unlike Dostoevsky's Idiot, a partial Christ story set in
        a place the author knew well, Faulkner's A Fable fails be-
        cause it is too involved in its parallels to the gospels
        and set in too unfamiliar a place for Faulkner. The horse-
        thief section "probably symbolizes the human qualities
        that Faulkner wishes to celebrate" better than does the
        rest of the book.

55   MOHRT, MICHEL. "William Faulkner: ou, démesure du souvenir,"
        Preuves, IV (April), 8-14.
            Like Balzac and Proust, Faulkner is profuse, profound.
        His comedy is not unified nor written by plan like Bal-
        zac's. Surveying the work, the critic discusses Faulkner's
        style and other characteristics.

56   PAULDING, GOUVERNEUR. "A Note in Rejoinder," Reporter (14
        September), pp. 45-46.
            Denies (See Howe, 1954.B44) that A Fable is specifically
        a Christ fable; Faulkner is looking at man's suffering.
        Faulkner does not prejudge the General--who represents the
        wisdom of the world--but he uses him to raise the neces-
        sary questions about why war exists.

57   PEARSON, NORMAN HOLMES. "Faulkner's Three Evening Suns,"
        YULG, XIX (October), 61-70.
            The author compares a fragmentary MS draft at Yale, the
        version by Mencken at AMerc, and the These 13 version of
        "That Evening Sun," and quotes a portion of an unpublished
        introduction to Sartoris also at Yale (See 1973.B11), dis-
        cussing Faulkner's revisions. Compare Manglaviti,
        1972.B70.

58   PODHORETZ, NORMAN. "William Faulkner and the Problem of War,"
        Commentary, XVIII (September), 227-32.
            A Fable is dull, tortured, and pretentious; it may be
        one of Faulkner's worst books. Faulkner's work is harmed
        by the lack of the middle-class consciousness and the val-
        ues of the Enlightenment. Faulkner has no ideas. A Fable
        is a "religious" demonstration of the failure of nerve.
        See rejoinder, 1954.B78.
        Reprinted 1966.A8.

59 PRITCHETT, V. S. "Time Frozen," PR, XXI (September-October),
    557-61.
    A Fable explores the conflict "between the moral claims
    of war... and the anguish of man." Faulkner's myth is
    more powerful than his characters, and his style is often
    too obscure.
    Reprinted 1966.A8.

60 RAYMOND, BERNARD. "A Fable, by William Faulkner," ArQ, X
    (Winter), 361-63.
    Giving his impressions of an appreciative first reading,
    the reviewer points up musical analogies for the structure
    of A Fable, discusses ambiguities, and concludes that it
    is Faulkner's act of repentance for all he wrote to glorify
    war and violence in his earlier work. It is a "brilliant
    celebration" of man's ability to suffer and endure with
    courage. Like the Gospels, it requires the opposite of
    reason to be understood.

61 REAVER, J. RUSSELL. "This Vessel of Clay: A Thematic Com-
    parison of Faulkner's As I Lay Dying and Latorre's The Old
    Woman of Peralillo," FSUSt, No. 14. Tallahassee, Fla.:
    Florida State University, pp. 131-40.
    Comparing Faulkner's novel to the 1937 short story by
    Chilean Mariano Latorre, the author makes no claim for in-
    fluence or source; instead he compares the ways in which
    each author dramatizes the reaction to death and its emo-
    tional associations, arguing that Faulkner's farce is thin
    and crude by comparison, cheapening the theme of death.

62 RICE, PHILIP BLAIR. "Faulkner's Crucifixion," KR, XVI (Au-
    tumn), 661-70.
    A Fable is flawed and uneven, its philosophical import
    questionable; the action is too remote from Faulkner's ex-
    perience. The best parts are the familiar portions, like
    the horsethief episode.
    Reprinted 1960.A1.

63 ROBERTS, ERNEST F. "Faulkner," Commonweal (27 August), p. 514.
    A letter-writer explains the failures of A Fable as being
    caused by an age that has lost belief. It is a step for-
    ward in the search to find belief and restore God to modern
    life.

64 ROLO, CHARLES J. "Reader's Choice," AtlM, CXCIV (September),
    79-80.
    A Fable seems to be the "most inaccessible" novel Faulk-
    ner has written. Though "spurious and unreal," it is a
    "heroically ambitious" failure.

1954

65   RUBIN, HAROLD.   Review of A Fable, New Orleans Times-Picayune
      (1 August), Section II, p. 4.
           A Fable is Faulkner "at his best, readable, bitter, sa-
      tiric." It is a symbolic story of the false armistice.

66   RUNYAN, HARRY.   "Faulkner's Non-Fiction Prose: An Annotated
      Checklist," FauSt, III (Winter), 67-69.
           The author provides a selective checklist of Faulkner's
      prose sketches, introductions, and reviews.

67   _____. "Faulkner's Poetry," FauSt, III (Summer-Autumn),
      23-39.
           Faulkner's collected and uncollected published poetry is
      mostly either about Nature or about love; the style is
      often derivative or stereotyped. Mutability is the dom-
      inant theme. Swinburne and Housman are the chief models,
      but there are traces of Rossetti, Cummings and Eliot.
      There is a list of published poems.

68   SAWYER, KENNETH B.   "Hero in As I Lay Dying," FauSt, III
      (Summer-Autumn), 30-33.
           The quest in As I Lay Dying is not heroic but brutal and
      meaningless. Jewel, the character upon whom so much atten-
      tion is focused, manages to reach tragic proportions.

69   SCOTT, ARTHUR L.   "The Myriad Perspectives of Absalom, Absa-
      lom!," AQ, VI (Fall), 210-20.
           The calculated confusion of Absalom, Absalom! is the re-
      sult of shifts in viewpoint or perspective used for aes-
      thetic purposes: the creation of suspense, variety. But
      Faulkner also has the motives of the modern artist, such
      as cubistic point of view and futuristic interest in mo-
      tion, behind his techniques. Difficulties with the novel
      are the reader's, not the author's, fault.

70   SHERWOOD, JOHN C.   "The Traditional Element in Faulkner,"
      FauSt, III (Summer-Autumn), 17-23.
           Faulkner uses a number of traditional literary forms and
      themes: Gothicism, incest, the lost child, buried treas-
      ure, the trickster, the beautiful girl disguised as a man.
      Faulkner uses the grossest form of naturalism in conjunc-
      tion with the most excessive kinds of romance, and his work
      contains "serious weaknesses."

71   SMITH, FRANK ELLIS.   The Yazoo River, illustrated by Janet E.
      Turner. New York: Rinehart, pp. 297-304.
           Smith quotes extensively from Faulkner's work to set the
      mood of rural Mississippi for his Rivers of America series
      piece.

72   *STEWART, RANDALL. Review of A Fable, Providence Sunday Jour-
       nal (1 August). Reprinted under the title "Faulkner Tells
       a Wartime Fable," edited by George Core, GaR, XXII (Spring
       1968), 128-30.
          In one of the early reviews of A Fable, Stewart says the
       claim that it is Faulkner's greatest work is absurd. It
       lacks the dramatic presentation of human tragedy that is
       in his best fiction.

73   SWIGGART, PETER. "Two Faulkner Critics," SR, LXII (Autumn),
       696-705.
          Reviewing Howe (1952.A1) and O'Connor (1954.A2), the
       critic lists the inadequacies of both, then goes on to
       call "The Old Man" a novel and to assert that Gavin Stevens
       is Faulkner's spokesman. He thinks O'Connor's background
       material is accurate.

74   THOMPSON, LAWRANCE R. "Faulkner's The Sound and the Fury:
       Introduction," EIE 1952. New York: Columbia University
       Press, pp. 3-4.
          Each essay in the symposium on The Sound and the Fury
       attempts close analysis of a single technical element of
       the novel. For the essays, See 1954.B16, 1954.B25,
       1954.B49, and 1954.B75.

75   _____. "Mirror Analogues in The Sound and the Fury,"
       EIE 1952. New York: Columbia University Press,
       pp. 83-106.
          Mirrors as image, symbol, and structural principle per-
       form a major role in The Sound and the Fury. For Benjy,
       the missing mirror in the Compson house is an analogue of
       the absent Caddy; Quentin's obsession with his shadow, his
       reflection in the water, and similar images depicts his
       self-absorption and prepares for his suicide. The Macbeth
       soliloquy of the title mirrors the actions of Quentin,
       Quentin's parents, and Jason. The four sections are like
       a hinged mirror, reflecting certain peculiar visions of
       reality, which work in pairs.
       Reprinted 1966.A8, 1973.A9.

76   VICKERY, OLGA W. "The Sound and the Fury: A Study in Per-
       spective," PMLA, LXIX (December), 1017-37.
          The sections of The Sound and the Fury are static, focus-
       ing on character, providing different perspectives on
       Caddy, the loss of her virginity, and what it means to
       each character. The novel progresses from Benjy's uncon-
       nected world of shapes through increasingly public images
       to the omniscient fourth section. Incorporated into
       1959.A4.

1954

77   WAGNER, GEOFFREY. "Faulkner's Contemporary Passion Play,"
      TC, CLVI (December), 527-38.
          Primarily violent and horrifying, Faulkner's work has
      recently taken on a change for the moral and religious
      which is reflected fully in A Fable. The British reviewer
      finds A Fable to be "literary evangelism" which fails to
      dramatize its message.

78   WASSER, HENRY. "Faulkner as Artist," Commentary, XVIII (De-
      cember), 569-70.
          Taking issue with Norman Podhoretz's review of A Fable
      (1954.B58), the writer argues that Faulkner is a "minor
      writer" not because he "does not recognize the enlight-
      ened qualities...brought into the world by the middle
      class," but because "he is unaware of the middle class,
      its taste, its moderation." Podhoretz does not evaluate
      Faulkner on literary terms. Faulkner may be criticized
      for his carelessness, his indifference to the reader, his
      "inability to portray the complexity of the human being in
      respect to self and in relation to society."

79   WATKINS, FLOYD C. "The Structure of 'A Rose for Emily,'"
      MLN, LXIX (November), 508-10.
          A five-part structure defined by visits to Emily from
      the outside world gives "A Rose for Emily" a symmetry un-
      usual for Faulkner. The central section signifies the in-
      domitableness of the old order, for in it no one enters
      the house.

80   *WEST, ANTHONY. "William Faulkner: A Critical Consensus,"
      Study of Current English (Tokyo), X (September), 28-29.
          Bassett (1972.A2), Item GG31.

81   WEST, RAY B., JR. "The Modern Writer," CE, XV (January),
      207-15.
          The Sound and the Fury, among other novelists' work, il-
      lustrates the writer's comments about the difficulty of
      modern writing and how it may be understood. Faulkner's
      method resembles musical composition "where themes are in-
      troduced in isolation or in simple combinations, then de-
      veloped...in a series of movements."

82   WHICHER, STEPHEN E. "The Compsons' Nancies: A Note on The
      Sound and the Fury and 'That Evening Sun,'" AL, XXVI (May),
      253-55.
          The writer corrects misapprehensions (in Cowley, Campbell
      and Foster, and O'Connor) about the identity of "Nancy" of
      "That Evening Sun" and The Sound and the Fury. In the

(WHICHER, STEPHEN E.)
   novel the children refer to an animal destroyed because of
   a broken leg, not to the Negro cook of the short story.

83   ZINK, KARL E. "William Faulkner: Form as Experience," SAQ,
     LIII (July), 384-403.
        Faulkner's formal devices--including syntactic as well
     as overall structure--seek to communicate precise, immedi-
     ate experience. The article investigates Faulkner's use
     of point of view and flashback as structure and suspended
     syntax as style. Incremental repetition, from different
     points of view, achieves an increased sense of complexity:
     for example, reports of Joe Christmas's death in Light in
     August, accounts of Eula's growing up in The Hamlet, the
     versions of the Sutpen story in Absalom, Absalom!

1955 A   BOOKS

1   ANON. William Faulkner: Bibliography and Criticism, 1951-54.
     Supplement, 1951-54. Eugene, Oregon: Oregon University
     Library.
        Two alphabetical listings of published work on Faulkner
     and his fiction.

1955 B   SHORTER WRITINGS

1   ANON. "Fight to the Finish," TLS (10 June), p. 313.
        A Fable belies its title by failing to be simple. It
     fails because the tone is unvarying and the structure too
     complex. Faulkner shows man's martyrdom not his redemp-
     tion.

2   ANON. "Scenes from America," TLS (19 August), p. 473.
        Faulkner's County (London: Chatto & Windus, 1955), an
     English version of the Faulkner Reader with different con-
     tents, is a good arrangement with ample evidence of Faulk-
     ner's merits as a short story writer.

3   ANON. Review of Big Woods, NY (19 November), p. 236.
        A Christmas book with a "certain unity."

4   BECK, WARREN. "The New Faulkner," CE, XVII (December), 183-
     84.
        The preludes to the stories in Big Woods come unacknowl-
     edged from Requiem, "Red Leaves," "A Justice," and "Missis-
     sippi," and the epigraph is adapted from "Delta Autumn."
     The book seems to "water down" Faulkner's brilliant fic-
     tion.

5   BREIT, HARVEY. "In and Out of Books--Youth," NYTBR (20
     March), p. 8.
        Students at Brown University have a little review which
     acts just like a big one; it claims that A Fable has been
     universally misunderstood.

6   ____. "A Walk with Faulkner," NYTBR (30 January), p. 4.
        Faulkner clarifies his famous rating of modern authors,
     mentions going to Europe for the U. S. Government, and
     announces Big Woods.
        Reprinted 1956.B9 and 1968.A6.

7   BRENNAN, DAN. "Journey South," UKCR, XXII (Autumn), 11-16.
        As a young college student, Brennan arrived unannounced
     at Faulkner's Oxford home, was received cordially and
     granted some conversations recorded here. See 1962.B1.
     Reprinted 1968.A6.

8   *BRIERRE, ANNIE. "Faulkner Parle," NL (6 October), pp. 1, 16.
     Reprinted, revised, as "Dernière rencontre avec Faulkner,"
     NL (12 July 1962); reprinted, 1968.A6.
        In a 1955 interview, Faulkner admits his pleasure in
     Paris, where he would not live because he would not be
     able to work; criticizes his great-grandfather's White
     Rose of Memphis; and gives Sherwood Anderson credit for
     his beginnings as a writer. He has been to the theatre
     five times in his life: three times for Hamlet, once for
     Ben Hur, and once for Midsummer Night's Dream.

9   BROWN, ANDREW. "The First Mississippi Partisan Rangers,
     C.S.A.," CWHi, I (December), 371-99.
        A documented account of Col. W. C. Falkner's war experi-
     ences.

10   BRUMM, URSULA. "Wilderness and Civilization: A Note on Wil-
     liam Faulkner," PR, XXII (Summer), 340-50.
        In A Fable, Faulkner has advanced his belief that all of
     human history and achievement is the product of rapacity,
     pitting the passive resistance of his Corporal against the
     whole tide of life. Faulkner's deep-seated distrust of
     civilization and its benefits or horrors is revealed in Go
     Down, Moses. Faulkner may be compared to Cooper; like his
     Natty Bumppo, Faulkner's Sam Fathers represents wilderness
     against civilization. Faulkner is a humanist not a primi-
     tivist: his characters reject the trappings of civiliza-
     tion but they represent the "archetype of man suffering"
     and renouncing "the power and the privilege."

11   CARTER, THOMAS H. "Dramatization of an Enigma," WR, XIX
      (Winter), 147-58.
            The "fable" in Faulkner's A Fable is correct, but much
      of the writing associated with other matters is quite
      wrong. At its best it dramatizes the enigma of man's in-
      volvement in terrible but sometimes necessary wars to pre-
      serve his frail and partly absurd civilization.

12   CHAPSAL, MADELEINE. "A Lion in the Garden," Reporter (3 No-
      vember), p. 40.
            At a cocktail party given by Faulkner's French publisher
      in Paris, Faulkner reveals his personal strengths and so-
      cial discomfort to a sympathetic observer.
      Reprinted 1968.A6.

13   CORKE, HILARY. "Bad Conscience," Encounter, V (October), 85-
      87.
            A Fable is a good conception, but the style and form are
      discouraging. The early pieces in Faulkner's County, an
      author's selection, seem far better.

14   COWLEY, MALCOLM. "Life of the Hunter," NYTBR (16 October),
      pp. 4, 44.
            Big Woods is a unified integrated book, but its virtues
      have been achieved at the expense of Go Down, Moses and
      the theme of black-white relationships so important there.

15   *D'AGOSTINO, NEMI. "William Faulkner," SA, I, pp, 257-308.
            The "first long article" on Faulkner in Italy, according
      to Materassi (1971.B60), sees Faulkner in terms of "nega-
      tive" aspects of the "aesthetic traditionalism" espoused
      by the Southern Agrarians. Faulkner's close relation to
      the formalists is responsible for his overly complex struc-
      tural experiments. Culturally disadvantaged, Faulkner
      created a limited poetics which is mannerist and gratui-
      tously vague. Faulkner is at his best when his "choral
      poetry" coincides with his subject matter, as it does in
      the last two sections of The Sound and the Fury.

16   EDEL, LEON. The Psychological Novel 1900-1950. Philadelphia:
      Lippincott, pp. 147-53.
            The three stream-of-consciousness sections of the four-
      part The Sound and the Fury are differentiated by each
      character's concept of time. In them, Faulkner has given
      a dramatization of the tragedy of the South, where time
      and the past are an obsession and also both out of joint.
      Faulkner's European experience in World War I in Oxford,
      England, helped to show him the way to the timelessness of

1955

(EDEL, LEON)
his fiction.
Reprinted 1961.B22, and, with the addition of 1962.B22, in
1964.B21.

17   FADIMAN, CLIFTON. "Party of One," Holiday, XVIII (December),
6-19.
The columnist briefly mentions Faulkner's essay in
Harper's on privacy and the American Dream ("On Privacy
The American Dream: What Happened to It?").

18   _____. "William Faulkner," Party of One. Cleveland: World
Publishing Co., pp. 98-125.
A "case study of the non-Faulknerian mind," the essay
records, with some humility, Fadiman's twenty-five years
of public dismay and doubt concerning Faulkner's fiction,
revealed through selections from his reviews in Nation and
NY.

19   FLINT, R. W. "What Price Glory?," HudR, VII (Winter), 602-06.
A Fable is artificial and flat, an idea conceived in
Hollywood which should have remained there. It is not
satisfactory as a "martial elegy" or as a "symbolic parable."

20   FRIEDMAN, MELVIN J. Stream of Consciousness: A Study in
Literary Method. New Haven: Yale University Press, pp.
8-11, 252-55.
The narratives of The Sound and the Fury move from childhood to age, from confusion to awareness, bringing an increasing perceptiveness that the reader actually experiences. As I Lay Dying is less ambitious, and does not have
the same kind of structural development. Faulkner's later
work is a reaction against the stream-of-consciousness
method.

21   GALHARN, CARL. "Faulkner's Faith: Roots from The Wild
Palms," TCL, I (October), 139-60.
Faulkner began as a "Southerner devout in most of the
facets" of his traditional society, became disillusioned,
and worked through to a new faith. Sexuality was a "source
of abhorrence" in the early novels. The Wild Palms represents a change; there is hope as well as abhorrence in the
sexuality of that novel. The convict is heroic, tested
and found not wanting.

22   HALSBAND, ROBERT. "Faulkner and the Critics," SatR (26
March), p. 19.

130

(HALSBAND, ROBERT)
The best Faulkner criticism has been written by other
creative writers.

23   HARTT, JULIAN N. "Some Reflections on Faulkner's Fable," Religion in Life, XXIV (Fall), 601-07.
A Fable is not blasphemous; it is Faulkner's attempt to
come to grips on his own terms with a story which has repeatedly lured artists. It "witnesses" to man, not God.
It is not a very good or successful work.
Reprinted 1963.B42.

24   HEINEY, DONALD W. "William Faulkner," Essentials of Contemporary Literature. Great Neck, N. Y.: Barron's Educational
Series, pp. 133-43.
In a brief overview of Faulkner's life and work for the
young student, the author stresses the Sartoris/Snopes
dichotomy and Faulkner's regionalism, violence, and uncon-
ventionality.
Reprinted Recent American Literature (Great Neck, N. Y.:
Barron's, 1958), pp. 208-27.

25   HOFFMAN, FREDERICK J. The Twenties. New York: Viking Press,
pp. 213-16.
The Sound and the Fury is a successful use of the sub-
conscious because of the way Faulkner limits and blends
his perspectives and facts. Each brother monitors Caddy's
moral life on his own terms; the monologues prepare us,
however, for the external view through Dilsey.

26   HOPKINS, VIOLA. "William Faulkner's The Hamlet: A Study in
Meaning and Form," Accent, XV (Spring), 125-44.
Symbolism, characterization, humor, and meaning all give
formal richness and complexity to The Hamlet. Flem is central, though generally off-stage; his antagonists are rep-
resented by Ratliff, whose moral view and commentary give
one level of unity. Scenes and characters are carefully
balanced and contrasted. Humorous incidents, in parallel
and in contrast, and repeated humorous language help unify
the book.

27   HUBBELL, JAY BROADUS. "Who Are the Best American Writers? A
Study of Some Critical Polls Sponsored by American Magazines," Anglo-Americana (Vienna-Stuttgart), No. 70,
pp. 80-91.
The essay, which discusses how the ebb and flow of literary reputations are reflected in polls, anthologies, literary histories, literary prizes, and other forms of ranking

1955

(HUBBELL, JAY BROADUS)
our authors, is the germ of Hubbell's Who Are the Major American Writers? (1972.B54). Faulkner is included.

28   KAZIN, ALFRED. "Faulkner in His Fury," The Inmost Leaf. New York: Harcourt, Brace, pp. 257-73.
The words and ideas of the Nobel address are germinal for all Faulkner's work. A long quote from Intruder in the Dust shows how the flowing periods of Faulkner's style create a world and individuals with troubled souls. Includes material from 1951.B36.

29   KENNER, HUGH. "A Fable," Shenandoah, VI (Spring), 44-53.
A Fable is, in some respects, a reductio ad absurdum of how to write a profound book by larding it with significance. Faulkner has abased the language shockingly, leaving us, in this case, not some of the usual illuminations, but a contrived myth.

30   KING, ROMA, JR. "The Janus Symbol in As I Lay Dying," UKCR, XXI (June), 287-90.
The theme of As I Lay Dying is frustration. Contradictory states of being, symbolized by the horse (man's animal state) and the fish (female fertility and a Christian image) are never resolved.

31   KOHLER, DAYTON. "A Fable: The Novel as Myth," CE, XVI (May), 471-78.
A Fable is not simple reenactment of the Christ story nor an account of a second coming, but a modern application of mythology to "contemporary conflict and disaster." It is a moral symbolism in which events or characters are heightened by association with an ancient, accredited account of fundamental human problems. The Corporal is not Christ but a man "willing to assume the risks of humanity." The novel is central to Faulkner; criticism has only skimmed it.

32   _____. "A Fable: The Novel as Myth," EJ, XLIV (May), 253-60.
Same article as 1955.B31.

33   LEAVER, FLORENCE. "The Structure of The Hamlet," TCL, I (July), 77-84.
The Hamlet has a narrative as well as a thematic structure--the drama of Snopes versus the community which reaches its turning point in the spotted horses episode. Mrs. Littlejohn is at the head of a hierarchy of minds set in different kinds of opposition to Snopesism, and only she is invulnerable to Snopeses.

34   LEWIS, R. W. B. The American Adam: Innocence, Tragedy, and
      Tradition in the Nineteenth Century. Chicago: University
      of Chicago Press, p. 199.
           Ike McCaslin is tantalized into a lifelong quest for the
      innocence which once existed in the New World.

35   LIND, ILSE DUSOIR. "The Design and Meaning of Absalom, Absa-
      lom!," PMLA, LXX (December), 887-912.
           Individual and social error combine in monumental form
      and with great artistry to create a new myth in Absalom,
      Absalom! Faulkner makes mythic, tragic, and biblical as-
      sociations with his characters to create an "atmosphere of
      doom." The narrators are the center of the novel, reflect-
      ing the dramatic events of Sutpen's history, providing a
      synthesis in the reader, and ultimately illuminating Quen-
      tin Compson's personal tragedy. Each narrator has two
      voices: conversational and bardic.
      Reprinted 1973.A9.

36   _____. "The Teachable Faulkner," CE, XVI (February),
      284-87, 302.
           The Sound and the Fury, while a challenge to the teacher,
      may prove too complex for the student; in order to teach
      it, attention must be given to the four styles and view-
      points, to changes of mood and symbolism, and the whole
      book should be assigned for re-reading after close analy-
      sis. Race relations, psychology, and religious symbolism
      make Light in August inherently engaging to students;
      teaching it should concentrate on unity, contrast, social
      symbolism, and charting time sequences. As I Lay Dying
      and Absalom, Absalom! do not teach well. Sanctuary is a
      poor risk. The stories are useful introductions to Faulk-
      ner.

37   LYTLE, ANDREW. "The Son of Man: He Will Prevail," SR, LXIII
      (Winter), 114-37.
           The Generalissimo as a young man learns all a man can
      know, a knowledge he eventually shares with the Quarter-
      master (his John the Baptist) and the Corporal (his son).
      A summary discussion of Faulkner's achievement through The
      Unvanquished points up the failure of technique in A Fable.
      Reprinted 1966.B48.

38   MACLAREN-ROSS, JULIAN. "A Fable, by William Faulkner,"
      LonMag, II (November), 84-87.
           It is paradoxical that Faulkner should put his apparent
      credo--a paraphrase of the Nobel speech--in the mouth of
      the devil's advocate in A Fable. The horsethief episode

1955

(MACLAREN-ROSS, JULIAN)
seems the only misplaced portion of the narrative, though
the Gospel parallels are overelaborately exploited.

39 MIZENER, ARTHUR. "The Thin Intelligent Face of American Fiction," KR, XVII (Autumn), 507-24.
Gavin Stevens, an intelligent, sensitive, educated man,
has the problem of finding a place for his own ideals in
democratic society. In "Go Down, Moses," the concluding
story of the like-named novel, he illustrates the "innocence and incongruity of the community's solidarity," unable to participate in the homely ritual which satisfies
Mollie and Miss Worsham. Gavin and Faulkner are identified
together especially in Knight's Gambit and Intruder in the
Dust.

40 MOHRT, MICHEL. "William Faulkner: ou, Une religion du
temps" and "A Fable, 'nouveau testament' de Faulkner," Le
nouveau roman américain. Paris: Gallimard, pp. 80-118,
119-23.
Massey (1968.A4), Items 1955 and 1960.

41 *O'CONNOR, WILLIAM VAN. "William Faulkner and the Spirit of
Protestantism," Frontiers (April), 7-10.
Bassett (1972.A2), Item AA93.

42 ONIS, HARRIET de. "William Faulkner," Torre, III (October-
December), 11-26.
Faulkner's work is calvinistic and, in his dislike of
women, in the tradition of St. Paul and St. Augustine.
Faulkner's fiction is surveyed in a discussion of style,
character, and structure.

43 PENICK, EDWIN A., JR. "The Testimony of William Faulkner,"
ChrSch, XXXVIII (June), 121-33.
Faulkner's work deepens our understanding of the human
condition. His characters yearn for the assurances of
meaning in life we all seek. Pride, selfishness, and hard-
ness are inextricable from evil in Faulkner's characters.
He should not be labeled superficially: humanism, deism,
stoicism, nature mysticism, and fatalism are all found in
his work.

44 PHILLIPS, WILLIAM L. "Sherwood Anderson's Two Prize Pupils,"
UChiMag, XLVII (January), 9-12.
Faulkner's Yoknapatawpha is an elaboration of Anderson's
method in Winesburg, Ohio. The author gives an account of
personal and literary relations between the two men.

45   PUSEY, WILLIAM WEBB, III. "William Faulkner's Works in Ger-
      many to 1940: Translations and Criticism," GR, XXX (Octo-
      ber), 211-26.
         German translations of Faulkner's work are listed and
      evaluated. The 1935 translation of Light in August was
      the beginning of his critical fame there.

46   RICHARDSON, MAURICE. Review of A Fable, NewSt, XLIX (18
      June), 863-64.
         A Fable is the weekly reviewer's bane, too long, with
      "intermittent corpse-flares of genius." There is no char-
      acter for the reader to identify with.

47   *ROMANOVA, ELENA. "Antivoyennyie motivy v tvorchestve Uilyama
      Folknera," Inostrannaya literatura, VI, 170-76.
         The essay, "Anti-War Themes in the Work of William Faulk-
      ner," is summarized in Brown, Soviet Attitudes Toward Amer-
      ican Writing (1962.B29), pp. 180-81.

48   ROSENBERGER, COLEMAN. "Four Faulkner Hunting Stories, Rich
      in Narrative and Symbol," NYHTB (16 October), pp. 1, 16.
         As a tribute to Malcolm Cowley's "perception" that "The
      Bear" as a hunting story omits part IV, Faulkner publishes
      it with that omission in Big Woods. Virtue prevails only
      in the very young and the very old.

49   ROTA, BERTRAM. "Contemporary Collections, 7: The George
      Lazarus Library (The William Faulkner Collection)," BC, IV
      (Winter), 279-84.
         The bookman describes the George Lazarus Faulkner collec-
      tion, which includes first editions and manuscripts, in-
      cluding "Bench for Two" (a version of "Pennsylvania Sta-
      tion") and "Light in August," a portion of the novel er-
      roneously described as a short story apparently "unrelated"
      to the novel of that title; and a full holograph MS of Ab-
      salom, Absalom!, which, along with other material in this
      collection, is now at the University of Texas. (See the
      catalogue of an exhibition at Texas, 1959.B48; and Lang-
      ford's partial transcription of the Absalom MS, 1971.A4.)

50   ROUSSEAUX, ANDRÉ. "L'enfer de Faulkner," Littérature du
      vingtième siècle, 5th series. Paris: Editions Albin
      Michel, pp. 115-33.
         The biblical story of Amnon, Absalom, and Tamar explains
      the events of Faulkner's Absalom, Absalom! before we open
      the book. Incest evaded only by fratricide and the doomed
      family reaping the horrors of a carnal life are emblems of
      what happens to Faulknerian man when he puts a blind faith

1955

(ROUSSEAUX, ANDRÉ)
in temporal things. Faulkner's work is a beautiful cry
thrown at the walls of the prison of existence.

51   SARTRE, JEAN-PAUL. "William Faulkner's Sartoris," Literary
and Philosophical Essays, translated by Annette Michelson.
New York: Criterion, pp. 73-78.
Translation of 1938.B14 and 1947.B8.

52   _____. "On The Sound and the Fury: Time in the Work of
Faulkner," Literary and Philosophical Essays, translated
by Annette Michelson. New York: Criterion, pp. 79-87.
Translation of 1939.B28 and 1947.B7.

53   SCHWARTZ, DELMORE. Review of A Fable, Perspectives USA, X
(Winter), 126-36.
   Faulkner's use of the Gospel account of Christ's passion
functions simply and only as an example of "supreme nobility." The real point of the novel is to question whether
human beings, caught in a characteristic posture--i.e.,
war--deserve supreme nobility. Typical mistaken readings
will see the book as a cruel and heretical parody or a
simplistic religious affirmation. Problems of style, once
their deliberate difficulty is mastered, dissolve. The
book is Faulkner's masterpiece. The interview between the
supreme commander and the Corporal is the key to the meaning of the book.
Reprinted 1970.B70.

54   SMITH, THELMA M. and WARD L. MINER. "Faulkner," Transatlantic
Migration: The Contemporary American Novel in France.
Durham, N. C.: Duke University Press, 122-45.
   From the first, Faulkner was regarded by the French as
one of the greatest and most philosophical of twentieth
century writers. Many essays published in the wake of the
Nobel Prize award, however, essentially echoed earlier remarks and were journalistic in nature. The authors list
translations of Faulkner's novels, stories, speeches,
poems, extracts, and other material; provide a bibliography
of 64 critical articles in French periodicals; and give a
brief list of reviews of Faulkner's books.

55   SPILLER, ROBERT E. "The Uses of Memory: Eliot, Faulkner,"
The Cycle of American Literature. New York: Macmillan,
pp. 291-300.
   Faulkner shared Steinbeck's social concerns, his "faith
in the primitive as the seat of truth," his ethical bent
and his humor. He lived his art intensely, uncompromising

136

(SPILLER, ROBERT E.)
   in both style and technique, and he made of his local scene
   an "objective correlative" for human experience.
   Reprinted New York: New American Library, 1957, pp. 208-
   28.

56   STAVROU, CONSTANTINE N. "William Faulkner's Apologia: Some
      Notes on A Fable," ColQ, III (Spring), 432-39.
         Faulkner's philosophy recognizes man's limitations while
      it believes in man's potential for sacrifice and endurance.
      It is neither pessimistic nor overly romantic, but merely
      realistic. Intruder in the Dust and Requiem for a Nun are
      inferior to novels for which they represent "solutions"--
      that is, Light in August or Sanctuary. A Fable, however,
      rises above the deliberately polemical and is an eloquent
      statement of Faulkner's philosophy.

57   STEWART, RANDALL. "The Outlook for Southern Writing: Diag-
      nosis and Prognosis," VQR, XXXI (Spring), 252-63.
         Faulkner is the greatest Southern writer; he embraces
      all levels of society, language, and point of view.

58   SWIGGART, PETER. "Time in Faulkner's Novels," MFS, I (May),
      25-29.
         Faulkner makes a point of emphasizing the time-sense of
      such characters as Benjy, Quentin, Jason, Dilsey, Lena
      Grove, Joe Christmas, and Darl Bundren; Eula Varner defies
      time, is timeless. Possible sources for the conscious ex-
      ploitation of time exist in Eliot, Joyce and Bergson.
      Faulkner seems to divide his world between those who seek
      to separate past and present, and those who accept time as
      a continuum.

59   TILLEY, WINTHROP. "The Idiot Boy in Mississippi: Faulkner's
      The Sound and the Fury," American Journal of Mental Defi-
      ciency, LIX (January), 374-77.
         Benjy is not accurately an idiot nor imaginatively
      brought to life. The Sound and the Fury is an interesting
      failure.

60   UNTERMEYER, LOUIS. "William Faulkner," Makers of the Modern
      World. New York: Simon and Schuster, pp. 702-11.
         A survey of Faulkner's career reveals his work to be
      violent, innovative, filled with catastrophe and agony,
      concerned with the "rotting" civilization of the Old South.
      Later work like Requiem for a Nun is "embarrassing" because
      it shows Faulkner's old prejudices.

1955

61   VALLETTE, JACQUES. "Lettres anglo-saxonnes--Un apologue à la
      gloire de l'homme," Mercure de France (1 October), pp. 330-
      34.
           No clearer than any of Faulkner's other work, A Fable is
      mysterious on a grand scale in its retelling of the Christ
      story. All Faulkner's work, past and future, "est un acte
      du foi en homme."

62   VICKERY, JOHN B. "William Faulkner and Sir Philip Sidney?,"
      MLN, LXX (May), 349-50.
           The author wonders if a passage in Sidney's Apology for
      Poetry is the source for Faulkner's "Nilebarge clatter-
      falque" and "Momus' Nilebarge clatterfalque" in Pylon.

63   WELTY, EUDORA. "Place in Fiction," The Archive, LXVII
      (April), 5-7, 9-11, 13-14.
           Humor, of "all forms of fiction, entirely accepts place
      for what it is," a point illustrated by Faulkner's "Spotted
      Horses." Faulkner is the "triumphant example" of the mas-
      tery of place in fiction.
      Reprinted SAQ, LV (January 1956), 57-72. Reprinted
      1957.B68.

64   WYKES, ALAN. "The Perceptive Few and the Lost Generation,"
      A Concise Survey of American Literature. New York: Li-
      brary Publishers, pp. 165-74.
           The style, with all its excesses, is inseparable from
      the work which, despite violence and ugliness, is a com-
      plex treatment of the human condition.

1956 A BOOKS

1   ANON., compiler. Faulkner on Truth and Freedom. Manila:
      Philippine Writers' Association.
           In excerpts from tape-recorded remarks made during a
      stopover in the Philippines when he was returning from
      Japan, Faulkner is represented by statements about writing,
      life, and himself.
      Reprinted 1968.A6.

2   JELLIFFE, ROBERT A., ed. Faulkner at Nagano. Tokyo:
      Kenkyusha.
           A preface explains the nature of Faulkner's visit to
      Japan in 1955; and the text records interviews with facul-
      ty, students and newsmen. Faulkner is polite, candid, and
      informative about his writing.
      Reprinted 1968.A6.

1956 B   SHORTER WRITINGS

1   ALLEN, CHARLES A. "The Spectator's Appraisal: William Faulk-
    ner's Vision of Good and Evil," Pacific Spectator, X (Sum-
    mer), 236-41.
        Faulkner's later heroes, like Gavin Stevens in Intruder
    in the Dust, are didactic and symbolic, spokesmen for truth
    and justice. Ike McCaslin and the Corporal are examples,
    but Cash Bundren, the tall convict, and Ratliff, in the
    earlier fiction, although comic, have the virtues of the
    didactic hero, too. Faulkner emphasizes that man is not
    innately good or bad; he is the product of his past, and
    he may be good or evil depending on how he deals with it.

2   ARBAN, DOMINIQUE. "En attendant Requiem pour une nonne,"
    FigLit (22 September), p. 4.
        Camus took Requiem for a Nun because much of the work of
    adaptation to the stage was already done.

3   ARCHER, H. RICHARD. "The Writings of William Faulkner: A
    Challenge to the Bibliographer," PBSA, L (3rd Quarter),
    229-42.
        Faulkner's work presents typical difficulties for the
    bibliographer of modern writing because he worked in so
    many categories and because of the innumerable secondary
    materials which surround his work, including nonprint
    media and interviews. The author compares passages from
    different printed versions of the Nobel address and com-
    pares them with related phrases in Notes on a Horsethief
    and A Fable to show some textual problems.

4   BACKMAN, MELVIN. "Faulkner's Sick Heroes: Bayard Sartoris
    and Quentin Compson," MFS, II (Autumn), 95-108.
        Bayard Sartoris the younger is a modern "sick" hero
    driven to self-destruction partly by family heritage and
    partly by present guilt and inadequacy. Benbow, yielding
    to Belle Mitchell in Sartoris, suffers a similar fate.
    And Quentin Compson in The Sound and the Fury is a Prufrock
    figure, impotent, half in love with death, more like an
    Ophelia than a Hamlet. These heroes are compared to other
    Faulkner characters and to characters from the work of
    Hemingway, Dos Passos, and Kafka.
    Reprinted 1957.B14, 1966.A1.

5   BALDWIN, JAMES. "Faulkner and Desegregation," PR, XXIII
    (Fall), 568-73.
        Baldwin challenges Faulkner's "go slow" remarks on de-
    segregation with several questions about Southern history,

1956

(BALDWIN, JAMES)
Southern character, and the Negro's long wait for equality.
Not the white South but the Negro's constant pressure has
brought whatever changes have occurred in society.
Reprinted Nobody Knows My Name (New York: Dial, 1961),
pp. 117-26.

6   BEEBE, MAURICE. "Criticism of William Faulkner: A Selected
Checklist with an Index to Studies of Separate Works,"
MFS, II (Autumn), 150-64.
A secondary bibliography of general treatments and spe-
cific essays on individual works.
Reprinted 1957.B14; expanded 1967.B4.

7   BONGARTZ, ROY. "Give Them Time: Reflections on Faulkner,"
Nation (31 March), p. 259.
The author makes a satirical commentary upon remarks at-
tributed to Faulkner in the Russell Warren Howe interview
(See 1956.B26).

8   BREIT, HARVEY. "In and Out of Books," NYTBR (14 October), p.
8.
Faulkner has been active as head of an Eisenhower project to get American writers involved in image-building
abroad; he has traveled for the State Department.

9   _____. "Walk with Faulkner," The Writer Observed. Cleveland: World Publishing Co., pp. 281-84.
Reprint from 1955.B6; reprinted 1968.A6.

10   BROWN, DEMING. "American Best-Sellers in Soviet Bookstores,"
Reporter (29 November), pp. 36-38.
In a two-paragraph summary of Russia's increasing interest in Faulkner--because of his "anti-militarism"--the author reports that the Leningrad public library has a supply
of English versions of his books.

11   BROWN, MAUD. "William C. Falkner, Man of Legends," GaR,
X (Winter), 421-38.
A long-time resident of Oxford sketches the Falkner family history and provides anecdotes about the novelist's
great-grandfather.

12   CARPENTER, RICHARD C. "Faulkner's Sartoris," Expl, XIV
(April), Item 41.
Sartoris explores the "Christian myth of sin, guilt, and
redemption" as in A Fable. Parallels with Cantos XXXII
and XXXIII of Dante's Inferno--imagery of cold--suggest

(CARPENTER, RICHARD C.)
    that young Bayard is punished for his egotism. Faulkner
reveals his "Protestantism."

13   COINDREAU, MAURICE E. "From Bill Cody to Bill Faulkner,"
    PULC, XVII (Summer), 185-90.
        The influence of American writing in Europe has been im-
mense. Recalling his own experience as reader and translator, Coindreau recalls the impact of the technique of
moderns like Faulkner upon the French consciousness. Writers have not given a distorted picture of American life to
the European; they have shown a true world, with both good
and evil, and have balanced unfavorable characters with
admirable ones like Dilsey.
    Reprinted 1971.B18.

14   COTTRELL, BEEKMAN W. "Christian Symbols in _Light in August_,"
    MFS, II (Winter), 207-13.
        Parallels between Christ and Joe Christmas include the
names Faulkner gives other characters: Simon McEachern
can be Simon Peter; Joanna Burden can be John the Baptist;
Percy Grimm resembles the Roman soldier who speared Christ.
Lena and Byron parallel Mary and Joseph the carpenter.
Hightower is associated by name and deed with Pontius Pi-
late. The theme is that the mingling of good and evil can
bring Hope.

15   EINSIEDEL, WOLFGANG von. "Revolte des Menschensohnes--zu
    William Faulkners _Eine Legende_," _Merkur_, X, 282-90.
        The gist of Faulkner's message in his modern passion
story, _A Fable_, is that man, if he wants salvation, must
help himself. The novel uses a complex chiaroscura of
contrasted characters.

16   FAULKNER, WILLIAM. "Mr. Faulkner Writes," _Reporter_ (19
    April), p. 7.
        Faulkner, in one of several such statements, denies say-
ing that, in 1956, one state would challenge the Union or
that he would fight against the United States. Russell
Warren Howe (_See_ 1956.B26), who had printed the statement,
replies that his notes were transcribed verbatim from
shorthand.

17   FLYNN, ROBERT. "The Dialectic of _Sanctuary_," _MFS_, II (Au-
    tumn), 109-13.
        Analogues and allusions to Greek tragedy and medieval
Christian civilization, as well as Jungian archetypes, are
found in the characters and events of _Sanctuary_. The

1956

(FLYNN, ROBERT)
"dialectic" of the title occurs in the contrast between
Greek and medieval Christian conceptions which produces a
synthesis of bizarre machine-age Christianity. It offers
no "sanctuary" to a person in distress.
Reprinted 1957.B14.

18   FRAZIER, DAVID L. "Gothicism in Sanctuary: The Black Pall
and the Crap Table," MFS, II (Autumn), 114-24.
Somewhat like Flynn (1956.B17), the author sees a dialectic between tradition and modernism symbolized in the
movement from such things as the black pall of Red's funeral to the crap table underneath, from the Old Frenchman's Place to the corn crib and the Memphis "crib" house.
The traditional elements in Sanctuary are Gothic convention, while the modern ones are horrific in more appalling
ways. The book is not sensational but critical.
Reprinted 1957.B14.

19   GRENIER, CYNTHIA. "The Art of Fiction: An Interview with
William Faulkner--September, 1955," Accent, XVI (Summer),
167-77.
Interviewed in Paris, Faulkner answers questions about
his early work, the young writer, criticism, his philosophy, his characters, and his reading.
Reprinted 1957.B24 and 1968.A6.

20   GRIFFIN, WILLIAM J. "How to Misread Faulkner: A Powerful
Plea for Innocence," TSL, I, 27-34.
The author satirizes Bache (1954.B8) for his overzealous
interpretation of "Dry September" and criticizes others
for seeing Faulkner only as a "Southern traditionalist,"
notably O'Donnell (1939.B26) and Davidson (See 1953.B31
and 1957.B15).

21   GUÉRARD, ALBERT J. "William Faulkner, ou le fardeau de
l'Homme Noir," RN, XXIV, 331-38.
A Fable emphasizes that man must found his being not on
the special gifts that occasionally mark the superior individual but on his ordinary human qualities. Faulkner's
message is his work; it is not merely in it.

22   HAFLEY, JAMES. "Faulkner's 'Fable': Dream and Transfigura-
tion," Accent, XVI (Winter), 3-14.
The basic conflict dramatized in A Fable by the Generalissimo and the Corporal is that between the material
world, with its harsh demanding realities, and the spiritual realm, with its hopes. The Corporal is more the

(HAFLEY, JAMES)
simple martyr than he is a Christ; he is son of God and of
man, and the general's role is that of earthly, not heaven-
ly, father. The crowd, and the armies, signify the inevitable failure of democracy, which is choked by its own un-
gainly numbers in the very act of asserting its single
will against tyranny.

23   HETTICH, BLAISE. "A Bedroom Scene in Faulkner," Renascence,
VIII (Spring), 121-26.
Ike McCaslin's wife abuses their marriage contract by
using sex to make Ike break his vow of repudiation. The
scene is key to the meaning of "The Bear." She represents
the corruption of the earth that Ike is trying to correct.

24   HOWE, RUSSELL WARREN. "New Civil War if Negro Claims Are
Pressed," London Sunday Times (4 March), p. 7.
Account of 22 February 1956 interview with Faulkner in
which he is reported as saying that the South will fight
again if Northern interference on the racial issue per-
sists. See 1956.B25, 1956.B26, and 1968.A6 for perspective on the interview, which Faulkner later disputed.

25   _____. "Prejudice, Superstition and Economics," Phylon,
XVII (Third Quarter), 215-26.
Mentions the Reporter interview (1956.B26): it is
filled with contradictions common to Southerners when they
talk about race. Racism is a dangerous and outdated attitude in the Cold War world. He quotes from Faulkner's
statements about the Negro's potential.

26   _____. "A Talk with William Faulkner," Reporter, (22 March),
18-20.
Faulkner's statements on race here are sympathetic and
understanding; he did not like racial injustice or persecu-
tion and he believed racial intermarriage would solve the
problem in 300 years once and for all. He believed himself in a numerical liberal minority in Mississippi, with
even most blacks against his views in favor of equality.
Naturally "Negroes are right--make sure you've got that--
they're right" to want equal rights and opportunities.
Faulkner's comment on another Civil War and his part in it
are replied to by Faulkner in 1956.B16.
Reprinted 1968.A6. For the London version of this interview, See 1956.B24.

27   JUIN, HUBERT. "L'univers clos de William Faulkner," Esprit,
No. 244 (November), 704-15.
Faulkner's world is unique, operating on laws of its own

1956

(JUIN, HUBERT)
that have nothing to do with the region he lives in. Go Down, Moses expresses the nature of this fictional South best. There are those who exploit the land and those who suffer and renounce to expiate the sin.

28 KING, ROMA A., JR. "Everyman's Warfare: A Study of Faulkner's A Fable," MFS, II (Autumn), 132-38.
A Fable is not specifically a reworking of the Christ story, but an allegory of the eternal warfare between the forces of dark and light, good and evil, in Everyman. The Generalissimo is a composite character, associated with both sides of man's nature; the Corporal is a Christ figure, pivotal in the novel, although, like the runner who is his St. Paul, not fully satisfying as a character. The ending is handled ironically--baffling a simple acceptance of the Corporal's resurrection--and the impression is clear that good and evil do coexist. There is hope in the battered runner's claim that he will never die.
Reprinted, with commentary, 1972.B58.

29 KRUTCH, JOSEPH WOOD. "In These Days Our Literature in All Its Might Came of Age," NYTBR (7 October), pp. 6-9, 40.
Faulkner belongs to a later literary period than Hemingway. He is a writer of the heart while Hemingway is a writer of the glands.

30 LEVIN, HARRY. Symbolism and Fiction. Charlottesville, Va.: University of Virginia Press, pp. 7-8.
In a paragraph on "The Bear" as a story of initiation, Levin criticizes the "Kenyon critics" for overallegorizing it.

31 McCLENNEN, JOSHUA. "Why Read William Faulkner?," Quarterly Review of the Michigan Alumnus, LXII, 342-45.
The difficulties of Faulkner's language and form are overcome by familiarity. He is a Christian writer, contrasting man's evil with his potential for good.

32 *____. "William Faulkner and the Christian Complacency," PMASAL, XLI, 315-22.
Bassett (1972.A2), Item AA 109.

33 MacLURE, MILLAR. "William Faulkner: Soothsayer of the South," QQ, LXIII (Autumn), 334-43.
The history of Yoknapatawpha County is divided into three periods: ancient, medieval, and modern; the Indian, the aristocrat, and the poor white; the bear, the centaur, and

1956

(MacLURE, MILLAR)
the automobile. The whole work is a dark allegory; a foreground of unconscious motives from the human past plays
against the ancient, soiled image of the earth. A survey
of the novels demonstrates their dream-world qualities.

34   MASSEY, LINTON. "Notes on the Unrevised Galleys of Faulkner's
      Sanctuary," SB, VIII, 195-208.
      An account of the publication of Sanctuary precedes a
      study of the original, unrevised galley proof. Tables
      list differences between galleys and the published book;
      they are listed in two orders so that a reader can roughly
      reconstruct the original. The author concludes that Faulk-
      ner greatly improved the book. See also Millgate's study
      (1963.B65) and Langford's (1972.A5).

35   MAYHEW, PAUL [pseud.]. "Giving Racism the Sanctity of Law,"
      NRep (7 May), pp. 13-16.
      A "distinguished Southern jurist and writer" quotes
      Faulkner on the South's strong feelings in an essay on
      Southern apologies for segregation and independence.

36   MINER, WARD L. "Faulkner and Christ's Crucifixion," NM, LVII,
      260-69.
      Faulkner's works are experienced, not read. After sum-
      marizing the use of the Christ story in The Sound and the
      Fury, Light in August, and A Fable, the author concludes
      that Faulkner's novels are most successful when the
      symbolic pattern is less dominant.

37   MOSES, W. R. "The Unity of The Wild Palms," MFS, II (Autumn),
      125-31.
      The Wild Palms is a single story with two mirror-image
      plots. The author offers three parallels between "Wild
      Palms" and "Old Man" as examples.
      Reprinted 1957.B14.

38   O'FAOLAIN, SEAN. "William Faulkner, or More Genius than Tal-
      ent," The Vanishing Hero: Studies in Novelists of the
      Twenties. London: Eyre and Spottiswoode, pp. 73-111.
      American edition: Boston: Little, Brown, 1957.
      Faulkner is unconscious and helpless before his own
      genius, unaware of the nuances of language, groping at
      strange forms. O'Faolain gives unique summaries of The
      Wild Palms and The Sound and the Fury in the course of ar-
      guing that Faulkner's books are unreadable. Faulkner
      writes of a corrupted, destroyed tradition that he does
      not know, since he is not a true old Southern aristocrat.

1956

39   PARKS, EDD WINFIELD. "Hemingway and Faulkner: The Pattern
of Their Thought," Dagens Nyheter (12 February), 4-5.
An English version of this essay in Danish is annotated
at 1957.B52.

40   SANDEEN, ERNEST. "William Faulkner: His Legend and His
Fable," Review of Politics, XVIII (January), 47-68.
Faulkner's exploration of Yoknapatawpha prepared him to
make the exploration of World War I in A Fable far different from what he had done in Soldiers' Pay. A Fable is an
Iliad, not an Odyssey. It is broader than Faulkner's previous work. His symbolic dialogues present age-old conflicts between conservatism or tradition and reform, for
which a moderate position is the recommended antidote.

41   _____. "Out of a Wasteland, William Faulkner," Books on
Trial, XIV (March), 281-82, 325-27.
Faulkner has moved from a large and undefined wasteland
to a concentration on the geography and mythology of the
South. No author deserves or requires so much to be read
in toto.

42   SILVER, MARGARET. "McCalls Visits 'Miss Maud,'" McCalls (October), 21-22, 25.
Reproductions of paintings by Faulkner's mother accompany a story on her and her work.

43   S[MITH], H[ARRISON]. "William Faulkner vs. the Literary Conference," SatR (7 July), p. 16.
Faulkner's interview in the Paris Review (1956.B44) is a
masterpiece of the form and good advice for all aspiring
writers.

44   STEIN, JEAN. "William Faulkner," Paris Review, XII (Spring),
28-52.
Faulkner answers questions about his contemporaries and
himself and his work, with a number of illuminating comments upon The Sound and the Fury, A Fable, and Light in
August. The piece includes a self-portrait and a repro-
duction of a MS page of As I Lay Dying. Reprinted, slightly expanded by an answer on his youthful religious background, in Writers at Work: The Paris Review Interviews,
edited by Malcolm Cowley (New York: Viking Press, 1959),
pp. 119-41.
Reprinted 1960.A1 and 1968.A6.

45   STEWART, RANDALL. "American Literature and the Christian Tradition," Peabody Reflector, XXIX (February), 33-38.
Too often misunderstood as a mere sociologist, Faulkner

146

(STEWART, RANDALL)

    is a great, elemental, symbolical writer whose concepts, like "prevail," are often biblical in origin, not modern and technological.

46   _____. "Hawthorne and Faulkner," CE, XVII (February), 258-62.

    Faulkner and Hawthorne are both allegorical, working in an orthodox religious tradition that recognizes original sin; man's struggle toward redemption is their common subject. They share a common view of the human condition, regional similarities (changing societies, the sense of history), and family backgrounds. "The Wild Palms of Hester Prynne," at the end of the article, prints a passage from The Scarlet Letter on "Shame, Despair, Solitude!." Essay reprinted CE, XXII (November 1960), 128-32.

47   STONESIFER, RICHARD J. "Faulkner's Old Man in the Classroom," CE, XVII (February), 254-57.

    "Old Man" has sufficient seriousness and poetic density to make it a suitable class assignment. It was "sandwiched" with "Wild Palms" for "some obscure Faulkner purpose." Thanks to the Signet paperback edition which puts the two together, but not alternately, "this tiresome and unrewarding puzzle-game can stop." It depicts Faulkner's "cosmic pessimism."

48   *STRAUMANN, HEINRICH. "Eine Americanische Seinsdeutung: Faulkners Roman, A Fable," Anglia, LXIII, 484-515. Translated in 1960.A1.

    Faulkner's most important novel for the European, A Fable, may have to wait a decade or two for a full appreciation. The seriousness of the main story is leavened with humor to emphasize clearly Faulkner's belief that in a world where suffering is inevitable men can bear what they must. It is pervaded by a persistent subtle irony. The theme of "the Crowd and the Stranger" repeats throughout. All-embracing in its philosophy and subject, it is an example of the "symbolic mimesis" which is characteristic of American writing. Incorporated into 1968.A8. Reprinted, translated, 1973.A9.

49   TAYLOR, WALTER FULLER. The Story of American Letters. Chicago: Henry Regnery, pp. 471-81.

    A summary of Faulkner's work shows his immense variety and talent, but he has never been able to treat the large middle class of respectable people and he distorts the South.

1956

50   *VIERTEL, TOM. "Faulkner's Position on Equality," Coastlines,
      V (Summer), 33–43.
      Bassett (1972.A2), Item BB29.

51   WESTON, JOHN C., JR. "Faulkner as Anthologist," CarQ, VIII
      (Fall), 69–70.
      Big Woods is a commercial book modified to be less dif-
      ficult; it still shows Faulkner's artistic integrity in
      the quality of the stories and the unity of the collection.
      The reviewer regrets the separation of the racial theme
      from the wilderness theme.

52   ZINK, KARL E. "Faulkner's Garden: Woman and the Immemorial
      Earth," MFS, II (Autumn), 139–49.
      Prime reality for Faulkner is the "mysterious enduring
      process of Life." Ranging Faulkner's canon, the critic
      concentrates on the imagery Faulkner uses to set forth his
      regard for the forces of the earth and the identification
      he makes between the earth and women or Negroes. Faulk-
      ner's men may respond to Nature, and those who do not have
      a proper relation to it usually fear and hate both women
      and the earth.

53   _____. "Flux and the Frozen Moment: The Imagery of Stasis
      in Faulkner's Prose," PMLA, LXXI (June), 285–301.
      There is persistent imagery of stasis in Faulkner's work
      from Soldiers' Pay onward. Faulkner has always believed
      that Time is a function of consciousness. The past is not
      dead, but "recurs whenever it crosses the mind."

1957 A BOOKS

1   *HOFFMAN, FREDERICK J., and OLGA W. VICKERY. William Faulkner:
      Venti anni di critica, translated by Annina Coppini and Levi
      della Vida. Parma, Italy: Guanda 1957.
      This translation of Two Decades of Criticism (1951.A2)
      also includes two Italian essays, Elio Vittorini, "Faulkner
      come Picasso?" (from La Stampa [8 December 1950]) and
      Emilio Cecchi, "Note sur William Faulkner" (from Pros-
      pettive, No. 7 [Spring 1954]), not in the original collec-
      tion, according to Vickery (1951.A2).

2   MALIN, IRVING. William Faulkner: An Interpretation. Stan-
      ford, California: Stanford University Press.
      In a psychoanalytic study of the father-son relationship
      in Faulkner's work, the author finds a psychological rigid-
      ity in Faulkner's tragic or violent characters, male or

(MALIN, IRVING)
female, which seems to depend upon some mutation of father-
son myth. Faulkner uses the Bible and either borrows or
duplicates Freud and Jung to develop the recurrent story
of the son's rebellion as he attempts to discover himself.
The author suggests a personal psychological source in
Faulkner's grappling with his own family past, the "inadequacy" of his father and the "towering proportions" of a
complex great-grandfather.

3   ROBB, MARY COOPER. William Faulkner: An Estimate of His Con-
     tribution to the Modern American Novel. Pittsburgh: Uni-
     versity of Pittsburgh Press.
          A moralist, Faulkner has a positive conception of life
     which requires him to explore character from the inside,
     making it necessary for him to employ experimental stylis-
     tic devices and points of view. Yoknapatawpha is more
     than a regionalist's tool; it is part of his meaning. His
     "horrors" have a moral value. Pathos, repose, humor, na-
     ture, religion all play roles in Faulkner's view of life.

1957 B   SHORTER WRITINGS

1   ANON. "Qui est Faulkner?," Réforme (16 February), p. 7.
          Faulkner is far better than his interpretation by André
     Malraux would suggest, and he is not to be identified with
     Malraux.

2   ANON. "Meet the Author--And His Editor," Books From the
     U. S. A. (November), pp. 504-06.
          Saxe Commins, Faulkner's editor at Random House, talks
     about Faulkner briefly, in an essay which depends heavily
     on Cowley and other secondary materials.

3   ABEL, DARREL. "Frozen Movement in Light in August," BUSE,
     III (Spring), 32-44.
          Faulkner's use of symbol in Light in August is best ex-
     plained by reference to Henri Bergson's theories of intui-
     tion and art. The stories of Joanna Burden and Joe Christ-
     mas are given in "cuttings" superimposed against the image
     of the static and eternal earth; their stories are expres-
     sions of universal human reality. Comparison with the
     image and meaning of John Keats' urn is appropriate. High-
     tower's final vision is a full enlightenment, in imagery
     appropriate to both Bergson and Christian iconography.
     Ranged against it is the more readily available human at-
     tainment of peace and harmony with the earth which Lena
     Grove represents.
     Reprinted 1971.A3.

1957

4   ANGOFF, ALLAN, ed. American Writing Today: Its Inde-
          pendence and Vigor. New York: New York University Press.
          From a special number of TLS, there are numerous refer-
          ences to Faulkner and his work, and a reprinting of
          1930.B2. Faulkner is the giant of Southern and American
          writing.

5   *BEALE, BETTY. "William Faulkner Lambastes Press," Washington
          Evening Star (12 June), 1-B.
              Bassett (1972.A2), Item DD24; reprinted 1968.A6. In
          another society page piece (See also Beale 1954.B12), the
          author interviews Faulkner at a party given by his daugh-
          ter's in-laws; he expresses hostility toward those who in-
          vade his privacy.

6   BLOTNER, JOSEPH L. "As I Lay Dying: Christian Lore and
          Irony," TCL, III (April), 14-19.
              The author cites biblical allusions in As I Lay Dying--
          as many to the Old Testament as to the New--in the course
          of suggesting that the novel is built·on the ironies of in-
          verse correspondence.

7   BRUMM, URSULA. "The Figure of Christ in American Literature,"
          PR, XXIV (Summer), 403-13.
              Faulkner, along with many other American writers, works
          in a tradition which uses Christ in tragic terms. Fic-
          tional heroes achieve Christ's passions, "while Christ
          signifies not only his own individual fate but that of all
          humanity." Innocence, sure of its purity, is defeated by
          adversity and evil.

8   CAMUS, ALBERT. "Avant-propos," Requiem pour une nonne, trans-
          lated by Maurice E. Coindreau. Paris: Gallimard, ix-xiv.
              Faulkner has received a glory in France denied him in
          his own country. In Requiem for a Nun, the courtroom is
          like a temple, the governor's office like a confessional,
          the jail like a convent, and Faulkner's historical intro-
          ductions give a full sense of the human and historical sig-
          nificance of these settings. Faulkner created a noble
          language suitable for tragedy in the prose of his novel.
          Camus briefly discusses the differences between the novel
          and his adaptation.

9   CARTER, HODDING. "Faulkner and His Folk," PULC, XVIII
          (Spring), 95-107.
              Faulkner was disliked by his fellow citizens for his
          outspokenness on the race and education issues. Despite
          popular charges against him, however, he was a Southerner

(CARTER, HODDING)
through and through in his pride, ancestry, clannishness, and ambivalent love of his region.
Reprinted 1963.B20.

10   CHASE, RICHARD. "Faulkner--the Great Years," The American Novel and Its Tradition. Garden City, N. Y.: Doubleday, pp. 205-36.
By nature a novelist, Faulkner, in the period 1929-1932, demonstrated his genius and proved to be one of the two or three greatest American novelists. Joe Christmas, a "marginal man," endures his self-doubts, insists on his right to be human, and runs a good race; he is tragic but without the illusion of a chance to survive. The Sound and the Fury shows the impact of history in a modern ironic mind; it maintains tragic consistency

11   COINDREAU, MAURICE E. "On Translating Faulkner," PULC, XVIII (Spring), 108-13.
One must work hard to keep Faulkner's style and rhythms when translating his work, but in French it is not so easy to be obscure as in English, so The Sound and the Fury, for example, is clearer in its French version than in the English one. Faulkner's titles and dialectical speech present special problems for the translator, but not insuperable ones. His work is good training for the translator.
Reprinted 1960.B17.

12   COLLINS, CARVEL. "Folklore and Literature: A Symposium. 3. Folklore and Literary Criticism," JAF, LXX (No. 1), 9-10.
In light of increasing awareness that literature and folklore are related, the author makes a plea for folklorists' help with criticism. The suggestive relationships between T. B. Thorpe's "The Big Bear of Arkansas" and Faulkner's "The Bear" are given as an example.

13   _____. "The Pairing of The Sound and the Fury and As I Lay Dying," PULC, XVIII (Spring), 114-23.
The Sound and the Fury uses Christian lore from the Easter story; As I Lay Dying uses classical mythology--both of them adapting several techniques of Joyce's Ulysses. The title of As I Lay Dying comes from Book XI of the William Morris translation of The Odyssey. Freud, Frazer, and Joyce are all very much in evidence in these early Faulkner novels.

1957

14   Configuration Critique de William Faulkner, Part I, RLM,
      IV (2^e trimestre).
         A collection of essays, chiefly translated from English:
      1956.B4, 1956.B17, 1956.B37, 1958.B58, 1956.B18, 1956.B14,
      1956.B28, 1956.B52, 1956.B6; and two pieces on Faulkner's
      reception in France, an essay (1957.B71) and a bibliog-
      raphy (1957.B72).

15   DAVIDSON, DONALD. "Why the Modern South Has a Great Litera-
      ture," Still Rebels, Still Yankees, and Other Essays.
      Baton Rouge, La.: Louisiana State University Press,
      pp. 159-79.
         In a speech first given at Mississippi State College
      during the 1950 Southern Literary Festival, Davidson takes
      a satirical thrust at the social scientists' view of the
      South: Mississippi, at the bottom of every index of
      wealth, culture, education, and social amenity, has pro-
      duced the greatest writer in America. Also printed in
      Volume I of Vanderbilt Studies in the Humanities (1951).
      For a reply by Chapel Hill sociologist Howard Odum, See
      1953.B31.

16   DOUGLAS, HAROLD J., and ROBERT DANIEL. "Faulkner and the
      Puritanism of the South," TSL, II, 1-13.
         After a brief introduction to the sources and influences
      of Southern Puritanism, the authors turn to Faulkner
      through consideration of W. V. O'Connor's studies of Faulk-
      ner's Puritanism (See, e.g., 1954.A2), which they dispute,
      saying Faulkner is a Calvinist much like Joe Christmas,
      hating the harshness but accepting the view of man's in-
      nate evil. They discuss As I Lay Dying in terms of The
      Scarlet Letter. Relations between races and sexes in
      Faulkner symbolize the human condition.
      Reprinted 1972.A1, with comment 1972.B35.

17   ENGLAND, MARTHA WINBURN. "Teaching The Sound and the Fury,"
      CE, XVIII (January), 221-24.
         Rhetorical analysis of every section of The Sound and
      the Fury shows that Benjy's thoughts are essentially con-
      crete and declarative and nonallusive; Quentin's are ab-
      stract, convoluted with qualifications and subordinates;
      Jason's are egocentric, frequently self-quoting, and full
      of cause and effect. A brief chronology of the Benjy sec-
      tion is appended.

18   FIEDLER, LESLIE A. "From Clarissa to Temple Drake," Encoun-
      ter, VIII (March), 14-20.
         In a discussion of the blonde and the dark women of
      American fiction, the author identifies Temple Drake of

(FIEDLER, LESLIE A.)
Sanctuary as "the final avatar of the Female Savior in
America." Translated 1962.B45.

19   FREEDMAN, MORRIS. "Sound and Sense in Faulkner's Prose," CEA,
XIX (September), 1, 4-5.
Edmund Wilson's criteria for judging Faulkner a failure
as prose stylist (1948.B28) are irrelevant. Faulkner's
prose is not to be measured, as Wilson measures it, against
Conrad, Proust, or Joyce; it is the result of his concern
for the "essence" of the thing, not its idea. He is no
craftsman, but an inspired first-draft writer. He should
be studied on his own terms.

20   FROHOCK, W. M. "William Faulkner: The Private Vision," The
Novel of Violence in America, 2nd ed., revised, Dallas,
Texas: Southern Methodist University Press, 144-65.
A revision of 1949.B9.

21   GALPHIN, BRUCE. Review of The Town, Atlanta Journal (5 May),
Section E, p. 16.
Faulkner is smiling at his neighbor's foibles in The
Town. Gavin Stevens has "the misfortune to make a fool of
himself twice."

22   GARRETT, GEORGE P., JR. "An Examination of the Poetry of
William Faulkner," PULC, XVIII (Spring), 124-35.
Faulkner's poetry is imitative only in the sense that
most beginning poetry is; it still has a vision of its own
and The Marble Faun is constructed on an ambitious, well
worked-out structural and thematic scheme. His poetry
shows the same kind of experimentation as his prose. Between pages 128 and 129 are illustrations from Faulkner's
manuscripts and typescripts.
Reprinted 1973.A9.

23   GREET, T. Y. "The Theme and Structure of Faulkner's The Hamlet," PMLA, LXXII (September), 775-90.
Patterns of theme, image, and mythological allusion give
meaning and form to The Hamlet. The self-consciousness
and conventional morality of the characters prevent the
gestures which might redeem Frenchman's Bend from the curse
of greed and materialism. Counterpoint, humor, and a rich
style give the book its fine complexity.
Reprinted 1960.A1.

24   GRENIER, CYNTHIA. "L'art du roman, Dialogue de William Faulkner avec Cynthia Grenier," TaRd, No. 109 (January), 36-46.
See 1956.B19; Reprinted 1968.A6, 1973.A9.

1957

25   GUNTER, JAMES. Review of The Town, Memphis Commercial Appeal
        (12 May), Section V, p. 10.
        The "word labyrinths" of The Town would make Faulkner
      unfit to be a good journalist. This book is not as clear
      as some of the great books of the past.

26   GWYNN, FREDERICK L., and JOSEPH L. BLOTNER. "Faulkner in the
        University: A Classroom Conference," CE, XIX (October),
        1-6.
        Faulkner answers questions on writing, on visiting Eu-
      rope, on Hollywood, on his reading and his goals as a writ-
      er, and on such fiction as Absalom, Absalom!, "A Rose for
      Emily," "The Bear," and The Sound and the Fury. "I knew
      Joyce, I knew of Joyce." See also 1959.A1 for other
      Faulkner conferences at the University of Virginia.

27   HALE, WILLIAM HARLAN. "Every Man an Ambassador," Reporter
        (21 March), pp. 18-22.
        The author includes several paragraphs on Faulkner in an
      account of Eisenhower's people-to-people cultural exchange
      program. Faulkner's letter to fellow writers suggesting
      what America could do to counter Communist influence in
      the world is reprinted in part: bring 10,000 Communists
      to America and let them buy a car on the installment plan;
      smuggle Johnson grass across the Iron Curtain.

27.5 HENNECKE, HANS. "Zu Faulkners Gedichte," [Afterword to] Ein
        Grüner Zweig, translated by Hans Hennecke. Zurich:
        Fretz & Wasmuth Verlag, pp. 67-81.
        Not much appreciated in America or elsewhere, Faulkner's
      poetry yet contains, in compressed form, many themes and
      ideas more fully expressed in his fiction, as a comparison
      of poems from A Green Bough and passages from The Wild
      Palms illustrates. The background of the poems, including
      a biographical error about study at England's Oxford Uni-
      versity, is discussed; several of the lyrics receive high
      marks.

28   HOADLEY, FRANK M. "Folk Humor in the Novels of William Faulk-
        ner," TFSB, XXIII (September), 75-82.
        Nineteenth-century American humor, oral and written, cul-
      minated in Mark Twain and found its way into Faulkner's
      fiction in almost all its forms.

29   HOGAN, PATRICK G., JR. "Critical Misconceptions of Southern
        Thought," MissQ, X (January), 19-28.
        A rejoinder to Campbell and Foster (1951.A1), this essay
      denies "cosmic pessimism" in Faulkner's work. Faulkner's

(HOGAN, PATRICK G., JR.)
    public statements, as well as his fictional ones, show his
high regard for love, fidelity, honesty and compassion and
demonstrate a difficult but nevertheless real optimism.

30   JACOBS, ROBERT D. "How Do You Read Faulkner?," Provincial,
      I (April), 3-5.
      Faulkner's style and structure create the most difficulty
for his would-be readers. His devices are deliberately designed to involve one in the process of history and fiction
as discoverer.

31   JONES, LEONIDAS M. "Faulkner's 'The Hound,'" Expl, XV
      (March), Item 37.
      The moral complexity of "The Hound" is inherent in the
symbolism of the story, where Cotton, the lowly sharecrop-
per, is a cowardly murderer but also a man driven to extremes in order to preserve dignity, a struggle he contin-
ues even after the murder. Pride is both virtue and sin.

32   KAZIN, ALFRED. "Mr. Faulkner's Friends, the Snopeses," NYTBR
      (5 May), pp. 1, 24.
      The Snopeses are unlike the aristocrats whom Faulkner
depicts "out of his anguished sense of decline" or the
Negroes of his fiction. They are symbols of the destruction of the old order, and they have declined to comic-
strip creations in Faulkner's imagination. The Town is
also so loosely constructed that one doubts Faulkner's interest in writing novels.

33   _____. "The Stillness of Light in August," PR, XXIV
      (Autumn), 519-38.
      Faulkner's roots in place, his contrast of earth-figures,
like Lena and Byron, with the rootless and nameless, like
Joe and Lucas Burch, are characteristic of the best American writing and prove we are not a homogeneous people.
Christmas is an abstraction trying to become a person but
doomed by a race-mad society to failure; we see him from a
distance, always in profile, brooding, still--caught in
nonbeing, carried forward by Fate to his particular end.
Reprinted 1960.A1 and 1966.A8.

34   KÖHLER, MATHILDE. "Ein Herr aus den Südstaaten: Besuch bei
      William Faulkner," Hamburger Abendblatt (15/16 June), p. 9.
      The director of the paper's New York bureau recounts a
visit to one of Faulkner's conferences at the University
of Virginia.

1957

35   LIND, ILSE DUSOIR. "The Calvinistic Burden of <u>Light in Au</u>-
      <u>gust</u>," <u>NEQ</u>, XXX (September), 307-29.
           Analyzing the Christmas narrative alone, one finds the
      central situation to be his conflict with Joanna Burden,
      who like Joe is a victim of a harsh puritan heritage. De-
      fiance, revolt, and sexual perversity caused by authori-
      tarian repression cause the tragedy. A broader, more sym-
      pathetic view of Southern religion is included in the por-
      traits of Lena and Byron.

36   LIVELY, ROBERT. <u>Fiction Fights the Civil War: An Unfinished</u>
      <u>Chapter in the Literary History of the American People</u>.
      Chapel Hill: University of North Carolina Press, pp. 178-79.
           <u>Sartoris</u> and <u>The Unvanquished</u> are mentioned in a survey
      of literature about the Civil War. In <u>The Unvanquished</u>,
      Bayard becomes <u>the</u> Sartoris, but also a man without a
      family.

37   *LOMBARDO, AGOSTINO. "Il primo e l'ultimo Faulkner," <u>Realismo</u>
      <u>e simbolismo</u>. Rome: Edizioni di Storia e Letteratura,
      pp. 207-21.
           Based on Lombardo's reviews, but unified when collected,
      this essay is, according to Materassi (1971.B60), an ac-
      count which emphasizes Faulkner's humanity. Novels like
      <u>A Fable</u>, which may not satisfy the critic, still satisfy
      the human being in us. The Snopes-Sartoris conflict is a
      metaphor for the struggle with Time. Faulkner is a puri-
      tan writer who sees the soul as a battlefield for good and
      evil.

38   LONGLEY, JOHN L., JR. "Joe Christmas: The Hero in the Mod-
      ern World," <u>VQR</u>, XXXIII (Spring), 233-49.
           A comparison of Oedipus and Joe Christmas shows that
      <u>Light in August</u> meets the requirements of both classical
      and modern tragedy. Joe's quest for self-knowledge brings
      him in a tragic circle.
      Reprinted 1960.A1, 1966.A8, 1971.A3. <u>See also</u> 1963.A6.

39   _____. "Galahad Gavin and a Garland of Snopeses," <u>VQR</u>,
      XXXIII (Autumn), 623-28.
           <u>The Town</u> concerns Flem's discovery of respectability.
      Faulkner has deliberately made Gavin foolish, but he is
      human and rejects Snopesism as a personal means to victory.

40   LOPEZ, EMILIO SOSA. "El problema de mal en William Faulkner,"
      <u>Sur</u>, No. 247 (July-August), 55-63.
           Faulkner's characters manifest evil as a kind of congeni-
      tal disability. His work penetrates the depths of the

(LOPEZ, EMILIO SOSA)
human heart and reveals the old eternal verities. He does not reproach man's evils but comprehends them.

41   LYTLE, ANDREW. "The Town: Helen's Last Stand," SR, LXV (July-September), 475-84.
An Agrarian essay on the values of a pious aristocracy and a monolithic religion is preliminary to a discussion of the Sartoris-Snopes dichotomy Lytle finds in Faulkner's work. Ab Snopes was left in the unmoral condition of the passing frontier; he could only prey on the stable society that had grown up around him. The Town, with the bank as its subtle symbol of usury, dramatizes the loss of meaning in life. Respectability is the only virtue; acquisition the only goal.
Reprinted 1968.B48.

42   McCLENNEN, JOSHUA. "Absalom, Absalom! and the Meaning of History," PMASAL, XLII, 357-69.
Absalom, Absalom! is not, as Poirier claims (1951.B46), about Quentin's view of history but about the meaning of history for everyone in the novel and for Faulkner himself. Quentin brings love and its power of intuition to his explanation, making his view superior to Rosa's hateful version and his father's cynical indifference, but even he cannot transcend a harsh view of Sutpen, and so he, too, fails of complete understanding and ends by hysterically denying his feelings about the South.

43   McCORMICK, JOHN. Catastrophe and Imagination: A Reinterpretation of the Recent English and American Novel. London: Longmans Green, pp. 257-60.
Though guilty of tasteless gallows humor in some work, indicating an obsession with death, Faulkner creates shattering irony and stark tragedy in As I Lay Dying and Light in August. His technique "exempts him from" success.

44   MALCOLM, DONALD. "Faulkner Returns to Yoknapatawpha," NRep (27 May), pp. 20-21.
A strong element of magic in the way Faulkner characterizes and chronicles the Snopeses in The Town is marred by bad style lacking conviction.

45   MARCUS, STEVEN. "Snopes Revisited," PR, XXIV (Summer), 432-41.
Faulkner's most interesting book in fifteen years, The Town "revives the direct, dramatic mode of As I Lay Dying." The reviewer regrets Ratliff's eclipse by Gavin Stevens

1957

(MARCUS, STEVEN)
(who wrote the Nobel Prize speech). The greatest quality
of the novel is its demonstration of Faulkner's myth-making
ability; he goes back to events he has already created and
accepts them as real.
Reprinted 1960.A1.

46   *MAYES, MARTHA. "Faulkner's Juvenilia," new campus writing
No. 2, edited by Nolan Miller. New York: Putnam's,
pp. 135-44.
Reprinted New York: Bantam Books, 1957, pp. 135-44.
Massey (1968.A4), Items 1912, 1913.

47   MERIWETHER, JAMES B. "The Snopes Revisited," SatR (27 April),
pp. 12-13.
A funny book and one of Faulkner's best, The Town seriously treats the further rise of Flem Snopes. It clarifies, for the less attentive reader, the fact that Gavin
Stevens is not Faulkner's spokesman.

48   _____. "William Faulkner: A Check List," PULC, XVIII
(Spring), 136-58.
A list of Faulkner's American publications: books and
pamphlets; short stories; poems; nonfiction prose; speeches
and published letters; and contributions to University of
Mississippi student publications.
Reprinted in pamphlet form (Princeton: Princeton Univer-
sity Library, 1957).

49   MERWIN, W. S. "William Faulkner," Nobel Prize Winners, ed.
L. J. Ludovici. Westport, Conn.: Associated Booksellers,
pp. 43-60.
"Time and place"--as Faulkner dramatizes them--are both
blind urges working within and incomprehensible forces
working outside the individual. Biographical material is
interlaced with brief comments on the books.

50   MOLONEY, MICHAEL F. "The Enigma of Time: Proust, Virginia
Woolf, and Faulkner," Thought, XXXII (Spring), 69-85.
Renaissance concepts of space and time, which have bound
and haunted man, have been modified in the modern world.
Limitations of space are breaking down; the enslavement to
time and causality has been challenged by such ideas as
the philosophy of Bergson and the experiments and ideas of
modern novelists. For Proust, though one cannot arrest
time's flow, there is yet triumph in "recapturing" time
after it has been swept away. Woolf was interested in the
discrepancy between clock time and "mind" time. She is

(MOLONEY, MICHAEL F.)
  increasingly defeated by time. Faulkner's is yet a different view: man cannot escape time, as Absalom, Absalom!
  and The Sound and the Fury illustrate. Sutpen is tragic;
  Quentin pitiable. Faulkner's work displays an all-embrac-
  ing somberness; Faulkner's "man will endure" is inspired
  by compassion, not conviction.

51 O'CONNOR, WILLIAM VAN. "Hawthorne and Faulkner, Some Common
    Ground," VQR, XXXIII (Winter), 105-23.
      Hawthorne and Faulkner both lived under the spell of fam-
    ily history; shared a common view of Puritanism; had simi-
    lar views on Catholicism's acceptance of human weakness;
    used the incest theme similarly. Both were stylized writ-
    ers preoccupied with gloomy wrongs. O'Connor quotes a let-
    ter from Phil Stone where it is claimed that Faulkner never
    read much Hawthorne or anything else and that Hawthorne's
    The Marble Faun had nothing to do with the title of Faulk-
    ner's first book of peoms. Stone claims to have provided
    the title.
    Reprinted 1962.B92.

52 PARKS, EDD WINFIELD. "Faulkner and Hemingway--Their Thought,"
    SAB, XXII (March), 1-2.
      Hemingway and Faulkner both demonstrate changed philos-
    ophies. From the early belief in scientific determinism
    they have come to assert a humanistic view of man. Faulk-
    ner's shift becomes apparent in Absalom, Absalom! Orig-
    inally in Danish, 1956.B39.

53 PAULDING, GOUVERNEUR. "Book Notes: Many Souths," Reporter
    (19 September), 47-48.
      The general northern suspicion of books from a "literary
    South"--and this occurs in Italy and France as well as in
    the United States--forces "Southern writers" to write bet-
    ter. Faulkner has "breathed new life into traditional
    Southern figures." The Town is an example.

54 PODHORETZ, NORMAN. Review of The Town, NY (1 June), pp. 110-
    16.
      As in A Fable, Faulkner is trying to force an irrelevant
    meaning out of his material. The fears expressed about
    the Snopeses are out of proportion to what the Snopeses do.
    Faulkner has lost the courage of his honesty.

55 PRESCOTT, ORVILLE. "Books of the Times," NYT (1 May), p. 35L.
      "Faulknerians--on college campuses, in the ivory towers
    and in the...offices of little magazines" will be

1957

(PRESCOTT, ORVILLE)
  happy that Faulkner is back in Yoknapatawpha County. The
  Town is above his average, though he still indulges stylistic eccentricities and structural infelicities.

56 RIEDEL, FREDERICK C. "Faulkner as Stylist," SAQ, LVI (Autumn), 462-79.
  Attacking several long sentences in Faulkner's later
  writings, the author argues for the inadequacy of the involved and confused syntax. A sentence from "Old Man"
  shows how Faulkner achieves the effect of action without
  numerous verbs. Faulkner misuses even his favorite words,
  but also puts his vocabulary to bold and effective use.
  Faulkner fails to exercise proper control over what is a
  remarkable, excellent style.

57 ROGERS, THOMAS H. "Farce and Anecdote," ChiR, XI (Autumn),
  110-14.
  The Town is sociological, not artistic, marred by bad
  language, trifling plot, and enfeebled characters. The
  decline is due to Faulkner's having "completed" the Yoknapatawpha works; the rest is anticlimax.

58 RUBIN, LOUIS D., JR. "Snopeslore: or, Faulkner Clears the
  Deck," WR, XXII (Autumn), 73-76.
  One of Faulkner's funniest books, The Town centers on
  Flem Snopes and his antagonists. It sets the stage for a
  satisfactory finale to come, in which Faulkner must answer
  some questions about which side of human nature will
  triumph.

59 RUGOFF, MILTON. "Faulkner's Old Spell in a New Novel of Yoknapatawpha," NYHTB (5 May), p. 1.
  Though the "macabre humor" of the Snopes stories still
  exists, they have suffered a diminution in scale in The
  Town: instead of being monstrous, as in The Hamlet, they
  are "in a university town merely queer."

60 SCOTT, NATHAN A., JR. "The Vision of William Faulkner,"
  ChrCent, LXXIV (18 September), 1104-06.
  The Town belongs with Faulkner's best work, a chronicle
  of the triumph of positivism and the success creed, personified by Snopes. As a poet with a large and complex
  vision, Faulkner dramatizes the burden of being human.
  His Snopes novels are, on one level, "an abstract of that
  underworld of the human spirit . . . called Hell."

61 SIMMONS, MABEL C. Review of The Town, New Orleans Times-
  Picayune (25 April), Section III, p. 8.

(SIMMONS, MABEL C.)
The story in The Town "emerges painfully...from the confusing and oblique reports" of Ratliff, Gavin Stevens, and Chick Mallison. Long and abstruse sentences and paragraphs discourage the reader.

62   SLATOFF, WALTER JACOB. "The Edge of Order: The Pattern of Faulkner's Rhetoric," TCL, III (October), 107-27.
Many of Faulkner's suspensions of meaning are never resolved; he deliberately "seems very anxious to keep pieces from fitting together." One sign of this is the frequent use of arrested motion or oxymoronic states; another is the marathon sentence. Faulkner's work shows an "active quest for 'failure,'" an internal conflict between ideas of order and ideas of disorder. Faulkner cannot make the choice.
Reprinted 1960.A1, 1973.A9.

63   TAYLOR, WALTER FULLER. "William Faulkner: The Faulkner Fable," ASch, XXVI (Autumn), 471-77.
Even in A Fable, which critics have seen as proof of Faulkner's moral view, a preponderance of the human characters are reprehensible and morally corrupt. The novel focuses on evil--more the evil of "filth and unawareness" than the traditional sin of pride. Faulkner's is a plain, bleak humanism. He is akin to Swift, Voltaire, Twain at his darkest. The real Faulkner fable is one erected by critics who see a "Christian allegory" in his 1954 novel. See reply 1958.B51.

64   VICKERY, OLGA W. "Faulkner's First Novel," WHR, XI (Summer), 251-56.
Soldiers' Pay is badly structured, too mannered, shallow in its humor, but it shows Faulkner's ambition to use time as "a source of motives" and gradual revelation as a dramatic method. It foreshadows the work to come.

65   *VITTORINI, ELIO. Diario in pubblico. Milan: Bompiani, pp. 97, 145.
According to Materassi (1971.B60), the collection includes early essays on Faulkner's fiction.

66   WAGGONER, HYATT H. "William Faulkner's Passion Week of the Heart," The Tragic Vision and the Christian Faith, edited by Nathan A. Scott. New York: Association Press, pp. 306-23.
Faulkner's work, which shows Paul Tillich's "ultimate concern" about life, is religious, though his public remarks are ambiguous. His work inspires piety, but not

1957

(WAGGONER, HYATT H.)
faith and hope. It is existential.
Reprinted as Chapter 11 of 1959.A5, "A Passion Week of the
Heart."

67   WATT, DAVID. "Down South Again," Spectator (6 December),
pp. 791-793.
A plot summary is a real service to the theatre-goer in
the case of Faulkner's Requiem for a Nun at the Royal
Court in London. The story has great subtlety, but it is
not really a play; it is too obscure. Under the circumstances, however, it is played rather well.

68   WELTY, EUDORA. Place in Fiction. New York: House of Books.
Of all fictional forms, humor "entirely accepts place
for what it is," a point illustrated wonderfully by Faulkner's "Spotted Horses." Faulkner is the "triumphant example" of the mastery of place in fiction.

69   WESTBROOK, JOHN T. "Twilight of Southern Regionalism," SWR,
XLII (Summer), 231-34.
Faulkner's work is familiar and right to the native
Southerner, even though the world he creates is not a real
one. The regional South of fiction is now so far passed
away that an aspiring Southern writer who wants to treat
that kind of world had better live elsewhere. The South
is increasingly urban, industrial, and sophisticated.

70   WOLFE, DON MARION. "Faulkner and Hemingway: Image of Man's
Desolation," The Image of Man in America. Dallas: Southern Methodist University Press, pp. 344-61.
The evil that men do, as Faulkner shows it, comes not
from their treatment of the land or the black man, but
from the hot, wild blood of man himself. His novels all
treat sexual obsession or deviation. The author agrees
with Hardwick (1948.B16) that Faulkner is possessed by his
genius in the old Romantic sense; the reader cannot identify with his characters because their situations are so
bizarre. Thomas Wolfe is more in touch with life than
Hemingway or Faulkner.

71   WOODWORTH, STANLEY D. "La critique Faulknerienne en France:
Essai de synthèse," in Configuration Critique de William
Faulkner I, RLM, IV (2e trimestre), 178-90 (1957.B14).
The author discusses major trends of Faulkner criticism
in France and lists essays and reviews in 1957.B72.
Reprinted 1959.A6.

72   . "Sélection bibliographique d'ouvrages ou d'articles
sur William Faulkner en France, 1931-1952," in Configuration Critique de William Faulkner I, RLM, IV (2e trimestre), 191-96 (1957.B14).
    Essays and reviews of Faulkner's books in France.
Reprinted 1959.A6.

73   WORSLEY, T. C. "Redemption," NewSt (7 December), p. 773.
    Reviewing the London production of Requiem for a Nun
starring Ruth Ford, the critic finds that Temple is
"less . . . redeemed than made respectable." The play is
unconvincing.

1958 A   BOOKS - NONE

1958 B   SHORTER WRITINGS

1   ANON. "Faulkner's Cruse," TLS (7 February), p. 74.
    Faulkner's books are not sections of a roman fleuve but
parts of an imaginative world revealed. He is best compared with Thomas Hardy. The Hamlet is composed like a
symphony in a series of movements. The Town is a series
of voices.

2   ANON. "Faulkner: Advice to a Young Writer," Daily Prince-
tonian (19 March), p. 2.
    An "excerpted, condensed text" of an interview which
Faulkner gave a Princeton undergraduate; Faulkner's remarks are printed as a single narrative statement: write
for pleasure, write about people, read everything, don't
worry about symbols or plots. "I usually build around one
quick action that is sharp and definite. Then I show how
it affects people and how they react to it."

3   ADAMS, ROBERT M. "Romantic Openness and the Unconscious,"
Strains of Discord: Studies in Literary Openness. Ithaca,
N. Y.: Cornell University Press, pp. 180-200.
    "Romantic openness," in which the mind seeks to remain
unresolved in the face of experience, characterizes much
of Faulkner's work, where "his characters barely emerge"
from passion to affirm life as "meaningless and incommuni-
cable." The Sound and the Fury, though patterned on the
Christ story, is strongly nihilistic, and so is As I Lay
Dying. When Faulkner diminishes his structural complexities, as in recent years, he overstates a moral position
and loses his characteristic power.

1958

4   AIKEN, CONRAD. "William Faulkner," A Reviewer's ABC. New
       York: Meridian Books, pp. 197-207.
       Reprints 1927.B1 and 1939.B3.

5   ALLEN, WALTER. "Snopes on the March," NewSt (1 February),
       p. 143.
       The Hamlet is a masterpiece, but The Town is clumsy and
     without the grand humor of the earlier work.

6   APPLEWHITE, DAVIS. "The South of Light in August," MissQ, XI
       (Fall), 167-72.
       For the historian, Faulkner's most vivid quality is his
     ability to depict the North Mississippi hill country, ru-
     ral and small town, where his fiction is set. Characters
     and speech are well done, although the middle class is re-
     grettably omitted, and his negative view of Southern re-
     ligion is deplorable. The author questions the validity
     of Faulkner's "racial views," especially the "guilt" at-
     tributed to the South.

7   BACKUS, JOSEPH. "Names of Characters in Faulkner's The Sound
       and the Fury," Names, VI (December), 226-33.
       Candace goes back to "Canace" in Ovid's Heroides and un-
     derscores the incest theme, confirming Caddy's affair with
     Benjy, whose original name, Maury, may have evolved from
     Macarius, Canace's brother. Quentin comes from "quaint
     honor" in a line of Marvell's "To His Coy Mistress."
     Jason is classical and also derived from Jacob Thompson of
     Oxford. Other names in the novel are similarly dealt with.

8   BERNBERG, RAYMOND E. "Light in August: A Psychological
       View," MissQ, XI (Fall), 173-76.
       The characters of Light in August are psychologically
     well motivated; sexuality is used believably. The Byron-
     Lena plot satirizes the main plot, its characters antithe-
     ses to the figures in the main plot.

9   BLÖCKER, GÜNTER. "William Faulkner," Die Neuen Wirklich-
       keiten: Linien und Profile der modernen Literatur. Ber-
       lin: Argon Verlag, pp. 112-23.
       In the modern world with all its division and meaning-
     lessness, the artist seeks order and gives significance to
     existence. Of almost all modern artists, Faulkner is the
     most natural. Against the self-consciousness and intellec-
     tuality of the rest, he sets his savage creative power.
     He is at home with the mythology others must learn. The
     Sound and the Fury marks a real advance on Proust and
     Joyce. His distortions are as soundly based as Picasso's.

(BLÖCKER, GÜNTER)
Sartre's strictures about Faulkner's concept of time
(1939.B28) are not applicable.
Reprinted 1966.A8.

10 BLUM, IRVING D. "The Parallel Philosophy of Emerson's Nature
and Faulkner's The Bear," ESQ, No. 13 (4th Quarter), 22-25.
Faulkner followed an Emersonian design and principle in
creating the nature-philosophy of "The Bear." When Ike repudiates the symbols of the exploitation of nature, he
achieves harmony with existence.

11 BLUMENBERG, HANS von. "Mythos und Ethos Amerikas im Werk
William Faulkners," Hochland, L, 234-50.
Faulkner's books are filled with the terrible burden of
human freedom and responsibility. Harry Wilbourne's choice
in The Wild Palms--grief over nothing--is typical of Faulkner's point of view.

12 BOWLING, LAWRENCE E. "Faulkner and the Theme of Innocence,"
KR, XX (Summer), 466-87.
The Sound and the Fury is about innocence. Benjy personifies the humanist view of innocence as want of knowledge; Quentin personifies the puritan view, as freedom
from sin or evil. Quentin's obsession with innocence leads
him to a state close to Benjy's; his inner life becomes so
real he cannot distinguish reality. Jason, guilty and innocent, suffering without receiving any truth, is a naturalist. Caddy also remains innocent, for all her misad-
ventures, and she never acquires "spiritual depth." Mrs.
Compson, in her passivity and rationalization, is also innocent. Only Dilsey has knowledge and truth. Benjy's
flower symbolizes two crucifixions; he offers a faint ray
of hope in the novel--love is the way to salvation.

13 BRAEM, HELMUT M. "Das scandalon William Faulkner: Die meta-
physische Kampfstatt und ein sadistischer Jehova," DeuRs,
LXXXIV (October), 944-50.
The "scandalous" Faulkner's fiction, full of horror,
violence, perversion, idiocy, and his philosophy of man's
endurance, shows that he believes in a sadistic God.

14 BREADEN, DALE G. "William Faulkner and the Land," AQ, X (Autumn), 344-57.
A profound Agrarian realist, Faulkner depicts agricul-
tural life as it is, and his work displays a land philosophy that is "brilliant and humanitarian." It is based on
natural law--as set down by Locke, the Physiocrats, and

1958

(BREADEN, DALE G.)
Henry George. Ike McCaslin is a symbol of natural rights, with ideas very similar to those of Henry George. The author discusses the way land title and ownership are presented in Faulkner's work.

15 BROWN, JAMES. "Shaping the World of Sanctuary," UKCR, XXV (Winter), 137-42.
The first three chapters of Sanctuary use structural, thematic, imagic, and other means to shape the "moral dimensions" in which Temple's story unfolds: desecration, involvement, and ultimate compromise with the world's evil.

16 CANTWELL, ROBERT. "Faulkner's 'Popeye,'" Nation (15 February), 140-41, 148.
Neil Karens Pumphrey, alias Popeye, a Memphis gangster of the twenties, is apparently the model for the character in Sanctuary.

17 COANDA, RICHARD. "Absalom, Absalom!: The Edge of Infinity," Renascence, XI (Autumn), 3-9.
Faulkner's style in Absalom, Absalom! is like that of the Jacobean "essayists who fused in prose the techniques of baroque and mannerist art," playing over a compounded biblical theme. His view of man is essentially orthodox, though not theologically identifiable. Man exists in precarious balance between heaven and hell.

18 COLLINS, CARVEL. "About the Sketches," William Faulkner: New Orleans Sketches. New Brunswick, N. J.: Rutgers University Press, pp. xi-xxxiv.
Faulkner's literary friendships in New Orleans in the mid-twenties provide the background to the writing he did there. Reprinted as "Introduction" (New York: Grove Press, 1961) and in a revised edition (New York: Random House, 1968), which adds Faulkner's essay "Sherwood Anderson" from the Dallas (Texas) Morning News, 26 April 1925.

19 _____. "William Faulkner's The Sound and the Fury," Expl, XVII (December), Item 19.
Scott's novel Quentin Durward is the possible source of the given names in The Sound and the Fury; Scottish ancestry and the valuation of "honor in an age which had abandoned it" are common to both characters.

20 DOSTER, WILLIAM C. "The Several Faces of Gavin Stevens," MissQ, XI (Fall), 191-95.
As his characterization changes slightly between Knight's Gambit, Intruder in the Dust, Requiem for a Nun, and The

(DOSTER, WILLIAM C.)
Town, Gavin Stevens deteriorates as a man--he grows weaker,
more garrulous, and capitulates in his struggles against
modern rapacity.

21   FLANAGAN, JOHN T., and A. P. HUDSON. Folklore in American
      Literature. Evanston, Ill., and White Plains, N. Y.:
      Row, Peterson and Co., pp. 275-304.
         A one paragraph introduction which discusses use of folk
      materials precedes a reprint of "Spotted Horses."

22   FLANAGAN, JOHN T. "Folklore in American Literature," The Fam-
      ily Saga and Other Phases of American Folklore, edited by
      Harold Lancess. Urbana, Ill.: University of Illinois
      Press, pp. 49-65.
         The Hamlet is almost without parallel in American litera-
      ture in its use of folk material, folk point of view, and
      backcountry life.

23   FRAZIER, DAVID L. "Lucas Burch and the Polarity of Light in
      August," MLN, LXXIII (June), 417-19.
         The character Lucas Burch makes the moral viewpoint in
      Light in August triangular, since he has no values at all,
      in contrast to the negative and positive values contrasted
      in the other characters. Amidst the tragedy and comedy of
      the novel, his life is a satire.

24   GARRETT, GEORGE PALMER. "The Earliest Faulkner," PrS, XXXII
      (Fall), 159-60.
         In a review of New Orleans Sketches, poet and novelist
      Garrett praises the editing by Carvel Collins, but regrets
      the failure to mention "Elmer," Faulkner's novel partially
      about New Orleans and Paris, written, but not completed,
      in the mid-twenties. See 1973.B59.

25   _____. "Some Revisions in As I Lay Dying," MLN, LXXIII
      (June), 414-17.
         Drawing on reproductions in print of first and last pages
      of the As I Lay Dying holograph MS, Garrett shows that
      Faulkner revised the book considerably, contrary to his
      famous statement about not changing a word.

26   GEISMAR, MAXWELL. "William Faulkner: Before and After the
      Nobel Prize," American Moderns: From Rebellion to Con-
      formity. New York: Hill and Wang, pp. 91-106.
         Geismar's reviews of Intruder in the Dust, Requiem for a
      Nun, A Fable, and The Town are reprinted.

1958

27   GOING, WILLIAM T.   "Faulkner's 'A Rose for Emily,'" Expl, XVI
      (February), Item 27.
          Rose has several referents, including its traditional
      function as symbol of love, the "rose by any other name"
      passage in Romeo and Juliet, and a rejected stanza from a
      poem in Faulkner's A Green Bough.

28   GREER, SCOTT.   "Joe Christmas and the 'Social Self,'" MissQ,
      XI (Fall), 160-66.
          Light in August explores "the meaning of race-identifica-
      tion" in a small southern town.   The Lena-Byron plot re-
      flects the values of folk-society; the religious plot em-
      phasizes the harshness of Southern Calvinism.   Joe Christ-
      mas is the "marginal man" produced when two societies in-
      terpenetrate--he cannot identify with either white or
      black, but society will not allow him abiguity.   Histori-
      cally and sociologically, he is a potential messiah, with
      a "call" to bring two systems together, but in actuality
      he is no messiah, only a man seeking self-identity in a
      Godless world.   The story is only incidentally Southern;
      it is universal.

29   GWYNN, FREDERICK L.   "Faulkner's Raskolnikov," MFS, IV (Sum-
      mer), 169-72.
          Quentin Compson resembles Rodion Raskolnikov: he is a
      university student and unstable; he carries out a murder
      (his own); he takes his father's watch to a "shopkeeper";
      he is compulsive and searching for identity; and he has
      family relationships similar to those of Dostoevsky's char-
      acter.   Crime and Punishment may have helped release Faulk-
      ner's creativity for The Sound and the Fury.

30   HANOTEAU, GUILLAUME.   "Faulkner, il s'est battu à Verdun et
      se souvient," Paris Match (10 May), 14-17, 19, 32.
          An account of Faulkner's visit to Verdun, with photo-
      graphs, includes references to A Fable and biographical
      supposition.

31   HARDER, KELSIE B.   "Proverbial Snopeslore," TFSB, XXIV (Sep-
      tember), 89-95.
          I. O. Snopes' jumbled proverbs establish him in the tra-
      dition of the "counterfeit schoolmaster."   Faulkner's ar-
      tistic adaptation of folk materials creates a Snopeslore,
      a dark handbook of behavior appropriate for a Snopes.

32   HOLMAN, C. HUGH.   "The Unity of Faulkner's Light in August,"
      PMLA, LXXIII (March), 155-66.
          Faulkner models the lives of his characters in Light in

(HOLMAN, C. HUGH)
August upon the story of Christ to "unify" his novel and
express his themes. Joe Christmas's life parallels
Christ's in many particulars, but he also resembles the
"suffering servant" of Isaiah. Religion, sex, and race
are linked in the novel by Joe's early life and later obsessions, and they are recalled in his affair with Joanna.
The Lena-Byron plot celebrates a new annunciation and
birth which rejuvenates the defrocked minister. Hightower
dies at the end. Expanded from a paper read at the December 1956 MLA meeting, "Christian Allegory in Faulkner's
Light in August," a 13-page TS of which is in the Massey
collection at Virginia (Item 1653).
Reprinted 1971.A3, 1972.B49.

33 HOWELL, ELMO. "A Note on Faulkner's Negro Characters," MissQ,
XI (Fall), 201-23.
Faulkner's minor Negro characters provide a touchstone
for his treatment of the race, as for example Job in The
Sound and the Fury, who gets the best of Jason Compson yet
preserves the required decorum between the races demanded
in his place and time.

34 HYMAN, STANLEY EDGAR. "Some Trends in the Novel," CE, XX
(October), 1-9.
Trying to give Temple Drake some grandeur in Requiem for
a Nun, Faulkner succeeds in making her ridiculous. A Fable
is "ham-handed," a ponderous reworking of the Passion story
so well handled in Light in August. These are examples of
"unattractive" trends in recent work by major writers: the
tendency of Hemingway, Steinbeck, and Faulkner to rewrite
their earlier successes in "parody."

35 INGE, TOM [M. THOMAS]. "Faulkner Answers Student Questions
at University of Virginia Session," The Yellow Jacket (23
May), pp. 2, 4.
A student reporter from Randolph-Macon College, Ashland,
Va., gives his version of the 12 May 1958 session with
Faulkner at the University of Virginia also reproduced,
somewhat differently, in Faulkner in the University
(1959.A1, 1965.A1), pp. 279-80. Faulkner discusses humor--
"an attitude of optimism toward man's predicament"--the
Negro, movies, and success in remarks which do not appear
in the book-length compilation; conversely, some remarks
recorded in the book are omitted from this account.

36 *JOBE, PHYLLIS. "'The Bear,'" Nimrod, II (Winter), pp. 27-30.
Sleeth (1962.B109) and Bassett (1972.A2), Item N82.

37   KAZIN, ALFRED. "Faulkner Forecast," NYTBR (2 March), pp. 4-5.
      Faulkner has more in common with Mark Twain than with the
      literary agrarians, as some of the early pieces printed in
      New Orleans Sketches prove. The sketches also demonstrate
      that whatever Faulkner's youthful excesses, he had the true
      literary artist's genuine love of words.

38   KNOLL, ROBERT E. "The Unvanquished for a Start," CE, XIX
      (May), 338-43.
      The Unvanquished, which is a considerable achievement de-
      spite some critical attempts to dismiss it, provides a sub-
      stantial, characteristic, but still simpler work for stu-
      dents' first exposure to Faulkner. Faulkner's theme is
      that an act cannot be judged outside its accompanying cir-
      cumstances. Points worth special attention are listed.

39   LAMONT, WILLIAM H. F. "The Chronology of Light in August,"
      MFS, III (Winter), 360-61.
      Questioning the often stated belief that Joe Christmas
      dies at the Christological age of 33, the author suggests
      that Joe and Hightower both die in 1932 and that Joe is 36.

40   LEAVER, FLORENCE. "Faulkner: The Word as Principle and
      Power," SAQ, LVII (Autumn), 464-76.
      The "myth" in Faulkner's work is supported not only by
      the connecting narrative element but also by style, es-
      pecially diction. Faulkner finds words for his mythos by
      using many abstract nouns, special intensives, coined com-
      pounds, and repetition from chapter to chapter and book to
      book: examples are given.
      Reprinted 1960.A1.

41   McELDERRY, B. R., JR. "The Narrative Structure of Light in
      August," CE, XIX (February), 200-07.
      The Lena-Byron story moves in straight chronology, giving
      forward motion to Light in August, while Christmas's story
      comes in extremely nonchronological form on three levels:
      present, immediate past, and remote past. The author gives
      a schematic of the book's narrative structure and an out-
      line of the two plots chronologically arranged.

42   _____. "The Narrative Structure of 'Light in August,'"
      MissQ, XI (Fall), 177-87.
      The same article as 1958.B41.

43   MONTEIRO, GEORGE. "Bankruptcy in Time: A Reading of William
      Faulkner's Pylon," TCL, IV (April-July), 9-20.
      Pylon is filled with images and events that repeat or

(MONTEIRO, GEORGE)
reinforce the theme of the human failure to communicate
and the theme of time. The reporter becomes the central
figure, a tragic character.

44   _____. "Initiation and the Moral Sense in Faulkner's
Sanctuary," MLN, LXXIII (November), 500-04.
Sanctuary is about an initiation which is not efficacious. Temple goes from innocence to experience without
changing. Popeye, incapable of initiation, represents
what Temple becomes.

45   MORRIS, WRIGHT. "The Function of Rage: William Faulkner,"
The Territory Ahead. New York: Harcourt, Brace, pp. 171-
84.
Faulkner is an expressionist, like Van Gogh; his great
power comes from the controlled rage of the impotence of
man before the mystery of life. Yet in characters like
Lena Grove and the wilderness, where Dav_d Hogganbeck and
the Indian vie for Herman Basket's sister and lose her ("A
Courtship"), he presents the calm mythic center which is
the world of our past, our dreams, and our aspirations.

46   O'CONNOR, WILLIAM VAN. "Rhetoric in Southern Writing:
3. Faulkner," GaR, XII (Spring), 83-86.
Faulkner displays a "high rhetoric," the heritage of
Ciceronian Southern oratory; an elegant fin de siècle poetic style; and "folk language" from the native nineteenth-
century humorists. Passages from "The Bear," Absalom, Absalom! and The Hamlet illustrate.

47   *ORLOVA, RAISA, and LEV KOPELEV. "Mify i pravda amerikanskovo
yuga," Inostrannaya literatura, III, 206-20.
"Myth and Truth About America's South" mentions Faulkner,
according to Brown (1962.B28).

48   REED, JOHN Q. "Theme and Symbol in Faulkner's Old Man," EdLr,
XXI (January), 25-31.
Greater than the "Wild Palms" section of The Wild Palms,
"Old Man" is critically neglected; it is a "savage indictment" of the modern world and a celebration of man's
strength and endurance, carried out by the use of symbols.
The chief symbol is the anonymous convict; the second is
the penal farm which represents "modern industrial society"; the river, a force of nature, is set in opposition
to the penal farm. Because plot and meaning are inade-
quately presented, however, we are left in doubt concerning Faulkner's thematic intentions.

1958

49   ROBSON, W. W. "William Faulkner," Spectator (14 February),
     p. 206.
        At his best, Faulkner is more the heir of Twain than of
     Joyce and Sartre; his naïveté, his country simplicity,
     often overlooked by his cult, are the staple of his best
     work. His early reputation was in part sensational, and
     his style was bent on obscuring the things he dared to say.
     He is generally overrated, but The Town is not up to stan-
     dard; it is more inspired by the desire to create a saga
     than by the desire to write a satisfactory book.

50   ROLLE, ANDREW F. "William Faulkner: An Inter-disciplinary
     Examination," MissQ, XI (Fall), 157-59.
        A brief introduction to a Faulkner symposium held by the
     Southern California American Studies Association, 1955,
     where Faulkner was discussed from four points of view:
     sociological (1958.B28), historical (1958.B6), psychologi-
     cal (1958.B8), and literary critical (1958.B20). See also
     1958.B52.

51   SEBOLD, JANE. "The Reader Replies," ASch, XXVII (Winter),
     135.
        Replying to Taylor (1957.B63), the writer notes that A
     Fable, though an artistic failure because of its obvious
     moralizing, helps one understand Faulkner's greater work
     by showing that his multiplicity and complexity are re-
     ducible to a single theme.

52   SMITH, HALLETT. "Summary of a Symposium on Light in August,"
     MissQ, XI (Fall), 188-90.
        Summarizing the four papers on Light in August (1958.B6,
     1958.B8, 1958.B20, and 1958.B28), the author suggests top-
     ics for further exploration.

53   STEWART, GEORGE R., and JOSEPH M. BACKUS. "'Each in its Or-
     dered Place': Structure in 'Benjy's Section' of The
     Sound and the Fury," AL, XXIX (January), 440-56.
        Accepting Benjy's section of The Sound and the Fury as
     a puzzle, the authors present the expanded result of a
     classroom project to solve it. Two tables show 106 units
     for 13 time levels, and a map attempts to delineate the
     Compson property. Commentary explains the process used
     to determine scenes and time-levels, a job complicated by
     the discovery of inconsistencies in the use of roman and
     italic type (See Meriwether, 1962.B85, for textual informa-
     tion). They believe incest occurred between Caddy and
     Benjy and are puzzled by the last sentence in the book.

54   STEWART, JAMES T.   "Miss Havisham and Miss Grierson," FurmS,
      VI (Fall), 21-23.
         Several parallels between the characters in "A Rose for
      Emily" and Dickens' Great Expectations are offered.

55   STEWART, RANDALL.   American Literature and Christian Doctrine.
      Baton Rouge: Louisiana State University Press, pp. 136-42.
         Because of his effective dramatization of "the basic
      Christian concepts," Faulkner is "one of the most pro-
      foundly Christian writers of our time."   Man in Faulker's
      work is heroic and tragic; capable of greatness, troubled
      by Original Sin; at war within himself, spirit versus
      flesh; and aware of the value of discipline, sacrifice,
      and redemption.

56   STONESIFER, RICHARD J.   "Faulkner's The Hamlet in the Class-
      room," CE, XX (November), 71-77.
         Books I and IV of The Hamlet are carefully and complexly
      parallel, with similar events heightened and made more
      darkly important in the closing episodes, by contrast to
      relatively innocent events in Book I.   Books II and III
      are likewise balanced; the theme is love, and Flem and
      Eula, who are otherwise not frequently portrayed in the
      novel, are raised to a higher plane.   Eula is the earth
      itself, ripe for exploitation, handed over to the barren
      Snopes, the reductio ad absurdum of the modern commercial
      man.

57   THOMPSON, HOWARD.   "Faulkner Chides U. S. on Education," NYT,
      Late Edition (8 March), p. 19.
         Talking at Princeton, Faulkner says education takes a
      back seat to everything, including athletics; that it is
      glorified baby-sitting.   Black and white cultures will
      never get together without integrated schools, and it is
      the white man's responsibility to make this happen.

58   TORCHIANA, DONALD T.   "Faulkner's Pylon and the Structure of
      Modernity," MFS, III (Winter 1957-58), 291-308.
         The real force behind the activities of the pilots and
      the reporter in Pylon is finance capitalism, which bru-
      tally arranges the events described in the book for the
      profit of New Valois.   The urban setting is hellish, op-
      pressive; the Mardi Gras is a depraved wasteland ritual.
      The chief symbol is the pylon, sign of Godhead as of man's
      brutality and a reminder of the limits within which man
      must operate.   Pylon is a condemnation of the death-in-
      life of modernity and an affirmation of love, sacrifice,
      and discipline.
      Reprinted 1957.B14.

1958

59 TORCHIANA, DONALD T. "The Reporter in Faulkner's Pylon,"
    HistIdN, IV (Spring), 33-39.
        An explanation of why Pylon has been critically ne-
    glected, this essay notes Faulkner's heavy reliance on
    T. S. Eliot's poetry, which has rendered his humor inef-
    fective, and his "glorification of life," which is blurred
    by the contradictory strains from Eliot.

60 VICKERY, OLGA W. "Faulkner and the Contours of Time," GaR,
    XII (Summer), 192-201.
        Paradoxically, man is both in time and yet contains time
    within himself by virtue of memory. Natural time--as pro-
    cess, continuation, the causal sequence--must be joined
    with human time--the product of memory and hope--to achieve
    a successful existence: one must accept change while pre-
    serving identity and continuity. "Doom" for Faulkner is
    the annihilation of individuality. Included in 1959.A4
    and 1964.A10.

61 _____. "Faulkner's Mosquitoes," UKCR, XXIV (Spring),
    219-24.
        The tour de force, Mosquitoes, with its echoes of Joyce,
    Huxley, and Firbank, does not succeed; the "heartless stu-
    pidity of words" overcomes, instead of informs, the work.
    Character and event are never pulled together. Included
    in 1959.A4, 1964.A10.

62 _____. "The Making of a Myth: Sartoris," WR, XXII (Spring),
    209-19.
        Sartoris was the first book where Faulkner dramatized
    the emptiness of words by creating the domineering Sartoris
    myth and exploring its effect on several generations. The
    Civil War and World War I are contrasted; the legend of
    the past is what dominates, and the Sartoris worship of
    old and glamorous disasters dooms the family, makes them
    mere pawns of a fatality they have invented. Included in
    1959.A4, 1964.A10.

63 WAGGONER, HYATT H. "William Faulkner: The Definition of
    Man," BBr, XVIII (March), 116-22.
        Faulkner's definition of man--which appears compositely
    in the characters of The Sound and the Fury, Light in Au-
    gust, Absalom, Absalom! and A Fable--is that he is a crea-
    ture with a soul. So many of his lost characters seek
    this soul, a few of them successfully.

64 WARREN, ROBERT PENN. "William Faulkner," Selected Essays.
    New York: Random House, 59-79.
        Central to Faulkner's thought, and one of the things

(WARREN, ROBERT PENN)
that generalizes his work beyond its Southern setting is
the notion that love is the only true relation of man to
men and nature. Exploitation in any form--from slavery to
real estate deals--is a curse which will reap its punishment on the lives and spirits of the perpetrators of the
act. Faulkner's best characters are those who can recognize "the common human bond"; his tragic failures, his mean
or whining cynics, and his monsters are those who can not
or will not.
Reprinted 1959.B20; 1960.A1; 1961.B71; 1973.A9.

65   WILDER, AMOS N. "Faulkner and Vestigial Moralities," Theology and Modern Literature. Cambridge, Mass.: Harvard
University Press, pp. 113-31 (2nd ed., 1967).
Unlike many modern writers who emphasize the individual
alone, Faulkner puts his characters into an historical and
social situation and persistently studies "the moral
forces by which men endure." Quentin in The Sound and the
Fury perverts a vestigial Christian morality to punish
himself. By contrast, Dilsey has an uncorrupted Christianity. The Sound and the Fury illustrates how Faulkner can
show the results of a secularized society; but it also
shows the vigor of a prevailing faith.
Reprinted 1972.A1, with commentary, 1972.B111.

66   YOUNG, THOMAS D., and FLOYD C. WATKINS. "Faulkner's
Snopeses," MissQ, XI (Fall), 196-200.
It is a distortion to assume that all Snopeses are im-
moral, rapacious, and self-interested. Essentially a cor-
rective to George Marion O'Donnell's Sartoris-Snopes dichotomy (1939.B26), the essay traces Snopes history to The
Town.

1959 A   BOOKS

1   GWYNN, FREDERICK L., and JOSEPH L. BLOTNER, eds. Faulkner in
the University: Class Conferences at the University of
Virginia 1957-1958. Charlottesville: University of Virginia Press.
A compilation of selected interviews and class sessions
tape-recorded during Faulkner's residence at the University
of Virginia. The 1965 Vintage paperback (1965.A1) is a
corrected version.

2   O'CONNOR, WILLIAM VAN. William Faulkner (Minnesota Pamphlets
on American Writers). Minneapolis, Minn.: University of

1959

(O'CONNOR, WILLIAM VAN)
Minnesota Press. (Revised ed. 1964; reprinted in O'Connor, Seven Modern American Novelists. Minneapolis: University of Minnesota Press, 1964, pp. 118-52.)
An updated version (including The Town; 1964 version adds The Mansion and The Reivers) of material condensed from The Tangled Fire of William Faulkner (1954.A2), this brief treatment summarizes Faulkner's novels and discusses him as a non-orthodox Christian humanist without literary or intellectual sophistication.

3   *POULSSEN, MARIE NICHOLAAS JOSEPH. Onirische Taal: Gaston Bachelard's theoriöen over de "Dromende" literaire berbeeldung, getoest aan het oeuvre van William Faulkner. Nijmegen, Netherlands: Drukkerij Gebr. Janssen N. V.
National Union Catalogue, Author List, 1958-1962, Volume 36, p. 524.

4   VICKERY, OLGA W. The Novels of William Faulkner. Baton Rouge, La.: Louisiana State University Press.
Critical readings of all Faulkner's novels up through The Town (1957) and a concluding section that summarizes Faulkner's techniques, themes, and his philosophy of man. The truth of the human heart, different from knowledge and from both history and legend, is the most important thing for a Faulkner character to know. Likewise important is a conception of the continuity of time. Faulkner's theory of language is that it invokes what "is already present in the memory of all men," and the literary artist's task is to reveal to man his nature and his potential. Man's touchstone is the immemorial and abiding land which affirms universal brotherhood. Includes material from 1957.B64, 1958.B61, 1958.B62, 1954.B76, 1959.B26, 1958.B60. Revised ed. 1964.

5   WAGGONER, HYATT H. William Faulkner: From Jefferson to the World. Lexington, Kentucky: University of Kentucky Press.
The author discusses Faulkner's fiction, including an overview of the stories, in chronological order. The readings are formalist in nature, but there are general remarks on Faulkner's moral and religious views as seen in his fiction and an overall evaluation of the achievement. Go Down, Moses and The Unvanquished are not considered as novels. The falling spires in Soldiers' Pay prefigure "the dominant theme" of Faulkner's best work: "his tortured and ambiguous mixture of religious denial and affirmation." After Intruder, he is the artist preaching. Though he takes the moral and psychological insights of American Christianity, he is "existentialist."

6   WOODWORTH, STANLEY D. William Faulkner en France (1931-1952).
     Paris: Lettres Modernes.
     A survey of the translation and critical reception of
     Faulkner's fiction in France and its influence upon modern
     French literature, this brief study includes bibliograph-
     ical information on essays published in France. Includes
     1957.B71 and 1957.B72.

7   *ZAVALETA, CARLOS EDUARDO. William Faulkner, novelista tragico
     (Publicaciones del Instituto de Literatura de la Facultad
     de Letras de la Universidad Nacional Mayor de San Marcos.
     Massey, Item 2500.

1959 B   SHORTER WRITINGS

1   ANON. "Visit with the Author," Newsweek (9 February), p. 58.
     A reporter accosts Faulkner in Oxford and questions him
     on his failure to attend the New York opening of the dra-
     matic version of Requiem for a Nun.

2   ANON. "Guides to Yoknapatawpha County," TLS (10 July),
     p. 408.
     Summary review of several books on Faulkner and his work:
     1959.A6, 1959.B20, New Orleans Sketches (See 1959.B18), and
     the 1959 edition of Miner (1952.A2).

3   ANON. "The Limits of the Possible: Accepting the Reality of
     the Human Situation," TLS (6 November), p. xvi.
     Faulkner's greatness is in the way he transcends all the
     stock characteristics of the American novel. He has a
     "superior grasp of reality."

4   ALLEN, WALTER ERNEST. "The Worldwide Influence of William
     Faulkner: Reports from Six Capitals: Report from London,"
     NYTBR (15 November), p. 52.
     In London Faulkner is still appreciated by only a mi-
     nority of readers, but with great impact on those who read
     him. He has had little influence upon English writers.

5   ALPERT, HOLLIS. "Old Times There are Not Forgotten," SatR (7
     March), p. 28.
     A review of the 1959 film of The Sound and the Fury
     treats it on its own terms and not as it portrays Faulk-
     ner's novel.

6   ARNAVON, CYRILLE. "Absalon! Absalon! et l'histoire," Con-
     figuration Critique de William Faulkner II, RLM, V (Win-
     ter), 250-70.
     Absalom, Absalom! plunges us directly into the center of

1959

(ARNAVON, CYRILLE)
Faulkner's conception of the South, where all the evils
one sees are related to the racial problem which is the
result of slavery. The "police inquest" which Quentin and
Shreve undertake becomes a holy quest. The novel dramatizes twentieth-century man's confrontation with a vanished
culture. Faulkner retains traits of the decadent writers,
especially with regard to pictorial quality in his work.
He modifies Conrad's method with the techniques of Joyce.
His view of history, like that of Camus or Pasternak, is
tragic, fateful; man's place is not to understand but to
endure it. See 1959.B20.

7   ASSELINEAU, ROGER. "Faulkner, moraliste puritain," Configuration Critique de William Faulkner II, RLM, V (Winter), 231-
49.
Faulkner, who is as personally mysterious as his fiction,
is neither psychologist nor sociologist; he is not developing a systematic study of the mores of a stratified society. He is neither realist nor naturalist. Though a
complete artist, he is also a moralist in the tradition of
Hawthorne and the Calvinist puritans, disturbed by everything that touches on the sexual, as Light in August demonstrates. See 1959.B20.

8   BACKMAN, MELVIN. "Tandis que j'agonise," Configuration Critique de William Faulkner II, RLM, V (Winter), 309-30.
In As I Lay Dying, Faulkner seems to have come out of the
shadows of obsession that dominate Sartoris, The Sound and
the Fury, and Sanctuary, into the light of a normal humanity. Backman interprets the symbols he finds in the novel
and calls it a fable of salvation and family loyalty where
love does not express itself in words but in deeds. See
1959.B20.

9   BAKER, CARLOS. "William Faulkner: The Doomed and the
Damned," The Young Rebel in American Literature, edited by
Carl Bode. London: Heinemann, pp. 143-69.
Faulkner's rebels are often inarticulate, unaware of the
forces which have shaped their rebellious spirit. Baker
divides the type into two forms: the "savers" and the
"sinners," the Doomed and the Damned, discussing their appearance in a range of Faulkner's novels. These characters
remind us of "the immanent presence of grace" and support
Faulkner's stated belief in man's ability to prevail over
his own folly.

10   BALDANZA, FRANK. "Faulkner and Stein: a Study in Stylistic
     Intransigence," GaR, XIII (Fall), 274-86.
         Faulkner and Gertrude Stein shared, perhaps merely as
     psychological coincidence, stylistic peculiarities, as a
     comparison of Absalom, Absalom! and The Making of Americans
     demonstrates. Both ignore linguistic convention in order
     to convey stasis within an emotional continuum. They in-
     terrupt, repeat, create positives by negating negatives.
     Both convey "primitive intransigent possession."

11   BECK, WARREN. "Faulkner et le Sud," Configuration Critique
     de William Faulkner II, RLM, V (Winter), 271-91.
         See 1959.B20; reprinted from 1941.B3, "Faulkner and the
     South."

12   _____. "Le style de William Faulkner," Configuration
     Critique de William Faulkner II, RLM, V (Winter), 365-84.
         See 1959.B20; reprinted from 1941.B4, "William Faulkner's
     Style."

13   BERTIN, CELIA. "The Worldwide Influence of William Faulkner:
     Reports from Six Capitals. Report from Paris," NYTBR (15
     November), p. 52.
         Faulkner has a large audience in France, as sales fig-
     ures indicate. His work is represented by good transla-
     tions. He has been a strong influence on contemporary
     French writers.

14   BROOKS, CLEANTH, and ROBERT PENN WARREN. Understanding Fic-
     tion, 2nd ed. New York: Appleton-Century-Crofts,
     pp. 350-54.
         A consideration of "A Rose for Emily" as a horror story,
     the commentary here omits comparison with Poe's "Fall of
     the House of Usher" (See 1943.B2). The story has a tragic
     undercurrent. Emily's "madness" is a function of her pride
     and disillusionment; she acts solely on her own terms in
     the face of community opposition. Reprint, with revi-
     sions, 1943.B2.

15   CARPENTER, FREDERIC J. "'The American Myth': Paradise (To
     Be) Regained," PMLA, LXXIV (December), 599-606.
         In a discussion which synthesizes previous attempts to
     describe a single American Myth into the vision of para-
     dise lost and, hopefully, to be regained, the author de-
     votes three final paragraphs to "The Bear," where, he says,
     Ike gains a newer, wiser innocence and a view of paradise
     to be regained in his loss of the wilderness he has helped
     to destroy.

1959

16   CECCHI, EMILIO. "The Worldwide Influence of William Faulkner:
      Reports from Six Capitals: Report from Rome," NYTBR (15
      November), p. 53.
          Faulkner is well-known in Italy since Sanctuary; he has
      had a strong influence on young Italian writers.

17   CHAPMAN, ARNOLD. "Pampas and Big Woods: Heroic Initiation
      in Güiraldes and Faulkner," CL, XI (Winter), 61-77.
          Faulkner's "The Bear" and Don Segundo Sombra by the Ar-
      gentine author Ricardo Güiraldes have many similarities,
      though not due to any influence or borrowing; both cele-
      brate the vanishing paradisal frontier, both depict ini-
      tiation.

18   COHEN, B. BERNARD. "Study Aids for Faulkner's Intruder in
      the Dust," Exercise Exchange, VII (October), 12-13.
          Numerous viewpoints and questions are offered as guides
      to appreciating the style and content of Intruder in the
      Dust. It differs from many other Faulkner works by not
      relying on "decadent elements" and by concentrating on a
      young boy's moral growth.

19   COLLINS, CARVEL. "Foreword," The Unvanquished, by William
      Faulkner. New York: New American Library, vii-xii.
          The Unvanquished is the story of Bayard's growth to ma-
      turity and courage. It is built on firm structural prin-
      ciples. Drawing partly on family legend, Faulkner takes
      deliberate liberties with history in order to create his
      effects. Like all Faulkner's art, it records man's dura-
      bility and hope.

20   Configuration Critique de William Faulkner II, RLM, V (Win-
      ter).
          A collection of essays, some original and some trans-
      lated from previously published essays in American journals
      and books. Includes 1941.B3, 1941.B4, 1958.B64, 1959.B6,
      1959.B7, 1959.B8, 1959.B25, 1959.B40, 1959.B79. There is
      a cumulative index of references to Faulkner's work in Con-
      figuration Critique I (1957.B14) and II.

21   CONNOLLY, THOMAS E. "Faulkner's Fable in the Classroom," CE,
      XXI (December), 165-71.
          An outline-map of the presentation of character in A
      Fable shows how Faulkner uses time to characterize and to
      structure. Characters of the various plots are listed by
      order of appearance; major events in each life are traced
      through the novel.

22   DELGADO, F. "El mundo complejo de William Faulkner," Razon y
      fe (Madrid), CLX, 323-34.
           Faulkner's work has traits of Greek tragedy and medieval
      epic; he transcends his regionalism. He illuminates the
      man at our side. The author discusses Faulkner's major
      novels.

23   EBY, CECIL D. "Faulkner and the Southwestern Humorists,"
      Shenandoah, XI (Autumn), 13-21.
           Faulkner paralleled the Southwestern writers of the nine-
      teenth century, such as Joseph Glover Baldwin and Johnson
      Jones Hooper, because his material and techniques came from
      conditions of life which had remained essentially the same
      for 100 years. The Hamlet, especially, shows parallels.

24   FRANKEL, MAX. "The Worldwide Influence of William Faulkner:
      Reports from Six Capitals: Report from Moscow," NYTBR (15
      November), pp. 52-53.
           Faulkner is very little known in Russia, where he is dis-
      trusted because of the apolitical nature of his novels.

25   FRIEDMAN, MELVIN. "Le monologue intérieur dans As I Lay Dy-
      ing," Configuration Critique de William Faulkner II, RLM,
      V (Winter), 331-44.
           Unlike most contemporary novelists, Faulkner puts a pre-
      mium on form while he also makes use of the most modern
      techniques of fiction, orchestrating stream-of-conscious-
      ness sections with great virtuosity. The combination of
      the free-flowing interior monologue with formal design is
      a strong feature of As I Lay Dying. Darl is the only con-
      sciousness which sees its own condition; the rest are lost
      in their fixed ideas. It is compared with Virginia Woolf's
      The Waves.

26   GARRETT, GEORGE P., JR. "Faulkner's Early Literary Criti-
      cism," TSLL, I (Spring), 3-10.
           Faulkner's early criticism in the University of Missis-
      sippi student newspaper reveals some of his early influ-
      ences and aesthetic development as well as a number of
      lifelong conceptions, such as his interest in form, char-
      acter, the variety of the American scene, and the use of
      art as a positive gesture against anarchy and chaos.

27   *GIANNITRAPANI, ANGELA. "Wistaria: Le immagini in Faulkner,"
      SA, No. 5 (1959), 243-80.
           Included in Wistaria (1963.A4).

1959

28   HAGOPIAN, JOHN V. "Style and Meaning in Hemingway and Faulk-
      ner," JA, IV, 180-90.
          The distinctive literary styles of Faulkner and Hemingway
      are juxtaposed in order to "illuminate" their work. Faulk-
      ner's complicated sentences are nearly uniform as his dom-
      inant, lifelong style, while Hemingway moves from a machine-
      gun simplicity to a more complex style in three stages.
      Faulkner's involvement, fictionally and really, is with the
      community, as his work demonstrates. By contrast, Heming-
      way deals with isolatoes. Faulkner is the greater writer.

29   HAMILTON, EDITH. "Faulkner: Sorcerer or Slave?" Saturday
      Review Gallery, edited by Jerome Beatty. New York: Simon
      and Schuster, pp. 419-29.
          Reprints 1952.B19.

30   HANDY, WILLIAM J. "As I Lay Dying: Faulkner's Inner Report-
      er," KR, XXI (Summer), 437-51.
          The tension between Darl Bundren's actions and his per-
      ceptions characterizes his sensitivity as reporter in As I
      Lay Dying and validates his perceptions. Other characters
      have similarly valid inner lives which they follow, includ-
      ing Anse. Addie gets her wish by playing on Anse's inner
      world, his high regard for the word.
      Reprinted 1971.B35.

31   HARDER, KELSIE B. "Charactonyms in Faulkner's Novels," BuR,
      VIII (April), 189-201.
          The author makes random identification of character names
      in some Faulkner novels, using traditional name-lore and
      subjective associations.

32   HEWES, HENRY. "Faulkner and the Fallen Idle," SatR (14 Feb-
      ruary), p. 32.
          Reviewing the dramatic version of Requiem for a Nun, the
      critic notes that "divine omniscience" has nothing to do
      with the punishment meted out to the characters in the
      play. Ruth Ford's performance is too mature for the part.
      He prefers the Camus adaptation to the American one.

33   HICKS, GRANVILLE. "The Last of the Snopeses," SatR (14 Novem-
      ber), pp. 20-21.
          The Mansion is not one of Faulkner's great novels, yet
      it contains some good writing. It proves, if we need
      proof, that O'Donnell's Sartoris/Snopes dichotomy
      (1939.B26) is an inadequate approach to Faulkner's work.
      Faulkner, losing his genius, has learned to respect human
      endurance.

34   HOWE, IRVING. "Faulkner: End of a Road," NRep (7 December),
       pp. 17-21.
          On the occasion of reviewing The Mansion, Howe surveys
       Faulkner's career since the novelist's powers began to "de-
       cline," blaming overreliance upon rhetoric, improbable
       plotting, and "disengagement" from the matter of Yoknapa-
       tawpha County. Gavin Stevens is Faulkner's alter ego; The
       Mansion is hurt by his musings.

35   HOWELL, ELMO. "Colonel Sartoris Snopes and Faulkner's Aristo-
       crats," CarQ, XI (Summer), 13-19.
          "Barn Burning" shows that Faulkner is a traditional mor-
       alist. Because his name represents the right sort of aris-
       tocracy, Sarty Snopes affirms principle over family. See
       rejoinder 1968.B25.

36   _____. "Faulkner's Sartoris," Expl, XVII (February),
       Item 33.
          Dr. Alford's office and the officious professionalism of
       his nurse, Myrtle, in Sartoris dramatize "new and untried
       ways" encroaching on a traditional community.

37   _____. "The Quality of Evil in Faulkner's Sanctuary," TSL,
       IV, 99-107.
          The thesis of Sanctuary appears in the "discrimination
       among the evil impulses of man"--there are degrees of evil
       in the novel, many of them not grandiose but no less of-
       fensive. Benbow holds to the truth, though he fails.

38   HUTCHERSON, DUDLEY R. "El mundo novelesco y real de William
       Faulkner," Arbor, XLIII (January-April), 72-83.
          Translated from the English by Sofia M. Gamero. The
       creation and characteristics of Faulkner's mythical county
       are discussed in terms of social and racial strata: the
       aristocrats, the "Rednecks," and the Negroes, whom Faulk-
       ner most admires, make up his material. When he writes of
       other matters, he is less successful.

39   LABOR, EARLE. "Faulkner's The Sound and the Fury," Expl, XVII
       (January), Item 30.
          Mr. Labor suggests that the knife scene in The Sound and
       the Fury does not signify wished-for incest but an at-
       tempted hysterectomy. Quentin wants to assume Caddy's
       identity and become a Tiresias whose suicide purges her
       sin. In the context, incest would be a relatively positive
       element, something which Quentin lacks. See 1960.B14.

1959

40   LeBRETON, MAURICE. "La thème de la vie et de la mort dans As
      I Lay Dying," Configuration Critique de William Faulkner
      II, RLM, V (Winter), 292-308.
          As I Lay Dying is in the tradition of the American tall
      tale, joining the macabre to the humorous and disregarding
      verisimilitude, but it transcends this popular genre to
      become a serious poetic reflection on the mysteries of
      life and death. It contains numerous affinities with The
      Sound and the Fury, not merely method and style but char-
      acter and theme as well. Each figure in the novel explores
      the meaning of self.

41   LEMAY, HARDING. "Faulkner and His Snopes Family Reach the
      End of Their Trilogy," NYHTB (15 November), pp. 1, 14.
          The "plot serves merely as a point of entry into [Faulk-
      ner's] multi-mirrored exploration of the universal conflict
      between integrity and evil." The Mansion has less exuber-
      ance than The Hamlet and less of the sinister humor of The
      Town, but there is a "compensating warmth of sympathy" for
      the characters. Linda Snopes is one of Faulkner's great-
      est women characters.

42   LEWIS, FLORA. "The Worldwide Influence of William Faulkner:
      Reports from Six Capitals: Report from Bonn," NYTBR (15
      November), p. 53.
          Germans see Faulkner as the most "European" of American
      writers. He is gaining a broader public. Publishers' fig-
      ures are given.

43   LEWIS, R. W. B. "William Faulkner: The Hero in the New
      World," The Picaresque Saint: Representative Figures in
      Contemporary Fiction. Philadelphia: Lippincott, pp. 179-
      219. Includes 1951.B40.
          Europeans were the first to recognize Faulkner because
      they were more capable than American critics of seeing the
      human condition dramatized in his works, especially the
      darker view that appears up to 1940. With Go Down, Moses
      and "The Bear" Faulkner ventures "into a world of light
      like that following the Incarnation." Lewis also discusses
      A Fable.
      Partially reprinted 1966.A8.

44   McGREW, JULIA. "Faulkner and the Icelanders," SS, XXXI (Feb-
      ruary), 1-14.
          Faulkner's novels and stories show the survival of
      themes, values, and events that make for epic structure,
      particularly when compared with Icelandic lore and the
      sagas produced out of it.

45   MERCER, CAROLINE, and SUSAN J. TURNER. "Restoring Life to
        Faulkner's The Hamlet," CEA, XXI (December), 1, 4-5.
            Arguing for renewed attention to the human rather than
        symbolical elements of fiction, the essay uses The Hamlet
        to illustrate the value of getting students to notice the
        passions, the tall tales, the characters' language.

46   MERIWETHER, JAMES B. "The Snopes Trilogy Completed," CarQ,
        XII (Winter), 30-34.
            The Mansion is the story of the fate which finally over-
        takes Flem Snopes, the "bitter and implacable" cousin Mink.
        The ending, where Mink submits to the earth, is a fitting
        close to the trilogy. The hardships which drive Mink are
        the same ones that, in the beginning, had driven Flem to
        his corrupt and unfeeling commercialism.

47   _____. "William Faulkner," Shenandoah, X (Winter), 18-24.
            Part of a symposium on "Modern Novelists and Contemporary
        American Society," the essay sketches Faulkner's relations
        with his own community and compares his work chiefly with
        Hemingway's. Hemingway's books have no duration, only mo-
        ments of time; no families; but Faulkner's books show plen-
        itude and humor, and they do not concern themselves with
        writers of the Leftist movement of the thirties. In The
        Town, Chick Mallison receives the nineteenth-century code
        from his ineffective uncle and has the ability to act,
        though how he would appear in The Mansion could not be
        foreseen.

48   _____, compiler. William Faulkner: An Exhibition of Manu-
        scripts. Austin: The Research Center, University of
        Texas.
            An exhibition catalogue with a brief introduction, de-
        scriptive annotation of the items on exhibit, and illus-
        trations from the revised galleys of Sanctuary, a MS page
        of Light in August, and revision of A Green Bough. The
        exhibit contains examples of Marionettes and other Univer-
        sity writings, Sanctuary, A Green Bough, Go Down, Moses,
        As I Lay Dying, Absalom, Absalom!, Light in August, Pylon,
        The Marble Faun, These 13, and Doctor Martino.

49   MOSES, W. R. "Water, Water Everywhere: Old Man and A Fare-
        well to Arms," MFS, V (Summer), 172-74.
            Supplementing Richardson's article on the "Wild Palms"
        section of The Wild Palms (1959.B56), Moses offers paral-
        lels between A Farewell to Arms and the "Old Man" plot.
        Water imagery is central to both; escapes by water are

1959

(MOSES, W. R.)
prominent. The women in both are pregnant. Failure of ex-
act parallels at the end of the two stories leads one naturally back to "Wild Palms," with which "Old Man" is
strongly connected.

50   MUELLER, WILLIAM R. "The Theme of Suffering: William Faulkner's The Sound and the Fury," The Prophetic Voice in Modern Fiction. New York: Association Press, pp. 110-35.
Dilsey is the "center of sacrifice and suffering" in The
Sound and the Fury, the symbol of that faith in man's endurance which Faulkner would later express in the Nobel
Prize acceptance speech.

51   NISHIKAWA, MASAMI. "The Worldwide Influence of William Faulkner: Reports from Six Capitals: Report from Tokyo,"
NYTBR (15 November), p. 53.
Faulkner is not as popular as Hemingway or Steinbeck, but
there is a strong academic interest in his work in Japan.

52   O'CONNOR, WILLIAM VAN. "The Grotesque in Modern American Fiction," CE, XX (April), 342-46.
Taking his conception about grotesque from an essay by
Thomas Mann--it is the great antibourgeois style and the
result of the disappearance of simple categories of comic
and tragic in modern art--O'Connor briefly compares the
work of Warren, Capote, McCullers, Sherwood Anderson,
Flannery O'Conner, and Faulkner, mentioning Light in August
and As I Lay Dying.

53   _____. "Faulkner on Broadway," KR, XXI (Spring), 334-36.
The dramatic production of Requiem for a Nun in New York
emphasizes the theme of redemption through suffering. Compared to T. S. Eliot's The Family Reunion, it is both more
specific in its message and more dramatic. Weaknesses of
character and language, however, mar the play.

54   PAULDING, GOUVERNEUR. "Right Wind, Right Rain," Reporter, XXI
(26 November), 41-42, 44.
Faulkner is looking back over his previous work in The
Mansion, revising earlier judgments. The method, which is
akin to Proust's and to human memory as well, is valid and
an important expression of what makes Faulkner a significant writer. His characters "appear in the full stature."

55   PRESCOTT, ORVILLE. "Books of the Times," NYT (13 November),
p. 27, "city edition."
Equating "Faulknerian" with a variety of stylistic and

186

(PRESCOTT, ORVILLE)
structural faults, the reviewer finds The Mansion a "bore,"
lacking interest, structure, or character motivation.

56   RICHARDSON, H. EDWARD. "The 'Hemingwaves' in Faulkner's Wild
Palms," MFS, IV (Winter), 357-60.
The thematic and plot parallels between A Farewell to
Arms and the "Wild Palms" plot of Faulkner's The Wild
Palms suggest that Faulkner is expressing his gratitude to
Hemingway--seen as McCord in the novel--for suggesting the
plot or that it is satire against the more successful writ-
er. See also 1959.B49 and 1972.B66.

57   ROSENTHAL, M. L. "On Teaching Difficult Literary Texts," CE,
XX (January), 155-63.
Suggesting the benefits of a close reading of As I Lay
Dying, the essayist believes that the "I" of the novel's
title may refer to each of the narrators and, by extension, to the family and perhaps even to a kind of society
as a whole. Once the reader realizes the various mythological and Biblical parallels, the symbolic function of
characters and names, then the novel's difficulties begin
to disappear. The opening scene is key to the pattern of
the book. It interprets the defeat of love and feeling by
life's harsh realities.

58   SCOTT, NATHAN A., JR. "Man in Recent Literature" and "Beneath the Hammer of Truth," Modern Literature and the Religious Frontier. New York: Harper, pp. 65-83, 103-15.
Along with other modern writers, Faulkner depicts alienation and despair, using his South to dramatize "the central predicament of modern man"--the necessity of living
in a transitional time. The "dialectical entanglements of
his fiction" dramatize an "inclinatory Christian" viewpoint.

59   SEWALL, RICHARD B. "Absalom, Absalom!," Vision of Tragedy.
New Haven: Yale University Press, pp. 133-47.
The action in Absalom, Absalom! belongs to Sutpen, whose
fate is moral not tragic. Quentin, as commentator, creates
tragedy by his involvement with Miss Rosa and his obsession
with Sutpen's story. His vision of the good and evil in
human affairs communicates the precarious life of man.
"We have no hope, yet we hope. It is tragic."

60   STAVROU, C. N. "Ambiguity in Faulkner's Affirmation," Person,
XL (Spring), 169-77.
"In Faulkner, as in Shelley, the Prometheus motif is

1959

(STAVROU, C. N.)
 everpresent." Faulkner's "beliefs" center on individual
courage, compassion and sacrifice as ideals. His work
also contains much "negation and depression," and his de-
tractors, mistaking what he denounced for what he advo-
cated, can be forgiven for being wrong because Faulkner
has not yet found a "fictive receptacle" to articulate his
confidence in man's survival. A Fable, which receives
most attention, is called at best "cold," lacking the
power to impart the compassion it preaches.

61 STONE, PHIL. "Faulkner Publication," SatR (27 June), p. 23.
 After New Republic had taken Faulkner's first poem, ac-
cording to his friend Stone, they refused others, where-
upon Faulkner and Stone sent a poem by John Clare and
Coleridge's "Kubla Khan," with equal lack of success.
Adds to 1959.B64.

62 STONESIFER, RICHARD J. "In Defense of Dewey Dell," EdLr,
 II (1 July), 27-33.
 Dewey Dell's self-absorption is expected, given her condition and age. She is "more sinned against than sinning"
in As I Lay Dying. She should be regarded with compassion;
her acts and desires are a product of her fears and needs.

63 STEWART, RANDALL. "A Doctrine of Man," MissQ, XII (Winter),
 4-9.
 One of several papers on religious trends in contemporary
America, from the American Studies Association of the Lower
Mississippi's 1958 meeting, the essay mentions Eliot, Warren, and Faulkner as writers who, one way or another and
without the need for labels, have affirmed the presence of
sin and the need for grace in man. Contrary to Faulkner's
critics, the grace is there in his works, along with the
sin, though it is not an easy grace. "We mustn't look for
happy endings... The Crucifixion itself was a great
failure when looked at through worldly eyes."

64 STRAUSS, GERALD H. "Faulkner's First Appearance," SatR (30
 May), p. 25.
 The writer corrects the statement (SatR 9 May) that the
New Orleans Double Dealer first published Faulkner, pointing out that "L'Après-Midi d'un Faune" appeared in NRep
6 August 1919. See Phil Stone's additional comment,
1959.B61.

65 TATE, ALLEN. "The Novelist in the American South," NewSt,
 LVII (13 June), 831-32.
 Faulkner's maturity in the mid-thirties is used for

(TATE, ALLEN)
purposes of fixing "an historical moment for the climax of
what has been called the Southern Renaissance."

66   TAYLOR, WALTER F., JR. "Let My People Go: The White Man's
Heritage in Go Down, Moses," SAQ, LVIII (Winter), 20-32.
Ike is the hero, the Edmonds men are the villains in the
drama of race and land that appears in Go Down, Moses.
Cass fails to understand the "truths shown him through
Ike's repudiation," and he repeats the sin of old
Carothers. Ike has countered the sin by adopting "primi-
tive virtues of the Negro and Indian."

67   THONON, ROBERT. "William Faulkner: From The Hamlet to The
Town," ESA, II (September), 190-202.
The Town has a more hopeful outlook than The Hamlet.
From the irresistible progress of the rodentlike Snopeses
we arrive at a point where more effective opposition to
Flem can be mounted. Snopesism appears to be self-
destructive.

68   TYNAN, KENNETH. Review of Requiem for a Nun at the John
Golden Theatre, NY (7 February), pp. 82, 84-85.
The dramatic version of Requiem for a Nun is "dense and
prolix." The characters are poorly done, the construction
is primitive, and it does not redeem any of its mechanical
faults by going to the roots of the human condition. The
acting is also poor in Ruth Ford's production.
Reprinted and expanded in Curtains. New York: Atheneum,
1961, pp. 276-78, 299-301.

69   VALVERDE, JOSÉ MARÍA. "Faulkner," Historia de la Literatura
Universal. Barcelona: Editorial Wagner, S.A., pp. 551-
57.
Faulkner's work is thoroughly modern in its demands upon
the reader's attention and involvement. It reads like poetry. Neither inspiration nor "tricks" have created
Faulkner's fiction; it comes from artistry and continuous
hard work.

70   WALD, JERRY. "Faulkner & Hollywood," Films in Review,
X (March), 129-33.
Faulkner's relationship with Hollywood was purely a fi-
nancial one. His novels present a number of special difficulties to the director who wants to adapt them for
film.

1959

71   WARREN, ROBERT PENN. "William Faulkner," Configuration Cri-
        tique de William Faulkner II, RLM, V (Winter), 429-54.
        Reprinted from 1958.B64. See 1959.B20.

72   WASIOLEK, EDWARD. "Dostoevsky and Sanctuary," MLN, LXXIV
        (February), 114-17.
            Crime and Punishment and The Brothers Karamazov may con-
        tain sources for two passages in Sanctuary about the cor-
        ruption of innocence.

73   _____. "As I Lay Dying: Distortion in the Slow Eddy
        of Current Opinion," Critique, III (Spring-Fall),
        15-23.
            Previous critics have been unable or unwilling to deal
        with the comic irony in As I Lay Dying. Addie represents
        Faulkner's point of view, and the children are epitomes of
        her states of mind at their moment of conception. Darl is
        the only one who seeks answers to life's most terrible
        questions.

74   WATKINS, FLOYD C. "The Gentle Reader and Mr. Faulkner's
        Morals," GaR, XIII (Spring), 68-75.
            Reviewing some of the things which the "average" reader
        objects to in Faulkner's work, the author discusses Faulk-
        ner's "reasons" for writing what and as he does. Posterity
        may forgive Faulkner his peculiarities. He writes of human
        weakness and folly because it is there.

75   _____. "William Faulkner in His Own Country," EmUQ,
        XV (December), 228-39.
            Mississippians and other mid-Southerners have strong
        opinions and a number of misconceptions about Faulkner.
        Quotes some favorable comments as well.

76   WEIGEL, JOHN A. "Teaching the Modern Novel: From Finnegan's
        Wake to A Fable," CE, XXI (December), 172-73.
            A Fable is the climax of an ambitious course in the in-
        ternational modern novel, where the students were found
        capable of appreciating complex fiction. The students
        voted A Fable the "most important book" they had read in
        the course.

77   WEST, ANTHONY. "Dying Fall," NY (5 December), pp. 236-43.
            The Mansion is an "appalling" last act to what should
        have been the tragedy of Flem Snopes. Instead of Mink as
        sole agent of Flem's destruction, Linda Snopes and Gavin
        Stevens are the real and callous manipulators from behind
        the scenes. Ratliff descends to the point of embracing

(WEST, ANTHONY)
Madison Ave. in the form of Myra Allanovna's expensive
ties. The best is still good--the words that deal directly
with Mink.

78   WHEELER, OTIS B. "Faulkner's Wilderness," AL, XXXI (May),
127-36.
Dealing with all the "Ike McCaslin stories," from "Lion"
to Big Woods, the author identifies two themes--the wilderness as victim, the wilderness as teacher--which fuse in
the Go Down, Moses version of "The Bear" and in Big Woods.
Ike learns the code of the hunter and receives knowledge
of the mysterious unity of life. He also participates with
his fellow initiate, Sam, and with the uninitiated, like
his cousin Cass, in the chase which makes the wilderness a
victim. Sam contrives the death of the wilderness to save
it from a worse fate. There is no hope or promise in the
stories. Faulkner is a believer in the "decline of the
West,"

79   WOODWORTH, STANLEY D. "Problèmes de traduction," Configuration Critique de William Faulkner II, RLM, V (Winter),
569-88.
Up through 1952, Faulkner has had eight translators putting his work into French, of whom R. N. Raimbault and
Maurice E. Coindreau are the most significant. Coindreau
is also an important interpreter of Faulkner to the French
audience. The essay discusses the problems of putting a
contemporary American novel into contemporary French with
examples from several other writers before taking up problems peculiar to Faulkner work. Allusions, sentence
rhythms, slang, strong verbs of action for which there are
no French equivalents, Faulkner's personal style and his
regionalism are all difficult to translate. The "Legend
of the South" so prominent in American criticism of Faulkner may not exist in France because the "South" in Faulkner's work does not translate.

80   *WYLD, LIONEL. "Faulkner and Yoknapatawpha: Out of the 'Waste
Land,'" American Literary Review (Japan), XXX (December),
4-12.
Bassett, Item AA133.

81   ZOELLNER, ROBERT H. "Faulkner's Prose Style in Absalom, Absalom!," AL, XXX (Winter), 486-502.
Faulkner's stylistic innovations, as in Absalom, Absalom!, are intentional, complex, meaningful, and effective.
A classification of certain devices and a discussion of

1959

(ZOELLNER, ROBERT H.)
their effects on the reader shows how Faulkner forces the
reader into a new relationship with time and history, giving immediacy to his narrative, stressing the eternality
of evil, showing the accumulation of tradition, and de-
stroying merely spatial considerations--the total effect
is to universalize Sutpen's story and to communicate Faulkner's "metaphysic."

1960 A   BOOKS

1   HOFFMAN, FREDERICK, and OLGA W. VICKERY, eds. William
     Faulkner: Three Decades of Criticism. East Lansing,
     Michigan: Michigan State University Press.
         Contains 1939.B3, 1939.B26, 1939.B28, 1941.B4, 1946.B2,
     1946.B16, 1952.B8, 1952.B33, 1954.B75, 1955.B10, 1956.B44,
     1957.B62, 1958.B40, 1960.B36, an excerpt on As I Lay Dying
     from 1953.B30, 1954.B62, 1955.B35, 1956.B48, 1957.B23,
     1957.B38, 1957.B45, 1959.A4, plus Faulkner's Nobel Prize
     address, an original article: Joseph J. Moldenhauer, "Uni-
     ty of Theme and Structure in The Wild Palms" (See 1960.B48),
     and a "Selective Bibliography" by Vickery. Hoffman's intro-
     duction (1960.B36) surveys the critical reception of Faulk-
     ner's work. Second edition pub. New York: Harcourt, Brace
     and World, 1963.

2   SLATOFF, WALTER J. Quest for Failure: A Study of William
     Faulkner. Ithaca, New York: Cornell University Press.
         This study, done through close reading in the manner of
     the New Critics, discerns a repeated emphasis upon motion
     and immobility, sound and silence, "quiescence and turbu-
     lence" in Faulkner's fiction from The Sound and the Fury
     through The Town (excluding The Unvanquished and Knight's
     Gambit). Tension is the chief ingredient of Faulkner's
     fictional world; he has "polar imagination" and tends to
     view all experience as composed of things at variance.
     Faulkner is unwilling to resolve any of these tensions, so
     that reading his fiction is an endless struggle. With an
     apparently Bergsonian view of self and knowledge, Faulkner
     attempts to engage the reader's intuition in the process
     of understanding his characters. But the high degree of
     deliberate disorder in the fiction indicates that he has
     sought failure deliberately, repeatedly, to elevate the
     significance of his efforts.

1960 B   SHORTER WRITINGS

1   ADAMS, PERCY G.   "The Franco-American Faulkner," TSL, V, 1-13.
        A brief comment on Woodworth (1959.A6) leads to general
     discussion of Faulkner criticism in France.   French critics
     do not compare Faulkner to Hawthorne, Melville, or James,
     as Americans do, but to Balzac, Proust, Joyce, Hardy, Dos-
     toevsky, Dickens, Zola, Mann or Cervantes.   The French
     like several of Faulkner's supposedly "lesser" novels:
     Pylon and Sanctuary, for example, though they generally
     prefer the ones generally acknowledged great.   They have
     always seen him as primarily a novelist.   French and Amer-
     ican responses to Faulkner's techniques and themes (Time,
     Humor, Race, Puritanism, etc.) are compared briefly.

2   ALLEN, CHARLES A.   "William Faulkner: Comedy and the Purpose
     of Humor," ArQ, XVI (Spring), 59-69.
        Faulkner's comedy is for the purpose of revealing "with
     satire, respect and compassion man's comic futility."
     Among the works discussed, chiefly by summary, are "A Rose
     for Emily," As I Lay Dying, "Old Man," and The Hamlet.

3   ALLEN, WALTER ERNEST.   The Novel Today.   New York: Longmans,
     Green, pp. 111-24.
        Faulkner's genius is evident in the power and complexity
     of novels that are at once brilliant and obscure.   He is
     Southern literature.   His achievement is not Balzacian,
     however.   He is a combination of his great European sources
     and the American tall tale tradition from A. B. Longstreet
     to Twain.   The author discusses Faulkner's concept of Time
     in The Sound and the Fury and Intruder in the Dust; his
     sympathetic treatment of poor whites in As I Lay Dying and
     Light in August; and the doom of Thomas Sutpen.   Repub-
     lished as Tradition and Dream: The English and American
     Novel from the Twenties to Our Time.   London: Phoenix
     House, 1964.

4   ALTENBERND, LYNN.   "A Suspended Moment: The Irony of History
     in William Faulkner's 'The Bear,'" MLN, LXXV (November),
     572-82.
        Discussing "The Bear" as a novelette, the author says
     section four reinforces the parable of Southern history in
     the remaining four sections.   The skills learned in the
     hunt are the very ones that destroy the hunt.   Lion, a
     tame creature gone wild, represents the attributes of the
     hunters without their humanity.   Indian, Negro, and White
     are equally guilty of creating the situation which destroys
     the wilderness.   The serpent in the wilderness is evil,

1960

(ALTENBERND, LYNN)
which Ike acknowledges; and Ike himself is redeemed, though
the world around him must wait.

5   ALVAREZ, ALFRED. "The Difficulty of Being South African,"
     NewSt (4 June), pp. 827-28.
        The book under review, Dan Jacobson's The Evidence of
     Love, is compared with Faulkner's work, which has never
     made Jacobson's "step from private intensity to public re-
     sponsibility."

6   ASHRAF, S. A. "Faulkner in '57," Venture (Karachi), I
     (March), 13-17.
        An Indian scholar who visited in America recounts an
     interview with Faulkner at the University of Virginia in
     April 1957. A testy Faulkner emphasizes his interest in
     creativity over philosophy and claims to write because he
     wants to "excel Balzac, Dostoevsky, and Shakespeare."

7   BARTH, J. R. "Faulkner and the Snopes Trilogy," America, CII
     (27 February), pp. 638-40.
        The Snopes trilogy ranks with Twain's work "in the genre
     of the American folk tale." The episodic structure, paral-
     lel to folk tradition, gives free play to Faulkner's imag-
     ination. The plots are summarized and the conclusion of
     the trilogy is discussed as Calvinist: evil can be de-
     feated but not destroyed or redeemed, and good and evil,
     as personified in Gavin Stevens and Snopes, seem preor-
     dained, a matter of election.

8   BECK, WARREN. "Faulkner in 'The Mansion,'" VQR, XXXVI
     (Spring), 272-92.
        Realism and the grotesque, combined in a structure that
     lets us see all sides of the "object" from several view-
     points and tempered with a deep humanity, makes The Mansion
     one of Faulkner's great novels about the tragedy called
     life.

9   BERGER, YVES. "Présence et signification chez William Faulk-
     ner," NRF, VIII (May), 951-60.
        Reviewing the new translation of The Hamlet, the author
     finds that it lacks coherence and force; it is inconsis-
     tent. Faulkner's characters are disquieting. Labove and
     Eula are the most richly symbolic.

10   BIGELOW, GORDON E. "Faulkner's Snopes Saga," EJ, XLIX (Decem-
     ber), 595-605.
        Summarizing the Snopes novels and discussing the members

194

(BIGELOW, GORDON E.)
of the family, the critic finds that Faulkner's meaning is
not localized but broad--a condemnation of modern man's
mechanistic, sterile existence and of the results of this
way of life on people and the land. In The Mansion, Faulkner displays pity even for Flem, who is, after all, just
another "poor son of a bitch."

11   BOUVARD, LOÏC. "Conversation with William Faulkner," translated by Henry Dan Piper, MFS, V (Winter), 361-64.
Translation of 1954.B14. Reprinted 1966.A6.

12   BRENNAN, JOSEPH X., and SEYMOUR L. GROSS. "The Problem of
Moral Values in Conrad and Faulkner," Person, XLI (Winter),
60-70.
Faulkner and Conrad differ from writers like Zola,
Dreiser, and Hemingway, who portray a world without the
possibility of triumph or defeat. Both have sought moral
values through fiction, but Faulkner believes in both God
and immortality, while Conrad does not. Faulkner's early
work depicts only social decay, but beginning with Intruder in the Dust there is hope and belief. His later
work, though least convincing fictionally, strongly embodies the "belief" of the Nobel speech.

13   BRISSENDEN, R. F. "Outrage, Impotence and Honour in the
World of William Faulkner," CR, III, 31-40.
Faulkner depicts a world in which the old verities can
exist only when men believe and will that they exist. Outrage and impotence in the face of immorality and the preservation of honor in defeat mark many of Faulkner's characters and novels. After Go Down, Moses, the work is more
baldly and less dramatically moralistic.

14   BRODERICK, JOHN C. "Faulkner's The Sound and the Fury," Expl,
XIX (November), Item 12.
Following Labor's note on the knife scene in The Sound
and the Fury as an attempted "hysterectomy" (1959.B39),
the author calls attention to Jason's remark that when
they castrated Benjy they should have rendered Caddy and
Miss Quentin barren, too.

15   BUTOR, MICHEL. "Les relations de parenté dan 'L'ours' de
William Faulkner," Répertoire: Études et conférences,
1948-59. Paris: Éditions de Minuit, pp. 250-61.
Faulkner writes for his Southern readers and only approaches the outsider through them, for he wants to show
them their history in order to free them from the evils of

1960

(BUTOR, MICHEL)
the past. "The Bear" demonstrates: the complex parental relations, where white and black lines of the McCaslins are dramatically juxtaposed, along with the spiritual parentage of Sam Fathers, against a wilderness where pure lineage is also important, reveal the importance of genealogy. The ultimate genealogical reference is the lineage of the serpent.

16   CAMUS, ALBERT. "Camus' Illuminating Answers to Searching Questions," NYHTB (21 February), p. 1.
Answering questions submitted by editors of Venture, Camus evaluates American authors: "Faulkner remains for me your great living creator. I have just read 'A Fable.' Since Melville, none of your writers has spoken about suffering as Faulkner does."

17   COINDREAU, MAURICE E. "On Translating Faulkner," Princeton Alumni Weekly (29 April), pp. 3-4.
Reprints 1957.B11; included in The Time of William Faulkner (1971.B18).

18   COLE, DOUGLAS. "Faulkner's Sanctuary: Retreat from Responsibility," WHR, XIV (Summer), 291-98.
Society is ironically portrayed in Sanctuary, where corruption is widespread even among those who condemn the obvious criminal element. Faulkner sets up parallels between respectable and criminal society, showing that there is little difference between them.

19   COLLINS, CARVEL. "Miss Quentin's Paternity Again," TSLL, II (Autumn), 253-60.
Evidence in The Sound and the Fury refutes the often repeated contention that Caddy commits incest with Benjy or Quentin and disputes the claim that Dalton Ames fathers Miss Quentin. The "Appendix" to the Portable Faulkner is of questionable value and usefulness to a reading of the novel.
Reprinted 1970.A6.

20   CONNOLLY, THOMAS E. "The Three Plots of A Fable," TCL, VI (July), 70-75.
The horse-racing plot is parallel and complementary to the main plot of A Fable. Both stories split into two parts: idealistic and realistic. The other plot, involving Levine, also reflects the main plot. A Fable is tightly organized. The struggle of idealism and realism is basic to Faulkner's work.

21   COOK, ALBERT S. "Plot as Discovery," The Meaning of Fiction.
      Detroit: Wayne State University Press, pp. 232-41.
        History, not suffering, binds Faulkner's characters.
      They exist fictionally only when they move in a widened
      plot often constructed out of "allegorical situations."
      Faulkner's work seeks to define the intangible mysteries
      of an ever-present past.
      Reprinted 1973.

22   COUCH, JOHN PHILIP. "Camus and Faulkner: The Search for the
      Language of Modern Tragedy," YFS, No. 25 (Spring), 120-25.
        Camus' adaptation, Requiem pour une nonne (1956), is a
      commentary on Faulkner. His preface to the 1957 transla-
      tion of the novel observes that Faulkner was able to formu-
      late a language for modern tragedy in Requiem for a Nun,
      but his adaptation seems to use the language of Sanctuary
      and Pylon, two Faulkner novels which Camus greatly admired.

23   CROSS, BARBARA M. "The Sound and the Fury: The Pattern of
      Sacrifice," ArQ, XVI (Spring), 5-16.
        As one of three related novels unified by the ritualiza-
      tion of character and event (the others being As I Lay Dy-
      ing and Sartoris), The Sound and the Fury is "informed
      with a pervasive symbolism," not exclusively Christian but
      reflecting James G. Frazer's The Golden Bough. Primitive
      ritual as recorded in the 12-volume Golden Bough is
      searched for sources of The Sound and the Fury.

24   DILLISTONE, F. W. The Novelist and the Passion Story. Lon-
      don: Constable, pp. 92-118 (also New York: Sheed and
      Ward).
        Faulkner's A Fable emphasizes that the twentieth century
      must understand the Passion in terms of its own cata-
      strophic times; it must realize that individuals are ca-
      pable of compassion and sacrifice, and that through such
      men all men become truly human. It takes on the twin
      Juggernauts of the age, Greed and Warfare, and affirms that
      integrity and sacrifice and hope can overcome them.

25   FADIMAN, CLIFTON. "Reading I've Liked," Holiday, XXVII (Janu-
      ary), 23.
        The reviewer admits, grudgingly and in one paragraph,
      that against all his expectations from Faulkner, The Man-
      sion had held his attention.

26   FIEDLER, LESLIE. Love and Death in the American Novel. New
      York: Criterion Books, pp. 309-15.
        Faulkner is afraid of "castrating women" and sexuality.
      His later work, like Requiem for a Nun and The Town, seems

1960

(FIEDLER, LESLIE)
to attempt redemption of his "anti-virgins," but his art
fails when he attempts sentimentality instead of nausea
and despair. Revised edition New York: Stein and Day,
1966, pp. 320-25.

27 _____. "William Faulkner, Highbrows' Lowbrow," No! In
Thunder: Essays on Myth and Literature. Boston: Beacon
Press, pp. 111-18.
Reprinted from "William Faulkner: An American Dickens"
(1950.B8).

28 FISHER, MARVIN. "The World of Faulkner's Children," UKCR,
XXVII (October), 13-18.
Faulkner is a master of limited point of view, especially
in stories that deal with children, where the device takes
on great power. "Barn Burning" and "That Evening Sun"
demonstrate: neither is about initiation, though both show
children exposed in their innocence to adult complexities.
In "Barn Burning" the child escapes a world of fear and
despair; in "That Evening Sun" the children, failing to
understand, reduce adult events to the absurd.

29 *FUKUDA, R. "Bibliography of William Faulkner in Japan,"
Hikaku bungaki, III, 122-31.
Bassett (1972.A2), Item GG44.

30 GARDINER, HAROLD C. "Two Southern Tales" and "William Faulkner's A Fable," In All Conscience: Reflections on Books
and Culture. Cambridge, Mass.: Harvard University Press,
pp. 129-31.
Requiem for a Nun (as reviewed in America, 6 October
1951) is one of Faulkner's less successful books; A Fable
(reviewed in America, 21 August 1954) is a riddle without
a key, and probably a book without a treasure to be un-
locked.

31 GARRETT, GEORGE P. Review of New Orleans Sketches, GaR, XIV
(Summer), 215-16.
Faulkner's early stories, which show "only a slight prom-
ise," should encourage the young writer who is overawed by
The Sound and the Fury. He praises the few scholars work-
ing in the Faulkner field, like Collins and Meriwether.

32 *GIANNITRAPANI, ANGELA. "Il procedimento dello stupore in
Faulkner," SA, No. 6, 275-305.
In Wistaria, 1963.A4.

33   GOLD, JOSEPH. "The Humanism of William Faulkner," Humanist,
      XX (March-April), 113-17.
          Faulkner's fiction has always depicted a hopeful view of
      man and a realistic view of the imperfections of society.
      Faulkner prefers the single human voice to man's institu-
      tions, including the church; he puts a high value on in-
      dividual responsibility; and he believes that man is re-
      sponsible for his own fate.

34   _____. "Truth or Consequences: Faulkner's The Town,"
      MissQ, XIII (Summer), 112-16.
          Flem's defeat comes through the harmony of accord
      between Tom Tom and Turl; elsewhere in the novel divisive-
      ness allows him to triumph: dishonesty, moral cupidity,
      pride. Ratliff, by being honest and generous, keeps out
      of Snopes's clutches. The final Snopes image in the book
      is a terrible warning: the children who are half Snopes
      and half Indian represent the ultimate corruption of the
      promise of the New World. It is less good artistically
      than The Hamlet: Gavin is too intrusive, Eula is not fully
      realized, and the structure is flawed.

35   GUTTMANN, ALLEN. "Collisions and Confrontations," ArQ, XVI
      (Spring), 46-52.
          A large number of physical collisions in Faulkner's
      earlier novels (from Sartoris to Absalom, Absalom! and in-
      cluding "The Bear") are characteristic and appropriate
      images for Faulkner's violent characters.

36   HOFFMAN, FREDERICK J. "William Faulkner: An Introduction,"
      in William Faulkner: Three Decades of Criticism (1960.A1),
      pp. 1-50.
          Taken in part from the introductory essay in Two Decades
      of Criticism (1951.A2) and partly previously published in
      1960.B37, this is a survey of Faulkner's critical recep-
      tion, in two parts, with the Nobel Prize used as the divid-
      ing point. The essay discusses reviews and criticism, in-
      cluding some foreign criticism.

37   _____. "William Faulkner: A Review of Recent Criticism,"
      Renascence, XIII (Autumn), 3-9, 32.
          Since 1950, Faulkner has "taken a hand in the evaluation
      of his own work" by virtue of his public remarks. Recent
      criticism has reflected this. Incorporated into 1960.B36.

38   HOWARD, LEON. Literature and the American Tradition. New
      York: Doubleday, pp. 318-23.
          By the late 1930s, Faulkner's prevailing attitudes,

1960

(HOWARD, LEON)
obscured heretofore by his dazzling experimentation,
emerged as a strong sense of the past and a dramatization
of its dangerous effects; a preoccupation with the forces
of greed and materialism; and a belief in the simple power
of mankind to endure its own folly.

39   HOWELL, ELMO.   "Faulkner's Jumblies: The Nonsense World of
As I Lay Dying," ArQ, XVI (Spring), 70-78.
As I Lay Dying, like the Jumblies by Edward Lear, is
chiefly nonsense, and criticism which reads heroism or
tragedy into it must be challenged. The major novels preceding it were dark studies of the failure of traditional
society; As I Lay Dying contains the same theme, but the
Bundrens' futile and insincere gestures are turned to
sport.

40   JORDAN, ROBERT M.   "The Limits of Illusion: Faulkner, Fielding, and Chaucer," Criticism, II (Summer), 278-305.
Modern criticism and fiction put idea over image and use
literature as a means to an end. New Critics and Faulkner
demonstrate organic theories of formal unity ignore fiction
written by plan or design. The critic then discusses The
Sound and the Fury as an example of organic but jumbled
structure demanding that the reader order temporal and
logical relations for himself. The opening of Intruder in
the Dust presents something of the same effect, while
Light in August shows Faulkner treating Joe Christmas much
as the modern novel treats the reader: he is a puzzled man
responding to a story he does not understand. Illusion
and the suppression of fictiveness are Faulkner's chief
devices. Chaucer and Fielding are examples of the opposite practice.

41   KERR, ELIZABETH M.   "Snopes," WSCL, I (Spring-Summer), 66-83.
A rambling cursory overview of character, image, theme,
and narrative technique in the Snopes trilogy, the article
concludes that "final evaluation of Snopes as part of the
Yoknapatawpha Saga must be postponed until the saga is
completed."

42   LORD, JOHN B.   "A Study of Faulkner's Revisions," Exercise Ex-
change, VII (February), 6-7.
Two passages from the Saturday Evening Post version of
"Raid" are compared to the version in The Unvanquished,
and students are asked to write essays on the purpose of
the "revisions" which the differences indicate.

43   McKEAN, KEITH F. "Southern Patriarch: A Portrait," VQR,
      XXXVI (Summer), 376-89.
          Faulkner's novels show the Southern concern with "blood,"
      kinship, and a long history in the land. Only one para-
      graph is devoted to Faulkner.

44   MacLACHLAN, JOHN M. "Southern Humor as a Vehicle of Social
      Evaluation," MissQ, XIII (Fall), 157-62.
          A paragraph on The Hamlet and one on As I Lay Dying put
      Faulkner into the "Longstreet tradition" of Southern humor.

45   MacLURE, MILLAR. "Allegories of Innocence," DR, XL (Summer),
      145-56.
          Lord of the Flies, The Fall, and Absalom, Absalom! demon-
      strate the use the modern writer has made of the theme of
      man's innocence. Sutpen can accept the world only in terms
      of his own plans; and Quentin, hearing his story, can ac-
      cept the story of Sutpen only in terms of his own fate.
      Innocence is a captivity within a limited vision of one's
      own destiny.

46   _____. "Snopes: A Faulkner Myth," CanF, XXXIX (February),
      245-50.
          A sociological or a tragic reading of the Snopes trilogy
      in inadequate. Faulkner has changed his mind about Flem,
      trying to put him into a tragic role for which he is fic-
      tionally unready. The "ironic genius" presides over The
      Hamlet; the Trickster over The Town; and Athene over The
      Mansion. The Jefferson jail is the "hieroglyph of a cursed
      kingdom"--the central symbol of man's fate in the trilogy,
      a fact underlined by "The Jail" episode of Requiem for a
      Nun, which presents the multifold meaning of the symbol:
      a recognition of man's sinfulness, his hope for order, and
      his inexhaustible self-assertion: "This was I."

47   MERIWETHER, JAMES B. "The Literary Career of William Faulk-
      ner: Catalogue of an Exhibition in the Princeton Univer-
      sity Library," PULC, XXI (Spring), 111-64.
          An overview of Faulkner's work in the form of an exhibi-
      tion catalogue with annotated entries on the books and man-
      uscripts and other Faulkneriana on display. Included in
      1961.A4.

48   MOLDENHAUER, JOSEPH J. "Unity of Theme and Structure in The
      Wild Palms," Faulkner: Three Decades of Criticism
      (1960.A1), pp. 305-22.
          Both sections of The Wild Palms are subject to allegori-
      cal and symbolic interpretation. They are intricately

1960

(MOLDENHAUER, JOSEPH J.)
related studies on the theme of puritanism and its effects.
The love story is an inverted Scarlet Letter; the river
story resembles Huckleberry Finn. The two sections are
compared in detail for parallels and antitheses.

49   MOONEY, STEPHEN L. "Faulkner's The Town: A Question of
Voices," MissQ, XIII (Summer), 117-22.
An analysis of the twenty-four "dramatic monologues"
which make up the book reveals that Gavin, who is grammat-
ically correct and occasionally rhapsodic, sees events and
wants to express them in simultaneous order; that Ratliff
is ungrammatical, homely, and acutely perceptive; and that
Chick Mallison is midway between them and thus qualifies
as "voice" of Jefferson. Chick's telling of the first and
last tales in The Town frames the action. The three voices
fuse to represent the synthesis of "We," the whole of the
town's view.

50   MOORE, GEOFFREY. "Mink Agonistes," KR, XXII (Autumn), 519-22.
The depiction of Mink as one of the faceless tribe of
dirt farmers is praiseworthy. There are three Faulkners:
the "county" Southern gentleman; the farmer and hunter; the
modern bohemian and experimentalist of New Orleans and the
1920s. The Mansion was written by number two; it ranks
high among Faulkner's works.

51   NATHAN, MONIQUE. "Un Sartoris chez les Snopes," Critique, XVI
(March), 222-27.
The reviewer likes The Hamlet but not René Hilléret's
French translation.

52   O'CONNOR, WILLIAM VAN. "The Old Master: The Sole Proprie-
tor," VQR, XXXVI (Winter), 147-51.
The reviewer objects to Gavin Stevens' role and to the
middle of The Mansion, but sees the "Old Master" in the
portrait of Mink Snopes.

53   PERLUCK, HERBERT A. "'The Heart's Driving Complexity': An
Unromantic Reading of Faulkner's 'The Bear,'" Accent, XX
(Winter), 23-46.
Ike McCaslin is not a hero in "The Bear." Part Four is
deeply ironic in tone and matter; it undercuts Ike's
slightly insincere claim of freedom. McCaslin (Cass)
slowly discovers and drives home Ike's weakness for life--
going back to the scene with the fyce in the hunting narra-
tive--and reveals the inadequacy of renunciation as an approach to the problem of existence.

(PERLUCK, HERBERT A.)
    Partially reprinted in 1964.A9; reprinted 1972.A1, with
    comment at 1972.B87.

54   RAINES, CHARLES. "Faulkner and Human Freedom," ForumH, III
        (Summer), 50-53.
        Freedom is the "major theme" of Faulkner's work. His
    characters have responsibility; they can choose their
    lives; and they must bear the burden of the sometimes para-
    doxical situations these conditions create. The two images
    of freedom in the fiction are the primitive forest and
    flight, as in The Wild Palms, Absalom, Absalom!, and Light
    in August. Time, with which Faulkner is so concerned, is
    the great threat to freedom.

55   ROBERTS, JAMES L. "The Individual and the Community: Faulk-
        ner's Light in August," Studies in American Literature,
        edited by Waldo McNeir and Leo B. Levy. Baton Rouge:
        Louisiana State University Press, pp. 132-53.
        The circle image is used to characterize Lena Grove's
    role in Light in August; she is involved in the endless
    round of nature; she opens and closes the book. The image
    connects her with Joe Christmas, whose life runs in a
    circle, too. Hightower, the "moral reflector" of the nov-
    el, is the spokes of the wheel, connecting the two main
    actions. Joe is the center or axle. Each character is
    isolated within the community; each produces an appropriate
    response from the community. It is Faulkner's most diffi-
    cult novel.

56   _____. "The Individual and the Family: Faulkner's As I Lay
        Dying," ArQ, XVI (Spring), 26-38.
        The Sound and the Fury condemns Southern aristocracy,
    while As I Lay Dying condemns "backward hill people," and
    the two reveal many similarities: like Benjy, Vardaman
    Bundren is an idiot. The trip in As I Lay Dying is an-
    other of Addie's acts of violence, done to force an aware-
    ness of her self on the family; character by character,
    the family fails her. Darl is a sane observer in an absurd
    world; much of the action is through his eyes.

57   SCHOLES, ROBERT. "The Modern American Novel and the Mason-
        Dixon Line," GaR, XIV (Summer), 193-204.
        Sutpen's innocence of the knowledge of good and evil in
    Absalom, Absalom! precipitates his downfall. He lives in
    a perpetual isolation from the realities of his world, act-
    ing as if only his dream exists. In The Wild Palms, Harry
    takes the blame for his actions, unlike Frederick Henry of

1960

(SCHOLES, ROBERT)
the similar story, A Farewell to Arms, who blames the im-
personal cosmos. Writers like Hemingway, Fitzgerald, and
James G. Cozzens diminish man's stature; Faulkner exalts
it. In The Great Gatsby an ideal has failed; in Absalom,
Absalom! a man has failed to meet the ideal.

58 SLABEY, ROBERT M. "Joe Christmas, Faulkner's Marginal Man,"
Phylon, XXI (Fall), 266-77.
All the major characters of Light in August are not only
outsiders in the community but strangers to themselves as
well. Using sociological vocabulary, the author argues
that Joe, Joanna, Hightower, Lena and Byron are all outcasts and "marginal," but Joe Christmas is the "marginal
man," totally without status, and representative of the
problem of trying to be human.

59 _____. "Myth and Ritual in Light in August," TSLL,
II (Autumn), 328-49.
Though Faulkner uses Christian parallels in Light in August, Joe Christmas is not a Christ figure but more properly an avatar of the dying and resurrected god of world
mythology as treated in Frazer's The Golden Bough. Mythic,
existential, mystic, and Jungian parallels in Joe's life
reveal the novel as a "cycle of ritualistic repetition"
emblematic of life. Hightower's "dying" vision of the
wheel image is a mandala, and the use of Lena at the very
end is a "concrete personification of tranquility."
Reprinted 1971.A3.

60 SOUTHERN, TERRY. "Dark Laughter in the Towers," Nation (23
April), pp. 348-50.
As I Lay Dying is used to illustrate "absurd or grotesque" literature, of which it is a precursor; it is an
example of a "strong existentialist writing full of dark
laughter."

61 SPRINGER, ANNE M. The American Novel in Germany: A Study of
the Critical Reception of Eight American Novelists Between
the Two World Wars. Hamburg: Cram, de Gruyter, pp. 84-87.
In 1932, with Light in August, Faulkner was introduced
to the German audience in the wake of his mention by Sinclair Lewis at the 1930 Nobel Prize ceremonies. The novel
was translated in 1935. Before the war, Pylon, Absalom,
Absalom!, and many stories appeared in German and an
English version of The Unvanquished--all were generally
favorably received. A bibliography of translations of
Faulkner is appended.

62   STEENE, BIRGITTA. "William Faulkner and the Myth of the Amer-
     ican South," Moderna Sprak, LIV (No. 3), 270-79.
       The Southern myth, which Faulkner opposes as much as he
     accepts, differs markedly from the general American myth.
     Absalom, Absalom!, The Hamlet, Sanctuary, and "The Bear"
     are used to show how fully Faulkner has explored the myth
     and even tested it by "Christian morality."

63   STEIN, WILLIAM BYSSHE. "The Wake in Faulkner's Sanctuary,"
     MLN, LXXV (January), 28-29.
       The wake for Red in Sanctuary travesties Christian rit-
     ual, parodies the crucifixion, and ends with the woman in
     red as Whore of Babylon urging that the gambling be re-
     sumed. Anti-Christ has converted the world to pandemonium.

64   STEWART, DAVID H. "Absalom Reconsidered," UTQ, XXX (October),
     31-44.
       As a corrective to criticism of Absalom, Absalom! one
     must see that Faulkner is trying to make the reader be-
     lieve that the South is not responsible for the attitudes
     and conditions which have made it what it is. The novel
     devolves from Rosa to Mr. Compson to Quentin and Shreve,
     and finally to Faulkner himself, who tries to manipulate
     the reader into accepting his own erroneous view of South-
     ern history. His symbolism is confused and arbitrary. He
     tries to persuade us that docile Negroes are better than
     violent, aggressive ones.

65   STONE, EDWARD. "Usher, Poquelin, and Miss Emily: The Prog-
     ress of Southern Gothic," GaR, XIV (Winter), 433-43.
       There are more similarities between "A Rose for Emily"
     and G. W. Cable's "Jean-ah Poquelin" than between it and
     Poe's "The Fall of the House of Usher" (See 1943.B2).
     Like Poe's, Faulkner's Gothicism is "not of the Rhine, but
     of the Soul."
     Reprinted, under a new title, 1969.B78.

66   SWIGGART, PETER. "The Snopes Trilogy," SR, LXVIII (Spring),
     319-25.
       The Town and The Mansion are not as vital nor as good
     fictionally as The Hamlet. Gavin Stevens is admired but
     still represents Faulkner's "denigration" of rationality
     and intellect in favor of primitive intelligence. The
     Jefferson and Yoknapatawpha of these two novels are too
     well documented socially and not imaginatively alive.
     Reprinted Modern American Fiction: Essays in Criticism,
     edited by Walton Litz. New York: Oxford University
     Press, 1963, pp. 194-200.

1960

67   THORP, WILLARD. "Mr. Faulkner in the Classroom," NYHTB (31
      January), pp. 1, 11.
         Faulkner in the University as published could be dis-
      tilled to fifty pages of useful information, but Faulkner
      occasionally comes to grips with real questions and gives
      real answers. The reviewer points out what no longer needs
      to be asked, what might get a good answer, and a list of
      questions Faulkner did not like.

68   _____. "Southern Renaissance: William Faulkner," American
      Writing in the Twentieth Century. Cambridge, Mass.:
      Harvard University Press, pp. 263-74.
         Faulkner's "theory of the South" is that it was blessed
      by God, cursed by slavery, and ruined by men. He is the
      "best and truest historian of his region" and its con-
      science, too. A survey of the novels illustrates.

69   TRITSCHLER, DONALD. "The Unity of Faulkner's Shaping Vision,"
      MFS, V (Winter), 337-43.
         The manipulation of symbol, myth, point of view, and Time
      allow Faulkner to shape the materials of his fiction into
      an overall unity. Sex and violence, as in Light in August,
      are not gratuitous or sensational, but thematically and
      structurally related to myth and ritual from the past,
      which depict similar human actions in symbolical terms.
      His formal devices are intimately related to considerations
      of theme.

70   VICKERY, OLGA W. "A Selective Bibliography," in Three Decades
      of Criticism (1960.Al), pp. 393-428.
         A list of Faulkner's main book-length works; of bibliog-
      raphies and checklists, interviews and other biographical
      essays; and of critical works on Faulkner, including books
      and articles, both general and, arranged alphabetically
      by subject, specific.

71   WATKINS, FLOYD C. "Delta Hunt," SWR, XLV (Summer), 266-72.
         The author participated in a deer hunt with men from Ox-
      ford, Miss., whom Faulkner had frequently accompanied.

72   _____. "William Faulkner, the Individual and the World,"
      GaR, XIV (Fall), 238-47.
         Faulkner's essays, public letters, interviews, and a few
      of his books form the text of a sermon on individualism.
      "Old Man," considered alone, illustrates the value of in-
      dividualism. Faulkner is Southern and Agrarian.

73   WATKINS, FLOYD C., and WILLIAM B. DILLINGHAM. "The Mind of
      Vardaman Bundren," PQ, XXXIX (April), 247-51.
         Identification of Vardaman in As I Lay Dying as an idiot
      or a moron, as well as interpretations which make him a
      pure symbol, ignore the evidence that he is simply a very
      confused young child suffering bereavement.

74   WATKINS, FLOYD C., and THOMAS DANIEL YOUNG. "Revisions of
      Style in Faulkner's The Hamlet," MFS, V (Winter), 327-36.
         Differences between the Snopes short stories of the 1930s
      and The Hamlet are used as evidence of Faulkner's revision
      from the folk tale, the humorous story and the local color
      fiction to a more complex, more ambitious form. The tone
      of the novel is uniformly more elevated, more formal and
      universal than that of the tales, though there were some
      losses, as well as gains, in the process of transformation.

75   WEST, RAY B., JR. "Faulkner's Light in August: A View of
      Tragedy," WSCL, I (Winter), 5-12.
         The tragedy of Joe Christmas is the tragedy of society--
      arrogance and isolation cause it. The parallels to the
      biblical scheme of death and resurrection, however, offer
      hope that evil can be overcome by good. Lena Grove is
      symbolic assurance that man can achieve regeneration
      through coming to know nature. Life is a struggle between
      the demands of our dreams--the heroic world of isolation--
      and the demands of Nature--the "real" world where we live.

76   WILLIAMS, AUBREY. "William Faulkner's 'Temple' of Innocence,"
      Rice Institute Pamphlets, LXVII (October), 51-67.
         After reviewing standard opinions of Sanctuary, the au-
      thor analyzes the function of children in a world of adult
      evil as a major theme. Temple's experience is the ultimate
      extension of the view that maturation is learning one's own
      involvement in evil. Popeye is not "modernism" but evil.
      The novel is set in a mournful world of hopeless darkness;
      there is no sanctuary.

77   YOUNG, JAMES DEAN. "Quentin's Maundy Thursday," TSE, X, 143-
      51.
         Literal and symbolic parallels between Quentin's last
      day and Maundy Thursday of Holy Week underscore Faulkner's
      use of the passion of Christ. The symbolic structure or-
      ganizes Quentin's monologue and ties it to the other sec-
      tions of the book. Jason represents the Father; Quentin
      the Son; and Benjy the Holy Ghost.

1961

1961 A   BOOKS

1   BECK, WARREN. Man in Motion: Faulkner's Trilogy. Madison,
     Wisconsin: University of Wisconsin Press.
         Faulkner's ethical concerns are behind the conception of
     all his work--most especially the Snopes trilogy, a study
     of "ubiquitous evil and its opposition." The trilogy, the
     "crown" of Faulkner's achievement, is analyzed by close
     reading to show how Faulkner achieves the "illumined sus-
     tained embodiment of an epically conceived legend, popu-
     lous, circumstanced...projected through all its intri-
     cate recapitulations and extensions."

2   CULLEN, JOHN B., in collaboration with FLOYD C. WATKINS. Old
     Times in the Faulkner Country. Chapel Hill, N. C.: Uni-
     versity of North Carolina Press.
         Cullen, a near contemporary of Faulkner in Oxford and
     environs, engages in reminiscences about Faulkner, the an-
     nual deer hunt and bear hunt he was associated with, and
     related matters. Professor Watkins explains that Cullen
     began reading some of Faulkner's work after he formed his
     recollections, and that one of his intentions is to "re-
     tell the folk tales used by Faulkner in his fiction."

3   HOFFMAN, FREDERICK J. William Faulkner. New York: Twayne.
         An introductory survey of Faulkner's major work, with
     less attention to the post-1936 fiction, which is judged
     lesser, this brief study takes issue with Malcolm Cowley's
     oversimplifications (1946.B2). Faulkner's province is the
     time-haunted realm of human psychology; except for Sanc-
     tuary, he rarely treats a pure present or past but instead
     the continual interaction between the two. In his later
     work he moves toward "good strong" heroes like Gavin Ste-
     vens and explicit moral pronouncements. He is a moralist.
     Revised edition, 1966.A4.

4   MERIWETHER, JAMES B. The Literary Career of William Faulkner:
     A Bibliographical Study. Princeton, N. J.: Princeton
     University Press.
         Based in part on the catalogue of the 1957 Princeton
     exhibit (1960.B47), this compilation includes, besides
     Faulkner's MSS, TSS, and first editions, lists of English
     editions, translations, writing for motion pictures, and a
     a short story sending schedule which Faulkner kept in the
     early 1930s.

5   MILLGATE, MICHAEL. William Faulkner. Edinburgh: Oliver
     and Boyd.
         A general treatment, Millgate's book contains essays on

(MILLGATE, MICHAEL)
Faulkner's background, development and achievement, chapters on the novels, and an overview of Faulkner and his critics. It is not to be confused with the later, more comprehensive The Achievement of William Faulkner (1966.A6).
Reprinted New York: Grove Press; New York: Capricorn Books, 1971.

1961 B SHORTER WRITINGS

1   ANON. "Flem Snopes is Dead," TLS (13 January), p. 21.
     The best parts of The Mansion are those in the folk tradition of Longstreet.

2   ADAMS, JAMES DONALD. "It is a Nightmare World, Wearing a Mask of Reality," The Idea of an American Novel, edited by Louis D. Rubin, Jr., and John Rees Moore. New York: Thomas Y. Crowell, pp. 352-54.
     Reprints 1944.B1.

3   ADAMS, RICHARD P. "Faulkner and the Myth of the South," MissQ, XIV (Summer), 131-37.
     Faulkner's concern with motion makes it inevitable that he have a strong interest in Time. His theme of endurance and his belief that man will prevail suggest that for him life is the "assimilation of the experience of the past" and duty is, "by action in the present, to create the future." Change, good or bad, is inevitable. Faulkner's myth of the South is not a simplistic or primitivistic one such as charted by O'Donnell (1939.B26) and Cowley (1946.B2); the South is merely the particular social environment which Faulkner uses to express the "way it feels to be alive."

4   AIKEN, CONRAD. "Inventiveness of the Richest Possible Sort," The Idea of an American Novel, edited by Louis D. Rubin, Jr., and John Rees Moore. New York: Thomas Y. Crowell, pp. 354-59.
     Reprints 1939.B3.

5   BACKMAN, MELVIN.A. "Faulkner's 'An Odor of Verbena': Dissent from the South," CE, XXII (February), 253-56.
     The Unvanquished is a collection of stories, the first six sections lacking depth and moral complexity. "An Odor of Verbena," the last episode, is a serious treatment of the Reconstruction South. Drusilla is a priestess of the Old South and its values. Resisting her demands for

1961

(BACKMAN, MELVIN A.)
revenge, which contain the promise of "incest," Bayard
achieves a moral rebirth. He denies the hysteria and violence and the old code of behavior associated with the ancient order. Included in 1966.A1.

6   _____. "The Wilderness and the Negro in Faulkner's 'The
Bear,'" PMLA, LXXVI (December), 595-600.
"Division" between treatment of race and treatment of
the wilderness, noted as a fault by some critics of "The
Bear," is resolved when one reads it in the full context
of Go Down, Moses, of which it is "heart" and "climax."
Ike is torn between the need for atonement and the desire
to escape, paralyzed, as in the hunt of the Bear, and unable to act. Truth confronts him in "Delta Autumn," while
a larger hopelessness is the theme of "Go Down, Moses."
Included in 1966.A1.

7   BALDANZA, FRANK. "Faulkner's '1699-1945: The Compsons,'"
Expl, XIX (May), Item 59.
All the land transactions recorded in Faulkner's appendix to the Portable Faulkner are handled by men named
Jason. The classical Jason sought the Golden Fleece to
regain his father's land. Allusion and intention explain
the presence of "brothers" both named Jason. See correction, 1962.B107.

8   BARKSDALE, RICHARD. "White Tragedy--Black Comedy: A Literary Approach to Southern Race Relations," Phylon, XXII
(Fall), 226-33.
Faulkner sees two tragic elements in the South: the
"tragic inevitability" of his white heroes, who have a
death wish, and the black man's ability to endure hardship.

9   BASS, EBEN. "Meaningful Images in The Sound and the Fury,"
MLN, LXXVI (December), 728-31.
Caddy's wedding slipper, fondled by Benjy but despised
·by Miss Quentin, stands for Caddy in the Compson house,
where her name is not spoken. The pear tree, Benjy's weed,
the mirror and the fire are among other objects in the
novel which recur and take on meaningful associations.

10   BAUMGARTEN, MURRAY. "The Language of Faulkner's 'The Bear,'"
WHR, XV (Spring), 180-82.
The words "scared" and "afraid" are differentiated and
used with significance, though opaque, in "The Bear."

11   BLONSKI, JAN. "Americans in Poland," KR, XXIII (Winter), 32–
      51.
          Faulkner and Hemingway are accepted in Poland as the two
      greatest American writers. Faulkner "fascinates the young
      most of all," who greet him with "frightened admiration."
      The Polish intellectual identifies with Faulkner because
      he also feels that he is emerging from the death of a cul-
      ture.

12   BOWDEN, EDWIN T. "William Faulkner: Light in August," The
      Dungeon of the Heart: Human Isolation and the American
      Novel. New York: Macmillan, pp. 124–38.
          Similar to Sherwood Anderson's grotesques, the characters
      in Faulkner's Light in August seek to break out of their
      isolation. They are larger than life, as if viewed under
      a microscope. Both Joe Christmas and Hightower end isola-
      tion and find peace at the close of the novel.

13   BREYER, BERNARD. "A Diagnosis of Violence in Recent Southern
      Fiction," MissQ, XIV (Spring), 59–67.
          Violence is a reflection of human nature, which, what-
      ever name it is called by, is divided, prone to guilt, anx-
      iety and fear and reactions to these emotions. Sanctuary's
      violence represents a nightmare revelation of human nature.
      It also dramatizes the contradictions and polarities of
      human experience: Popeye contrasts sharply and ironically
      with Benbow.

14   BUCKLEY, G. T. "Is Oxford the Original of Jefferson in Wil-
      liam Faulkner's Novels?" PMLA, LXXVI (September), 447–54.
          Oxford, Mississippi, is not the principal source for the
      geography of Faulkner's mythical town, Jefferson; there
      are good reasons for accepting Ripley, the Falkner family
      seat, and Holly Springs, depending on the novel one is
      reading. Faulkner drew on the history and geography of
      north Mississippi widely. See reply, 1962.B27.

15   BURROWS, ROBERT N. "Institutional Christianity as Reflected
      in the Works of William Faulkner," MissQ, XIV (Summer),
      138–47.
          A survey of the way Faulkner treats the church, its min-
      isters and laity, in his "saga" forces one to conclude
      that the church has not been a wholesome spiritual force
      in Yoknapatawpha County. Faulkner's view of the failure
      of religion has become, in fact, more incisive and con-
      demnatory in his later work.

16   CAMBON, GLAUCO. "Stile e percezione del numinoso in un rac-
         conto di Faulkner," SA, VII, 147-62.
         An investigation of the "noumenal element" in "The Old
         People." Translated 1965.B13.

17   CHAZE, ELLIOTT. "Visit to Two-Finger Typist," Life (14 July),
         pp. 11-12.
         A brief interview, with photographs, gotten under false
         pretenses in Charlottesville, Va., with a very reluctant
         Faulkner.

18   CIANCIO, RALPH A. "Faulkner's Existentialist Affinities,"
         CaSE, No. 6, 69-91.
         The existential views of Sartre, Camus and Heidegger are
         used to explore Faulkner's possible philosophical kinship.
         Faulkner's work is godless, absurd, without useful value
         symbols, and his characters are unwanted, searching for
         identity and faced by the "absurd terminus," Death. There
         are almost no heroes in his works who live "authentically."
         Instead, his characters seek to become "things" or erect
         barriers to consciousness of their plights. Faulkner is
         closest to Heidegger in that his aim is to allow Being, as
         Heidegger defines it, to reveal itself "through the con-
         sciousness of his characters."

19   COTTRELL, BEEKMAN W. "Faulkner's Cosmic Fable: The Extraor-
         dinary Family of Man," CaSE, No. 6, 17-28.
         Mankind's faith in itself and its ability "to unite and
         believe and act" is the subject of A Fable. Faulkner is
         at his best in long flashback sequences and epiphanic
         scenes. It is the kind of "Cosmic Novel" many literary
         artists write to state their whole belief and may be fruit-
         fully compared to Kazantzakis' The Greek Passion. Problems
         with the novel's difficulty generally vanish upon second
         and additional readings.

20   CROSS, BARBARA. "Apocalypse and Comedy in As I Lay Dying,"
         TSLL, III (Summer), 251-58.
         In a ritual fashion, As I Lay Dying moves from the expul-
         sion of the scapegoat to feast and bridal, but there is no
         redemption; the manifold symbolic actions of the book mis-
         carry, every triumph is a defeat. It would be terrible if
         it were not also humorous, a parody of myth.

21   DAY, DOUGLAS. "The War Stories of William Faulkner," GaR,
         XV (Winter), 385-94.
         Faulkner's five war stories--"Ad Astra," "All the Dead
         Pilots," "Crevasse," "Turnabout," and "Victory"--are

(DAY, DOUGLAS)
deeper, more satisfactory stories than critics have real-
ized. "Turnabout" is intentionally romantic, while the
earlier stories show the destructive effect of wartime
values. The author discusses the relationship of Elliott
White Springs' War Birds (1926).

22   EDEL, LEON. The Modern Psychological Novel, revised edition.
London: Hart-Davis.
Reprints 1955.B16. Revised and enlarged edition, with
new introduction, New York: Grosset & Dunlap, 1964.

23   ENGLAND, MARTHA WINBURN. "Quentin's Story: Chronology and
Explication," CE, XXII (January), 228-35.
The Sound and the Fury tells the story of Caddy and her
daughter in four modes: lyric, dramatic, satiric, and
epic. Quentin's section is explicated, including sources
for allusions there.

24   GAUNT, ROGER. "The Magic World Within the Mind," Debonair,
I (February), 57-64.
The article summarizes the careers of Joyce and Faulkner.

25   GERSTENBERGER, DONNA. "Meaning and Form in Intruder in the
Dust," CE, XXIII (December), 223-25.
Taking some issue with Edmund Wilson (1948.B28), the author argues for clear and meaningful design in Intruder in
the Dust. Its meaning moves far beyond simple mystery
story; freeing Lucas from jail still does not free him
from a polarized society which resents his perpetual challenge of established patterns.

26   GERSTENBERGER, DONNA, and GEORGE HENDRICK. The American
Novel 1789-1959: A Checklist of Twentieth-Century Criticism. Denver: Alan Swallow, pp. 71-89.
The section on Faulkner lists criticism alphabetically
by book title and closes with sections devoted to "general"
studies and to bibliography.

27   GOLD, JOSEPH. "Delusion and Redemption in Faulkner's A
Fable," MFS, VII (Summer), 145-56.
A "drab grey work," A Fable is nonetheless ambitious,
challenging the reader and critic. It contributes to a
general understanding of Faulkner. In "Tomorrow," the final section, the body of Corporal/Christ is bought with a
watch and becomes the unknown soldier, proving that man
can redeem himself from Time and a life without value.
The moral is that man may choose to act out his best nature

1961

(GOLD, JOSEPH)
   instead of perishing in self-torment. Humanistic, it still
   advocates Christian ethics.

28   GOLD, JOSEPH. "Faulkner's The Sound and the Fury," Expl, XIX
      (February), Item 29.
         Allegorically, the ending of The Sound and the Fury pre-
      sents a white innocent and a black on a life journey con-
      fronting the dead symbol of the Civil War, the monument;
      by trying to emulate "the quality," the white man's worst
      attributes, the Negro causes chaos to ensue. Quentin,
      clinging to the past, has left Jason, the modern spirit,
      in control.

29   GREENE, THEODORE M. "The Philosophy of Life Implicit in
      Faulkner's The Mansion," TSLL, II (Winter), 401-18.
         Using the Nobel Prize address as a starting point, the au-
      thor argues the presence of the verities in the third and
      last volume of the Snopes trilogy. Faulkner's novels blend
      empirical detail and moral vision. The Mansion is his most
      mature book in style, analysis of character, and philoso-
      phy. His belief is reserved for man alone: the righteous
      individual doing his best.

30   HAGOPIAN, JOHN V. "The Aydt and the Maze: Ten Years of
      Faulkner Studies in America," JA, VI, 134-51.
         Criticism of Faulkner since the Nobel Prize has illumi-
      nated his work, though left-wing critics like Irving Howe
      (1952.A1) are too obsessed with social matters to appreci-
      ate Faulkner's art. Some critics, like Campbell and Fos-
      ter (1951.A1) and Malin (1957.A2), overuse psychological
      terms. The reviewer deals chiefly with books.

31   HARDING, D. W. "Revenger's Tragedy," Spectator (27 January),
      pp. 110-11.
         Simple in structure and narrative style, The Mansion
      shows Faulkner living "into every incident," skimping
      nothing. It is compared to Light in August in style and
      matter.

32   HART, JOHN A. "That Not Impossible He: Faulkner's Third-
      Person Narrator," CaSE, No. 6, 29-42.
         In "The Bear" and Intruder in the Dust, Faulkner uses a
      third-person limited point of view narration that confines
      itself exclusively to the inner thoughts of the central
      intelligence. In "The Bear," the effect is to contrast
      the old with the young Ike McCaslin and to give both depth
      and immediacy to the presentation. In Intruder in the

(HART, JOHN A.)
Dust, the technique is similar. Gavin Stevens' speeches, by contrast to Chick Mallison's moral coming of age, reveal his prejudice, his ignorance, his human distance from Chick.

33   HAUGH, ROBERT F. "Faulkner's Corrupt Temple," ESA, IV (March), 7-16.
Between Sanctuary and Requiem for a Nun, Temple Drake moves "from the world of the glands to the world of the heart." In the early novel she has no moral nature; she is driven, helpless, acquiescent. Requiem for a Nun demonstrates on both narrative and dramatic levels how law arises by social contract and moral awareness develops through recognition of sin and personal responsibility.

34   HAYS, ANN L. "The World of The Hamlet," CaSE, No. 6, 3-16.
The Hamlet is a fictional demonstration of the effects of a complete absence of morality on a town and its people. In contrast to Flem's opportunism, Faulkner sets up V. K. Ratliff as an ethical adversary; the conflicts between these two forces, along with other episodes that run parallel, develop the single idea that unifies the novel.

35   HOAR, JERE R. "William Faulkner of Oxford, Mississippi," WrD, XLI (July), 15-16, 77-78, 80.
The writer briefly summarizes some of Faulkner's communications to the weekly newspaper of Oxford, Miss., with examples.

36   HOWELL, ELMO. "Faulkner's 'A Rose for Emily,'" Expl, XIX (January), Item 26.
There is no evidence of necrophilia in "A Rose for Emily." It is a moral tale, not a morbid one. See replies, 1962.B23, 1962.B35, and 1964.B32.

37   _____. "Faulkner's Sartoris and the Mississippi Country People," SFQ, XXV (June), 136-46.
The most memorable scenes of Sartoris are drawn from the lives of the back country people: drinking, hunting, folk remedies, and other lore. Faulkner had a high regard for his region and its plain people.

38   ISAACS, NEIL D. "Faulkner with a Vengeance: The Grass is Greener," SAQ, LX (Autumn), 427-33.
The influence of American writing on the modern French novel may be seen in Claude Simon's The Grass, which is compared to Faulkner's As I Lay Dying, though without examples.

1961

39   JACOBS, ROBERT D. "William Faulkner: The Passion and the
      Penance," South: Modern Southern Literature in its Cul-
      tural Setting, edited by Louis D. Rubin, Jr. and Robert D.
      Jacobs. Garden City, N. Y.: Doubleday, pp. 142-76.
         Faulkner's fiction is surveyed in a general overview.

40   JEWKES, W. T. "Counterpoint in Faulkner's The Wild Palms,"
      WSCL, II (Winter), 39-53.
         A chapter by chapter investigation of parallels, con-
      trasts, and thematic "counterpoint" between the major and
      minor plots of The Wild Palms. Faulkner develops comple-
      mentary "issues and emphases"--subject and countersubject--
      in a way that fits the musical analogy Faulkner often used
      to describe the structure of the novel. "Wild Palms" is
      the main story; judgments about "Old Man" alone are criti-
      cally impertinent and incomplete. Harry is capable of
      sacrifice; he emerges as a real man at the end.

41   KAZIN, ALFRED. "Big Chips Off the Old Block," Griffin (New
      York), May, pp. 2-7.
         A review of Collected Stories in the monthly advertising
      pamphlet of the Readers' Subscription book club.

42   LANGSTON, ALBERT DOUGLAS BEACH. "The Meaning of Lena Grove
      and Gail Hightower in Light in August," BUSE, V (Spring),
      46-63.
         As Joe Christmas is a suffering servant, so is Lena Diana
      of the Grove at Nemi and Hightower the Buddha or a Bodhi-
      sattva, all of them "avatars." The Lena-Byron story finds
      parallels in The Golden Bough and is also converted, like
      pagan myth, to Christian lore. Hightower receives enlight-
      enment and sets the wheel of law into motion. All charac-
      ters find self-knowledge, but do not create salvation for
      the world, and we are left with hope, Lena's baby, still
      traveling the earth.

43   LEE, JIM. "The Problem of Nancy in Faulkner's 'That Evening
      Sun,'" SCB, XXI (Winter), 49-50.
         If we assume that Jesus is in fact not coming back,
      Nancy's behavior in "That Evening Sun" reflects insanity
      produced by guilt. Her confrontation of Stovall, her at-
      tempted suicide, neither caused by Jesus, support the con-
      jecture. It is a story of guilt and retribution; the name
      Jesus is thereby appropriate.

44   LEVINE, PAUL. "Love and Money in the Snopes Trilogy," CE,
      XXIII (December), 196-203.
         The Hamlet is a mythic world in which the land is a

(LEVINE, PAUL)
chief symbol; it is exploited and man dispossesed of Eden.
The bank is the center of The Town, which depicts a real,
not mythic, world, where Flem destroys social morality.
The Mansion is a panorama of life between the wars, a
götterdämmerung of Yoknapatawpha. Linda, Mink, and Ratliff, isolated, heroic and philosophical in order, constitute the central images.

45   LONGLEY, JOHN L., JR.   "Faulkner's Byron Bunch," GaR, XV
(Summer), 197-208.
Byron is unfallen Adam; Lena the fallen Eve whom he fol-
lows out of his well-ordered and rigidly maintained garden.
It is a fortunate fall; he becomes Lena's companion and
protector. The concluding scene of Light in August is deliberate undercutting of an unrealistic, romantic hope for
Byron to win Lena's love easily, though it does not altogether deny the possibility that he will.

46   *MATERASSI, MARIO.   "Faulkner e la presentazione del personag-
gio," SA, VII, 163-93.
Materassi (1971.B60), p. 85.

47   MERIWETHER, JAMES B.   "Discussion Group I: Bibliographical
and Textual Studies of Twentieth-Century Writers," Ap-
proaches to the Study of Twentieth-Century Literature.
Proceedings of the Conference on the Study of Twentieth-
Century Literature, first session, East Lansing, Michigan:
Michigan State University, pp. 35-51.
Faulkner's texts are discussed, including information
about his reworking of The Mansion.

48   _____. "Faulkner and the South," The Dilemma of the
Southern Writer, edited by Richard K. Meeker. Farmville,
Va.: Longwood College, pp. 143-63.
A full treatment of Faulkner and the South is a project
for the future, but one can discuss Faulkner's fate as a
Southern literary artist, under fire from Marxist and
right-wing critics alike. The treatment of "Skirmish at
Sartoris," an episode of The Unvanquished, is used as an
example of critical mayhem on Faulkner's work.
Reprinted Southern Writers: Appraisals in Our Time, ed-
ited by R. C. Simonini, Jr. Charlottesville, Va.: University of Virginia Press, 1964, pp. 142-61.

49   _____. "Some Notes on the Text of Faulkner's Sanctuary,"
PBSA, LV (3rd Quarter), 192-206.
The article is concerned "with some corrections that

1961

(MERIWETHER, JAMES B.)
have been made in America in the published text of...
Sanctuary, with some apparent errors which are still un-
corrected in that text, and with some changes made in the
text by the novel's English publishers."

50   MILLGATE, MICHAEL. "Faulkner Criticism: An Annotated Bibliography," Venture, II (June), 128-34.
A selective critical bibliography of books devoted exclusively or in part to Faulkner, with lengthy appraisals;
written for Pakistani schools.

51   MILLS, RALPH J., JR. "Faulkner's Essential Vision: Notes on
A Fable," ChrSch, XLIV (Fall), 187-98.
Man lives in a present often not of his own making; when
it overwhelms him, he can attempt to escape into the past,
which only deepens his problems, or he can face life and
bear it. This is Faulkner's philosophy in Light in August,
The Sound and the Fury and A Fable, where an image of
Christ brings men to the necessity of choice. The horsethief episode of A Fable parallels the main plot and advocates perseverance and nobility.

52   MORRISON, SISTER KRISTIN. "Faulkner's Joe Christmas: Character Through Voice," TSLL, II (Winter), 419-43.
Following a discussion of voice in fiction and Faulkner's
practice, the article takes up Light in August specifically. Faulkner is closest to Joyce in method. Joe Christmas
is revealed through the often conflicting narrative voices
and styles of the book, and our final view is a combined
recital of all voices that "speak him."

53   MURPHY, FRANK. "New Southern Fiction: Urban or Agrarian,"
CarQ, XIII (Spring), 18-26.
Almost alone of the older twentieth-century Southern
writers, Faulkner has shown his awareness of the changed
order of Southern life. He wisely reminds us of how the
"New South" evolves out of the old, without dwelling on
the impact of industrial and urban influences.

54   O'BRIEN, FRANCES BLAZER. "Faulkner and Wright: Alias S. S.
Van Dine," MissQ, XIV (Spring), 101-07.
There are suggestive parallels between the works of Willard Huntington Wright (who wrote mysteries under the name
of S. S. Van Dine) and Faulkner. The author operates from
a claim that Faulkner was influenced by Wright's Creative
Will.

55   PATERSON, JOHN. "Hardy, Faulkner and the Prosaics of Trag-
        edy," CentR, V (Spring), 156-75.
            Because of changes in the novel, Faulkner's Absalom, Ab-
        salom! is a lesser tragedy than Hardy's Mayor of Caster-
        bridge, though it is a "more formidable" work of art.
        Reprinted 1971.A2.

56   PINEDA, RAFAEL. "Yoknapatawpha, el condado de William Faulk-
        ner," Farol (Caracas), XXII (May-June), 9-12.
            Faulkner's work and reputation are surveyed.

57   RIBEIRO, LEO GIBSON. "Brazil: Between Dogpatch and Yoknapa-
        tawpha," KR, XXIII (Summer), 394-407.
            Faulkner's influence on young Brazilian writers is
        briefly mentioned.

58   ROBERTS, JAMES L. "Snopeslore: The Hamlet, The Town, The
        Mansion," UKCR, XXVIII (October), 65-71.
            The Town and The Mansion do not measure up imaginatively
        or artistically to The Hamlet. We are not prepared for
        the diminution of character nor for the new sympathy to-
        ward some Snopeses. The symbolic value of Snopes has been
        diluted. Faulkner seems to have been overcome by the de-
        sire to moralize about man's potential greatness.

59   SHAW, JOE C. "Sociological Aspects of Faulkner's Writing,"
        MissQ, XIV (Summer), 148-52.
            Faulkner is capable of taking all points of view toward
        the South in his fiction, but he "would call all change a
        curse." There are four given conditions in Faulkner's
        work: upper-class rule; Negro and poor white subjugation;
        Southerners as the only able interpreters of the Negro;
        and the belief that a martyred South deserves special
        treatment.

60   SIDNEY, GEORGE. "An Addition to the Faulkner Canon: The
        Hollywood Writings," TCL, VI (January), 172-74.
            The checklist records Faulkner's film scripts, produced
        and unproduced.

61   _____. "William Faulkner and Hollywood," ColQ, IX (Spring),
        367-77.
            The author excerpts an account of Faulkner's screen-
        writing career from his more detailed dissertation, mostly
        anecdotal, with reference to the properties Faulkner worked
        on while in Hollywood (See 1961.B60). Despite the fact
        that he worked on films from 1932 to 1945, Faulkner was not
        a good screenwriter.

1961

62 SLABEY, ROBERT M. "Faulkner's 'Waste Land': Vision in Absa-
    lom, Absalom!," MissQ, XIV (Summer), 153-61.
        Sutpen and Quentin Compson, who will relive the life of
    the planter and his sons, are opposites. Sutpen is a ra-
    tional positivist who exploits people, reminiscent of Haw-
    thorne's Aylmer or Ethan Brand. His preoccupation with
    racial purity symbolizes man's attempt to escape the con-
    sequences of original sin. Quentin is the other side of
    divided man, feeling, incapable of action. Faulkner has
    come to an "ethical" position of affirmation that resembles
    Eliot's, although "Faulkner lacks Eliot's philosophical
    training."

63 SOWDER, WILLIAM J. "The Concept of Endurance in the Charac-
    ters of William Faulkner," HPCS, I (Spring), 15-30.
        Faulkner attaches the concept of endurance to many char-
    acters and makes it a value. Homogeneity is the basis of
    endurance. Faulkner's use of the term is traced, and pro-
    gressively Faulkner's faith in man is found to become more
    general.

64 STALLMAN, ROBERT WOOSTER. "A Cryptogram: As I Lay Dying,"
    The Houses That James Built and Other Literary Studies.
    East Lansing, Michigan: Michigan State University Press,
    pp. 200-214.
        Addie Bundren is the overall consciousness in As I Lay
    Dying, where Faulkner uses the reflectors of Henry James
    and the impressionistic backing and filling operation of
    Ford Madox Ford and Conrad to create a grotesque tragi-
    comedy. Time, the recurrence of events, is the subject.

65 STEIN, WILLIAM BYSSHE. "Faulkner's Devil," MLN, LXXVI (De-
    cember), 731-32.
        Abner Snopes in "Barn Burning" is the Devil in human
    form, according to Faulkner's imagery, which contains all
    the traditional descriptions and associations which make
    the characterization work. He is deformed, rootless, an
    arsonist. He is also appropriately modern: robot-like;
    he is a symbol of materialism.

66 STEWART, DAVID H. "The Purpose of Faulkner's Ike," Criti-
    cism, III (Fall), 333-42.
        Ike McCaslin in "The Bear" is presented sympathetically
    but with a number of reservations; it is possible that
    Faulkner's characterization is deliberately negative and
    critical, but Faulkner is to be judged harshly for failing
    to clearly decide the issue against Ike and the status quo.
    Reprinted 1964.A9.

67   STONESIFER, RICHARD J. "Faulkner's 'The Bear': A Note on
      Structure," CE, XXIII (December), 219-23.
          "The Bear," written for the Saturday Evening Post, should
      be criticized in its Big Woods version; each of the four
      sections is made of seven parts with elaborate parallels.
      The divisions are outlined and summarized.

68   SULTAN, STANLEY. "Call Me Ishmael: The Hagiography of Isaac
      McCaslin," TSLL, III (Spring), 50-66.
          Arguing the unity of Go Down, Moses, the critic discusses
      the function of each section. Faulkner goes from an "anti-
      romance of the Old South" in "Was" to the tragic results of
      old L. Q. C. McCaslin's heritage. The book is an "indict-
      ment of civilization" and a plea for a deliverer.

69   TURNER, ARLIN. "William Faulkner, Southern Novelist," MissQ,
      XIV (Summer), 117-30.
          One strength of Faulkner's work is its well-documented
      location in a real place (the novels outside Yoknapatawpha
      suffer for the lack of this). He is, however, an "untradi-
      tional traditionalist" vis-à-vis the South, for he portrays
      it in every conceivable mood, time, and mutation without
      laying down unwarranted praise or blame. His fiction is
      critical, skeptical of accepted "Southernisms," but his
      very independence of mind may be particularly Southern.
      He is sophisticated and well-read, as well as acquainted
      with the native American tradition of humor.

70   TYNAN, KENNETH. "Requiem for a Nun, by William Faulkner, at
      the Royal Court, London" and "Requiem for a Nun...at
      the Golden," Curtains. New York: Athenaeum, pp. 276-78,
      299-300.
          The first review is a satire done in the style of Our
      Town; it observes that Requiem for a Nun as a play is writ-
      ten backwards, is too melodramatic, and is sophomorically
      philosophical. The second finds the style enraging, the
      handling of Nancy the "basic flaw," the direction "limp."
      Faulkner does not seem to know that "suffer the little
      children" means allow.

71   WARREN, ROBERT PENN. "Within the traditional world there had
      been a notion of truth," The Idea of an American Novel,
      edited by Louis D. Rubin, Jr. and John Rees Moore. New
      York: Thomas Y. Crowell, pp. 359-63.
          Taken from "William Faulkner," 1958.B64.

72   WAY, BRIAN. "William Faulkner," CritQ, III (Spring), 42-53.
          Faulkner's canon is appreciatively surveyed, concentrat-
      ing on his large view of the human condition and his major

1961

(WAY, BRIAN)
themes: aristocratic ideal and its decadence; moral vision
and the horror and fascination of evil; and the fanatic as
hero. Faulkner's vision of the Negro has matured. The
Wild Palms is "probably" his finest work.

73   WEBER, ROBERT. "Aspekte der Faulkner-Kritik in Frankreich,"
      JA, VI, 152-67.
          Since 1952, Faulkner studies in France have been con-
      cerned with Bewusstseinsrealismus in Faulkner. After a
      review of specific critical articles, the author concludes
      that the French are involved in phenomenological criticism.

74   WOODRUFF, NEAL, JR. "'The Bear' and Faulkner's Moral Vision,"
      CaSE, No. 6, 43-68.
          Although "The Bear" marks a change in Faulkner's fic-
      tional manner, it does not mark a change in his philosoph-
      ical or religious outlook. From first to last, Faulkner
      has been consistently a humanistic writer, but in his post-
      1948 work he is merely more explicit about his values. The
      central issue, a study of character reveals, is exploita-
      tion of self or others.

75   WRIGHT, AUSTIN M. The American Short Story in the Twenties.
      Chicago: University of Chicago Press, pp. 42-43 and
      passim.
          Comparison with stories by other major writers of the
      1920s--Anderson, Porter, Fitzgerald and Hemingway--shows
      Faulkner's typicality in the creation of theme, character,
      and treatment. Chief among Faulkner's themes is alienation
      and the need and fear of love. These 13 is used, but the
      stories are not discussed in detail.

76   YORKS, SAMUEL A. "Faulkner's Women: The Peril of Mankind,"
      ArQ, XVII (Summer), 119-29.
          Faulkner's women are often destructive forces, but
      chiefly as they surmount and render ridiculous the male
      world of rhetoric and codified action. Woman is a source
      of value and a force to be fled. Lena Grove embodies these
      paradoxical qualities, and Light in August derives theme
      and form from Joe Christmas's confrontations with women.
      The writer notes "Faulkner's fear and distrust of women."

1962 A   BOOKS

1   CHRISTADLER, MARTIN. Natur und Geschichte im Werk von William
      Faulkner. (Supplement 8, JA.) Heidelberg: Carl Winter
      Universitäts-Verlag.

1962

(CHRISTADLER, MARTIN)
   Man's relationships to Nature and to history are touch-
stones of character and important themes in Faulkner's fiction. Primitive characters--the feeble-minded, women, Ne-
groes--and simple virtues like patience, compassion, and
endurance are set at a premium. History is the antithesis
of Nature, as Time is the enemy of life. A goal of many
Faulkner characters is to leave some ineffaceable mark that
will survive the ravages of Time. The two themes are discussed in detail. Faulkner sees art as the transcendent
occupation.

2   HOWE, IRVING. William Faulkner, rev. ed. New York: Vintage.
     See 1952.A1 and correction at 1972.B59.

3   NILON, CHARLES H. Faulkner and the Negro. Boulder, Colo.:
     University of Colorado Press.
        Lucas Beauchamp in Intruder in the Dust is the "defini-
     tive" portrait of the Negro in Faulkner's work; and the
     novel is an allegory of how the South can achieve racial
     justice and spiritual peace. Throughout his fiction,
     Faulkner depicts the Negro as superior victim of white
     misunderstanding or violence. He reiterates that "the
     South must assume moral responsibility toward the Negro."
     Reprinted New York: Citadel Press (1965.A3).

4   SEYPPEL, JOACHIM. William Faulkner. Berlin: Colloquium
     Verlag.
        A capsule survey of Faulkner's work.
     Reprinted, translated by the author, New York: Frederick
     Ungar, 1971.

5   SWIGGART, PETER. The Art of Faulkner's Novels. Austin,
     Texas: University of Texas Press.
        Faulkner's narrative technique is characterized by the
     use of stylized characters, symbolic imagery, and struc-
     tural and perceptual innovations. Though a realist,
     Faulkner uses his novel methods of narration and charac-
     terization to allegorize his moral and social views and to
     involve the reader in the process of exploring the psycho-
     logical conditions which "make human reality and truth
     possible." The Sound and the Fury, As I Lay Dying, Light
     in August, and Absalom, Absalom! receive detailed analysis
     from this perspective; other novels are examined less
     thoroughly. Later printings add a note on The Reivers.
     Puritanism, with its accompanying rigidity, is discovered
     in the actions and tragedies of Faulkner's major charac-
     ters. See review, 1964.B9.

1962

1962 B   SHORTER WRITINGS

1   ANON. "Une vie de livres," "Faulkner l'universel," FigLit
     (14 July), p. 8.
         A brief account of some of the major events in Faulkner's
     life.

2   ANON. "Faulkner's Legacy: 'Honor, Pity, Pride,'" Life
     (20 July), p. 4.
         An editorial on Faulkner at the time of his death.

3   ANON. "A Great-hearted Writer Belongs to the Ages," Life
     (20 July), pp. 36-36B.
         Photographs of Faulkner's funeral and burial.

4   ANON. "The Last of William Faulkner," TLS (21 September),
     p. 726.
         Faulkner had the "elementary gift of spinning a story"
     and a true instinct for comedy, both of which are put to
     good use in The Reivers. Part of the pleasure derived
     from Faulkner's work is our sense of the living world he
     created, a world found piece by piece in the novels--which
     the reviewer briefly surveys. The canon gives a rich con-
     text to his last book on the human comedy.

5   ANON. "Disparitions William Faulkner," Livres choisis, LXXXI
     [N. S. No. 19], 1-2.
         Faulkner's death occasions reflections upon the loss to
     literature and upon Faulkner's resistance to critical and
     intellectual approaches.

6   ADAMS, RICHARD P. "The Apprenticeship of William Faulkner,"
     TSE, XII, 113-56.
         Faulkner served his apprenticeship principally in wide
     reading which is discoverable in the allusions one finds
     everywhere in his writing. He was aware of modernist
     painting and poetry. Not only a poet, as a young man he
     produced a limited amount of astute criticism and thought
     of himself as something of a graphic artist. Not even the
     most miraculous genius could have duplicated Faulkner's
     literary achievement without "the hardest kind of study,
     thought, and labor."
     Reprinted 1973.A9.

7   ALLEN, GAY WILSON. "With Faulkner in Japan," ASch, XXXI (Au-
     tumn), 566-71.
         Allen, in Japan in 1955 on a cultural exchange program
     himself, recounts some of Faulkner's movements and utter-

1962

(ALLEN, GAY WILSON)

ances during his Japan trip. Faulkner's behavior and remarks lead the biographer of Whitman to surmise that perhaps Faulkner's literary creations were unconscious, that
"the intricate patterns and baroque style were the super-
abundance of imaginative vitality, not cultivated deliberately."

8   ATKINSON, BROOKS. "Faulkner's Style Part of Nature," Richmond
(Va.) Times-Dispatch (19 July), p. 51.
If all the Snopes saga is published, Faulkner's death
makes it necessary that it be published without fixing the
inconsistencies. The critic comments on the Snopes trilogy
and recalls a visit with Faulkner twenty years previously.

9   AURY, DOMINIQUE. "William Faulkner," NRF, N. S., X (August),
315-16.
Wherever Faulkner is laid to rest and whatever strange
American funerary rites have been conducted, his true rest-
ing place is in the cemetery of Jefferson, the town of his
imagination. Faulkner was no more gentle with his creation than the maker of Cain and Abel; he saw men and women
in all their complexity, pride, shame and courage; he saw
them revolting against the human condition.

10   BACKMAN, MELVIN. "Faulkner's The Wild Palms: Civilization
Against Nature," UKCR, XXIX (Spring), 199-204.
The counterpoint of The Wild Palms is thematic--"sick
modernity" versus "primitivism." The novel fails to create
an adequate vision of modern society, however, and instead
gives us a stereotype. Included in 1966.A1.

11   BALDWIN, JAMES. "As Much Truth as One Can Bear," NYTBR (14
January), pp. 1, 38.
As an admirer of Faulkner, Baldwin is upset by his state-
ments on race, the "soupy rhetoric" of the Nobel Prize
speech, and the obfuscation of Intruder in the Dust and
Requiem for a Nun.

12   BASSO, HAMILTON. "William Faulkner: Man and Writer," SatR
(28 July), 11-14.
Recounting his memories of the New Orleans literary bo-
hemia of the 1920s, the author derides any suggestions
that Faulkner was ever debilitated or unmannerly because
of drink. He gives his impressions of Faulkner's wide
reading and self-education, tells an account of some barn-
storming aviators of the period ("Gates' Flying Circus"),
and praises Faulkner for his vision of the South, which

1962

(BASSO, HAMILTON)
was the main subject of Faulkner's work. The hope was always there.

13   BATES, OPHELIA. "Faulkner: Assessment," Books and Bookmen
(September), pp. 16-17.
Faulkner's difficult style is a burden for Englishmen.
He has been an obvious influence on other Southern writers.
Following the article is an account of a brief "Interview"
by Nils Dahlgren (pp. 17-19) in which some of Faulkner's
remarks about himself, his writing, and Hollywood are re-
corded.

14   BEAUVOIR, SIMONE de. The Prime of Life, translated by Peter
Green. Cleveland, Ohio: World Publishing Co., pp. 149-51.
She and Sartre discovered Faulkner through As I Lay Dying and Sanctuary; they particularly admired the way Faulkner showed the realities beneath appearances.

15   BECK, WARREN. "Faulkner: A Preface and a Letter," YR, LII
(Autumn), 157-60.
Sanctuary, which Faulkner conceived to make money, was
deliberately redeemed by Faulkner's revisions; the preface
to the Modern Library text, vexatious and cynical in part,
affirms Faulkner's "fidelity to vocation." Beck quotes a
letter Faulkner wrote him in 1941, replying to the gift of
three articles on Faulkner's work, where Faulkner displays
his positive humanism and his artistic purposes long before the Nobel Prize speech.

16   _____. "Told with Gusto," VQR, XXXVIII (Autumn), 681-85.
The Reivers is a raucous moral tall tale about the difficult struggle between virtue (with its ally, meaningful
traditional value) and nonvirtue. It may be ranked with
Faulkner's best work.

17   BELL, H. H., JR. "A Footnote to Faulkner's 'The Bear,'" CE,
XXIV (December), 179-82.
The author discusses the genealogy and chronology of the
McCaslin story and comments upon the final scene of "The
Bear." Boon's role as killer of Old Ben leaves Ike "un-
sullied" to participate in the ritual of Sam Fathers' bur-
ial, to become the guardian of the wilderness, and to re-
pudiate his shameful inheritance.

18   BERLAND, ALWYN. "Light in August: The Calvinism of William
Faulkner," MFS, VIII (Summer), 159-70.
Joe Christmas's "blackness"--never certainly estab-

226

1962

(BERLAND, ALWYN)
lished--is "original sin" in the Calvinist sense. It is
significant because and only when he believes in it. It
is invariably associated with sex. Joe's self-torment
comes from his ultimate refusal to believe in anything but
his blackness, his refusal to accept the amelioration offered by women and love. Joe's maiming at the end brings
peace. The theme of sex is presented almost everywhere in
Faulkner's work as negative in value.

19 *BIANCHI, RUGGERO. "Faulkner e The Unvanquished," SA, VIII,
129-50.
On the occasion of Faulkner's death, the writer remarks
According to Materassi (1971.B60), p. 76, this is a
"thorough examination of the semantic function of syntax"
in the first six chapters of The Unvanquished.

20 BOUSSARD, LEON. "William Faulkner," RDM (1 August), pp. 424-
30.
On the occasion of Faulkner's death, the writer remarks
upon the paradoxes and enigmas of his life and art.

21 BRADFORD, MELVIN E. "Faulkner's 'Tall Men,'" SAQ, LXI (Winter), 29-39.
Faulkner's yeoman hill farmers represent a favorable economic and social condition. Owsley's Plain Folk of the
Old South (1949) provides background. The writer summarizes the role yeomen play in Faulkner's fiction, including Byron Bunch and the tall convict of "Old Man" in The
Wild Palms, adding that their qualities are found in aris-
tocrats like Buck and Buddy McCaslin. The yeoman plays
such a relatively small role in Faulkner's work because
Faulkner's view and preoccupation are essentially tragic.

22 BRENNAN, DAN. "Invasion of Faulkner's Sanctuary," Off Campus,
I (No. 3), 20-22, 45, 68.
Seen in an undated clipping at the University of Vir-
ginia; essentially the same as 1955.B7. See also 1949.B28.

23 BRIDE, SISTER MARY. "Faulkner's 'A Rose for Emily,'" Expl,
XX (May), Item 78.
Agreeing with Howell (1961.B36) that "A Rose for Emily"
does not have necrophilia as its subject, the writer interprets the story as an allegory of Faulkner's ambivalent,
paradoxical attitude toward the South, which he admires
for its indomitable spirit but hates for its "couching
with a corrupt materialism."

1962

24   BRIERRE, ANNIE. "Dernière rencontre avec Faulkner," <u>NL</u> (12
      July), p. 3.
          From a clipping at the University of Virginia; reprinted
      from 1955.B8; in 1968.A6.

25   BROCKI, SISTER MARY DAMASCENE. "Faulkner and Hemingway: Val-
      ues in a Modern World," <u>MTJ</u>, XI (Summer), 5-9, 15.
          The writer accepts the concept of the Sartoris/Snopes
      dichotomy and regards Ike McCaslin as Faulkner's spokesman
      in a note comparing Faulkner and Hemingway as critics of
      the modern world. "The Bear" is an attempt to show man's
      reorientation to the world; like Hemingway in <u>The Old Man</u>
      <u>and the Sea</u>, Faulkner depicts life as a struggle.

26   BROOKS, CLEANTH. "Faulkner's Vision of Good and Evil," <u>MassR</u>,
      III (Summer), 692-712.
          Attempting a slight corrective to Randall Stewart's view
      (1958.B55), the essayist does not see Faulkner himself as
      necessarily Christian, though "profoundly religious" in
      his fiction, where his characters reflect a Christian en-
      vironment and Christian concerns, including original sin,
      the conflict between spirit and flesh, the need for sacri-
      fice, for suffering, and for redemption. Faulkner's con-
      cept of man is not romantic; it corresponds to T. E.
      Hulme's exposition of the classical attitude. Faulkner
      believed in discipline, not natural goodness, as a com-
      parison of characters in his work shows. Evil, for Faulk-
      ner, "involves the violation of the natural and the denial
      of the human." It can be resisted, and it must be, a les-
      son man learns through suffering.
      Reprinted <u>The Hidden God</u> (1963.B14), and also 1972.B14,
      with commentary.

27   _____. "Southern Literature: The Well-Springs of Its Vi-
      tality," <u>GaR</u>, XVI (Fall), 238-53.
          Family, community, the concrete experience of life and
      other qualities set Southern life and literature apart.
      Faulkner's "An Odor of Verbena" dramatizes the "hard
      choices" of the Southern experience. <u>Light in August</u> and
      <u>Absalom, Absalom!</u>, among other works, show the importance
      of community.
      Reprinted in <u>A Shaping Joy</u> (1971.B12).

28   BROWN, CALVIN S. "Faulkner's Geography and Topography," <u>PMLA</u>,
      LXXVII (December), 652-59.
          Replying to Buckley (1961.B14) as a man who grew up in
      Oxford, Miss., the author offers numerous parallels between
      Oxford and Lafayette County and Faulkner's fictional geog-
      raphy and history. Includes maps.

29   BROWN, DEMING. <u>Soviet Attitudes Toward American Writing</u>.
         Princeton, N. J.: Princeton University Press, pp. 180-83.
         Serious treatment of Faulkner in the Soviet Union did
      not begin until mid-1950s. Previously if he was mentioned
      at all, he was denounced as a decadent reactionary. His
      "anti-militarism" in <u>Soldiers' Pay</u>, "Victory," and <u>A Fable</u>
      first attracted attention. He continued to be misunder-
      stood, however, by "Soviet literary political science"
      throughout the 1960s.

30   BROWN, RUTH. "The Falkners of Mississippi," <u>SatR</u> (28 July),
         p. 17.
         A brief summary of Faulkner's family background and life
      accompanies obituary material.

31   BUTOR, MICHEL. "Son pays a mis longtemps à le comprendre,"
         "Faulkner l'universel," <u>FigLit</u> (14 July), p. 8.
         Faulkner's great contribution was to realize that the
      European tradition of the novel was not sufficient to ren-
      der American realities. Then his South became one of the
      universal regions of the human spirit.

32   CARTER, HODDING. "William Faulkner: The Man, the Writer,
         the Legend," <u>NYHTB</u> (15 July), pp. 4-5.
         Listing the stereotypical views of Faulkner in his home
      state, Carter, the Greenville newspaperman, corrects the
      opinion that Faulkner was a non-Southern renegade. He was
      Southern "by every standard," including his sense of "love
      and outrage."

33   *CLAXTON, SIMON. An interview with Faulkner, <u>The Cate Review</u>
         (June). Reprinted <u>Lion in the Garden</u> (1968.A6), pp. 270-
         81.
         An English schoolboy, then at Cate School in California,
      walks in on Faulkner and questions him about New Orleans,
      his current work, writing in general, and other topics.

34   CLEMENTS, ARTHUR L. "Faulkner's 'A Rose for Emily,'" <u>Expl</u>,
         XX (May), Item 78.
         Replying to Howell (1961.B36), the writer argues that
      Faulkner prepares us to believe that Emily did lie with
      the body of her lover, long after he was dead, by refer-
      ence to the graying of her hair in the period after the
      "smell" episode.

35   COLLINS, CARVEL. "Faulkner at the University of Mississip-
         pi," <u>William Faulkner: Early Prose and Poetry</u>. Boston:
         Little, Brown, pp. 3-33.
         A detailed undocumented account of Faulkner's literary

1962

(COLLINS, CARVEL)
activities at the University of Mississippi from 1916 to
1925 written as preface to a collection of juvenilia from
the period. See also Faulkner's University Pieces (Tokyo:
Kenkyusha, 1962), which does not contain one of Faulkner's
poems from the university period and omits the Appendix
that contains two essays and two poems published in the
New Orleans Double Dealer.

36   CORKE, HILARY. "Faulkner Across the Water," NRep (16 July),
      pp. 20-21.
          Lucius Priest in The Reivers hangs between two worlds
      during his adventures with Boon and Ned. "Nemesis is the
      fourth passenger." Without mentioning Leslie Fiedler, the
      author writes of the nonsexual "homosexuality" of the
      novel.

37   CURLEY, THOMAS F. "Faulkner Smiles," Commonweal, LXXVI
      (22 June), 331-32.
          The Reivers is mellow; its "language is supple, plain,
      vigorous." Whatever the critics may say, the reader will
      enjoy it.

38   CYPHER, JAMES R. "The Tangled Sexuality of Temple Drake,"
      AI, XIX (Fall), 243-52.
          Temple can be explained as motivated by an Electra com-
      plex. Her surname--male duck--indicates her confusion
      about the sex role; and her behavior, which is dreamlike,
      can be understood in Freudian terms as a wish to return to
      the womb. The ending is wish-fulfillment. She is united
      in a close relationship with her father.

39   DIRKSEN, SHERLAND N. "William Faulkner's Snopes Family: The
      Hamlet, The Town, and The Mansion," ESRS, XI (December),
      5-45.
          The rise of Snopesism is the destruction of the old or-
      der, an "allegory of power" which destroys society from
      within. Flem's success comes easily against people who
      are tempted to adopt his rapacious morality.

40   DORSCH, ROBERT L. "An Interpretation of the Central Themes
      in the Work of William Faulkner," ESRS, XI (September), 5-
      42.
          The philosophy of the 1950 Nobel Prize speech is con-
      sistently in all of Faulkner's work. Representative fic-
      tion from before and after 1949 is used to argue that
      Faulkner's central themes are belief and understanding of
      the old universal truths and demonstration of man's spirit
      of compassion.

41   DROIT, MICHEL. "Écartons l'homme pour apprécier l'écrivain,"
      "Faulkner l'universel," FigLit (14 July), p. 8.
         During a conversation in New Orleans in 1952, Faulkner
      insisted that he was a farmer, that his literary agent
      came down to harvest his fictional crop now and then. He
      affected not to recall the name of the Swedish prize which
      he had won.

42   EBY, CECIL D., JR. "Ichabod Crane in Yoknapatawpha," GaR,
      XVI (Winter), 465-69.
         The Hamlet is a reworking of Irving's "Legend of Sleepy
      Hollow." Labove, Eula, and McCarron are patterned after
      Ichabod, Katrina, and Brom von Blunt.

43   EDEL, LEON. "How to Read The Sound and the Fury," Varieties
      of Literary Experience: Eighteen Essays in World Litera-
      ture, edited by Stanley Burnshaw. New York: New York
      University Press, pp. 241-57.
         The Compson Appendix only compounds the difficulty of
      reading The Sound and the Fury. We must approach Benjy's
      section on its own terms and not try to rearrange it.
      Faulkner confronts us with a world which reveals itself in
      its own way through "intensities of feeling." The novel
      symbolizes the "tortured inner life" of the South.
      Reprinted as part of 1964.B21.

44   FASEL, IDA. "Spatial Form and Spatial Time," WHR, XVI (Sum-
      mer), 223-34.
         Modern literary art has ceased being Lessing's "sound in
      time"--historical event--and has adapted to itself the
      techniques of painting and musical structure to gain im-
      mediacy, to halt time. Bergson's conception of Time as
      "durée" has been a great influence. The four parts of The
      Sound and the Fury are like pure color tones used in Im-
      pressionist painting, and the parts are internally "frag-
      mentized" past and present juxtaposed. Faulkner's meta-
      physic is Bergsonian; his "endured" may be understood in
      terms of Bergson's "durée."

45   *FIEDLER, LESLIE. "Le Viol des Temple, De Richardson à Faulk-
      ner," Preuves, No. 138, 75-81.
         Translation of 1957.B18.

46   *FONTAINE, JOHN E. "Never the Ordinary Genius," Jackson
      (Miss.) Clarion-Ledger, Jackson Daily News (15 July).
         Reprinted Webb and Green (1965.A5), pp. 30-37. A writer
      who had known Faulkner at the University of Mississippi
      remembers him in an obituary essay.

1962

47   FORD, ARTHUR L. "Dust and Dreams: A Study of Faulkner's
      'Dry September,'" CE, XXIV (December), 219-20.
         Dust imagery characterizes "Dry September," a tale of
      September dreams and lynching. Dust and dreams are symp-
      toms of the hysteria that causes the lynching and they are
      the illusions behind which the real causes are masked.

48   FREEDMAN, WILLIAM A. "The Technique of Isolation in The Sound
      and the Fury," MissQ, XV (Winter), 21-26.
         A number of images in The Sound and the Fury heighten
      the effect of isolation: fences, gates, walls, doors--a
      device begun in the novel's first sentence. Benjy is cut
      off from communication. Quentin is intellectually im-
      prisoned. Jason, a hoarder, imprisons himself. Miss Quen-
      tin literally escapes. Dilsey "absorbs walls; only thus
      can we endure." The discussion relies heavily on the Comp-
      son Appendix.

49   FROHOCK, W. M. "Faulkner and the 'Roman Nouveau': An In-
      terim Report," BuR, X (March), 186-93.
         Faulkner has affected the content and form of such French
      New Novel writers as Claude Simon, Michel Butor, Alain
      Robbe-Grillet, Nathalie Sarraute.

50   GIBBONS, KATHRYN G. "Quentin's Shadow," L&P, XII (Winter),
      16-24.
         Shadow is the key word in Quentin's section of The Sound
      and the Fury, where it is used with psychological signifi-
      cance. The imagery is in accord with Jungian psychology
      and it indicates that Faulkner made Quentin an unsympa-
      thetic character. Jungian terminology is used to interpret
      Quentin's relationship to his memories of his own family,
      and Jung and James G. Frazer are used to discuss the water,
      mirror and shadow images in the novel. Quentin never ma-
      tures, never integrates his personality; he "desires death
      and rejects life."

51   GILMAN, RICHARD. "Faulkner's Yes and No," Commonweal, LXXVI
      (10 August), 449-58.
         An obituary paean to Faulkner as America's greatest writ-
      er, the essay warns agains oversimplifications, efforts to
      sum up the work in a word, and the saga theory. Using a
      phrase from Lionel Trilling, the critis says Faulkner was
      able to present his society's "yes and no"--its contradic-
      tory affirmations and denials.

52   GOFORTH, DAVID. "William Faulkner Found Sanctuaries for Him-
      self" and "Filming Intruder in the Dust Exciting Time in

(GOFORTH, DAVID)
Oxford," Jackson (Miss.) Daily News (14 July), p. 15.
A reporter's obituary surveys discuss aspects of Faulkner's impact on Oxford, Miss. The same reporter had a 19
July piece on Jill Faulkner Summers in the Daily News (an
incomplete clipping is in the Massey Collection, University
of Virginia, but not catalogued in "Man Working" (1968.A4).

53   GOLD, JOSEPH. "The 'Normality' of Snopesism: Universal
Themes in Faulkner's The Hamlet," WSCL, III (Winter), 25-
34.
Flem Snopes is no out-and-out villain, but a reflection
of a corrupt, insensitive materialistic society from which
he has learned most of his tricks. His successes in The
Hamlet are due to the cupidity of his victims, not to their
innocence. He is a mirror of the other villagers.
Reprinted 1973.A9.

54   _____. "William Faulkner's 'One Compact Thing,'" TCL,
VIII (April), 3-9.
Faulkner always affirms human values and criticizes the
evils of extreme materialism. Soldiers' Pay, Mosquitoes,
Sartoris, and The Unvanquished are used to demonstrate how
Faulkner depicts those who have lost human values and those
who honor them. Man, not some cosmic meaninglessness, is
responsible for the ruined world of modern times. Snopesism is the result, not the cause, of the Sartoris's failure.

55   GREER, DOROTHY D. "Dilsey and Lucas: Faulkner's Use of the
Negro as a Gauge of Moral Character," ESRS, XI (September),
43-61.
Dilsey and Lucas Beauchamp represent Faulkner's concept
of endurance. They show the dignity of humankind. Dilsey
is unequivocally good. Lucas's story in Intruder in the
Dust indicts racism and mob violence and extols brotherly
love.

56   GRENIER, ROGER. "La ténébreuse malédiction faulknérienne,"
"Faulkner l'universel," FigLit (14 July), p. 8.
The writer, a novelist, prefers the "Wild Palms" section
of The Wild Palms and Pylon to the rest of Faulkner's work
and could not have written his novel "Les Monstres" without them.

57   GUERESCHI, EDWARD. "Ritual and Myth in William Faulkner's
Pylon," Thoth, III (Spring), 101-10.
Use of myth and ritual in Pylon extols Christian virtues

1962

(GUERESCHI, EDWARD)
of submission, sacrifice, and courage. The ritualized
lives and sacrifices of the aviators, interpreted by the
reporter, reveal the frequent disparity between traditional
values and the way they are debased by language.

58   HAGAN, JOHN. "Fact and Fancy in Absalom, Absalom!" CE, XXIV
(December), 215-18.
Charles Bon's Negro heritage is fact, not uncertainty,
in Absalom, Absalom! Quentin's knowledge has come from
his meeting with Henry Sutpen on the day he accompanies
Rosa to the Sutpen house.

59   HAHN, OTTO. "Le second Faulkner (À propos du Hameau et du
Domaine)," TM, No. 195 (August), 347-57.
Beginning with The Wild Palms, Faulkner changed his point
of view, became godlike toward his characters, set his work
in timeless, unhistorical contexts, in terms of myth, or in
terms of the gospels. He became political, preacherlike,
but because he could not free himself from the old South,
his art from here on is confused. Having nothing to say,
he wrote of characters who had nothing to say.

60   HAPPEL, NIKOLAUS. "William Faulkners 'A Rose for Emily,'"
NS, N. F. XII, 396-404.
Comic, tragic, macabre, and ironic, "A Rose for Emily"
plays upon the "smell" about which the town does not dare
address a "lady." In the conflict between the individual
and the community, she wins, ironically, a greater battle
than the community knows until the story's end. Like much
Faulkner work, the story is built on polarities, often
ironic.
Reprinted 1970.A1.

61   HEALD, WILLIAM F. "Morality in 'Spotted Horses,'" MissQ, XV
(Spring), 85-91.
Dante's moral vision in The Inferno--as interpreted by
Dorothy Sayers--is used to discuss Faulkner's moral vision
in the Hamlet version of "Spotted Horses." All the men
who let themselves be used by Flem are guilty, as guilty
as Snopes himself. The analogue in Dante is the assignment
of degrees of sin, due to lack of will, to different levels, although sin remains Sin, regardless of degree.
Faulkner is an uncompromising moralist.

62   HICKS, GRANVILLE. "Building Blocks of a Gentleman," SatR
(2 June), p. 27.
The Reivers is not a major novel, but it moves well.
The style is mannered but restrained.

63 HOWE, IRVING. "Time Out for Fun in Old Mississippi," NYTBR
    (3 June), pp. 1, 24-25.
        Faulkner's novels are acts of creative passion; he is a
    brilliant comedian. The Reivers evades some of the moral
    issues plaguing Faulkner, but it is a pleasant work.

64 _____. "Yoknapatawpha County Was a World That Was Complete
    in Itself," NYTBR, (22 July), pp. 7, 24.
        A summary view of Faulkner's career written at Faulkner's
    death.

65 HOWELL, ELMO. "Reverend Hightower and Southern Adversity,"
    CE, XXIV (December), 183-87.
        The adversities of Southern history are reflected in
    Rev. Hightower's vision of an ironic heroism; when he un-
    dergoes a kind of regeneration, he does not lose the ideal
    which had heretofore been his chief "reality," but he
    comes back into the world with the ideal intact, having
    survived and finding peace.

66 _____. "William Faulkner and the Concept of Honor," NwRev,
    V (Summer), 51-60.
        Faulkner's writing is a reaction to the drabness of mod-
    ern existence and the indifference to moral values like
    the concept of honor. The Unvanquished dramatizes honor
    by virtue of Faulkner's humanism, not by virtue of motiva-
    tion in the novel. Faulkner's chief device to show honor
    is the premium he puts on telling the truth, as in "Barn
    Burning" and "Old Man."

67 _____. "William Faulkner and the Plain People of Yoknapa-
    tawpha County," JMH, XXIV (April), 73-87.
        Faulkner's view of poor, plain people in Yoknapatawpha
    County is sympathetic, especially by contrast to others
    who write about the region.

68 _____. "William Faulkner and Tennessee," THQ, XXI
    (September), 251-62.
        Southern disloyalty during the Civil War was widespread.
    Faulkner seems to draw on knowledge of this in "Mountain
    Victory," but he deliberately sets the story in Tennessee,
    out of his own South, in order to preserve the ideal.

69 HUNTER, MARJORIE. "Faulkner Sensed Impending Crisis," NYT
    (7 October), p. 61.
        Passages from Faulkner's books and public statements
    show that he forecast a fight like that which took place
    in 1962 at the University of Mississippi over the admis-
    sion of James Meredith.

1962

70   HYMAN, STANLEY EDGAR.   "Taking a Flyer with Faulkner," NewL,
      XLV (9 July), 18-19.
          The Reivers is a bad piece of juvenile fiction, with tor-
      tured prose, a ridiculous sub plot ("The Magdalen's Redemp-
      tion").

71   IGOE, W. J.   "Faulkner's Swan Song," The Tablet, CCXVI (24
      November), 1135-36.
          The Reivers is the tale of a youth's initiation, better
      than Twain, by the lord and master of Yoknapatawpha.
      Faulkner was by no means the provincial he pretended to be.

72   INGE, M. THOMAS.   "William Faulkner and George Washington Har-
      ris: In the Tradition of Southwestern Humor," TSL, VII,
      47-59.
          Faulkner's admission that he had read George Washington
      Harris's Sut Lovingood stories is the basis of a discussion
      of similarities and alleged parallels between the two au-
      thors' work, especially pointed in The Hamlet and As I Lay
      Dying.

73   JACKSON, ESTHER MERLE.   "The American Negro and the Image of
      the Absurd," Phylon, XXIII (Winter), 359-71.
          Faulkner uses black characters as a "frieze, a continuous
      image of humanity in barest relief" which discourages iden-
      tification and leaves humanity exclusively to the whites.
      Joe Christmas is the "tragic mulatto" involved in an "ab-
      surd odyssey," an abstraction of modern man like Kafka's
      Joseph K.

74   JUSTUS, JAMES H.   "The Epic Design of Absalom, Absalom!"
      TSLL, IV (Summer), 157-76.
          Regarding Absalom, Absalom! as tragedylike leaves the
      Judith-Henry-Bon plot, to which so much attention is di-
      rected, out of proper consideration.   There is no single
      tragic protagonist.   The novel is better discussed as epic.
      Using E. M. W. Tillyard's guidelines, Justus attempts to
      show how this may be done.   Epic stature is provided by
      the narrative points of view, all of which make the story
      of Sutpen, the apotheosis of the self-made man, larger
      than life.   If they tend to obscure his admirable quali-
      ties, they still give a "bardic" framework and provide a
      "stately" style.

75   KANTERS, ROBERT.   "Son oeuvre est le negro spiritual de
      l'homme blanc," "Faulkner l'universel," FigLit (14 July),
      p. 8.
          There is an Old Testament quality to Faulkner's works
      and very little of hope in his view of man.

76 KAZIN, ALFRED. "The Stillness of Light in August" and "William Faulkner: More Snopeses," Contemporaries. Boston: Little Brown, pp. 130-49, 150-54.
Reprints 1957.B32, 1957.B33.

77 ____. "William Faulkner: The Short Stories," Contemporaries. Boston: Little Brown, pp. 154-58.
Faulkner writes stories to relax; he is not the typical perfectionist in short fiction, but he has some good stories: "Race at Morning," "That Evening Sun," "Beyond," and others. His talent, and his interest in character, is too large for the form.

78 KERR, ELIZABETH M. "As I Lay Dying as Ironic Quest," WSCL, III (Winter), 5-19.
Romance, especially the literature of the quest, provides parallels for As I Lay Dying. Using Northrop Frye's Anatomy of Criticism as a guide to romance, the author finds Faulkner's method to be ironic inversion. The "epiphany" occurs with Darl's "yeses," which signify acceptance of the insane world to which he is being transported, a mockery of the concept of life's meaningfulness.
Reprinted 1973.A9.

79 ____. "William Faulkner and the Southern Concept of Woman," MissQ, XV (Winter), 1-16.
Relying on popular sociology for generalizations about Southern womanhood, the author compares the derived "concept" to Faulkner's treatment of women. Faulkner disapproves of this ideal and "doubts the genuineness of women who seem to exemplify it." Faulkner has scorn and pity for hypocritical characters like Narcissa Benbow and Temple Drake; admiration for simple or natural or rebellious ones like Lena Grove, Eula Varner, or Caddy Compson. His positive ideal is the courageous unselfish character like Miss Jenny DuPre. He is not a misogynist.

80 LAMBERT, J. W. "Faulkner's World," London Sunday Times (8 July), Magazine Section, p. 25.
Faulkner created a world rich in terror and pity and "appalling comedy" that has not been equaled by any except the giants of the nineteenth century. His real life is relatively unimportant. "Time will overcome the common reader's bewilderment." The old world of the defeated South, for all the burdens, was preferable to a "soulless future."

1962

81   LAURAS, ANTOINE. "Paradoxal Faulkner," Études, CCCXV (Octo-
       ber-December), 87-93.
          An obituary survey of Faulkner's career.

82   LEIBOWITZ, HERBERT A. "The Snopes Dilemma and the South,"
       UKCR, XXVIII (Summer), 273-84.
          Theme, not structure, unifies the Snopes trilogy, and it
       represents, besides a work of art, an important cultural
       document. The conflict between the Dionysian and the Apol-
       lonian man, the raising of human acts to mythic stature,
       recourse to medieval analogies--all play a role in the mak-
       ing of the trilogy, especially The Hamlet and The Mansion.
       Linda's deafness isolates her from human folly and anguish
       so she can act.

83   LEITER, LOUIS. "Faulkner," CE, XXIV (October), 66.
          In the light of Faulkner's death, the writer recalls a
       conversation with Faulkner in the summer of 1957 at the
       University of Virginia. Faulkner talked about sailing in
       the Gulf in 1928 and 1929; about eating 'possum and 'coon;
       and about violence, which Faulkner is quoted as describing
       "characteristic of the poor" because it is the only means
       of expression for people unable to comprehend their psycho-
       logical conditions.

84   MARSHALL, LENORE. "The Power of Words," SatR (28 July),
       pp. 16-17.
          The writer stakes her claim to have discovered The Sound
       and the Fury for its publisher.

85   MERIWETHER, JAMES B. "Notes on the Textual History of The
       Sound and the Fury," PBSA, LVI (3rd Quarter), 285-316.
          The author recounts the publishing history of The Sound
       and the Fury, from the first editing and correction at Cape
       and Smith through subsequent editions, including the impor-
       tant French translation. Included as illustration is the
       reproduction of a page from a sample gathering showing the
       publisher's revisions of form in the Benjy section which
       Faulkner strongly rejected. Tables list errors in English
       and American editions, including the Modern Library text.
       Revised, reprinted 1970.A6.

86   _____., ed. "Sartoris and Snopes: An early Notice,"
       LCUT, VII (Summer), 36-39.
          Phil Stone's announcement of Mosquitoes, which includes
       reference to forthcoming Faulkner work, is reprinted from
       a carbon TS at the University of Texas; it was apparently
       written for the Oxford Eagle.

87   MILLGATE, MICHAEL. "William Faulkner," BAASBull, N. S. No. 5
       (December), 43-46.
           The British reaction to The Reivers has been overpraise,
       denoting the general discomfort British critics have felt
       with Faulkner's more important and more difficult work.
       Obituary notices demonstrated hostility toward Faulkner in
       a marked degree. Faulkner uses the Southern legend in his
       fiction, but he never treats it uncritically; his work
       does show, however, an "almost unconscious assumption of
       Negro inferiority."

88   MITCHELL, JULIAN. "Chronicler," Spectator (21 September),
           p. 409.
           "Greed and dignity in the face of a usually intolerable
       human condition are the moral poles of Faulkner's world."
       His work possesses an "enormous range of feeling," and it
       is obscure at times only because he tries to reconcile
       time and space on the written page. The Reivers is a fit-
       ting last work.

89   MOHRT, MICHEL. "Le voici couché sur ce sol qu'il a tant
           aimé," "Faulkner l'universal,' FigLit (14 July), p. 8.
           Faulkner and his characters are inseparable.

90   MOSES, W. R. "The Limits of Yoknapatawpha County," GaR, XVI
           (Fall), 297-305.
           Writing before The Reivers and Faulkner's death, Moses
       approaches The Mansion as Faulkner's "Golden Book" or
       "Doomsday Book." Surveying the "doom" met by the heroes
       of Faulkner's fiction, he compares the fate of Flem Snopes,
       whose murder is fateful. In death Flem becomes another of
       the poor sons of bitches and thus a member of the human
       race, the "limit" of the article's title.

91   O'CONNOR, WILLIAM VAN. "Faulkner's One-Sided 'Dialogue' with
           Hemingway," CE, XXIV (December), 208, 213-15.
           Faulkner and Hemingway were always aware of each other.
       Faulkner did not hit his stride as soon as Hemingway, but
       when he did he kept experimenting in a way that the other
       did not. The Wild Palms is Faulkner's "reply" to A Fare-
       well to Arms; it is not "loaded" and does not emphasize
       "defeat and dejection" the way Hemingway's novel does.

92   _____. "Hawthorne and Faulkner: Some Common Ground," The
       Grotesque, An American Genre, and Other Essays. Carbon-
       dale, Ill.: Southern Illinois University Press, pp. 59-77.
           Reprinted from 1957.B51

1962

93 PAULDING, GOUVERNEUR. "Running Away," Reporter (5 July),
    p. 38.
        Lucius Priest in The Reivers is brought out of childhood
    by discovering that those who possess courage and loyalty
    are more vulnerable than those who do not. Though it
    creates a dream world, the novel deserves to be accepted
    on its own terms for the magic in it.

94 PAVESE, CESARE. "William Faulkner: Un angelo senza cura
    d'anima," La Letteratura americana e altri saggi. Torino:
    Giulio Einaudi editore, pp. 167-70.
        According to Materassi (1971.B60), a reprinting, under
    new title, of 1934.B21; the book is another edition of
    1953.B33.

95 PEARSON, NORMAN HOLMES. "The American Writer and the Feeling
    for Community," ES, XLIII (October), 403-12.
        The longing for community is one of the chief character-
    istics of American writing. The Sound and the Fury, Ab-
    salom, Absalom!, and Light in August offer examples of the
    continuation of this tradition and are perfectly in accord
    with the work of a writer like Hawthorne.

96 PLIMPTON, GEORGE. "The Reivers, by William Faulkner," NYHTB
    (27 May), p. 3.
        The Reivers is a classic "boy's adventure story," almost
    parodic in its use of stock elements, but out of the genre
    by virtue of language, settings, and occasionally subject.

97 PRESCOTT, ORVILLE. Review of The Reivers, NYT (4 June), Late
    edition, p. 27.
        Eager for the Yoknapatawpha Saga to end, Prescott finds
    The Reivers good, surprised that the "longest sentence is
    only twenty-six lines." The humor is "gay, engaging and
    kindly." Faulkner demonstrates that he is "on the side of
    the angels."

98 PRITCHETT, V. S. "Autumn Books--That Time in the Wilderness,"
    NewSt (28 September), pp. 405-06.
        Faulkner is the only American novelist since James. He
    had a dense European strain from Balzac, Dostoevsky, and
    Joyce. The rootless modern writers compare unfavorably
    with him. The "primitive absurdity" that lay in the back-
    ground of his world attracted the existentialists. He was
    always a humanist. The dangers to Faulkner's art were not
    in his ethical bent but in his "mysticism," as reflected
    in A Fable.

99   RICHARDSON, H. EDWARD. "Faulkner, Anderson, and Their Tall
      Tale," AL, XXXIV (May), 287-91.
         The tall tale of the Jackson family in Mosquitoes is ba-
      sically by Anderson and posits hidden Anderson influence
      on Faulkner. See Rideout and Meriwether (1963.B69) for
      the facts which contradict this view.

100   ROSENBERG, JESSIE. "William Faulkner: The Wild Palms,"
      CORADDI (Woman's College of the University of North Caro-
      lina) (Fall), pp. 6-8.
         The stories of The Wild Palms complement each other.
      Harry is destroyed while the convict accepts oblivion.

101   ROSENFELD, ISAAC. "Faulkner's Two Styles," An Age of Enormi-
      ty: Life and Writing in the Forties and Fifties, edited
      by Theodore Solotaroff. New York: World, pp. 268-72.
         Reprints, under a new title, 1951.B55.

102   ROSSKY, WILLIAM. "As I Lay Dying: The Insane World," TSLL,
      IV (Spring), 87-95.
         The novel is a serio-comic vision of life's "terrible
      incongruities." The world is absurd, but the mode is
      richly comic. Like Quentin Compson and Horace Benbow,
      Darl, who has the clearest vision of the horror of exis-
      tence, fails to survive his perceptions. Faulkner will
      wait for Ratliff in The Hamlet to find a character who can
      face the world with "humor and dignity."

103   _____. "Faulkner: The Image of the Child in The Mansion,"
      MissQ, XV (Winter), 17-20.
         Our growing sympathy for Mink Snopes in The Mansion is
      due to his figurative identification with Faulkner's "child
      myth," a myth expressed in Faulkner's novels by the journey
      from innocence to knowledge of evil, the fall of adulthood.
      Child imagery applied to adult characters contributes to
      the reader's sense of the person's innocence: Mink is fre-
      quently surrounded by such imagery. Contrasted with his
      vengeance and "venom," it gives a "just picture" of the
      human condition.

104   RUBIN, LOUIS D., JR. "The South and the Faraway Country,"
      VQR, XXXVIII (Spring), 444-59.
         Most Southern writers, including Faulkner, have needed
      but also remained detached from the Southern community
      life, living in "another country," the realm of fiction.

105   SANDEEN, ERNEST E. Review of The Reivers, The Critic, XX
      (June-July), 62-63.
         Lucius Priest in The Reivers learns that he already has

1962

(SANDEEN, ERNEST E.)
the built-in qualities of the gentleman. It is a book
bathed in "one jolly, sentimental, nostalgic glow."

106   SCHOLES, ROBERT E.   "Myth and Manners in Sartoris," GaR, XVI
(Summer), 195-201.
Sartoris does not contrast sharply with "Snopes." It
represents an archaic code in a recognizable society under-
going radical change. Sartoris shows the conflict between
the romantic past and the sordid present presented as a
novel of manners.

107   SIMPSON, HASSELL A.   "Faulkner's The Sound and the Fury, Appendix," Expl, XXI (December), Item 27.
The author corrects Baldanza's statement about two brothers named Jason (1961.B7); they are father and son.   Also
corrects the erroneous listing of the generations in
O'Faolain's The Vanishing Hero (1956.B38).

108   *SLABEY, ROBERT M.   "Faulkner's Mosquitoes and Joyce's Ulysses," RLV, XXVIII, 435-37.
According to American Literary Scholarship 1963, p. 76,
the note argues that Joyce's work is demonstrably an influence on Faulkner's early writing.

109   SLEETH, IRENE.   "William Faulkner: A Bibliography of Criticism" TCL, VIII (April), 18-43.   Also: Denver: Alan Swallow.
A bibliography of criticism of Faulkner's work from the
1920s to early 1961 based chiefly on already published
bibliographies, and including selected foreign criticism.
Arranged as books and articles, alphabetically by author.

110   SOUTHERN, TERRY.   "Tom Sawyer in the Brothel," Nation (9
June), pp. 519-21.
The story of The Reivers is treated with a "child-like
heavy handedness."   But objections disappear when one
realizes that it is written as a sophisticated juvenile, a
young person's book, not for adults.

111   SOWDER, WILLIAM J.   "Colonel Thomas Sutpen as Existentialist
Hero," AL, XXXIII (January), 485-99.
Sutpen's failure in Absalom, Absalom! may be discussed
in existentialist terms as the result of free choice.
When Sutpen tries to determine where he made the wrong
choice, he errs in assigning the event to his first marriage to the woman with Negro blood.   Sowder argues that
the really determinate choice was Sutpen's decision to

1962

(SOWDER, WILLIAM J.)
become a gentleman planter. Using Sartre's terms, he discusses the events which led to that choice, Sutpen's "bad faith" and ultimate despair.

112   STEWART, RANDALL. "Poetically the Most Accurate Man Alive,"
       ModA, VI (Winter), 81-90.
       Accepting O'Donnell's categories (1939.B26) as valid outlines of Faulkner's allegory and Cowley's remarks about frontier humor and psychological horror in Faulkner as a proper perspective for viewing Faulkner's antecedents, Stewart suggests modifications, focusing on Longstreet and Poe and adding as a third influence the tidewater plantation fiction. Faulkner also has affinities with Hawthorne.

113   STONE, EDWARD. "William Faulkner's Two Little Confederates,"
       OhioUR, IV, 5-18.
       Comparison of the Saturday Evening Post stories later revised for The Unvanquished with Thomas Nelson Page's Two Little Confederates (1888) shows how far Faulkner "soared above" Page's work.

114   STYRON, WILLIAM. "As He Lay Dead, a Bitter Grief," Life (20
       July), 39-42.
       Faulkner "detested more than anything the invasion of his privacy." Styron records events surrounding Faulkner's funeral in Oxford.

115   TAILLEFER, ANNE. "As Faulkner Lies Dead," Catholic Worker,
       XXIX (September), 2, 8.
       Unlike most Americans, Faulkner knew the past, its meanings, and saw clearly the effects of injustice and rapacity in a supposedly Christian nation. His legacy is his revelation of human possibility, of the nobility of simple souls.

116   TALMEY, ALLENE, and HENRI CARTIER-BRESSON. "Faulkner at West
       Point," Vogue (July), pp. 70-73, 114, 116.
       A photographic and brief verbal record of Faulkner's 1962 visit to the U. S. Military Academy at West Point.
       See also 1964.A5.

117   TATE, ALLEN. "William Faulkner," NewSt (28 September), p.
       408.
       This "recollection and appreciation" of Faulkner begins with an anecdote about Faulkner's effrontery in signing his name like a member of the English nobility. Faulkner wrote "at least five masterpieces"--The Sound and the Fury,

1962

(TATE, ALLEN)
As I Lay Dying, Sanctuary, Light in August, and The Hamlet.
He will be recognized as one of the last great Impression-
ist novelists. A vast background and a rich imagination
were his assets.
Reprinted 1963.B84.

118   TAZEWELL, WILLIAM L. "Faulkner and the Negro Stereotype,"
Norfolk Virginian Pilot (4 July), p. 4.
    Speaking at Hampton Institute "last spring," novelist
Ralph Ellison acknowledged Faulkner's humanity and artistry. "Without distorting the human reality he has done
more to explore the Negro's humanity than any other writer
in the United States."

119   THOMPSON, RAY M. "Mississippi's William Faulkner," Down
South on the Beautiful Gulf Coast, XII (September-October),
7, 16, 26.
    A summary of Faulkner's career in a tourist-oriented
magazine.

120   TICK, STANLEY. "The Unity of Go Down, Moses," TCL, VIII
(July), 67-73.
    Theme, development, and other factors indicate that Go
Down, Moses is a novel blended of six closely interdepen-
dent units (though "Pantaloon in Black" remains, for the
author, an anomaly). Old L. Q. C. McCaslin's sin comes
full circle to the "present" in "Delta Autumn." "Go Down,
Moses," the final story, provides the final context; Gavin
Stevens is positive, a "new" Southerner who directs the
townsfolk in doing the right thing.
Reprinted 1973.A9.

121   VICKERY, JOHN B. "Ritual and Theme in Faulkner's Dry September," ArQ, XVIII (Spring), 5-14.
    The scapegoat ritual is dramatized in this ironic story
of lynching and its aftermath. There are parallels to
Frazer and Jane Harrison which help identify the roles of
the main characters. The ritual is performed to end the
"dry September," but it is not efficacious.

122   WEATHERBY, W. J. "The Not-So-Mythical Town of Jefferson,
Miss.," Manchester Guardian Weekly (18 October), p. 13.
    An obituary survey of Faulkner's work and a look at his
country.

123   WELTY, EUDORA. "He Created Life in Fictional County," Washington Post (7 July).
    An obituary tribute by one Mississippi novelist for an-

1963

(WELTY, EUDORA)
other, distributed by the Associated Press from Jackson; seen in a clipping in the Massey Collection, University of Virginia.

124 WERTENBAKER, THOMAS J., JR. "Faulkner's Point of View and the Chronicle of Ike McCaslin," CE, XXIV (December), 169-78.
       The author argues that "The Bear" must be read in all five sections and in conjunction with "Was," "The Old People," and "Delta Autumn." Part four of "The Bear" is the crucial kernel to which the surrounding tale of initiation is but a prelude. A chronology and genealogy of the McCaslins and a schematization of the narrative sequence of part four of "The Bear" is included.

125 WHITBREAD, THOMAS. "The Snopes Trilogy: The Setting of The Mansion," Six Contemporary Novels: Six Introductory Essays, edited by William O. S. Sutherland, Jr. Austin, Texas: University of Texas Department of English, pp. 76-88.
       A summary of the Snopes trilogy, with long quotations, this essay concludes that The Mansion is not up to the standard of the other two volumes, but is still good.

126 WILSON, COLIN. "William Faulkner," The Strength to Dream: Literature and the Imagination. Boston: Houghton Mifflin, pp. 36-40.
       Faulkner's imagination seems to seek escape from a reality he prefers not to view. For him the present is full of horrors, sadism.

127 YODER, EDWIN M. "Faulkner: Brooding History, Single Combat in Camelot," Greensboro (N. C.) Daily News (5 August), Section C, p. 3.
       The conflict between compassion and its absence lies at the heart of Faulkner's novels. He saw the South in delicately refined shadings of good and evil. Time--the brooding presence of the past--is his essential medium.

1963 A BOOKS

1   BROOKS, CLEANTH. William Faulkner: The Yoknapatawpha Country. New Haven, Conn.: Yale University Press.
       Faulkner's Yoknapatawpha novels (excluding, thus, Soldiers' Pay, Mosquitoes, Pylon, The Wild Palms, and A Fable) receive close readings from the point of view that Faulkner's fiction is informed by provinciality, a sense of

1963

(BROOKS, CLEANTH)
real community values, knowledge of the strata of Southern
society, and a Puritan sense of man's fall from nature.
The novels are taken up in thematic rather than chronological order. Extensive notes provide genealogies, background information, and discussion of secondary points.
There is an abbreviated character index; a general index;
and a reprinting of the map from Absalom, Absalom!

2 FAULKNER, JOHN. My Brother Bill. New York: Trident Press.
An autobiographical reminiscence of the Falkner family
and the novelist by his youngest surviving brother pictures
the hectic normality of a house full of boys growing up in
a small Southern town.
Reprinted New York: Pocket Books, 1964.

3 FORD, MARGARET, and SUZANNE KINCAID. Who's Who in Faulkner.
Baton Rouge, La.: Louisiana State University Press.
An index to Faulkner's characters. See also 1963.A5.

4 GIANNITRAPANI, ANGELA. Wistaria: Studi Faulkneriani.
Napoli: Istituto Universitario Orientale, Casa Editrice
Cymba.
The first book-length study of Faulkner's fiction in
Italy contains three previously printed essays: one on
Faulkner's early work, his relationship to Sherwood Anderson, his "New Orleans novels," and the stories and novels
where New Orleans is the typical "Babylon"--including Absalom, Absalom! and Go Down, Moses; one primarily on Absalom, Absalom!; one primarily on Requiem for a Nun. Also
reprinted is an account, from reviews, of Faulkner's critics. 'Wistaria' is the predominant color in Faulkner's
palette; it represents objective reality.
Reprints 1959.B27, 1960.B32, and "La New Orleans e la
Louisiana de Faulkner," Annali dell' Istituto Universitario
Orientale di Napoli, 1959. Summarized in Materassi,
(1971.B60), p. 74.

5 KIRK, ROBERT W., and MARVIN KLOTZ. Faulkner's People: A
Complete Guide and Index to the Characters in the Fiction
of William Faulkner. Berkeley: University of California
Press.
Some 1200 characters in Faulkner's long and short fiction are indexed and identified. Novels are arranged in
order of publication; short stories and sketches (including Go Down, Moses) are listed in order of their book publication. Appendices give a list of characters presented
inconsistently and genealogies of Sartoris, Burden, and

1963

(KIRK, ROBERT W., and MARVIN KLOTZ)
McCaslin families. The work is based on dissertations by
the two authors supplemented by a 1955 MA thesis by Mrs.
Mason Altiery (Hawaii).

6 LONGLEY, JOHN L. The Tragic Mask: A Study of Faulkner's
Heroes. Chapel Hill, N. C.: University of North Carolina
Press.
Faulkner's "comic" heroes--the tall convict, Chick Mal-
lison of Intruder in the Dust, Gavin Stevens and V. K.
Ratliff of the Snopes trilogy, Byron Bunch and Ike McCas-
lin--are, in general, idealists of varying degree who pay
a price in anguish and even in defeat for their beliefs.
Faulkner's "villains" are Popeye, Jason Compson, and Flem
Snopes, from whom his tragic heroes, like John Sartoris,
Joe Christmas, and Thomas Sutpen, must be differentiated.
Elements of the tragic appear in all Faulkner's work and
characters, even among his villains. Loss, isolation, human limitation, the pressure of circumstances, pride, and
other factors shape portions of the lives of all his characters, with tragic implications. The meaning is found in
Faulkner's overall legend of the South--a tragic view of
life of which his best characters are symbolic. Time and
impermanence are man's perpetual antagonists; only the artist can defeat them. Includes 1957.B38 and 1961.B45.

7 NATHAN, MONIQUE. Faulkner par lui-même. Collections micro-
cosme. Écrivains de toujours 65. Paris: Éditions de
Seuil.
Extracts from Faulkner's interviews, public statements,
etc., are arranged as a discussion of his career and work.

8 RAIMBAULT, RENÉ-NOËL. Faulkner. Paris: Éditions Universi-
taires.
An account in French of the laconic and mysterious little farmer--part genius and part whiskey--who has become
one of the world's most important writers, the book begins
with Faulkner's spiritual and literal biography and then
briefly discusses the novels, "Les années de silence," the
Nobel award, and Faulkner's death. Faulkner's interviews
and fiction are used to depict him.

9 THOMPSON, LAWRANCE. William Faulkner: An Introduction and
Interpretation. New York: Barnes and Noble.
Faulkner's peculiar achievement has been extravagantly
praised and unwarrantedly blamed. The Yoknapatawpha chron-
icle, in which Faulkner is at his best, universalizes the
South. Faulkner uses the "mythical method" of Joyce and

1963

(THOMPSON, LAWRANCE)
Eliot, a musical-like counterpoint, aspects of modern psychology, as well as more conventional symbolism to create
meaningful analogies to situations and characters in his
work. Faulkner's moral vision includes both fate and free
will and adopts the passion of Christ to dramatize the redeeming power of love.

1963 B   SHORTER WRITINGS

1   ANON. "'The Bear' and Huckleberry Finn: Heroic Quest for
    Moral Liberation," MTJ, XII (Spring), 12-13, 21.
       Novels of education, "The Bear" and Huckleberry Finn are
    compared for the ways they "mirror the formula of the ini-
    tiation rite." Both end affirmatively.

2   ANDERSON, CHARLES ROBERTS. "The Universal Truths of the Latin
    Humanists Form the Moral Center of His Fiction: William
    Faulkner," Johns Hopkins Magazine, XIV (February), 17-18,
    24-27.
       Faulkner was not a humanitarian but a humanist in the
    classical sense, "concerned with those classical principles
    of conduct formulated by the Latin moralists of the late
    Republic and early Empire of Rome: virtus, gloria, pietas,
    and integritas. See 1954.B1.

3   ATKINSON, JUSTIN BROOKS. "Faulkner and Comedy," Tuesdays and
    Fridays. New York: Random House, pp. 244-46.
       Faulkner's characters in The Reivers "inadvertently rep-
    resent the philosophy of comedy."
    Reprinted from NYT (5 June 1962).

4   BERINGAUSE, A. F. "Faulkner's Yoknapatawpha Register," BuR,
    XI (May), 71-82.
       The Bible, name-lore, Jung's psychological theories, and
    other sources are used to discuss the significance of some
    of the names in Faulkner's fiction. Sartoris, for example,
    is a "partial anagram" for aristocrat.

5   BJÖRK, LENNART. "Ancient Myths and the Moral Framework of
    Faulkner's Absalom, Absalom!" AL, XXXV (May), 196-204.
       Faulkner fuses Hebrew, Greek, and Christian myth in Ab-
    salom, Absalom! The stories of Agamemnon and King David
    are appropriate parallels to Sutpen's fall; Faulkner im-
    plies the need for the Christian's "grace, charity, love,
    and pity." The fusion provides a broad moral framework
    from which Sutpen can be viewed.

6   BLOTNER, JOSEPH. "William Faulkner's Name Was in the Books
     He Loved Best," NYTBR (8 December), pp. 4-5, 45.
          The books in Faulkner's library tell us what he liked to
     read. Included in the introduction to 1964.A2.

7   BORGAL, CLÉMENT. "William Faulkner: La ville, traduit de
     l'anglais par J. et L. Bréant," TaRd, No. 183 (April),
     140-41.
          Epical in many qualities, The Town is not as striking a
     novel as Faulkner's earlier work, but it still demonstrates
     his power to capture his characters through the depiction
     of their universal drives and attitudes.

8   BOWLING, LAWRENCE E. "William Faulkner: The Importance of
     Love," DR, XLIII (Winter), 474-82.
          All Faulkner's work is about the importance of love.
     Where love is absent, depravity and desperation reign;
     where it is present, there is harmony and order. His great
     lovers are not the couple in The Wild Palms but Ike McCas-
     lin, Chick Mallison, Lena Grove, Dilsey, Ruby Lamar, and
     Lucius Priest.
     Reprinted 1973.A9.

9   BRADBURY, JOHN M. Renaissance in the South: A Critical His-
     tory of the Literature, 1920-1960. Chapel Hill, N. C.:
     University of North Carolina Press, pp. 50-57.
          Along with the Fugitives, Faulkner inaugurated a "new
     tradition of symbolic naturalism" in Southern writing.
     The Yoknapatawpha novels are concerned with the evils of
     exploitation of men and land and the consequences in guilt
     and violence. They are written in a "portentous style"
     and aspire to myth. His best work is found in the novels
     from The Sound and the Fury through Absalom, Absalom! (ex-
     cluding Pylon). He is a master of the short story.

10   BROOKS, CLEANTH. "The Community and the Pariah," VQR, XXXIX
     (Spring), 236-53.
          Stating his notion of the importance of community as a
     touchstone, "the essential ether" of Faulkner's fiction,
     Brooks discusses the problems of relationship which iden-
     tify each main character of Light in August. Lena is the
     only character not suffering from alienation; she redeems
     Byron from his "pallid" regimented life. The novel closes
     with a comic version of man's difficult and perpetual ef-
     forts to fulfill himself. Included in 1963.Al.

11   _____. "Faulkner's Sanctuary: The Discovery of Evil," SR,
     LXXI (Spring), 1-24.
          The power of evil is the novel's theme. Temple discovers

1963

(BROOKS, CLEANTH)
her capacity for evil and submits to it until she is list-
less and bored. Benbow is defeated by his discovery of
evil and ends in a condition much like Temple's. Included
in 1963.A1.

12 _____. "Faulkner's Savage Arcadia: Frenchman's Bend," VQR,
XXXIX (Autumn), 598-611.
A mythicized genre picture set at a comfortable aesthetic
distance, The Hamlet poetically presents the conflicts between the provincial inhabitants of a traditional community
and the forces of greedy and indifferent materialism loosed
by the advent of Flem Snopes. Faulkner's sympathy for his
characters and his sense of wonder at human possibility
make the book a believable fiction. Honor and love are major themes. Included in 1963.A1.

13 _____. "History, Tragedy and the Imagination in Absalom,
Absalom!" YR, LII (March), 340-51.
Faulkner's most brilliant novel combines a masterful and
serious detective story with a dramatization of the difficulty of truly apprehending and comprehending history.
Judith Sutpen is one of Faulkner's greatest--and noblest--
characters. The key to Quentin's full knowledge of Bon's
past is his visit to Sutpen's Hundred with Miss Rosa,
though exactly how he gets his knowledge is not certain.
Included in 1963.A1.

14 _____. "William Faulkner: Vision of Good and Evil," The
Hidden God: Studies in Hemingway, Faulkner, Yeats, Eliot,
and Warren. New Haven, Conn.: Yale University Press,
pp. 22-43.
Reprinted from 1962.B26. Reprinted 1973.A9.

15 BRUMM, URSULA. Die Religiöse Typologie im Amerikanischen
Denken: Ihre Bedeutung für die Amerikanische Literatur-
und Geistesgeschichte. Leiden: E. J. Brill, pp. 175-83.
No writer has made more significant use of the Christ
figure than Faulkner. In general, his critics have not
understood what he is trying to do, even in The Sound and
the Fury and Light in August, but especially in A Fable,
which holds civilization in general responsible for rapacity and foolishness that create war. Christianity is "rapacity's masterpiece." Faulkner's practice adopts standard
typology; A Fable is about the tragic fate of a single,
peace-loving mankind, symbolized in the Corporal, the un-
heroic hero so typical of American literature.

16   BUNGERT, HANS. "William Faulkners letzter Roman," NS, N. F.
      XI (November), 498-506.
          The Reivers, Faulkner's greatest comedy, is in the tra-
      dition of the picaresque novel. Apparently autobiographi-
      cal, it is clearer in style and form than any previous work
      and like all his Yoknapatawpha novels presents several new
      facets of characters who have appeared before. It also
      expresses the final stage in Faulkner's treatment of the
      Negro, for here Lucius does not need to endure Chick Mal-
      lison's soul-searching, while Ned and Uncle Parsham are
      both presented simply as potent and wise men and not as
      members of a class or race with special status. The book
      is marred by its sentimentality, but it throws light on
      all Faulkner's pre-1940 fiction and contributes to our pic-
      ture of him as one of America's great humorists.

17   _____. "William Faulkner on Moby Dick: An Early Letter,"
      SA, IX, 371-75.
          Remarks on Faulkner's note to the book editor of the Chi-
      cago Tribune precede a transcription of the note. Faulkner
      praises Melville's novel and also Moll Flanders and Milne's
      When We Were Very Young.

18   CALLEN, SHIRLEY. "Planter and Poor White in Absalom, Absa-
      lom!, 'Wash,' and The Mind of the South," SCB, XXIII (Win-
      ter), 24-36.
          Cash's Mind of the South is used as an index of Faulk-
      ner's sociology of poor white-planter relationship in Ab-
      salom, Absalom! and "Wash." Sutpen, no "new man," but,
      according to Cash, a typical planter, and Wash Jones,
      whose relationship with Sutpen is close and not class-
      conscious, prove basic accord between Faulkner and Cash,
      though Faulkner is granted more subtlety.

19   *CAMBON, GLAUCO. "'Assalonne, Assalonne!': Il demone della
      memoria," La Lotta con Proteo. Milan: Bompiani, 215-22.
          According to American Literary Scholarship, 1963, p. 77,
      the article notes how the circumstances of Sutpen's life
      are forecast or ironically reflected by the succeeding
      events of the novel.

20   CARTER, HODDING. "Faulkner and His Folk," First Person Rural.
      Garden City, N. Y.: Doubleday and Co., pp. 71-85.
          Reprinted from 1957.B9.

21   CHIKAMORI, KAZUE. "Unity of Theme and Technique in Absalom,
      Absalom!" Ei-Bei Bungaku Hyoran (Essays and Studies in
      British and American Literature), XI (Summer), 65-88.
          The mood of Absalom, Absalom! is shadowy, a fact empha-

1963

(CHIKAMORI, KAZUE)
sized by both the setting and the times of day used in the
novel. Throughout, Faulkner uses special imagery to unite
themes and characters.

22   CHURCH, MARGARET. "William Faulkner: Myth and Duration,"
Time and Reality: Studies in Contemporary Fiction.
Chapel Hill, N. C.: University of North Carolina Press,
pp. 227-50.
Faulkner uses both the transcendent idea of time as non-
existent and Bergson's notion of durée, that being endures
and, in a sense, creates time. In his use of myth and
archetypal symbols, whether general or merely out of the
Southern past, he abolishes time to create timeless, never-
fading moments. But in instances where his characters
feel the rush of the past and relive it, the combination
is a fault and causes some of Faulkner's novels, like Soldiers' Pay and Pylon, to fail. Each of Faulkner's novels
is discussed for its dramatization of time concepts.

23   COINDREAU, MAURICE E. "Faulkner tel que je l'ai connu,"
Preuves, No. 144 (February), 9-14.
Critical of those who willfully misunderstand Faulkner
or claim knowledge they do not possess in obituary essays,
Coindreau sets some of the record straight and recounts
his own thirty-year relationship with Faulkner and his
work, including portions of Faulkner letters and conversa-
tions with Coindreau. Translated as "The Faulkner I
Knew," Shenandoah (1965.B19); also translated, with introductory paragraph restored, 1971.B18.

24   *____. ["One Year After His Death Faulkner is Still Mis-
judged in the United States"], Arts (10 July and
23 July).
In French; translated 1971.B18. Misunderstood and unap-
preciated in his lifetime, Faulkner, a year after his
death, remains terra incognita to most Americans, who cannot bring themselves to see that the horrors Faulkner depicts are part of their own history and their own psyches.
In a country of exhibitionists, he refused to pander either
to popular taste or to popular curiosity.

25   CONNOLLY, THOMAS E. "A Skeletal Outline of Absalom, Absalom!" CE, XXV (November), 110-14.
A character list and a genealogy of the Sutpen family
from Absalom, Absalom! does not differentiate between characters who have objective fictional being and those invented or elaborated upon by other characters in the novel.
Reprinted 1971.A2.

26   DONNELLY, WILLIAM and DORIS. "William Faulkner: in Search
      of Peace," Person, XLIV (Autumn), 490-98.
         Faulkner's post-Nobel prize work indicates that he had
      found meaning in life; The Reivers, especially, is a fit-
      ting climax to his career. Incest, rape, idiocy, fratri-
      cide, suicide, and prostitution dominate the early novels.
      Discussing Faulkner's changing point of view after Go Down,
      Moses the author assumes that the later works were the
      product of new insights into the nature of man.

27   DOS PASSOS, JOHN. "William Faulkner, 1897-1962," Proceedings
      of the American Academy of Arts and Letters, 2nd Series,
      No. 13, pp. 289-90.
         A tribute to Faulkner's memory. Reading Faulkner brings
      back the "lost world" of a Southern childhood and native
      storytellers whose gift Faulkner possessed. Faulkner's
      characters are real because true to life.
      Reprinted as "Faulkner," NatRev (15 January 1963), p. 11;
      reprinted 1964.B19.

28   EISINGER, CHESTER E. "William Faulkner: Southern Archetype,"
      Fiction of the Forties. Chicago: University of Chicago
      Press, pp. 178-86.
         Faulkner's fiction of the forties embodies the myth of
      the South: exploitation of the land and the Negro have
      cursed the South. Only eccentrics like Ike McCaslin,
      children like Chick Mallison, and old ladies can perceive
      and expiate the Southern guilt. Community, its traditions
      and families, is Faulkner's center of value and responsi-
      bility. Folk life and humor are important. Modern society
      is condemned. Faulkner is one of those conservatives who
      would preserve the good of the past and acknowledge and
      expiate its evils.

29   FARMER, NORMAN, JR. "The Love Theme: A Principal Source of
      Thematic Unity in Faulkner's Snopes Trilogy," TCL, VIII
      (January), 111-23.
         Eula, as spirit of nature and fecundity, triumphs pas-
      sively over the spirit of exploitation. The events set
      into motion by her pregnancy will eventually destroy the
      exploiting spirit. Gavin and DeSpain together make up a
      single appropriate counterpoint to Eula in The Town: vi-
      rility and idealism. In The Mansion, Gavin and Linda
      dramatize the love theme, which is allied to the theme of
      nature by Mink Snopes's apotheosis at the novel's end, re-
      turning us full circle to Eula as earth goddess before
      exploitation.

1963

30   FISHER, RICHARD E.   "The Wilderness, the Commissary, and the
      Bedroom: Faulkner's Ike McCaslin as Hero in a Vacuum,"
      ES, XLIV (February), 19-28.
          Ike becomes a hero in a vacuum when the third element of
      his education--his marriage, which follows his discovery
      about slavery and hunting--creates disillusion and he re-
      pudiates "vocation." Ike fails to understand love, as he
      is charged, because he has failed to understand that mixed
      blood--as in Sam, Boon, and Lion--is nothing to be hated
      or feared. He ends a failure, having taught no one.

31   FLANAGAN, JOHN T.   "Faulkner's Favorite Word," GaR, XVII (Win-
      ter), 429-34.
          "Implacable," used epithetically, is Faulkner's favorite
      and, in the early fiction, most often used word.

32   GOLD, JOSEPH.   "The Two Worlds of Light in August," MissQ,
      XVI (Summer), 160-67.
          Joe Christmas is a mirror of the society he moves in;
      his perversions and problems are those of the major and
      minor antagonists he meets. By contrast, Lena Grove ac-
      cepts and overcomes the unreasonable forces of life. Dis-
      cusses each of the characters of the novel in terms of
      their inhumanity--the result of racial guilt, perverted
      religiosity, or immersion in an unreal past.

33   GOLDSTEIN, MELVIN.   "A Source for Faulkner's 'Nobel Prize
      Speech of Acceptance': Or, Two Versions of a Single Mani-
      festo," BSTCF, IV (Spring), 78-80.
          Dylan Thomas's "In My Craft and Sullen Art" is offered
      as a source.

34   GRAHAM, MARY WASHINGTON.   "Article on Faulkner Held a Misap-
      praisal," Charlottesville (Va.) Daily Progress (2 August),
      p. 4.
          A letter to the editor takes issue with Nancy Hale's es-
      say on Faulkner and Charlottesville in Vogue (1963.B40),
      suggesting that Ms. Hale disliked Faulkner because he did
      not behave like a writer. The followers of the hunt were
      a more varied and intelligent crew than Ms. Hale repre-
      sents.

35   GRAHAM, PHILIP.   "Pattern in Faulkner's Sanctuary and Requiem
      for a Nun," TSL, VIII, 39-46.
          Both Sanctuary and Requiem for a Nun use a similar struc-
      tural pattern as well as similar characters, setting, and
      theme; in each there is a three-part movement from the
      physical, to the social, to the moral--Nature, society,

(GRAHAM, PHILIP)
abstract Truth. In Sanctuary, the death of an innocent
person (Tommy, Red, Godwin) punctuates each stage. Requiem for a Nun, concerned with regeneration, breaks into
three dramatic units, each preceded by a narrative introduction, each ending with a "death": Temple's baby, the
governor (a metaphysical death which occurs when he disappears), and Nancy.

36   GREEN, MARTIN. "Faulkner: The Triumph of Rhetoric," Re-
Appraisals: Some Commonsense Readings in American Literature. London: Hugh Evelyn, pp. 167-95. American edition
New York: Norton, 1965.
Faulkner's language is rhetorical to a fault, substitut-
ing sound for sense, dulling the reader's perceptions with
inaccuracies or even absurdities. His devices, like in-
direct narrative; his characterizations; and his plots are
all equally excessive, never involving our intelligence.

37   GRESSET, MICHEL. "Faulkner par lui-même," Mercure de France,
CCCL (November), 622-28.
Reviewing Nathan's Faulkner par lui-même (1963.A7), the
author briefly reviews the history of Faulkner criticism
in France and its preoccupations, as, for example, time in
the novels.

38   GRIFFIN, ROBERT J. "Ethical Point of View in The Sound and
the Fury," Essays in Modern American Literature, edited by
Richard E. Langford. Deland, Fla.: Stetson University
Press, pp. 55-64.
The four narratives of The Sound and the Fury display an
ethical progression from amorality to absolute idealism,
to moral hypocrisy, to humanistic sympathy and acceptance.

39   HAGAN, JOHN. "Déjà Vu and the Effect of Timelessness in
Faulkner's Absalom, Absalom!" BuR, XI (March), 31-52.
Chapters 1-6 of Absalom, Absalom! present the "Jefferson
phase" of Sutpen's story; 7 and 8 show the causes of what
eventually happened to bring the house of Sutpen to a ruin;
chapter 9 reveals "the hidden existence" of Henry, Quentin's final authority, and rounds out his tragedy with
fire. The effect of the structure on the reader is compared to déjà vu as defined out of Bergson's philosophy.
The sins and suffering of the father are repeated in subsequent generations.

40   HALE, NANCY. "Colonel Sartoris and Mr. Snopes," Vogue (1 August), pp. 112-13, 135-36, 139.
Anecdotes from local people make up an account of

1963

(HALE, NANCY)
Faulkner in Charlottesville, especially his relationship
to the fox hunting gentry. See rejoinders 1963.B34,
1963.B57.

41   HARRIS, WENDELL V. "Faulkner's The Sound and the Fury," Expl,
      XXI (March), Item 54.
         Quentin, Jason, and Caddy each mirror one dominant trait
      of Mr. Compson: his mordant explanations of phenomena
      his caustic wit at Maury's expense, his true affection for
      all his children. Benjy is the result of a streak of fam-
      ily insanity and the "ultimate reduction" of Bascomb help-
      lessness.

42   HARTT, JULIAN N. The Lost Image of Man. Baton Rouge, La.:
      Louisiana State University Press, pp. 109-11.
         In his use of the Christian model of expiation, Faulkner
      fails to convince because he venerates man too highly:
      his men do not need the sacrifice of the Son of God.
      Reprinted from 1955.B23.

43   HOGAN, PATRICK G., JR. "Faulkner's 'Female Line': 'Callina'
      McCaslin," SSF, I (Fall), 63-65.
         "Callina," the name given to the short-lived child of
      Tennie and Tomey's Turl, is evidence that the sister of
      Buck and Buddy is named "Caroline."

44   _____. "Faulkner Scholarship and the CEA," CEA, XXVI (Octo-
      ber), 1, 5, 7-8, 12.
         The author points out errors in Charles Nilon's Faulkner
      and the Negro (1962.A3).

45   HOWE, IRVING. "The Quest for Moral Style," A World More At-
      tractive: A View of Modern Literature and Politics. New
      York: Horizon Press, pp. 59-76.
         The writers of the post-World War I generation, coming
      into a world without value, searched for a style which
      would give value or replace moral outlook. Faulkner had
      the advantage of Protestant background, a sense of histor-
      ical meaning, and the roots of kinship. Though critical
      of the South, its ways and institutions, which turned out
      to be one with the rest of the valueless modern world,
      Faulkner had hill folk, poor farmers, Negroes, and chil-
      dren to turn to for a moral core, an embodiment of good-
      ness and charity. Then, through exploration, he discovered
      these figures incomplete as moral guides--for example,
      Ratliff.

46   HUGHES, RICHARD. "Faulkner and Bennett," <u>Encounter</u>, XXI (September), 59-61.
     The author of <u>A High Wind in Jamaica</u> tells how he chanced to arouse Arnold Bennett's interest in Faulkner and recites some of the results, including excerpts from Bennett's early reviews and an account of how Faulkner came to be published by Chatto & Windus in England. Comparing <u>Mosquitoes</u> and <u>The Reivers</u>, he criticizes the sentimentality of the more recent work.

47   HUTCHISON, E. R. "A Footnote to the Gum Tree Scene," <u>CE</u>, XXIV (April), 564-65.
     Agrees with Bell (1962.B17) and suggests as parallels to the scene in "The Bear" two additional scenes where Boon guards trees--in the anecdote about the bear cub and the railroad and at Sam's burial. He suggests that Boon is deliberately destroying his gun in frustration and grief over the loss of the wilderness.

48   ISAACS, NEIL D. "Götterdämmerung in Yoknapatawpha," <u>TSL</u>, VIII, 47-55.
     In "Wash," Sutpen is an earthly horse-god to Wash Jones and a fitting symbol of all the poor white can never be. The story concerns the falling apart of Wash's reason for being. Images of a world gone awry dominate the last part of the story. The ending is ritualized. A comparison with the revised material in <u>Absalom, Absalom!</u> is useful; especially provocative is the identification between Quentin and Wash.

49   KAZIN, ALFRED. "Young Man, Old Man: 2. Faulkner: Back into the Havoc," <u>Reporter</u> (19 December), pp. 36-40.
     Though he had not played the hermit--Hollywood, <u>Saturday Evening Post</u>, Latin America and Europe, the Nobel address, the lectures and interviews prove that he "had never been like anyone else"--he had remained personally inaccessible. Faulkner cuts off the future, "his only significant fault." "The Bear" is discussed as a novelette; Faulkner's work is generalized upon as a "reflection of human destiny."

50   KERN, ALEXANDER C. "Myth and Symbol in Criticism of Faulkner's 'The Bear,'" <u>Myth and Symbol: Critical Approaches and Applications</u>, edited by Bernice Slote. Lincoln, Neb.: University of Nebraska Press, pp. 152-61.
     A survey of mythological and symbolic criticism of "The Bear" and an account of Faulkner's use of Chickasaw customs, Christian symbolism, and "the American myth" in the five-part version of the story concludes that Ike's act is a failure, though one which is well-meant and tragic.

1963

51   KILLINGER, JOHN. The Failure of Theology in Modern Litera-
      ture. Nashville, Tenn.: Abingdon, pp. 46-47, 54-57, 89-
      94.
          From the Christian point of view, Faulkner's obvious hu-
      manistic outlook in A Fable is unfortunate, but it remains
      his best novel. God is absent--though he exists not far
      away--from Faulkner's world. This explains the chaos and
      dementia, for neither human nor divine order is possible.
      as, for example, is dramatized in Sanctuary, The Sound and
      the Fury, and Light in August. Only the negro church in
      The Sound and the Fury is vital.

52   KILLINGSWORTH, KAY. "Au-delà du déchirement: L'héritage
      méridional dans l'oeuvre de William Faulkner et d'Albert
      Camus," Esprit, N. S. No. 13 (September), 209-34.
          Faulkner's philosophy corresponds to Camus'. Man is
      alienated in his universe, unhappy, subject to fate, but
      able to bear his burdens and love creation, even to attain
      a kind of immortality.

53   KREUZ, HIERONYMO. "Book Reviews," Ramparts, I (January), 90-
      93.
          When Faulkner wrote as a "cerebral" writer, he was de-
      rivative and weak. His early poetry and reviews in Early
      Prose and Poetry smack of Huneker and Saltus and the Smart
      Set. His failure as a poet gave us a great novelist.

54   LINNEMAN, WILLIAM R. "Faulkner's Ten-Dollar Words," AS,
      XXXVIII (May), 158-59.
          An investigation of the vocabularies of Faulkner and
      Hemingway shows that there is little difference in their
      use of native as opposed to borrowed words, but that Faulk-
      ner uses more abstract words than Hemingway.

55   LINSCOTT, ROBERT. "Faulkner Without Fanfare," Esquire, LX
      (July), 36, 38.
          The Random House editor tells anecdotes about Faulkner's
      impassivity in social situations and recounts some personal
      good times together.

56   LITTLE, GAIL B. "Three Novels for Comparative Study in the
      Twelfth Grade," EJ, LII (October), 501-05.
          Intruder in the Dust, Huckleberry Finn, and Catcher in
      the Rye are usefully compared as three perspectives on the
      way a society is tested by a "child's interior code of
      ethics." Stylistic differences and characterization are
      discussed. Gavin Stevens is hard to defend.

57   LONGLEY, JOHN LEWIS, JR. "Miss Hale's Faulkner Caricature
        Explained," Vogue (6 August), p. 4.
          Tongue-in-cheek explanation is offered for Nancy Hale's
        Vogue article (1963.B40): it was written in a patronizing,
        cute way because that is what the magazine, which Ms. Hale
        used to edit, requires.

58   *McDONALD, W. U., JR. "The Time-Scheme of The Hamlet," MidR,
        V, 22-29.
        American Literary Scholarship 1963, p. 75.

59   *MATERASSI, MARIO. "Le immagini in Soldiers' Pay," SA, IX,
        353-70.
          According to American Literary Scholarship 1964, p. 77,
        Materassi "analyzes the use of imagery to characterize
        Cecily Saunders" and shows how Faulkner's later style is
        foreshadowed.
        Reprinted 1968.A5.

60   MAXWELL, DESMOND ERNEST STEWART. American Fiction: The In-
        tellectual Background. New York: Columbia University
        Press, pp. 275-78.
          Faulkner has taken the novel about gangsterism and crime
        detection and made of it something artistic. Sanctuary is
        one extreme example, but Intruder in the Dust goes beyond
        the recording of decadence and violence to assure that a
        traditional community and its lasting values do exist and
        can be, in however odd or small a way, mobilized for good.
        Where "fortitude and loyalty remain, so does the hope of
        order."

61   MERIWETHER, JAMES B. "Faulkner and the New Criticism," BA,
        XXXVII (Summer), 265-68.
          Part of a symposium on explication du texte, Meriwether's
        remarks are to the effect that by and large the New Critics
        ignored Faulkner's work, the explication and sale of which
        they might have helped, in the 1930s and 1940s. Comment
        by Wolfgang Fleischmann (pp. 268-69) offers the defense
        that the failure to consider Faulkner's work was not lack
        of perception so much as a general situation; no one was
        reading Faulkner's work very much at this time. Meriwether
        suggests that Faulkner himself was a kind of New Critic in
        his interest in all the elements of modern fiction.

62   _____. "The Text of Faulkner's Books: An Introduction and
        Some Notes," MFS, IX (Summer), 159-70.
          Citing examples of inconsistency and error in the use of
        texts for quotation in critical articles on Faulkner, Meri-
        wether argues for more textual sophistication by literary

1963

(MERIWETHER, JAMES B.)
  critics and provides a list of the most reliable texts of
  Faulkner's books then available.

63   MILLEDGE, LUETTA UPSHUR. "Light Eternal: An Analysis of Some
  Folkloristic Elements in Faulkner's Go Down, Moses," TFSB,
  XXIX (December), 86-93.
    Humor, exaggeration, ribaldry--all in a form akin to the
  practice of folk literature--appear throughout Faulkner's
  work. Go Down, Moses, besides these elements, contains
  the folk exemplum, folk speech, legend, customs, and
  ritual.

64   MILLER, DOUGLAS T. "Faulkner and the Civil War: Myth and
  Reality," AQ, XV (Summer), 200-09.
    A summary of Faulkner's use of the Civil War, the article
  finds Faulkner to be antebellum traditionalist with a high
  regard for individualism, never totally rejecting the popular view of the South.

65   MILLGATE, MICHAEL. "'A Fair Job': A Study of Faulkner's
  Sanctuary," REngLit, IV (October), 47-62.
    In revising and restructuring the galleys of the first
  version of Sanctuary, Faulkner de-emphasized the Benbow-
  Sartoris material and made the book more the story of
  Temple Drake; he actually did not reduce the so-called hor-
  rific element.

66   MOSELEY, EDWIN M. "Christ as Social Scapegoat: Faulkner's
  Light in August," Pseudonyms of Christ in the Modern Novel:
  Motifs and Methods. Pittsburgh, Pa.: University of Pittsburgh Press, pp. 246-59.
    Lena Grove in Light in August is the springlike goddess
  of love renewing the land; Christmas is the scapegoat perishing in the winter for the restoration of love and sacrifice. Loveless forms of Christianity are held up to
  violent criticism. The book, in its eclectic pursuit of
  the ideal of suffering and renewal, reminds us of the
  "king of the wood" section of Frazer's The Golden Bough.

67   MUELLER, WILLIAM RANDOLPH. "The Reivers: William Faulkner's
  Valediction," ChrCent (4 September), pp. 1079-81.
    Living with human dignity, which includes regard for
  others as well as self, is a touchstone in The Reivers and
  in many other Faulkner books. A young boy's coming to
  knowledge is seen through the gentle and wise perspective
  of the boy as a 67 year old grandfather. Faulkner's comedy does not say "all is well," but it does exalt human

(MUELLER, WILLIAM RANDOLPH)
capacity for growth and endurance. Faulkner is a humanist in whose recent works there is a touch of theism.

68   NEMEROV, HOWARD. "Calculation Raised to Mystery: The Dialectics of Light in August," Poetry and Fiction: Essays. New Brunswick, N. J.: Rutgers University Press, pp. 246-59.
Light in August is built on the related polarities of black and white, male and female, and their "marriage combat" as dramatized in all the novel's characters. Joe Christmas and Hightower are opposites, related by plot and other devices. The form of the book is deliberate, poetic, successful.

69   RIDEOUT, WALTER B., and JAMES B. MERIWETHER. "On the Collaboration of Faulkner and Anderson," AL, XXXV (March), 85-87.
Replying to 1962.B99, the authors give the facts about the Al Jackson tales which Faulkner and Sherwood Anderson swapped in the 1920s. In Mosquitoes, Faulkner drew upon his own contributions to the legend, not upon Anderson.

70   ROBERTS, JAMES L. "Experimental Exercises--Faulkner's Early Writings," Discourse, VI (Summer), 183-97.
Faulkner's early work up through Mosquitoes is interesting both for its presentation of the world he would depict later and for its experimental technique.

71   ROLLINS, RONALD G. "Ike McCaslin and Chick Mallison: Faulkner's Emerging Southern Hero," WVUPP, XIV (October), 74-79.
Two young Southerners, both effectively "fatherless," undergo moral initiation at the hands of racially hybrid mentors, both through hunting trips. "The Bear" and Intruder in the Dust show the young men dying in their old societies and being reborn into new ones. The stories have many similarities.

72   RUBIN, LOUIS D., JR. "Chronicles of Yoknapatawpha: The Dynasties of William Faulkner," The Faraway Country: Writers of the Modern South. Seattle, Washington: University of Washington Press, pp. 43-71.
In the novels of the "Yoknapatawpha chronicle," Faulkner presents a three-part history of the South from the wilderness days to the present century. His technique is to use a central consciousness as focus--sometimes the reader himself--and to demand the reader's participation in the unfolding of the drama. In Absalom, Absalom!, Sutpen's fall

1963

(RUBIN, LOUIS D., JR.)
is the "fall of civilization." In The Sound and the Fury,
Quentin represents the specific breakdown that dooms the
family to tragedy. Faulkner is not lost in the past, however, nor devoted to a chronicle of the South's evolution;
he is a moral writer who repeatedly dramatizes the result
of the absence of love in human relationships.

73 _____. "The Difficulties of Being a Southern Writer or, Getting Out from Under William Faulkner," JSoH, XXIX (November), 486-94.
A new South needs new writers with new views and new materials. What Faulkner saw in Southern experience is no
longer true today, a fact which helps to explain his failure with Gavin Stevens in Intruder in the Dust and The
Mansion. A comparison of Faulkner's work with Madison
Jones's The Buried Land is used to illustrate the argument.

74 SEIDEN, MELVIN. "Faulkner's Ambiguous Negro," MR, IV (Summer), 675-90.
Absalom, Absalom! is a melodrama with Charles Bon's
blackness the quality which makes him a dangerous, intrusive force. He remains enigmatic even to the reader, who
has a superior view of the novel's events. Faulkner uses
racism to undercut racism, and he has spoken with truth
about a real American condition. The forms which flawed
love take characterize the narrative viewpoints.

75 SIMON, JOHN K. "Faulkner and Sartre: Metamorphosis and the
Obscene," CL, XV (Summer), 216-25.
Sartre's debt to Faulkner has not been fully explained
or understood. Philosophically different as he believed
himself, Sartre yet used an imagery common with Faulkner's
in his early work, as in La Nausée. Sanctuary and As I Lay
Dying are particularly instructive for comparison with
Sartre's fiction. Both writers have a predilection for
images and words which underscore the "anguish" of the relationship between consciousness and the inhuman world.

76 _____. "What Are You Laughing At, Darl? Madness and Humor
in As I Lay Dying," CE, XXV (November), 104-10.
Darl's laughter at the close of his final scene is a
product of the division of his personality into self and
not-self, consciousness and being. It is a final outside
comment upon the absurdity of a world that includes his
own betrayed, maddened self.
Reprinted 1973.A9.

77   SLABEY, ROBERT M. "As I Lay Dying as an Existential Novel,"
      BuR, XI (December), 12-23.
          As I Lay Dying dramatizes differences between those with
      "courage to be" and those without, using the metaphor of
      the life-journey, which is reduced to an image of the ab-
      surdity of human existence. The form remains dynamic and
      is itself an affirmation of the artist's ability to face
      existence and express what he sees.

78   _____. "Faulkner's Sanctuary," Expl, XXI (January), Item 45.
          Hermes, the divine messenger of classical mythology, is
      a prototype for Popeye in Sanctuary; the novel should be
      given consideration in the light of Eliot and Joyce.

79   _____. "The 'Romanticism' of The Sound and the Fury," MissQ,
      XVI (Summer), 146-59.
          Soldiers' Pay and Mosquitoes prefigure The Sound and the
      Fury, though marred by "lost generation" attitudes and
      themes. Sartoris is closer, more involved with its mate-
      rial, but still "Romantic," particularly in the view of
      the Old South era as a gallant time. The Sound and the
      Fury is distinguished by its critical examination and im-
      plied moral commentary of the Romantic Southern tradition.
      Quentin is an unreconstructed romantic obsessed by visions
      of purity and by the past, unable to accept human complex-
      ity.

80   SOWDER, WILLIAM J. "Faulkner and Existentialism: A Note on
      the Generalissimo," WSCL, IV (Spring-Summer), 163-71.
          The Generalissimo, a living emblem of the human propen-
      sity for rapaciousness and endurance, resembles the high-
      est element in Jean Paul Sartre's trinity of existential
      modes, être-pour-autres. A Fable is not an allegory of
      Christ, however, though it uses Christian lore; it is a
      celebration of man, who wills to live, rather than die,
      for a cause.

81   _____. "Lucas Beauchamp as Existential Hero," CE, XXV (No-
      vember), 115-18, 127.
          In contrast to Sutpen (See 1962.B111) who is an example
      of Sartre's être-pour-autres and a failure, Lucas Beau-
      champ is an existential hero, master of all situations.
      He refuses to accept his objectivity by others and he en-
      dures the freedom that such a posture affords him.

82   STANFORD, RANEY. "Of Mules and Men: Faulkner and Silone,"
      Discourse, VI (Winter), 73-78.
          Qualities of endurance, patience, and indomitability are

1963

(STANFORD, RANEY)
"made flesh" in Faulkner's mules and Ignazio Silone's don-
keys. The article discusses several parallels between the
work of the two writers.

83   SWIGGART, PETER. "Faulkner's The Sound and the Fury," Expl,
       XXII (December), Item 31.
          Shreve's allusion to Byron's "wish" in Absalom, Absalom!
       is identified as a reference to Don Juan, Canto 6, and an
       obscene evocation of the poet's desire for sexual posses-
       sion of all women at once. See also 1966.B55.

84   TATE, ALLEN. "William Faulkner, 1897-1962," SR, LXXI (Win-
       ter), 160-64.
          Reprinted from 1962.B117.

85   TAYLOR, NANCY DEW. "The River of Faulkner and Twain," MissQ,
       XVI (Fall), 191-99.
          The article compares the importance of the Mississippi
       River to Faulkner and Twain and Faulkner's treatment in the
       subplot of The Wild Palms ("Old Man") with Twain's writing
       on the river, noting parallels, especially with Huckle-
       berry Finn. In both works the river is a symbol of free-
       dom.

86   *THOMPSON, LAWRANCE. "A Defense of Difficulties in William
       Faulkner's Art," Carrell, IV (December), 7-19.
          According to American Literary Scholarship 1964, the ar-
       ticle, though pitched at an elementary level, justifies
       Faulkner's fictional methods, especially in Absalom, Absa-
       lom! and Go Down, Moses.

87   TOOLE, WILLIAM B., III. "Faulkner's 'That Evening Sun,'"
       Expl, XXI (February), Item 52.
          Mr. Compson is the only worthy white character in "That
       Evening Sun," but he does not measure up to his own sym-
       pathy for Nancy, who, as a consequence, is elevated in the
       story to a greater height. The father's diminution is
       figured in the elevation of little Jason to his shoulders.

88   WEISS, DANIEL. "William Faulkner and the Runaway Slave,"
       NwRev, VI (Summer), 71-79.
          Negroes are ritual objects, not humans, in Faulkner's
       work, and the question of his social morality is irrelevant
       to his use of the Negro. The Negro is the South's "luck"
       misused; he brings misfortune. In "Was" and "Dry Septem-
       ber" the Negro is used to reawaken sexuality, but because
       he is misused, the efforts are abortive or cataclysmic.

89   WELTY, EUDORA. "Presentation to William Faulkner of the Gold
      Medal for Fiction," Proceedings of the American Academy of
      Arts and Letters, 2nd Series, #13, pp. 225-26.
          The Mississippi writer praises Faulkner; the gold would
      find its way to his pocket like a puppy. Faulkner's re-
      ply, pp. 226-27.

90   *WISNIOWSKI, BRONISLAW. "William Faulkner," William Faulkner,
      Ernest Hemingway, John Steinbeck. Warsaw: Czytelnik, pp.
      11-104.
          Library of Congress National Union Catalogue, 1956-1967,
      Vol. 123, p. 245.

1964 A BOOKS

1   AGUILAR, ESPERANZA. Yoknapatawpha, Propriedad de William
      Faulkner. Santiago de Chile: Cuadernos del Centro de in-
      vestigaciones de literatura comparada, Universidad de
      Chile.
          This handbook approach to Faulkner contains maps, geneal-
      ogies of the principal fictional families, a brief biog-
      raphy of Faulkner, and summaries and discussions of the
      novels in chronological order.

2   BLOTNER, JOSEPH, compiler. William Faulkner's Library: A
      Catalogue. Charlottesville, Va.: University Press of
      Virginia.
          The compilation lists, under national categories, the
      books in Faulkner's library at the time of his death.
      Blotner's introduction, which appeared in the NYTBR
      (1936.B6), argues that Faulkner's signature in a book in-
      dicates special regard for it. An appendix lists books
      purchased in the 1920s by Phil Stone. See review,
      1966.B50.

3   *BRASIL, ASSIS. Faulkner e a tecnica do romance. Rio: Edi-
      tôra Leitura.
          Massey (1968.A4), Item 1174.

4   DAIN, MARTIN. Faulkner's County. New York: Random House.
          Black and white photographs óf people and places in and
      around Faulkner's home county, Lafayette; reproductions of
      Faulkner family pictures; and a series of shots of Faulk-
      ner with his horses.

5   FANT, MAJOR JOSEPH L., and LT. COL. ROBERT P. ASHLEY. Faulk-
      ner at West Point. New York: Random House.
          Faulkner's April 1962 visit to the U. S. Military

(FANT, MAJOR JOSEPH L., and LT. COL. ROBERT P. ASHLEY)
Academy at West Point is briefly recounted, with photographs, in a volume that also contains the text of The
Reivers passage he read, a transcription of question and
answer sessions with cadets, copies of Faulkner's letters
of acceptance and thanks, and the Nobel address.

6 HICKERSON, THOMAS FELIX. The Falkner Feuds. Chapel Hill,
N. C.: The Colonial Press.
An account, by a collateral descendant of R. J. Thurmond,
of the circumstances before and after Thurmond's shooting
of Col. W. C. Falkner, the novelist's great-grandfather,
including biographical material on the Falkner family.

7 RUNYAN, HARRY. A Faulkner Glossary. New York: The Citadel
Press.
An index to Faulkner's work, the volume claims to contain "all titles, characters, and places" in the published
writing, excluding actual people and places. Seven appendices provide a short biographical sketch; checklists of
poetry, nonfiction prose, and fiction; histories of principal families of Yoknapatawpha (Indian, black, and white);
the geography of the mythical county; and a list of the
"documents"--i.e., the relevant fiction--of Yoknapatawpha
history.

8 TUCK, DOROTHY. Crowell's Handbook of Faulkner, with an introduction by Lewis Leary. New York: Crowell.
Leary provides a sketch of Faulkner's background, his
symbolic style, and his influences. The handbook has chapters on the history of Yoknapatawpha County; on Faulkner's
style; summaries of the novels and stories; a dictionary
of characters; a brief biography of Faulkner; a selected
bibliography; and genealogical charts of major families
of the fiction. See correction in 1972.B59.

9 UTLEY, FRANCIS L., LYNN Z. BLOOM, and ARTHUR F. KINNEY.
Bear, Man, and God: Seven Approaches to William Faulkner's
"The Bear." New York: Random House.
A casebook for the younger student which treats the five-
part "The Bear" as a novella and reprints criticism from
books and articles on various aspects of the piece, including background material and Faulkner's own work.
Reprinted, with additional material, as . . . Eight Approaches . . . (Random House, 1971).

10 VICKERY, OLGA W. The Novels of William Faulkner, revised ed.
Baton Rouge: Louisiana State University Press.
A reprinting of 1959.A4 with additional material on The

1964

(VICKERY, OLGA W.)
Mansion and The Reivers and a summary chapter, "William
Faulkner and the Figure in the Carpet" (1964.B73), which
sees as the "unifying principle" of Faulkner's works the
endlessly changing formal arrangement of complexly imagined
human characters. Faulkner had a "quizzical, reflective"
mind eager to probe both the known and unknown.

11   VOLPE, EDMOND L.   A Reader's Guide to William Faulkner.   New
     York: Noonday Press.
       Following a brief biographical essay, Volpe presents a
     general overview of Faulkner's fiction which stresses the
     theme of initiation into manhood; studies of individual
     novels; genealogies, outlines and chronologies. Faulkner's
     characters require·initiation because they are too oriented
     toward the past, too idealistic and puritanical, too sensi-
     tive and introspective. His main themes, coming from the
     hero's encounter with the modern world, are individualism,
     the wasteland, the problems of race, the power of social
     forces, the virtues of primitivism.

1964 B   SHORTER WRITINGS

1   ANON. "A Faulknerian Gnat-Bite," TLS (22 October), p. 953.
       Richard Hughes's introduction to Mosquitoes gives the
     history of his association with Faulkner's publication in
     England, which ironically delayed Mosquitoes until 1964.
     It is reminiscent of the 1920s Huxley, and it is not as
     comic as the publisher claims.

2   ANON. "Col. Falkner Killed 75 Years Ago Today; Old Papers
     Turned Up In Frisco Freight Depot Tell Story," broadside
     published by and reprinted from the New Albany (Miss.)
     Gazette, 5 November.
       An account of the finding of telegrams filed by a corres-
     pondent for several Memphis, Tenn., newspapers at the time
     Faulkner's great-grandfather was shot in Ripley, Miss.; an
     account of the murder and subsequent trial; and reprinting
     of the telegrams, now housed in the Mississippi Collection,
     University of Mississippi Library.

3   ADAMS, PERCY G. "Humor as Structure and Theme in Faulkner's
     Trilogy," WSCL, V (Autumn), 205-12.
       The comedy of the Snopes trilogy is ironic, parodic, and
     employed about evenly in all three volumes. There is the
     Heleniad, concerning Eula, and a strong comic resemblance
     to Paradise Lost that fits the general theme of the tril-
     ogy: evil recoils upon and destroys itself. Balanced

1964

(ADAMS, PERCY G.)
     comic scenes in The Town and The Mansion support this in-
     terpretation.

4   ALLEN, WALTER ERNEST. "Literary Letter from London," NYTBR
        (15 November), p. 54.
          Faulkner's Mosquitoes, published for the first time in
        England, has an introduction by Richard Hughes discussing
        his early interest in Faulkner. Hughes's criticism of
        Faulkner is worthwhile. See 1963.B46.

5   BARTH, J. ROBERT. "Faulkner and the Calvinist Tradition,"
        Thought, XXXIX (Spring), 100-120.
          Faulkner's world is not merely protestant, but strictly
        Calvinist: Sartoris, The Sound and the Fury, Light in Au-
        gust, Absalom, Absalom!, Go Down, Moses, The Town all de-
        pict characters whose lives are rigidly determined, whether
        for good or evil. Requiem for a Nun and A Fable, however,
        offer hope through suffering, which can give man a sense
        of peace. The Reivers shows "man sinful, but striving for
        the good...struggling to be free."
        Reprinted 1972.A1.

6   BASSAN, MAURICE. "Benjy at the Monument," ELN, II (Septem-
        ber), 46-50.
          The courthouse "circle" at the end of The Sound and the
        the Fury is like the face of Quentin's watch. Benjy's ex-
        perience in the final scene of the novel is an expression
        of an attitude toward time. Benjy must go counterclock-
        wise, against the movement of time.

7   BEJA, MORRIS. "A Flash, A Glare: Faulkner and Time," Renas-
        cence, XVI (Spring), 133-41, 145.
          More than in the works of other moderns, Faulkner's char-
        acters must have special qualifications for experiencing
        an epiphany or illumination. They must have sensitivity
        and a special orientation toward the past. Light in Au-
        gust provides the best example; Joe's invovlement with
        time seems an index of his near victimization by his il-
        luminations. In Requiem for a Nun, Faulkner tries to give
        the reader an "illumination of his whole vision."

8   BOWLING, LAWRENCE E. "Faulkner and the Theme of Isolation,"
        GaR, XVIII (Spring), 50-66.
          The theme of isolation in The Sound and the Fury is the
        link between its regional, familial significance and a
        more universal meaning. Benjy is behind barriers (key
        word: Fence). Quentin seeks isolation (key word: wall).

1964

(BOWLING, LAWRENCE E.)
Jason is naturalistic: all men are dogs (key word:
bitch). The fourth section shows an alternative in
Dilsey's "communion" and spiritual renewal and dedication
to others.

9   BRADFORD, MELVIN E. "Faulkner Among the Puritans," SR, LXXII
(Winter), 146-50.
Swiggart's book on Faulkner (1962.A5) is typical of approaches which link Faulkner to the American Romance, as
in Hawthorne and Melville, and to Puritanism as a cause of
the inward-looking of that form. Swiggart's terminology
is incomplete and confusing.

10   _____. "Faulkner and the Great White Father," LaS, III,
323-29.
"Lo!" is satirically critical of Federalism and the notion that a single government can comprehend and serve the
varied local elements which make up the country. It reaffirms Faulkner's faith in "genuine communities."

11   BROOKS, CLEANTH. "The American 'Innocence': In James, Fitzgerald, Faulkner," Shenandoah, XVI (Autumn), 21-37.
Like the heroes of The American and The Great Gatsby,
Thomas Sutpen of Absalom, Absalom! comes from nowhere, is
uneducated, and creates a new persona for himself. Each
hero is innocent in typically American ways. Sutpen's innocence is his inability to comprehend what sin is; he believes the world can be manipulated to his own ends.
Faulkner presents the community with which his character
is at odds more sympathetically than James or Fitzgerald,
reflecting a truer view of American history. "Natural"
innocence is insufficient unless augmented by custom and
ceremony, the fruits of a disciplined life.
Reprinted in A Shaping Joy (1971.B12).

12   BURGER, NASH K. "A Story to Tell: Agee, Wolfe, Faulkner,"
SAQ, LXIII (Winter), 32-43.
In the context of longer comments on Agee and Wolfe, the
author comments on Faulkner's relationship to the South as
material, milieu, and homeland.

13   CANTWELL, ROBERT. "Introduction," Sartoris, by William Faulkner. New York: Signet, pp. vii-xviii.
A condensed version of the earlier introduction to this
book (1953.B8).

1964

14   CAREY, GLENN O. "Social Criticism in Faulkner's 'Dry September,'" _EngR_, XV (December), 27-30.
      Faulkner dramatizes the complexity of racism by playing it against social disapproval and human weakness to create a lynching that need not have occurred. Hawkshaw the barber is weak because he does not have the courage of his convictions about human freedom.

15   CONNOLLY, THOMAS E. "Fate and 'the Agony of Will': Determinism in Some Works of William Faulkner," _Essays on Determinism in American Literature_, edited by Sydney J. Krause. Kent, Ohio: Kent State University Press, pp. 36-52.
      Environment and psychological factors are the agents of determinism in such early Faulkner works as _Sanctuary_, _The Sound and the Fury_, and _Light in August_, although in the last-named novel society also plays a very strong role in Christmas's fate. Sutpen, in _Absalom, Absalom!_, is unaware of the force he wars against and unconscious of his defeat. A religious element enters, especially in "The Bear," where God's curse is operative and Ike repudiates the land to become a Messiah, a role that is only personally successful. In _Intruder in the Dust_, Chick goes beyond Ike, repudiating the curse and bringing redemptive action into the world. Faulkner's view of man changes from heavily deterministic to a trust in man's ability to effect change.

16   *CRONIN, MARY A. "Mississippi Revisited," _Lit_, No. 5, 11-14.
      Cited in Beebe (1967.B4), p. 147. Not in Massey or Bassett. Review of _The Reivers_.

17   DANIEL, BRADFORD. "William Faulkner and the Southern Quest for Freedom," _Black, White and Gray: Twenty-one Points of View on the Race Question_, edited by B. Daniel. New York: Sheed & Ward, pp. 291-308.
      Faulkner was outspoken on the racial issue, demanding equality of education and opportunity. Daniel reprints six letters Faulkner wrote to the Memphis (Tenn.) _Commercial Appeal_, portions of two public addresses, and some commentary on Faulkner's position.

18   DICKERSON, MARY JANE. "_As I Lay Dying_ and _The Waste Land_--Some Relationships," _MissQ_, XVII (Summer), 129-35.
      There are apparent parallels of theme, event, and language between _The Waste Land_ and _As I Lay Dying_. The endings of both works are compared. Darl is identified with Teresias, the narrator of Eliot's poem.

19   DOS PASSOS, JOHN. "Faulkner," Occasions and Protests. Chi-
      cago: Henry Regnery, pp. 275-77.
      Reprinted from 1963.B27.

20   DURRETT, FRANCES B. "The New Orleans Double Dealer," Reality
      and Myth: Essays in American Literature in Memory of
      Richard Croom Beatty, edited by William E. Walker and
      Robert L. Welker. Nashville, Tenn.: Vanderbilt University
      Press, pp. 212-36.
          Faulkner is the most famous of the people who were con-
      nected with the New Orleans little magazine, the Double
      Dealer, in the mid-1920s. His contributions are noted,
      some reprinted and discussed, in a brief overview of the
      magazine's history.

21   EDEL, LEON. The Modern Psychological Novel. New York: The
      Universal Library, Grosset & Dunlap, pp. 97-102, 162-76.
      A revision of 1955.B16 by the addition of 1962.B43.

22   ELLISON, RALPH. "Twentieth Century Fiction and the Black
      Mask of Humanity," Shadow and Act. New York: Random
      House, pp. 24-44.
          Reprinted from 1953.B16. Reprinted New York: New Amer-
      ican Library, 1966.

23   EMERSON, O. B. "Prophet Next Door," Reality and Myth: Es-
      says in American Literature in Memory of Richard Croom
      Beatty, edited by William E. Walker and Robert L. Welker.
      Nashville, Tenn.: Vanderbilt University Press, pp. 237-
      74.
          Southern reviewers, many of them writers and critics,
      generally accorded Faulkner's books the praise and under-
      standing they deserved. Only a minority of Southern re-
      views of Faulkner's works were hostile. Sanctuary and As
      I Lay Dying were both better received South than North.

24   FIEDLER, LESLIE. "The Death of the Old Men," Waiting for the
      End. New York: Stein and Day, pp. 9-19.
          An impressionistic speculation on the meaning of Faulk-
      ner's literary career. His dramatization of the race
      problem accounts for his lasting influence.

25   FOSTER, RUEL E. "From Yoknapatawpha to Charlottesville:
      Faulkner's Late Migration to a Pleasant Life Among the
      Snobs," National Observer (3 February), p. 22.
          A brief account of Faulkner's activities in Charlottes-
      ville, Va., including an account, by an "intimate friend"
      and riding companion, of Faulkner's reaction to Hemingway's
      death.

1964

26   FRENCH, WARREN. "The Background of Snopesism in Mississippi
          Politics," MASJ, V (Fall), 3-17.
          A comparison of the history of Mississippi politics with
          Faulkner's fictional portrayal suggests that Frenchman's
          Bend in The Hamlet is a microcosm of Mississippi geography
          and demography.

27   FULLER, JOHN. "Novel of the Twenties," NewSt (27 November),
          p. 844.
          Faulkner's sense of comedy, but not his brilliant style,
          shows through in Mosquitoes.

28   GARRETT, GEORGE P., JR. "The Influence of William Faulkner,"
          GaR, XVIII (Winter), 419-27.
          Novelist and poet Garrett comments appreciatively on the
          influence which Faulkner represents for the young writer,
          particularly the Southern writer, and he lists critical
          misconceptions about Faulkner and his "primitivism," his
          "message," and the overemphasis of symbolism. Faulkner's
          film work is proof of his toughness, his craft, and it
          should be studied for influence on his fiction.

29   GIBSON, WILLIAM M. "Faulkner's The Sound and the Fury," Expl,
          XXII (January), Item 33.
          Calling Quentin Faulkner's "last-created" character in
          The Sound and the Fury, the author suggests an origin in
          Dante's Inferno and The Scarlet Letter.

30   GRESSET, MICHEL. "Les larrons," MercdeFr, CCCLI (May), 153-54.
          The Reivers is a warm picaresque tale, minor in tone, a
          kind of benediction.

31   _____. "Temps et destin chez Faulkner," Preuves, No. 155,
          (January), 44-49.
          Taking off from the word "outrage," the essay studies
          how Faulkner builds his world--time is the place where
          history occurs. Faulkner's best passages are those con-
          cerned with movement. "La création d'un univers crucifié
          dans le temps, paradis géographique mué en enfer par
          l'histoire."

32   HAGOPIAN, JOHN V., and MARTIN DOLCH. "Faulkner's 'A Rose for
          Emily,'" Expl, XXII (April), Item 68.
          Replies to 1961.B36 and 1962.B34. The "strand of hair"
          in "A Rose for Emily" means something like a lock which
          Emily has put on the pillow by her lover as a ritual ges-
          ture of farewell (like the ancient Greeks) to her appro-
          priately named love, Homer Barron.

33   HARDY, JOHN EDWARD. "William Faulkner: The Legend Behind
      the Legend," Man in the Modern Novel. Seattle: Univer-
      sity of Washington Press, pp. 137-58.
          Faulkner's use of the Christ story in such books as The
      Sound and the Fury and Light in August is a way of showing
      that modern man carries only fragments of the Christian
      myth, which haunt him like a bad dream and challenge his
      moral consciousness with its potential and its failure.
      Absalom, Absalom! is a profound study of Time and the prob-
      lems of self-discovery in the human family.

34   HATHAWAY, BAXTER. "The Meanings of Faulkner's Structures,"
      EngR, XV (December), 22-27.
          Counterpoint, as in The Sound and the Fury and As I Lay
      Dying, correlates the many points of view in Faulkner's
      fiction. Faulkner must have planned Benjy's section,
      which contains "100" sections, to the point of scissoring
      longer scenes to reach an even number.

35   HILL, ARCHIBALD. "Three Examples of Unexpectedly Accurate
      Indian Lore," TSLL, VI (Spring), 80-83.
          According to comparison with a dictionary of Choctaw,
      Faulkner is probably giving an accurate sense of Choctaw-
      related Chickasaw words in his use of "Yoknapatawpha."

36   HORSCH, JANICE. "Faulkner on Man's Struggle with Communica-
      tion," KM, pp. 77-83.
          [Beebe (1967.B4) and Bassett (1972.A2) list this as
      1963, but Massey (1968.A4) and the Xerox in the Massey
      Collection at University of Virginia, from which the anno-
      tation is derived, have 1964.] Many Faulkner characters
      express different facets of the problem of communication,
      the seductive or deceptive power of words and their in-
      adequacy, and the need or ability to express certain
      things wordlessly.

37   HOVDE, CARL F. "Faulkner's Democratic Rhetoric," SAQ, LXIII
      (Autumn), 530-41.
          Tocqueville's remark that democratic style will be "fan-
      tastic, incorrect, overburdened and loose," because people
      accustomed to struggle require strong language, is easily
      applied to Faulkner's rhetoric. Characteristics of this
      style are a high percentage of superlatives, oxymoron,
      verbs of violent action, and characters who are narrow
      and thus dominated by one or two drives, "preternaturally
      clear." Faulkner's humor keeps these extremes from be-
      coming too strident.

38   HOWELL, ELMO. "William Faulkner and the New Deal," MQ, V
      (Summer), 323-32.
         Brief passages from "The Tall Men" and The Mansion are
      used in conjunction with W. J. Cash's The Mind of the South
      and Thomas Nelson Page, as well as John Faulkner's Men
      Working, to argue that Faulkner admired the yeoman farmer
      and did not like government bureaucracy.

39   HURT, LESTER·E. "Mysticism in 'Go Down, Moses,'" EngR, XV
      (December), 27-30.
         Faulkner's belief in the "reality of the spiritual life"
      is attested to by such stories as "Pantaloon in Black" and
      "The Old People" from Go Down, Moses. In "The Bear,"
      Faulkner asserts the principle of recurrent life, the tri-
      umph over death. Transcendental and Platonic notions
      abound in Faulkner's work.

40   INGE, M. THOMAS. "Faulkner, the Man and His Masks: A Bio-
      graphical Note," Southern Observer, II (March), 55-59.
         We can probably never know Faulkner the man, since none
      of his family or friends or acquaintances were capable of
      comprehending him. Faulkner himself used a variety of
      masks and poses to keep the head-hunting biographers away.
      Some of the poses are reviewed.

41   JANKOVIĆ, MIRA. "Faulknerova Alegoriya Moralne Svijesti,"
      Radovi, V (Winter), 256-65.
         According to an English summary, "Faulkner's Allegory of
      Moral Consciousness," pp. 265-66, Gavin Stevens is the
      chief figure in Faulkner's biblical and chivalric "alle-
      gories." He is the knight of Knight's Gambit, the Gawain
      his name implies.

42   JENSEN, ERIC G. "The Play Element in Faulkner's 'The Bear,'"
      TSLL, VI (Summer), 170-87.
         Accepting the views of Slatoff (1960.A2) and Arthos
      (1948.B1) that Faulkner is pushed by his paradoxical view
      of the incompatibility of art and life to deliberate fail-
      ures, the author sees a principle of unity in the "play
      principle" in Faulkner's work. "The Bear," by focusing on
      the child's initiation through "play" elements, creates
      meaningful ritual in a natural way and thus avoids the
      paradoxes of some of Faulkner's other work. Ike McCaslin's
      repudiation is interpreted in psychoanalytic terms; his
      identity crisis in inconclusive.

43   KALUZA, IRENA. "William Faulkner's Subjective Style," KN, XI
      (No. 1), 13-29.
         Faulkner is a "subjective" writer, presenting his world

(KALUZA, IRENA)
as experience and imposing it on the reader. Elements of style through which he achieves this are discussed. Though he uses abstractions, he projects physical perceptions so well we are involved in his view.

44   KARTIGANER, DONALD M. "The Role of Myth in Absalom, Absalom!" MFS, IX (Winter), 357-69.
        The story of Sutpen and his heirs in Absalom, Absalom! is like the myths of the god-king who must face and recognize his progeny and struggle to see if he must yield succession. The book is also a myth of the South in which Quentin has divided loyalties to the old and new orders.

45   KIMMEY, JOHN L. "The Good Earth in Light in August," MissQ, XVII (Winter), 1-8.
        Offering an antidote to criticism which turns Light in August into a collection of abstractions, particularly Christological ones, the article emphasizes a right relation to the natural world as a touchstone for the novel's characters. Lena, a figure out of the earth, is set against man's rape of the woods--the sawmills of the book-- and his rejection of nature. Lucas Burch, Joanna Burden, Joe Christmas and Hightower all fear, hate, or flee a nature for which they also truly long. Hightower, by his involvement with Joe and Lena, is transformed, and he does not perish at the end but survives.
        Reprinted 1971.A3.

46   KINNEY, ARTHUR F. "'Delta Autumn': William Faulkner's Answer for David H. Stewart," PMASAL, XLIX, 541-49.
        The Ike McCaslin of "Delta Autumn" may not be used to judge the Ike of "The Bear" because Go Down, Moses is not a unified book. The later Ike is merely a reconsideration, a more human and less saintly Ike.
        Reprinted in 1964.A9. See 1961.B66.

47   KLOTZ, MARVIN. "The Triumph Over Time: Narrative Form in William Faulkner and William Styron," MissQ, XVII (Winter), 9-20.
        Faulkner's innovations in The Sound and the Fury and Absalom, Absalom! were necessary to "defeat the intrinsically chronological nature of literary art." The difficulties of Benjy's section are perhaps not resolved even when a reader finishes the book; it must be read again to be fully appreciated, and if that is so, the violation of chronology has been rendered unnecessary. Quentin's section is more narration than stream-of-consciousness, changing to a tech-

1964

(KLOTZ, MARVIN)
nique like that in "The Bear," part four, where Faulkner
attempts to capture the "presentness" of the past. Absalom, Absalom! is likewise "reflexive, depending for final
resolution of disordered materials upon the completion of
the book and the final interworking of the material. There
is no redemption in Faulkner's work; his heroes are heroes,
his villains are villains from beginning to end.

48   LOUGHREY, THOMAS F.   "Aborted Sacrament in Absalom, Absalom!"
      Four Quarters, XIV (November), 13-21.
          Absalom, Absalom! is about the failure of love and the
      South's adherence to a "merciless code." The non-conduc-
      tivity of love in this world is depicted in images of
      stasis and airlessness, of ghastliness. The tombstones he
      is so concerned about become symbols of Sutpen's accom-
      plishment. The aborted ritual of his funeral is one of
      many in the novel and another image of discontinuity. The
      novel illuminates "the lost meaning of sacrament."

49   MacLURE, MILLAR.   Review of Cleanth Brooks, William Faulkner:
      The Yoknapatawpha Country [1963.A1], CanF, XLIX (Novem-
      ber), 188-89.
          Brooks overemphasizes community, does not write enough
      on Requiem for a Nun, and omits reference to the Indian
      stories.

50   MARKOVIC, VIDA.   "Interview with Faulkner," TSLL, V (Winter),
      463-66.
          Translation of a May 1962 interview by a visiting Yugo-
      slav scholar whose questions begin, "Do you like . . .?"
      Faulkner replies politely about minor personal matters and
      his reading.
      Reprinted 1968.A6.

51   MERIWETHER, JAMES B., ed.   "Early Notices of Faulkner by Phil
      Stone and Louis Cochran," MissQ, XVII (Summer), 136-64.
          In 1932, Cochran, who had known Faulkner at the Univer-
      sity of Mississippi, wrote a reminiscence that appeared in
      the Memphis Commercial Appeal (1932.B10). In 1934, Stone,
      Faulkner's friend, published three parts of a proposed
      longer reminiscence and commentary in the short-lived Ox-
      ford Magazine (1934.B26). Both pieces are reprinted, along
      with introduction, notes, and a letter from Stone to Coch-
      ran commenting on an early version of Cochran's essay.

52   MILLGATE, JANE.   "Short Story into Novel: Faulkner's Rework-
      ing of 'Gold is Not Always,'" ES, XLV (August), 310-17.
          A close study of the short story which was revised to

(MILLGATE, JANE)
become chapter two of "The Fire and the Hearth" section of
Go Down, Moses demonstrates the unity of the 1942 book.
"Gold is Not Always" is revised to make Lucas Beauchamp
speak more like the whites, underscoring his independence,
his kinship with the McCaslins, and his pride. The novel
version also clarifies Lucas's relationship with whites,
contributing to the black-white theme of the novel.

53 MILLGATE, MICHAEL. "Faulkner and the Air: The Background of
Pylon," MQR, III (October), 271-77.
The opening of Shushan Airport in New Orleans and the
air show which was held in commemoration lie behind Faulkner's novel Pylon. Included in 1966.A6.

54 MIZENER, ARTHUR. "The American Hero as Gentleman: Gavin
Stevens," The Sense of Life in the Modern Novel. Boston:
Houghton Mifflin, pp. 161-81.
Gavin Stevens, in Intruder in the Dust and Go Down
Moses, is Faulkner's version of the small-town gentleman-
intellectual, a character found in American fiction at
least since Twain's Pudd'nhead Wilson. Whether or not
Faulkner is treating him ironically is not clear. Gavin
struggles manfully to be at home in the small town to
which he is devoted.

55 NATHAN, MONIQUE. "Jeunesse de Faulkner," Preuves, No. 161
(July), 85-88.
White, black and red blood of Faulkner's characters
mingle themselves in The Reivers to do the right thing.

56 PODHORETZ, NORMAN. "Faulkner in the 50's," Doings and Un-
doings: the fifties and after in American writing. New
York: Farrar, Straus, pp. 13-24, 24-29.
Reprints 1954.B58 and 1957.B53.

57 PRICE, REYNOLDS. "Clearer Road Signs in His Country," Book
Week (12 January), p. 5.
Brooks (1963.A1) "underestimates" Faulkner's playfulness,
his solitary pleasure in doing as he pleased.

58 PRICE-STEVENS, GORDON. "Faulkner and the Royal Air Force,"
MissQ, XVII (Summer), 123-28.
Errors about Faulkner's military service are corrected:
he was a cadet in the Royal Flying Corps in Toronto and did
not get abroad or see combat. Faulkner's war fiction is
based on stories he heard and his imagination.

1964

59   RANALD, R. A. "William Faulkner's South: Three Degrees of
      Myth," Landfall, XVIII (September), 329-37.
         No mere regionalist or moderate Southern spokesman,
      Faulkner was the creator of a mythos of twentieth century
      man in terms of his own native soil. He held no brief for
      the old South myth; instead, he created the kind of myth
      that makes reality intelligible and bearable.

60   RICHARDSON, H. EDWARD. "Anderson and Faulkner," AL, XXXVI
      (November), 298-314.
         An account of some relationships between Sherwood Ander-
      son and Faulkner suggests parallels between Anderson's
      fiction and Faulkner's early work. Anderson is suggested
      as the source for the sugarcane grinding scene in Sartoris.
      See Richardson, 1962.B99, and Rideout and Meriwether,
      1963.B69.

61   _____. "The Ways That Faulkner Walked: A Pilgrimage,"
      CarQ, XVII (Fall), 55-66.
         An additional account of a trip to Oxford, Miss. (See
      also his 1965.B58 and 1965.B59) and conversations with
      Phil Stone and Mack Reed. Stone claimed extensive proof-
      reading and revision of Faulkner's work through Sanctuary.
      Reed corrected some impressions about Faulkner's "lounging
      around" the drugstore. Mr. Reed claimed that Faulkner did
      not own a dictionary.

62   RINALDI, NICHOLAS M. "Game Imagery and Game-Consciousness in
      Faulkner's Fiction," TCL, X (October), 108-18.
         Game imagery in Faulkner's work depicts his characters
      approaching life as if it were a contest. Intent on "win-
      ning" and opposing we use other "players." Faulkner's
      characters thereby violate or ignore the verities at the
      heart of the author's moral vision. Frequently they posit
      a fictional cosmic player who opposes them. The relation-
      ships reduced to the inhuman by game-consciousness are eco-
      nomic, sexual, racial, legal, and marital. Ike McCaslin
      is a hero who uses game-consciousness in the good sense.

63   RUBIN, LOUIS D., JR. "Notes on a Rear-Guard Action," The
      Idea of the South, edited by Frank E. Vandiver, Jr.
      Chicago: University of Chicago Press, pp. 27-41.
         Faulkner's theme was that love and courageous compassion
      could put an end to unnecessary human chaos and suffering.
      Since the world he lived in was what it is, Faulkner wrote
      tragedies about the failure of love. Joe Christmas in
      Light in August is trying to define himself on his own con-
      fused terms in a society that demands he be either black

(RUBIN, LOUIS D., JR.)
or white and behave according to the role assigned to one
or the other.

64   SILVER, JAMES WESLEY. Mississippi: The Closed Society. New
York: Harcourt, Brace & World, pp. xi-xiv.
Faulkner's speech to the Southern Historical Association
in Memphis, Tenn., November 1955 is recalled along with a
statement about Faulkner's enduring belief in social justice for all.

65   SLABEY, ROBERT M. "Faulkner's Geography and Hightower's
House," AN&Q, III (February), 85-86.
The author offers a correction to Calvin Brown
(1962.B28), who had erroneously stated that Hightower in
Light in August listened to music from the Presbyterian
Church, by noting that the passage is about two other
churches. The correction actually further corroborates
Brown's identification of Jefferson and Oxford, since
Hightower's back-street house--not the parsonage--is near
"The Ditch," a landmark in both real and fictional towns.

66   _____. "Quentin Compson's 'Lost Childhood,'" SSF, I (Spring),
173-83.
Quentin is narrating "That Evening Sun" (and "A Justice,"
which is not considered in detail) as he prepares to kill
himself in Cambridge. The story explains him and his
suicide. It is a story about the loss of innocence. Unlike Nancy, Quentin can never grasp reality.

67   _____. "Soldiers' Pay: Faulkner's First Novel," RLV, XXX
(No. 3), 234-43.
Joyce and Eliot are influences on the "mythical method"
of Soldiers' Pay.

68   SOWDER, WILLIAM J. "Christmas as Existential Hero," UR, XXX
(Summer), 279-84.
Joe Christmas kills Joanna Burden in Light in August because he cannot bear the idea of bringing a new life into
a meaningless world, although he knows Joanna cannot have
a child. Joe hates sex because it serves a base and use-
less purpose--an existential attitude.

69   SULLIVAN, WALTER. "The Decline of Regionalism in Southern
Fiction," GaR, XVIII (Fall), 300-08.
Faulkner's Snopes trilogy portrays "the decline of regionalism itself as reality and therefore as literary
source." Faulkner should have stopped with The Hamlet.

279

1964

(SULLIVAN, WALTER)
The Town and The Mansion are given over to "social and political clichés of our time."

70   THOMPSON, LAWRANCE.   "Afterword," Sartoris, by William Faulkner. New York: Signet, pp. 304-16.
The romanticism of both Benbows and Sartorises is treated
ironically and extends to Byron Snopes and the returned
black soldier, Caspey. The rhetoric of the novel is not
Faulkner's but lent to his characters. Faulkner's life in
the 20's gave him a detachment from the splendid literary
materials he rediscovered in writing Sartoris. He is not
celebrating the grand families of his novel, and he may be
satirizing their vainglory and destructive self-love.

71   TOMLINSON, T. B.   "Faulkner and American Sophistication," CR,
VII, 92-103.
Faulkner's reception, whether hostile or favorable, has
never seemed to reflect his true worth, which is not all
good. His "tendency towards hollowly sophisticated prose"
and "metaphysical banality" is especially deplored. Light
in August is the key to Faulkner's work.

72   VAHANIAN, GABRIEL.   "William Faulkner: Rendez-vous with
Existence," Wait Without Idols. New York: Braziller,
pp. 93-116.
Yoknapatawpha County is a microcosm of the human condition in the Christian tradition, a world of contingency
where hope nevertheless lives. The Sound and the Fury illustrates: as Easter gives meaning to Good Friday, the
sermon Dilsey hears gives meaning to the events in the
Compson family which precede it. Faulkner's work is an
example of how Christian thought has continued to develop
in a post-Christian world.

73   VICKERY, OLGA W.   "William Faulkner and the Figure in the
Carpet," SAQ, LXIII (Summer), 318-35.
The "possibilities inherent in character" and the problems of individual and common identity, laid out in "an
intricately related series of lyrical stases" in both the
novels and stories, seem to constitute Faulkner's "figure
in the carpet." The stories are briefly discussed in relation to Faulkner's other formal experiments in the "story
novel," the "novel of formal juxtaposition," the "counterpointed novel," and the "fused novel." Incorporated into
1964.A10.

74   WALKER, WILLIAM E. "The Unvanquished: The Restoration of
      Tradition," Reality and Myth: Essays in American Litera-
      ture in Memory of Richard Croom Beatty, edited by William
      E. Walker and Robert L. Welker. Nashville, Tenn.: Vander-
      bilt University Press, pp. 275-97.
          Beneath the incidents in The Unvanquished engendered by
      war--the lying and cheating and killing--are traditional
      human values which repeatedly transcend the chaos of the
      times. Though Granny Millard cultivates in the boys the
      values that will enable them to survive and overcome the
      war and its results, her flaw is that she loses sight of
      her role under God, takes the role of power instead of in-
      strument. Drusilla is also defeated, but by John's reluc-
      tance and Bayard's refusal to advance the cult of violence.

75   WARDLE, IRVING. "Faulkner in Fancy Dress," London Observer
      Weekend Review (25 October), p. 27.
          Mosquitoes is a period piece with stock and lifeless
      characters, but still contains some of Faulkner's powerful
      prose, as in the swamp trek of the young lovers.

76   WHEELER, OTIS B. "Some Uses of Folk Humor by Faulkner,"
      MissQ, XVII (Spring), 107-22.
          Faulkner's early books show relatively little influence
      of folk humor, with the exception of As I Lay Dying. The
      Snopes stories are a chief depository of folk humor. They
      are discussed in terms of point of view, subject matter,
      and humor.
      Reprinted 1973.A9.

77   WILLIAMS, PHILIP. "Faulkner's Satan Sutpen and the Tragedy
      of Absalom, Absalom!" ELLS, No. 45-46 (December), 179-99.
          Quentin is an Ishmael brought to destruction by Sutpen,
      the avatar of Satan at the center of Absalom, Absalom!
      Sutpen is not, as Brooks (1963.A1) thinks, "innocent," but
      fallen; not victim, but cause. The book is a biblical
      tragedy, "an archetypal story of evil."

78   WOLFE, RALPH HAVEN, and EDGAR F. DANIELS. "Beneath the Dust
      of 'Dry September,'" SSF, I (Winter), 158-59.
          Sexual maladjustment motivates the action of Minnie and
      the lynchers in "Dry September."

79   WYNNE, CAROLYN. "Aspects of Space: John Marin and William
      Faulkner," AQ, XVI (Spring), 59-71.
          Bergsonian influence on modern art produces new attitudes
      toward time. The artist John Marin is compared with Faulk-
      ner on the basis of the way both stop time. Curiously,

1964

(WYNNE, CAROLYN)
Faulkner's interest in time is laid to his being a Southerner. Impressionism and futurism provide techniques used
by both artists. No relationships or influences are suggested.

1965 A   BOOKS

1   GWYNN, FREDERICK L., and JOSEPH L. BLOTNER. Faulkner in the
     University: Class Conferences at the University of Vir-
     ginia, 1957-1958, revised edition. New York: Vintage.
        Originally published as 1959.A1; this version makes some
     corrections in transcriptions of the selected tapes of
     Faulkner's interviews and class conferences, etc., during
     his tenure as writer in residence at the University of
     Virginia.

2   HUNT, JOHN W. William Faulkner: Art in Theological Tension.
     Syracuse, N. Y.: Syracuse University Press.
        Faulkner's fiction--as well as his public remarks about
     it--invites attention to the theological implications of
     his work. His "moral vision," so often discerned, moves
     from what man must do to make his life meaningful to what
     God can do that man cannot, emphasizing that traditional
     human virtues must be transcended in order to be fulfilled
     in human existence. The tension in Faulkner's theological
     work is between the Stoic and Christian views; there is no
     dramatic pilgrimage toward meaning in Faulkner's work but
     a constant view, easily discernible in The Sound and the
     Fury, as well as Absalom, Absalom! and "The Bear." Ike
     McCaslin accurately diagnoses the human condition, but fal-
     laciously assumes stoic renunciation is the solution.

3   NILON, CHARLES. Faulkner and the Negro. New York: Citadel.
     Reprints 1962.A3.

4   SMART, GEORGE K. Religious Elements in Faulkner's Early Nov-
     els: A Selective Concordance. UMPEAL, No. 8. Coral
     Gables, Fla.: University of Miami Press.
        The introduction discusses Faulkner and religion and re-
     ligious language in Soldiers' Pay, Mosquitoes, and Sar-
     toris. The main section is a selective alphabetical list
     of religious terms, from Abraham to Zeal, found in these
     works. An appendix lists expletives of religious origin
     and includes statistical charts, and an essay on Christian
     allusions in "Mirrors of Chartres Street." Review by
     Kathleen Higgins, MissQ, XIX (Spring 1966), 90-92, points
     out errors and inaccuracies.

5   WEBB, JAMES W., and A. WIGFALL GREEN, eds. William Faulkner
        of Oxford. Baton Rouge: Louisiana State University Press.
        People in Faulkner's home town recollect him in essays
        and tape-recorded interviews. Early pieces by Phil Stone
        (See 1934.B26) and Louis Cochran (1932.B10) are reprinted
        (See also 1964.B51). Includes excerpt from John Faulkner's
        reminiscence (1963.A2) and an obituary piece by John Fon-
        taine (1962.B46).

1965 B   SHORTER WRITINGS

1   ABSALOM, H. P. "Order and Disorder in The Sound and the
        Fury," DUJ, LVII (December), 30-39.
        All the themes, characters, and events of The Sound and
        the Fury are complexly introduced or prefigured in Benjy's
        section. Even his mentality is a reflection of the family,
        its nature, its specific problems, and its individual re-
        actions. The book represents disciplined art, but control
        never interferes with the reader's sense of its immediacy
        or vitality.

2   ADAMS, RICHARD P. "Faulkner," American Literary Scholarship,
        an annual, 1963, edited by James Woodress. Durham, N. C.:
        Duke University Press, pp. 72-80.
        Adams begins his essay in the first volume in this series
        of compilations of criticism with a brief summary of the
        history of serious treatment of Faulkner's work, which he
        says begins in 1939. He evaluates much of the criticism
        done in 1963, in the process correcting several entries in
        the MLA bibliography. He warns especially against taking
        Faulkner's characters as his spokesmen and applying sim-
        plistic thematic approaches to the fiction.

3   _____. "Recent Scholarship on Faulkner and Hemingway," The
        Teacher and American Literature: Papers Presented at the
        1964 Convention of the NCTE, edited by Lewis G. Leary.
        Champaign, Ill.: National Council of Teachers of English,
        pp. 149-56.
        Adams analyzes briefly "some of the more interesting and
        promising directions" of criticism and research on Faulkner
        and Hemingway.

4   ANTRIM, HARRY T. "Faulkner's Suspended Style," UR, XXXII
        (Winter), 122-28.
        Faulkner's work is filled with the recreation of was, the
        past. Bridging the gap between was and the violent present
        results in Faulkner's difficult language and style, espe-
        cially "parenthetical suspension" and "involuted recapitu-

1965

(ANTRIM. HARRY T.)
lation." Faulkner's failures, when they occur, come from
the often impossible nature of the task he has set himself.

5   BACKMAN, MELVIN. "Sutpen and the South: A Study of <u>Absalom,</u>
<u>Absalom!</u>" <u>PMLA</u>, LXXX (December), 596-604.
The "fact and legend of Southern history" and parallels
to themes in Thomas Sutpen's life are examined, using
W. J. Cash's <u>The Mind of the South</u> and other works, to
show that the "new man," Sutpen, is typical of those who
built the great South and brought about its demise. There
is no simple Sartoris-Snopes division in Faulkner's work.
Quentin, who has sought an answer to modern impotence in
the past, is left unfulfilled; the dilemma of the Southern
present is unsolved. Included in 1966.A1.

6   BELL, HANEY H., JR. "A Reading of Faulkner's <u>Sartoris</u> and
'There Was a Queen,'" <u>ForumH</u>, IV (Fall, Winter), 23-26.
After <u>Sartoris</u> and "There Was a Queen" the Sartoris family is gone forever; their degeneration has been told in
three stages. Includes a genealogy of the family.

7   BOWLING, LAWRENCE E. "Faulkner: The Theme of Pride in <u>The</u>
<u>Sound and the Fury</u>," <u>MFS</u>, XI (Summer), 129-39.
The events of Quentin's last days in <u>The Sound and the</u>
<u>Fury</u> can be analyzed in terms of the way they present par-
allels to his past; they acquire symbolic value--the trout
in the river equals ideality, for example. Quentin's
pride consists in his refusing the various emblems of life
and benison which existence offers him on his last day.
He remains impenitent, rejects life, and dies without understanding.

8   BRADFORD, MELVIN E. "Escaping Westward: Faulkner's 'Golden
Land,'" <u>GaR</u>, XIX (Spring), 72-76.
Faulkner's story of the unreality, corruption, and de-
spair of life in urban California documents his view of
America in mid-passage and shows his affinities with the
Nashville Agrarians. Nature and religion, which go to-
gether, are absent from the life of people who have moved
from the farm to the Golden West.

9   _____. "Faulkner and the Jeffersonian Dream: Nationalism
in 'Two Soldiers' and 'Shall Not Perish,'" <u>MissQ</u>, XVIII
(Spring), 95-100.
"Two Soldiers" and "Shall Not Perish" concentrate on the
plain people and affirm Faulkner's patriotism and the
"Jeffersonian conception of the Republic," which is made

(BRADFORD, MELVIN E.)
up of independent men like the Griers of the two stories.
They are in the mainstream of American experience, "still
powerful and still dangerous and still coming."

10   _____. "Faulkner's 'Tomorrow' and the Plain People," SSF,
II (Spring), 235-40.
"Tomorrow" from Knight's Gambit is an example of Faulk-
ner's sympathetic treatment of the "plain people," the
Southern yeomen, and a statement about their ability to
hope and endure.

11   BRIDGMAN, RICHARD. "As Hester Prynne Lay Dying," ELN, II
(June), 294-96.
The families and lives of Hester Prynne in Hawthorne's
The Scarlet Letter and Addie Bundren in As I Lay Dying are
similar, but Faulkner's story is grimly nihilistic by con-
trast.

12   CABANISS, ALLEN. "A Source of Faulkner's Fable," UMSE, VI,
87-89.
The ancient "Jewish canard, the Taldoth Jesu," a blasphemous gospel parody, is a source for A Fable. Faulkner
may have been projecting a full-scale attack upon Christianity. Appeared as "Eine Quelle zu Faulkners' Die
Fabel,'" in Schweitzer Monatshefte, December 1975.

13   CAMBON, GLAUCO. "Faulkner's 'The Old People': The Numen-
Engendering Style," SoR, N. S. I (January), 94-107.
As in "Pantaloon in Black," the ghostly appearance in
"The Old People" is given as a real datum. Ike is the
Christ who redeems the world from Doom--Adam's fall--
validating Sam's shameful last name, "Fathers," by becom-
ing the symbolic son. Stylistically, by ambiguous pro-
noun reference, Faulkner achieves identification between
Ike, Sam, and the deer. By changing from "he" to "it" in
reference to the ghostly deer later, he accentuates its
mystery and its association with the personified wilderness. Faulkner's style achieves the reestablishment of
Nature as mysterium tremendum in all its mythic richness.
Translation of 1961.B16.

14   CAREY, GLENN O. "William Faulkner as a Critic of Society,"
ArQ, XXI (Summer), 101-08.
Faulkner's fiction demonstrates a lifelong social awareness. He criticizes man and society for their abuse of
institutions and rights, their rapacity and inhumanity.
He contrasts primitivism and modernism, though he remains,
first and last, an artist.

1965

15 CARPENTER, ROBERT ALLEN. "Faulkner 'Discovered,'" Delta Review, II (July-August), 27-29.
The reporter sets down portions of Malcolm Cowley's talk to the 1965 Southern Literary Festival at the University of Mississippi, subsequently printed as part of The Faulkner-Cowley File (1966.A2).

16 CARTER, HODDING. "The Forgiven Faulkner," JIAS, VII (April), 137-47.
A reminiscence by the Greenville, Miss., editor of his first meeting with Faulkner in New Orleans and an account of resentment towards Faulkner's racial views in Mississippi, including letters to newspapers.

17 CLERC, CHARLES. "Faulkner's The Sound and the Fury," Expl, XXIV (November), Item 29.
Faulkner's allusions to St. Francis in The Sound and the Fury are appropriate and knowledgeable, particularly in linking sister-water and bodily death. The allusion is to a canticle by St. Francis.

18 COFFEE, JESSIE. "Faulkner's The Sound and the Fury," Expl, XXIV (October), Item 21.
Nancy, whose bones are mentioned as being in the ditch in The Sound and the Fury, is not, as some have assumed, the prostitute of "That Evening Sun," killed and left unburied, but some large domestic animal.

19 COINDREAU, MAURICE E. "The Faulkner I Knew," Shenandoah, XVI (Winter), 27-35.
A translation, by James S. Patty, of 1963.B23; reprinted 1971.B18.

20 COLLINS, CARVEL. "Faulkner's The Sound and the Fury," The American Novel from James Fenimore Cooper to William Faulkner. New York: Basic Books, pp. 219-28.
The complex and rich under-patterns of The Sound and the Fury, like the Christ story, allusions to Frazer's Golden Bough, to Freud's psychology, and to Macbeth, make it a novel well worth the third reading that will bring it fully alive to the attentive reader. Like Joyce and Eliot, Faulkner built his fiction on a firm and learned structure of references to the literature and ideas of both present and past.

21 FALKNER, MURRY. "The Day the Balloon Came to Town," AH, XVII (December), 46-49.
Reprinted from 1965.A5.

22   FARNHAM, JAMES F. "Faulkner's Unsung Hero: Gavin Stevens,"
        ArQ, XXI (Summer), 115-32.
            Stevens in the Snopes trilogy is one of Faulkner's human
        heroes, like Nancy Mannigoe, V. K. Ratliff, and the Cor-
        poral. They are all "realists"--they accept existence.
        At the end of The Town, Stevens is defeated and puzzled;
        but at the end of The Mansion his eyes are opened to man's
        lot; he sees that man can only do the best he can, doomed
        to lose many of his battles for the good.

23   *FINKELSTEIN, SIDNEY. Existentialism and Alienation in Amer-
        ican Literature. New York: International Publishers,
        pp. 184-97.
            Given the author's definitions, according to American
        Literary Scholarship 1965, "almost everybody" is "existen-
        tialist, alienated, or both"; Marxism is his solution.

24   FLANAGAN, JOHN T. "The Mythic Background of Faulkner's Horse
        Imagery," Folklore Studies in Honor of A. P. Hudson.
        Chapel Hill, N. C.: North Carolina Folklore Society,
        pp. 135-45.
            Horses and riders have a significant mythic and histori-
        cal background, as well as a rich literary tradition in
        Faulkner's work. S. V. Benét's John Brown's Body, D. H.
        Lawrence's St. Mawr, and Robinson Jeffers' Roan Stallion
        are the background.

25   *FOSTER, RUEL E. "Social Order and Disorder in Faulkner's
        Fiction," Approach, No. 55 (Spring), 20-28.
            Bassett, Item AA189.

26   FRADY, MARSHALL. "The Faulkner Place," FurmS, N. S. XIII
        (November), 1-6.
            Account of a visit to Rowan Oak, Faulkner's Oxford,
        Miss., home.

27   GILLEY, LEONARD. "The Wilderness Theme in Faulkner's 'The
        Bear,'" MQ, VI (July), 379-85.
            "The Bear" is not a Romantic elegy for a lost Edenic
        wilderness; all his life Ike exploits the wilderness, and
        the killing of Old Ben is a part of it. Life is destruc-
        tive and man unwittingly hurries the world to its death.
        The serpent at the end--the image of death--represents no-
        bility of spirit and self-transcendence.

28   GIORGINI, J. "Faulkner and Camus," Delta Review, II (July-
        August), 31, 74-79.
            Camus agreed philosophically with Faulkner's remarks on
        man and on young writers.

1965

29   GOSSET, LOUISE Y. Violence in Recent Southern Fiction. Dur-
      ham, N. C.: Duke University Press, pp. 29-47.
         Faulkner's violence is an index of his horror at human
      baseness; it de-romanticizes the South. Faulkner presents
      violence in an almost classical manner; the effect of his
      language and style is to place it off-stage. He proves
      "how much men can endure."

30   GRANT, DOUGLAS. "The Last of William Faulkner," Purpose and
      Place. London: Macmillan, pp. 183-88.
         Faulkner's power to give us his world is demonstrated
      again in The Reivers. Surveying his career, one sees how
      he excels in comedy as in tragedy, and with perhaps greater
      naturalness and ease. The matter of Yoknapatawpha, evoked
      for the last time, illuminates the South and the whole hu-
      man comedy.

31   GREEN, A. WIGFALL. "William Faulkner's Flight Training in
      Canada," UMSE, VI, 49-57.
         Information in this article is supplemented and cor-
      rected by 1964.B58, 1966.B53, and 1968.B47.

32   GREENBERG, ALVIN. "Shaggy Dog in Mississippi," SFQ, XXIX
      (December), 284-87.
         Lena's portion of Light in August is a kind of "shaggy
      dog story" in which incredible adversity is capped by un-
      derstatement and anticlimax. The same method is in "Old
      Man." The method is proof of Faulkner's concept of the
      human ability to bear and transcend any difficulties.

33   HALL, SUSAN CORWIN. "William Faulkner," Hawthorne to Heming-
      way: An Annotated Bibliography of Books from 1945 to 1963
      about nine American Writers, edited by Robert H. Woodward.
      New York: Garrett Publishing Co., pp. 51-56.
         Annotations are abstracts of book reviews published in
      American Literature; the books range from studies to col-
      lections of essays to anthologies of original material by
      Faulkner.

34   HAMBLEN, ABIGAIL ANN. "Faulkner's Pillar of Endurance:
      Sanctuary and Requiem for a Nun," MQ, VI (July), 369-75.
         Sanctuary and Requiem for a Nun depict evil and traf-
      ficking in evil with unalloyed repulsiveness, but at the
      same time they show that the existence of evil does not
      eradicate the existence of good. Ruby and Nancy, Horace
      and Gavin, despite weakness, show the lengths to which
      men and women can go to help other human beings and see
      that justice is done. Evil, unlike good, is self-destruc-
      tive.

288

35   HAWKINS, E. O. "Faulkner's 'Duke John of Lorraine,'" AN&Q,
      IV (September), 22.
           The reference in Absalom, Absalom! to Duke John of Lor-
      raine who married his sister must be to John V, Count of
      Armagnac, whose history includes an incestuous marriage.

36   _____. "Jane Cook and Cecilia Farmer," MissQ, XVIII (Fall),
      248-51.
           An event which Faulkner uses in The Unvanquished, In-
      truder in the Dust, and Requiem for a Nun comes from the
      history of Oxford, Miss.: the story of a young girl who
      carves her name in a window with her ring while watching
      Confederate troops pass by.

37   HORNBACK, VERNON T., JR. "The Uses of Time in Faulkner's The
      Sound and the Fury," PLL, I (Winter), 50-58.
           Function of time in the Jason and "Dilsey" sections of
      The Sound and the Fury is best understood in light of Flem
      Snopes and "The Bear," respectively. Quentin, as Sartre
      correctly saw, is trapped in the past. Jason is obsessed
      with time as an economic factor--time is money. Dilsey
      sees time as duration and accepts it as lived.

38   HOWARD, EDWIN. "Anecdote: The Faithful Smith," Delta Review,
      II (July-August), 35.
           Report of an interview with Earl Wortham of Oxford,
      Miss., who shoed Faulkner's horses, including some infor-
      mation about Chester Carruthers driving young Col. Falk-
      ner's car to Memphis.

39   _____. "Foote-note on Faulkner," Delta Review, II (July-
      August), 37, 80.
           The author reports reactions to Faulkner's death by two
      younger writers and friends, Shelby Foote and Joan Wil-
      liams.

40   HOWELL, ELMO. "In Ole Mississippi: Faulkner's Reminiscence,"
      KM, pp. 71-81.
           In The Reivers, Faulkner reaffirms his faith in the old
      Southern standards, though his Mississippi South is not
      exactly like the Virginia South of Thomas Nelson Page.

41   _____. "William Faulkner and the Andrews Raid in Georgia,
      1862," GHQ, XLIX (June), 187-92.
           Faulkner's "account of the Andrews Raid" and the Great
      Locomotive Chase in The Unvanquished shows his "casual at-
      titude toward facts." He changes place, time and circum-
      stances.

1965

42 HOWELL, ELMO. "William Faulkner and the Chickasaw Funeral,"
    AL, XXXVI (Winter), 523-25.
        In the burial rites of Sam Fathers in "The Bear" Faulk-
    ner confuses Chickasaw and Choctaw practice. Included in
    1967.B45.

43 HOWORTH, LUCY SOMERVILLE. "The Bill Faulkner I Knew," Delta
    Review, II (July-August), 38-39, 73.
        One of the members recounts the forming of the student
    drama club, The Marionettes, at the University of Missis-
    sippi in 1920, and Faulkner's part in the group.

44 KARTIGANER, DONALD M. "Faulkner's Absalom, Absalom!: The
    Discovery of Values," AL, XXXVII (November), 291-306.
        Sutpen outrages Jefferson because he is a raw version of
    its own principles. Sutpen's quest is to achieve, in even
    less time than one generation, all the symbols of aristo-
    cratic Southern "valley" society. Charles Bon is the moral
    center of the novel; the ability to fully believe in him
    is the imaginative act that places Sutpen's design in
    proper perspective. Bon seeks a true communion; Sutpen
    uses everyone to achieve respectability.

45 KIRK, ROBERT W. "Faulkner's Anse Bundren," GaR, XIX (Winter),
    446-52.
        Though not central to As I Lay Dying, Anse Bundren re-
    mains one of Faulkner's best comic creations. His mock
    heroism is applied not to fulfilling Addie's wish but to
    satisfying his own desires. The ending of the novel is
    good low comedy.

46 KLOTZ, MARVIN. "Procrustean Revision in Faulkner's Go Down,
    Moses," AL, XXXVII (March), 1-16.
        Klotz argues the superiority of the short-story versions
    of material in Go Down, Moses. His view is that Faulkner
    sacrificed aesthetics to economics by trying to make a
    novel out of short story material.

47 KUNKEL, FRANCIS L. "Christ Symbolism in Faulkner: Prevalence
    of the Human," Renascence, XVII (Spring), 148-56.
        Joe Christmas is an inverted Christ figure and the Cor-
    poral in A Fable is a secular, not a divine Christ. For
    Faulkner the Christ story was simply the "best-known reve-
    lation of...love and honor...compassion and sacrifice."

48 LAWSON, LEWIS A. "The Grotesque-Comic in the Snopes Trilogy,"
    L&P, XV (Spring), 107-19.
        The grotesque-comic characterization of the threatening

(LAWSON, LEWIS A.)

Snopeses is a form of meiosis, belittling, done in order
to render them less powerful. This diminution occurs by
virtue of Faulkner's depicting Flem and other Snopeses in
deformed, comic, or physically reduced terms.

49 LEHAN, RICHARD. "Faulkner's Poetic Prose: Style and Meaning
in 'The Bear,'" CE, XXVII (December), 243-47.

Language identifies Lion and Boon as alike in "The Bear";
both are natural forces tamed by man and, hence, mechanistic. They are turned against pristine Nature and destroy
it. Ike is the Christlike hero. The story is a myth of
the post-Civil War South.

50 LONGSTREET, STEPHEN. "My Friend, William Faulkner," Part I,
Cavalier, XV (April), 58-61; Part II, Cavalier, XV (May),
50-52, 85-86.

A friend and one-time screenwriter, novelist Longstreet
reminisces about Faulkner in Hollywood, his antipathies to
screenwriting, his love of Mississippi and horses. Faulkner maintained he only wrote about people, not ideas.

51 MACLAREN-ROSS, JULIAN. Memoirs of the Forties. London: Alan
Ross, p. 10.

The author remembers a meeting with British publisher
Jonathan Cape who claimed close acquaintance with Faulkner
and the publishing history of Sanctuary. Cape said Faulkner had forgotten to put in the part about Popeye's childhood and "went back to his nightwatchman's shack and over
a jug of corn liquor got out the missing chapter." Since
the book was in press, Faulkner said, "Let's put it in
last and the hell with them." Cape noted that Faulkner
was polite and had only one foot as a result of a war in-
jury.

52 MERIWETHER, JAMES B. "Editor's Preface," Essays, Speeches
and Public Letters of William Faulkner. New York: Random
House, pp. vii-ix.

Faulkner himself once planned a collection of essays,
though smaller and less inclusive than this compilation.
Many pieces of his nonfiction prose reflect his sense of
responsibility to society in the latter part of his career.
Where possible, original texts or manuscripts have been
used.

53 MELLARD, J. M. "Faulkner's 'Golden Book': The Reivers as
Romantic Comedy," BuR, XIII (December), 19-31.

Northrop Frye's types of comic character are used to

1965

(MELLARD, J. M.)
explicate figures in The Reivers; Frye's concept of the
structure and purpose of comedy and romance are used to
discuss the form of the book--a romantic comedy. The novel
fulfills Faulkner's comment that he would someday write a
"Golden Book."

54   MITCHELL, CHARLES. "The Wounded Will of Faulkner's Barn
      Burner," MFS, XI (Summer), 185-89.
         In "Barn Burning," Ab Snopes' wounded heel is emblematic
      of his satanic unsubmissiveness and it is also the explana-
      tion of why he is a barn burner. The barn, containing a
      planter's harvest, is an equivalent of the Garden of Eden.
      Sarty is, by contrast to his father, whom he effectively
      destroys, a proper union of love and will, a union of child
      and man created by his act in the story.

55   MUSTE, JOHN M. "The Failure of Love in Go Down, Moses," MFS,
      X (Winter), 366-78.
         Contrary to much criticism which has been puzzled by Go
      Down, Moses or which has been content to concentrate on
      the five-part "The Bear," Muste argues for the book's vital
      and thoroughly prepared unity. The first three stories in-
      troduce the theme of love and its concomitants; the next
      three, on hunting, underline parallels between the white's
      treatment of the Negro and the wilderness. It is not the
      loss of a hunting preserve for the privileged but the fail-
      ure to understand and appreciate a way of life, an older
      order, that is the tragedy here. Ike's repudiation of his
      heritage is bad and foolish; even his occupation as a car-
      penter allies him with the lumbering outfit that rapes the
      woods. See corrections, 1966.B35.

56   PRATT, J. NORWOOD. "Faulkner's The Sound and the Fury," Expl,
      XXIII (January), Item 37.
         Quentin's attention to the sparrow in the opening of his
      section of The Sound and the Fury is a reference to two
      poems by Catullus about Lesbia's sparrow and a connection
      to St. Francis. The sparrow is, thus, Caddy and death,
      both objects of Quentin's unnatural love. See comment,
      1966.B24.

57   PRICE-STEPHENS, GORDON. "The British Reception of William
      Faulkner, 1929-1962," MissQ, XVIII (Summer), 119-200.
         A chronological narrative account of the reception of
      Faulkner's novels in the British press and intellectual
      journals fills this issue of MissQ. The compiler evaluates
      the criticism, notes trends, misconceptions. Appendices

(PRICE-STEPHENS, GORDON)
provide publication dates of Faulkner's books in England,
a list of reviews of the novels in British papers, and a
list of general articles and sections in books.

58 RICHARDSON, H. EDWARD. "The Ways That Faulkner Walked: A
Pilgrimage," ArQ, XXI (Summer), 133-45.
Previously published, 1964.B61.

59 _____. "Oxford, Mississippi," Books and Bookmen (February),
pp. 39-40, 48, 33.
Impression of a visit to Oxford, two weeks after Faulkner's death. See also 1964.B61 and 1965.B58.

60 RODRIGUES, EUSEBIO L. "Time and Technique in The Sound and
the Fury," Literary Criterion, VI, 61-67.
Faulkner's vision is of despair; he does not seek the
root of evil in the world. The Sound and the Fury exhibits
his technique of recreating time in terms of space.

61 ROSSKY, WILLIAM. "The Reivers and Huckleberry Finn: Faulkner
and Twain," HLQ, XXVIII (August), 373-87.
The boy narrator, the relationship between Lucius, Boon
and Ned, the fear of capture, the "shrewd practice," the
struggle with conscience, and more all make The Reivers
similar to Huckleberry Finn. The most important similarity
is the "out-of-time" experience in both--Huck and Jim on
the raft, the "reivers" in their car.

62 _____. "The Reivers: Faulkner's Tempest," MissQ, XVIII
(Spring), 82-93.
The Reivers roams easily in Faulkner's own early life
and through almost all his previous fiction, creating,
with the repeatedly emphasized "grandfatherly" voice of
the narrator an easy, content, philosophical tone like
Shakespeare's The Tempest: an overview of life that recog-
nizes evil but displays faith in man's powers of regeneration. It represents a firm statement of Faulkner's final
acceptance of life.
Reprinted 1973.A9.

63 RYAN, JACK. "The Lady of the Dakota," Delta Review, II (July-
August), 44-45, 71-72.
Ruth Ford, interviewed in New York, talks briefly about
Faulkner; article illustrated with a letter from Faulkner
to Ben Wasson of Greenville, Miss., Faulkner's one time
agent in New York.

1965

64   SADLER, DAVID F. "The Second Mrs. Bundren: Another Look at
      the Ending of As I Lay Dying," AL, XXXVII (March), 65-69.
         Evidence in As I Lay Dying leads to the conclusion that
      Anse Bundren has not married the "new Mrs. Bundren." The
      duck-shaped woman represents the triumph of an attitude to
      life totally different from Addie's and of the ignoble mo-
      tives of Anse and the other family members.

65   SANDERSON, JANE. "A Kind of Greatness," Delta Review, II
      (July-August), 15-17.
         Account of the author's "crashing" of Jill Faulkner's
      wedding as a reporter for the Memphis Commercial Appeal
      and of Faulkner's reaction when she identified herself.

66   SIMON, JOHN K. "The Scene and the Imagery of As I Lay Dying,"
      Criticism, VII (Winter), 1-22.
         Faulkner uses synaesthesia, images of chaos, and empha-
      sizes the interrelationship between place and people and
      events to create the physical world of As I Lay Dying.

67   SIMPSON, LEWIS P. "Isaac McCaslin and Temple Drake: The
      Fall of New World Man," Nine Essays in Modern Literature,
      edited by Donald E. Stanford. Baton Rouge, La.:
      Louisiana State University Press, pp. 88-106.
         The fable of hope and failure which the European lived
      in America is shadowed starkly in Faulkner's work. "The
      Bear" especially depicts the hope of the wilderness life
      and the second Fall in its exploitation by technology.
      The story of Temple Drake in Sanctuary and Requiem for a
      Nun depicts the far-flung result in the modern world of
      the second fall, but suggests a new redemption in the form
      of accepting the destructive along with the merciful in
      human nature.

68   STEINBERG, AARON. "Absalom, Absalom!: The Irretrievable Bon,"
      CLAJ, IX (September), 61-67.
         We can never know for sure if Charles Bon in Absalom,
      Absalom! is Negro because Quentin Compson as informant is
      changed by the story he uncovers and may change the story
      by his efforts to know. If Henry Sutpen is the source of
      Quentin's knowledge, Henry is himself suspect. Lacking
      objective guides to the validity of Bon's race, we are left
      with a novel seriously faulted in the second half, where
      an essentially unreal story is being told.

69   _____. "Intruder in the Dust: Faulkner as Psychologist of
      the Southern Psyche," L&P, XV (Spring), 120-24.
         A depth psychology study of racism in Detroit, Michigan,

(STEINBERG, AARON)
is used to evaluate and explain Faulkner's "profound understanding of the Southern psyche." Chick Mallison's digging
up the grave in Intruder in the Dust is symbolically a
probing of the white psyche. Gavin Stevens' speeches are
white rationalizations provoked by Charles's discoveries.

70   STERN, RICHARD G. "Faulkner, at Home Abroad," BA, XXXIX (Autumn), 408-11.
Faulkner's Italian reception is reviewed briefly; what
Italian critics find most notable in Faulkner's work is his
ocean-like passion and control, his experimentation with
form, and the greatness of his fiction.

71   STONE, EMILY WHITEHURST. "Faulkner Gets Started," TQ, VIII
(Winter), 142-48.
Phil Stone's widow recounts aspects of her late husband's
relationship with Faulkner, quoting Stone's statements
about his hand in Faulkner's early writing.

72   _____. "How a Writer Finds His Material," Harper's, CCXXXI
(November), 157-61.
Phil Stone's widow recounts some family anecdotes from
her late husband which formed the basis of some of Faulkner's fiction, especially "The Bear."

73   STRANDBERG, VICTOR. "Faulkner's Poor Parson and the Technique
of Inversion (or William Faulkner: An Epitaph)," SR,
LXXIII (April-June), 181-90.
Disputing Tate (1963.B83), the author sees the biblical
practice of "inversion," the "technique of offering one's
followers the absolute antithesis of what reason and experience would predict" as central to Faulkner's work, not
the Greco-Trojan Myth of Yankees versus cultivated Southerners. The setting of Rev. Shegog's sermon in The Sound
and the Fury and the preacher's appearance are prime examples of the technique. The ending of the novel is
"Isaianic: the last shall be first"--and thus positive.

74   TERREY, JOHN. "Faulkner and Hemingway: Implications for
School Programs," The Teacher and American Literature:
Papers Presented at the 1964 Convention of the NCTE. Cham-
paign, Ill.: NCTE, pp. 157-62.
The writer urges a more sophisticated approach to Faulk-
ner's work; Faulkner is international, not regional.

75   TISCHLER, NANCY P. "William Faulkner and the Southern Negro,"
SUS, VII (June), 261-65.
Faulkner never felt able to penetrate the Negro mind; he

1965

(TISCHLER, NANCY P.)
believed the white man could never understand the black. He believed in social justice achieved by black evolution and Southern good will. He speaks for the "best of Southern conservatism."

76   TOLLIVER, KENNETH R. "Truth and the Poet," Delta Review, II (July-August), 48, 67-69.
The writer reports on Robert Penn Warren's talk at the Southern Literary Festival at the University of Mississippi in the spring of 1965. See also 1965.B78.

77   TUCK, DOROTHY. "Faulkner: Light in August: The Inwardness of the Understanding," Approaches to the Twentieth Century Novel, edited by John Unterecker. New York: Crowell, pp. 79-107.
The least experimental of Faulkner's great novels (those between 1929 and 1936), Light in August still achieves the aim of the experiments in the others by involving the reader in the story. Repeatedly falling from innocence-- in each of the three cases a woman and sexuality are involved--Joe does not achieve self-awareness. For the participants, and especially the townspeople of the novel, there are chiefly antinomies of character and experience, but for the reader Faulkner has brought the disparate elements together into a timeless evocation of life's complexity.

78   WARREN, ROBERT PENN. "Faulkner: The South and the Negro," SoR, N. S. I (July), 501-29.
Following a general discussion of Faulkner's South and how it is presented--the variety, the change from a society where there was the occasional hope of meaningful action-- Warren writes of racism, specifically slavery, as the "doom" to truth and the ideal. The Negro is the central character in Faulkner's work. The black man's struggle-- and he is seldom simply black but more often black-white, to emphasize his common ancestry with the uncomprehending whites--is not so much for social equality as with fate, the human condition.
Reprinted 1966.A8.

79   WEBB, JAMES W. "Rowan Oak, Faulkner's Golden Bough," UMSE, VI, 39-47.
The history of Faulkner's home in Oxford is recounted, including some anecdotal account of how he bought and named it.

80   WEBER, ROBERT. "Raskol'nikov, Addie Bundren, Meursault: Sur
      la continuité d'un mythe," Archiv, CCII (#2), 81-92.
         The myth of "Byronism" is studied in Dostoevsky, Camus,
      and Faulkner's As I Lay Dying, where it is Addie Bundren
      who suffers from the illusions of appearance. She suffers
      from the inability to achieve union with others except in
      conventional ways and through conventional words, like
      love, which deceive. The myth of Byronism is alive in mod-
      ern literature.

81   WEISGERBER, JEAN. "Faulkner et Dostoëvski: The Sound and the
      Fury," RLC, XXXIX (July-September), 406-21.
         Characters, events, and themes in The Sound and the Fury
      are compared with those in Dostoevsky's Crime and Punish-
      ment and The Brothers Karamazov.

82   WELTY, EUDORA. "The Humanities: Something More On Camera:
      Welty on Faulkner," Major Notes (Millsaps College Alumni
      Magazine), VI (April), 25-27.
         Miss Welty and two of her creative writing students at
      Millsaps College, Jackson, Miss., discuss Faulkner and
      "Spotted Horses" on a television program, of which this
      publication is a transcription.

83   WEST, PAUL. The Modern Novel. New York: Hilary House,
      Vol. II, pp. 253-58.
         Rebellious in form and content, Faulkner's work is "non-
      literary"; the best of his work, that between 1929 and
      1936, depicts an unexplainable world of mystery inhabited
      by characters who are responsible for their own fates.
      Later work is episodic or composed of previously published
      stories.

84   WIDMER, KINGSLEY. The Literary Rebel. Carbondale, Ill.:
      Southern Illinois University Press, pp. 118-20.
         Joe Christmas in Light in August is the epitome of the
      "American Joe," the generic domestic rebel in a land of
      repression and hate, his condition emphasized by his puta-
      tive blackness and a circular determinism.

85   WYNN, LELIA CLARK. "A Bookman's Faulkner," Delta Review, II
      (July-August), 33-35, 57.
         A collector recounts how a collection of Faulkner's books
      and related material was assembled. Illustrations include
      book title pages, an inscription, and a letter from Faulk-
      ner.

1966

1966 A   BOOKS

1   BACKMAN, MELVIN. Faulkner: The Major Years. Bloomington,
       Indiana: Indiana University Press.
         Close reading is the basis of essays on ten Faulkner nov-
       els from Sartoris through Go Down, Moses, excluding Pylon.
       Backman concludes that there is an acute spiritual and bio-
       graphical link between Faulkner and his work which demon-
       strates his isolation and introspection, his "identifica-
       tion" with Quentin Compson. With As I Lay Dying he shows
       sympathy and humor. His social involvement increases in
       Light in August and Absalom, Absalom! Six of the essays
       were published in some form previously (See 1956.B4,
       1959.B8, 1961.B5, B6, 1962.B10, and 1965.B5).

2   COWLEY, MALCOLM. The Faulkner-Cowley File: Letters and Mem-
       ories, 1944-1962. New York: Viking Press.
         Cowley gives his version of the compiling and editing of
       The Portable Faulkner, including letters exchanged with
       Faulkner, and also recounts subsequent dealings between
       Faulkner and himself.

3   GOLD, JOSEPH. William Faulkner: A Study in Humanism from
       Metaphor to Discourse. Norman, Oklahoma: University of
       Oklahoma Press.
         Faulkner's fiction falls into two periods, before and
       after World War II, with correspondences to his own con-
       trasting of the Old and New Testaments of the Bible. Like
       the Old Testament, his early work is powerfully imagistic,
       folkloristic, and mythical. After the war and the Nobel
       Prize, his work, like the New Testament, is philosophical,
       filled with ideas and arguments, his characters become sym-
       bols, ideas not human archetypes. "The Bear" is pivotal,
       showing Faulkner's tendency to rhetorical discourse, while
       at the same time it deals in archetypes and myths. Ike is
       a pathetic failure, as Faulkner's reference to his lack of
       posterity repeatedly emphasizes, whereas Faulkner's heroes
       are those who act, like the children in Intruder in the
       Dust and The Reivers. Faulkner is religious but not ortho-
       dox, and humanistic, but without a "rational dialectic."

4   HOFFMAN, FREDERICK J. William Faulkner, revised edition.
       New York: Twayne.
         Adds to 1961.A3 a section on The Reivers, one on the
       overall achievement, and an updated bibliography.

5   HOLMES, EDWARD M. Faulkner's Twice-Told Tales: His Re-Use
       of His Material. The Hague: Mouton.
         A brief (98 pages) discussion of differences between

(HOLMES, EDWARD M.)
versions of material Faulkner incorporated eventually into
the Snopes trilogy, The Unvanquished, Go Down, Moses, or
other books is coupled with a consideration of his reuse
of other fictional materials. The appendix lists "many of
the repeated uses of characters, episodes, and...
phraseology" in the novels and stories.

6   MILLGATE, MICHAEL. The Achievement of William Faulkner. New
     York: Random House. London: Constable.
     A full critical study of Faulkner's career, the book be-
     gins with a documented biographical essay and discusses the
     novels chronologically, summarizing the critical tradition
     and analyzing with the help of Faulkner's manuscripts and
     typescripts, including unpublished material. A separate
     chapter is devoted to the short stories. Faulkner's "ma-
     jor concerns, like those of all great artists, were ulti-
     mately moral." He has been misread because he has been
     underestimated. His solid provinciality of subject matter
     was a base for his exploration of universal human themes.
     He is to be ranked alongside Dickens.
     Reprinted New York: Vintage, 1971.

7   PEPER, JÜRGEN. Bewusstseinseinlagen des Erzählens und Er-
     zählte Wirklichkeiten dargestellt an Amerikanischen Roman-
     en des 19. und 20. Jahrhunderts insbesondere am Werk Wil-
     liam Faulkners. Leiden: E. J. Brill.
     The work of Joseph Conrad is a reference point for a
     discussion of Faulkner's use of narrative point of view.
     In novels like Pylon and Absalom, Absalom! the observers
     find, like Marlow in Lord Jim, that facts bring confusion
     while an imaginative response to the mystery of character
     has better results and produces more truth. Sutpen, who
     believes in facts and plans, is defeated by truths of the
     human heart he does not comprehend. Absalom, Absalom! is
     analyzed for language and structure, while Faulkner's other
     novels are discussed in passing.

8   WARREN, ROBERT PENN, ed. Faulkner: A Collection of Critical
     Essays. Englewood Cliffs, N. J.: Prentice-Hall.
     A new essay by Warren (See 1966.B75) introduces a selec-
     tion of previously published essays, and excerpts from es-
     says and books. Includes 1939.B3, 1939.B26, 1939.B28,
     1941.B4, 1946.B2, 1946.B9, 1948.B20, chapter six of
     1954.B75, 1958.B9, 1966.A6, portions of chapter seven of
     1934.B15, 1957.B33, 1957.B38, 1959.A4, portions on Absalom,
     Absalom! from 1959.A5 and from 1963.A1, material from
     1948.B16, 1948.B28, 1949.B20, 1954.B58, 1954.B59, 1959.B43,

1966

(WARREN, ROBERT PENN)
1965.B78, and also brief pieces from 1933.B11, 1933.B13,
1936.B9, 1937.B9, 1942.B7, 1949.B36, 1950.B1, 1951.B13,
1951.B16, 1951.B22, 1951.B52, 1952.A1, 1955.B19, 1960.B26,
1963.B84, and genealogies of fictional families from
1963.A1 and the map of Yoknapatawpha from Absalom, Absalom!

1966 B   SHORTER WRITINGS

1   ADAMS, RICHARD P.   "Faulkner," American Literary Scholarship
     an annual, 1964, edited by James Woodress.   Durham, N. C.:
     Duke University Press, pp. 73-81.
        Adams surveys and evaluates Faulkner criticism for 1964,
     and corrects several listings in the MLA Bibliography.

2   ALTER, JEAN V. "Faulkner, Sartre, and the New Novel," Sym-
     posium, XX (Summer), 101-12.
        Along with Dostoevsky, Proust, and Kafka, Faulkner is
     recognized by the French "new novelists" as one of the lib-
     erators of the form and as a specifically important in-
     fluence on their own work. Sartre (See 1938.B14 and
     1939.B28) is mediator through his existential analysis of
     Faulkner's work. Sartre's essays are analyzed for the im-
     pact they may have had on young writers.

3   BENSON, WARREN R. "Faulkner for the High School: 'Turn-
     about,'" EJ, LV (October), 867-69, 874.
        Violence and stylistic difficulties make Faulkner hard
     to teach at the high school level. He writes as a "nega-
     tivist," demonstrating man's good qualities by their more
     frequent absence. "Turnabout" is a good story to teach,
     because it demonstrates the virtues Faulkner venerated and
     the qualities he urged on young people in the Nobel Prize
     Speech.

4   BLEIKASTEN, ANDRÉ. "Faulkner et le nouveau roman," Les
     Langues Modernes, LX (July-August), 422-32.
        Despite the fact that Faulkner's structural experiments,
     his use of time, and his rhetoric are anathema to the "new
     novel," Faulkner's work, especially Absalom, Absalom!, has
     been a real influence on writers like Robbe-Grillet,
     Nathalie Sarraute, and Claude Simon.

5   BLOTNER, JOSEPH. "William Faulkner: Roving Ambassador," In-
     ternational Educational and Cultural Exchange, Summer, pp.
     1-22.
        The author recounts Faulkner's trips abroad on behalf of
     the U. S. Department of State, his feelings about the
     trips, and their impact upon the peoples he visited.

6   BRADFORD, MELVIN E. "Brotherhood in 'The Bear': An Exemplum
     for Critics," ModA, X (Winter), 278-81.
          Faulkner's view that the human condition implies ines-
     capable responsibilities is dramatized in "The Bear." Ike
     McCaslin is wrong to deny his obligations to his family and
     land. Brotherhood requires "elder brothers," too, a role
     Ike is not willing to play.

7   _____. "Faulkner, James Baldwin, and the South," GaR,
     XX (Winter), 431-43.
          Bradford argues against Baldwin (1962.B11) that Faulk-
     ner's position on race is consistent; he places Faulkner
     in a philosophical context related to Southern ideas of
     community, individual responsibility, and distrust of le-
     galistic ukase.

8   _____. "Faulkner's 'That Evening Sun,'" CEA, XXVIII (June),
     1, 3.
          Nancy's reference to herself as "nigger" means that she
     is recognizing her own weak character and her responsibil-
     ity, rather than the community's, for her plight. The story
     is about "the potential for tragedy in the human condition."
     See rejoinder, 1966.B33.

9   BROWN, CALVIN S. "Faulkner's Manhunts: Fact Into Fiction,"
     GaR, XX (Winter), 388-95.
          The author recounts paper-chases in the woods around Ox-
     ford, Miss., directed for teen-agers by the young Faulkner,
     and speculates about their relation to Faulkner's fiction:
     the manhunts in "Red Leaves," Light in August, Absalom,
     Absalom!, "Was," and minor episodes elsewhere.

10   CAPPS, JACK L. "West Point's William Faulkner Room," GaR, XX
     (Spring), 3-8.
          The memorial room at the U. S. Military Academy at West
     Point, a replica of Faulkner's writing room at his Oxford
     home, is described along with dedication ceremonies, in-
     cluding a reprinting of Joseph Blotner's speech on Faulk-
     ner's family and his personal relationships to the mili-
     tary. The collections of books and secondary material in
     the room are described briefly.

11   CHAPMAN, ARNOLD. "William Faulkner: The Demonic Novel," The
     Spanish American Reception of United States Fiction, 1920-
     1940. Berkeley: University of California Press, pp. 127-
     50, 216-20.
          From 1933, with Lino Novas Calvo's "El demonio de Faulk-
     ner" (1933.B16), there has been a steady Spanish-American

1966

(CHAPMAN, ARNOLD)
    interest in Faulkner. The reception of Faulkner's work is
discussed; a bibliography lists translations and criticism.
Many critics found him too obscure or violent.

12   COINDREAU, MAURICE E. "Preface to The Sound and the Fury,"
    translated by George M. Reeves, MissQ, XIX (Summer),
    107-15.
       Reeves's brief introduction gives the background to
Coindreau's influential work on Faulkner, both his articles on the novels or his prefaces and the translations
he has done.
    Reprinted from 1938.B7; included in 1971.B18.

13   COWLEY, MALCOLM. "A Fresh Look at Faulkner," SatR (11 June),
    pp. 22-26.
       Based on material in 1966.A2.

14   _____. "Introduction," The Viking Portable Faulkner, revised
    and expanded edition. New York: Viking, pp. vii-
xxxiii.
       Revision of 1946.B2.

15   _____. "The Solitude of William Faulkner," AtlM, CCXVII
    (June), 97-98, 101-06, 108-15.
       A prepublication extract from 1966.A2.

16   DICKERSON, MARY JANE. "Some Sources of Faulkner's Myth in As
    I Lay Dying," MissQ, XIX (Summer), 132-42.
       The Demeter-Persephone story is a basis for the waste-
land tale of sterility and crippled family relationships
in As I Lay Dying. As corn spirit, Addie Bundren is linked
to pig and horse as was the goddess in Frazer's Golden
Bough. She is the dying goddess and Dewey Dell represents
the thwarted rebirth. Poems from A Green Bough are used
to underscore the argument.

17   DILLINGHAM, W. B. "William Faulkner and the 'Tragic Condi-
    tion,'" Edda, LIII, 322-35.
       Both self-deception and the nature of things, the evil
which simply exists, can destroy man's identity, creating,
in Faulkner's words, the "most tragic condition that an individual can have--to not know who he is." The Sound and
the Fury and Absalom, Absalom! illustrate the power of illusion.

18   DOYLE, CHARLES. "The Moral World of Faulkner," Renascence,
    XIX (Fall), 3-12.
       Faulkner's attitude, though not orthodox, is religious
in that he insists on man's fallen state, on the objective

(DOYLE, CHARLES)
value of ethics, and on the possibility of moving from sin toward perfection. The worst evil is the failure to love. Alienation is one of his chief themes. "The Bear" is pivotal. Faulkner's work is an "example of the transformation of the aesthetic consciousness into the moral consciousness."

19   DUNN, RICHARD J. "Faulkner's Light in August, Chapter 5," Expl, XXV (October), Item 11.
Joe Christmas murders Joanna Burden when her treatment of him brings together the forces which have already misshaped his life: misdirected religious belief and frustrated human love. Joe's "It's because she started praying over me...." is the key statement.

20   EDEL, LEON. The Modern Psychological Novel. New York: Grosset and Dunlap, pp. 97-102, 162-76.
The impressionism of Faulkner's stream of consciousness style is a poetic evocation of images not heretofore possible for prose fiction. Dilsey's true time sense in The Sound and the Fury emphasizes the decay of the Southern gentry and the South's fantasy life devoted to the dead past. "That Evening Sun" demonstrates Faulkner's theme: the childhood discovery of the adult world of death, suffering, bigotry, and evil.
Reprints 1955.B16 with 1962.B43.

21   FRANKLIN, ROSEMARY. "Animal Magnetism in As I Lay Dying," AQ, XVIII (Spring), 24-34.
Cash makes Addie's coffin in As I Lay Dying with beveled seams to counteract the forces of animal magnetism which radiate from the corpse's longitudinal center through 360 degrees. Nineteenth-century pseudo-science is used to explain the context. The "magnetism" is a fitting description of the influence Addie, even dead, exerts on her family. It is also a metaphor for clairvoyance.

22   FREDRICKSON, MICHAEL A. "A Note on 'The Idiot Boy' as a Probable Source for The Sound and the Fury," MinnR, VI, 368-70.
Wordsworth's ballad is a probable source for the characterization of Benjy Compson who has the same birth date (April 7) as Wordsworth's idiot. Parallels are argued.

23   FRENCH, WARREN. "A Troubled Section--'A Little Sweetening for the Chaps,'" The Social Novel at the End of an Era. Carbondale, Ill.: Southern Illinois University Press, pp. 18-41.
The Hamlet can be seen as a social novel depicting the rise of "Snopesism" from the end of Reconstruction to the

1966

(FRENCH, WARREN)
Depression. The Hamlet is not about the demagogic politics
which developed in the South but it does depict the culture
which produced the politicians and their followers.

24   GARMON, GERALD M. "Faulkner's The Sound and the Fury," Expl,
XXV (September), Item 2.
The sparrow identified as from Catullus (1965.B56) is too
common a figure for sex and death to be so explicitly identified. An alternative from Absalom, Absalom! is offered
as explanation.

25   GATLIN, COL. JESSE C., JR. "Of Time and Character in The
Sound and the Fury," HAB, XVII (Autumn), 27-35.
Time in Faulkner is unmeasurable and uncapturable because
it is a flux, a continuum, like Bergson's durée. In the
four characters of The Sound and the Fury Faulkner shows
us that to be aware of duration alone is to be a slave to
perception, while to be aware of social time alone is to
be a slave to conception. Overbalance either way is bad.
Benjy is the extreme, conscious only of duration; Quentin
finds time to be an enigma; Jason has no conception of duration. Dilsey strikes the balance. Faulkner differs
from Bergson in that his duration seems to exist in a cir-
cular track, not a constantly new forward line.

26   GLICKSBERG, CHARLES I. Modern Literature and the Death of
God. The Hague: Martinus Nijhoff, pp. 119-21.
Faulkner is "neither Christian nor anti-Christian"; he
can identify with all his characters and all points of
view because he is a great fabulist. His tragic vision
offers no redemption, only the human ability to bear suffering with courage.

27   GOLD, JOSEPH. "No Refuge: Faulkner's Sanctuary," UR, XXXIII
(Winter), 129-35.
An indictment of modern society on all fronts, Sanctuary
remains tour de force, its characters unbelievable as hu-
mans and many of its scenes unnecessary.

28   GORMAN, THOMAS R. "Faulkner's Ethical Point of View," CEA,
XXVIII (June), 4-6.
In some 75 short stories, Faulkner shows the complexity
and sincerity of his moral viewpoint, repeating the Calvary
of the human heart, reiterating that man must know and fear
himself and that the meek shall endure.

29   GRESHAM, JEWELL H. "Narrative Technique of William Faulkner's
        Form," NassauR, I (Spring), 103-19.
            Irrationality and violence are twin "structural motifs"
        in Faulkner's work. He uses three devices--a special hand-
        ling of time, special language to circumvent linguistic
        limitations in contemporary English, and multiple perspec-
        tives in point of view. Examples are discussed.

30   GRESSET, MICHEL. "Psychological Aspects of Evil in The Sound
        and the Fury," MissQ, XIX (Summer), 143-53.
            Each element of character in The Sound and the Fury dem-
        onstrates the presence of evil in a world which is both
        linear--decadent--and cyclic--subject to fatality. The
        Negro characters, who live in horizontal instead of ver-
        tical, downward time, are a foil to the whites, but they
        do not save a world that ends with Benjy's howling.
        Reprinted, revised, 1970.A6.

31   _____, ed. "Valéry Larbaud et les débuts de Faulkner en
        France," Preuves, CLXXXIV, 26-28.
            An introduction and a series of letters from Valéry Lar-
        baud to Maurice E. Coindreau from 1932-33 about translating
        Faulkner and about the preface to the French translation of
        As I Lay Dying.

32   HARRISON, ROBERT. "Faulkner's 'The Bear': Some Notes on
        Form," GaR, XX (Fall), 318-27.
            Discussions of myth and archetypal patterns in "The Bear"
        are illuminating but should not be extended to create
        statements about theme, making everything a Christ allegory
        or its equivalent. The distorted chronology of the story
        gives historical density. Intellectual key to the story
        is section four, where Ike's inheritance in all its forms
        is presented.

33   HOGAN, PATRICK G. "Faulkner: A Rejoinder," CEA, XXVIII
        (June), 3.
            The author questions Bradford (1966.B8) on his claim that
        the community and the Compsons "fail" Nancy in "That Eve-
        ning Sun" and discusses the relationships between them.

34   _____. "Faulkner's New Orleans Idiom: A Style in Embryo,"
        LaS, V, 171-81.
            A study of the language of Faulkner's New Orleans writ-
        ing points out its peculiar qualities and the way it fore-
        shadows the writing to come.

1966

35   HOGAN, PATRICK G., DALE A. MYERS, and JOHN E. TURNER.
      "Muste's 'Failure of Love in Faulkner's Go Down, Moses,'"
      MFS, XII (Summer), 267-70.
      The authors correct errors in Muste's article (1965.B55).

36   HOLMAN, C. HUGH. "William Faulkner: The Anguished Dream of
      Time," Three Modes of Southern Fiction. Athens, Ga.: Uni-
      versity of Georgia Press, pp. 27-47, 73-82.
      The Deep South, different from Glasgow's Tidewater and
      Wolfe's mountains, is Faulkner's literary province. The
      histories of his fictional families, especially McCaslin,
      Compson, Sartoris, Sutpen and Snopes, reflect the histori-
      cal experience of the area. Discussing Absalom, Absalom!,
      the author wonders if Faulkner will have the same appeal
      and power when his great issue, race, is not such a pub-
      licly volatile one. A concluding chapter summarizes the
      contrasts between Glasgow, Faulkner and Wolfe, and is re-
      printed 1972.B49.

37   HOWELL, ELMO. "Mark Twain, William Faulkner, and the First
      Families of Virginia," MTJ, XIII (Summer), 1-3, 19.
      Faulkner's ambivalent attitude toward his Virginia "ori-
      gin" is compared to Mark Twain's feeling for Virginia as
      expressed in Huckleberry Finn and Pudd'nhead Wilson.

38   _____. "A Note on Faulkner's Presbyterian Novel," PLL,
      II (Spring), 182-87.
      Light in August is unsatisfactory because the characters
      are not drawn from life in North Mississippi but are alle-
      gorical. Its extreme Calvinism is also misplaced, since
      that is actually alien to the South where Faulkner lived.
      McEachern especially is artificial, a stage character.

39   _____. "A Note on Faulkner's Emily as a Tragic Heroine,"
      Serif, II (No. 3), 13-15.
      Emily in "A Rose for Emily" murders Homer because her
      finer Southern nature reasserts itself; he is a vulgar,
      common Yankee and her affair with him is wrong, so she
      puts a clear end to it. There is no evidence of necro-
      philia. The killing is mad, but a moral act which keeps
      Emily's ideal intact.

40   _____. "William Faulkner's New Orleans," LaHist, VII,
      229-40.
      The author gives an anecdotal account of Faulkner's per-
      sonal and literary relationships with New Orleans.

41   HOWELL, JOHN M. "Hemingway and Fitzgerald in Sound and Fury,"
      PLL, II (Summer), 234-42.
            Faulkner parodies Hemingway and Fitzgerald in The Sound
      and the Fury; there are parallels between Benjy and Jake
      Barnes of The Sun Also Rises and images similar to those
      in The Great Gatsby.

42   INGE, M. THOMAS. "Donald Davidson on Faulkner: An Early Rec-
      ognition," GaR, XX (Winter), 454-62.
            Introduces and reprints reviews of Faulkner's first three
      books which appeared in Davidson's book page in the Nash-
      ville Tennessean. See 1929.B3, 1927.B4, 1926.B5.

43   KAPLAN, HAROLD. "The Inert and the Violent: Faulkner's Light
      in August," The Passive Voice: An Approach to Modern Fic-
      tion. Athens, Ohio: Ohio University Press, pp. 111-30.
            Dualities of mind and body, opposing dual aspects of
      characters like Joanna or Joe and opposites like Joanna and
      Lena, Bunch and Burch, Hightower and Christmas, create the
      thematic and dramatic conflicts of Light in August. In the
      end, the natural triumphs, "the recompense of tragedy," but
      tragedy itself is not understood. Hightower has felt pity
      but remains outside the mystery.

44   KOWALCZYK, RICHARD L. "From Addie Bundren to Gavin Stevens,"
      CEJ, II (No. 1), 45-52.
            Faulkner's dissatisfaction with the communicative power
      of language expresses itself in two ways in his novels:
      in his intervention in a monologue with heavily rhetorical
      forms to force a meaning and in characters who flee reality
      by substituting words for meaning.

45   LEACH, MACEDWARD. "Folklore in American Regional Literature,"
      JFI, II (December), 376ff.
            Faulkner, in a brief discussion, is cited for creating
      the "finest regional humorous situations in American liter-
      ature," especially The Hamlet and The Reivers.

46   LEVITH, MURRAY J. "Unity in Faulkner's Light in August,"
      Thoth, VII (Winter), 31-34.
            Unity in Light in August, with its many plots, is
      achieved by the physical and thematic connections between
      characters.

47   LYDENBERG, JOHN. "Nature Myth in Faulkner's The Bear," Myth
      and Literature: Contemporary Theory and Practice, edited
      by John B. Vickery. Lincoln, Nebraska: University of
      Nebraska Press, pp. 257-64.
      Reprinted from 1952.B29.

1966

48   LYTLE, ANDREW. "The Son of Man: He Will Prevail," "Regenera-
     tion for the Man," "The Town: Helen's Last Stand," The
     Hero With the Private Parts. Baton Rouge, La.: Louisiana
     State University Press, pp. 103-28, 129-36, 137-47.
     Reprints 1955.B37, 1949.B20, and 1957.B51.

49   McHANEY, THOMAS L. "Faulkner Borrows from the Mississippi
     Guide," MissQ, XIX (Summer), 116-20.
        In the narrative introduction to the second act of Req-
     uiem for a Nun, Faulkner baldly borrowed his guidebook ter-
     minology about Jackson, Miss., from Mississippi: A Guide
     to the Magnolia State, one of the state guides created by
     the WPA Federal Writers' Project and published in 1938.
     Passages are presented for comparison.

50   _____. Review of Joseph Blotner, William Faulkner's Library:
     A Catalogue (1964.A2), MissQ, XIX (Winter), 44-48.
        The review notes the absence from Faulkner's library of
     many books he had acknowledged as influential or had other-
     wise identified as important to him. The form and lack of
     annotation of the catalogue are questioned and several er-
     rors noted.

51   *MATERASSI, MARIO. "Le prime prove narrative di William Faulk-
     ner," Paragone, XVII (June), 74-92.
        American Literary Scholarship 1966, p. 82; reprinted
     1968.A5.

52   MILLGATE, MICHAEL. "William Faulkner, Cadet," UTQ, XXXV (Jan-
     uary), 117-32.
        Records in Toronto and interviews with men who trained
     at the same time as Faulkner provide further information
     about Faulkner's service in the Royal Air Force in Canada.
     Faulkner's stories of the RAF and of combat apparently
     came from his reading, his imagination, and his sense of
     the way things are, based on some personal participation
     in training for World War I.

53   *MINER, WARD L. "The Southern White-Negro Problem Through the
     Lens of Faulkner's Fiction," Journal of Human Relations,
     XIV, 507-17.
        Bassett, Item AA209.

54   MORILLO, MARVIN. "Faulkner's The Sound and the Fury," Expl,
     XXIV (February), Item 50.
        Swiggart's explanation of Byron's "wish" (1963.B83) is
     expanded by discovering revealing allusions to the relevant

(MORILLO, MARVIN)
passage from Don Juan in Sartoris, "Divorce in Naples,"
and A Fable. The meaning of the allusion in The Sound and
the Fury is extended to include a reference by Shreve to
incest.

55   MOSES, W. R. "Victory in Defeat: 'Ad Astra' and A Farewell
to Arms," MissQ, XIX (Spring), 85-89.
The author suggests parallels between A Farewell to Arms
and Faulkner's story "Ad Astra."

56   *MOTYLEVA, TAMARA L. Zarubezhnyi roman segodnia [The Foreign
Novel Today]. Moscow: Sovietsky Pisatel, pp. 176-212.
Faulkner's work and career is surveyed in the context of
other foreign writers. One photograph.

57   MULLEN, PHIL. "William Faulkner, Great Novelist, Also a Great
and Gentle Man," Osceola (Ark.) Times (22 December), pp.
1-4, 6-7.
The former associate editor of the Oxford (Miss.) Eagle,
in a new editorial position, reminisces about his relationship with Faulkner, and reproduces Faulkner material from
the Oxford paper, including photographs and letters.

58   NESTRICK, WILLIAM V. "The Function of Form in 'The Bear,'
Section IV," TCL, XII (October), 131-37.
Stylistically a fragment, Section IV of "The Bear" sus-
pends time and action while it brings the whole of human
history behind Ike McCaslin's act of repudiation and, by
its rhetoric and punctuation, forces in the reader a repudiation, formal in this case, of life's conventions.

59   O'CONNOR, WILLIAM VAN. "Faulkner, Hemingway, and the 1920's,"
The Twenties: Poetry and Prose, edited by Richard E.
Langford and William E. Taylor. Deland, Fla.: Everett
Edwards Press, pp. 95-98.
Comments on the similarities between Faulkner and Heming-
way, with emphasis on A Farewell to Arms and The Wild
Palms, follow a brief biographical introduction.

60   PEARCE, RICHARD. "Faulkner's One Ring Circus," WSCL, VII (Autumn), 270-83.
Light in August is, in form, comic, its characters like
those of the comic strip. Bergson's Laughter helps explain
how Faulkner is shocking us out of established notions.
The novel is not strictly naturalistic, for we do not know
the truth of Christmas's heredity. The rigidity of social
roles creates the predicament of the novel.
Reprinted 1970.B60.

1966

61 PEAVY, CHARLES D. "An Early Casting of Benjy: Faulkner's
    'The Kingdom of God,'" SSF, III (Spring), 347-48.
       The author points out parallels of theme and description
    between "The Kingdom of God," one of Faulkner's New Orleans
    sketches, and The Sound and the Fury. The idiot, in both
    places, is used to show the inhumanity, or love, of others.

62 _____. "The Eyes of Innocence: Faulkner's 'The Kingdom of
    God,'" PLL, II (Spring), 178-82.
       Flower names, flower symbolism, biblical references point
    up parallels between Faulkner's New Orleans sketch and The
    Sound and the Fury. In both pieces the idiot is used to
    symbolize both innocence and a warning against self-love.

63 _____. "Faulkner's Use of Folklore in The Sound and the
    Fury," JAF, LXXIX (July-September), 437-47.
       Flower-lore, superstition, folk expressions and beliefs
    are found in The Sound and the Fury.

64 POIRIER, RICHARD. A World Elsewhere: The Place of Style in
    American Literature. New York: Oxford University Press,
    pp. 78-83.
       "The Bear," an example of uniquely American writing in
    which the "reader's assumptions about reality" are dis-
    placed, is about "relinquishment," a fact reflected in the
    demands the style makes on Faulkner's readers, who are
    forced to perceive intuitively much as Ike does.

65 POMMER, HENRY F. "Light in August: A Letter by Faulkner,"
    ELN, IV (September), 47-48.
       Replying to a query about an apparent textual crux in
    Light in August, Faulkner said that the "Him" on p. 222
    of the Modern Library text should be "Ham," but the expla-
    nation was later revealed to be false on the basis of ex-
    amination of MS and TS of the novel. Faulkner had origi-
    nally written simply "him."

66 PRICE, LAWRENCE MARSDEN. The Reception of United States Lit-
    erature in Germany. Chapel Hill, N. C.: University of
    North Carolina Press, pp. 152-57, 217-18.
       Faulkner's reception in Germany is discussed in narra-
    tive form; a separate bibliography of important German ar-
    ticles is included.

67 ROGERS, KATHARINE M. The Troublesome Helpmate: A History of
    Misogyny in Literature. Seattle, Washington: University
    of Washington Press, pp. 252-57.
       Faulkner presented women as either too self-assertive or

1966

(ROGERS, KATHARINE M.)
as mindless animals, distrusting both types at one time or
another. Faulkner projects his own dread of women onto
his characters.

68   *SCHMIDTBERGER, LOREN F. Faulkner's Absalom, Absalom! A Critical Commentary. New York: Barrister Publishing Company.
A study aid to the Faulkner novel from a firm specializ-
ing in bar notes, literature study and examination guides.
Listed in the National Union Catalogue Author List, 1968-
72, Vol. 84.

69   SPRATLING, WILLIAM. "Chronicle of a Friendship: William
Faulkner in New Orleans," TQ, IX (Spring), 34-40.
Spratling, the artist and draftsman who was Faulkner's
roommate in New Orleans and companion to Europe, reminisces
about their lives, including parties, story-telling, an ac-
count of the production of Sherwood Anderson & Other Famous
Creoles and anecdotes from the trip to Europe.
Reprinted in File on Spratling, 1967.B93.

70   SUTHERLAND, RONALD. "As I Lay Dying: A Faulkner Microcosm,"
QQ, LXXIII (Winter), 541-49.
Devices of style and technique, themes and ideas in As I
Lay Dying provide a key to the reading of all Faulkner's
work. It may be his most perfect work.

71   TeSELLE, SALLIE McFAGUE. Literature and the Christian Life.
New Haven: Yale University Press, pp. 181-85.
In the historical world of Absalom, Absalom!, Faulkner
reflects and creates human experience in all its difficulty, giving the kind of awareness of life which is important
to the Christian if he is to understand and love his followers.

72   TURAJ, FRANK. "The Dialectic in Faulkner's A Fable," TSLL,
VIII (Spring), 93-102.
A Fable dramatizes the conflict between orthodoxy, order
at all costs, and a simple humanity, with the masses of men
in between. Orthodoxy takes many forms, and may be idealistic. Platitudes like "for God and country" will be man's
epitaph if man does not follow the simple messages of some
corporal Christ. The Runner offers the glimmer of hope.

73   WALTERS, THOMAS N. "On Teaching William Faulkner's 'Was,'"
EJ, LV (February), 182-88.
"Was" is the best introduction to Faulkner for eleventh
grade students. Chief subjects for consideration are

1966

(WALTERS, THOMAS N.)
Faulkner's use of time, humor, parallel structure, narrative form, and symbolism. "Was" is a humorous tale of a
better time from an old family memory, with a number of
symbolic images given prominent display.

74   WARREN, JOYCE W. "Faulkner's 'Portrait of the Artist,'"
      MissQ, XIX (Summer), 121-31.
         Gordon of Faulkner's Mosquitoes seems modeled on Joyce's
      Daedalus, and passages from the novel suggest Faulkner's
      knowledge of Joyce's Portrait of the Artist. Gordon has
      Stephen's silence, exile, and cunning; he seems to be aware
      of Stephen's notions of epiphany and the "Passion week of
      the heart." Faulkner's artist figure emphasizes the "ag-
      ony" of life, while Joyce's character seeks the "ecstasy."

75   WARREN, ROBERT PENN. "Introduction: Faulkner: Past and Fu-
      ture," Faulkner: A Collection of Critical Essays, edited
      by R. P. Warren. Englewood Cliffs, N. J.: Prentice-Hall,
      pp. 1-22.
         Though in the sense that he is a genius Faulkner is un-
      explainable, it is also demonstrable that aspects of his
      art are due to the fact that he grew up in a "cut-off,
      inward-turning, backward-looking" South caught in the com-
      plexities of the twentieth century. He had both the ele-
      giac vision of what had been and of what might have been,
      and the sure sense of latent violence and catastrophe. He
      explored his visions with technical virtuosity and lacked,
      for a long time, both a proper hearing and a proper under-
      standing. Cowley's Portable Faulkner and the post-World
      War II generation discovered him and gave him an audience.
      Now a little overpraised, his work needs sensible and dis-
      cerning criticism to illuminate individual items among the
      canon.

76   WEBB, JAMES W. "Faulkner Writes A Fable," UMSE, VII, 1-13.
         Anecdotes about Faulkner's knowledge of World War I and
      his writing habits precede an account of the writing of A
      Fable. Faulkner's outline of the novel, written on the
      wall of his "office" at Rowan Oak, is given in transcrip-
      tion.

77   *WILNER, HERBERT. "Aspects of American Fiction: A Whale, a
      Bear, and a Marlin," Americana-Austriaca, edited by Klaus
      Lanzinger. Vienna: W. Braumiller, pp. 229-46.
         Bassett (1972.A2), Item N122.

1967 A   BOOKS

1   FALKNER, MURRY C.   The Falkners of Mississippi: A Memoir.
     Baton Rouge, La.:   Louisiana State University Press.
          Reminiscences by one of Faulkner's brothers about the
     family background, their growing up, and later years of
     his own and his brothers' lives.

2   KALUZA, IRENA.   The Functioning of Sentence Structure in the
     Stream-of-Consciousness Technique of William Faulkner's
     "The Sound and the Fury":   A Study in Linguistic Stylis-
     tics.   Krakow: Jegellonian University Press.
          A linguistic and stylistic examination of nonverbal pas-
     sages in the first three sections of The Sound and the Fury
     is used to explore the nature and function of Faulkner's
     stream-of-consciousness technique in the novel.   Assuming
     as true Luster's claim that Benjy is congenitally "deaf and
     dumb," the author finds Benjy's "ideolect" to be "ritualis-
     tic stylized language," monolithic in perception; he does
     not realize his own existence.   Quentin's ideolect distorts
     standard patterns of language; he is "complex, quick, in-
     telligent and sensitive, but emotionally unstable."   His
     language seems to epitomize Faulkner's own subjective lan-
     guage.   Jason's ideolect is nervous, colloquially careless,
     a "common speech medium" appropriate to the fact that it
     is more monologue than stream-of-consciousness.
     Reprinted Philadelphia: Folcroft Press, 1970.   See essay
     review by Gunter, 1969.B38.

3   RICHARDSON, KENNETH E.   Force and Faith in the Novels of Wil-
     liam Faulkner.   The Hague: Mouton.
          In all Faulkner's novels destructive and creative forces
     struggle for mastery over the individual and the community.
     The passive, rigid, unresponsive father (Sartoris, The
     Sound and the Fury, Light in August, and Absalom, Absalom!)
     is opposed by the spiritual wilderness father ("The Bear");
     the lustful entrapping female by the mother figure; the
     Snopeses by the defenders of community.   Faulkner's view
     of man has changed, beginning with "The Bear" and culminat-
     ing most clearly in the Nobel Prize speech and A Fable,
     where he dramatizes his belief in man's toughness, his
     fight against evil, his "immortal soul."

1967 B   SHORTER WRITINGS

1   BALDANZA, FRANK.   "The Structure of Light in August," MFS,
     XIII (Spring), 67-78.
          Faulkner's principal structural method is closely akin

313

1967

(BALDANZA, FRANK)
to the short-story anthology--the grouping of individual
stories into a whole by thematic repetitions; Sartoris,
The Sound and the Fury and Absalom, Absalom! are offered
as examples, and Light in August is given detailed study
to illustrate the point. The principal theme is the outcast: Hightower and Burden as pariahs, Lena and Joe as
orphans and wanderers. Pursuit and flight, religious and
racial dogma, and a score of additional themes--using the
word in a musical sense--are examined. Faulkner was most
comfortable writing short, static scenes which he stitched
together by thematic repetition.

2   BARNETT, SUZANNE B. "Faulkner's Relation to the Humor of the
Old Southwest," JOFS, II (Winter), 149-65.
Faulkner's fullest use of material out of the tradition
of frontier humor is in The Hamlet and other Snopes books.
Some of Faulkner's writing may be compared to George Wash-
ington Harris's Sut Lovingood stories.

3   BAUM, CATHERINE B. "'The Beautiful One': Caddy Compson as
Heroine of The Sound and the Fury," MFS, XIII (Spring),
33-44.
The four sections of The Sound and the Fury trace Caddy
through the stages of her life and the impact she has at
each stage upon members of the Compson family. Her childhood affects Benjy; her adolescence and loss of innocence
affects Quentin; her adulthood, when she is an economic in-
teger, affects Jason. Defeated by Jason, Caddy disappears
altogether at last; the events of section four are the result. Critics have been too harsh on her; her actions are
a natural result of her own self-less love, the family's
deterioration, and Jason's machinations.

4   BEEBE, MAURICE. "Criticism of William Faulkner: A Selected
Checklist," MFS, XIII (Spring), 115-61.
Books and shorter writings on Faulkner are divided into
a long general section and sections organized alphabetically for books and stories. Revision of 1956.B6.

5   *BLACKWELL, LOUISE. "Faulkner and the Womenfolk," KM, pp. 73-
77.
According to American Literary Scholarship 1967, the author finds that Faulkner's women characters are not easily
characterized because they are individualized.

6   BLEIKASTEN, ANDRÉ. "L'espace dans Lumière d'aout," BFLS,
XLVI (December), 406-20.
Faulkner manipulates space as well as time in his fic-

314

(BLEIKASTEN, ANDRÉ)
    tion. An idea of space--Yoknapatawpha County--lies at the
base of Faulkner's discovery of his fictional material, and
either journeys or established places figure prominently in
the novels. Lena and Joe, opposites, both move in space,
but Lena orders and compares as she travels, while Christmas is always victim, at the mercy of his vain searching.
"La route" and "la rue"--the pastoral and the hell of the
cities--characterize the different journeys in Light in
August. The ideas of Gaston Bachelard are used to discuss
images of space and enclosure, of entry and exit, which
play important roles throughout the novel.

7   BLOTNER, JOSEPH. "Faulkner in Hollywood," Man and the Movies,
      edited by W. R. Robinson. Baton Rouge, La.: Louisiana
      State University Press, pp. 261-303.
         Faulkner's Hollywood years are recounted, including his
film work, his attitude toward movie writing and west coast
life. Faulkner knew he had to compromise some, but he used
Hollywood to keep his own work going; he survived and suc-
ceeded where many others failed.
      Reprinted Baltimore, Md.: Pelican Books, 1969.

8   BLUESTEIN, GENE. "The Blues as a Literary Theme," MassR,
      VIII (No. 4), 593-617.
         Though far from understanding blues and black American
music, Faulkner observed much of it accurately and comes
closer than any writer up to his time to a true use of it.
Rev. Shegog's sermon in The Sound and the Fury is a fine
example of the "singing sermon."

9   BOSWELL, GEORGE W. "Folkways in Faulkner," MissFR, I (Fall),
      83-90.
         Folk language, folk literature, folk action, folk sci-
ence, and "folk honor" in Faulkner's fiction are discussed,
with examples.

10   BRADFORD, MELVIN E. "All the Daughters of Eve: 'Was' and
      the Unity of Go Down, Moses," ArlQ, I (Autumn), 28-37.
         The obligations men have to land and women, and the so-
cial relations which the "two together compel men to sustain" are central to Go Down, Moses. "Was" introduces
these themes: women involve men in life, complicate their
existence and end their idealism. By defying nature, Buck
postpones the inevitable. Women bring community, provide
for continuation.

1967

11   BRADFORD, MELVINE E. "The Gum Tree Scene: Observations on
       the Structure of 'The Bear,'" SHR, I (Summer), 141-50.
           The last two pages of "The Bear," concerning Boon and the
       squirrels, predict an ominous future for the impiety of the
       present age. Ike's error earlier is to take the route of
       humility alone in his approach to life, thus denying the
       necessary stewardship that preserves proper existence.
       Boon takes pride, manifested by aggression. The ideal is
       a balance of the two.

12   _____. "On the Importance of Discovering God: Faulkner and
       Hemingway's The Old Man and the Sea," MissQ, XX (Summer),
       158-62.
           Faulkner's laudatory review of The Old Man and the Sea
       reveals his metaphysic--that creation implies a creator
       who rewards "endurance" by giving man "pity" to see and af-
       firm the difficult common mortal lot. Bradford refers to
       the piece as Faulkner's only review (See Early Prose and
       Poetry and Essays, Speeches, and Public Letters).

13   BRIEN, DOLORES E. "William Faulkner and the Myth of Woman,"
       RS, XXXV, 132-40.
           Faulkner's men and women are estranged because the old
       code of spotless Southern womanhood has broken down. His
       fictional women are largely abstractions seen through the
       eyes of male characters who have created a mythic cult.
       His men may be characterized by their attitudes to women.
       Neither hater nor worshipper of women, Faulkner is a sympa-
       thetic observer of the dilemma of beings caught between the
       need for self-identity and man's myth of womanhood.

14   BROSS, ADDISON C. "Soldiers' Pay and the Art of Aubrey
       Beardsley," AQ, XIX (Spring), 3-23.
           Beardsley's influence on Faulkner's Soldiers' Pay in-
       cludes the role and descriptions of Januarius Jones, Mar-
       garet Powers, and Cecily Saunders. The play of light and
       dark in descriptions and imagery of clothed figures and
       gesturing hands are also Beardsleyesque.

15   BROWN, WILLIAM R. "Faulkner's Paradox in Pathology and Salva-
       tion: Sanctuary, Light in August, Requiem for a Nun,"
       TSLL, IX (Autumn), 429-49.
           Contrary to some opinion (e.g., Canby, 1936.B5 and Geis-
       mar, 1942.B7), Sanctuary is moral; a pervasive imagery of
       evil and uncleanness describes the perpetrators of modern
       immorality. Popeye, like Joe Christmas in Light in August,
       is a "sociopath," an asocial, aggressive, guiltless man.
       In Requiem for a Nun, Nancy has Popeye's role of illuminat-

(BROWN, WILLIAM R.)
ing Temple's evil, with the important difference that Nancy
is consciously a redeemer.

16   BRUCCOLI, MATTHEW J. "A Source for Sartoris?" MissQ, XX
      (Summer), 163.
          The twins Dolly and Polly Sartoris who were in the
      1922-23 Broadway play Two Little Girls in Blue could have
      suggested the surnames of the twin characters in Faulk-
      ner's 1929 novel.

17 · BRUMM, URSULA. "Geschichte als Geschehen und Erfahrung: Eine
      Analyse von William Faulkners Absalom, Absalom!" Archiv,
      CCIV (May), 26-50.
          As most critics have noted, Absalom, Absalom! is con-
      cerned with the meaning and nature of history. There is a
      dialectic in the novel--interaction between history as
      fact and history as "observation." Henry and Quentin, in
      their final confrontation, which is the dropping into place
      of the last key to the mystery, represent the coming to-
      gether of fact and speculation. Chapters six through eight
      reveal the results of that meeting.

18   BUTLER, FRANCELIA, and R. H. W. DILLARD. "Parnassus in the
      1920's: Floyd Dell Contemplates His Own Period," TSL, XII,
      131-48.
          In a 1960 interview, Dell mentions his dislike of Faulk-
      ner's work.

19   CARPENTER, THOMAS P. "A Gun for Faulkner's Old Ben," AN&Q,
      V (May), 133-34.
          Ben is hard to kill in "The Bear" because the hunters are
      undergunned, perhaps a deliberate expression by Faulkner of
      the thoughtlessness and cruelty of the Southern hunter.

20   CLARK, WILLIAM G. "Is King David a Racist?," UR, XXXIV, 121-
      26.
          Sutpen in Absalom, Absalom! is not a stereotyped Southern-
      er; he is not concerned with social disapproval when he
      acts to prohibit his daughter's marriage to a man who is
      partly black. He acts because of his life experience,
      chiefly the encounter with the Negro butler which sends
      him on his search for a dynasty.

21   COFFEE, JESSIE A. "Empty Steeples: Theme, Symbol and Form
      in Faulkner's Novels," ArQ, XXIII (Autumn), 197-206.
          Church bells, spires, and steeples are major images in
      selected Faulkner novels: Soldiers' Pay, The Sound and the

1967

    (COFFEE, JESSIE A.)
        Fury, Light in August, and Intruder in the Dust. Empty or
        falling steeples, for example, denote a wasteland condi-
        tion, one which seems to predominate in Faulkner's pictures
        of churches.

22   COOPERMAN, STANLEY. "A World Withdrawn: Mahon and Hicks,"
        World War I Literature and the American Novel. Baltimore,
        Md.: Johns Hopkins Press, pp. 159-62.
        Faulkner's Mahon is one of the "spiritual sleepwalkers"
        of post-World War I fiction; his work pictures the "culture
        which made the absurdity possible." Each character in Sol-
        diers' Pay is identified by a peculiar futility, and the
        novel is a cycle of impotence. Faulkner's book is compared
        with Thomas Boyd's Through the Wheat.

23   COWLEY, MALCOLM. "Faulkner: Voodoo Dance," "Faulkner by Day-
        light," Think Back on Us. Carbondale, Ill.: Southern Il-
        linois University Press, pp. 268-71, 358-60.
        Reprints 1935.B13 and 1940.B5.

24   CROSS, RICHARD K. "The Humor of The Hamlet," TCL, XII (Janu-
        ary), 203-15.
        Humor, especially as a function of narrative voice, plays
        a large role in unifying The Hamlet. The plot of the novel
        is still weak.

25   FALKNER, MURRY C. "The Falkners of Oxford: The Enchanted
        Years," SoR, N. S. III (April), 357-86.
        Faulkner's next younger brother reminisces about family
        history and the boys' childhood. Included in 1967.A1.

26   FASEL, IDA. "A 'Conversation' Between Faulkner and Eliot,"
        MissQ, XX (Fall), 195-206.
        Lines and phrases from The Waste Land are compared with
        passages from The Sound and the Fury.

27   FEASTER, JOHN. "Faulkner's Old Man: A Psychoanalytic Ap-
        proach," MFS, XIII (Spring), 89-93.
        "Old Man," taken in isolation from The Wild Palms, drama-
        tizes a search for self, cast in psychological terms. The
        convict's acts are admirable, but his withdrawal at the
        end, when he embraces a longer prison sentence, demon-
        strates "some psychic disorder," and Feaster relates this
        to symbolic repetition of the birth trauma in the convict's
        experience.

28   FEUERLICHT, IGNACE. "Christ Figures in Literature," Person,
         XLVIII (October), 461-72.
            A brief survey of modern "Christ figures" in the novel
         is used to show how loosely the term is applied. Deriva-
         tive comments are made on Joe Christmas, Benjy Compson,
         and the Corporal from A Fable, who, the author says, have
         been called Christ figures but are in reality satanic or
         merely inarticulate.

29   FRANKLIN, R. W. "Narrative Management in As I Lay Dying,"
         MFS, XIII (Spring), 57-65.
            Narrative method in As I Lay Dying is designed to remove
         distance between reader and the experiences of fictional
         characters. Some devices--typography in some sections and
         Cash's list of 13 reasons for the way he builds the cof-
         fin--break the illusion which the method seeks to create.
         Using pre-publication forms of the novel as evidence, the
         author argues that the novel shows the haste in which it
         was written. See rejoinder, 1972.B80.

30   FREDERICK, JOHN T. "Anticipation and Achievement in Faulk-
         ner's Soldiers' Pay," ArQ, XXIII (Autumn), 243-49.
            Physical setting, character, and theme in Soldiers' Pay
         deserve more attention than they have received because of
         the ways in which they point to Faulkner's later work.

31   FRENCH, WARREN. "William Faulkner and the Art of the Detec-
         tive Story," The Thirties: Fiction, Poetry, Drama.
         Deland, Florida: Everett Edwards, pp. 55-62.
            Light in August, Absalom, Absalom!, "The Bear," "A Rose
         for Emily," and other Faulkner fictions partake of the
         elements of detective fiction, but in a serious, thought-
         ful, and powerful way. One of the objects of Faulkner's
         "detection" was the pride which was the secret cause of
         the self-destruction of so many of his characters and fam-
         ilies.

32   FROHOCK, W. M. "Continuities in the New Novel," Style and
         Temper: Studies in French Fiction, 1925-1960. Cambridge,
         Mass.: Harvard University Press, pp. 118-37.
            Faulkner's influence in France has gone through four dis-
         tinct stages, the most recent of which is the effect his
         style has had on the writers of the "New Novel."

33   GIDLEY, MICK. "William Faulkner," N&Q, XIV (January), 25-26.
            The author poses a query, seeking information on Faulk-
         ner's knowledge of philosophy, saying an "undocumented"
         assertion in a thesis mentions Faulkner's acknowledgment
         of Bergson. (See Bouvard's interview, 1954.B14.)

1967

34   GRESSET, MICHEL. "Faulkner Essayiste," NRF, XV (February),
      309-13.
         "Mississippi" and two essays on the American Dream of
      privacy are the most interesting pieces in Essays, Speeches
      and Public Letters. "My country" always had for Faulkner
      a double meaning that included his fictional creation with
      his native state.

35   GRUEN, JOHN. "Ruth Ford: A Tomorrow Kind of Woman," Status
      & Diplomat (July), pp. 54-57, 73.
         In an interview, Ruth Ford recounts her meeting Faulkner
      and the work on Requiem for a Nun.

36   GUETTI, JAMES. "Absalom, Absalom! The Extended Simile," The
      Limits of Metaphor: A Study of Melville, Conrad, and
      Faulkner. Ithaca, N. Y.: Cornell University Press, pp.
      69-108.
         Like Ahab, Sutpen in Absalom, Absalom! is both monomaniac
      perishing in his folly and cosmic hero daring the order of
      the universe; the telling of the story correlates with the
      story itself by virtue of parallels between Quentin's at-
      tempts to tell and understand and Sutpen's design, both
      arising from a conception of the world as meaningless. The
      novel's theme is the inability to make experience meaning-
      ful. Quentin is like Ishmael and Conrad's Marlow. Faulk-
      ner's style is an extension of Melville's and Conrad's:
      metaphor is used to express the inexpressible. But since
      no meaning exists, no metaphor is possible.
      Reprinted 1971.A2.

37   GUTTMANN, ALLEN. The Conservative Tradition in America. New
      York: Oxford University Press, pp. 71-74.
         Though conservative in some respects, Faulkner is not
      plainly in the conservative tradition because of the Faust-
      ian drives and ambition and the violence in his novels.

38   HAGOPIAN, JOHN V. "Nihilism in Faulkner's The Sound and the
      Fury," MFS, XIII (Spring), 45-55.
         A study of section four of The Sound and the Fury reveals
      that Faulkner denies the meaning of Dilsey's Christianity
      and produces a book in which the title, as Cleanth Brooks
      claims, is an accurate key to the meaning of the world por-
      trayed there. The last chapter contains four movements:
      a prologue and a recapitulation in reverse order of the
      principal foci of the book--Quentin's religious focus;
      Jason's economic one; and Benjy's nihilistic one. See re-
      joinder, 1970.B74.

39   HAMMOND, DONALD. "Faulkner's Levels of Awareness," FQ, I
        (ii), 73-81.
        In Light in August and Absalom, Absalom!, Faulkner dif-
        ferentiates what a character can say, what he can think in
        words, and what he can conceptualize wordlessly. Faulkner
        adds dimension and depth to his characters by these levels
        of expression. The deepest voice is his own, expressing
        what the character cannot say.

40   HARKNESS, BRUCE. "Faulkner and Scott," MissQ, XX (Summer),
        164.
        A scene in The Talisman suggests a source for an image
        in The Hamlet.

41   HIRANO, NABUYUKI. "Reconsideration of Moral Order and Dis-
        order in Faulkner's Works," HitJA&S, VIII (September),
        7-32.
        Ambiguous characters in Soldiers' Pay and Sartoris make
        it difficult to judge the novels. Both The Sound and the
        Fury and As I Lay Dying dramatize moral problems. Light
        in August is an advance on the earlier books, a monument
        toward the positive theme of the wilderness.

42   HOFFMAN, FREDERICK J. The Imagination's New Beginnings:
        Theology and Modern Literature. Notre Dame and London:
        University of Notre Dame Press, pp. 92-102.
        A Fable is not a novel but a compilation of Faulkner's
        post-Nobel Prize humanistic pronouncements. It fails as a
        novel because the hero suffers no anguish and the identifi-
        cation with Christ is blunted.

43   HOWELL, ELMO. "Faulkner's Wash Jones and the Southern Poor
        White," BSUF, VIII (Winter), 8-12.
        Wash Jones is a true representative of the Southern poor
        white; his tragedy is linked with Sutpen's, in whose orbit
        he is inevitably pulled to doom. The story of this tragedy
        is a "challenge" to those who by birth or wealth stand in
        positions of trust. "Wash" version is used.

44   _____. "Inversion and the 'Female' Principle: William
        Faulkner's 'A Courtship,'" SSF, IV (Summer), 308-14.
        In "A Courtship" Hogganbeck and Ikkemotubbe compete for
        the hand of Herman Basket's sister and lose the girl but
        come to love one another in a manly way. Both the outcome
        and the girl are typical in Faulkner's work. She takes
        the available chance and lets the idealism of the two other
        men go.

1967

45 HOWELL, ELMO. "President Jackson and William Faulkner's Choc-
    taws," ChrOk, XLV (Autumn), 252-58.
        In "Lo!" Faulkner draws on real visits to Washington by
    Indian chiefs Greenwood Leflore and Pushmataha, though he
    does not let the facts control his imagination. 1965.B42
    printed as an appendix.

46 _____. "Sam Fathers: A Note on Faulkner's 'A Justice,'"
    TSL, XII, 149-53.
        In "A Justice," Sam Fathers is apparently the son of
    Crawford, but he knows that in truth (as Faulkner made him
    in Go Down, Moses) he is the son of Doom, old Ikkemotubbe.
    Quentin, who also learns the truth of Sam's parentage in
    the course of hearing Sam's story, is exposed to the ter-
    rifying adult world into which he soon must pass.

47 _____. "William Faulkner's Caledonia: A Note on Intruder in
    the Dust," SSL, III (April), 248-52.
        Faulkner deliberately uses Scottish names to draw paral-
    lels between the hill country South and the Scottish high-
    lands and to remind the reader of the virtues of the fron-
    tier ideal.

48 _____. "William Faulkner's 'Christmas Gift!'" KFR, XIII
    (April-June), 37-40.
        Faulkner's use of the expression "Christmas Gift" in The
    Sound and the Fury shows his debt to Southern folklore.
    (Same observation in 1966.B63.)

49 _____. "William Faulkner and the Mississippi Indians," GaR,
    XXI (Fall), 386-96.
        Faulkner lacked specific knowledge about Indians, but the
    effects he attempts and the quality of his imaginative
    achievement are great anyway.

50 _____. "William Faulkner and Pro Patria Mori," LaS, IV (Sum-
    mer), 89-96.
        Faulkner's gentle pacifism is expressed in the paradoxi-
    cal heart and mind conflict in his soldiers who abhor war
    but honor courage and loyalty to country. "Shall Not Per-
    ish" and "Two Soldiers" are examples.

51 _____. "William Faulkner's Southern Baptists," ArQ, XXIII
    (Autumn), 220-26.
        Faulkner is not always accurate in his depiction of
    Southern fundamentalist protestant religion, especially the
    Baptists. He seems to stress those who degrade the heri-
    tage rather than those--like Byron Bunch or the tall con-

(HOWELL, ELMO)
vict--who ennoble it. Faulkner's attitude is essentially
"Anglican."

52   HUNT, JOEL A. "Thomas Mann and Faulkner: Portrait of a Ma-
gician," WSCL, VIII (Summer), 431-36.
Mann's story "Mario and the Magician" is similar to
Faulkner's "An Error in Chemistry."

53   IZSAK, EMILY K. "The Manuscript of The Sound and the Fury:
The Revisions in the First Section," SB, XX, 189-202.
In revisions between the MS of the Benjy section of The
Sound and the Fury and the published version, Faulkner put
greater emphasis upon the Christian parallels, the circus,
and Luster's problems with money. The published version
contains more italicized passages.

54   JACKSON, NAOMI. "Faulkner's Woman: 'Demon-Nun and Angel-
Witch,'" BSUF, VIII (Winter), 12-20.
Leslie Fiedler's view that Faulkner feared "castrating
women" is untenable when one regards the fiction as a
whole. Faulkner was especially fond of the "White Goddess," the Muse, the eternally feminine, the life-giver
and destroyer, a major touchstone for women in his work.

55   JENNINGS, ELIZABETH. "Full of Magic," Spectator (3 November),
pp. 541-42.
Typical Faulkner in spite of being a children's fantasy,
The Wishing Tree will delight the young reader.

56   KAY, WALLACE G. "Faulkner's Mississippi: The Myth and the
Microcosm," SoQ, VI (October), 13-24.
In creating his apocrypha, Faulkner has taken real events
and places and formed them into emblems of reality. Faulkner concentrates on the time of greatest change in Mississippi; he transforms the significant events of this period
into myth by making them representative and larger than
life.

57   KERR, ELIZABETH M. "The Reivers: The Golden Book of Yoknapatawpha County," MFS, XIII (Spring), 95-113.
The Reivers is the book anticipated by Faulkner in the
Paris Review interview (See 1956.B44) when he referred to
his Doomsday Book or Golden Book of Yoknapatawpha, after
which he would cease to write. It ties the saga together
and caps it. Lucius Priest is the success that Ike McCaslin in Go Down, Moses failed to be. See rejoinder 1970.B54.

1967

58   KIRK, ROBERT W. "Faulkner's Lena Grove," GaR, XXI (Spring),
     57-64.
          Like the author's essay on Anse Bundren (1965.B45), this
     character study recounts the events of the novel concerned,
     in this case Light in August.

59   LARSEN, ERIC E. "The Barrier of Language: The Irony of Lan-
     guage in Faulkner," MFS, XIII (Spring), 19-31.
          Because words are inadequate to communicate experience,
     Faulkner creates "experiential truth" by exploring the
     limits of language. Absalom, Absalom! demonstrates the
     technique: the "true" story exists only in the reader's
     full perception of the pattern of the novel.

60   LEVIN, DAVID. "Absalom, Absalom! The Problem of Recreating
     History," In Defense of Historical Literature: Essays on
     American History, Autobiography, Drama, and Fiction. New
     York: Hill and Wang, pp. 118-39.
          Faulkner makes fundamental questions about history and
     its interpretation a part of the narrative of Absalom,
     Absalom! Quentin makes the effort to understand his re-
     gion, reviewing its history from 1833 to 1910. Slavery
     is a metaphor for inhumanity and ruthless acquisition.
     Each narrator has some value for us, however prejudiced
     the viewpoint.

61   LORCH, THOMAS M. "Thomas Sutpen and the Female Principle,"
     MissQ, XX (Winter), 38-42.
          Sutpen and his dynasty are both sustained and destroyed
     by the female "principle"--the passive, enduring, indomi-
     table life force represented by women who do not limit
     themselves by devotion to abstractions. The "vessels"
     Sutpen chooses to perpetuate his unrealizable dream in
     Absalom, Absalom! finally absorb and stifle him. Male-
     female conflicts in Faulkner represent a body-soul duality
     which, ideally, ought to be resolved into a unity.

62   *McDONALD, WALTER R. "Faulkner's 'The Bear': The Sense of Its
     Structure," EngR, XVIII (December), 8-14.
          Bassett (1972.A2), Item N133.

63   MALCOLM, JANET. Review of The Wishing Tree, NY (16 December),
     178, 181.
          There is some humor, but The Wishing Tree is primarily
     a "staggeringly dull" account of a childish quest for a
     magic tree.

64 MARSHALL, SARAH L. "Fathers and Sons in Absalom, Absalom!"
    UMSE, VIII, 19-29.
        Sutpen does not have the biblical David's human concern
    for his children in Absalom, Absalom!; he does not even
    recognize the irony of his death at the hands of Wash
    Jones, who plays a role like the one which started Sutpen
    on his dream.

65 MASON, ROBERT L. "A Defense of Faulkner's Sanctuary," GaR,
    XXI (Winter), 430-38.
        Sanctuary has a serious purpose and is artfully written;
    characters and events are motivated and prepared for.
    Temple, the center, acts out of a fascination with evil,
    which is a stimulus to her, sexually and otherwise. This
    explains her perjury at the end.

66 *MATERASSI, MARIO. "Il primo grande romanzo di Faulkner: The
    Sound and the Fury," Convivium, XXXV (May-June), 303-24.
    In 1968.A5.

67 MATHEWS, JAMES W. "The Civil War of 1936: Gone With the Wind
    and Absalom, Absalom!" GaR, XXI (Winter), 462-69.
        Margaret Mitchell's Gone With the Wind and Faulkner's
    Absalom, Absalom! had very different receptions the year
    they appeared; they have both become present-day classics.

68 MELLARD, JAMES M. "The Biblical Rhythm of Go Down, Moses,"
    MissQ, XX (Summer), 135-47.
        Go Down, Moses gets unity by repetition and counterpoint
    of theme, pattern, mode, and structure, moving from life
    in an unfallen Eden through the fall, the exile, and
    death, and on to a suggestion of redemption. Romance,
    epic, ironic statement, and coda characterize the movement
    of the book.

69 _____. "Faulkner's Philosophical Novel: Ontological Themes
    in As I Lay Dying," Person, XLVIII (October), 509-23.
        Faulkner's work approaches the major philosophical ques-
    tions of being and reality which may be resolved by ideal-
    ism, nominalism, or realism. All three points of view are
    contrasted in As I Lay Dying; Darl and Addie are the an-
    tipodes of idealism and nominalism, while other characters
    align with one of them. Cash is the only realist, prob-
    ably Faulkner's spokesman.

70 MERIWETHER, JAMES B. "A Source in Balzac for The Unvan-
    quished," MissQ, XX (Summer), 165-66.
        The titles of chapters one and five of The Unvanquished
    seem to come from Balzac's Les Chouans.

1967

71   MERTON, THOMAS. "'Baptism in the Forest': Wisdom and Initia-
      tion in William Faulkner," Mansions of the Spirit: Essays
      in Literature and Religion, edited by George Panichas.
      New York: Hawthorn, pp. 17-44.
          Camus' fascination with Faulkner rested in part upon
      his belief that Faulkner's themes were given religious
      treatment in the novels by being raised to tragedy.
      Faulkner has "sapientia"--the wisdom of ultimate causes,
      a metaphysical and moral awareness of what it means to be
      man in the world. Go Down, Moses and The Wild Palms are
      used to illustrate, one dramatizing initiation in the
      forest, the other isolation in the modern world. Both
      show "monastic" solutions.
      Reprinted 1968.B45.

72   MILLER, DAVID. "Faulkner's Women," MFS, XIII (Spring), 3-17.
          Faulkner's women are either "ghosts" or "earth mothers,"
      and the latter are joined with "seed bearers" like Dalton
      Ames in The Sound and the Fury or Prufrocks, like Quentin
      Compson. Faulkner's message seems to be that sex is both
      bad and good; the violence of human passion destroys and
      creates.

73   MILLER, JAMES E., JR. "William Faulkner: Descent into the
      Vortex," Quests Surd and Absurd: Essays in American Lit-
      erature. Chicago: University of Chicago Press, pp. 41-66.
          Faulkner's complex exploration of a character's past re-
      moves the possibility of simple judgments; his most tor-
      tured and evil characters are victims of their past lives,
      of their families. Faulkner depicts an absurd world,
      where action is frantic and without goal, where all men of
      whatever persuasion are essentially alike. Individual
      truths like honesty, compassion, and courage ennoble human
      effort. Faulkner has passed his contemporaries; he con-
      tinues to speak to the more modern mind.

74   MILLGATE, MICHAEL. "William Faulkner: The Problem of Point
      of View," Patterns of Commitment in American Literature,
      edited by Marston LaFrance. Toronto: University of To-
      ronto Press, pp. 181-92.
          Faulkner's almost life-long experiments with form were
      chiefly concerned with strategies for deploying narrative
      point of view. Only two novels use pure first person nar-
      rative, The Unvanquished and The Reivers. He used stream-
      of-consciousness and interrupted monologue, the device
      that predominates after Absalom, Absalom! He joined these
      monologues by "ironic juxtaposition" allowing physical or
      dramatic context to serve as a reflector which ordered the

(MILLGATE, MICHAEL)
> speakers' meanings. The Town may be the novel in which
> Faulkner most satisfactorily solved the problems of point
> of view he had explored throughout his career, for it has
> unity and complexity, representative narrators and indi-
> viduals, bound in a matrix that puts the kinds of demands
> upon the reader Faulkner always sought.
> Reprinted, in part, 1970.A6; reprinted 1973.A9.

75   MUEHL, LOIS. "Faulkner's Humor in Three Novels and One
> 'Play'," LC, XXXIV, 78-93.
> Faulkner's early work, such as Sartoris, Absalom, Absa-
> lom!, and Intruder in the Dust, while not generally humor-
> ous, shows Faulkner's ability to use lightness as a nar-
> rative variation as he does in The Reivers, the "play."

76   NAUMAN, HILDA. "How Faulkner Went His Way and I Went Mine,"
> Esquire, LXIII (December), 173-75.
> The author recounts a distant memory of an evening with
> Faulkner after the publication of Sanctuary and a literary
> tea given by "Ben Wasserman" (possibly Ben Wasson?) at the
> Algonquin.

77   NISHIYAMA, TAMOTSU. "As I Lay Dying: A Strange Comedy," EWR,
> III (February), 19-30.
> Predominantly comic, As I Lay Dying is a kind of Don
> Quixote in which the whole Bundren family represents the
> knight of La Mancha's efforts to do his best in a shabby
> world.

78   PAGE, RALPH. "John Sartoris: Friend or Foe," ArQ, XXIII
> (Spring), 27-33.
> The Bayard-John story in Sartoris is compared with the
> biblical tale of Cain and Abel. Bayard's guilt is due to
> symbolic fratricide.

79   PALMER, WILLIAM J. "The Mechanistic World of Snopes," MissQ,
> XX (Fall), 185-94.
> Flem Snopes is associated, directly or implicitly, with
> machinery; his rise symbolizes the gradual triumph of
> mechanistic forces over the fecund rural world he enters.
> The characters who survive and "endure" Flem's rapacity
> are not mechanistic.

1967

80 PEAVY, CHARLES D. "Faulkner and the Howe Interview," CLAJ,
       XI (December), 117-23.
       A false portrait of Faulkner's views on race have come
       from disregard of his letters and public utterances. The
       Howe interview (1956.B26) has been given an inordinate
       amount of attention. While Howe maintains the accuracy of
       his report, Faulkner repudiated the remarks attributed to
       him and a Time reporter indicated later that Faulkner had
       been upset and drinking heavily because of a racial argu-
       ment with his brother John at the time of the interview.

81 *POWERS, LYALL H. "Hawthorne and Faulkner and the Pearl of
       Great Price," PMASAL, LII, 391-401.
       Bassett (1972.A2), Item E124.

82 REEVES, CAROLYN H. "The Wild Palms: Faulkner's Chaotic Cos-
       mos," MissQ, XX (Summer), 148-57.
       Landscape and characterization in The Wild Palms are
       both used to depict a world in chaos. The four primal
       elements of the ancient world--earth, air, fire, and
       water--all appear in ambiguous states to underline the
       chaotic atmosphere of the book. Faulkner presents a
       "timeless, primeval, chaotic world"--a world where man is
       paradoxically alien and at home.

83 RUBIN, LOUIS D., JR. "The Difficulties of Being a Southern
       Writer Today or, Getting Out from Under William Faulkner,"
       The Curious Death of the Novel: Essays in American Lit-
       erature. Baton Rouge, La.: Louisiana State University
       Press, 282-93.
       Reprinted from 1963.B73.

84 _____. "Notes on a Rear-Guard Action," The Curious Death of
       the Novel: Essays in American Literature. Baton Rouge,
       La.: Louisiana State University Press, pp. 131-51.
       Reprinted from 1964.B63.

85 _____. The Teller in the Tale. Seattle, Washington: Univer-
       sity of Washington Press, pp. 211, 213-14.
       In a "Postscript" to his discussion of the inevitable
       presence of the true author in any tale, the author prints
       the opening of Absalom, Absalom! and argues that it is
       given, "coldly and objectively," by Faulkner himself and
       not by any character in the book. All novels are the
       product of an argument between reader and author to accept
       the author's way of telling his tale.

86 RUTLEDGE, WILMUTH S. "How Colonel Falkner Built His Railroad," MissQ, XX (Summer), 166-70.
A newly discovered letter from Col. W. C. Falkner, great grandfather of the novelist, reveals something about the methods he used to finance and build his narrow-gauge railroad.

87 SANDERS, BARRY. "Faulkner's Fire Imagery in 'That Evening Sun,'" SSF, V (Fall), 69-71.
The "life-force" in Nancy of "That Evening Sun" has gone out, first symbolized in the story by images of extinguished fire and the absent "Jesus," whose name is ironic. At her cabin are images of extreme fires, symbolizing her impending utter destruction.

88 SANDSTROM, GLENN. "Identity Diffusion: Joe Christmas and Quentin Compson," AQ, XIX (Summer), 207-23.
Joe Christmas of Light in August and Quentin Compson of Absalom, Absalom! and the identity theories of psychologist Erik Erikson are used to discuss the theme of the search for selfhood in Faulkner's work. Faulkner isolated and dramatized identity problems which were itemized and analyzed only later by psychologists.

89 SARGENT, ROBERT. "New Albany, Mississippi," GaR, XXI (Winter), 448.
A poem by a New Orleanian living in Washington, D. C. about the failure of New Albany, Miss., to erect a monument to Faulkner, who was born there.

90 SINGLETON, MARVIN K. "Personae at Law and Equity: The Unity of Faulkner's Absalom, Absalom!" PLL, III (Fall), 354-70.
Legal terms from English common law and from chancery proceedings provide a relationship between character and narrative technique in Absalom, Absalom! and illuminate the meaning of the novel. Sutpen is feudalistic and speaks in terms of medieval common law to justify or explain his actions (including terms of chivalry, doublets). Shrevelin, whose name may derive from "shire-reeve," the old term for sheriff, uses many legal archaisms. Rosa's story is an equity plea. None of Faulkner's legal material is so obtrusive as to become allegorical.

91 SMITHEY, ROBERT A. "Faulkner and the Status Quo," CLAJ, XI (December), 109-16.
Roth Edmonds' racially motivated rejection by his black playmate Henry in "The Fire and the Hearth" is not dealt with honestly by Faulkner, who attributes it to something

1967

(SMITHEY, ROBERT A.)
innate, the "curse," rather than to the indoctrination by
Roth's elders which is the real cause. Henry's reaction
is part of the emasculated black's way of life--unques-
tioning acceptance. Faulkner's guilt makes him transfer
the responsibility to nature.

92 SOLOMON, ERIC. "Joseph Conrad, William Faulkner, and the
Nobel Prize Speech," N&Q, XIV (July), 247-48.
Passages from Joseph Conrad's "Henry James: An Appreciation" echo in Faulkner's Nobel Prize address. In both
instances the words reflect the artists' "hopeful views of
man's chances in a doom-ridden world."

93 SPRATLING, WILLIAM. File on Spratling. Boston: Little,
Brown and Co., pp. 21-34.
Reprints 1966.B69.

94 STROZIER, ROBERT. "Some Versions of Faulkner's Pastoral,"
ForumH, V (Summer), 35-40.
A man of many styles and a master of no single one,
Faulkner is not a great stylist. In his short stories he
uses five basic methods of revelation. "Barn Burning,"
"A Bear Hunt," "Centaur in Brass," "Uncle Willy" are used
to illustrate Faulkner's technique in the pastoral or
rural tale.

95 TAYLOR, NANCY DEW. "The Dramatic Production of Requiem for a
Nun," MissQ, XX (Summer), 123-34.
The author recounts the events surrounding Faulkner's
adaptation of his novel Requiem for a Nun for the stage
and the ten-year delay in getting it produced in New
York. Camus' adaptation for the French stage and its reception are also discussed.

96 TAYLOR, WALTER. "The Freedman in Go Down, Moses: Historical
Fact and Imaginative Failure," BSUF, VIII (Winter), 3-7.
Faulkner's Southern loyalties, which ran to paternalism
and a doctrine of Northern non-interference, create artistic problems visible in Go Down, Moses. The Negro
caricatures Faulkner uses to dramatize the Freedman's in-
capacities for self-discipline are flat and uncritical;
they weaken Ike's arguments and strain the reader's belief
in Faulkner's "hero" and his "climactic act of renunciation." Faulkner's imagination failed him.

97   TRILLING, LIONEL. The Experience of Literature: A Reader
         with Commentaries. Garden City, N. Y.: Doubleday & Co.,
         pp. 745-48.
            "Barn Burning" dramatizes the Sartoris-Snopes dichotomy
         in Faulkner's work. Abner is a great and even appealing
         force in Sarty's struggle with conscience. Against the
         somewhat childish DeSpain, Abner shows up monstrous but
         large because he has more at stake.

98   UNDERWOOD, HENRY J., JR. "Sartre on The Sound and Fury: Some
         Errors," MFS, XII (Winter), 477-79.
            Sartre's "Time in Faulkner" (1939.B28) posits a meta-
         physic for Faulkner by identifying the author's thought
         literally with statements by his characters. Sartre also
         errs by confusing as Quentin's, words spoken in The Sound
         and the Fury by his cynical father. In another context,
         Sartre attributes a quote from The Sound and the Fury to
         Joe Christmas of Light in August. Sartre's case is seri-
         ously undermined, if not totally destroyed by these
         misunderstandings.

99   WALTERS, PAUL S. "Theory and Practice in Faulkner: The Sound
         and the Fury," ESA, X (March), 22-39.
            In The Sound and the Fury, Faulkner starts us at the
         farthest point from the truth, giving us, through Benjy,
         pure experience. There are paradoxes of perception in
         that Benjy is more acute, in a certain sense, than his
         more intellectual brothers. Quentin cannot apply his
         sensitivity to any useful end; Jason's sanity is harsh and
         inhumane. The objectivity of section four is restorative.
         Dilsey's endurance is active, not passive, and in a gen-
         eral sense Christian. The gist of the novel's technique
         is that we must know the sound and the fury before we
         know peace.

100   WATKINS, FLOYD C. "What Happens in Absalom, Absalom!" MFS,
         XIII (Spring), 79-87.
            A large number of inconsistencies of "fact" in Absalom,
         Absalom!--dates, ages, length of occurrences, the nature
         of events themselves--are apparently Faulkner's intention
         and show the discrepancies between the four unreliable
         narrators. Some inconsistencies continue to puzzle the
         reader, however, and may be accidental. Contrary to
         Faulkner, there is not even a fourteenth way of seeing the
         truth in Absalom, Absalom! It remains indefinite--and
         thereby richer--for everyone.

1967

101   WEATHERBY, H. L.   "Sutpen's Garden," GaR, XXI (Fall), 354-69.
      Pervasively employing Christian imagery, Faulkner yet
      displays surprising "ignorance" of Christian theology,
      confusing the reader at the point where these character-
      istics intersect, the images creating expectations which
      the bad theology only thwarts.   The glowing December gar-
      den at Sutpen's is compared to the Christian garden alle-
      gory, and the author shows what Faulkner might have done
      with his material if he had understood Christianity.

102   WIGGINS, ROBERT A.   "Faulkner," American Literary Scholarship
      an annual, 1965, edited by James Woodress.   Durham, N. C.:
      Duke University Press, pp. 82-89.
      This survey of Faulkner criticism has the overall view
      that 1965 was "not a vintage year."

103   WOLPERS, THEODORE.   "Formen Mythisierenden Erzählens in der
      modernen Prosa: Joseph Conrad im Vergleich mit Joyce,
      Lawrence, und Faulkner," Lebende Antike: Symposium für
      Rudolph Suhnel.   Berlin: E. Schmidt, passim.
      Faulkner's style and his use of time and space is dis-
      cussed in relation to other modern writers.

104   BEVINGTON, HELEN.   "A Present for Victoria," NYTBR (7 May),
      p. 38.
      The Wishing Tree is a "curiosity," not a book for a
      child to read; it does not display Faulkner's "shining
      talent."   The tale is summarized.

105   CIARDI, JOHN.   "Faulkner and Child, Faulkner and Negro,"
      Harper's, CCXXXIV (May), 114.
      Faulkner's "talent was never for sweetness," and his
      black caricatures in The Wishing Tree are unforgivable.
      It is an "offensively bad" children's book.

1968 A   BOOKS

1   ADAMS, RICHARD P.   Faulkner: Myth and Motion.   Princeton,
    N. J.:   Princeton University Press.
    In a study of Faulkner's early writing and all his nov-
    els, Adams explores the development of style, structural
    strategies, and ethical point of view through Faulkner's
    career.   Myth and motion--the repeated use of the mytho-
    logical method as developed by Joyce and described by
    Eliot and a preoccupation with the motion of life--are
    primary elements in Faulkner's work.   Extended readings
    of The Sound and the Fury and Absalom, Absalom!, using

(ADAMS, RICHARD P.)
the insights of the general overview, occupy separate
chapters.

2   BRYLOWSKI, WALTER. Faulkner's Olympian Laugh: Myth in the
Novels. Detroit: Wayne State University Press.
Faulkner's use of myth extends from allusion and thematic counterpoint to plot itself, when the stories become
mythological on their own terms; it includes a "mythic
mode of thought," an epistemology which, when understood,
helps to reveal the meaning of both Faulkner and his characters and the overall design of the saga itself with its
use of the Old South myth. The author discusses the
levels of myth in Faulkner's work with emphasis on the
major novels, finding that Faulkner's sophisticated--if
perhaps intuitive--knowledge and use of myth allows him to
reconcile a world of suffering and evil with a faith in
man's ability to bear and transcend his condition.

3   COWAN, MICHAEL, ed. Twentieth-Century Interpretations of
The Sound and the Fury. Englewood Cliffs, N. J.: Prentice-Hall.
The introduction to this anthology of articles and excerpts from articles and books, etc., discusses the background of the writing, publication, and reception of The
Sound and the Fury and surveys some of the questions of
meaning and technique which the novel raises. The an-
thologized criticism is almost invariably cut, edited,
and retitled; the basic text used is the 1946 Modern Library edition of the novel.

4   MASSEY, LINTON R. William Faulkner: "Man Working, 1919-
1962": A Catalogue of the William Faulkner Collections at
the University of Virginia. Charlottesville, Va.: Bibliographical Society of the University of Virginia.
The primary emphasis in this catalogue is upon material
gathered and donated to the library by Mr. Massey, primarily editions and translations of Faulkner's work and
secondary material, including association items, but also
including some prepublication forms of material. Faulkner's own MSS and TSS, also on deposit at Virginia, are
briefly catalogued.

5   *MATERASSI, MARIO. I romanzi di Faulkner. (Biblioteca di
Studi Americani 17.) Rome: Edizioni di Storia e Letteratura.
According to Millgate in American Literary Scholarship
1970, pp. 117-18, this is a good survey for the Italian

1968

(MATERASSI, MARIO)
reader, though it omits consideration of The Unvanquished
and Go Down, Moses as novels.
Reprints 1966.B51, 1963.B59, 1967.B66; "Il razzisme di
William Faulkner," Il Nuovo Osservatore, IV (November
1963), 1062-64; and "Ultima critica faulkneriana," Il
Ponte, XXIII (November 1967), 1495-1501. The chapter surveying Faulkner's Italian reception appears in translation, 1971.B60.

6   MERIWETHER, JAMES B., and MICHAEL MILLGATE, eds. Lion in
the Garden: Interviews with William Faulkner: 1926-1962.
New York: Random House.
A collection of interviews, previously published, with a
three-part index of references to other authors, to Faulkner's own work, and to themes and subjects. Includes
1926.B1, 1931.B2, 1931.B4, 1931.B23, 1931.B29, 1931.B30,
1932.B20, 1937.B1, 1939.B4, 1939.B24, 1948.B18, 1948.B26,
1951.B5, 1951.B37, 1953.B3, 1954.B12, 1954.B14, 1955.B6,
1955.B7, 1955.B8, 1955.B12, 1956.A1, 1956.A2, 1956.B9,
1956.B19, 1956.B26, 1956.B44, 1957.B5, 1962.B33, 1964.B50.

7   O'CONNOR, WILLIAM VAN. The Tangled Fire of William Faulkner.
New York: Gordian Press.
Reprints 1954.A2.

8   STRAUMANN, HEINRICH. William Faulkner. Frankfurt am Main and
Bonn: Athenäum Verlag.
A critical study, in German, devotes eight chapters to
Faulkner's background, his breakthrough to mastery, problems of alienation in the fiction, the short stories, the
investigation of time, themes of wilderness and ancestry,
"Seinsdeutung" in A Fable, and the diminution in powers
reflected in The Reivers. Chapter on A Fable previously
published at 1956.B48 and in 1960.A1.

1968 B   SHORTER WRITINGS

1   ADAMS, RICHARD P. "Some Key Words in Faulkner," TSE, XVI,
135-48.
There is deliberate enrichment of meaning in the way
Faulkner plays upon some of his favorite words--doom,
terrific (with its derivatives like terrible), wait. As
with other elements of his fiction, Faulkner manipulates
these and other words to allow them to acquire multiple
meanings.

2   ANGELL, LESLIE E. "The Umbilical Cord Symbol as Unifying
Theme and Pattern in Absalom, Absalom!" MSE, I, 106-10.
    Three scenes in Absalom, Absalom! where the umbilical
cord is used as image and symbol, along with the contex-
tual significance of Jim Bond, create a pattern of meaning
which shows connections between past and present, between
characters in the novel, and between the reader and the
book.

3   ASALS, FREDERICK. "Faulkner's Light in August," Expl, XXVI
(May), Item 74.
    The three stages of Joe's relationship with Joanna par-
allel the three temptations of Christ in Matthew IV: 1-11.
Joanna is not only temptress, however; like Joe, she is an
ambivalent paradoxical figure. They share a Janus-like
doubleness--reflected in their names--and irreconcilable
qualities. Neither can accept the other's ambivalence.
There is both hellishness and apotheosis in the death of
each.

4   ASWELL, DUNCAN. "The Puzzling Design of Absalom, Absalom!"
KR, XXX (Issue I), 67-84.
    Faulkner takes deliberate precautions to prevent a read-
er from objectively proving many of the "facts" of Absalom, Absalom! The search for meaning parallels the efforts of the book's characters, who seek meaning in their
own lives. The chronology is not only no help, but a deliberate further confusion, fair warning from Faulkner
that a simple "answer" is not available. The book is
about the relation between the body's capacity for endurance and the mind's search for "purpose, meaning and
truth."

5   _____. "The Recollection and the Blood: Jason's Role in The
Sound and the Fury," MissQ, XXI (Summer), 211-18.
    Far from being unique or free from his past, young Jason
Compson in The Sound and the Fury shares many of the obsessions and faults of the members of his family, especially Quentin, but also his father and Benjy. He has
both "recollection" and "blood" that tie him to his
sources.

6   *BASHIRUDDIN, ZEBA. "The Lost Individual in Absalom, Absalom!" Newsletter Number 11, American Studies Research
Centre, Hyderabad, 1967, pp. 49-52.
    1969 MLA International Bibliography, Volume I, Item 83.

7   BEDIENT, CALVIN. "Pride and Nakedness: <u>As I Lay Dying</u>,"
     <u>MLQ</u>, XXIX (March), 61-76.
          <u>As I Lay Dying</u> is an opaque aesthetic object in which
     the isolation of the characters is underscored by the form
     of the book. Pride--a sustaining sense of self-worth--
     supports these isolated characters and, in an existential
     sense, makes it possible for them to exist in a world that
     leaves everyone naked and alone. Darl is the most naked;
     Cash has the most pride and therefore is the most human.

8   BEIDLER, PETER G. "Faulkner's Techniques of Characterization:
     Jewel in <u>As I Lay Dying</u>," <u>EA</u> XXI (July-September), 236-42.
          Since no authorial intrusion occurs in <u>As I Lay Dying</u>,
     Faulkner must characterize by indirect means. Jewel, an
     example of Faulkner's skill, is characterized by appear-
     ance, speech, thoughts, foils to him, the opinions of
     others, and his actions.

9   BELLMAN, SAMUEL I. "Hemingway, Faulkner, and Wolfe...and the
     Common Reader," <u>SoR</u>, N. S. IV (Summer), 834-49.
          Academic criticism of Faulkner and other modern writers
     asks the wrong questions; a criticism which could gener-
     alize upon "gut" responses by ordinary readers is needed.
     Reviewing several books on Faulkner and the republished
     poetry, the writer finds little to admire, especially in
     <u>A Green Bough</u>, but admits the validity of the conception
     of <u>The Marble Faun</u>.

10   BORGSTRÖM, GRETA I. "The Roaring Twenties and William Faulk-
     ner's <u>Sanctuary</u>," <u>Moderna Språk</u>, LXII (No. 3), 237-48.
          <u>Sanctuary</u> is a commentary upon the "roaring twenties."
     Context, narrative technique, and pictorial style are
     appropriate to the period. It is a Dantesque world, with
     Popeye as Devil and Temple as his high priestess, captur-
     ing the evil beneath the romance of the times.

11   BOSWELL, GEORGE W. "Picturesque Faulknerisms," <u>UMSE</u>, IX,
     47-56.
          In his stories, novels, and titles, Faulkner uses dia-
     lect, neologisms, and imaginative distortions of words
     and names, a few of which are surveyed.

12   _____. "Traditional Verse and Music Influence in Faulkner,"
     <u>NMW</u>, I (Spring), 23-31.
          Faulkner's possible familiarity with mythology, folk
     music, and traditional religious songs is surveyed.

13   BRADFORD, MELVIN E. "Certain Ladies of Quality: Faulkner's
      View of Women and the Evidence of 'There Was a Queen,'"
      ArlQ, I (Winter), 106-39.
           Narcissa Benbow, as developed from Sartoris, Sanctuary,
      and "There Was a Queen," is foil to Miss Jenny DuPre;
      along with Elnora, a kind of female Lucas Beauchamp, both
      lead us to an understanding of Faulkner's view of women.
      He put a premium on the high-class, enduring females of
      the old order, to whom Narcissa is in complete contrast.

14   _____. "Faulkner's 'Elly': An Exposé," MissQ, XXI (Summer),
      179-87.
           The 1934 short story, "Elly," is an "exposé" of the
      "flapper" and of the disregard of "verities" which typi-
      fied the twenties and early thirties. Elly is selfish,
      self-deluded, unable to love, and she deliberately commits
      a double murder as a final act of revenge.

15   _____. "Spring Paradigm: Faulkner's Living Legacy," ForumH,
      VI (Spring), 4-7.
           "Brotherhood" for Faulkner did not mean levelling but
      duty and consciousness of place. Characters in Faulkner's
      work who "endure" by virtue of a strong sense of self and
      duty emerge more strongly by The Unvanquished (1938) and
      Go Down, Moses (1942). Critics who ignore this sense of
      value do so at their peril.

16   BROOKS, CLEANTH. "Faulkner as Poet," SLJ, I (Autumn), 5-19.
           Housman and Swinburne were major influences on Faulk-
      ner's poetry, Housman especially evident in A Green
      Bough. The Marble Faun represents a literary, not a north
      Mississippi nature; it is filled with the flora and fauna
      of England, not America. Faulkner was able to develop and
      employ his poetic skills in his fiction. Poetry and relat-
      ed prose passages are compared.
      Reprinted 1971.B12.

17   _____. "Introduction," Light in August. New York: Modern
      Library, pp. v-xxv.
           Faulkner weaves an intricate story out of the lives of a
      series of outcasts in a traditional community in Light in
      August by balancing character against character. Joe
      Christmas and Lena Grove are polarities of humankind, one
      alienated from, one at peace with all that is natural.
      Giving Faulkner credit for knowing what he is doing, an
      attentive reader need not be puzzled by the meaningful
      intricacy of the book.

1968

18   BROWN, CALVIN S.   "Faulkner's Use of the Oral Tradition,"
         GaR, XXII (Summer), 160-69.
         Faulkner was brought up in a tradition where oral tales
     out of family and regional history were a staple augmented
     by the tall tale tradition of the old Southwestern yarn-
     spinners and the skaz (inside narratives) of late nine-
     teenth century literary humor. He blended oral and liter-
     ary traditions. Also in 1969.B10.

19   CAMERINO, ALDO.   "Novilá de William Faulkner," Scrittori di
         lingua inglese. Milan and Naples: Ricciardi, pp. 208-15.
         Reprints 1934.B4.

20   CASSILL, R. V.   "Introduction," The Wild Palms. New York and
         Scarborough, Ontario: New American Library, pp. v-xvii.
         Charlotte, incandescent and unforgettable, is the center
     of The Wild Palms. Wilbourne's decision to live and re-
     member is made in the face of every pressure to forget.
     The story of the convict, which Faulkner wanted to alter-
     nate with the love story, is an appropriate "consort,"
     and the convict's acquiescence in prison routine is power-
     fully countered by Harry's "Promethean decision" to re-
     member at the price of agony.

21   CLARK, CHARLES C.   "'Mistral': A Study in Human Tempering,"
         MissQ, XXI (Summer), 195-204.
         The Americans in "Mistral" reveal to one another the
     story of the priest's lust, which is symbolically inces-
     tuous, and his murder of the rich fiancé. They are ini-
     tiated into the evil of the Old World, which they must,
     like Hawthorne's characters Robin in "My Kinsman, Major
     Molineux" or Young Goodman Brown, recognize as their own
     world. Imagery of earth, air, fire, and water pervades,
     given hellish associations.

22   CLARK, WILLIAM G.   "Faulkner's Light in August," Expl, XXVI
         (March), Item 54.
         Joe Christmas's dealings with white prostitutes in Light
     in August are designed to provide assurance for him that
     there is a meaningful difference between being black and
     being white. When the northern prostitute does not re-
     spond to his "revelation," he becomes violent because she
     has denied the meaning of his lifelong search for an
     "answer," an answer he does get when Percy Grimm kills
     and emasculates him in a manner "appropriate" to Joe's
     blackness.

1968

23   COLLINS, CARVEL. "Introduction," <u>New Orleans Sketches</u>, re-
        vised edition. New York: Random House, pp. xi–xxxiv.
           Reprints 1958.B18, with revised introduction and the ad-
        dition of "Sherwood Anderson," an essay by Faulkner that
        first appeared in the Dallas (Tex.) <u>Morning News</u> in April
        1925.

24 *____. "On William Faulkner," <u>Talks with Authors</u>, edited by
        Charles F. Madden. Carbondale, Ill.: Southern Illinois
        University Press, pp. 39–55.
           Conference-call-taught class featuring questions by stu-
        dents. Bassett, Item AA227.

25   FRANKLIN, PHYLLIS. "Sarty Snopes and 'Barn Burning,'" <u>MissQ</u>,
        XXI (Summer), 189–93.
           Replies to Howell (1959.B35), disputing any mere Sar-
        toris/Snopes dichotomy in "Barn Burning." The story is
        Sarty's, showing the causes and the ambiguity of his moral
        dilemma and its resolution. "Barn Burning" was omitted as
        the first chapter of <u>The Hamlet</u> perhaps because Sarty is
        "too normal" for the exaggerated world of that novel.

26   GATES, ALLEN. "The Old Frenchman Place: Symbol of a Lost
        Civilization," <u>IEY</u>, XIII, 44–50.
           The chief thematic value of the old Frenchman's Place in
        <u>The Hamlet</u> is as a "symbol of a bygone era." It drama-
        tizes the need for urban renewal in Yoknapatawpha County
        and the South.

27   GREINER, DONALD J. "Universal Snopesism: The Significance of
        'Spotted Horses,'" <u>EJ</u>, LVII (November), 1133–37.
           "Spotted Horses" universalizes the theme of greed and
        rapacity of the Snopes trilogy by demonstrating the gener-
        al lust for acquisition. By virtue of its thematic im-
        portance and its origin as the germ of <u>The Hamlet</u> in the
        early "Father Abraham," "Spotted Horses" is the "central
        episode" of that novel. It also sets up the final combat
        between Ratliff and Snopes which brings Ratliff's fall.

28   GRESSET, MICHEL. "Weekend, Lost and Revisited," <u>MissQ</u>, XXI
        (Summer), 173–78.
           Charles Jackson's popular novel of 1944, <u>The Lost Week-</u>
        <u>end</u>, is compared with a Faulkner story published in 1965
        as "Mr. Arcarius" but also titled, in a TS at the Univer-
        sity of Virginia, "Weekend Revisited." There is influence,
        and "Mr. Arcarius" is a serious, though not first rate, ex-
        pression of Faulkner's philosophy.

1968

29   GROSS, BEVERLY. "Form and Fulfillment in The Sound and the
     Fury," MLQ, XXIX (December), 439-49.
          The final scene of The Sound and the Fury is a poetic
     resolution of both theme and form in the novel. The end-
     ing shatters the equilibrium toward which the novel has
     apparently been working, restoring the novel to its "trag-
     ic beginnings." While not a conventional conclusion, it
     nevertheless provides a suitable, though unusual termina-
     tion for the book.

30   HALL, JAMES. "Play, the Fractured Self, and American Angry
     Comedy: From Faulkner to Salinger," The Lunatic Giant in
     the Drawing Room: The British and American Novel Since
     1930. Bloomington, Ind.: Indiana University Press,
     pp. 56-77.
          Faulkner's "last major novel," The Hamlet, reveals the
     effects of simplification and universality Faulkner
     achieves by concentrating on what we are prepared to be-
     lieve about country people. It also advances the possible
     roles of the hero in the modern novel from frustration to
     irritation. The fractured self pulls together and oper-
     ates toward a goal, but stays loose in the process, shows
     "steadiness in the face of threat."

31   HARRIS, WENDELL V. "Of Time and the Novel," BuR, XVI (March),
     114-29.
          In a discussion of time in modern novels, the author
     argues that The Sound and the Fury, instead of changing
     the reader's sense of time, causes the reader to comment
     upon and judge as insufficient the time sense of each of
     the three narrators. Faulkner's technique demanded om-
     niscience instead of interior monologue for Dilsey's sec-
     tion to strengthen the sense that she has escaped the
     chaos to which the other three are given over.

32   HOFFMAN, FREDERICK J. "William Faulkner," American Winners of
     the Nobel Literary Prize, edited by W. O. French and W. E.
     Kidd. Norman, Okla.: University of Oklahoma Press,
     pp. 138-57.
          A survey of Faulkner's career notes that Faulkner did
     seem to change after the Nobel award. He was not "a pre-
     cise or an imaginative intellectual."

33   HOWELL, ELMO. "Mink Snopes and Faulkner's Moral Conclusions,"
     SAQ, LXVII (Winter), 13-22.
          Faulkner's later writing--post-1940--is weak and preachy.
     Mink Snopes, however, as portrayed in The Town and The
     Mansion, is one of his most powerful characters. His

(HOWELL, ELMO)
criminal impulses contrast strikingly with Faulkner's high regard for him. Faulkner has "thrown...off...his Southern ethic," and substituted a rapacious humanism.

34   . "A Name for Faulkner's City," Names, XVI (December), 415-21.
Named for an obscure mail rider, as Faulkner reveals in Requiem for a Nun, Jefferson represents not homage to the great liberal Virginia revolutionary but homage to the independent spirit of the frontier South.

35   . "Faulkner's Country Church: A Note on 'Shingles for the Lord,'" MissQ, XXI (Summer), 205-10.
Faulkner is unfamiliar with the country church displayed in the 1943 story "Shingles for the Lord," because he has given his "Methodist" minister an uncharacteristic baptizing gown.

36 HUTCHINSON, JAMES D. "Time: The Fourth Dimension in Faulkner," SDR, VI (Autumn), 91-103.
Reality, like the psychological sense of time, is only a condition of consciousness for Faulkner. Bergson and William James offer instructive parallels to Faulkner's use of time and memory in his fiction.

37 ISRAEL, CALVIN. "The Last Gentleman," PR, XXXV (Spring), 315-19.
Israel, then a senior at City College of New York, met Faulkner in Washington Square Park. A reticent Faulkner did not respond very much to the young man's comments and questions.

38 *JÄGER, DIETRICH. "Die Darstellung des Kampfes bei Stephen Crane, Hemingway, Faulkner, und Britting," Amerikanische Erzählungen von Hawthorne bis Salinger: Interpretationen. KBAA, VI, 112-54.
MLA International Bibliography 1969, Item F 76.

39   . "Der 'verheimlichte Raum' in Faulkners 'A Rose for Emily' und Brittings 'Der Schneckenweg,'" LWU, I, 108-16.
Attention to the exterior of the house, then detailed views inside leading gradually to the secret of the "hidden" room in "A Rose for Emily" are paralleled by a gradually more revealing look at Emily's motives for the murder.

1968

40   KEARFUL, FRANK J.   "Tony Last and Ike McCaslin: The Loss of a
      Usable Past," UWR, III (Spring), 45-52.
         Ike McCaslin's paradoxical failure is compared to the
      similar fate of a character in Evelyn Waugh's A Handful of
      Dust.   Each is separated from the source of his virtue;
      each survives into an inimical world.   Both reveal "the
      absurdity, nobility, and sinfulness of seeking in the
      ideal a better world than that which can be lived in."

41   *LANATI, BARBARA.   "Il primo Faulkner: As I Lay Dying," Sigma,
      XIX, 83-119.
         According to American Literature Scholarship 1969,
      p. 116, this article is "appreciative" and makes some "sug-
      gestive stylistic comments" about As I Lay Dying.

42   LANDOR, MIKHAIL.   "William Faulkner: New Translations and
      Studies," SovL, VIII (No. 242), 180-85.
         The Snopes trilogy and short stories have attracted a
      Faulkner audience in Russia.   Soldiers' Pay was translated
      in 1966 in a "provincial journal."   Intruder in the Dust
      was published almost in reply to critics like Maxwell
      Geismar who say Faulkner's work after Absalom, Absalom! is
      not as good as his earlier work.   Eisenstein was interest-
      ed in Faulkner's techniques.   Faulkner criticism in Russia
      and translations of his work are reviewed.

43   McDONALD, WALTER R.   "Coincidence in the Novel: A Necessary
      Technique," CE, XXIX (February), 373-88.
         A short discussion of the way Faulkner prepares and uses
      coincidence in Light in August and Absalom, Absalom! notes
      that comic or grotesque coincidence add to the sense of
      Calvinist predestination, in the former case, or to Greek-
      like fatality in the latter.   Coincidence, skillfully han-
      dled, is the staple of fiction and the quality in it which
      keeps the fascinated reader coming back.

44   MERIWETHER, JAMES B., and MICHAEL MILLGATE.   "Introduction,"
      Lion in the Garden: Interviews with William Faulkner,
      1926-1962.   New York: Random House, pp. ix-xvi.
         Faulkner believed an artist's work should stand for it-
      self, without publicity about his private life.   By and
      large he resisted the limelight by various means, includ-
      ing silence, misinformation, and outright hostility to
      prospective interviewers.   But, under the right circum-
      stances, and with an understanding audience, he could also
      be quite revealing about his work.   Following the awarding
      of the Nobel Prize, he made himself more available, not
      only through his public speeches but also through more
      frequent interviews.

45   MERTON, THOMAS. "'Baptism in the Forest': Wisdom and Initia-
     tion in William Faulkner," CathW, CCVII (June), 124-30.
     Reprinted from 1967.B71.

46   MILLGATE, JANE. "Quentin Compson as Poor Player: Verbal and
     Social Clichés in The Sound and the Fury," RLV, XXXIV,
     40-49.
         In The Sound and the Fury, Quentin Compson uses romantic,
     sentimental clichés from melodrama in his reactions to
     life, a characteristic prefigured in his childhood. His
     suicide, a fitting gesture, in the context, is an attempt
     to impose his own order on existence.

47   MILLGATE, MICHAEL. "Faulkner in Toronto: A Further Note,"
     UTQ, XXXVII (January), 197-202.
         Further evidence from men who trained with the RAF in
     Toronto at the same time as Faulkner continues to affirm
     that Faulkner would have had little chance to fly and that
     he exaggerated his exploits to his family in Oxford.

48   MUEHL, LOIS. "Word Choice and Choice Words in Faulkner's
     Sartoris," LC, XXXV (Winter-Spring), 58-63.
         Young Bayard Sartoris in Sartoris is characterized by
     the use of monosyllables and the infrequent use of the
     first person pronoun, an appropriate device.

49   MULQUEEN, JAMES E. "Foreshadowing of Melville and Faulkner,"
     AN&Q, VI (March), 102.
         A story on "Metaphysics of Bear-Hunting," which by title
     suggests the chapter on Indian-hating in Melville's The
     Confidence-Man, suggests in substance the hunt in Go Down,
     Moses.

50   *NICOLAISEN, PETER. "Hemingways 'My Old Man' und Faulkners
     'Barn Burning': Ein Vergleich," Amerikanische Erzählungen
     von Hawthorne bis Salinger: Interpretationen. KBAA, VI,
     187-223.
         American Literary Scholarship 1969, p. 128.

51   NOBLE, DAVID W. "After the Lost Generation," The Eternal Adam
     and the New World Garden: The Central Myth in the Ameri-
     can Novel Since 1830. New York: George Braziller,
     pp. 163-76.
         After three lost generation novels, in two of which the
     hero expects the world to respect his innocence and dis-
     covers instead corruption and disillusion, Faulkner turned
     to a larger social order, to greater psychological depth
     in his characters, and to an assertion of the universality

1968

(NOBLE, DAVID W.)
of alienation. He discovers, as in Sanctuary, that alienation is not tragic but pathetic. Joe Christmas of Light in August is alienated because society has inculcated values of perfection he cannot meet.

52 O'BRIEN, MATTHEW C. "A Note on Faulkner's Civil War Women," NMW, I (Fall), 56-63.
Granny Millard and Drusilla in The Unvanquished are "victims" of the "total war" concept of the Civil War, one through moral blindness, the other through over-reaction. Faulkner admires the courage of his Civil War women, but criticizes them for maintaining old customs.

53 O'DEA, RICHARD J. "Faulkner's Vestigial Christianity," Renascence," XXI (Autumn), 44-54.
Faulkner puts positive emphasis in his work on human virtues which also happen to be the bedrock of Christianity. It is not dogmatically Christian, but preparatory. The author reviews the critical treatment of Christian thought in Faulkner's work.

54 OTTEN, TERRY. "Faulkner's Use of the Past: A Comment," Renascence, XX (Summer), 198-207, 214.
Absalom, Absalom!, "The Bear," The Unvanquished, and Requiem for a Nun give a full range of Faulkner's treatment of the past, his use of history. He used the past to universalize the moral problems he approached. Requiem for a Nun is not as successful as the earlier work.

55 PATE, WILLARD. "Benjy's Names in the Compson Household," FurmS, XVI (May), 37-38.
The names by which another character addresses or refers to Benjy in The Sound and the Fury is an index to that character's personality and to the relationship with the idiot.

56 PEAVY, CHARLES D. "A Note on the 'Suicide Pact' in The Sound and the Fury," ELN, V (March), 207-09.
Later comment by Faulkner about Caddy proves she would not have agreed to a suicide pact with Quentin. It is one of his fantasies.

57 _____. "'Did You Ever Have a Sister?'--Holden, Quentin, and Sexual Innocence," FQ, I, 82-95.
Faulkner's high regard for Catcher in the Rye and obvious similarities between Holden Caulfield of that novel and Quentin Compson of The Sound and the Fury invite com-

(PEAVY, CHARLES D.)
parison of the two novels. Both young men recognize awak-
ening sexuality as a threat to what they are trying to
preserve. Holden is driven into a sanitarium, Quentin to
suicide by the inability to prolong childhood and the fear
of life.

58 PRESLEY, DELMA EUGENE. "Is Reverend Whitfield a Hypocrite?"
RS, XXXVI (March), 57-61.
Though an adulterer, Whitfield of As I Lay Dying is not
technically a "hypocrite," as he has been called. He is
"a simple and honorable man of the cloth." He endures.

59 PRICE, REYNOLDS. "Pylon: The Posture of Worship," Shenandoah,
XIX (Spring), 49-61.
Pylon is about the three flyers at its center, but they
are essentially silent and shadowy as characters and we
are not meant to understand them. The reporter--a figure
for the poet--is fascinated by them and the novel takes up
this fascination of poet for hero, a mystery not fully to
be resolved. It is more a psalm to the mystery than a
conventional novel.

60 RICHARDSON, DALE. "A Literary Letter from Southern Ken," Mid-
South, Memphis Commercial Appeal Sunday Magazine,
(13 October), pp. 6-9, 11-13.
Comments on Faulkner and on changes in Southern literature since his death are taken from Walker Percy, Shelby
Foote, and Peter Taylor, who were interviewed for the
piece.

61 RICHARDSON, H. EDWARD. "The Decadence in Faulkner's First
Novel: The Faun, the Worm, and the Tower," EA, XXI (July-
September), 225-35.
Fin de siècle decadence in Faulkner's poetry and first
novel is used to contrast the worlds of soldiers and ci-
vilians. Images used to carry some of the themes of decadence are the worm (death), the tower (transcendence), and
the faun (man's animality).

62 RIESE, UTZ. "Das Dilemma eines dritten Weges: William Faulkners widerspruchlicher Humanismus," ZAA, XVI (No. 2),
138-55; (No. 3), 257-73.
Faulkner's work shows a progressive move toward a solution to modern alienation, seen in this essay in Marxist
terms. From Light in August to Intruder in the Dust,
Faulkner changes from a praise of nature as a source of
meaning to a new humanistic awareness as the solution.

1968

(RIESE, UTZ)
Faulkner has difficulty not seeing nature as commodity.
He uses Bergsonian time, but not exclusively. A sociolog-
ical interpretation of Faulkner's work.

63 ROBINSON, CECIL. "The Fall of 'The Big House' in the Literature of the Americas," ArQ, XXIV (Spring), 23-41.
Faulkner, among other writers, and Absalom, Absalom!,
among other books, are used in a discussion of recognizable similarities between Latin American treatments of the
plantation in fiction and North American treatments.

64 SANDERSON, JAMES L. "'Spotted Horses' and the Theme of Social
Evil," EJ, LVII (May), 700-04.
Farce and pathos combine to create a poignant view of
"social evil" in "Spotted Horses." Rapacity preys on a
permissive society, harming the gullible and the innocent.

65 SMITH, JULIAN. "A Source for Faulkner's A Fable," AL, XL
(November), 394-97.
Humphrey Cobb's Paths of Glory (1935), a copy of which
was in Faulkner's library, may be a source for A Fable.
Parallels are listed.

66 STEVENS, ARETTA. "Faulkner and 'Helen,'--A Further Note," PN,
I (October), 31.
An image from Poe's "Helen" found in "A Rose for Emily"
(1968.B69) is also in The Hamlet, where it links Eula to
Helen of Troy.

67 STEWART, JACK. "Apotheosis and Apocalypse in Faulkner's
'Wash,'" SSF, VI (Fall), 586-600.
As one of the betrayed, Wash Jones achieves revenge in
"Wash" as apotheosis of Apocalypse: Time, Death,
Judgment.

68 STEWART, RANDALL. Review of A Fable, edited by George Core.
GaR, XXII (Spring), 128-30.
Reprints 1954.B72.

69 STRONKS, JAMES. "A Poe Source for Faulkner? 'To Helen' and
'A Rose for Emily,'" PN, I (April), 11.
Poe's poem "To Helen" is a possible source for recurrent
images in "A Rose for Emily" describing Emily as like an
idol in a niche. See also 1968.B66.

70   TATE, ALLEN. "Faulkner's Sanctuary and the Southern Myth,"
      VQR, XLIV (Summer), 418-27.
           Faulkner, a master of observation and the inner conflict
      which is the essence of the art of fiction, is ranked with
      the writers who used, not invented, an existing Southern
      mythos to create great imaginative literature.

71   TURNER, ARLIN. "William Faulkner and the Literary Flowering
      in the American South," DUJ, LX (March), 109-18.
           Faulkner's late discovery, even by the other writers of
      the Southern Renaissance so-called, is a result of his de-
      termination to stick to his place, follow his own artistry.
      Much better read than people have imagined, Faulkner was
      steeped in his region's history. His books assess the
      traditions of the South; he was master, not victim, of the
      tradition. His greatness is due to his prolific oeuvre,
      his mastery of technique, and his ability to draw charac-
      ters and tell stories.

72   TUSO, JOSEPH F. "Faulkner's 'Wash,'" Expl, XXVII (November),
      Item 17.
           The mare 'Griselda' in "Wash" is, after its name, pre-
      dictably faithful, bearing a male colt, while ironically
      Milly Jones bears Sutpen a daughter. In Absalom, Absalom!,
      which seems to originate in "Wash," Faulkner changed the
      mare's name to "Penelope," another tag for faithfulness
      and a reference appropriately epical, like the novel into
      which it fits.

73   UCHINO, TAKAKO. "The Pattern and Devices in Light in August,"
      Maekawa Shunichi Kyoju Kanreki Kinen-ronkunshu (Essays and
      Studies in Commemoration of Professor Shunichi Maekawa's
      Sixty-First Birthday). Tokyo: Eihosha, 155-63.
           Contrast between Lena and Joe in Light in August creates
      a pattern. A chart and explanation describe how other
      characters fit the scheme. It dramatizes the intersection
      of life and death.

74   VAN NOSTRAND, ALBERT D. "The Poetic Dialogues of William
      Faulkner," Everyman His Own Poet: Romantic Gospels in
      American Literature. New York: McGraw-Hill, pp. 175-96.
           Faulkner's poetic quality in the novels consists of the
      reiteration of events, images, and themes through various-
      ly shaded impressions arranged in formal patterns. His
      myth is the legend of divine retribution wreaked on the
      South for its sins, a myth which his characters accept as
      an explanation of the forces of circumstance. The myth is
      explored in "poetic dialogues" like The Sound and the Fury,

1968

(VAN NOSTRAND, ALBERT D.)
Intruder in the Dust, Light in August, Absalom, Absalom!,
and "The Bear," where the form is self-interruptive,
filled with dramatic dialogues of different kinds, and
where the central situation is a character's attempt to
find and exorcise the complex causes of his personal
predicament.

75   WALL, CAREY. "Drama and Technique in Faulkner's The Hamlet,"
      TCL, XIV (April), 17-23.
         Themes alone do not write or explain The Hamlet. Faulk-
      ner's "private vision" is revealed by the way he depicts
      the "individual human spirit battling...in a doomed at-
      tempt to wrest happiness and satisfaction from human life."
      The episodes of the novel repeatedly depict this struggle
      in dramatic terms. Yoknapatawpha lives, in general, de-
      pict man's response to the injustice of deprivation.

76   WARREN, JOYCE W. "The Role of Lion in Faulkner's 'The Bear':
      Key to a Better Understanding," ArQ, XXIV (Autumn),
      252-60.
         Lion is not associated with mechanistic civilization or
      Anglo-Saxon rapacity. Like Old Ben, the bear, he is an
      elemental force of nature; there are many similarities be-
      tween the two animals. The conflict between the two
      teaches Ike that "the spirit of nature can never die."
      This in turn prepares him to repudiate the plantation.
      Ike has insight and compassion which his cousin McCaslin
      will never possess.

77   WATKINS, FLOYD C. "Faulkner and His Critics," TSLL, X
      (Summer), 317-29.
         The article lists a number of critical inaccuracies in
      articles and books about Faulkner and his work, from
      Soldiers' Pay to Absalom, Absalom! but excluding Pylon.

78   WEISGERBER, JEAN. "Faulkner et Dostoëvski, confluences et in-
      fluences," Travaux de la Faculté de Philosophie et Lettres
      Université Libre de Bruxelles, XXXIX. Brussels: Univer-
      sity of Brussels.
         A parallel study of Faulkner and Dostoevsky which at-
      tempts to judge Faulkner in the light of the Russian. The
      first part discusses common preoccupations and themes,
      parallels between the writers' uses of places and times;
      the second part discusses Faulkner's books, including sto-
      ries, in chronological order. Finds more "confluence" than
      "influence."

79 _____. "Faulkner's Monomaniacs: Their Indebtedness to Raskolnikov," CLS, V (June), 181-93.
Raskolnikov, as monomaniac, influences Faulkner's portraits of Bayard Sartoris, Quentin Compson, Joe Christmas,
Thomas Sutpen, and Mink Snopes. They share his madness,
his tendency to abstraction, his estrangement, his pride.

80 WEISS, MIRIAM. "Hell Creek Bottom Is: A Reminiscence," JMH,
XXX (August), 196-201.
A description of Hell Creek Bottom, and an auto trip
through it in 1915 are recalled in view of Faulkner's fictional treatment in The Reivers. The real place is on the
road between Tupelo, Miss., and Memphis, Tenn., not between Oxford and Memphis. Faulkner moves the site for his
purposes.

81 WIGGINS, ROBERT A. "Faulkner," American Literary Scholarship
an annual, 1966, edited by James Woodress. Durham, N. C.:
Duke University Press, pp. 79-84.
The annual survey of Faulkner criticism.

82 WILLIAMS, JOHN S. "'The Final Copper Light of Afternoon':
Hightower's Redemption," TCL, XIII (January), 205-15.
Light in August moves structurally from the humor and
buoyancy of Lena Grove's travels into increasing darkness
in the lives of Hightower and Christmas. At the end it
reverses the pattern, but Hightower, who mediates between
the extremes, has been changed by contact with both sides
and redeemed from a life in bondage to the past. He is
drawn out of his isolation back into the human community.

1969 A BOOKS

1 *ALEXANDRESCU, SORIN. William Faulkner. Bucharest: Editura
pentru Literatură Universală.
An introduction to Faulkner for the Romanian reader and
a structuralist study of the fiction viewed as a "continuum." See review, MissQ, XXII (Summer 1970), 336-38. A
portion translated in 1970.B3.

2 EVERETT, WALTER K. Faulkner's Art and Characters. Woodbury,
N. Y.: Barron's Educational Series, Inc.
This handbook includes a brief biographical summary and
an overview of Faulkner's career as introduction; discussions of the novels in alphabetical order; discussions of
the stories in alphabetical order; a dictionary of charac-

1969

(EVERETT, WALTER K.)
ters with identifications by race and by relative importance in the work in question.

3 KERR, ELIZABETH M. Yoknapatawpha: Faulkner's "Little Postage
Stamp of Native Soil." New York: Fordham University
Press.
The author attempts to demonstrate often minute correspondences between the places and people of Faulkner's
fictional city or county and Oxford and Lafayette County,
Miss. New Deal sociology and contemporary social and political commentary are used to paint a picture of a reac-
tionary, benighted South, more violent than Faulkner's
fiction. Gavin Stevens is identified as Faulkner's personal representative. Twenty photographs illustrate the
book. Appendices discuss the Oxford/Jefferson courthouse,
ruined mansions in the area, the preservation and demythol-
ologization of the cavalier tradition, the Mississippi
plantation, and Faulkner's great grandfather, Col. W. C.
Falkner. The Reivers is the Golden Book of Yoknapatawpha.
(See her article, 1967.B57, and reply 1970.B54.) Extensive reviews at 1969.B9 and 1970.B64.

4 *LYRA, FRANCISZEK. William Faulkner. Warsaw: Wiedza Pow-
szechna.
A study of Faulkner which includes a bibliography of
translations and reviews in Poland. Library of Congress
National Union Catalogue, Author List 1968-1972, Vol. 58.

5 MINTER, DAVID L. Twentieth-Century Interpretations of Light
in August. Englewood Cliffs, N. J.: Prentice-Hall.
Minter's introduction to this collection of excerpts
from criticism of Light in August suggests the value of
certain viewpoints and approaches toward the novel and indicates some of the adverse criticism which Light in August and Faulkner's work in general has received. Includes material from 1957.B10, 1957.B1, 1959.A4, 1963.A1,
1966.A6, and short extracts from other critics and from
Faulkner's own statements about the novel. Appendix includes material from 1958.B41.

6 RICHARDSON, H. EDWARD. William Faulkner: The Journey to
Self-Discovery. Columbia, Mo.: University of Missouri
Press.
Faulkner's eccentric behavior in young manhood and the
poetry he wrote then were misguided efforts to create and
express expectations of glory; like his faun in The Marble
Faun, Faulkner felt imprisoned in his own Southern place.

(RICHARDSON, H. EDWARD)
Gradually moving toward prose and "regional realism" under
the influence of Sherwood Anderson, Faulkner comes "home
to his roots" in Sartoris, the culmination of his
apprenticeship.

7   WEBER, ROBERT WILHELM. Die Aussage der Form: Zur Textur
und Struktur des Bewusstseinsromans. Dargestellt an W.
Faulkners The Sound and the Fury. Beihefte zum JA, Bd.
XXVII. Heidelberg: Carl Winter Verlag.
The techniques of modern structural criticism are used
to investigate The Sound and the Fury. The author adopts
methods from Russian, American, and German formalists, the
psychological and linguistic critics, and the French
phenomenologists to produce a reading of the novel.

1969 B   SHORTER WRITINGS

1   ARPAD, JOSEPH J. "William Faulkner's Legendary Novels: The
Snopes Trilogy," MissQ, XXII (Summer), 214-25.
The unresolved juxtaposition of the legendary and the
real makes the Snopes trilogy a "legendary novel." The
effect is created and heightened by the narrators' unre-
liability, including that of the authorial voice. The
purpose of such an approach to fiction is to explain the
unknowable and enigmatic in human existence.

2   ATKINS, ANSELM. "The Matched Halves of Absalom, Absalom!"
MFS, XV (Summer), 264-65.
Chapters I-V and VI-IX of Absalom, Absalom! present a
matched, almost mirrored parallelism. Both begin with
two people (of whom Quentin, in each case, makes one) and
a note (Miss Rosa's summons; Mr. Compson's letter). The
"cold" tale is told in a Mississippi September; the "hot"
one is recounted in a New England December and both the
tellings and retellings last about the same amount of
time. This balance may be the key to more subtle
parallels.

3   BLAIR, JOHN G. "Camus' Faulkner: Requiem for a Nun," BFLS,
XLVII (January), 249-57.
Although Camus did not himself initiate the adaptation
of Faulkner's Requiem for a Nun, it remains revealing for
Camus' art and a commentary upon Faulkner's novel. The
novel was not very "playable." Nancy's skin is the nun's
habit, but the white community sees her as worthless.
The novel is designed to involve the reader in "the difference between two levels of right or wrong." Nancy's

1969

(BLAIR, JOHN G.)
act is right under a higher morality. Camus' changes in
the material are discussed.

4   BLAKE, NELSON M. "The Decay of Yoknapatawpha County," Novelists' America: Fiction as History, 1910-1940. Syracuse,
N. Y.: Syracuse University Press, pp. 75-109.
One of several essays by a historian on the historical
uses of fiction, this chapter discusses the South that appears in Faulkner's novels, noting parallels between
Faulkner's real home town and county and the fictional
ones and giving a capsule history of the fictional county
out of the novels. Faulkner accepted the New South and
its commercial and social effects while he lamented the
passing of the virtues of the older society.

5   BLOTNER, JOSEPH. "Speaking of Books: Faulkner's 'A Fable,'"
NYTBR (25 May), pp. 2, 34, 36, 38, 39.
Blotner draws upon his research for the biography of
Faulkner to give a brief account of the sources and com-
position of Faulkner's A Fable.

6   _____. "William Faulkner: Committee Chairman," Themes and
Directions in American Literature: Essays in Honor of
Leon Howard, edited by Ray B. Brown and Donald Pizer.
Lafayette, Ind.: Purdue University Press, 200-19.
Faulkner's involvement in President Eisenhower's People-
to-People program is recounted, including letters,
speeches.

7   BRADFORD, MELVIN E. "'New Men' in Mississippi: Absalom, Ab-
salom! and Dollar Cotton," NMW, II (Fall), 55-66.
A comparison of stories of the parvenu in Faulkner's
Absalom, Absalom! and his brother John's 1942 novel Dollar
Cotton. John's book castigates a system, and like his Men
Working (1941) is conservative. Faulkner's book is tragic,
concentrating on the man.

8   BROUGHTON, PANTHEA R. "Masculinity and Menfolk in The Hamlet," MissQ, XXII (Summer), 181-89.
False notions of masculinity, dominated by the need to
conquer and possess another human being, make The Hamlet
a more trenchant commentary upon Yoknapatawpha society
than has been supposed. Flem Snopes is not that much
worse than the other men of the book, who exploit people--
in this case, women--as though they were objects. Even
Mink, Ike Snopes, and Ratliff, the most sympathetic men in
the book, represent different forms of the failure to
achieve a harmonious, human love relationship with women.

9   BROWN, CALVIN. "A Dim View of Faulkner's Country," GaR, XXIII
     (Winter), 501-11.
          This review of Kerr's book (1969.A3) takes issue chiefly
     with her sociology, but also with some of her identifica-
     tions of Faulkner's fictional places.

10   _____. "Faulkner's Use of the Oral Tradition," Proceedings of
     the Vth Congress of the International Comparative Litera-
     ture Association, Belgrade, 1967, edited by Nikola Bana-
     šević. Amsterdam: Swets & Zeitlinger, pp. 519-26.
          Appeared first in 1968.B18.

11   BRUMM, URSULA. "Thoughts on History and the Novel," CLS, VI
     (September), 317-30.
          In Absalom, Absalom! Faulkner takes up the "epistemo-
     logical problem" of history, dramatizing the way history
     becomes a function of subjective consciousness and imagi-
     nation. It is a historical novel and a novel about his-
     tory. The "historian and the writer are one," seeking the
     truth of the past.

12   CAMUS, ALBERT. "William Faulkner: Foreword to Requiem for a
     Nun," "On Faulkner," "Excerpts from Three Interviews,"
     Lyrical and Critical Essays, translated by Ellen Conroy
     Kennedy. New York: Knopf, pp. 311-20.
          The introduction to a combined edition of Camus' play
     version and a translation of Faulkner's novel discusses
     the difficulties of adaptation: Camus left to the scene
     designers, he says, the job of interpreting the prose
     narratives which set the "religious" character of each
     setting, while he redistributed the novelistic dialogue
     into more actable form, preserving, if sparingly, the mar-
     velous tragic soliloquies of Faulkner's novel. A program
     note to the play version praises Faulkner for creating a
     modern high tragedy out of the stuff of the daily papers.
     Interviews from 1956 include answers to questions about
     Requiem for a Nun. Taken from Albert Camus, Théâtre, Ré-
     cits, Nouvelles (Paris: Gallimard, 1967), pp. 1863-81,
     with the omission of Camus' 1951 letter to the Harvard
     Advocate (1951.B13).

13   CLARK, WILLIAM J. "Faulkner's Light in August," Expl, XXVIII
     (November), Item 19.
          Joe Christmas's "ritual" behavior during the time before
     he kills Joanna includes his sleeping in an old stable on
     the place. He questions his desire to go there himself,
     wondering why he wants to "smell horses." The key is his
     association of the place and its "man-smell" with punish-

1969

(CLARK, WILLIAM J.)
ment, which he subconsciously desires as a release from
responsibility.

14   COBAU, WILLIAM W.   "Jason Compson and the Costs of Specula-
        tion," MissQ, XXII (Summer), 257-61.
        Jason Compson's Good Friday speculations on the cotton
     futures market are explained, and normal practice is com-
     pared to what Faulkner does with the material. The state
     of the actual market on that day is given. The conclusion
     is that Faulkner has created an "expressive device" to de-
     pict Jason's character.

15   COMMINS, DOROTHY B.   "William Faulkner in Princeton," Journal
        of Historical Studies, II (Autumn), 179-85.
        Mrs. Saxe Commins recounts Faulkner's visits in Prince-
     ton with her and her husband, Faulkner's editor at Random
     House, including impressions of the novelist and remarks
     on the editing of The Town.

16   CORE, GEORGE, ed.   "The State of Southern Fiction," South-
        ern Fiction Today: Renascence and Beyond. Athens, Ga.:
        University of Georgia Press, pp. 58-60, 82-85.
        Walter Sullivan, Louis D. Rubin, Hugh Holman, Core, and
     others participate in a symposium and discuss the effect
     of Faulkner's influence and the merits of his later work.

17   CRANE, JOHN K.   "The Jefferson Courthouse: An Axis Exsecra-
        bilis Mundi," TCL, XV (April), 19-23.
        The mythological roots of Yoknapatawpha County, as de-
     lineated in Faulkner's books, explain his characters.
     Mircea Eliade's theories of human organization help ex-
     plain that the Jefferson courthouse is an axis mundi, the
     center point which creates "sacred space," and outlying
     regions correspond to Eliade's concept of "profane space,"
     which is filled with demons, the unknown.

18   DARNELL, DONALD G.   "Cooper and Faulkner: Land, Legacy, and
        the Tragic Vision," SAB, XXXIV (March), 3-5.
        Cooper and Faulkner share a tragic view of the American
     experience as a missed second chance. Both dramatize the
     paradox that the beautiful new world fails to inspire its
     inhabitants with new and better behavior. Both show the
     values inherent in dynasty and stewardship, but Faulkner
     sees the ownership of the land as producing a curse. Both
     are aware of the guilt--Cooper applying it to the dispos-
     session of the Indians and Faulkner to slavery--which
     taints the American experiment.

19   DeVILLIER, MARY ANNE G. "Faulkner's Young Man: As Reflected
      in the Character of Charles Mallison," LauR, IX (No. 2),
      42-49.
          Charles Mallison, briefly characterized in several
      Faulkner fictions, is, in Intruder in the Dust, the "in-
      itiate" who succeeds in gaining "identity through knowl-
      edge of self." In The Town and The Mansion, he "endures."

20   DITSKY, JOHN. "From Oxford to Salinas: Comparing Faulkner
      and Steinbeck," StN, II (Fall), 51-55.
          There are more similarities between Faulkner and Stein-
      beck than critics have seen: their view of man; their
      regionalism; their view of nature. Steinbeck confirms
      Faulkner's values, mentioning him by name in his own Nobel
      speech.

21   DOVE, GEORGE N. "Shadow and Paradox: Imagery in The Sound
      and the Fury," Essays in Memory of Christine Burleson in
      Language and Literature by Former Colleagues and Students,
      edited by Thomas G. Burton. Johnson City, Tenn.: Resi-
      dent Advisory Council, East Tennessee State University,
      pp. 89-95.
          Quentin's section of The Sound and the Fury, richest in
      imagery, centers on time, honeysuckle, water, and Quen-
      tin's shadow; throughout is an emphasis on the shadow
      world that prefigures his concern with time and death.
      Many of the images reflect the imagery of other sections,
      showing Faulkner's rhetorical control.

22   DUNLAP, MARY M. "Sex and the Artist in Mosquitoes," MissQ,
      XXII (Summer), 190-206.
          Most characters of both sexes in Mosquitoes depict the
      sterility of sex and art in the modern world. Gordon, the
      sculptor, is exceptional, yet he sacrifices love and the
      sexual conquest in order to concentrate on creating a
      lasting art.

23   DUSSINGER, GLORIA R. "Faulkner's Isaac McCaslin as Romantic
      Hero Manqué," SAQ, LXVIII (Summer), 377-85.
          "The Bear" dramatizes a modern version of the "Romantic
      Quest." Ike goes into the wilderness, finds his essential
      self, but refuses the Return. "The Old People" is Pre-
      lude; "Delta Autumn" shows the results in the life of "a
      man who has developed only one side of his being." The
      fourth part of "The Bear" is crucial to an understanding
      of Ike's failure in the novel. The weakness of Ike's
      position is his need to justify it by obviously lame
      arguments.

1969

24 EIGNER, EDWIN M. "Faulkner's Isaac and the American Ishmael," JA, XIV, 107-15.
Faulkner's typical hero, which he shares with many American writers before him, is no more accurately described than these other characters by the biblical Ishmael whose name many have borrowed. The American wanderer is not, however he may be identified, an outcast or exile forced from home; he has chosen to wander. Faulkner's Ike, named for the biblical Isaac, is more to the point. Go Down, Moses, shows that playing the role of Ishmael, fleeing responsibility, is no answer.

25 *EMERSON, O. B. "Faulkner, the Mule, and the South," Delta Review, VI (November-December), 108-10.
Bassett, Item AA238.

26 FARNHAM, JAMES F. "A Note on One Aspect of Faulkner's Style," Lang&S, II (Spring), 190-92.
Faulkner's difficult style deliberately reflects the difficulties his characters encounter as they attempt to know reality. His books are filled by references to this difficulty and with "not...but" constructions. Another difficulty is his reliance upon oral forms, hence the absence of formal prose structure in the work.

27 FERRIS, WILLIAM R., JR. "William Faulkner and Phil Stone: An Interview with Emily Stone," SAQ, LXVIII (Autumn), 536-42.
The widow of Faulkner's early friend and literary adviser, Phil Stone, answers questions about Faulkner and the background of the relationship between the two men when they were young.

28 FETZ, HOWARD W. "Of Time and the Novel," XUS, VIII (Summer), 1-17.
A discussion of Faulkner's use of time in the context of a general analysis of time in representative modern novels. Faulkner uses objects and images as bridges between time levels.

29 FLANAGAN, JOHN T. "Folklore in Faulkner's Fiction," Studies in American Literature in Honor of Robert Dunn Faner, edited by Robert Partlow. PLL, V, Supplement (Summer), 119-44.
All categories and subjects of folklore and folk language are found in Faulkner's writings; they are surveyed briefly.

30 FRANKLIN, PHYLLIS. "The Influence of Joseph Hergesheimer upon
   Mosquitoes," MissQ, XXII (Summer), 207-13.
      The three Joseph Hergesheimer novels Faulkner reviewed
   in 1922 for the University of Mississippi student newspaper, The Bright Shawl, Linda Condon, and Cytherea, appear
   to have influenced technique and characterization in Mosquitoes. In some sense, Faulkner satirizes Hergesheimer's idealism. The real world's demands intrude throughout Mosquitoes.

31 GARMON, GERALD M. "Mirror Imagery in The Sound and the Fury,"
   NMW, II (Spring), 13-24.
      Mirrors are image, symbol, and motif in The Sound and
   the Fury, emphasizing Benjy's separateness and Quentin's
   egocentric brooding. See also 1954.B75.

32 GELFANT, BLANCHE H. "Faulkner and Keats: The Ideality of Art
   in 'The Bear,'" SLJ, II (Fall), 43-65.
      Ike's entrance into the wilderness is like the repeated
   theme of Keats' poems: escape to a better world, return,
   and the accompanying sense of loss. But Ike rejects the
   return, longs for the timeless, and his life is affected
   by his belief that he can live in the ideal. He does not
   shoot the bear, he repudiates the plantation, and he seeks
   to escape the human condition.

33 GÉRARD, ALBERT. Les Tambours du Néant: Essais sur le pro-
   blème existentiel dans le roman américain. Brussels: La
   renaissance du livre, pp. 79-92.
      Post-war disillusion and despair in American fiction has
   little to do with the war and much to do with the repeatedly broken American Dream of perfection. Faulkner's
   Soldiers' Pay shows the war as catalyst. The Yoknapatawpha fiction uses the "legend of the South" also to depict
   the vacuity of modern existence. Faulkner's use of debased sexuality in several novels merely dramatizes the
   lack of faith and hope in the future. But Faulkner's men
   are not victims of some cosmic absurdity. Men themselves
   have created the injustice and folly from which other men
   suffer.

34 GIERMANSKI, JAMES R. "William Faulkner's Use of the Confes-
   sional," Renascence, XXI (Spring), 119-23, 166.
      In Requiem for a Nun, Faulkner explores the value of
   "sin-telling" as a cathartic and penitential art as it has
   been used in the Catholic Church for 2000 years.

1969

35   GOLD, JOSEPH. "Dickens and Faulkner: The Uses of Influence,"
      DR, XLIX (Spring), 69-79.
            Faulkner's admission of his interest in Charles Dickens'
      fiction leads one to see that the English novelist is a
      major influence on Faulkner. There are sources for
      scenes, names and characters in almost all Faulkner's work
      which come from Dickens; there are interesting parallels
      in the careers of the two writers.

36   _____. "The Faulkner Game: or, Find the Author," SLJ, I
      (Spring), 91-97.
            Reviewing Adams' Myth and Motion (1968.A1), Gold also
      makes a complaint about critical clichés in work on Faulk-
      ner and the failure to use existing scholarship.

37   GRESSET, MICHEL. "Un Faulkner féerique," NRF, N. S. XVII
      (September), 437-40.
            The Wishing Tree, published in France as L'arbre aux
      souhaits, is not unique or even a pure version of the
      fairy tale Faulkner prepared in several versions for
      children of his acquaintances from the early twenties to
      the late forties. It bears a relationship to "That Eve-
      ning Sun" and The Sound and the Fury; there is a sophis-
      ticated symbolism in the story.

38   GUNTER, RICHARD. "An Essay-Review" of The Functioning of
      Sentence Structure in the Stream-of-Consciousness Tech-
      nique of William Faulkner's "The Sound and the Fury": a
      Study in Linguistic Stylistics, by Irena Kaluza [1967.A2].
      MissQ, XXII (Summer), 264-79.
            Kaluza's attempt to analyze the "linguistic facts" which
      the style of the dramatic interior monologues of The Sound
      and the Fury present to an attentive reader explores
      largely unexamined fields of research. Gunter explains
      the theory and practice behind Kaluza's study and sum-
      marizes some of her observations and conclusions. A dif-
      ficult and valuable book, the study is the first step in
      a useful way to analyze literary works.
      Reprinted 1970.A6.

39   HOFFMAN, DANIEL. "William Faulkner, 'The Bear,'" Landmarks
      of American Writing, edited by Hennig Cohen. New York:
      Basic Books, pp. 341-52.
            In a series of essays originally prepared for presenta-
      tion over the Voice of America, Hoffman's piece argues
      that parts I, II, III, and V of "The Bear" identify Ike as
      a transcendental hero using the mythology and folklore of
      the hunt. Part IV takes up the quest for truth and the

(HOFFMAN, DANIEL)
　　need for initiation, paralleling the hunt tales, and ex-
　　plores his proper renunciation of the sins of his fathers.
　　He becomes the hero, but not the leader of a people.

40　HOWELL, ELMO. "William Faulkner's Mule: A Symbol of the
　　　Post-War South," KFR, XV (October-December), 81-86.
　　　　The mule is a symbol of Southern intransigence and
　　　doggedness.

41　　　　　. "William Faulkner: The Substance of Faith," BYUS, IX
　　　(Summer), 453-62.
　　　　Faulkner's fiction embodies the same faith in God and
　　　country present at the creation of America. Though aware
　　　of decay, he had the ability to make the best of his world,
　　　where he still found among the folk and the remnant of
　　　aristocracy vestiges of old times and old values.

42　HUME, ROBERT D. "Gothic Versus Romantic: A Revaluation of
　　　the Gothic Novel," PMLA, LXXXIV (March), 282-90.
　　　　Sanctuary and Moby Dick are used in a discussion and
　　　definition of the Gothic novel. Sanctuary creates a
　　　unique world, an atmosphere of terror, isolation in time
　　　and space (the South), and sets up, in the Benbows, a
　　　"normal" morality as reflector. It is about the perva-
　　　siveness of moral evil. Like the Gothic novel it presents
　　　evil as bound up with the good, providing no answers about
　　　why, and thus it portrays the insufficiency of reason to
　　　explain life's complexities.

43　HUNT, JOEL A. "William Faulkner and Rabelais: The Dog Sto-
　　　ry," ConL, X (Summer), 383-88.
　　　　In The Mansion Faulkner elaborates an episode from
　　　Rabelais' Pantagruel; Ratliff's humiliating Clarence
　　　Snopes with the help of the dogs. Like Rabelais, Faulkner
　　　is in tune with the folk idiom. See rejoinder and Hunt's
　　　reply, 1970.B63.

44　KAEL, PAULINE. Review of The Reivers [film version], NY, XLV
　　　(27 December), 47.
　　　　The film of The Reivers benefits from the Faulkner ma-
　　　terial behind it. It is a reminder that the young are
　　　people, too.

45　KEEFER, T. FREDERICK. "William Faulkner's Sanctuary: A Myth
　　　Examined," TCL, XV (July), 97-104.
　　　　Claiming that there has been "nearly universal condem-
　　　nation" of Sanctuary, the author believes himself to be

1969

(KEEFER, T. FREDERICK)
evaluating the novel seriously "for the first time." Internal evidence in the novel suggests Faulkner had a "calendar" of events for it, which proves his care and seriousness.

46 *KEITH, DON LEE. "Faulkner in New Orleans," Delta Review, VI (May), 46-49.
Bassett, Item BB109.

47 KIBLER, JAMES E., JR. "William Faulkner and Provincetown Drama, 1920-22," MissQ, XXII (Summer), 226-36.
Stark Young may have introduced Faulkner to the work of the Provincetown Playhouse in the 1920's. Faulkner demonstrates knowledge of O'Neill, Millay, Kreymborg in 1922 reviews for the University of Mississippi student newspaper. The article discusses the nature of Faulkner's knowledge and some applications found in Faulkner's writing.

48 KING, FRANCES H. "Benjamin Compson--Flower Child," CEA, XXXI (January), 10.
Benjy in The Sound and the Fury is, by current definition, a "flower child"--the fun-loving, free-living street person of the hippie movement. The point is argued.

49 KLINKOWITZ, JEROME F. "The Thematic Unity of Knight's Gambit," Critique, XI (No. 2), 81-100.
The stories in Knight's Gambit are united by the theme of conflict between outsider and community. Analysis of each story according to this thesis demonstrates the point. The author argues against paying too much attention to Gavin Stevens.

50 KULSETH, LEONARD I. "Cincinnatus Among the Snopes: The Role of Gavin Stevens," BSUF, X (Winter), 28-34.
Despite his oft-noted faults, Gavin Stevens becomes "Faulkner's favorite character," and, as a Cincinnatus devoted to justice, he comes to play a significant role in the fiction. His educational achievements, which some have seen as fatuous, are Faulkner's way of characterizing him as an intellectual capable of understanding human nature and society. He struggles against Snopesism and "for justice and truth."

51 LEHAN, RICHARD. "American Fiction and French Existentialism," Themes and Directions in American Literature, edited by Ray B. Brown and Donald Pizer. Lafayette, Ind.: Purdue University Press, pp. 186-99.

(LEHAN, RICHARD)
French interest in the "tragic world of American fiction" brought them to Faulkner's work. Though not himself an existentialist, Faulkner was capable of interpretation by writers like Sartre and Camus for their own purposes. The author discusses Faulkner's humanism and his focus on redeeming the past rather than living the present.

52 LEWIS, CLIFFORD L. "William Faulkner: The Artist as Historian," MASJ, X (No. 2), 36-48.
James Silver's book on Mississippi (1964.B64) is used to discuss the accuracy of the social picture in Intruder in the Dust. The novel is visionary of "the agony of attempting to unlock the doors and windows of the closed society."

53 *LINSCOTT, ELIZABETH. "Faulkner in Massachusetts," NEGalaxy, X (No. 3), 37-42.
The wife of one of Faulkner's Random House editors, Bob Linscott, recounts Faulkner's visits to their home, according to American Literary Scholarship 1970, p. 117.

54 *LITVIN, RINA. "William Faulkner's Light in August," Hasifrut, I, 589-98.
[In Hebrew, with English summary p. 768.] According to Millgate, American Literary Scholarship 1970, p. 124, the article sees the image of the wagon wheel as symbolically central to Light in August and discusses character in terms of static and dynamic views of reality.

55 McGLYNN, PAUL D. "The Chronology of 'A Rose for Emily,'" SSF, VI (Summer), 461-62.
Time, the "unseen character" in "A Rose for Emily," is the victor, marking the townspeople. The chronology is listed. Corrections are suggested in 1971.B73.

56 McHANEY, THOMAS L. "Robinson Jeffers' 'Tamar' and The Sound and the Fury," MissQ, XXII (Summer), 261-63.
Faulkner may have drawn some of the themes, images, characterizations, and events of The Sound and the Fury from Jeffers' long poem, "Tamar." Examples of striking parallels are given.

57 McLUHAN, MARSHALL. "The Southern Quality," The Interior Landscape: The Literary Criticism of Marshall McLuhan, 1943-1962. New York: McGraw-Hill, pp. 185-209.
Reprinted from 1947.B5.

1969

58 MELLARD, JAMES M. "Jason Compson: Humor, Hostility, and the
      Rhetoric of Aggression," SHR, III (Summer), 259-67.
        The comic, wit, and humor in Jason's section of The
      Sound and the Fury are discussed in Freudian terms. His
      rhetoric is agressive, expressing "his need for recogni-
      tion and acceptance," but it also reveals his spiritual
      malignity. As satire, it makes one of four modes of nar-
      rative in The Sound and the Fury, along with Benjy's pas-
      toral, Quentin's tragic, Dilsey's comedic.

59 MERIWETHER, JAMES B. "William Faulkner," Fifteen Modern Amer-
      ican Authors: A Review of Research and Criticism, edited
      by Jackson R. Bryer. Durham, N. C.: Duke University
      Press, pp. 175-210.
        Faulkner criticism up through 1967 is evaluated and its
      salient points summarized in essay form; the emphasis is
      upon the useful books and articles. Reprinted, in Sixteen
      Modern American Authors, edited by Bryer. (New York:
      Norton, 1973), pp. 223-58, with a "Supplement" pp. 258-75.

60 MYRES, W. V. "Faulkner's Parable of Poetic Justice," LaS,
      VIII (Fall), 224-30.
        Poetic justice, compounded on Res Grier who tries to
      avoid the effects of natural law, is the central theme of
      "Shingles for the Lord."

61 NAGEL, JAMES. "Huck Finn and The Bear: The Wilderness and
      Moral Freedom," ESA, XII (March), 59-63.
        Faulkner and Twain both saw the South cursed by slavery.
      In Huckleberry Finn and "The Bear" both writers equate the
      escape to the wilderness with moral freedom. Faulkner's
      world is less hopeful because the wilderness is
      diminishing.

62 O'NAN, MARTHA. "William Faulkner's Benjy: Hysteria," The
      Role of Mind in Hugo, Faulkner, Beckett, and Grass. New
      York: Philosophical Library, pp. 13-22.
        Benjy in The Sound and the Fury is one example of hys-
      teria in Faulkner's fiction; the fear of loss is something
      even he cannot escape.

63 PARSONS, THORNTON. "Doing the Best They Can," GaR, XXIII
      (Fall), 292-306.
        In As I Lay Dying, theme not plot or character predomi-
      nates. Family unity is the norm of the novel; and, de-
      spite the grotesque events of the book, there is a
      "healthy accommodation to realities" in the end. Darl, who
      thinks too much, is sent away to save a lawsuit; ironical-

(PARSONS, THORNTON)
ly, he is the greatest threat to Bundren unity. The family has saved itself in a way of which it is ignorant.

64   PATE, WILLARD. "Pilgrimage to Yoknapatawpha," FurmMag
      (Winter), 6-13.
        The author recounts five days in the Oxford, Miss., area
    visiting sights of interest to the Faulkner enthusiast.
    Five photographs illustrate.

65   PAYNE, LADELL. "The Trilogy: Faulkner's Comic Epic in
      Prose," SNNTS, I (Spring), 27-37.
        Like Fielding, Faulkner uses epic tradition in much of
    his work, especially the Snopes trilogy, but he goes be-
    yond Fielding to make his epic materials organic elements
    of a larger artistic purpose and, for all their humor, se-
    rious and frequently dark dramatizations of humankind.
    The author enumerates episodes, allusions to mythological
    characters, and similar devices which give epic stature to
    the trilogy, comparing Faulkner's work to Fielding's defi-
    nition of the comic epic.

66   PRASAD, V. R. N. "The Pilgrim and the Picaro: A Study of
      Faulkner's The Bear and The Reivers," Indian Essays in
      American Literature: Papers in Honour of Robert E. Spil-
      ler. Bombay: Popular Prakashan, pp. 209-21.
        Two modes of behavior are depicted in "The Bear" and The
    Reivers. The story depicts a primal order with no excep-
    tions; the novel depicts a civilized order based on arti-
    fice. Initiation into either world denies the other. The
    Reivers depicts a more successful, satisfying result,
    leading to speculation about Faulkner's discovery of mean-
    ing in his later work.

67   PRINCE, JOHN. "Andre Dhotel, Steinbeck et Faulkner: quel-
      ques similitudes," Caliban, VI, pp. 85-90.
        A comparison of passages suggests to the author that the
    French novelist Dhotel was influenced by the Americans.

68   PRIOR, LINDA T. "Theme, Imagery, and Structure in The Ham-
      let," MissQ, XXII (Summer), 237-56.
        Waste, emotional impotence, and greed are the central
    themes of The Hamlet, chiefly embodied in Eula Varner, a
    symbol of love and fecundity denied, misused, rendered
    impotent by the life of the cut-off country community.
    Other characters who carry the theme are Ike and Mink
    Snopes--both ironically compared and contrasted to Eula
    and the men in her life. Imagery of ruin and desolation

1969

(PRIOR, LINDA T.)
versus rain and ripeness underline these themes and the
structural form of the book. Books II and III are balanced and contrasted with I and IV; the focal point is
Ratliff's imaginary vision of Flem in Hell.

69 ROSENBERG, BRUCE A. "The Oral Quality of Rev. Shegog's Sermon
in William Faulkner's The Sound and the Fury," LWU, II,
73–88.
Shegog's sermon in The Sound and the Fury is typical and
effective; it perfectly parallels authentic black oral
tradition as reflected in transcriptions of contemporary
Negro sermons.

70 SANDERLIN, ROBERT R. "As I Lay Dying: Christian Symbols and
Thematic Implications," SoQ, VII (January), 155–66.
On the basis of religious imagery--and encouraged by
Faulkner's use of Christian lore elsewhere in his work--
the author discusses As I Lay Dying as a family pilgrimage
with religious meaning, and interprets each character as
a facet of the Christian story: Dewey Dell as the Virgin
going to Bethlehem, Vardaman as the devout believer, Darl
as prophet, Jewel as a false idol, Cash as Christ. Only
Cash experiences affirmative change; the rest are failures.

71 SHOWETT, H. K. "Faulkner and Scott: Addendum," MissQ, XXII
(Spring), 152–53.
Faulkner may have taken the image of the sword severing
a veil in the spotted horses episode of The Hamlet from a
speech by L. Q. C. Lamar which referred to the passage in
Scott's novel (See 1967.B40) suggested as a source.
Faulkner's great grandfather was an admirer of Lamar; the
speech was widely reported; it is also contained in an
1896 biography of Lamar which Faulkner might have read.

72 SOLOMON, ERIC. "From Christ in Flanders to Catch-22: An Approach to War Fiction," TSLL, XI (Spring), 851–66.
World War I is an objective correlative for Faulkner's
view of the human condition. As in Catch-22, immorality
in A Fable prevails in the higher orders and battle is un-
pleasant. Faulkner's novel, like Heller's, is anti-war.

73 SORENSON, DALE E. "Structure in William Faulkner's Sartoris:
The Contrast Between Psychological and Natural Time,"
ArQ, XXV (Autumn), 263–70.
Without reference to its original form as "Flags in the
Dust," the author discusses the structure of Sartoris as
built on two kinds of time, psychological (the individual's

(SORENSON, DALE E.)
perception) and natural (independent of subjectivity and
identified with seasonal change). Young Bayard moves to
his doom haunted by the Sartoris past; but the novel is
filled with contrasting images of natural time flowing
forward.

74 SPATZ, JONAS. Hollywood in Fiction: Some Versions of the
American Myth. The Hague: Mouton, pp. 116-19.
"Golden Land" depicts a place in which the American
Dream of regeneration in the wilderness has become a "de-
nial of sin and time" and the triumph of illusion.

75 STAFFORD, T. J. "Tobe's Significance in 'A Rose for Emily,'"
MFS, XIV (Winter), 451-53.
Tobe, Miss Emily's servant in "A Rose for Emily," offers
a contrast that helps put the spinster's behavior in proper perspective. He is active, meets the world, performs
necessary functions that affect her life. His name suggests "to be"--a future. At the end he is freed from her
decayed world.

76 STAFFORD, WILLIAM T. "'Some Homer of the Cotton Fields':
Faulkner's Use of the Mule Early and Late (Sartoris and
The Reivers)," PLL, V (Spring), 190-96.
The mule passage in Sartoris is thematically functional,
offering a contrast to the romanticism of the novel. The
use of the mule in Sartoris prepares for The Reivers,
where the animal also appears as a "central symbol of
ideal behavior."

77 STEVENS, LAUREN R. "Sartoris: Germ of the Apocalypse," DR,
XLIX (Spring), 80-87.
Faulkner meant "apocalypse" not "apocrypha" when he
called Sartoris the germ of his work, meaning the germ of
his prophetic revelation. Hamlet is an important source:
Sartoris is dramatic, Simon is Polonius, Horace is Hora-
tio, Narcissa is Ophelia, and Bayard is the melancholy
young man haunted by a death in the family. The Elizabethan theme of order is important in the work.

78 STONE, EDWARD. "William Faulkner," A Certain Morbidness: A
View of American Literature. Carbondale, Ill.: Southern
Illinois University Press, pp. 85-120.
Reprinted from 1960.B65.

1969

79   SUGG, REDDING S., JR.   "Introduction," Cabin Road, by John
        Faulkner.   Baton Rouge, La.:   Louisiana State University
        Press, pp. vii–xxv.
            Reprints portions of "John's Yoknapatawpha," SAQ, LXVIII
        (Summer 1969), 343–62.   John Faulkner, Faulkner's brother,
        wrote five pot-boilers published as paperback originals.
        Suggs compares them to Faulkner's work, tries to place
        them in the tradition of frontier humor, suggests a con-
        spiracy of silence against them or against John, and
        argues for the seriousness of these minor works, of which
        Cabin Road was the first.   John's fiction is a "distinc-
        tive but complementary" version of the "Matter of Lafa-
        yette County."   See review MissQ, XXIII (Summer 1970),
        343–46.

80   SWANSON, WILLIAM J.   "William Faulkner and William Styron:
        Notes on Religion," CimR, VII (March), 45–52.
            The contrast between Dilsey's true religion with the
        false religion of the blacks in Styron's Lie Down in Dark-
        ness is a clue to major differences between Styron's work
        and Faulkner's The Sound and the Fury, as well as a touch-
        stone by which to judge criticism of the two works.

81   THORNTON, WELDON.   "A Note on the Source of Faulkner's Jason,"
        SNNTS, I (Fall), 370–72.
            Faulkner's character, Jason, in The Sound and the Fury
        may be modeled on the ancient Hebrew high priest, Jason,
        in the Apocryphal II Maccabees and in Josephus' Antiq-
        uities of the Jews.

82   TRIMMER, JOSEPH F.   "The Unvanquished: The Teller and the
        Tale," BSUF, X (Winter), 35–42.
            Understanding The Unvanquished is helped when we realize
        the limitations of Bayard's willingness or ability to re-
        port all the events of his youth.   Taking the author's
        vantage, however, we see the gaps in Bayard's story as
        meaningful.   Only gradually does Bayard come to see the
        bravado and inadequacy of the Sartoris code.   In "An Odor
        of Verbena" he stands against it.   His act, nevertheless,
        is boyish bravado.

83   VORPAHL, BEN M.   "Moonlight at Ballenbaugh's: Time and Imag-
        ination in The Reivers," SLJ, I (Spring), 3–26.
            The author raises the possibility of The Reivers being
        Faulkner's "Doomsday Book" (See also 1970.B54) because it
        was Faulkner's last novel and because it demonstrates his
        conception of time, history, and recollection as meaning-
        ful only in terms of the present moment.

84 WALTON, GERALD W. "Tennie's Jim and Lucas Beauchamp," AN&Q,
    VIII (October), 23-24.
        A continuing error in a footnote of the Norton American
    Tradition in Literature text identifies Lucas Beauchamp as
    Tennie's Jim's son, when he is, in fact, his brother.

85 WEST, ANTHONY. "Remembering William Faulkner," Gourmet: The
    Magazine of Good Living (January), 22-23, 74-75.
        West remembers meeting Faulkner with his Random House
    editor Robert Linscott; at parties; or in Oxford, with a
    food angle; Faulkner would thaw out over a good meal. He
    recounts a story about the theft of the MS of As I Lay Dy-
    ing by one of Faulkner's kinswomen for the purpose of ex-
    purgating it; she threw it out of Faulkner's car.

86 WIGGINS, ROBERT A. "Faulkner," American Literary Scholarship
    an annual, 1967, edited by James Woodress. Durham, N. C.:
    Duke University Press, pp. 86-95.
        The annual survey of work on Faulkner.

87 WINN, JAMES A. "Faulkner's Revisions: A Stylist at Work,"
    AL, XLI (May), 231-50.
        A consideration of revisions in the MSS and TSS of
    Faulkner's books gives specific examples from Absalom,
    Absalom!, The Wild Palms, The Hamlet, As I Lay Dying, and
    The Sound and the Fury that demonstrate Faulkner's stylis-
    tic and thematic improvements at the level of the word,
    phrase, sentence, and paragraph. Faulkner improves sense,
    image, rhythm in his careful revisions.

88 WOODWARD, ROBERT H. "Poe's Raven, Faulkner's Sparrow, and
    Another Window," PN, II (April), 37-38.
        There are possible parallels between "The Raven" and the
    opening of Quentin's section of The Sound and the Fury,
    with the possibility of a related allusion in Absalom,
    Absalom! where Quentin regards the dormitory window and
    repeats "Nevermore."

89 ZOLLA, ELÉMIRE. The Writer and the Shaman: A Morphology of
    the American Indian, translated by Raymond Rosenthal. New
    York: Harcourt Brace Jovanovich, pp. 200-02.
        Faulkner's cycle of Indian tales is "Baroque," his Indi-
    ans corrupted by their association with European ways.
    "A Courtship," "A Justice," "Red Leaves," "The Old People,"
    and "The Bear" are summarized briefly for their Indian
    content.

1970

1970 A   BOOKS

1   INGE, M. THOMAS, ed. William Faulkner: A Rose for Emily.
       Merrill Casebooks. Columbus, Ohio: Charles E. Merrill.
       This casebook on Faulkner's story, "A Rose for Emily,"
       includes the story; articles and excerpts of criticism by
       various hands, including a parody; G. W. Cable's "Jean-Ah
       Poquelin"; and a modern short story in the "tradition."
       The collection of criticism includes, according to Michael
       Millgate in American Literary Scholarship 1970, p. 130,
       "almost everything, good or bad, which has ever been writ-
       ten" about the story.

2   IZARD, BARBARA, and CLARA HIERONYMUS. Requiem for a Nun: On-
       stage and Off. Nashville: Aurora Publishing, Inc.
       Interviews with some of the principals, anecdotes, and
       similar information are used to create an account of the
       stage versions of Requiem for a Nun in America, France,
       England and elsewhere. See essay-review, 1971.B81.

3   JARRETT-KERR, FR. MARTIN. William Faulkner. Grand Rapids,
       Michigan: William B. Eerdmans.
       A survey of Faulkner, very brief. A review in MissQ,
       XXVI (Summer 1973), 465-66, indicates that the work is
       derivative and out-of-date.

4   KALUZA, IRENA. The Functioning of Sentence Structure in the
       Stream of Consciousness Technique of William Faulkner's
       'The Sound and the Fury': A Study in Linguistic Stylis-
       tics. Philadelphia: Folcroft Press.
       See review 1969.B38.
       Reprints 1967.A2.

5   MERIWETHER, JAMES B. Checklist of William Faulkner. Columbus,
       Ohio: Charles E. Merrill.
       Faulkner's book-length publications and selected schol-
       arship about Faulkner are listed in this brief checklist.
       See also 1957.B48.

6   MERIWETHER, JAMES B., ed. The Merrill Studies in The
       Sound and the Fury. Columbus, Ohio: Charles E. Merrill.
       A selection of criticism on The Sound and the Fury con-
       tains revised versions of 1962.B85, 1954.B25, 1960.B19,
       1966.B30; portions of chapters one and three of 1968.A2;
       1967.B38; portions of 1967.B74; and an original essay,
       1970.B34.

7   PITAVY, FRANÇOIS, and ANDRÉ BLEIKASTEN. William Faulkner: As
     I Lay Dying, Light in August, introduction by Michel Gres-
     set. Paris: Arman Colin. [In French; for trans., re-
     vised edition, See Pitavy (1973.A6) and Bleikasten
     (1973.A1).]
          Gresset's introduction discusses problems central to
     Faulkner studies. There is a chronology of Faulkner's
     life and work in the context of world events, and an ap-
     pendix with reproductions of MSS pages from both books.

8   WATSON, JAMES GRAY. The Snopes Dilemma: Faulkner's Trilogy.
     Coral Gables, Fla.: University of Miami Press.
          The unifying theme of the Snopes trilogy comes out of
     the conflict between the truths of the human heart and
     the amoral machinations of Snopesism. Every character
     must choose between these poles. This straight-forward
     reading relies heavily on Beck (1961.A1), Vickery
     (1964.A10), and Brooks (1963.A3). Mink's apotheosis, fig-
     ured in astrological language at the end of The Mansion,
     is appropriately placed in the context of Linda's love and
     Gavin's morality, and brings to an end Faulkner's best
     statement of the nature and outcome of man's struggle
     against the inhuman and amoral.

1970 B   SHORTER WRITINGS

1   ANON. "The Postmaster," NY (21 November), p. 50.
          Faulkner's career and retirement as postmaster at the
     University of Mississippi is partially explained by the
     official letter, dated 2 September 1924, from a postal in-
     spector listing the seven charges against Faulkner's man-
     agement: neglect, mistreatment of mail, unauthorized per-
     sons in workrooms, and others.

2   ADAMS, RICHARD P. "Focus on William Faulkner's 'The Bear':
     Moses and the Wilderness," American Dreams, American
     Nightmares, edited by David Madden. Carbondale and Ed-
     wardsville, Ill.: Southern Illinois University Press,
     pp. 129-35.
          Ike McCaslin is no hero, and his dream is a dream of
     death, a nightmare, which is fulfilled in the scene with
     Roth's mistress in "Delta Autumn." He says "No" to life.
     Adams relates Faulkner's "The Bear" to Hawthorne, Mel-
     ville, Poe, Cooper, and Twain to suggest "the breadth and
     depth" of Faulkner's deliberate context. The theme is
     that the boy who has the American Dream must outgrow his
     innocence.

3   ALEXANDRESCU, SORIN. "William Faulkner and the Greek Tragedy,"
      RoR, XXIV (No. 3), 102-10.
        A translation, in part, of 1969.A1. Similarities be-
      tween the slave-culture of the pre-Civil War South and
      fifth-century Greece lie behind similarities between Greek
      tragedy and Faulkner's fiction. Absalom, Absalom!, Light
      in August, The Unvanquished, the Snopes trilogy, and "A
      Rose for Emily" are used in the discussion of similarities
      and differences.

4   ANDERSON, HILTON. "Colonel Falkner's Preface to The Siege of
      Monterey," NMW, III (Spring), 36-40.
        A brief introduction gives some background on a preface
      written by Faulkner's great-grandfather for a book-length
      poem he wrote about the Mexican War.

5   BEAUCHAMP, GORMAN. "The Unvanquished: Faulkner's Oresteia,"
      MissQ, XXIII (Summer), 273-77.
        Aeschylus and Faulkner are, in similar ways and with
      similar moral vision, dealing with radical societal
      change. Both the Oresteia and The Unvanquished are about
      the inadequacy of the primitive lex talionis. Like Aes-
      chylus, Faulkner has his character rise above conflicting
      demands and end the code of revenge. The novel is a kind
      of commedia, a bildungsroman in which the styles of the
      episodes reflect the stages of Bayard's development.
      Reprinted 1973.A9.

6   BIER, JESSE. "The Romantic Coordinates of American Litera-
      ture," BuR, XVIII (Fall), 16-33.
        Taking the writer's unwillingness or inability to "ac-
      cept a realistic measurement of human limitations" as a
      touchstone of Romanticism inherited from the Transcenden-
      talists and Poe, we see Faulkner applying "Thoreau to
      fiction," though there was in Faulkner also a "triumphant
      realist."

7   BLANCHARD, MARGARET. "The Rhetoric of Communion: Voice in
      The Sound and the Fury," AL, XLI (January), 555-65.
        The narrative "voice" of the fourth section of The Sound
      and the Fury is not omniscient or objective. It is sub-
      jective, limited, conjectural, with privileged access into
      one mind only--Jason's. It thus characterizes no one so
      much as the reader himself, whose involvement in the nov-
      el, forced by the first three sections, is given objective
      form.

8   BOSWELL, GEORGE. "The Legendary Background in Faulkner's
     Work," TFSB, XXXVI (September), 53-63.
        Faulkner used and created legends, sometimes disguising
     them as tall tales.

9   _____. "Notes on the Surnames of Faulkner's Characters,"
     TFSB, XXXVI (September), 64-66.
        Many of Faulkner's character names seem significant and
     meaningful when traced to their roots.

10   BRADFORD, MELVIN E. "Addie Bundren and the Design of As I Lay
     Dying," SoR, N. S. VI (Autumn), 1093-99.
        Addie, the "I" of the title of As I Lay Dying, is audi-
     tor of all the reveries which make up the novel, includ-
     ing her own. Her will is strong and she will not rest un-
     til "saved" from the Bundrens in her family plot in Jef-
     ferson. Outside voices, less under Addie's control and
     static against the moving Bundrens, provide perspective
     and document the journey. Addie seeks being by repeatedly
     violating others and ends by saying "No" to life, because
     she cannot control it, as opposed to her family, who un-
     consciously affirm.

11   _____. "Brother, Son, and Heir: The Structural Focus of
     Faulkner's Absalom, Absalom!" SR, LXXVIII (Winter)
     76-98.
        Charles Bon is his father's son in more than the literal
     way. Like Sutpen he is single-minded and eventually de-
     structive. He should not be "angelized." Henry, by con-
     trast, "breaks the inherited mold," he "puts human values
     ahead of theories" (his sister's future life). The topic
     of discussion between Shreve and Quentin has, however, all
     along been Quentin, not so much the South. Quentin repre-
     sents a failure to accept his responsibilities, and he is
     directly opposite the equally but differently faulted
     Sutpen. The novel thus uses its characters to explore
     the meaning of endurance.

12   BROOKS, CLEANTH. "Faulkner's First Novel," SoR, N. S. VI
     (Autumn), 1056-74.
        Mahon's experience, which gives structure to the novel,
     has more importance for Faulkner than for other charac-
     ters or a reader. Januarius Jones seems undigested into
     the story. The setting of Soldiers' Pay, though akin to
     later Jefferson, is not strongly localized.

1970

13   BROOKS, CLEANTH. "The Poetry of Miss Rosa Canfield [sic],"
      Shenandoah, XXI (Spring), 199-206.
          Miss Rosa Coldfield's unseen and doubtless hackneyed
      newspaper verse extolling the Confederate soldiers aside,
      Chapter V of Absalom, Absalom! qualifies her as a real
      poet. Lacking knowledge and understanding of the full
      course of events which have ruined her family, Rosa demon-
      izes Sutpen by a dramatic rendition of her own version of
      his behavior. However Baroque, it is striking and
      powerful.

14   BRUMM, URSULA. American Thought and Religious Typology. New
      Brunswick, N. J.: Rutgers University Press, pp. 206-20.
          In her chapter on "Christ and Adam as 'Figures' in Amer-
      ican Literature," Brumm discusses Faulkner's use of the
      crucifixion as an "archetypal human tragedy" in The Sound
      and the Fury and Light in August and argues for a broad
      interpretation of A Fable as a condemnation of the rapac-
      ity of civilization and of "rapacity's masterpiece,"
      Christianity.

15   CABANISS, ALLEN. "To Scotch a Monumental Mystery," NMW, III
      (Fall), 79-80.
          The report in Murry Falkner's book (1967.A1) which
      places the Confederate statue in the Oxford square in 1902
      is in error; it was erected in 1907.

16   CAMPBELL, HARRY M. "Faulkner's Philosophy Again: A Reply to
      Michel Gresset," MissQ, XXIII (Winter), 64-66.
          Michel Gresset's remarks about Campbell and Foster's
      book (1951.A1) in his review of Joseph Gold's book [MissQ,
      XX (Summer 1967), pp. 177-81] are challenged; "cosmic
      pessimism," Campbell and Foster's term, is still useful to
      describe the "myth that prevails in most of" Faulkner's
      fiction.

17   CATE, HOLLIS L. "Faulkner's V-shaped Land in 'Delta Au-
      tumn,'" RS, XXXVIII (June), 156.
          Faulkner wanted the reader to see the "funnel-shaped"
      symbol, instead of a Delta with the base down, in order to
      reinforce the impression that things in "Delta Autumn" are
      at an end for Ike and his world.

18   CECIL, L. MOFFIT. "A Rhetoric for Benjy," SLJ, III (No. 1),
      32-46.
          Faulkner uses several rhetorical strategies to create a
      believable "voice" for Benjy in The Sound and the Fury
      and, at the same time, to tell his part of the story in an

(CECIL, L. MOFFIT)
    artistic way. Benjy has a 500-word "vocabulary"; his
nouns are concrete, but "bright shapes" is both concrete
and an abstract concept for feelings.

19   COLLINS, R. G. "The Game of Names: Characterization Device
      in 'Light in August,'" EngR, XXI, 82-87.
      The thematic significance of all the names in Light in
August is discussed, using possible allusions and parano-
masia as keys to hidden meaning.

20   COOLEY, THOMAS W., JR. "Faulkner Draws the Long Bow," TCL,
      XVI, 268-77.
      Fairchild's tall tales in Mosquitoes, along with comment
by the author, point up Anderson's midwestern limitations.
In Faulkner's "tall tale" Snopes stories of the 1930's,
Faulkner moves into the literary form of the oral stage
and shows supreme mastery. The third stage is the conver-
sion of the tradition into the complex novel form, accom-
plished through voice (Ratliff).

21   DAVENPORT, F. GARVIN, JR. "William Faulkner," The Myth of
      Southern History: Historical Consciousness in Twentieth-
      Century Southern Literature. Nashville: Vanderbilt Uni-
      versity Press, pp. 82-130.
      Faulkner's sense of history was nearly unique in America
and the South; he related the Southern dilemma to "national ideals and universal history." He is not to be identified with the Agrarians. Absalom, Absalom! is used to illustrate the argument; The Sound and the Fury and Intruder
in the Dust are often mentioned.

22   DITSKY, JOHN M. "Faulkner's Carousel: Point of View in As I
      Lay Dying," LauR, X (No. 1), 74-85.
      Multiple point-of-view in As I Lay Dying allows Faulkner
to give several thematic perspectives for the events of
the book, while his skill allows him to weave the whole
together tightly.

23   DUNLAP, MARY M. "William Faulkner's 'Knight's Gambit' and
      Gavin Stevens," MissQ, XXIII (Summer), 223-40.
      Knight's Gambit, though a collection of stories, has a
unity and structure of its own. There is a progressive
enrichment of Gavin Stevens; and the title story, put last
in the book, seems designed to pull the pieces together.
The essay discusses the title story, "Knight's Gambit."

24   DURANT, WILL and ARIEL. "William Faulkner," Interpretations
      of Life: A Survey of Contemporary Literature. New York:
      Simon and Schuster, pp. 11-27.
          A brief overview of Faulkner's life and literary career
      gives praise: Faulkner's art is "a splendor of illumina-
      tion and originality."

25   EARNEST, ERNEST. The Single Vision: The Alienation of Ameri-
      can Intellectuals. New York: New York University Press,
      pp. 189-91.
          Faulkner's unrelievedly dark view of Southern decadence
      does not fulfill his expressed wish to uplift the hearts
      of men and puts him in with Hemingway and Jeffers and
      others of the second American renaissance who produced a
      "paranoid vision" of America.

26   EMERSON, O. B. "Bill's Friend Phil," JMH, XXXII (May),
      135-45.
          A summary of some of Phil Stone's early remarks upon
      Faulkner come, in large part, from Emerson's earlier piece
      (1964.B23).

27   FAULKNER, JIM. "The Picture of John and Brother Will," Delta
      Review, VII (Fall), 12-14.
          An account, by Faulkner's nephew, of how Faulkner and
      his brother John came to have their pictures taken in
      1949.

28   FICKEN, CARL. "The Christ Story in A Fable," MissQ, XXIII
      (Summer), 251-64.
          Christ-imagery is attached to many characters and events
      besides the Corporal and his mutiny in A Fable. The
      Christ story is often used ironically, and Faulkner seems
      to be warning the reader to make a little less of it than
      first glance invites, while he expands the function of
      other characters and enlarges the tragic scope of his
      complex story.

29   GERSTENBERGER, DONNA, and GEORGE HENDRICK. "Faulkner, Wil-
      liam," The American Novel: A Checklist of Twentieth-
      Century Criticism on Novels Written Since 1789. Volume II.
      Criticism 1960-68. Chicago: Swallow Press, pp. 84-116.
          A list of criticism on Faulkner and his work.

30   GIDLEY, MICK. "Faulkner and Children," Signal: Approaches to
      Children's Books, III (September), 91-102.
          The Wishing Tree is placed into the context of Faulkner's
      reputation as a writer of "adult" fiction. Similarities

(GIDLEY, MICK)
and contrasts between the children's tale and Faulkner's
other work is discussed. Alice is a preliminary sketch
for Dilsey.

31 _____. "One Continuous Force: Notes on Faulkner's Extra-
Literary Reading," MissQ, XXIII (Summer), 299-314.
Faulkner's library, comments by Phil Stone, and internal
evidence in Faulkner's work are the background to a discussion of his extra-literary reading in aesthetics, philosophy, history, psychology, and social matters. It is
possible that Faulkner knew Elie Faure, Henry Morton Robinson, Mencken's American Language, Henry Adams, and
others, including derivative acquaintance with Plato,
Bergson and other philosophers.
Reprinted 1973.A9.

32 _____. "Some Notes on Faulkner's Reading," JAmS, IV (July),
91-102.
Using Faulkner's early writing as source, Gidley lists
literary works Faulkner alludes to or demonstrates familiarity with: Huxley, Joyce, Housman, Eliot, Poe, Rostand,
Fielding, Horace, Taine and others.

33 GOLUB, LESTER S. "Syntactic and Lexical Problems in Reading
Faulkner," EJ, LIX (April), 490-96.
Faulkner defies traditional lexical and syntactical convention in Light in August; to understand his work properly, the student must be taught the nature, purpose, and
effect of Faulkner's deviations from the norm. The differences between speaking and thinking voices allows
characters to express thoughts they would not verbalize.
Faulkner's repetition of key adjectives or other terms
helps to identify his characters like leit motifs.

34 GREGORY, EILEEN. "Caddy Compson's World," The Merrill Studies
in The Sound and the Fury, edited by James B. Meriwether.
Columbus, Ohio: Charles E. Merrill, pp. 89-101.
Caddy's despair is proved by her acceptance of Quentin's
ineffectual suicide pact; she accepts her femininity as
sinful on Quentin's terms and marries Herbert Head the
"blackguard," a worthless person. Like Emma Bovary, Anna
Karenina, or Faulkner's own Eula Varner, she inhabits a
world where there is no man worthy of her. See 1970.A6.

1970

35   HAUCK, RICHARD B. "The Comic Christ and the Modern Reader,"
         CE, XXXI (February), 498-506.
            Hunting Christ figures, a popular critical and pedagogi-
         cal sport, may be enlivened by seeking versions of a
         "comic Christ," as in As I Lay Dying, or the ironic
         Christ, Joe Christmas of Light in August. Jewel, Cash and
         Darl all have credentials.

36   HEMENWAY, ROBERT. "Enigmas of Being in As I Lay Dying," MFS,
         XVI (Summer), 133-46.
            Almost every event in As I Lay Dying calls the certainty
         of existence into question; states of being and non-being
         are evoked by playing upon the verb "to be." Time is the
         measure of existence; one can live only in the present,
         "is," to which the alternative is not "was" but "is not,"
         or oblivion. Obsession with the past is doomed to
         tragedy.

37   HERMANN, JOHN. "Faulkner's Heart's Darling in 'That Evening
         Sun,'" SSF, VII (Spring), 320-23.
            Caddy is the center of the story, "That Evening Sun."
         Her questions confront the other members of the family
         with their own cowardice.

38   HOUGHTON, DONALD E. "Whores and Horses in Faulkner's 'Spotted
         Horses,'" MQ, XI, 361-69.
            The spotted horses episode of The Hamlet, called the
         "later version" of the story, mingles pathos with humor to
         achieve greater seriousness. The key element in under-
         standing the piece is to observe that the horses and the
         women of the story have swapped roles--the horses repre-
         sent a kind of sexual desire while the women have become
         drab, animal-like, and unpursued.

39   HOWELL, ELMO. "Faulkner's Elegy: An Approach to 'The Bear,'"
         ArlQ, II (Winter), 122-32.
            A "surface" reading of the four-part "The Bear" shows it
         to be a paean and lament for a lost time when men lived in
         peace and order. The hunting camp is a microcosm of the
         South, though simplified to an all-male society in which
         class and race have their appropriate and proper roles.

40   _____. "William Faulkner's Chickasaw Legacy: A Note on 'Red
         Leaves,'" ArQ, XXVI (Winter), 293-303.
            Background on Indian ownership of slaves is used in dis-
         cussing Faulkner's departure from the facts in "Red
         Leaves." It is a wilderness horror tale like Conrad's
         Heart of Darkness but different in that it portrays a time
         when men and nature were one.

41 _____. "William Faulkner's General Forrest and the Uses of
History," THQ, XXIX, 287-94.
Faulkner is off by two years in his dating, but uses a
real incident in Nathan B. Forrest's career in "My Grandmother Millard and General Bedford Forrest and the Battle
of Harrykin Creek." The story marks a point in Faulkner's
career when he moved away from history, with consequent
diminution in his powers.

42 IRVINE, PETER L. "Faulkner and Hardy," ArQ, XXVI (Winter),
357-65.
Several parallels between Faulkner and Thomas Hardy are
discussed: the importance of time, history and place (the
land itself); their use of unconventional literary forms;
their distrust of intellect; their depiction of cultures
disturbed by the "outsider." Further subjects for discussion are tragedy, folklore and humor, their use of the
grotesque, use of the Bible.

43 KARTIGANER, DONALD M. "The Sound and the Fury and Faulkner's
Quest for Form," ELH, XXXVII (December), 613-39.
Bergsonian "distrust of 'concept' and modern emphasis
upon the centrality of self and mind" have forced literature to seek new strategies. Absalom, Absalom! is a key
to the way Faulkner ordered his "supreme fiction" and it
shows just what is missing in the fragmented wasteland
world of The Sound and the Fury. Benjy's vision is too
clear to be "truth." It is pure, in Bergson's sense, and
without either reflection or imagination to make human
reality. Quentin and Jason are at the opposite pole, too
warped by imagination. Dilsey's religious order is merely
another form of order, not a specially valid one, and it
is "tragically irrelevant" to the modern world as depicted
here.

44 KIBLER, JAMES E., JR. "A Possible Source in Ariosto for Drusilla," MissQ, XXIII (Summer), 321-22.
The name and nature of Drusilla in The Unvanquished may
come from a character in Canto 37 of Ariosto's Orlando
Furioso.

45 KINNEY, ARTHUR F. "Faulkner and the Possibilities for Heroism," SoR, N. S. VI (Autumn), 1110-25.
"The Old People," "The Bear," and "Delta Autumn" form a
"trilogy" that is the "fundamental" portion of Faulkner's
"last major novel," Go Down, Moses. The sin Ike has
sought to exorcise by a penance which has cost him nothing
comes full circle back to confront him. Yet his gift of

1970

(KINNEY, ARTHUR F.)
  the hunting horn is "cathartic," a union of his old sense
  of honor with his cherished hunting ritual. He alone is
  "aware of the paradoxes of life."

46 LEAF, MARK. "William Faulkner's Snopes Trilogy: The South
      Evolves," The Fifties: Fiction, Poetry, Drama, edited by
      Warren French. Deland, Fla.: Everett Edwards, pp. 51-62.
        The events of The Town and The Mansion are deliberately
      presented through the biased and psychologically inter-
      esting viewpoints of a frustrated V. K. Ratliff, a roman-
      tic Gavin Stevens, and an immature and often prurient
      Chick Mallison. Even the occasional omniscient voice is
      suspect because it seems to agree with Ratliff. Flem's
      rapacity is perhaps a necessary though extreme corrective
      to the old South's easy-going exploitation.

47 LEVINS, LYNN G. "The Four Narrative Perspectives in Absalom,
      Absalom!" PMLA, LXXXV (January), 35-47.
        Interrelationships of style and language are as impor-
      tant in the narrative perspectives of Absalom, Absalom! as
      in The Sound and the Fury and As I Lay Dying. The chro-
      nology at the end is Faulkner's signification that the
      events did "happen," fictionally. Each of the four "nar-
      rators" uses different information to tell a version of
      the story in unique style. Rosa uses Gothic mystery; Mr.
      Compson uses Greek tragedy; Quentin uses chivalric ro-
      mance; and Shreve uses the "ludicrous humor of the tall
      tale." Each perspective is a comment upon the other--and
      the different perspectives are at the center of the novel,
      ranking above Sutpen.

48 LHAMON, W. T., JR. "Pylon: The Ylimaf and New Valois," WHR,
      XXIV, 274-78.
        Pylon reverses normal procedures in order to depict the
      new world of speed and cities in which all values are
      turned upside down.

49 McCANTS, MAXINE. "From Humanity to Abstraction: Negro Char-
      acterization in Intruder in the Dust," NMW, II (Winter),
      91-104.
        Lucas Beauchamp becomes so superhuman that he is atypi-
      cal, an abstraction, in Intruder in the Dust. Gavin Ste-
      vens' speeches throw up too strong a contrast in "Sambo."
      It is not a novel of "lasting value."

50   McHANEY, THOMAS L. "A Deer Hunt in the Faulkner Country,"
        MissQ, XXIII (Summer), 315-20.
            Reprints a 1934-35 account from a Ripley, Miss., news-
        paper of a deer hunt near the camp Faulkner frequented in
        this period. The piece is written by a hunter apparently
        unaware of Faulkner or his reputation.

51   *MADEYA, ULRIKE. "Interpretationen zu William Faulkners 'The
        Bear': Das Bild des Helden und die Konstellation der
        Charakters," LWU, III, 45-60.
            Millgate, American Literary Scholarship 1970, calls this
        survey of American criticism of "The Bear" "undiscriminat-
        ing."

52   MELLARD, JAMES M. "Caliban as Prospero: Benjy and The Sound
        and the Fury," Novel: Forum on Fiction, III (Spring),
        233-48.
            Benjy's innocence identifies his section of The Sound
        and the Fury as romance; he is comparable to Caliban in
        The Tempest. Benjy is accorded a sexuality and a prob-
        lematical desire for Caddy and the little girl of the
        "rape" attempt. He is also Prospero, if not as cause of
        action at least as point of view. The end of Benjy's
        section is compared to the ending of Shakespeare's play.
        Dilsey's innocence is a vision, and is more fitting to
        end the novel.

53   _____. "The Sound and the Fury: Quentin Compson and Faulk-
        ner's 'Tragedy of Passion,'" SNNTS, II (No. 1), 61-75.
            Images of time, death, and sex, in a variety of forms,
        recur in Quentin's section of The Sound and the Fury.
        These images are archetypes of the tragic vision of life.
        Tragic action is also present, though disjunctive because
        of Caddy. Jason represents the "residue of tragedy's
        disillusionments." Frye's Anatomy of Criticism is a
        source in this criticism.

54   MERIWETHER, JAMES B. "The Novel Faulkner Never Wrote: His
        Golden Book or Doomsday Book," AL, XLII (March), 93-96.
            The Reivers, contrary to Kerr (1967.B57 and 1969.A3),
        is not the Golden Book which Faulkner referred to as
        something he was saving for the end of his career. His
        conception of that never-written volume was apparently to
        be like an extended version of the "Compson Appendix" to
        the Viking Portable Faulkner. It would have been a com-
        mentary upon his previous work, filled with afterthoughts,
        and additions, not a summary. See also 1969.B83.

1970

55　MERIWETHER, JAMES B.　"Notes on the Textual History of The
Sound and the Fury," Art and Error:　Modern Textual Edit-
ing, edited by Ronald Gottesman and Scott Bennett.
Bloomington, Ind.:　Indiana University Press, pp. 219-53.
Reprints 1962.B85.　Also reprinted, revised, 1970.A6.

56　MICHEL, LAURENCE.　"Faulkner:　Saying No to Death," The Thing
Contained:　Theory of the Tragic.　Bloomington, Ind.:
Indiana University Press, pp. 107-30.
Faulkner presents full tragedy in his best work by
balancing the yea to life with the no, by recognizing the
implacable adversary and witnessing to man's ability to
endure the perpetual conflict.　Though comic-tragic works
like Intruder in the Dust and The Reivers depict victory,
the victory is solely Faulkner's and can occur only because the tragic vision is real.　"The protean tragic
daemon has met its match in Faulkner's inexhaustible ability to spin an enveloping cocoon."

57　MILLER, WAYNE CHARLES.　An Armed America, Its Face in Fiction:
A History of the American Military Novel.　New York:　New
York University Press, 119-22.
Soldiers' Pay is pretentious, derivative.　Faulkner's
war fiction depicts his young men as deceived victims of
a pointless carnage and shows the survivors as divided
between those who understand the horror of war and those
who do not.

58　NEBEKER, HELEN E.　"Emily's Rose of Love:　Thematic Implica-
cations of Point of View in Faulkner's 'A Rose for
Emily,'" BRMMLA, XXIV, 3-13.
The true meaning of "A Rose for Emily" hides behind the
identity of the narrator.　The "we" of the story carefully
differentiates itself from the "they" of the town.　It
knows Emily's crime, abets her hiding it, but is itself
surprised by the hair on the pillow.　The "we" represents
Emily's old suitors.　The story contains a metaphor for
the South.　Chronological tables list the scheme of action
and point of view.

59　PAVESE, CESARE.　"Faulkner, A Bad Pupil of Anderson," American
Literature:　Essays and Opinions, translated by Edwin Fus-
sell.　Berkeley:　University of California Press,
pp. 142-45.
Reprints, translated, 1934.B21.

60   PEARCE, RICHARD. "Faulkner's One Ring Circus, Light in Au-
      gust," Stages of the Clown: Perspectives on Modern Fic-
      tion from Dostoevsky to Beckett. Carbondale and Edwards-
      ville: Southern Illinois University Press, pp. 47-66.
      Reprints 1966.B60.

61   PEAVY, CHARLES D. "Jason Compson's Paranoid Pseudocommunity,"
      HSL, II, 151-56.
          The "paranoid pseudocommunity"--a psychologist's con-
      ception--is used to characterize the human relationships
      of Jason Compson the younger. His paranoia, produced by
      his unhappy childhood, knows no bounds.

62   PITAVY, FRANÇOIS L. "The Landscape in Light in August,"
      MissQ, XXIII (Summer), 265-72.
          Landscape is a function of character in Light in August;
      it partakes of the qualities assigned to major characters.
      Faulkner emphasizes dream-like, almost imperceptible mo-
      tion and mutations of pale colors or of shades of light in
      a way that suggests the furious immobility of the charac-
      ters' lives, often using the same words for scene and
      character.

63   POCHMAN, HENRY A., and JOEL A. HUNT. "Faulkner and His
      Sources," ConL, XI, (Spring), 310-12.
          In an exchange of letters, Pochman writes to say that
      Hunt's article on Faulkner and Rabelais (1969.B43) is
      specious, since the anecdote is something Faulkner would
      have learned on the courthouse lawn in Oxford. Hunt re-
      plies that Pochman offers no support for the presence of
      such a tale in Mississippi oral tradition.

64   POLK, NOEL. "The Critics and Faulkner's 'Little Postage
      Stamp of Native Soil,'" MissQ, XXIII (Summer), 323-35.
          In the course of offering correctives to the too-close
      identification of Faulkner's fictional world with the
      county and town where he lived, the author comments fre-
      quently upon the work of Kerr (1969.A3), Brown (1969.B9
      and 1962.B2), Miner (1952.A2) and others who have con-
      centrated upon Faulkner's hometown as the sole prototype
      of his imaginative creation.

65   REA, J. "Faulkner's 'Spotted Horses,'" HSL, II, 157-64.
          The theme of "Spotted Horses" is man's love for poetry,
      represented by the horses. Chasing the ponies is proof
      that man will prevail because he "will try for poetry and
      will fail."

1970

66 RINALDI, NICHOLAS M. "Game Imagery in Faulkner's Absalom,
    Absalom!" ConnR, IV (October), 73-79.
        The three points-of-view toward Sutpen in Absalom, Absa-
    lom! present a clear image of him and his rough assault on
    respectability. Sutpen conceives himself a player in a
    game; game imagery abounds in the book, and Sutpen sees
    good only in victory. He is defined as a man who stakes
    his life on the gamble that he can become an aristocrat in
    one generation. Similar imagery is in Faulkner's other
    work.

67 RODNON, STEWART. "The House of the Seven Gables and Absalom,
    Absalom!: Time, Tradition and Guilt," StH, I (No. 2),
    42-46.
        Six parallels exist between The House of the Seven Ga-
    bles and Absalom, Absalom!, three of them substantive:
    concern with the effect of the past upon the present; ex-
    ploration of the decline of a tradition; a special view of
    good and evil. In both books, a character is corrupted
    and affects life around him.

68 ROSSKY, WILLIAM. "The Pattern of Nightmare in Sanctuary: or
    Miss Reba's Dogs," MFS, XV (Winter), 503-15.
        Slow motion, futile motion, static images and silent
    screams in Sanctuary denote a nightmare world of intense
    horror. Temple's failure to escape is explained by this
    atmosphere, which depicts not merely the baseness of mod-
    ernism but a larger cosmic terror. Miss Reba's dogs, at
    the center of the book, underscore this atmosphere and
    meaning, and serve a symbolic representation of the des-
    perate lives of the novel's central characters. The arti-
    cle also mentions some parallels between Faulkner's novel
    and Madame Bovary.

69 SAMWAY, PATRICK. "War: A Faulknerian Commentary," ColQ,
    XVIII (Spring), 370-78.
        A Fable dramatizes that freedom is a condition which
    must be struggled for. The actions of each character de-
    flect the actions of all the others. The Corporal gives
    hope to all men by his human example while the General
    fails to gain freedom even for himself.

70 SCHWARTZ, DELMORE. Selected Essays of Delmore Schwartz, edit-
    ed by Donald A. Dike and David H. Zucker. Chicago: Uni-
    versity of Chicago Press, pp. 274-89, 290-304.
        Reprints 1941.B10 and 1955.B53.

71 *SMITH, LEWIS A. "William Faulkner and the Racist Virus,"
    Annual Reports of Studies (Doshisha Women's College,
    Kyoto, Japan), XXI, 388-98.
    1971 MLA International Bibliography, Volume I, Item 8942.

72 SMITH, RALEIGH W., JR. "Faulkner's 'Victory': The Plain Peo-
    ple of Clydebank," MissQ, XXIII (Summer), 241-49.
    "Victory," one of Faulkner's stories of World War I,
    concerns the "rise" and fall of a young Scotsman who
    leaves his family and tradition for a life in the army and
    London. The theme of failure as a result of denying tra-
    dition prefigures Faulkner's use of the yeomanry of Yok-
    napatawpha as normative characters.

73 SPILKA, MARK. "Quentin Compson's Universal Grief," ConL, XI
    (Autumn), pp. 451-69.
    Caddy in The Sound and the Fury, like her daughter later,
    inherits the defunct Compson boldness and acts according-
    ly. The men, like Quentin, are failures and weak. But
    Quentin does have a vision of the family's failure, which
    is dramatized in Caddy's life and repeated for the last
    time in her daughter's, who is the "last brave Compson."
    Quentin sees a world so beset with lovelessness, lust and
    commercial greed that even Dilsey's children and grand-
    children falter and fail in it. His suicide is a desper-
    ate gambit, a rejection of his father's world and a ges-
    ture of the hope of union in dissolution.

74 STEEGE, M. TED. "Dilsey's Negation of Nihilism: Meaning in
    The Sound and the Fury," RS, XXXVIII (December), 266-75.
    Disagreeing with both Hagopian (1967.B38) and Hunt
    (1965.A2) on The Sound and the Fury, the author argues
    that there is no general triumph in the book, only one
    for Dilsey, who, true to her own view of things, sees the
    beginning and ending, accepts her own existence, and en-
    dures. The book will not solve a reader's spiritual prob-
    lems, though it may clarify them.

75 STEPHENS, ROSEMARY. "Ike's Gun and Too Many Novembers,"
    MissQ, XXIII (Summer), 279-87.
    There are several discrepancies in dates, chronology,
    and ages of characters in "The Bear."

76 *STERNBERG, MEIR. "The Compositional Principles of Faulkner's
    Light in August and the Poetics of the Modern Novel," Ha-
    sifrut, II, 498-537.
    [In Hebrew with English summary pp. 687-91.] The nar-
    rative structure of Light in August defies conventional
    expectations forcing the reader to concentrate on recurring
    images and motifs.

1970

77 STEVICK, PHILIP. The Chapter in Fiction: Theories of Narra-
      tive Division. Syracuse, New York: Syracuse University
      Press, pp. 113-14.
         A discussion of alternating double plots in fiction be-
      gins with the remark that there is no "explicit relation"
      between "Wild Palms" and "Old Man" in The Wild Palms, and
      no similarity of dramatic structure. Although each read
      independently is "slightly disappointing," this kind of
      structure puts great demands upon the reader.

78 TAYLOR, WALTER. "Faulkner: Social Commitment and The Artis-
      tic Temperament," SoR, N. S. VI (Autumn), 1075-92.
         An overview of Faulkner's statements and interviews on
      the race question finds him moral, moderate, often puzzl-
      ing by virtue of "ambiguities," and a "failure" as a po-
      litical voice. Ike McCaslin's actions are heroic, though
      ambivalently viewed, in Go Down, Moses.

79 VANDEKIEFT, RUTH M. "Faulkner's Defeat of Time in Absalom,
      Absalom!" SoR, N. S. VI (Autumn), 1100-09.
         Though Sutpen's dynastic dreams are foiled by his ina-
      bility to read his own past actions, Time, the enemy which
      cuts him down, is also defeated by characters like Judith
      and by the novel itself, a work of art. Faulkner's voice
      permeates all the voices of the novel as the chronicler.

80 VICKERY, OLGA W. "Faulkner," American Literary Scholarship an
      annual, 1968, edited by J. Albert Robbins. Durham, N. C.:
      Duke University Press, pp. 100-06.
         In the annual survey of Faulkner criticism, Vickery sug-
      gests "more research in manuscripts" as one of the most
      fruitful avenues for Faulkner scholarship to take.

81 VINSON, AUDREY L. "Miscegenation and its Meaning in Go Down,
      Moses," CLAJ, XIV, 143-55.
         With "deliberate semantic intention," Faulkner has ap-
      plied the word "miscegenation" broadly in Go Down, Moses,
      including several kinds of relationships between blacks
      and whites, such as Sam's initiation of Ike, the town's
      sharing of grief over Sam Beauchamp, and, coupled with the
      rejection motif, Rider's crap game with the white man or
      Lucas's fight with Zack.

82 WAGGONER, HYATT H. "The Historical Novel and the Southern
      Past: The Case of Absalom, Absalom!" SLJ, II (Spring),
      69-85.
         Using Tuck's handbook to Faulkner (1964.A8) as typical
      of the critical misconceptions about Absalom, Absalom!--

(WAGGONER, HYATT H.)
that it reflects Southern history and a specific Southern fault--the article argues for universality in Sutpen's story, comparing it with Hawthorne's The House of the Seven Gables: for example, Absalom, Absalom! is profoundly concerned with the meaning of the past. Sutpen's story reflects general American qualities: using people as things and the rags to riches rise.

83 WALL, CAREY. "The Sound and the Fury: The Emotional Center," MQ, XI, 371-87.
The Sound and the Fury has an "emotional structure" compounded out of repeated references in images and events to the terrible pain of spiritual loss in the modern world, which is the Compson's primary malaise. Benjy's section is an emotional progression, memory by memory, from vague to specific consciousness of the enormity of his loss. The pattern repeats with Quentin and Jason, whose sections Benjy's part has taught us to read.

84 WHITE, HELEN, and REDDING S. SUGG, JR. "John Faulkner: An Annotated Checklist of His Published Works and His Papers," SB, XXIII, 217-29.
A checklist of the manuscripts and other papers of Faulkner's brother John on deposit at the J. W. Brister Library of Memphis State University; papers include published and unpublished fiction and the setting copy of My Brother Bill (1963.A2).

85 WILLIAMS, ORA G. "The Theme of Endurance in As I Lay Dying," LaS, IX, 100-04.
As I Lay Dying illustrates the three qualities--compassion, sacrifice, and endurance--which make up the basic theme of Faulkner's work as he expressed it in the Nobel Prize speech. The I of the title, Addie, is the center of the novel, but each of her children also manifests some form of endurance.

86 *WILSON, ROBERT R. "The Pattern of Thought in Light in August," BRMMLA, XXIV, 155-61.
According to Millgate, American Literary Scholarship 1971, p. 114, the article "offers minor but suggestive comments about the relationship between conscious and pre-conscious levels of mind" in Light in August.

1970

87   YONCE, MARGARET. "Faulkner's 'Atthis' and 'Attis': Some
      Sources of Myth," MissQ, XXIII (Summer), 289-98.
           The author finds suggestive sources for Faulkner's ref-
      erences to the goddess Atthis in Soldiers' Pay, in Faulk-
      ner's poetry, and in Swinburne, and identifies Labove of
      The Hamlet with the emasculate god Attis, whose story is
      in Frazer's Golden Bough and Catullus.

1971 A BOOKS

1   BUNGERT, HANS. William Faulkner und die humoristische Tradi-
     tion des amerikanischen Sudens. Heidelberg: Carl Winter
     Universitätsverlag.
          Faulkner's relationship to the humorous and realistic
     writers of the old Southwest frontier is studied in three
     parts. Bungert surveys the original literature and traces
     its demise in local color; considers its influence on
     Faulkner's fiction, especially the tall tale; and explores
     Faulkner's thematic and structural purposes in the use of
     comedy. There is a bibliography, an index, a brief
     English-language summary, and an appendix on the Al Jack-
     son letters Faulkner swapped with Sherwood Anderson in
     New Orleans in the 1920's.

2   GOLDMAN, ARNOLD, ed. Twentieth-Century Interpretations of
     Absalom, Absalom! A Collection of Critical Essays. En-
     glewood Cliffs, New Jersey: Prentice-Hall.
          A collection of excerpts from articles and books on Ab-
     salom, Absalom! with an introduction by Goldman (See
     1971.B30). Includes 1951.B46, 1961.B55, 1967.B36,
     1963.B25, and excerpts from 1966.A6, 1966.A1, 1963.A1,
     and a chronology.

3   INGE, M. THOMAS, ed. The Merrill Studies in Light in Au-
     gust. Columbus, Ohio: Charles E. Merrill.
          Reviews and criticism of Light in August and excerpts
     from Faulkner's interviews and from Old Times in the
     Faulkner Country (1961.A2). The anthology includes
     1932.B8, 1932.B11 (excerpt), 1932.B17, 1932.B26,
     1933.B11, 1948.B7, 1957.B1, 1958.B32, a revised version of
     1960.B59, 1964.B45, and 1957.B38.

4   LANGFORD, GERALD. Faulkner's Revision of Absalom, Absalom!
     A Collation of the Manuscript and the Published Book.
     Austin and London: University of Texas Press.
          Differences between the MS of Absalom, Absalom! and the
     1951 Modern Library edition of the book (omitting ref-

(LANGFORD, GERALD)
erence to the TS setting copy at the University of Virginia) are discussed and followed by a list of the differences. <u>See</u> essay-review 1972.B93.

5   MERIWETHER, JAMES B. <u>The Literary Career of William Faulkner</u>,
revised edition. Columbia, S. C.: University of South
Carolina Press.
    Reprints 1961.A4 with a new preface and a list of errata
in the first edition.

6   MILLGATE, MICHAEL. <u>William Faulkner</u>. New York: Capricorn
Books.
    An unrevised reissue of 1961.A5, this is not to be con-
fused with the more comprehensive 1966.A6.

7   MOTTRAM, ERIC. <u>William Faulkner</u>. London: Routledge and
Kegan Paul.
    A volume in the publisher's "Profiles in Literature"
series, this small book gives a brief introduction to
Faulkner, chiefly through his own work. Millgate, <u>Ameri-
can Literary Scholarship 1971</u>, observes that it "has
nothing to offer North American readers."

8   PEAVY, CHARLES D. <u>Go Slow Now: Faulkner and the Race Ques-
tion</u>. Foreword by Patrick G. Hogan, Jr. Eugene, Ore.:
University of Oregon Books.
    Many critics have misunderstood or misinterpreted Faulk-
ner's handling of slavery, miscegenation, and the whole
race question in his fiction. Examples from the criticism
of Faulkner's fiction and of his supposed philosophy are
set against historical accounts, more sympathetic interpretations of Faulkner, and Faulkner's own statements in
essays and public letters in order to argue a new interpretation. Peavy concludes that Faulkner's public statements are his true feelings on the race issue and that his
fiction, often contradictory of nonfiction remarks, is an
idealization. <u>See</u> essay-review by Leland Cox, <u>MissQ</u>,
XXVII (Summer 1974), 359-64.

9   *SACHS, VIOLA. <u>Le Sacré et le profane: "The Bear" de William
Faulkner</u>. Paris: Département Anglo-Américain, Université
de Paris.
    According to <u>American Literary Scholarship 1972</u>, p. 127,
this is a study of the four-part "The Bear" by 28 French
undergraduates.

1971

10   SEYPPEL, JOACHIM. William Faulkner, translated by the author
      from 1962.A4. New York: Ungar.
          See review MissQ, XXV (Summer 1972), 377-78.

11   UTLEY, FRANCIS L., LYNN Z. BLOOM, and ARTHUR F. KINNEY, eds.
      Bear, Man and God: Eight Approaches to William
      Faulkner's "The Bear." New York: Random House.
      A revised, enlarged version of 1964.A9.

12   *VICKERY, JOHN B., and OLGA W. VICKERY, eds. Light in
      August" and the Critical Spectrum. Belmont, California:
      Wadsworth.
          Fifteen previously published articles or book chapters
      on Light in August which, according to American Literary
      Scholarship 1972, make up a "useful if slightly unadven-
      turous collection" of criticism.

1971 B SHORTER WRITINGS

1   ADAMOWSKI, T. H. "Joe Christmas: The Tyranny of Childhood,"
     Novel, IV (Spring), 240-51.
         Christmas's enigmatic behavior in allowing himself to be
     captured in Mottstown can be explained by reference to his
     childhood. He gives up his struggle for identity and sub-
     mits to the manufactured role of "nigger" in order to get
     the peace which a lifetime of warring with society over
     his mixed nature had denied him.

2   ALEXANDRESCU, SORIN. "A Project in the Semantic Analysis of
     the Characters in William Faulkner's Work," Semiotica, IV,
     37-51.
         The author suggests a "typological systematization" of
     Faulkner's characters in the "saga of the South" which he
     created, using a scheme of semantic analysis. Charts,
     graphs, formulas fill out the argument.

3   *ANASTASJEW, N. "Faulkners Weg zum Roman 'Das Dorf,'" trans-
     lated from the Russian by Gerhard Sewekow, KuL, XIX,
     956-74. Original in VLit, XIV (No. 9,1970), 122-41.
         An "unoriginal" and "inaccurate" summary of realistic
     elements in The Hamlet, according to American Literary
     Scholarship 1971, p. 108.

4   ANDERSON, HILTON. "Two Possible Sources for Faulkner's Dru-
     silla Hawk," NMW, III (Winter), 108-10.
         Col. W. C. Falkner's two long poems, The Spanish Hero-
     ine and The Siege of Monterey, offer possible sources for
     Drusilla Hawk in The Unvanquished.

5 BASSETT, JOHN E. "William Faulkner's The Sound and the Fury:
   An Annotated Checklist of Criticism," RALS, I (Autumn),
   217-46.
       This checklist of criticism on Faulkner's fourth novel
   includes American and British receptions and general
   criticism from 1929 to 1970; there is an index to authors.
   See also 1972.A2.

6 BEJA, MORRIS. Epiphany in the Modern Novel. Seattle, Washington: University of Washington Press; London: Peter
   Owen, pp. 182-210.
       In an examination of the "sudden spiritual manifesta-
   tion...out of proportion to...whatever produces it" found
   in modern fiction, Beja discusses Faulkner's practice of
   keying flashbacks to present epiphanies or to memories of
   past epiphanies. Thus Faulkner presents events not in
   chronological but "visionary and psychological" order. He
   requires a "sensitive" character to experience these illuminations, chiefly characters who seem to dwell more in
   time than space. The Sound and the Fury, Light in August,
   and Absalom, Absalom! provide most examples.

7 BENSON, JACKSON J. "Quentin Compson: Self Portrait of a
   Young Artist's Emotions," TCL, XVII (July), 143-59.
       Quentin, representing "consciousness," gives moral focus
   to The Sound and the Fury. He has the artist's equipment,
   including autobiographical significance for Faulkner himself. He is an "extreme" Faulkner trying to create by art
   the thing he has lost. Caddy's marriage is related to the
   marriage of Estelle Oldham.

8 BLOTNER, JOSEPH. "The Life and Works of William Faulkner,"
   The Nobel Prize Library: William Faulkner, Eugene O'Neill,
   John Steinbeck. New York: Alexis Gregory, pp. 105-17.
       A brief biographical account of Faulkner's life and work.

9 BOWEN, JAMES K., and JAMES K. HAMBY. "Colonel Sartoris Snopes
   and Gabriel Marcel: Allegiance and Commitment," NMW, III
   (Winter), 101-07.
       The conflict developed in "Barn Burning" between family
   loyalty and mature commitment is parallelled by an ontological conflict depicted in the work of G. Marcel, contemporary French Catholic philosopher.

1971

10   BROOKS, CLEANTH. "American Literature: Mirror, Lens or
      Prism," A Shaping Joy: Studies in the Writer's Craft.
      New York: Harcourt, Brace, Jovanovich, pp. 166–80.
          Using Ratliff and his tall tale of Snopes in Hell to de-
      pict one aspect of the presentation of the poor white in
      American fiction, Brooks pleads for the acceptance of lit-
      erature on its own marvelous terms and not as a pure re-
      flector of actual social or specific human conditions.

11   _____. "Faulkner's Treatment of the Racial Problem: Typical
      Examples," A Shaping Joy: Studies in the Writer's Craft.
      New York: Harcourt, Brace, Jovanovich, pp. 230–46.
          A reading of "That Evening Sun" and Light in August
      shows how complex is Faulkner's characterization and his
      elaboration of theme. Most critics view his treatment of
      race in an oversimplified light, failing to read closely
      and to acquaint themselves with all the circumstances in
      a novel or story.

12   _____. A Shaping Joy: Studies in the Writer's Craft. New
      York: Harcourt, Brace, Jovanovich.
          Reprints 1964.B11, 1968.B16, 1962.B27; See also 1971.B10
      and 1971.B11.

13   BROWN, CALVIN S. "Faulkner's Three-in-One Bridge in The Reiv-
      ers," NCL, I (March), 8–10.
          Supplementing 1962.B28, the author notes correspondences
      between Lafayette county landmarks and places in The Reiv-
      ers. Three bridges across the Tallahatchie River in
      Faulkner's youth were used to create the Iron Bridge
      crossing in his last novel.

14   CANTRELL, FRANK. "Faulkner's 'A Courtship,'" MissQ, XXIV
      (Summer), 289–95.
          Faulkner's 1948 story "A Courtship" is a serious and
      comic treatment of young manhood, companionship, and com-
      petition, cast in mock-epic style. In relation to "A
      Justice" (1931), it shows how Faulkner's conception of
      Ikkemotubbe continued to fill out and develop.

15   CAREY, GLENN O. "Faulkner and Mosquitoes: Writing Himself
      and His Age," RS, XXXIX (December), 271–83.
          Mosquitoes is a broadside satire of almost everything in
      the "American scene" of the mid-1920's, but it indicates,
      through reiteration of man's habitual follies, that life
      is much the same at any place and in any period--the prod-
      uct of the same human desires and compulsions. Here the
      characters avoid their "human responsibility."

16 _____. "William Faulkner: The Rise of Snopesism," StTwC,
No. 8 (Fall), 37-64.
Attitudes toward Snopesism in Faulkner's fiction, in his
public statements, and in criticism of his work is surveyed to give a picture of Snopesism in larger perspective. The Snopes trilogy holds out hope that the South
may preserve its worthwhile values against the ravages of
Snopesism.

17 CHURCHILL, ALLEN. The Literary Decade. Englewood Cliffs,
N. J.: Prentice-Hall, pp. 292-95, 314-15.
Faulkner's literary activities in the second half of the
"literary decade," the 1920's, are surveyed in anecdotal
form.

18 COINDREAU, MAURICE E. The Time of William Faulkner: A French
View of Modern American Fiction: Essays by Maurice Edgar
Coindreau, edited and chiefly translated by George M.
Reeves. Columbia, S. C.: University of South Carolina
Press.
Reeves' introduction discusses the work and influence of
Coindreau, one of the premier French translators and in-
terpreters of American literature, whose essays on Faulkner and translations of several stories and six novels
were very important in building Faulkner's European reputation. Includes reprints and/or translations of
1931.B16, 1935.B9, 1935.B10, 1937.B5, 1938.B7, 1950.B4,
1950.B5, 1952.B11, 1952.B12, 1954.B22, 1956.B13, 1960.B17,
1963.B23, 1963.B24, 1965.B19. A checklist of Coindreau's
work is appended.

19 CORRINGTON, JOHN WILLIAM. "Escape into Myth: the Long Dying
of Bayard Sartoris," RANAM, IV, 31-47.
Only the "myth of the South," with Lee as the Olympian
and Col. Sartoris as the genius loci, sustains the people
of Faulkner's Yoknapatawpha from the end of the Civil War
to the end of World War I. After that, the myth is increasingly less important to the community, but no less so
to young Bayard, whose flirtations with death eventually
result in his own apotheosis as a Sartoris on the old
Mythic model.

20 COWLEY, MALCOLM. "A Letter from Malcolm Cowley," Fitzgerald /
Hemingway Annual, 1971, edited by Matthew J. Bruccoli and
C. E. Frazer Clark, Jr. Dayton, Ohio: NCR Microcard Edi-
tions, pp. 317-18.
In a 13 October 1970 letter from Cowley to Bruccoli, the
anthologist discusses the circumstances behind the crea-

1971

(COWLEY, MALCOLM)
    tion of the Portable Faulkner and Portable Hemingway vol-
umes for Viking and their sales. Cowley claims that
Faulkner's comment, "I don't think there's too much
Southern legend in it," refers to the Viking Portable introduction and is not a judgment on Faulkner's own work.

21   CRANE, JOAN ST.C. "Rare or Seldom-Seen Dust Jackets of American First Editions: IV," Serif, VIII, 21-23.
    Reproductions of dust jackets of Sartoris, The Sound and
the Fury, As I Lay Dying, and Sanctuary. See also Serif,
VII (1970), 64-66.

22   DEVLIN, ALBERT J. "Sartoris: Rereading the MacCallum Episode," TCL, XVII (April), 83-90.
    The MacCallums in Sartoris do not represent ideal or
even normal existence. The presence of six unmarried
sons, most beyond middle age, under the control of their
father, represents a kind of pathology at best. Virgin-
ius, the patriarch, is so formidable and aggressive the
boys have not found it easy, or even possible, to develop
their own masculinity.

23   *DITSKY, JOHN. "Faulkner Land and Steinbeck Country," Steinbeck: The Man and His Work. Corvallis, Oregon: Oregon
State University Press, pp. 11-23.
    Faulkner and Steinbeck can be differentiated by virtue
of Steinbeck's use of repeated devices and Faulkner's
"valid prior assumptions about man and the land." Steinbeck is less adequate as a writer. (Warren French, American Literary Scholarship 1971, p. 232.)

24   EDWARDS, C. H. "A Hawthorne Echo in Faulkner's Nobel Prize
Acceptance Speech," NConL, I (March), 4-5.
    Hawthorne's reference to "truth of the human heart" in
the preface to The House of the Seven Gables may be echoed
in phrases of the Nobel speech.

25   EMERSON, O. B. "Faulkner and His Friend: An Interview with
Emily W. Stone," Comment, II (Winter), 31-37.
    The writer records anecdotes and personal opinions from
the widow of Faulkner's early Oxford friend, Phil Stone.

26   ESCHLIMAN, HERBERT R. "Francis Christensen in Yoknapatawpha
County," UR, XXXVII (Spring), 232-39.
    An analysis of the style of samples from Faulkner's
novels using the scheme of Francis Christensen's rhetorical analysis. Faulkner uses a high percentage of Christensen's "cumulative" sentences, with a great many levels.

27   FROHOCK, W. M.   "Faulkner in France: The Final Phase," <u>Mosaic</u>,
      IV (No. 3), 125-34.
           Faulkner has had a marked influence on "recent" French
      fiction.   Many of the elements common to modern French
      novelists and Faulkner have reached the stage of simple
      coincidence rather than influence.   Claude Simon and Mi-
      chel Butor show most use of Faulkner, but even here the
      evidence is not conclusive.   Faulkner's influence in
      France is in the ultimate phase: his work has been as-
      similated and has created a minor tradition that is now
      part of French literature.

28   GIDLEY, MICK.   "Another Psychologist, a Physiologist and Wil-
      liam Faulkner," <u>ArielE</u>, II (October), 78-86.
           Faulkner had possibly read about Freud in three books
      which Phil Stone had ordered in 1922; work by James Harvey
      Robinson, Havelock Ellis, and Louis Berman is discussed.

29   GLICKSBERG, CHARLES I.   "Faulkner's World of Love and Sex,"
      <u>The Sexual Revolution in Modern American Literature</u>.   The
      Hague: Martinus Nijhoff, pp. 96-120.
           Beginning with some misattributions, Glicksberg asserts
      that Faulkner, while able to do justice to sexual passion,
      as in <u>The Wild Palms</u>, is able to create "no mystique of
      sex."   He examines his characters objectively.   The con-
      tradictions of "sex and death" are significantly prominent
      in Faulkner's fiction.   Sexuality in its more perverse
      forms he uses to display the human potential for evil.
      But love is neither panacea nor particular curse; it is
      simply part of the human condition.

30   GOLDMAN, ARNOLD.   "Introduction," <u>Twentieth-Century-Interpre-</u>
      <u>tations of Absalom, Absalom!</u>   Englewood Cliffs, N. J.:
      Prentice-Hall, pp. 1-11.
           There is no critical unanimity about the events or mean-
      ing of <u>Absalom, Absalom!</u>   Goldman summarizes the story and
      sketches some of the distinct critical views in the col-
      lection of excerpts from books and articles on the novel.

31   _____.   "Note" and "Faulkner and the Revision of Yoknapatawpha
      History," <u>The American Novel and the Nineteen Twenties</u>.
      (Stratford-upon-Avon Studies (No. 13).   London: Edward Ar-
      nold; New York: Crane, Russak, pp. 165-95.
           Cowley's theory of a Yoknapatawpha Saga (<u>See</u>, e.g.
      1946.B2) is untenable, particularly in the face of Faulk-
      ner's statements about his work and his practice.   As the
      novels Faulkner wrote developed, they created the necessi-
      ty of new interpretations, "even requiring new and differ-

1971

(GOLDMAN, ARNOLD)
ent 'facts,'" to meet his artistic demands. His Yoknapatawpha County tales are best described in his own terms
not as history or saga but as an "apocrypha"--that is,
uncanonical. They are literature, not history or legend.

32   GRESSET, MICHEL. "Foreword," The Time of William Faulkner: A
French View of Modern American Fiction: Essays by Mau-
rice Edgar Coindreau, edited and chiefly translated by
George M. Reeves. Columbia, S. C.: University of South
Carolina Press, pp. ix-xiv.
Gresset writes an appreciation of Coindreau as dean of
French translators of modern American fiction. Coindreau
"invented" Faulkner for the French by presenting his work,
not only in translations but through intelligent and sym-
pathetic reviews, essays, and prefaces, beginning in 1932.
He has continued to champion succeeding generations of
Southern American writers.

33   GRIFFITH, BENJAMIN W. "Faulkner's Archaic Titles and the Second Shepherd's Play," NMW, IV (Fall), 62-63.
"Reive" in the sense Faulkner uses it for the title The
Reivers and "light" in the sense of having delivered a
child can be found in Second Shepherd's Play. See correction in 1972.B57.

34   HAMILTON, GARY D. "The Past in the Present: A Reading of Go
Down, Moses," SHR, V (Spring), 171-81.
A consideration of time-consciousness in Go Down, Moses
supports an argument for the book's identity as a novel.
Unity is achieved by the constant contrast of past and
present. The final judgment of the book is pessimistic,
since no figure emerges with McCaslin's activity and Ike's
conscience.

35   HANDY, WILLIAM J. "Faulkner's As I Lay Dying," Modern Fic-
tion: A Formalist Approach. Carbondale, Illinois:
Southern Illinois University Press, pp. 75-93.
Reprints, under a shorter title, 1959.B30.

36   HARTER, CAROL C. "The Winter of Isaac McCaslin: Revisions
and Irony in Faulkner's 'Delta Autumn,'" JML, I (No. 2),
209-25.
The short story version of "Delta Autumn" has no crucial
family relationships; the difference in the novel version
from Go Down, Moses is crucial to the book's meaning and
unity. Ike is a failure.

37   HAUCK, RICHARD BOYD. "The Prime Maniacal Risibility: William
     Faulkner," A Cheerful Nihilism: Confidence and "The Ab-
     surd" in American Fiction. Bloomington, Indiana: Uni-
     versity of Indiana Press, pp. 167-200.
          In the context of Melville and Twain, As I Lay Dying is
     the "definitive" absurdist book of the American twentieth
     century; Faulkner is both absurdist and moralist. The
     chapter includes a summary of the Snopes trilogy and brief
     comment on other Faulkner works.

38   HAYS, PETER L.   The Limping Hero: Grotesques in Literature.
     New York: New York University Press, pp. 82-84.
          Like.many other writers of the 1920's and 30's--Eliot,
     Lawrence, and Hemingway--Faulkner uses "maimed" charac-
     ters to depict social or spiritual sterility. "Limping
     heroes" in his work include Ab Snopes and "Old Ben," the
     great bear.

39   HELLSTRÖM, GUSTAF. "Presentation Address [to William Faulk-
     ner]," Nobel Prize Library: William Faulkner, Eugene
     O'Neill, John Steinbeck. New York: Alexis Gregory,
     pp. 3-6.
          Faulkner's accomplishments are surveyed in the presenta-
     tion address at the Nobel Prize ceremony.

40   HEPBURN, KENNETH W.   "Faulkner's Mosquitoes: A Poetic Turning
     Point," TCL, XVII (January), 19-28.
          Mosquitoes and the creation of several aesthetic stra-
     tegies, rather than Sartoris and the origin of Yoknapa-
     tawpha County, is the turning point in Faulkner's art.
     The novel contrasts Gordon the sculptor and Fairchild the
     Anderson-like writer. The yacht trip is a hiatus in which
     these artists undergo a crucial change: Gordon moves from
     Romantic idealism to a solid realism, Fairchild from self-
     consciousness to a sense of wonder. Self-deprecation and
     irony in the novel are Faulkner's signs of a new kind of
     art.

41   HODGSON, JOHN A.   "Logical Sequence and Continuity: Some Ob-
     servations on the Typographical and Structural Consistency
     of Absalom, Absalom!" AL, XLIII (March), 97-107.
          Faulkner's methods in Absalom, Absalom! are consistent
     and meaningful. He uses typographical variation to dis-
     tinguish speech and thought; parenthesis to signal time
     shifts and interpolations. The anomalous chapter three
     is a deliberate presentation of temporal shift. The
     overall effect of these devices is to involve the reader
     in the novel's search for meaning.

1971

42   HOLMAN, C. HUGH. "Absalom, Absalom! The Historian as Detec-
      tive," SR, LXXIX (Autumn), 542-53.
         Shreve, the voice of an isolated and harmless ratiocina-
      tion, tries unsuccessfully to reduce Sutpen and the other
      actors in his tragedy to ordinary typical characters, re-
      presentative pawns of Southern American social forces.
      Equally false is the demonizing and romanticizing in
      Quentin's information. The resulting synthesis is art--
      the creation of the imagination of the artist--and a larg-
      er view of "man's enduring tragedy."
      Reprinted 1972.B49.

43   INGE, M. THOMAS. "Contemporary American Literature in Spain,"
      TSL, XVI, 155-67.
         Next to Hemingway, Faulkner is the best known major
      American writer in Spain. The author lists translations,
      beginning with Sanctuary in 1934, and points out noteworthy
      ones, like Jorge Luís Borges' version of the The Wild
      Palms and Amando Lázaro Ros's versions of The Sound and
      the Fury and Absalom, Absalom!

44   _____. "William Faulkner's Light in August: An Annotated
      Checklist of Criticism," RALS, I (Spring), 30-57.
         A compendium of criticism, grouped according to contem-
      porary reviews, 1932-1934, and criticism, 1935-1971, with
      annotation. Authors are indexed.

45   INGRAM, FORREST L. Representative Short Story Cycles of the
      Twentieth Century. The Hague: Mouton, pp. 106-42.
         The stories of The Unvanquished demonstrate progressive-
      ly how war intrudes with increasing force upon human con-
      sciousness and events, corrupting even the innocent. The
      book is not a novel but "a composed, mythically oriented
      short story cycle," with interrelationships and develop-
      ments of theme and character which provide unity. The
      author compares it with Sartoris.

46   JAMES, STUART. "Faulkner's Shadowed Land," DenvQ, VI (Autumn),
      45-61.
         Like Benjy, Faulkner, trying to say, expresses himself
      not directly but in the shadows, between the lines. His
      world is filled with meaningful ghosts. Light in August,
      ironically titled, is a good example of his method with
      shadows and night sounds and inner worlds revealed in a
      dark mingling.

47   KANE, PATRICIA. "Adaptable and Free: Faulkner's Ratliff,"
      NConL, I (May), 9-11.
          The "rat" in Suratt-Ratliff's name seems significant in
      view of Faulkner's statement that the animal has adapta-
      bility and the power to retain personal liberty.

48   KARTIGANER, DONALD M. "Process and Product: A Study in Mod-
      ern Literary Form, Part II," MassR (Autumn), 789-816.
          Faulkner is discussed along with Conrad as a fictional
      artist who is concerned in his narratives (for instance,
      Absalom, Absalom!) with the disparity between the struc-
      tured and the spontaneous products of imagination. The
      lives of the narrators take shape around their reactions
      to and explanations of Charles Bon's murder. The novel's
      triumph is the communion of Quentin and Shreve and their
      imaginative recapture of a lost past. The tragedy of
      life--that process must become product--is viewed by
      Faulkner with both affirmation and despair.

49   KRIEGER, MURRAY. "The Light-ening of the 'Burden' of History:
      Light in August," The Classic Vision: The Retreat from
      Extremity in Modern Literature. Baltimore, Maryland:
      Johns Hopkins Press, pp. 313-36.
          The "three" deaths in Light in August--Joanna's, Joe's
      and Hightower's--are brought about by the weight of his-
      tory and family heritage, symbolized by the name and sto-
      ry of Miss Burden. Lena and the baby break free in the
      end, beyond extremity, neither trapped in Joe's circle
      nor haunted by Hightower's wheel, and thus the book moves
      from tragic to classic, from inferno to paradise.

50   KULIN, KATALIN. "Reasons and Characteristics of Faulkner's
      Influence on Modern Latin-American Fiction," ALitASH,
      XIII, 349-63.
          Faulkner is the most powerful influence on modern Latin
      American fiction, but similarities between the Latin
      American novelists and Faulkner are not always due to fa-
      miliarity with his work. The imaginary world, the human-
      ism, the use of myth--characteristics of Faulkner's work--
      have all been useful devices discovered, sometimes quite
      independently, by Latin authors.

51   LAWSON, LEWIS A. "William Faulkner," The Politics of
      Twentieth-Century Novelists, edited by George A. Pani-
      chas. New York: Hawthorn Books, pp. 278-95.
          Faulkner repeatedly demythologizes the political phi-
      losophy of the South in his fiction. In Sartoris, Aunt
      Jenny deliberately transmits the tradition of gallantry

1971

   (LAWSON, LEWIS A.)
      which makes it impossible for "modern Southern manhood to
      shake off the burden of the past and live successfully."
      In The Sound the Fury, Southern womanhood is again the de-
      structive force, while black tradition is clearly superior
      to the white. Sanctuary attacks not only ordinary society
      but the judicial process as well. Light in August depicts
      religion in similar terms. In the political sense Faulk-
      ner's most important creation was his own vision and, fi-
      nally, after the Nobel Prize, himself as an active politi-
      cal man.

52   LEARY, LEWIS. "William Faulkner and the Grace of Comedy,"
      Southern Excursions: Essays on Mark Twain and Others.
      Baton Rouge, Louisiana: Louisiana State University Press,
      pp. 209-29.
      A general estimate of the nature of Faulkner's great-
      ness altered from Leary's introduction to Tuck's Crowell
      Handbook (1964.A8).

53   LLOYD, JAMES BARLOW. "An Annotated Bibliography of William
      Faulkner, 1967-1970," UMSE, XII, 1-57.
      Picking up where Beebe (1967.B4) ends, Lloyd lists and
      annotates selected books and articles on Faulkner. The
      scheme of organization follows Meriwether's survey of
      criticism (1969.B59): Bibliography, Biography, Criticism.
      Some foreign criticism is included. There is no index.

54   *LUEDTKE, CAROL L. "The Sound and the Fury and Lie Down in
      Darkness: Some Comparisons," LWU, IV, pp. 45-51.
      According to AES, XVII (November 1973), the article
      points out that geography and the social scene in both
      novels are similar.

55   McCORMICK, JOHN. The Middle Distance: A Comparative History
      of American Imaginative Literature, 1919-1932. New York:
      The Free Press, pp. 98-107.
      Faulkner's best work is notable for "certainty of tone
      and the most absolute sense of place in American fiction,"
      qualities mostly missing from his first two novels.
      Faulkner has a profound view of history and a more com-
      plex view of his characters, especially the women, than
      he has been granted.

56   McCULLERS, CARSON. "The Russian Realists and Southern Liter-
      ature," The Mortgaged Heart, edited by Margarita G. Smith.
      Boston: Houghton Mifflin, pp. 252-58.
      Reprinted from 1941.B9.

57   McHANEY, THOMAS L. "Jeffers' 'Tamar' and Faulkner's The Wild
      Palms," RJN, No. 29 (August), 16-18.
          Several parallels exist between the love story in The
      Wild Palms and Robinson Jeffers' long narrative poem
      "Tamar" (1924); they are evidence of further Jeffers in-
      fluence on Faulkner's work. See also 1969.B56 and
      1972.B45.

58   _____. "Sanctuary and Frazer's Slain Kings," MissQ, XXIV
      (Summer), 223-45.
          Possibly through Eliot's influential notes to The Waste
      Land, James G. Frazer's The Golden Bough became for Faulk-
      ner the inspiration behind many incidents and characters
      in Sanctuary. It is also the probable source of the nov-
      el's title. Horace is the Tiresias who is witness to the
      perverted and spiritually barren reenactment of the rites
      of Diana, Demeter, Isis, etc., in the human drama of mod-
      ern corruption.

59   MALBONE, RAYMOND G. "Promissory Poker in Faulkner's 'Was,'"
      EngR, XXII (Fall), 23-25.
          There are unresolvable inconsistencies in the betting of
      the poker game in "Was," the opening section of Go Down,
      Moses. They may be justified by the slightly comic char-
      acter of all the bets, which are promises to do one thing
      or another.

60   MATERASSI, MARIO. "Faulkner Criticism in Italy," IQ, XV
      (Summer), 47-85.
          Beginning with Mario Praz's essay in 1931, which saw
      Faulkner as a moralist and a successful stylist, Italian
      criticism preceded American criticism by some eight years
      in understanding Faulkner's seriousness. Materassi sur-
      veys the history of Faulkner's Italian reception in essay
      form. The notes make a selected bibliography. Materassi
      claims the Italians have produced some of the best anal-
      yses of Faulkner's work in Europe or America. He points
      out that Elio Vittorini's influential translation of
      Light in August, though by one of the best writers of the
      time, omits whole paragraphs and expurgates the Burden-
      Christmas love-making. Translated and reprinted from
      1968.A5.

61   MAUD, RALPH. "Faulkner, Mailer, and Yogi Bear," CRevAS, II
      (Fall), 69-76.
          Ike McCaslin's initiation in "The Bear," which paral-
      lels American Indian rites of passage, fails because his
      mentor, Sam, being part black, is denied membership in

1971

(MAUD, RALPH)
the "'tribe' into which Ike can realistically seek admission." In <u>Why Are We in Vietnam</u>? Mailer parodies this Faulkner episode into a successful initiation for his characters, D. J. and Tex.

62   MEATS, STEPHEN E.   "Who Killed Joanna Burden?" <u>MissQ</u>, XXIV (Summer), 271-77.
      Evidence in <u>Light in August</u> does not offer convincing proof of Joe Christmas's killing of Joanna Burden. the sheriff and townspeople accept his guilt because, as Burch tells them, he is black.

63   MELLARD, JAMES M.   "Type and Archetype: Jason Compson as 'Satirist,'" <u>Genre</u>, IV (June), 173-88.
      Like most satirists, Jason Compson has a conservative view of life, its values and institutions; he is even a "champion of virtue," of sorts, trying to save the Compson name. Several works of satire are used to discuss section three of <u>The Sound and the Fury</u> and the ways in which Jason fits the characteristics of both satirist and <u>satiric persona</u>.

64   MERIWETHER, JAMES B.   "A. E. Housman and Faulkner's Nobel Prize Speech: a Note," <u>JAmS</u>, IV (February), 247-48.
      Poem IX in A. E. Housman's <u>Last Poems</u> (1922) contains a phrase, "The flesh will grieve on other bones than ours," which may be a source for Faulkner's Nobel Prize acceptance speech and a small clue to Faulkner's meaning.

65   _____.   "A Prefatory Note by Faulkner for the Compson Appendix," <u>AL</u>, XLIII (May), 281-84.
      The author introduces and reprints a short introduction Faulkner apparently wrote for publication with the Modern Library double volume of <u>The Sound and the Fury</u> and <u>As I Lay Dying</u>. The introduction, never published before, is printed without emendation.

66   _____.   "The Short Fiction of William Faulkner: A Bibliography," <u>Proof 1</u>, pp. 293-329.
      A bibliography of "all textually significant forms" known to the author at this time of Faulkner's short fiction. <u>See also</u> 1971.B67.

67   _____.   "Two Unknown Faulkner Short Stories," <u>RANAM</u>, IV, 23-30.
      "Two Dollar Wife" in <u>College Life</u>, 1936, and "Sepulture South," are both short stories that should be listed in

400

(MERIWETHER, JAMES B.)
Meriwether's check list (1957.B48) and Literary Career
(1961.A4). The first was omitted and the second erroneously listed as an essay. Both pieces are summarized and
briefly discussed.

68   MILLGATE, MICHAEL. "Faulkner," American Literary Scholarship
an annual, 1969, edited by J. A. Robbins. Durham, N. C.:
Duke University Press, pp. 108-21.
The annual essay surveying Faulkner criticism.

69   _____. Thomas Hardy: His Career as a Novelist. New York:
Random House, pp. 345-50.
Hardy's deliberate vision of tragedy in the life of a
small rural region, his rootedness in place, his Words-
worthian regard for man and nature, and his moral viewpoint all find parallels in Faulkner, though the novels
which depict Faulkner's world have an interrelatedness
which Hardy's novels do not.

70   MONTEIRO, GEORGE. "'Between Grief and Nothing': Hemingway
and Faulkner," HemN, I (Spring), 13-15.
The author suggests that Hemingway borrowed the ending
of For Whom the Bell Tolls from The Wild Palms and discovers onanism in both novels.

71   MUIR, EDWARD H. "A Footnote on Sartoris and Some Speculation," JML, I (March), 389-93.
The experimental aeroplane in which young Bayard is
killed has a prototype and source in a similar aircraft
designed by W. W. Christmas and advertised widely in 1919
and 1920. Christmas's name would have been provocative
for Faulkner.

72   NASH, HARRY C. "Faulkner's 'Furniture Repairer and Dealer':
Knitting Up Light in August," MFS, XVI (Winter), 529-31.
The bawdy and comic dialogue between the furniture
dealer and his wife that ends Light in August is warm,
human, and sentimental in the finest sense. Coming as it
does at the end of a novel filled with Gothic events, it
is a positive comment on human possibility.

73   NEBEKER, HELEN. "Chronology Revised," SSF, VIII (Summer),
471-73.
There are possible discrepancies in McGlynn's chronology of "A Rose for Emily" (1969.B55); 1894 is not the date
of Emily's father's death but of the remission of her
taxes. She dies around 1928, not eight years after the

1971

(NEBEKER, HELEN)
> publication of the story. The bridal chamber is apparent-
> ly sealed shortly after the smell is noticed.

74 NELSON, MALCOLM A. "'Yr Stars Fell' in The Bear," AN&Q, IX,
> 102-03.
> > The spectacular Leonid meteor shower of 1833 is Faulk-
> > ner's reference in the McCaslin ledgers of part four of
> > "The Bear" in Go Down, Moses.

75 NEUFELDT, LEONARD N. "Time and Man's Possibilities in Light
> in August," GaR, XXV (Spring), 27-40.
> > Joe Christmas's struggle with time in Light in August is
> > Faulkner's central theme. Lena Grove, accepting and mov-
> > ing through time's flux; Byron living in a precise clock-
> > time world; and Hightower, inhabiting an aborted but on-
> > going past--they provide the context of Joe's struggle,
> > his self-destruction through the inability to accept time
> > and historical circularity.

76 NOLTE, WILLIAM H. "Mencken, Faulkner, and Southern Moral-
> ism," SCR, IV (December), 45-61.
> > Frederick Law Olmsted is used as a corrective to H. L.
> > Mencken's sympathies toward the culture and economy of the
> > Old South, and Faulkner's fiction is used to demonstrate
> > who is left in the South after the best and the brightest
> > have migrated Northward. Light in August, especially, is
> > an ironic indictment of fanatical Southern protestantism.
> > In The Sound and the Fury, Faulkner denies "Christianity
> > as a moral guide." As I Lay Dying is, like Jeffers' po-
> > etry, a commentary on the "curse" of self-consciousness.

77 PEARCE, RICHARD. "Pylon, 'Awake and Sing!' and the Apoca-
> lyptic Imagination of the 30's," Criticism, XIII (Spring),
> 131-41.
> > Pylon is compared to Odets' play and other work of the
> > 1930's for its exploration of the lack of organic struc-
> > ture or controlling center to depict the chaotic times.
> > The novel is "all movement, violent, indiscriminate,"
> > presenting a vision of the apocalypse.

78 PETERSON, RICHARD F. "Faulkner's Light in August," Expl, XXX
> (December), Item 35.
> > The note expands upon 1969.B13, arguing that Joe Christ-
> > mas's desire for punishment is related to his original and
> > continuing relationships with women (the dietitian, Mrs.
> > McEachern, Bobbie Allen, Joanna) who, in one form or
> > another, give food and love in an atmosphere of deception.

(PETERSON, RICHARD F.)
As with the dietitian's rewards to the guilty child who
has stolen and eaten the toothpaste, the gestures of all
these women constitute "punishment deferred."

79   PIERLE, ROBERT C.   "Snopesism in Faulkner's The Hamlet," ES,
LII (June), 246-52.
Reviewing the "three phases" of critical comment on
Snopesism--O'Donnell's Snopes/Sartoris dichotomy
(1939.B26), Warren's meliorist view that not all Snopes
are bad or "Sartorises" good (1946.B16), and the more recent opinion that "Snopesism" as such is a mirror of all
modern greed and social humanity--the author distills the
characterization of Flem to the essence of pure Snopes and
compares other characters by that standard, concluding
that Snopesism is a low materialistic frame of mind.

80   POLK, NOEL.   "Alec Holston's Lock and the Founding of Jefferson," MissQ, XXIV (Summer), 247-69.
The episode concerning the lock in the first narrative
section of Requiem for a Nun is germinal to an understanding of the novel and of Faulkner's thoughts on freedom,
law, and government.   Thomas Jefferson Pettigrew is the
voice of law and order; he wants simple compliance to the
letter of the law, regardless of other circumstances.
The naming of the city after him signifies the village's
entrance into history with all its burdens and hopes.

81   _____.   "The Staging of Requiem for a Nun," MissQ, XXIV (Summer), 299-314.
This essay-review on 1970.A2 discusses errors of fact,
judgment, and point of view which make the book unreliable
and adds information about the play version of Requiem for
a Nun.

82   *PORAT, TSFIRA.   "Sawdust Dolls: Tragic Fate and Comic Freedom
in Faulkner's Light in August," Hasifrut, II, 767-82; in
Hebrew, with English summary, pp. 884-85.
According to Millgate, American Literary Scholarship,
1971, the article contrasts Byron Bunch's escape from
Calvinist rigidity through self-knowledge with Joe Christmas's failure to free himself from McEachern's influence.

83   PUTZEL, MAX.   "What is Gothic about Absalom, Absalom!" SLJ,
IV (Fall), 3-19.
The decay of chivalry as theme and several narrative
viewpoints, especially Rosa's, lend a Gothic tone to Absalom, Absalom! Quentin's tortured search for the ulti-

1971

(PUTZEL, MAX)
mate disclosure, withheld until late in the novel, is
another Gothic element. The terror here is of the soul.

84 *RAMA ROA, P. G. "Faulkner's Old Man: A Critique," IJAS, I
(No. 4), 43-50.
According to Millgate, American Literary Scholarship,
1972, p. 126, this article's "miscellaneous comments need
not be sought out."

85 RANDEL, FRED V. "Parentheses in Faulkner's Absalom, Absalom!"
Style, V (Winter), 70-87.
Limiting "parenthesis" to mean material between upright
curves without grammatical connection to the passage it in-
terrupts, Randel studies some 600 such constructions in
Absalom, Absalom! The central crisis is that experienced
by a character "when he leaves a world of dream and confronts a world of limits." Parenthesis is a means of re-
inforcing this theme since it provides opportunity for subjective interpretation of "factual" reality and for dramatizing contradictions.

86 RAPER, J. R. "Meaning Called to Life: Alogical Structure in
Absalom, Absalom!" SHR V (Winter), 9-23.
Faulkner represents the major theme of Absalom, Absalom!
("the thwarted life") through cinematographic maneuvers
and an "alogical structure" both of which project a living
image of his theme. The technique is compared to Sergei
Eisenstein's montage. Chapter 5 of the novel throws together striking, conflicting scenes and images, chiaroscura, shifting perspective.

87 *RICHE, JAMES. "Pragmatism: A National Fascist Mode of
Thought," L&I, No. 9, 37-44.
AES, VII (November 1971) summarizes the article, which
argues that Faulkner's stream-of-consciousness technique
allows characters to see value only in self-interest,
typical of pragmatic heroes since Ben Franklin's time.

88 *SHARMA, P. P. "The Snopes Theme in Faulkner's Larger Context," IJAS, I (No. 4), 33-41.
According to Millgate, American Literary Scholarship
1972, p. 126, "an unimportant article."

89 SMITH, BEVERLEY E. "A Note on Faulkner's 'Greenbury Hotel,'"
MissQ, XXIV (Summer), 297-98.
Several sources in popular lore and literature suggest
that the "Greenbury Hotel" in Knight's Gambit is the Peabody Hotel in Memphis.

404

90 STANZEL, FRANZ. Narrative Situations in the Novel, translated
    by James P. Pusack. Bloomington, Indiana: Indiana Uni-
    versity Press, pp. 14, 56–58, 68, 112, 148.
        Several Faulkner works are mentioned briefly, including
    The Sound and the Fury, in discussions of different narra-
    tive methods. The most extensive comment is on the way
    the wheel image in Hightower's thoughts in Light in August
    moves from the narrator's realm into the character's
    consciousness.

91 STARKE, CATHERINE JUANITA. Black Portraiture in American Fic-
    tion: Stock Characters, Archetypes, and Individuals. New
    York: Basic Books, pp. 192–96.
        Lucas Beauchamp in Go Down, Moses and Intruder in the
    Dust is portrayed as an engaging, individualized human be-
    ing, not in any sense as a black stereotype.

92 STEPHENS, ROSEMARY. "Mythical Elements of 'Pantaloon in
    Black,'" UMSE, XI, 45–51.
        "Pantaloon in Black" is an archetypal ritual search for
    meaning in a hostile world. Rider's house is a Jungian
    mandala; Mannie the anima; liquor the mana, and so on.

93 STRÖMBERG, KJELL. "The 1949 Prize," translated by Dale McAdoo.
    Nobel Prize Library: William Faulkner, Eugene O'Neill,
    John Steinbeck. New York: Alexis Gregory, pp. 119–21.
        The writer gives an account of the 1949 and 1950 voting
    on the Nobel Prize which resulted in Faulkner's award and
    of the reaction.

94 SUGG, REDDING S., JR. "John Faulkner's Vanishing South," AH,
    XXII (April), 65–75.
        The author presents a brief account of John Faulkner,
    Faulkner's brother, as a painter, with several reproduc-
    tions of his work, including two which were intended to be
    scenes from Faulkner's books.

95 SULLIVAN, RUTH. "The Narrator in 'A Rose for Emily,'" JNT, I
    (September), 159–78.
        Previous criticism of "A Rose for Emily" ignores the
    narrative voice, failing to question its nature and func-
    tion. The narrator is an anonymous group who watch Emily
    with an intense curiosity, but not objectively. The
    narrator-group is voyeuristic, intrusive, and it commits
    a symbolic rape in the forced entry. It accepts Miss
    Emily, in an infantile way, as mother figure, and it ex-
    presses both desire and anguish over loss regarding her.

1971

96 *TANAKA, HISAO. "Quentin Doomed as a Southerner: A Study of
   Absalom, Absalom!" SALit, VII, 1-14.
   American Literary Scholarship 1971, p. 116.

97 WAGNER, LINDA WELSHIMER. "Faulkner's Fiction: Studies in
   Organic Form," JNT, I (January), 1-14.
   After a brief discussion of Faulkner's relation to modern movements in literature and painting, the author
   studies effective organic form--structure, point of view,
   language, as it grows out of a single story's requirements
   --in The Sound and the Fury, Light in August, and The Hamlet. The later Faulkner novels are extensions of the formal experiments in the early ones.

98 _____. "Jason Compson: The Demands of Honor," SR, LXXIX
   (Autumn), 554-75.
   A sympathetic look at Jason Compson in The Sound and the
   Fury reveals the breadth of Faulkner's characterization,
   which does not paint in simple terms of good and evil.
   Jason is a neglected, mistreated child. He is, like the
   other children, a product of the family that made him. He
   is proud of the family name and works to preserve it.
   There is a kind of heroism in the fact that he meets life
   and goes on living.

99 WALTER, JAMES. "Expiation and History: Ike McCaslin and the
   Mystery of Providence," LaS, X (Winter), 263-73.
   The discussion of Providence in part four of "The Bear"
   illuminates the function and meaning of "Go Down, Moses,"
   the last story in the novel Go Down, Moses. Ike McCaslin
   attempts to discover God's will in history, finding, he
   believes, that men generally have accepted bondage instead
   of freedom and have exploited the land and finally also
   other people. He repudiates an economic arrangement that
   perpetuates this exploitation. Cass is a Biblical liter-
   alist who rejects Ike's notion of Providence; he fails,
   not Ike. The shift of tone from "Delta Autumn," where
   Ike's failure to change the social order is emphasized, to
   "Go Down, Moses," where communal action is achieved to
   unite the old and new epochs, indicates Providence as active in history.

100 WATKINS, FLOYD C. "William Faulkner: The Unbearable and Un-
    knowable Truth in Faulkner's First Three Novels," The
    Flesh and the Word: Eliot, Hemingway, Faulkner. Nash-
    ville, Tenn.: Vanderbilt University Press, pp. 169-80.
    Ambivalent about the meaning of man's experience with
    war, religion, and love, Faulkner, in his first three

1971

(WATKINS, FLOYD C.)
novels, seems to waver between a romantic and a critical
view. He is an intrusive author and rhetorical, although
he condemns "words."

101   _____. "The Word and the Deed in Faulkner's First Great Novels," The Flesh and the Word: Eliot, Hemingway, Faulkner.
Nashville, Tenn.: Vanderbilt University Press,
pp. 181-202.
In Faulkner's great novels, he dramatized life and let
the reader find a moral; Addie Bundren would have been
embarrassed by the Nobel Prize speech and Faulkner's late,
overly moralistic manner. In The Sound and the Fury, As I
Lay Dying, and Sanctuary "users of the word" are false.
Reprinted 1973.A9.

102   _____. "Language of Irony: Quiet Words and Violent Acts in
Light in August," The Flesh and the Word: Eliot, Hemingway, Faulkner. Nashville, Tenn.: Vanderbilt University
Press, pp. 203-15.
Words of peace pervade Light in August, where Faulkner
uses a new technique--blending truth and irony--to dramatize Joe Christmas's confused mind. The novel is not as
good as the preceding three, because of Faulkner's
intrusiveness.

103   _____. "Thirteen Ways of Talking About a Blackbird," The
Flesh and the Word: Eliot, Hemingway, Faulkner. Nashville, Tenn.: Vanderbilt University Press, pp. 216-33.
The silence of the mysterious past and the "logorrhea of
a talkative present"--in the form of the narrators--is
central to Absalom, Absalom!, which is filled with abstractions. It dramatizes fully the failure of language.

104   _____. "Faulkner's Inexhaustible Voice," The Flesh and the
Word: Eliot, Hemingway, Faulkner. Nashville, Tenn.:
Vanderbilt University Press, pp. 234-53.
The Unvanquished, with its narrator, "signals the beginning" of Faulkner's excessive use of "talkative story-
telling characters." The "Old Man" section of The Wild
Palms focuses on a character who is all action, but the
author intrudes to explain him repeatedly. In novels after Absalom, Absalom!, Faulkner is wordy, less happy in
subject matter, too often creating books "not sufficiently unified" to be called novels, attempting to manipulate
the feelings and beliefs of his audience, and making in-
vidious comparisons of black virtue and white callousness.

1971

105   WATKINS, FLOYD C.   "The Truth Shall Make You Fail," The Flesh
          and the Word: Eliot, Hemingway, Faulkner.   Nashville,
          Tenn.:   Vanderbilt University Press, pp. 254-73.
              Malcolm Cowley made Faulkner conscious of his achieve-
          ment and helped turn him toward nonfiction and public
          statement, even in the novels, like Intruder in the Dust,
          Knight's Gambit, Requiem for a Nun, A Fable, and The
          Reivers.

106   WILSON, GAYLE EDWARD.   "'Being Pulled Two Ways':   The Nature
          of Sarty's Choice in 'Barn Burning,'" MissQ, XXIV (Summer),
          279-88.
              Colonel Sartoris Snopes, committing a betrayal of family
          yet a repudiation of his father's "Paranoid" way of life,
          opens the door for his entrance into the acceptance of
          community values which provide stability.   Significantly,
          his father's name, Abner, means "father of light."

107   WOODBERRY, POTTER.   "Faulkner's Numismatics: A Note on As I
          Lay Dying," RS, XXXIX (June), 150-51.
              Faulkner deliberately conflates the liberty and buffalo
          nickels in Darl's final monologue in As I Lay Dying to
          suggest the bestial coupling of the American symbol of
          Democratic idealism.   Darl is a disillusioned victim of
          World War I.   His one memento is obscene, the pornographic
          spyglass.

108   *YOSHIDA, MICHIKO.   "The Voices and Legends in Yoknapatawpha
          County," SELit (English Number), pp. 174-76.
              An English summary of a longer article in Japanese which
          Millgate, in American Literary Scholarship 1971, says "can
          reasonably be left untranslated."

1972 A   BOOKS

  1   BARTH, J. ROBERT, ed.   Religious Perspectives in Faulkner's
          Fiction: Yoknapatawpha and Beyond.   Notre Dame, Indiana:
          Notre Dame University Press.
              Essays and book chapters on Faulkner and religion, most
          of them previously published, are collected with a brief
          commentary on each by Fr. Barth.   See the "B" section of
          1972 entries in this Reference Guide for annotation and
          summaries of the commentary; See also 1972.B5, 1972.B6.

2 BASSETT, JOHN. William Faulkner: An Annotated Checklist of
   Criticism. New York: David Lewis.
      Articles, books and newspaper reviews on Faulkner's
   life and work, and reviews of work on Faulkner are listed,
   arranged primarily in the order of Faulkner's publications, with an author index. There are separate sections
   for books on Faulkner, studies of individual novels, studies of stories and miscellaneous materials, topical studies, and "other materials," including a list of some 200
   dissertations that concern Faulkner. Annotations are
   generally brief; reviews are coded as favorable or not by
   symbols.

3 BEDELL, GEORGE C. Kierkegaard and Faulkner: Modalities of
   Existence. Baton Rouge, La.: Louisiana State University
   Press.
      An attempt to illuminate Faulkner's fiction using cate-
   gories derived from a reading of Kierkegaard's philosophy;
   no direct influence is claimed. See essay-review
   1973.B112. L. B. Cebik, GaR, XXVI (1973), 286-91, questions the whole approach.

4 EARLY, JAMES. The Making of Go Down, Moses. Dallas, Texas:
   Southern Methodist University Press.
      Go Down, Moses lacks unity. In 1941-42, Faulkner could
   not find a complex form like that of Absalom, Absalom! for
   his McCaslin chronicle. The published stories grew into
   the novel, where they became more serious. Faulkner mixes
   "conventional pieties" and some deliberate obscurity
   about the Ku Klux Klan in Ike's dialogue with Cass. Ike's
   greeting the snake depicts his maturity and acceptance of
   evil. Faulkner is to be identified with Gavin Stevens in
   "Go Down, Moses." An appendix contains a genealogy and
   the spiritual, "Go Down, Moses."

5 LANGFORD, GERALD. Faulkner's Revision of Sanctuary: A Colla-
   tion of the Unrevised Galleys and the Published Book.
   Austin and London: University of Texas Press.
      The introduction discusses aspects of Faulkner's compo-
   sition and revision of Sanctuary. The author concludes
   that Faulkner did not do a very fair job. Langford compares the unrevised galley proofs of the book with a 1966
   Modern Library reprint of an editorially "corrected" 1962
   Random House edition of the book, leaving the MS and TS
   setting copy at the University of Texas and University of
   Virginia out of consideration. The major portion of the
   book is taken up with a reprinting of differences between

(LANGFORD, GERALD)
the unrevised galleys and the edition Langford uses. <u>See</u> review, <u>MissQ</u>, XXVI (Summer 1973), 458-65.

6   PAGE, SALLY R. <u>Faulkner's Women: characterization and mean-</u><u>ing</u>, introduction Cleanth Brooks. Deland, Florida: Everett Edwards.
Critics of Faulkner like Maxwell Geismar, Irving Howe, Leslie Fiedler, Irving Malin and others have been too quick to oversimplify women in the novels and to attribute views expressed by Faulkner's characters to the author himself. Some of his women, like Lena Grove of <u>Light in August</u> and Eula in the Snopes trilogy, characterize man's ability to survive his own folly and sustain valuable human existence. Others, like the three principal women of <u>Soldiers' Pay</u> are individually inadequate to the task, though taken as a whole they represent the qualities of man's ideal. Chiefly through women, Faulkner has been able to depict the central conflict of his work--that between creativity and destructiveness. <u>See</u> essay-review 1973.B78.

7   ULICH, MICHAELA. <u>Perspective und Erzählstruktur in William</u> <u>Faulkners Romanen von The Sound and the Fury bis Intruder</u> <u>in the Dust</u>, (Beihefte zum <u>JA</u>, XXXIV), Heidelberg: Carl Winter Universitätsverlag.
The nature and evolution of Faulkner's narrative practice--manipulation of point of view and the accompanying structural forms which accommodate various strategies of narration--are analyzed and discussed beginning with <u>The Sound and the Fury</u> and including <u>As I Lay Dying</u>, <u>Absalom, Absalom!</u>, "The Bear" (as novella), and <u>Intruder in the Dust</u>. The conclusion mentions Faulkner's later work and challenges the view of many that Faulkner's earliest work contains the optimism and belief of the Nobel Prize speech which, in the author's view, is developed after <u>Absalom, Absalom!</u>

8   ZINDEL, EDITH. <u>William Faulkner in den deutschsprachigen</u> <u>Ländern Europas: Untersuchungen zur Aufnahme seiner Werke</u> <u>nach 1945</u>. Hamburg: H. Lüdke.
The book analyzes translations, reviews, and criticism of Faulkner's stories and novels in post-war Germany and German-speaking countries. Tables, charts, graphs, and extensive bibliographies back up the narrative account of Faulkner's reception.

1972 B   SHORTER WRITINGS

1   ADAMOWSKI, T. H. "Dombey and Son and Sutpen and Son," SNNTS,
     IV (Fall), 378-89.
         The character, themes, and events of Dickens' novel are
     compared with Faulkner's Absalom, Absalom! Among suggest-
     ed similarities are the father's isolation, his plans for
     dynasty, his treatment of his wife; the conclusions of the
     two books differ.

2   AINSA, FERNANDO. "En el santuario de William Faulkner," Cua-
     dernos Hispanoamericanos, XC, #269 (November), 232-43.
         The author recounts a visit to Oxford, Miss.: impres-
     sions, anecdotes, photographs including a picture of a
     letter from Faulkner to John Webber, partly in Spanish,
     written after Faulkner's visit to Venezuela.

3   ANTONIADIS, ROXANDRA V. "Faulkner and Balzac: The Poetic
     Web," CLS, IX (September), 303-25.
         Faulkner and Balzac are similar not only in general ways,
     but also in their remarks about the function of the novel-
     ist. Each conceived himself as a poet expressing the
     whole of human experience. The article takes up simil-
     arities of design, expression, inspiration, meaning, and
     achievement.

4   BARNES, DANIEL R. "Faulkner's Miss Emily and Hawthorne's Old
     Maid," SSF, IX (Fall), 373-77.
         Hawthorne's "The White Old Maid" and Faulkner's "A Rose
     for Emily" are similar in setting, character, and the use
     of hair to bring home the Gothic horror.

5   BARTH, J. ROBERT. "Epilogue," Religious Perspectives in
     Faulkner's Fiction, edited by J. Robert Barth. Notre
     Dame, Indiana: University of Notre Dame Press,
     pp. 217-21.
         The final comment, after a series of essays by various
     hands on Faulkner and religion, is that Faulkner's fiction
     leaves the impression of a religious or theological di-
     versity far richer than the individual approaches in the
     anthology allow. The problem of man's freedom is an im-
     portant one in the books, as is alienation; also impor-
     tant is Faulkner's use of myth.

6   _____. "Faulkner and the Calvinist Tradition," Religious Per-
     spectives in Faulkner's Fiction, edited by J. Robert
     Barth. Notre Dame, Indiana: University of Notre Dame
     Press, pp. 11-31. "Commentary," pp. 32-34.

1972

(BARTH, J. ROBERT)
Essay reprint from 1964.B5; Barth's commentary is that the conception of God which lies behind Faulkner's morality has not been determined.

7 BEAUCHAMP, GORMAN. "The Rite of Initiation in Faulkner's The Bear," ArQ, XXVIII (Winter), 319-25.
Ike's initiation in "The Bear" is discussed in terms of true primitive ritual; he learns the "secrets and beliefs of the tribes" as he is taken from the plantation and made a "wilderness child of wilderness parents." Sam is priest and father. The steps in the process are recounted. Ike's putting aside gun and compass is a circumcision ritual.

8 BENSON, JACKSON J. "Quentin's Responsibility for Caddy's Downfall in Faulkner's The Sound and the Fury," NMW, V (Fall), 63-64.
Caddy is doomed, as Faulkner says in the Compson Appendix, and causes her own downfall with a deliberate self-will. Quentin, as some critics have declared, is not responsible.

9 *BORDEN, CAROLINE. "Characterization in Faulkner's Light in August," L&I, XIII, 41-50.
According to Millgate in American Literary Scholarship 1972, p. 124, the article is a "savage if not very coherent attack on Faulkner as 'bourgeois propagandist.'"

10 BRADFORD, MELVIN E. "Faulkner's Last Words and 'The American Dilemma,'" ModA, XVI (Winter), 77-82.
The last speech Faulkner made--the 1962 acceptance of the American Academy of Arts and Letters Gold Medal--expresses a political philosophy for reevaluating the documents and key words of the American Revolution.

11 BROGUNIER, JOSEPH. "A Housman Source in The Sound and the Fury," MFS, XVIII (Summer), 220-25.
The scene at the branch in The Sound and the Fury seems to borrow from poem LIII of A Shropshire Lad. The identification depends more on tone, setting and event than strict borrowing of Housman's lines.

12 _____. "A Source for the Commissary Entries in Go Down, Moses," TSLL, XIV (Fall), 545-54.
"Diary of a Mississippi Planter," published in the Publications of the Mississippi Historical Society in 1909,

(BROGUNIER, JOSEPH)
> is a possible source for the ledger entries in section
> four of "The Bear."

13   BROOKS, CLEANTH. "Faulkner and History," MissQ, XXV (Spring),
supplement, pp. 3-14.
> Faulkner resisted any abstract theory of history, wheth-
> er millenialist or gnostic, in favor of a view that empha-
> sized man and his active attempts to deal with the com-
> plexities of existence according to the dictates of the
> heart. Sutpen in Absalom, Absalom! dramatizes one form of
> erroneous view of history while the novel as a whole re-
> quires the reader's participating in the imaginative pro-
> cess of "writing" history and points up the subjective and
> limited truth of which history is composed.

14   _____. "Faulkner's Vision of Good and Evil," and "Commentary"
by J. R. Barth, Religious Perspectives in Faulkner's Fiction, edited by J. R. Barth. Notre Dame, Indiana: University of Notre Dame Press, pp. 57-75, 76-78.
> Essay reprint from 1962.B26. The commentary argues that
> the male-female dichotomy which Brooks notes in certain
> Faulkner books may be more widely applied. Few men in
> Faulkner succeed in choosing or creating good, however,
> and few seem to have what Brooks describes as freedom of
> choice: family history, original sin, innate goodness or
> something else seems to predispose them to act as they do.

15   _____. "The Tradition of Romantic Love and The Wild Palms,"
MissQ, XXV (Summer), 265-87.
> Charlotte and Harry fit the classical definition of ro-
> mantic lovers, in love with love and death; their failure
> comes because they move not in a community with estab-
> lished traditions but in a permissive society which
> raises no obstacles to their affair. Discussion from the
> audience which heard Brooks' remarks follows the tran-
> script of the talk.

16   BROUGHTON, PANTHEA. "Requiem for a Nun: No Part in Rationality," SoR, N. S. VIII (October), 749-62.
> The unconventional form of the novel Requiem for a Nun
> belies the critical view that it is a sermon. The narra-
> tive and dramatic sections blend and counterpoint theme
> and action. Faulkner dismisses the "ephemerae of facts"
> to urge a transcendence of the institutionalized morality
> which has come to dominate man's existence.

1972

17   BROWN, CALVIN S. "Faulkner's Idiot Boy: The Source of a Sim-
        ile in Sartoris," AL, XLIV (November), 474-76.
        A simile in Sartoris, "as paper blown drowsily by an
        idiot boy," may have its source in The House of Luck, a
        1916 novel by Vicksburg, Miss., author Harris Dickson.

18   BRUMM, URSULA. "Forms and Functions of History in the Novels
        of William Faulkner," Archiv, CCIX (August), 43-56.
        The words saga, legend, and myth have all been applied
        to Faulkner's fictional image of the South. Brumm inves-
        tigates the history of this application and discusses the
        nature and meaning of Faulkner's transformation of histo-
        rical material or point of view. Though Faulkner wrote a
        brief historical "saga" as an appendix to Cowley's Porta-
        ble Faulkner, in his fiction he actually wrote more about
        the present than the past. He was concerned with history
        as a "burden on the mind" in the present and with how the
        past can be imaginatively reconstructed.

19   CAMPBELL, JEFF H. "Polarity and Paradox: Faulkner's Light in
        August," CEA, XXXIV (January), 26-31.
        The well-known polarity of character and event in Light
        in August gains meaning by virtue of theological paradox
        filtered through Hightower's role. His apotheosis at the
        intersection of the polar events which bring the novel to
        a climax signifies his understanding and reconciliation of
        contraries in human life.

20   CAREY, GLENN O. "Light in August and Religious Fanaticism,"
        StTwC, No. 10 (Fall), 101-13.
        The destructive element in Light in August is religious
        fanaticism, studied in the lives of Joanna Burden, Euphe-
        us Hines, Simon McEachern and Gail Hightower. Faulkner
        preferred an individual religion to the vitiating organ-
        ized religion of the South.

21   _____. "William Faulkner: Man's Fatal Vice," ArQ, XXVIII
        (Winter), 293-300.
        Man's fatal vice is war; Carey takes excerpts from sev-
        eral Faulkner novels to build a case for Faulkner's de-
        piction of war in unfavorable terms, from Soldiers' Pay
        to The Mansion. A Fable is discussed briefly in terms of
        Faulkner's statements about it in interviews and as a
        positive pronouncement about man's unwillingness to accept
        the spiritual death of mankind.

22   CARR, JOHN. Kite-Flying and Other Irrational Acts. Baton
     Rouge, Louisiana: Louisiana State University Press.
        There is frequent but random mention of Faulkner in in-
     terviews with the 12 contemporary Southern writers col-
     lected in this volume. No index.

23   CHATTERTON, WAYNE. "Textbook Uses of Hemingway and Faulkner,"
     CCC, XXIII (October), 292-96.
        Their popularity as modern writers has led to the wide-
     spread use of Hemingway and Faulkner in English handbooks
     and texts for the teaching of writing, not always with the
     best results.

24   CLARK, EULALYN W. "Ironic Effects of Multiple Perspective in
     As I Lay Dying," NMW, V (Spring), 15-28.
        Irony in As I Lay Dying is provided by discrepant per-
     spectives, not only from character to character but within
     the several levels of consciousness of a single character.
     Reliability of narrators is undermined, as in the case of
     Cora Tull, to provide one form of irony. Outsiders give a
     perspective on the Bundrens.

25   CREIGHTON, JOANNE V. "The Dilemma of the Human Heart in The
     Mansion," Renascence, XXV (Autumn), 35-45.
        Flem, the loveless monster of greed, effectively domi-
     nates the first two books of the Snopes trilogy, and his
     spirit seems to rule the town of Jefferson. In The Man-
     sion, however, positions against Flem are consolidated; he
     is opposed and defeated. The toll on his enemies is
     large, but Faulkner demonstrates that the world is not
     fated; it is a human world where man's acts have repercus-
     sions. It is also a hopeful world.

26   _____. "Self-Destructive Evil in Sanctuary," TCL, XVIII
     (October), 259-70.
        Sanctuary offers an allegorical demonstration of Faulk-
     ner's belief that evil is self-destructive, a "central
     theme" of the fiction. Popeye--impotent, loveless, ir-
     reverent toward life--is the emblem of the theme. His de-
     fects are congenital, not caused by "modernism." He is
     the product of a loveless match, the perversion of love.
     Temple's rape is her union with evil.

27   CRUNDEN, ROBERT M. From Self to Society, 1919-1941. New
     York: Prentice-Hall, pp. 167-76.
        Faulkner's fiction during the period between the two
     wars is the triumph of conservatism in art, where it
     flourishes best. The proof is in his appeal for critics

1972

(CRUNDEN, ROBERT M.)
on both left and right and especially for the New Critics
and their cousins the myth critics. His approach to time,
tradition, and religion made him particularly appealing to
conservative critics. Faulkner's viewpoint is enhanced by
his thorough familiarity with American myth and religion,
his independence of mind, and his lack of personal belief.

28   DABNEY, L. M. "'Was': Faulkner's Classic Comedy of the
      Frontier," SoR, N. S. VIII (October), 736-49.
      A tall tale comedy of manners, "Was" satirizes aspects
      of the old South legend and at the same time preserves the
      humorous reality of a human situation.

29   DAVIS, SCOTTIE. "Faulkner's Nancy: Racial Implications in
      'That Evening Sun,'" NMW, V (Spring), 30-32.
      Nancy's failure is personal, a sign of her weakness and
      resignation, not, as many critics argue, a condition
      caused by the racism and indifference of the community.

30   DAVIS, WILLIAM V. "The Sound and the Fury: A Note on Benjy's
      Name," SNNTS, IV (Spring), 60-61.
      The Biblical sources of Benjamin Compson's name prove
      significant: Benoni means "son of my sorrow" and Benja-
      min, which was substituted for it in the Bible, means
      "son of the right hand" or "son of the South." The Comp-
      son Appendix is used in arguing the appropriateness of
      the name lore to Faulkner's intentions.

31   DETWEILER, ROBERT. "The Moment of Death in Modern Fiction,"
      ConL, XIII (Summer), 269-94.
      Deliberately indiscriminate in his use of phenomenolo-
      gical and structuralist approaches and terminology, Det-
      weiler examines the death moment in several modern fic-
      tions, including the death of Houston in Faulkner's The
      Hamlet. Characteristics of the death moment are dis-
      juncture (astonishment, disorientation); interiorization
      (intense self-consciousness); and fusion (the effort to
      join two things, as, for example, a divided self, or to
      unite with the instrument of death). Houston's death
      revelation is that these "two types of southerners" (him-
      self and Mink) will never be free of one another but will
      create a new unity.

32   DEVLIN, ALBERT J. "The Reivers: Readings in Social Psychol-
      ogy," MissQ, XXV (Summer), 327-37.
      The "psychological determinism" in The Reivers is a
      positive force for socialization, democratization and

(DEVLIN, ALBERT J.)
>   initiation into a mature sexuality for Lucius Priest. The
>   family, community, and normal human relationships are the
>   controlling forces.

33   DITSKY, JOHN. "Uprooted Trees: Dynasty and the Land in
>   Faulkner's Novels," TSL, XVII, 151-58.
>   A brief survey of Faulkner's novels comments on the
>   presence or absence of dynastic themes--the use of land
>   for familial purposes. The Snopeses, who have no family
>   use for land but only greed and the instincts of the pack
>   or swarm, represent the ultimate destruction of dynasty.
>   In his later work, Faulkner turns, too, from an interest
>   in dynasty and the land to the unpropertied and the search
>   for the country of one's heart.

34   DOUGLAS, HAROLD J., and ROBERT DANIEL. "Faulkner's Southern
>   Puritanism," and "Commentary" by J. R. Barth, Religious
>   Perspectives in Faulkner's Fiction, edited by J. R. Barth.
>   Notre Dame, Indiana: University of Notre Dame Press,
>   pp. 37-51, 52-54.
>   Essay reprint from 1957.B16; commentary notes the value
>   of the insight that American Calvinism is not as rigid as
>   its theological source and stresses that Faulkner's own
>   position was developmental, toward more hope and redemp-
>   tion. Is Faulkner's tragic vision the result of his im-
>   mersion in Christian love?

35   EDWARDS, DUANE. "Flem Snopes and Thomas Sutpen: Two Versions
>   of Respectability," DR, LI (Winter), 559-70.
>   The Snopes trilogy treats comically what Absalom, Absa-
>   lom! treats with high seriousness, the deliberate and
>   thwarted struggle of very common men for respectability.

36   FAULKNER, JIM. "Auntee Owned Two," SoR, N. S. VIII (Autumn),
>   836-44.
>   Faulkner's nephew recounts an anecdote about why there
>   are two Confederate monuments in Lafayette County.

37   FICKEN, CARL. "The Opening Scene of William Faulkner's Light
>   in August," Proof 2, pp. 175-84.
>   Fragments of MS indicate that Faulkner considered be-
>   ginning Light in August with a character other than Lena
>   Grove. A salesman's dummy of the book, reproduced at the
>   end of the article, gives the opening with Lena in what
>   may be its initial form, preceding even the final MS ver-
>   sion available for inspection at the University of Vir-
>   ginia Library.

1972

38   FUNK, ROBERT W. "Satire and Existentialism in Faulkner's
      'Red Leaves,'" MissQ, XXV (Summer), 339-48.
      "Red Leaves" is both a satire upon the debilitating ef-
      fects of slave-owning on Indian culture and by extension a
      condemnation of slavery in general, as well as a story
      which focuses sharply on the struggle for existence and
      its ramifications for all men.

39   GARZILLI, ENRICO. Circles Without Center: Paths to the Dis-
      covery and Creation of Self in Modern Literature. Cam-
      bridge, Mass.: Harvard University Press, pp. 52-65.
      In a study of the fragmentation of the individual in
      modern fiction, Garzilli studies Absalom, Absalom! and As
      I Lay Dying for their techniques of exploring, through
      several different consciousnesses, the identity of the
      individual. Sutpen is never known to us but exists in the
      gap between the stories of him told by the narrators of
      the novel or by Faulkner himself and the reader's con-
      sciousness. In As I Lay Dying the search for self is seen
      from an omniscient view as each voice gives its version of
      the quest. As long as word and experience coincide, as in
      the on-going fulfillment of the promise to bury Addie in
      Jefferson, Addie is alive.

40   GIORDANO, FRANK R., JR. "Absalom, Absalom! as a Portrait of
      the Artist," From Irving to Steinbeck: Studies of Ameri-
      can Literature in Honor of Harry R. Warfel, edited by
      Motley Deakin and Peter Lisca. Gainesville, Florida:
      University of Florida Press, pp. 97-107.
      Absalom, Absalom! is the story of a young man who is
      telling a story based on stories he has heard, and the
      central issue is Quentin's "shaping imagination." Quen-
      tin's confusion at the novel's end is caused by his ina-
      bility to accept either the art he has created, with its
      dark view of the South, or the South of his everyday life.

41   GRANT, WILLIAM E. "Benjy's Branch: Symbolic Method in Part I
      of The Sound and the Fury," TSLL, XIII (Winter), 705-10.
      Christian symbolism in Benjy's section of The Sound and
      the Fury is more prevalent than noted. The "branch" in
      the pasture, like the river of Quentin's section, is cen-
      tral: the events associated with it are baptismal trav-
      esties. Returning to Edenic purity is not only impossi-
      ble, it is wrong and life-denying, yet Benjy and Quentin
      both want to "purify" their Caddy.

42   GRESSET, MICHEL.   Introduction, "Miss Zilphia Gant," trans-
         lated by Maurice E. Coindreau, NRF, XXXIX (April), 1.
         The story, published in America only in the limited edi-
      tion from the Book Club of Texas in 1932, was difficult
      for Faulkner to place. It suggests several Faulkner wo-
      men, without leading specifically to any, despite Henry
      Nash Smith's announcement that it was part of a projected
      novel.

43   GRIBBIN, DANIEL V.   "Stories and Articles by William Faulkner
         in the Rare Book Room Collection of the University of
         North Carolina Library," Bookmark [an occasional offering
         of the Friends of the University of North Carolina Li-
         brary, Chapel Hill], September, pp. 23-27.
         Works by Faulkner in the Rare Book Room at the Universi-
      ty of North Carolina at Chapel Hill Library are listed.

44   HAND, BARBARA.   "Faulkner's Widow Recounts Memories Of College
         Weekends In Charlottesville," Cavalier Daily (21 April),
         pp. 1, 4.
         In an interview for the University of Virginia student
      newspaper, Faulkner's widow talks about herself (painting,
      dancing, music) and says Faulkner used her for a character
      in his first novel and "hurt my feelings terribly." When
      people ask her why Faulkner hated women, she replies "I
      wasn't aware that he did. I was scared he liked women a
      little too much."

45   HAURY, BETH B.   "The Influence of Robinson Jeffers' 'Tamar' on
         Absalom, Absalom!" MissQ, XXV (Summer), 356-58.
         Images, phrases, and characters in Robinson Jeffers'
      narrative poem "Tamar" (1924) seem to be reflected in
      Faulkner's Absalom, Absalom! Both works use the Tamar
      and Absalom story from the Bible.

46   HELLER, TERRY.   "The Telltale Hair: A Critical Study of Wil-
         liam Faulkner's 'A Rose for Emily,'" ArQ, XXVIII (Winter),
         301-18.
         The language and syntax of "A Rose for Emily" under-
      score the details of conflict between Emily and the town,
      which puts her into categories: aristocratic lady, face-
      less citizen, etc. Emily resists stereotyping and tri-
      umphs over the town's attempts to define, control, and
      dismiss her. The narrator is sympathetic to her.

1972

47 *HESELTINE, H. P. "Some Reflections on the Faulkner-Cowley
        File," Pacific Circle 2 (Proceedings of the Third Biennial
        Conference of the Australian and New Zealand American
        Studies Association). Queensland: University of Queens-
        land Press.

48 HOLLAND, NORMAN N. "Fantasy and Defense in Faulkner's 'A
        Rose for Emily,'" HSL, IV, 1–35.
        A psychological interpretation of the hidden meanings of
        "A Rose for Emily" sees it as dramatizing Emily's regres-
        sion to the anal stage because of her overbearing father.
        The town behaves much as she does, a fact revealing South-
        ern inhospitality to change. Psychological "information"
        from the story is applied, with the addition of biographi-
        cal anecdote, to Faulkner himself and to critics of the
        story.

49 HOLMAN, C. HUGH. "The Novel in the South," The Roots of
        Southern Writing: Essays on the Literature of the Ameri-
        can South. Athens, Georgia: University of Georgia
        Press, pp. 87–95.
        With Wolfe and Warren, Faulkner is one of the three
        great novelists the South has produced. Tracing the de-
        velopments that lead to the work of each, Holman compares
        their major styles and concerns, finding Faulkner's
        greatest strength in his almost cosmic view of history
        and his most remarkable effects in his use of Christian
        and other forms of symbolization. The essay was previous-
        ly printed in A Time of Harvest, edited by Robert E. Spil-
        ler (New York: Hill and Wang, 1962). Other essays in
        the collection on Faulkner are reprinted from 1958.B32,
        1971.B42, 1966.B36.

50 HOLMES, EDWARD M. "Requiem for a Scarlet Nun," Costerus, V,
        35–49.
        Similarities between Requiem for a Nun and Hawthorne's
        Scarlet Letter include subject, character, themes, and
        resolution. The "Custom House" essay resembles Faulkner's
        narrative prologues. The jail is symbolically important
        in both.

51 HOWARD, ALAN B. "Huck Finn in the House of Usher: The Comic
        and Grotesque Worlds of The Hamlet," SoRA, V, 125–46.
        The blending of extravagantly comic and grotesque ele-
        ments, in the tradition of such frontier humor as G. W.
        Harris's Sut Lovingood's Yarns, is what holds The Hamlet
        together structurally. Violence and cruelty are made
        relatively harmless by the oral gift of a raconteur like

(HOWARD, ALAN B.)
Ratliff, but they become increasingly powerful by the end, revealing "some fundamental derangement in the universe." Ratliff regains control when he makes a kind of joke of his own duping.

52 HOWELL, ELMO. "Faulkner and Scott and the Legacy of the Lost Cause," GaR, XXVI (Fall), 314-25.
Summaries of Scott's Jacobite novels, Waverley, Rob Roy, and Redgauntlet, and Faulkner's The Unvanquished are followed by suggestions of differences between them. The author prefers Scott.

53 _____. "William Faulkner's Graveyard," NMW, IV (Winter), 115-18.
Reproducing inscriptions on gravestones in St. Peters Cemetery, Oxford, the author argues for their bearing on Faulkner's life and fiction.

54 HUBBELL, JAY B. Who Are the Major American Authors? Durham, N. C.: Duke University Press, passim.
Faulkner is one of many major American writers whose reputation can be seen to fluctuate up and down. Consulting best-seller lists, anthologies, "best book" lists and similar material, Hubbell demonstrates the relativity of an age's evaluation of an author.

55 HUNT, JOHN W. "The Theological Center of Absalom, Absalom!" and "Commentary" by J. R. Barth, Religious Perspectives in Faulkner's Fiction, edited by J. R. Barth. Notre Dame, Indiana: University of Notre Dame Press, pp. 141-69, 170-71.
Essay reprinted from 1965.A2; the commentary notes that the portrayal by indirection of an ideal of love is common to much modern fiction. Sutpen, an innocent, cannot be condemned individually; only as the type he represents.

56 _____. "The Theological Complexity of Faulkner's Fiction," and "Commentary," by J. R. Barth, Religious Perspectives in Faulkner's Fiction, edited by J. R. Barth. Notre Dame, Indiana: University of Notre Dame Press, pp. 81-87, 88-89.
Essay reprinted from 1965.A2; the commentary notes that Hunt's contribution suggests the addition of "Stoic elements" to a consideration of Faulkner's use of religion and insists that Faulkner's fiction presents the possibility of redemption from his earliest work. Barth believes that Faulkner has become increasingly a believer in redemption.

1972

57   INGE, M. THOMAS. "Faulknerian Light," NMW, V (Spring), 29.
        Correcting Griffith (1971.B33), Inge presents evidence
        that Faulkner interpreted "light" in Light in August as a
        quality of lambence during autumn in Mississippi. Faulk-
        ner's own statement on the subject is the source.

58   KING, ROMA A., JR. "A Fable: Everyman's Warfare," and "Com-
        mentary" by J. R. Barth, Religious Perspectives in Faulk-
        ner's Fiction, edited by J. R. Barth. Notre Dame, Indi-
        ana: University of Notre Dame Press, pp. 203-10, 211-16.
        Essay reprinted from 1956.B28; Barth's comment invites
        expanded interpretation of the General in A Fable as not
        only God and Satan but as Christ, too, and as one with
        the Corporal in several ways--representing the earthly
        element in man as the Corporal represents the divine. The
        novel is a mythological use of the Christ story; the dis-
        ciples are more realistic than King's essay admits.

59   KNIEGER, BERNARD. "Faulkner's 'Mountain Victory,' 'Doctor
        Martino,' and 'There Was a Queen,'" Expl, XXX (February),
        Item 45.
        The author challenges interpretations of "Mountain Vic-
        tory," "Doctor Martino" and "There Was a Queen" in Cro-
        well's Handbook (1964.A8) on the grounds that plots are
        not correctly summarized, and also corrects Irving Howe
        (1952.A1) on Miss Jenny in "There Was a Queen."

60   KOBLER, J. F. "Lena Grove: Faulkner's 'Still Unravish'd
        Bride of Quietness,'" ArQ, XXVIII (Winter), 339-54.
        Lena in Light in August is the equivalent of Keats' urn,
        used symbolically throughout the novel; the symbol is key
        to the novel's unity. Light in August may be at the core
        of Faulkner's optimism about man. Parallels with Keats'
        "Ode" are discussed.

61   LANDOR, MIKHAIL. "Faulkner in the Soviet Union," Soviet
        Criticism of American Literature in the Sixties: An
        Anthology, edited and translated by Carl R. Proffer. Ann
        Arbor, Michigan: Ardis, pp. 173-80.
        Soviet criticism and translation of Faulkner are re-
        viewed, with summaries of important articles and judgments
        upon the quality of translations.

62   LANGFORD, GERALD. Review of Watkins, The Flesh and the Word
        (1971.B100, etc.), SNNTS, IV (Fall), 534-36.
        An attempt to create a new kind of criticism fails, and
        Watkins is "at his worst" in the section on Faulkner.

1972

63   McALEXANDER, HUBERT, JR. "William Faulkner--The Young Poet in Stark Young's The Torches Flare," AL, XLIII (January), 647-49.
     Eugene Oliver in Stark Young's novel, The Torches Flare, bears physical as well as genealogical resemblance to Faulkner, whom Young had known.

64   McDONALD, WALTER R. "Faulkner's 'The Bear': Part IV," CEA, XXXIV (No. 2), 31-32.
     Stories in part four of "The Bear" in Go Down, Moses provide another pattern of theme and structure to link the parts of the novel. The Beauchamp legacy to Ike, the silver cup, is an example; it reflects the folly of ownership and contrasts with Sam Fathers' "gift of understanding."

65   _____. "Sartoris: The Dauntless Hero in Modern American Fiction," Modern American Fiction: Insights and Foreign Lights, edited by W. T. Zyla and W. M. Aycock. (Proceedings of the Comparative Literature Symposium, V). Lubbock, Texas: Texas Tech University Press, pp. 107-20.
     Young Bayard of Sartoris is an example of recklessness in American fiction and is compared with other figures.

66   McHANEY, THOMAS L. "Anderson, Hemingway and Faulkner's The Wild Palms," PMLA, LXXXVII (May), 465-74.
     Faulkner draws on memories of Sherwood Anderson and his novel Dark Laughter, while parodying A Farewell to Arms, in his 1939 novel The Wild Palms. Faulkner agrees with Anderson and not Hemingway about the meaning of existence and the aims of art and reflects his philosophy in the novel.

67   _____. "The Falkner Family and the Origin of Yoknapatawpha County: Some Corrections," MissQ, XXV (Summer), 249-64.
     Most information available in print on the Falkner family, including accounts by the novelist's brothers and townspeople, requires correction. The essay surveys published accounts and corrects them, providing a summary of facts for which evidence exists. Faulkner's fictional county existed as a combination of imagination and a varied experience of people and places in several Mississippi counties.

1972

68 McWILLIAMS, DEAN. "William Faulkner and Michel Butor's Novel of Awareness," KRQ, XIX (No. 3), 387–402.
Butor's essay, "Les relations de parenté dans 'l'Ours' de William Faulkner" (1960.B15) is used to demonstrate the nature of the French writer's interest in Faulkner's work in Butor's L'Emploi du temps.

69 MAGNY, CLAUDE-EDMONDE. "Faulkner, or Theological Inversion," The Age of the American Novel: The Film Aesthetic of Fiction Between the Two World Wars, translated by Eleanor Hochman. New York: Frederick Ungar, pp. 178–223.
Translated from 1948.B20.

70 MANGLAVITI, LEO M. J. "Faulkner's 'That Evening Sun' and Mencken's 'Best Editorial Judgment,'" AL, XLIII (January), 649–54.
Opening of the Mencken papers in 1971 makes available Mencken's copy of Faulkner's "That Evening Sun" and his editorial correspondence about the story. Mencken suggested changes, for the sake of decorum, and made cuts in the story. Faulkner obliged him, though he restored the cuts when he published the story in his collection, These 13.

71 MAY, JOHN R. "Words and Deeds: Apocalyptic Judgment in Faulkner, West, and O'Connor," Toward a New Earth: Apocalypse in the Modern Novel. Notre Dame, Indiana: University of Notre Dame Press, pp. 92–144.
As I Lay Dying is one example of the "apocalyptic" imagination in American fiction. The events around Addie's death and burial are "types of the primitive religious symbolism of chaos." Faulkner "emphasizes the moment of judgment" and shows the creation of new life. Darl gains by being freed from his family.

72 MERIWETHER, JAMES B. "Faulkner's 'Mississippi,'" MissQ, XXV (Spring), supplement, pp. 15–23.
The essay, "Mississippi," which Faulkner published in Holiday in 1954 combines fiction, autobiography and history in a challenging form. It has received too little attention. Racial injustice is the main theme, as Faulkner regards Southern history; also important are Snopesism, Nature, and man's attitude toward change. Faulkner's final sentence, which affirms his love for "all of it" and his hate for "some of it," does not express a mingled love-hate relationship but a mature love.

73   _____. "A Proposal for a CEAA Edition of William Faulkner,"
      Editing Twentieth Century Texts, edited by Francess G.
      Halpenny. Toronto: University of Toronto Press,
      pp. 12-27.
          The need for good texts of Faulkner's work is self-
      evident: his work is badly edited and he is an important
      writer given close scholarly attention. The materials for
      textual work are available. Meriwether describes the
      ideal definitive text and the alternative, a practicable
      edition with definitive apparatuses printed separately.

74   _____, ed. "An Introduction for The Sound and the Fury," by
      William Faulkner, SoR, N. S. VIII (Autumn), 705-10.
          Meriwether introduces and reprints an introduction for
      The Sound and the Fury which Faulkner prepared for a pro-
      posed 1933 edition of the novel. Faulkner says that in
      writing the novel he "learned to read and quit reading,"
      that it was a novel written "without any accompanying
      feeling of drive or effort." The introduction gives de-
      tails of the writing and history of the piece.

75   MILLGATE, MICHAEL. "Faulkner," American Literary Scholarship
      An Annual 1970, edited by J. A. Robbins. Durham, N. C.:
      Duke University Press, pp. 116-31.
          The annual survey of critical work on Faulkner.

76   _____. "Faulkner and Lanier: A Note on the Name Jason,"
      MissQ, XXV (Summer), 349-50.
          Passages from Sidney Lanier's poem, "Corn," could have
      been suggestive in Faulkner's characterization of Jason
      Compson in The Sound and the Fury as a small-town cotton
      speculator.

77   _____. "'The Firmament of Man's History': Faulkner's Treat-
      ment of the Past," MissQ, XXV (Spring), Supplement,
      25-35.
          Ike McCaslin in Go Down, Moses misreads history when he
      fails to recognize the irrevocable 'pastness' of the acts
      of his grandfather. Like the narrators of Absalom, Absa-
      lom!, he makes history "a projection of his own person-
      ality." Sartoris, Absalom, Absalom!, and Requiem for a
      Nun are a kind of trilogy on the meaning of the past: in
      the first, it is alive; in the second, its existence is
      questioned; in the third, it is affirmed to be dead.
      Faulkner saw himself as the historian and genealogist of
      Yoknapatawpha County, a mythical place, and believed his
      conception was a valid conception of the world around him.

1972

78   MONAGHAN, DAVID M. "Faulkner's Absalom, Absalom!" Expl, XXXI
(December), Item 28.
    Sutpen's life is analagous to the history of several
ancient heroes, but ironically so. The scene where his
sister is forced off the road by a carriage driven by a
slave parallels Oedipus' encounter with King Laius and
his slaves. "Unlike Oedipus...who kills his tormentor,"
Sutpen achieves only vicarious revenge by hurling clods
of dirt.

79   _____. "Faulkner's Relationship to Gavin Stevens in Intruder
in the Dust," DR, LII (Autumn), 449-57.
    In the debate about whether Gavin Stevens is Faulkner's
official mouthpiece, defenders of Faulkner as artist and
humanist have taken too little account of real similarities between Faulkner and his character. Stevens' words
are very like Faulkner's public statements in the 1950's.
Fictionally, Stevens is demonstrably an ironic portrait.
The subtle differences between Faulkner and Stevens emphasize Faulkner's belief that one must react to individual
circumstances, not in the abstract.

80   _____. "The Single Narrator of As I Lay Dying," MFS, XVIII
(Summer), 213-20.
    Arguing against Franklin (1967.B29), the author believes
that "inconsistencies" in the chronology and narrative
tenses of As I Lay Dying are proof of a single outside
narrator for the whole book, Addie herself. The first
scenes are limited to what she sees and hears from her
deathbed, but at the moment of death her consciousness is
released and her imagination takes over to reveal the inevitable results of the journey to Jefferson, which is
Addie's vengeance on a family--Jewel excepted--that did
not receive or give love.

81   MORELL, GILIANE. "The Last Scene of Sanctuary," MissQ, XXV
(Summer), 351-55.
    Setting the last scene of Sanctuary in the Luxembourg
Gardens in Paris, Faulkner may have known the history of
the palace there, which served as a prison during the
French Revolution and as the French Senate afterwards, a
contrasting set of symbols like those Faulkner would use
later in the jail-courthouse association in Requiem for a
Nun.

82 MUEHL, LOIS. "Form as Seen in Two Early Works by Faulkner,"
    LC, XXXVIII (Spring), 147-57.
      Sartoris and Light in August both seem elaborately and
    deliberately structured in a "crisscross form." Faulkner
    uses common objects and experiences, relations between
    people and things, forebodings, repetition of language or
    event, and memories of the past as recurring elements to
    bind his larger fiction together, like an "armature around
    which to sculpture the work of his fiction."

83 MUHLENFELD, ELISABETH S. "Shadows with Substance and Ghosts
    Exhumed: The Women in Absalom, Absalom!" MissQ, XXV
    (Summer), 289-304.
      Critics like Leslie Fiedler (See, e.g., 1960.B26) could
    not be more wrong about Faulkner's women characters as
    amoral, vicious, domineering, and calculating, as a close
    look at the women in Absalom, Absalom! shows. Far from a
    ghost, Rosa is an active, romantic, frustrated human being
    whom environment and history have shaped into a stunted
    figure. Judith, like Rosa, struggled with life, and un-
    like her is not obsessed with the past. Others in the
    novel express the attempt to communicate with an uncompre-
    hending, hostile world.

84 OLSON, TED. "Faulkner and the Colossus of Maroussi," SAQ,
    LXXI (Spring), 205-12.
      An eyewitness, who worked for the United States Informa-
    tion Agency, gives an account of Faulkner in Greece, with
    anecdotal material, including a dinner where Faulkner fab-
    ricated stories about his World War I experience, with a
    straight face, for the benefit of George Katsimbalis, the
    ".colossus" of the title.

85 PALIEVSKY, PYOTR V. "Faulkner's Road to Realism," Soviet
    Criticism of American Literature in the Sixties: An
    Anthology, edited and translated by Carl R. Proffer. Ann
    Arbor: Ardis, pp. 150-68.
      Faulkner "rediscovered" Realism. Like Columbus sailing
    for a known India and discovering a New World, he made of
    his discovery something new. His stories of Yoknapatawpha
    County are part of an interrelated continuum which is
    fluid and ever-changing as new characters are introduced
    and find their way. Like the Russian Sholokov, he dis-
    covered the value of mother earth and the potential of old
    human truths. Essay originally in Znamya, III (1965).

1972

86   PERLIS, ALAN D.   "As I Lay Dying as a Study of Time," SDR, X,
      103-10.
          The different time-senses of the characters of As I Lay
      Dying help characterize them. Darl, with "retrospective
      vision," and Addie, with her negative view, are in con-
      trast to the forward-looking positive characters like Cash
      and Anse. Cash represents a view that seeks human under-
      standing.

87   PERLUCK, HERBERT A.   "'The Bear': An Unromantic Reading," and
      "Commentary" by J. R. Barth, Religious Perspectives in
      Faulkner's Fiction, edited by J. R. Barth. Notre Dame,
      Indiana: University of Notre Dame Press, pp. 173-98,
      199-201.
          Essay reprinted from 1960.B53. Commentary notes that
      Perluck's view of Ike's canonization as ironic is a valid
      reading, but so is the "Romantic" view of Ike.

88   PFEIFFER, A. H.   "Eye of the Storm: The Observer's Image of
      the Man Who Was Faulkner," SoR, N. S. VIII (October),
      763-73.
          It is difficult to match Faulkner the man of Oxford with
      Faulkner the writer. Using previous interviews and im-
      pressions of Faulkner, the author sets down a summary view
      of Faulkner of Oxford--his appearance, voice, and other
      characteristics.

89   PITAVY, FRANÇOIS L.   "A Forgotten Faulkner Story: 'Miss
      Zilphia Gant,'" SSF, IX (Spring), 131-42.
          A study of TSS and MS of "Miss Zilphia Gant" at the Uni-
      versity of Virginia suggests a new order of composition
      for the story. Relations between the story and other
      Faulkner work of the 1920's and 1930's are discussed,
      especially "A Rose for Emily," "Dry September," and Light
      in August. It is a thin, but revealing precursor of Light
      in August.

90   _____. [Note on Idyll in the Desert], NRF, XL (December),
      69-70.
          The afterword to Pitavy's translation, Idylle au désert,
      discusses the writing and publication of Idyll in the
      Desert. The oral tale framework casts doubt on the nar-
      rator, but reveals that he has been touched by the tragedy
      more than he wishes to show. The story is suggestive of
      the portrait of Charlotte Rittenmeyer in The Wild Palms.

91   PITTS, STELLA. "The Quarter in the Twenties," <u>Dixie</u>
     (26 November), pp. 42-46.
         Life in the New Orleans French Quarter of the mid-1920's
     is partially recreated by interviews with surviving mem-
     bers of the bohemian group which gathered there, many of
     them people caricatured in <u>Sherwood Anderson & Other Fa-</u>
     <u>mous Creoles</u>. Harold Levy claims he and Faulkner collab-
     orated on "L'Après-midi d'un Faune" and that Faulkner
     dedicated it to him.

92   POLK, NOEL E. "Faulkner's 'The Jail' and the Meaning of
     Cecilia Farmer," <u>MissQ</u>, XXV (Summer), 305-25.
         Cecilia, the girl whose memory is preserved in a pane
     of glass at the Jefferson jail where she scratched her
     name, is the "lowest common denominator" of human life,
     but her act of self-assertion signifies that man, the in-
     dividual, can and will find a means to endure. The con-
     text of the jail, the meaning of which is explored fully
     throughout <u>Requiem for a Nun</u>, emphasizes the relationship
     between past and present, between man's immutable charac-
     teristics and his view of himself at any given time.

93   _____. "The Manuscript of <u>Absalom, Absalom!</u>" <u>MissQ</u>, XXV
     (Summer), 359-67.
         Langford's study of differences between the MS of <u>Absa-</u>
     <u>lom, Absalom!</u> and the published book (1971.A4) is almost
     useless because of inaccuracies and its disregard of the
     revised and heavily edited TS setting copy available at
     the University of Virginia.

94 *PRASAD, THAKUR GURU. "Nihilism in <u>The Sound and the Fury</u>,"
     <u>PURBA</u>, III (No. 1), 35-43.
         <u>1972 MLA International Bibliography</u>, Volume I, Item
     9679.

95   PROFFER, CARL R., editor and translator. "Introduction:
     American Literature in the Soviet Union," <u>Soviet Criti-</u>
     <u>cism of American Literature in the Sixties: An Anthology</u>.
     Ann Arbor, Michigan: Ardis, pp. xiii-xxxii.
         The introduction surveys and lists major Soviet trans-
     lations, including Faulkner, from 1960 to 1972. The
     anthology also contains 1972.B61 and 1972.B85.

96   RAMSEY, ROGER. "Faulkner's <u>The Sound and the Fury</u>," <u>Expl</u>,
     XXX (April), Item 70.
         Damuddy's death is not the Compson children's first
     knowledge of death. The mare Nancy who broke a leg and
     had to be destroyed is the first experience; it is also

1972

(RAMSEY, ROGER)
likely that the rotting corpse, the buzzards, and the
flies "buzzing" in the ground around the carcass are the
source for Benjy's subsequent ability to "smell" death,
a first and traumatic memory vivid enough to provide him
always with certain sense referents.

97 RICHARDS, LEWIS A. "Sex Under The Wild Palms and a Moral
Question," ArQ, XXVIII (Winter), 326-32.
Observing that the world of Faulkner's novels is devoid
of love, while possessed by carnality, the author reads
The Wild Palms as an approbation of illicit love, then
suggests that the world of carnality which Faulkner depicts may simply be a true picture of "our world."

98 ROBINSON, CLAYTON. "Memphis in Fiction: Rural Values in an
Urban Setting," Myths and Realities: Conflicting Values
in America, edited by Berkley Kalin and Clayton Robinson.
Memphis, Tennessee: Memphis State University, pp. 29-38.
Memphis references in Faulkner's work are briefly
listed.

99 RUBIN, LOUIS D., JR. "The Writer in the Twentieth Century
South," The Writer in the South. Athens, Ga.: University
of Georgia Press, pp. 82-116.
The story of Sutpen in Absalom, Absalom! is very close
in nature to the history of the Deep South, and Quentin
Compson speaks for the Southern writer. Faulkner reen-
acted the history of his region in his soul.

100 RULE, PHILIP C. "The Old Testament Vision in As I Lay Dying,"
and "Commentary" by J. R. Barth, Religious Perspectives in
Faulkner's Fiction, edited by J. R. Barth. Notre Dame,
Indiana: University of Notre Dame Press, pp. 107-16,
117-18.
An original essay, Rule's piece argues that the values
and images of As I Lay Dying are Old Testament in nature,
concerned with sin, man's struggle to understand his existence in an enigmatic world, and the possibility of success through faith and endurance. The Book of Job is a
particularly apt analogue. Cash is perhaps the normative
character. Barth's commentary notes that the Calvinistic
protestantism of Faulkner's country encourages the Old
Testament view.

101   SKAGGS, MERRILL M. The Folk of Southern Fiction. Athens,
          Georgia: University of Georgia Press, pp. 221-34.
          The stock characters and situations of earlier Southern
       fiction dealing with the plain folk--from whatever sub-
       region--are in Faulkner's fiction. Ratliff in the Snopes
       trilogy is a splendid example of Faulkner's adaptation
       from Southern local color of the nineteenth century: the
       plain folk hero.

102   SKERRY, PHILIP J. "The Adventures of Huckleberry Finn and
          Intruder in the Dust: Two Conflicting Myths of the Ameri-
          can Experience," BSUF, XIII (Winter), 4-13.
          Similar in plot, structure, and their use of the theme
       of initiation, Huckleberry Finn and Intruder in the Dust
       differ strikingly in the way they interpret the American
       myth of innocence. Skerry contrasts the novels on the
       basic narrative level, and on sociological, psychological,
       and symbolic planes, to show how Huck retreats from soci-
       ety while Chick Mallison is reintegrated into it as a re-
       sult of his experience.

103   SPEARS, JAMES E. "William Faulkner, Folklorist: A Note,"
          TFSB, XXXVIII (December), 95-96.
          Examples of folklore in Sartoris include the wart cure,
       Negro superstitions, and other elements.

104   SPIEGEL, ALAN. "A Theory of the Grotesque in Southern Fic-
          tion," GaR, XXVI (Summer), 426-37.
          The author mentions several Faulkner characters in argu-
       ing that the "grotesque" refers not to mood or mode of ex-
       pression but to misshapen characters who startle the read-
       er and illuminate the lives they enter. Often a scapegoat
       figure, or an alienated being, like Benjy, Jim Bond, or
       Quentin Compson, the grotesque character in Southern fic-
       tion is differentiated by greater reader sympathy and the
       frequent use of the inside narrator, as in the oral
       tradition.

105   SWINK, HELEN. "William Faulkner: The Novelist as Oral Nar-
          rator," GaR, XXVI (Summer), 183-209.
          Faulkner's style creates "oral" effects in general ways:
       long uninterrupted sentences, a special diction, point-
       of-view characters, openings that create "voice" in a sto-
       ry, and digression. Faulkner's attempts to follow oral
       tradition and achieve these effects shaped his character-
       istic style.

1972

106 *TANAKA, HISAO. "The Significance of the Past for Gail High-
       tower: One Aspect of Light in August," SALit, VIII,
       24–38.
          1972 MLA International Bibliography, Volume I, Item
       9690.

107   TAYLOR, WALTER. "Faulkner's Curse," ArQ, XXVIII (Winter),
       333–38.
          Faulkner's characters live in a world where their acts
       are determined by outside forces but where they still suf-
       fer the pains of guilt for those acts. The determinant is
       often given in Faulkner's terms as the "curse" and vari-
       ously interpreted as slavery or ownership of the land.
       Taylor offers "false pride" as a more appropriate single
       heading for the curse, illustrating with Absalom, Absalom!
       and Go Down, Moses that this curse also visits the heirs
       of the original sinner and is centered on white treatment
       of Negroes. Ike is a hero.

108   _____. "Faulkner's Pantaloon: The Negro Anomaly at the Heart
       of Go Down, Moses," AL, XLIV (November), 430–44.
          Ike McCaslin is one of Faulkner's "most attractive he-
       roes." "Pantaloon in Black," in the McCaslin novel, Go
       Down, Moses, is anomalous because it is a full study of a
       mature successful man of African origin. It prepares us
       to accept Ike's romantic and radical paean to the Negro
       in "The Bear," but since Ike's understanding is based on
       a false impression, the novel is "in an important sense a
       failure." Faulkner's ambivalence about blacks is the
       cause.

109 *WAD, SØREN. "I. William Faulkner; II. Absalom, Absalom!"
       Six American Novels: From New Deal to New Frontier: A
       Workbook. Aarhus: Akademisk Boghandel, pp. 85–118.
          1972 MLA International Bibliography, Volume I, Item
       9694.

110   WAGGONER, HYATT H. "Light in August: Outrage and Compas-
       sion," and "Commentary," by J. R. Barth, Religious Per-
       spectives in Faulkner's Fiction, edited by J. R. Barth.
       Notre Dame, Indiana: University of Notre Dame Press,
       pp. 121–37, 138–39.
          Essay reprint from 1972.A1; commentary remarks on the
       aptness of Waggoner's interpretation of Lena and Byron in
       Light in August as creating a true religious center for
       the novel around which the abuses of other characters are
       seen.

111 WIGLEY, JOSEPH A. "Imagery and the Interpreter," Studies in
    Interpretation, edited by Esther M. Doyle and Virginia H.
    Floyd. Amsterdam: Rodopi N. V., pp. 171-90.
    Absalom, Absalom! is used to demonstrate the validity
    and value of interpretation by tracing the imagery of a
    work. The author cast through the novel seeking differ-
    ent classes of images under several headings and found
    five major schemes. "Man and Beast," of which there are
    373 images, is used to illustrate the process. The animal
    imagery intensifies "the problem of the Negro," and em-
    bodies "Sutpen's sin."

112 WILDER, AMOS N. "Vestigial Moralities in The Sound and the
    Fury," and "Commentary," by J. R. Barth, Religious Per-
    spectives in Faulkner's Fiction, edited by J. R. Barth.
    Notre Dame, Indiana: University of Notre Dame Press,
    pp. 91-102, 103-05.
    Essay reprint from 1958.B65; the commentary notes that
    without community, in Cleanth Brooks' view, man falls back
    on his own limited values, with the risk of fanaticism and
    distortion, "radical alienation" such as Wilder emphasizes
    in his essay. Though Wilder corrects Sartre's view of
    time in Faulkner (See 1939.B28), he does not show clearly
    how the Christian view of time functions in Dilsey's sec-
    tion. Quentin's problem is that he sees the Christian
    world of guilt and retribution without any sense of grace.

113 WILSON, G. R., JR. "The Chronology of Faulkner's 'A Rose for
    Emily' Again," NMW, V (Fall), 56, 44, 58-62.
    The chronology of "A Rose for Emily" must be revised;
    it is actually set in 1936, six years later than the year
    of the story's appearance, a projection which may suggest
    the timelessness of Miss Emily. A chronology is appended.

114 *ZELLEFROW, KEN. "Faulkner's Flying Tales--a View of the
    Past," Descant, XVI (Summer), 42-48.
    According to Abstracts of English Studies, XVII (Novem-
    ber 1973), Item 868, the article argues that Faulkner's
    stories present a fascinating picture of doomed figures
    with courage and a sense of the value of life, a type of
    the alienated man in modern literature.

115 ZIOLKOWSKI, THEODORE. Fictional Transfigurations of Jesus.
    Princeton, N. J.: Princeton University Press,
    pp. 270-98 passim.
    A travesty of the story of Christ's life, A Fable uses
    the passion story as myth, even when the events used are
    not psychologically motivated in the novel, and strains

1972

(ZIOLKOWSKI, THEODORE)
our credulity as well as our aesthetic sense. All the
works considered, from The True History of Joshua Davidson in 1872 to John Barth's Giles Goat-Boy, 1966, use
formal signals to reveal the Gospel analogy; they represent a sub-genre, with a discernible history and development.

116   BLAIR, WALTER. "'A Man's Voice, Speaking': A Continuum in
American Humor," Vein of Humor, edited by Harry Levin.
Cambridge, Mass.: Harvard University Press, pp. 185-204.
Faulkner's work is mentioned briefly ("Spotted Horses"
and Light in August) in a paean of praise to the oral tale
in American humorous writing.

1973 A   BOOKS

1   BLEIKASTEN, ANDRÉ. Faulkner's As I Lay Dying, translated by
Roger Little and the author. Bloomington, Indiana: Indi-
ana University Press.
Most of this study appeared in French in 1970.A7. As I
Lay Dying is studied in eight sections: genesis and
sources; language; style; technique; character; setting;
themes; and reception. Two illustrations from the MS and
TS of the novel and an annotated bibliography of criticism.

2   DABNEY, LEWIS M. The Indians of Yoknapatawpha. Baton Rouge,
Louisiana: Louisiana State University Press.
Faulkner's Indian stories are discussed in a blend of
historical observation, ethical generalization, and liter-
ary criticism. "Lo!," "A Courtship," "A Justice," "Red
Leaves," and material from Go Down, Moses are considered.

3   HARZIC, JEAN. Faulkner. Paris: Bordas.
A brief general account of Faulkner and his works, in
French, with critical remarks on style, themes, and relationships to the other arts is divided into four categories: "Les jours," "Les oeuvres," "L'art," and "La
technique."

4   HUNTER, EDWIN R. William Faulkner: Narrative Practice and
Prose Style. Washington, D. C. and Lothian, Maryland:
Windhover Press.
Beginning with an account of Faulkner's experimentation,
the author discusses "narrative practice" in the novels,
including different strategies, revisions from stories to
novels, sentence structure, length, and structural rela-

(HUNTER, EDWIN R.)
    tionships. Appendix has further comments on aspects of
    Faulkner's style, the style of Benjy's recall, and the
    narrative variety of Quentin's monologue.

5   LEARY, LEWIS. William Faulkner of Yoknapatawpha County. New
        York: Thomas Y. Crowell.
        The author presents a general treatment of Faulkner's
    life and work for the younger reader. For Faulkner, time
    and his fiction contain four great kinds of past: the
    mythical past of folk memory, an Edenic period when men
    and earth were in harmony; the historical past, full of
    great events like the Civil War, the building of towns and
    railroads; the legendary past transmitted by family tradi-
    tion; and the individual's own remembered past. In much
    of his fiction his concern was the past and "the pettiness
    of contemporary life." The Unvanquished and Go Down,
    Moses are discussed as story collections rather than as
    novels.

6   PITAVY, FRANÇOIS. Faulkner's Light in August, translated by
        Gillian E. Cook and the author. Bloomington, Indiana:
        Indiana University Press.
        Most of this study appeared in French in 1970.A7. A
    seven-part study of Light in August, the book examines
    background and composition, structure and technique, char-
    acter, landscape, themes, styles, and critical reception.
    There is a selected critical bibliography.

7   REED, JOSEPH W., JR. Faulkner's Narrative. New Haven, Conn.:
        Yale University Press.
        Faulkner's narrative strategies, at their best in a
    complexly-wrought novel like Light in August or in Absa-
    lom, Absalom!, which is a grand examination of the whole
    fictive process, can also "create a deliberate mare's nest
    of prose as readily as it can of plot" and cover up the
    weaknesses of over-blown rhetoric which mars such books as
    Intruder in the Dust, Requiem for a Nun, and A Fable.
    Faulkner's indirections are thus sometimes red herrings
    to keep us from getting too close to his unsophisticated
    arguments. Strategy in the manipulation of voice, render-
    ing, or time-structure also turn many of his characters,
    as in the short stories, from stereotypes into "one and
    only" figures. Faulkner is chiefly a narrator who
    searches for an easy relationship between manipulation and
    naturalness.

1973

8   SCHMITTER, DEAN MORGAN, ed. <u>William Faulkner: a collec-</u>
       <u>tion of criticism</u>. New York: McGraw-Hill Book Co.
          Schmitter's introduction briefly surveys Faulkner's ca-
       reer and the difficulties of his style and structures.
       The anthology contains excerpts from books and articles
       and a bibliogaphy of Faulkner's books and of books on him.

9   WAGNER, LINDA WELSHIMER, editor. <u>William Faulkner: Four</u>
       <u>Decades of Criticism</u>. East Lansing, Michigan: Michigan
       State University Press.
          Essays and excerpts from books, some of which were also
       published in <u>Two Decades</u> (1951.A2) and <u>Three Decades</u>
       (1960.A1), on Faulkner and his work: 1939.B3, 1939.B26,
       1941.B4, 1949.B14, 1949.B38, 1954.B13, 1954.B75, 1955.B35,
       1956.B48, 1957.B22, 1957.B23, 1957.B62, 1958.B64, 1962.B1,
       1962.B78, 1962.B120, 1963.B8, 1963.B14, 1964.B76, 1965.B62,
       1967.B74, 1970.B5, 1970.B31, 1971.B101.

<u>1973 B   SHORTER WRITINGS</u>

1   ANON. "Book Note," <u>AN&Q</u>, XI (May), 144.
          Mrs. Jill Faulkner Summers has given permission for the
       Faulkner Concordance Project, jointly sponsored and con-
       ducted at the University of South Carolina and West Point,
       to use unpublished MSS material.

2   ADAMOWSKI, T. H. "Bayard Sartoris: Mourning and Melan-
       cholia," <u>L&P</u>, XXIII (No. 4), 149-58.
          Young Bayard's actions in <u>Sartoris</u>, molded by the en-
       telechy of violence that characterizes Sartoris men, seem
       those of the classical Freudian melacholiac. A victim of
       "narcissistic ambivalence," Bayard loves and hates the
       ideal of Sartoris which his twin represents.

3   _____. "Isaac McCaslin and the Wilderness of the Imagina-
       tion," <u>CentR</u>, XVII (Winter), 92-112.
          An examination of Ike McCaslin's wilderness experience
       in <u>Go Down, Moses</u> indicates that it is not a world with
       values which can be applied to "life in the 'settle-
       ments.'" Even in the woods Ike is an isolato, estranged
       from the other hunters. He accepts an "imaginary" wil-
       derness, product of Sam Fathers' memory and desire and
       Ike's own will to believe. His rituals are private ones;
       he has no part of any real world.

4   ADAMS, PERCY G. "Faulkner, French Literature, and 'Eternal
        Verities,'" William Faulkner: Prevailing Verities and
        World Literature, edited by W. T. Zyla and Wendell M.
        Aycock. Lubbock, Texas: Interdepartmental Committee on
        Comparative Literature, Texas Tech University Press,
        pp. 7-24.
           French literature, especially Balzac, Flaubert, and
        Zola, had a demonstrable influence on Faulkner's fiction.
        Balzac's story Gobseck is very suggestive in theme, char-
        acter, and plot for the Snopes trilogy, especially The
        Mansion. Faulkner in turn has greatly influenced French
        literature in his time. There are interesting differences
        between French and American views of Faulkner.

5   ADAMS, ROBERT M. Proteus: His Lies, His Truth. New York:
        Norton, pp. 23-28.
           Maurice E. Coindreau's translation of Faulkner's The
        Sound and the Fury is a characteristic but not horrible
        example of the difficulties of putting a novel into
        another language. Coindreau misses an occasional idiom,
        as with Mason and Dixon, which he converts to Southern
        cities. Faulkner's syntax is often too difficult for
        Coindreau, and he does not do a good job with dialect; his
        translation is a "low-voltage" version of Faulkner.

6   AYTÜR, NECLA. "Faulkner in Turkish," William Faulkner: Pre-
        vailing Verities and World Literature, edited by W. T.
        Zyla and Wendell M. Aycock. Lubbock, Texas: Interde-
        partmental Committee on Comparative Literature, Texas Tech
        University Press, pp. 25-39.
           Faulkner's style and the purification of the Turkish
        language compound the difficulty of translating Faulkner
        into Turkish. The essay notes the failures and successes
        of various translators and includes, as an appendix, a
        list of translations. Faulkner is read chiefly by modern
        Turkish intellectuals and is appreciated now primarily for
        his social commentary.

7   BARBER, MARION. "The Two Emilys: A Ransom Suggestion to
        Faulkner?" NMW, V (Winter), 103-05.
           John Crowe Ranson's poem, "Emily Hardcastle, Spinster,"
        is a possible source for Faulkner's "A Rose for Emily."
        The same suggestion is in 1973.B63.

8   BEIDLER, PETER G. "A Darwinian Source for Faulkner's Indians
        in 'Red Leaves,'" SSF, X (Fall), 421-23.
           Situation, title, some characterization, and references
        to cannibalism in "Red Leaves" may have come from Darwin's
        journal of the voyage of the Beagle.

9   BELL, HANEY H., JR. "The Relative Maturity of Lucius Priest and Ike McCaslin," Aegis, II, 15-21.
       Because it represents a diminution of Faulkner's powers and lacks the symbolic character of his earlier work, The Reivers will never receive much serious attention. It is a novel of initiation, but chiefly an "escapade," and the level of maturity Lucius Priest reaches may be constructively contrasted to the more serious progress of Ike McCaslin in "The Bear." Ike is a mature hero.

10   _____. "Sam Fathers and Ike McCaslin and the World in Which Ike Matures," Costerus, VII, 1-12.
       An account of Ike McCaslin's initiation and maturation under the tutelage of Sam Fathers concludes that Ike's greeting to the serpent signifies his recognition that both civilization and the wilderness contain good and evil. He assumes responsibility for all sins and relinquishes his inheritance to make restitution.

11   BLOTNER, JOSEPH. "William Faulkner's Essay on the Composition of Sartoris," YULG, XLVII (January), 121-24.
       A brief account of the writing and publication of Sartoris introduces a previously unpublished, unfinished introduction to the novel which Faulkner apparently worked on in the early 1930's.

12   BORING, PHYLLIS Z. "Usmail: The Puerto Rican Joe Christmas," CLAJ, XVI (March), 324-33.
       Mention of Faulkner's general influence on Spanish-language authors precedes a discussion of his specific influence upon the Puerto Rican short story writer and novelist Pedro Juan Soto, including parallels between Soto's Usmail (1959) and Light in August.

13   BRADFORD, MELVIN E. "An Aesthetic Parable: Faulkner's 'Artist at Home,'" GaR, XXVII (Summer), 175-81.
       The story, "Artist at Home," about a young poet's brief entry into the lives of a middle aged writer and his wife, whom the young poet loves, is a parable showing that art and home can coexist, though only by virtue of struggle. The story is too intellectual, too artistic.

14   BROOKS, CLEANTH. "The British Reception of Faulkner's Work," William Faulkner: Prevailing Verities and World Literature, edited by W. T. Zyla and Wendell M. Aycock. Lubbock, Texas: Interdepartmental Committee on Comparative Literature, Texas Tech University Press, pp. 41-55.

(BROOKS, CLEANTH)
British critics have ignored, misunderstood, or mis-
judged Faulkner's fiction, partly because they have derived from Faulkner's least sympathetic or perceptive
American critics a point of view that prohibits their seeing him clearly. Erroneous British preconceptions of the
South seriously affect criticism of Faulkner, and general
amateurism contributes its share of problems. Examples
are cited, many centering on Light in August.

15   _____. "A Note on Faulkner's Early Attempts at the Short Story," SSF, X (Fall), 381-88.
Faulkner's New Orleans characters are like Sherwood
Anderson's grotesques, but the stories do not show the effect of Anderson's style; nor are they up to the mark of
Faulkner's achievement in his first novel, Soldiers' Pay.
Several parallels between the work of Irving S. Cobb and
Faulkner's later, better method in the stories published
in the 1930's are suggested, especially in the use of narrative point of view which reflects an uninvolved
community.

16   _____. "On Absalom, Absalom!" Mosaic, VII (Fall), 159-83.
A three-part reflection on Absalom, Absalom! considers
the evidence for Bon as Sutpen's son, for who knows this
and when they learn; whether Sutpen is a representative
Southern gentleman (he is not, says Brooks); and the nature of Sutpen's "innocence" and his "elephantiasis of the
personal will" as he pursues his vision of the American
dream.

17   _____. "When Did Joanna Burden Die? A Note," SLJ, VI (Fall),
43-46.
Wheeler's chronology (1973.B117) is used to date Joanna's murder on August 6.

18   BROWN, CALVIN S. "Dilsey: From Faulkner to Homer," William
Faulkner: Prevailing Verities and World Literature, ed-
ited by W. T. Zyla and Wendell M. Aycock. Lubbock, Texas:
Interdepartmental Committee on Comparative Literature,
Texas Tech University Press, pp. 57-75.
The author argues for the generality of Dilsey in The
Sound and the Fury as a portrait of the old, faithful
servant who may be found in the work of Homer, Shake-
speare, Dickens, Waugh, and other writers through the
ages.

1973

19 BROWN, CALVIN S. "Sanctuary: From Confrontation to Peaceful
Void," Mosaic, VII (Fall), 75-95.
Confrontations which move from an individual to an institutional level are the chief dramatic means in Sanctuary. At the end, Faulkner comes to an expression of despair or nihilism, a low point on the scale he traveled
from Soldiers' Pay. After Sanctuary, he moved upwards
toward increasing "affirmation of human values."

20 *BRUMM, ANNE-MARIE. "Authoritarianism in William Faulkner's
Light in August and Alberto Moravia's Il Conformista,"
RLMC, XXVI, 196-220.
1973 MLA International Bibliography, Volume I, Item
9830.

21 BURROUGHS, FRANKLIN G., JR. "God the Father and Motherless
Children: Light in August," TCL, XIX (July), 189-202.
Women are protagonists of the central conflict of Light
in August. Lena is both similar to and different from
Joe Christmas; they are both "banished" because of the
same kind of community values, but Lena receives help and
charity by virtue of her passive requests, while Joe is
denied and reviled, a form of treatment he seems to invite or demand. Hightower and Joanna are contrasts, too,
preserving very different heritages, living sterile lives
as outcasts. Hines, MacEachern and Grimm are similar as
impersonations of the stern conscience, while the women
who deal with Joe are subversive Eves who remind him of
his fault, the result of the transgressions of his mother.

22 BUTTERWORTH, KEEN. "A Census of Manuscripts and Typescripts
of William Faulkner's Poetry," MissQ, XXVI (Summer),
333-59.
The author lists published and unpublished poetry by
Faulkner, including fragments salvaged from Phil Stone's
burned Oxford home, and records the existence of newly
discovered MSS at Faulkner's home, Rowan Oak, not available for examination.

23 CAMBON, GLAUCO. "My Faulkner: The Untranslatable Demon,"
William Faulkner: Prevailing Verities and World Litera-
ture, edited by W. T. Zyla and Wendell M. Aycock. Lub-
bock, Texas: Interdepartmental Committee on Comparative
Literature, Texas Tech University Press, pp. 77-93.
The background to Faulkner's translation and reception
in Italy includes work by Mario Praz, Cesare Pavese, Elio
Vittorini, and Emilio Cecchi, among others, who lie behind
Cambon's own interest in and translation of Faulkner's
Absalom, Absalom! and Notes on a Horsethief.

24   CANTRELL, FRANK. "An Unpublished Faulkner Short Story:
      'Snow,'" MissQ, XXVI (Summer), 325-30.
          A story which is about the exposure of two innocents to
      evil that they cannot influence or reveal, "Snow," which
      dates from 1942, resembles the 1931 story "Mistral" in
      several respects. The weakness of the tale is that the
      subtlety of the villain's psychology makes it almost in-
      comprehensible as a complicated murder story.

25   CARLOCK, MARY SUE. "Kaleidoscopic Views of Motion," William
      Faulkner: Prevailing Verities and World Literature, ed-
      ited by W. T. Zyla and Wendell M. Aycock. Lubbock, Texas:
      Interdepartmental Committee on Comparative Literature,
      Texas Tech University Press, pp. 95-113.
          Woman as life-force--personified particularly by Caddy
      Compson, Addie Bundren, and Eula Varder as she appears in
      The Town--is a characteristic Faulkner creation. Faulkner
      moves this life-force from novel to novel, in each of the
      three cases cited allowing her to be reflected by "multi-
      ple reflecting planes." This "composite figure" has a
      lasting effect on the lives of other characters and is op-
      posed by one or more negative figures, courted by an ad-
      venturer, and sung but not saved by a "poet." Each bears
      an illegitimate child. Faulkner's celebration of woman as
      energy seems to parallel Henry Adam's interest in general
      American blindness to such a force as represented by the
      Virgin.

26   COLLINS, R. G. "Light in August: Faulkner's Stained Glass
      Triptych," Mosaic, VII (Fall), 97-157.
          Light in August is read as an "unconnected" Yoknapa-
      tawpha novel--one that is intrinsically unified but not
      joined by any simplifying nerve-connections with the "saga."
      Allegorically, Hightower is the obsessed Southern mythic
      past; Christmas the racially conflicting present, Lena and
      Byron are the clarifying light of natural man and his
      earth-mother mate. Other characters are discussed similar-
      ly.

27   COLLMER, ROBERT G. "When 'Word' Meets Palabra: Crossing the
      Border with Literature," William Faulkner: Prevailing
      Verities and World Literature, edited by W. T. Zyla and
      Wendell M. Aycock. Lubbock, Texas: Interdepartmental
      Committee on Comparative Literature, Texas Tech Universi-
      ty Press, pp. 153-64.
          The author gives his thoughts on the cultural antipathy
      or ignorance between Latin and North America. Latin Amer-
      ica discovers the United States' artists through France;

1973

(COLLMER, ROBERT G.)
North Americans come to Latin literature indirectly.
Faulkner's world is congenial to Latin American
perceptions.

28 CREIGHTON, JOANNE VANISH. "Revision and Craftsmanship in the
Hunting Trilogy of Go Down, Moses," TSLL, XV (Fall),
577-92.
Assuming that Faulkner first wrote short stories and
then, after conceiving a larger framework, augmented and
revised them, the author discusses differences between the
"hunting" trilogy in Go Down, Moses and "The Old People,"
"The Bear" (using Bear, Man, and God text), "Lion," and
"Delta Autumn" in different versions.

29 DAHL, JAMES. "William Faulkner on Individualism," WGCR, VI
(May), 3-9.
Excerpts from Faulkner's public statements are used to
depict his philosophy of individualism.

30 DAVIDSON, MARSHALL B., et al. The American Heritage History
of the Writer's America. New York: American Heritage,
pp. 338-41.
Faulkner's career is briefly surveyed with concentration
upon the idea of a saga and its legendary, imaginative
qualities. A photograph and an enlarged Yoknapatawpha map
are included.

31 DAVIS, WILLIAM V. "Quentin's Death Ritual: Further Christian
Allusions in The Sound and the Fury," NMW, VI (Spring),
27-32.
The scene at the bridge in The Sound and the Fury where
Quentin and the three boys regard the old trout contains
several symbolic references to Christian parallels: the
18 years from Quentin's death to the present corresponds
to the 18 "hidden" years in the life of Christ.

32 DAY, DOUGLAS. "Introduction," Flags in the Dust, by William
Faulkner. New York: Random House, pp. vii-xi.
A brief explanation of the editing of the novel, which
apparently represents a version of the book which was cut
down to make Faulkner's Sartoris. See reviews in FCN No. 2
(November 1973), pp. 7-8, and SoR, X (Autumn, 1974),
877-88; See also reply by Albert Erskine of Random House,
FCN, No. 3 (May 1974), 2-3.

33   DEGENFELDER, E. PAULINE. "The Film Adaptation of Faulkner's
      Intruder in the Dust," L/FQ, I (Spring), 138-48.
          The background and results of the filming of Intruder in
      the Dust are discussed along with changes between book and
      film and the film's reception. Two stills from the film
      are included.

34   _____. "Yoknapatawphan Baroque: A Stylistic Analysis of As
      I Lay Dying," Style, VII (Spring), 121-56.
          The style of As I Lay Dying is both colloquial and ba-
      roque; the colloquial establishes the solidity of the com-
      munity and the baroque defines individual alienation with-
      in Yoknapatawpha society. Darl predominates as point of
      view because of his sensitivity and his attempts to re-
      solve his problems with language. Style is analyzed using
      generative and transformational grammar to show the dif-
      ference between simple and complex speech in the novel.
      Cash, the character who learns and creates order, uses a
      style that is balanced between colloquial and baroque; he
      is the "sane artist." Other characters and their rela-
      tionships to one another are revealed by style.

35   DELAY, FLORENCE, and JACQUELINE DE LABRIOLLE. "Márquez est-il
      le Faulkner Colombien?" RLC, XLVII (January-March),
      88-123.
          Like Faulkner, Gabriel García Márquez has taken a single
      place for the setting of his novels and stories. Paral-
      lels and possible influence between Faulkner's work and
      that of the Colombian writer are discussed; there are
      genealogies of the fictional families of both writers.

36   DEVLIN, ALBERT J. "Faulknerian Chronology: Puzzles and
      Games," NMW, V (Winter), 98-101.
          There are discrepant dates for the death of Buck McCas-
      lin, Ike's father, in Go Down, Moses; they create confu-
      sion in the novel and put into question the integration of
      section four of "The Bear" into the whole.

37   _____. "'How Much It Takes to Compound a Man': A Neglected
      Scene in Go Down, Moses," MQ, XIV (Summer), 408-21.
          A scene in section four of "The Bear" delineates Ike
      McCaslin and his mother, Sophonsiba, and thus provides
      evidence for the "etiology" of what has increasingly been
      seen as Ike's failure in life. Sophonsiba drives her
      brother Hubert's mulatto mistress out of the Beauchamp
      house, and Ike, a witness, enjoys a secret identification
      with his uncle. The scene is repeated, in essence, in
      "Delta Autumn," when Ike sends Roth's mistress away.

1973

38   DILLON, RICHARD T. "Some Sources for Faulkner's Version of
        the First Air War," <u>AL</u>, XLIV (January), 629-37.
            Faulkner may have used the war stories of Elliott White
        Springs and James Warner Bellah in his own war fiction.

39   DUNCAN, ALASTAIR B. "Claude Simon and William Faulkner,"
        <u>FMLS</u>, IX, 235-52.
            Major areas of similarity between Faulkner and the
        French new novelist are discussed.

40   EMERSON, O. B. "Faulkner and His Bibliographers," <u>BB</u>, XXX
        (April-June), 90-92.
            Bibliographical work on Faulkner is reviewed and evalu-
        ated. The author has praise for Meriwether (1957.B48 and
        1961.A4), Daniel (1942.A1), and Starke (1934.B25). A
        list of the "most important" bibliographies and checklists
        of Faulkner material--primary and predominantly secondary
        --is appended.

41   ESSLINGER, PAT M. "No Spinach in <u>Sanctuary</u>," <u>MFS</u>, XVIII
        (Winter), 355-58.
            Expanding on Faulkner's apparent reference to E. C.
        Segar's "Thimble Theatre" comic strip and its characters
        Popeye and Olive Oyl (noted in 1971.B58), the author sug-
        gests possible wider use of comic strip allusions in <u>Sanc-
        tuary</u>, including Orphan Annie, Barney Google, Gasoline
        Alley, and others. Such allusions contribute to the over-
        all symbology of modernism and grotesquery in the novel.

42   <u>Faulkner Concordance Newsletter</u>, No. 2 (November), 9 pp.
            The second in a series of occasionally-issued mimeo-
        graphed newsletters, this publication reports on work at
        the U. S. Military Academy, West Point, and the University
        of South Carolina to compile computer concordances of
        Faulkner's works using corrected texts. This issue in-
        cludes a brief report on the text of <u>Flags in the Dust</u>
        (Random House, 1973) to which Albert Erskine, vice presi-
        dent and executive editor of Random House, replies in
        <u>Newsletter</u> No. 3 (May 1974)

43   FAULKNER, HOWARD. "The Stricken World of 'Dry September,'"
        <u>SSF</u>, X (Winter), 47-50.
            The moon serves as an important thematic image in "Dry
        September"--it is described as burdened and stricken, and
        in one instance a favorable image reflects on Hawkshaw the
        barber to indicate that he is not (as some interpret) one
        of the villains of the piece.

44   GIDLEY, MARK [Mick]. "Elements of the Detective Story in Wil-
         liam Faulkner's Fiction," JPC, VII (Summer), 97-123.
         Faulkner, a reader of detective fiction himself, saw
      examples of the form in the work of such writers as Dosto-
      evsky and Chekov and also wrote detective fiction on two
      levels. He wrote straightforward tales of detection and
      a few crime stories, but he also wrote "subversive" fic-
      tion like "Monk" and Sanctuary in which the reader's ex-
      pectations of justice are thwarted by overpowering circum-
      stance. Knight's Gambit, Intruder in the Dust, and Absa-
      lom, Absalom! receive attention. Willard Huntington
      Wright ("S. S. Van Dine") is seen as a possible influence
      on Faulkner (See also 1961.B54).

45   GOLD, JOSEPH. "'Sin, Salvation and Bananas': As I Lay Dy-
         ing," Mosaic, VII (Fall), 55-73.
         After a severe survey of previous As I Lay Dying criti-
      cism, the author reads it himself in religious terms, sug-
      gesting parallels to St. Anselm, to Bunyan, and to the
      Methodist evangelist Whitefield. Addie is a "witch that
      ...worships God's enemy." Faulkner must admire the Bun-
      dren's achievement in the face of so much nihilism; gramo-
      phone, bananas, new wife, teeth and all represent a cele-
      bration of life by simple people.

46   GRAY, RICHARD. "The Meanings of History: William Faulkner's
         Absalom, Absalom!" DQR, III, 97-110.
         The interrelatedness of events past, present, and fu-
      ture lies at the heart of the problem of understanding
      Absalom, Absalom!, both for the reader and the novel's
      narrators. Exploration of Sutpen's story brings moral
      discovery: we learn how to behave and how to understand
      the relationship between history and ethical behavior.
      None of the characters in the novel succeeds in achieving
      this understanding.

47   GREGORY, EILEEN. "Faulkner's Typescripts of The Town,"
         MissQ, XXVI (Summer), 361-86.
         Besides the setting copy of The Town, the University of
      Virginia Faulkner Collection contains a complete early TS
      draft of the novel, part of it now found on verso sheets
      of an early draft of the third Snopes novel, The Mansion.
      Some of the pages of The Town draft contain, on versos,
      portions of letters, essays, and short fiction by Faulk-
      ner which reveal much about his literary activities during
      the late 1950's. Gregory describes and quotes from ma-
      terial found on these pages and analyzes the differences
      between early and final versions of The Town. The "most

1973

(GREGORY, EILEEN)
important of the shorter pieces" found on the reverse
sheets of the drafts are reprinted.

48   G[RESSET], M[ICHEL].   Introduction to "Le Menteur," translated
      by Gresset from Faulkner's "The Liar," NRF, XLII (Decem-
      ber), 53.
          One of Faulkner's most interesting apprentice texts, the
      sketch "The Liar," which first appeared in the New Orleans
      Times-Picayune, 25 July 1925, makes good use of the oral
      tradition and the raconteur-figure who would eventually
      develop into V. K. Ratliff.   The translation is on
      pp. 53-64.

49   HAGOPIAN, JOHN V.   "Absalom, Absalom! and the Negro Question,"
      MFS, XIX (Summer), 207-11.
          A survey of the racial attitudes of Faulkner's charac-
      ters in Absalom, Absalom! proves that the book is not
      racist itself; it dramatizes the "tragic consequences of
      racism."

50   HARAKAWA, KYOICHI.   "Faulkner Hihyo no Doko," EigoS, CXIX,
      228-29.
          According to the 1973 MLA International Bibliography,
      Volume I, Item 9861, this short piece surveys trends in
      Faulkner criticism.

51   HEIMER, JACKSON W.   "Faulkner's Misogynous Novel: Light in
      August," BSUF, XIV (Summer), 11-15.
          Expressions by other characters and by the omniscient
      narrator, as well as events and characterization in Light
      in August, make it misogynistic from first to last.   Wo-
      men are characterized as perfidious and emasculating.

52   HOWELL, ELMO.   "Faulkner's Enveloping Sense of History: A
      Note on 'Tomorrow,'" NConL, III (March), 5-6.
          "Tomorrow" shows that Faulkner is "impregnated with his
      cultural heritage," specifically by his use of the name
      "Stonewall Jackson Fentry."

53   *HUTCHINSON, D.   "The Style of Faulkner's Intruder in the
      Dust," Theoria, XXXIX, 33-47.
          1973 MLA International Bibliography, Volume I, Item
      9865.

54   HUTTEN, ROBERT W.   "A Major Revision in Faulkner's A Fable,"
     AL, XLV (May), 297-99.
        Changing a prophetic speech on war from the lawyer in
     Notes on a Horsethief to the Marshall in A Fable, Faulkner
     improved his novel.

55   JACOBS, ROBERT D.   "Faulkner's Humor," The Comic Imagination
     in American Literature, edited by Louis D. Rubin, Jr.
     New Brunswick, N. J.:   Rutgers University Press,
     pp. 305-18.
        In a book of essays first given as lectures over the
     Voice of America, Jacobs' piece emphasizes the folk, mas-
     culine quality of Faulkner's humor, its inheritance from
     the writers of the old southwestern frontier, its fre-
     quently Rabelaisian qualities.   The Hamlet is the center
     of the discussion, though humor in other works is also
     mentioned.   The Hamlet is Faulkner's comic masterpiece.

56   JARRETT, DAVID.   "Eustacia Vye and Eula Varner, Olympians:
     The Worlds of Thomas Hardy and William Faulkner," Novel,
     VI (Winter), 163-74.
        There are general similarities between Faulkner's work
     and Thomas Hardy's, and specific correspondences between
     the characterization of Eula Varner in The Hamlet and
     Eustacia Vye in The Return of the Native.   Both women are
     in strong contrast to their bleak surroundings; both are
     surrounded by passionate action.   Admitting that there
     are also many differences, the author speculates on simi-
     larities between the husbands Flem Snopes and Clym Yeo-
     bright and compares Diggery Venn with V. K. Ratliff.

57   KAZIN, ALFRED.   "The Secret of the South: Faulkner to Percy,"
     Bright Book of Life: American Novelists and Storytellers
     from Hemingway to Mailer.   Boston: Little, Brown and Co.,
     pp. 23-42.
        Seen in an overview after his death, Faulkner's career
     proves to be praiseworthy and unusual; he was private,
     contrary, and he wrote brilliantly imaginative but obscure
     novels filled with havoc, violence, and the dominance of
     the irrational.   The Sound and the Fury is his master-
     piece.   In all of his work, because there is history--be-
     cause it is history--there is significance and meaning.
     Ike McCaslin is his saint.

58   *KEARNEY, J. A.   "Paradox in Faulkner's Intruder in the Dust,"
     Theoria, XL, 55-67.
        1973 MLA International Bibliography, Volume I, Item
     9870.

1973

59 LANG, BÉATRICE. "An Unpublished Faulkner Short Story: 'The
    Big Shot,'" MissQ, XXVI (Summer), 312-24.
      "The Big Shot," a slightly O. Henryesque tale of gang-
    sters and the fate of a Sutpen-like social climber, is
    worth serious consideration on its own merits as well as
    for its analogues for several characters, themes, and
    events in Faulkner's later work.

60 LANGFORD, BEVERLY YOUNG. "History and Legend in William
    Faulkner's 'Red Leaves,'" NMW, VI (Spring), 19-24.
      The human sacrifice in the burial ritual of "Red Leaves"
    has precedents in the history of the Natchez Indians in
    Mississippi, a remnant of which tribe mingled with the
    Chickasaws who had lived in Faulkner's own region before
    it was fully settled by whites. In Lafayette County Indi-
    an lore there is an analogue to the story and a local tale
    of buried Indian treasure as well.

61 LANGFORD, GERALD. "Insights into the Creative Process: The
    Faulkner Collection at the University of Texas," William
    Faulkner: Prevailing Verities and World Literature, ed-
    ited by W. T. Zyla and Wendell M. Aycock. Lubbock, Texas:
    Interdepartmental Committee on Comparative Literature,
    Texas Tech University Press, pp. 115-33.
      A list of Faulkner materials in the Humanities Research
    Center at the University of Texas is appended to a brief
    discussion of the nature and literary value of those
    materials.

62 LEHAN, RICHARD. A Dangerous Crossing: French Literary Exis-
    tentialism and the Modern American Novel. Carbondale,
    Ill.: Southern Illinois University Press, pp. 68-79.
      A moral error lies at the root of the loss of a harmo-
    nius, Edenic world in such Faulkner novels as Absalom,
    Absalom! and Go Down, Moses, but the punishment cannot be
    explained, and thus the world is absurd in the existential
    sense. In As I Lay Dying, Light in August, and Sanctuary,
    there is "motion without meaning," which is hopelessness.
    In other novels an inscrutable manipulator controls the
    action, and a "constant irony" pervades the fiction.
    Faulkner is, however, chiefly a humanist who believes that
    man is responsible for his own problems and can achieve
    his own salvation. Part of this material appeared in
    1965.B49.

63   LEVITT, PAUL. "An Analogue for Faulkner's 'A Rose for Emily,'"
      PLL, IX (Winter), 91-94.
         John Crowe Ransom's poem "Emily Hardcastle, Spinster"
      seems analogous to Faulkner's "A Rose for Emily" and may
      be a source. Event and character in the two works are
      compared. See a similar argument, 1973.B7.

64   LONGLEY, JOHN L., JR. "'Who Never Had a Sister': A Reading
      of The Sound and the Fury," Mosaic, VII (Fall), 35-53.
         The theme of The Sound and the Fury is love; the absent
      Caddy is the focus; the technique is difficult. Longley's
      reading relies on only the novel and the Compson Appendix,
      with some reference to Longley's book (1963.A6), though it
      assumes the validity of Quentin's experiences in Absalom,
      Absalom! for his behavior in the earlier novel. The end-
      ing of the novel shows that in Jefferson, at least, Jason
      has control of his own family.

65   *LUPAN, RADU. "In Jefferson, Acasa la Faulkner," Luceafarul
      [Romania] (21 April), p. 1.
      American Literary Scholarship 1973, p. 139.

66   McHANEY, THOMAS L. "The Elmer Papers: Faulkner's Comic Por-
      traits of the Artist," MissQ, XXVI (Summer), 281-311.
         "Elmer," the novel that Faulkner worked on during his
      1925 trip to Europe and drew on variously later in his
      career, reveals his attempt to go beyond the sources and
      methods of Soldiers' Pay, which preceded it. In several
      respects apparently autobiographical, "Elmer" also draws
      on Bergson's conceptions of time and perception and bor-
      rows the techniques of modern painting for structural and
      thematic purposes. It helps explain the structure of much
      of Faulkner's early work, from Soldiers' Pay to Light in
      August, and it has a special relation as source or ana-
      logue for The Wild Palms. The long unpublished story,
      "Portrait of Elmer" which Faulkner made from the Elmer ma-
      terials in the early 1930's, is also discussed along with
      his other attempts to make profitable use of the unfinished
      earlier work.

67   MacMILLAN, DUANE. "Pylon: From Short Stories to Major Work,"
      Mosaic, VII (Fall), 185-212.
         Each of four flying stories Faulkner published in the
      1930's--"All the Dead Pilots," "Ad Astra," "Death Drag,"
      and "Honor"--is suggestive for his 1935 novel Pylon. The
      stories illustrate what, in Faulkner's terms, man can en-
      dure. The reporter of the novel comes to understand that
      there are indestructible human virtues and values. Notes
      to the article survey reviews and criticism of Pylon.

1973

68   MARTIN, HAROLD. "Caravan to Faulkner Country...And Beyond,"
        SoLiv (May), 117-18, 120.
           Anecdotes and general information about Faulkner and his
        local backgrounds are presented from the viewpoint of a
        college class excursion to Ripley and Oxford, Mississippi.

69   MERIWETHER, JAMES B. "Faulkner's Correspondence with Scrib-
        ner's Magazine," Proof 3, pp. 253-82.
           A brief introduction precedes transcriptions of letters
        between Faulkner, his agents, and the editors of Scrib-
        ner's Magazine between 1928 and 1935 about short stories
        submitted for sale.

70   _____. Introductions to "And Now What's To Do," "Nympholepsy,"
        "An Introduction to The Sound and the Fury," and "A Note
        on A Fable," all by William Faulkner, MissQ, XXVI (Summer),
        399, 403, 410, 416.
           Brief historical and textual notes precede four previous-
        ly unpublished pieces included in the 10th anniversary is-
        sue of MissQ's annual Faulkner number. "Nympholepsy" is an
        expansion of Faulkner's sketch "The Hill," and "And Now
        What's To Do" is an autobiographical essay.

71   MERTON, THOMAS. "Time and Unburdening and the Recollection of
        the Lamb: The Easter Service in Faulkner's The Sound and
        the Fury," Katallagete Be Reconciled [Journal of the Com-
        mittee of Southern Churchmen], IV (Summer), 7-15.
           Reproduced from one of a series of lectures by Merton at
        the Abbey of Gethsemani, Kentucky, beginning in January
        1967 and entitled "The Classical Values in William Faulk-
        ner," this essay offers reflections on one of Faulkner's
        "greatest saints," Dilsey in The Sound and the Fury, who
        proves Faulkner's very positive view of women. Merton
        discusses the book's "five parts"--i.e., including the
        Compson Appendix to the Viking Portable Faulkner. Faulk-
        ner's sense of time is not linear and clock-measured but
        "biblical"; he describes a process of fruition, ripening
        toward an event. This sense of time is one measure of
        soundness for characters in the novel. Each character is
        dominated by a different sense of time. The Easter serv-
        ice is "an authentic example of the way in which the Word
        of God is preached" and made effective.

72   MILLGATE, MICHAEL. "Faulkner," American Literary Scholarship,
        An Annual/1971, edited by J. A. Robbins. Durham, N. C.:
        Duke University Press, pp. 104-19.
           "The quantity of writing about William Faulkner continues
        to increase year by year but, unhappily, it is impossible

(MILLGATE, MICHAEL)
to speak of a corresponding rise in quality." Millgate
goes on to preface the annual survey of Faulkner criticism
with the observation that too much of the work merely repeats what has already been done.

73 _____. "Faulkner on the Literature of the First World War,"
MissQ, XXVI (Summer), 387-93.
Reproducing an early (mid-1920's?) essay by Faulkner
entitled "Literature and War," Millgate comments on Faulkner's own war fiction, including his use of some of the
authors mentioned in the previously unpublished essay:
Sassoon, Stephen Crane, R. H. Mottram (The Spanish Farm),
and Henri Barbusse (Le Feu, translated as Under Fire: The
Story of a Squad). Millgate traces Faulkner's development
of a proper thematic use of war in his fiction from Soldiers' Pay to A Fable.

74 _____. "Starting Out in the Twenties: Reflections on Soldiers' Pay," Mosaic, VII (Fall), 1-14.
Soldiers' Pay is exploratory for Faulkner: allusive and
possibly autobiographical, it shows his acuteness toward
the contemporary literary scene and his own background as
sources of fictional art. It fails most in the matter of
controlling material through skillful use of point of
view. A number of Faulkner's possible sources are reviewed and discussed.

75 MILUM, RICHARD A. "'The Horns of Dawn': Faulkner and Meta-
phor," AN&Q, XI (May), 134.
Faulkner uses a passage from his poem "The Flowers That
Died" in the Ike Snopes/cow episode of The Hamlet.

76 MONTEIRO, GEORGE. "The Limits of Professionalism: A Sociological Approach to Faulkner, Fitzgerald and Hemingway,"
Criticism, XV (Spring), 145-55.
Using Talcott Parsons' sociological observation on the
"affective neutrality" of the physician--the setting aside
of personal feelings vis-à-vis patients--Monteiro discusses, among other American fiction, The Wild Palms as an illustration of the importance of such distance.

77 MOSES, EDWIN. "Faulkner's The Hamlet: The Passionate Humanity of V. K. Ratliff," NDEJ, VIII, 98-109.
Ratliff's involvement in the treasure-hunt scene at the
close of The Hamlet is preposterous, given the salesman's
gifts, but when we see that Ratliff connived in his own
downfall, deliberately lost by ceasing to try to outwit
Snopes, we see that he regains his humanity thereby.

1973

78   MUHLENFELD, ELISABETH. Essay-Review of Sally R. Page, Faulk-
     ner's Women: Characterization and Meaning [1972.A6],
     MissQ, XXVI (Summer), 435-50.
        Oversimplifying Faulkner's women characters, Page's
     book does not deal thoroughly with a number of themes,
     subjects, or kinds of characterizations of women in the
     fiction.

79   NADEAU, ROBERT L. "Morality and Act: A Study of Faulkner's
     As I Lay Dying," Mosaic, VI (Spring), 23-35.
        Bergson's philosophy of dynamism provides a touchstone
     for the interpretation of As I Lay Dying in existential
     terms. Addie has found the meaning of life in union with
     the flow of universal reality, the primal flux, and other
     characters in the novel may be understood by the ways in
     which they achieve or fail to achieve this union. Jewel,
     who can act spontaneously, is closest to Addie; Cash and
     Anse are static, hiding behind words. There is a kind of
     human triumph at the end of the novel, however, in the
     form of the family's relation to the self-perpetuating
     life process.

80   NELSON, MALCOLM A. "'Yr Stars Fell' in 'The Bear,'" AN&Q, XII
     (September), 4-5.
        "Yr stars fell" reference in the McCaslin ledgers in the
     fourth section of "The Bear" is to the great Leonid meteor
     show in November 1833. That it has a real source does not
     weaken the tonal value of the reference as portent. Iden-
     tical to 1971.B74.

81   NELSON, RAYMOND S. "Apotheosis of the Bear," RS, XLI
     (September), 201-04.
        One of Faulkner's favorite words, "apotheosis," is used
     "with decisive force" in "The Bear" section of Go Down,
     Moses. True to his own being, the Bear is an apotheosis;
     so, too, is Ike, who follows his heart to relinquish the
     plantation, though, as "Delta Autumn" indicates, he lives
     too long.

82   NOBLE, DONALD R. "Faulkner's 'Pantaloon in Black': An Aris-
     totelian Reading," BSUF, XIV (Summer), 16-19.
        "Pantaloon in Black" can be read profitably as a tragedy
     with Rider as the hero. Aristotle's Poetics is the frame
     of reference.

83 NORRIS, NANCY. "The Hamlet, The Town and The Mansion: A
     Psychological Reading of the Snopes Trilogy," Mosaic, VII
     (Fall), 213-35.
         The activities of Labove, Flem, Ike, Ratliff, and Gavin
     Stevens in the Snopes Trilogy may be "narrative displace-
     ments" for incestuous desires. Oedipal fear also plays a
     role in the trilogy. What the narrators learn is the pow-
     er of psychological healing--by enduring their primal
     fears they prove that endurance is "worth the agony and
     the sweat."

84 O'BRIAN, MATTHEW C. "William Faulkner and the Civil War in
     Oxford, Mississippi," JMH, XXXV (May), 167-74.
         Accounts, from various records, of Civil War activity in
     Oxford, Miss., and Lafayette County, are compared with
     Faulkner's fiction. The author concludes that Faulkner
     does not treat the actual war in great detail.

85 PEAVY, CHARLES D. "'If I Just Had a Mother': Faulkner's
     Quentin Compson," L&P, XXIII (No. 3), 114-21.
         Quentin's "neurosis" examined for symptoms, causes, and
     effects reveals that he is incapable of love, is Oedipal,
     and harbors an infantile attachment for his sister. He
     becomes pathologically obsessed with the dirtiness of sex-
     uality and demonstrates female traits of behavior.

86 PERRY, J. DOUGLAS, JR. "Gothic as Vortex: The Form of Horror
     in Capote, Faulkner, and Styron," MFS, XIX (Summer),
     153-67.
         Gothicism is characterized by distinctive narrative form
     as well as by the use of certain themes and images.
     Faulkner's work displays formal similarities to Melville,
     Poe, and the English Gothicists. Three structural prin-
     ciples coincide with Irving Malin's paradigms of Gothic
     theme--confinement, flight, and narcissism--and image--
     the room, the voyage, the mirror: concentricity, pre-
     determined sequence, and character repetition. Faulkner's
     practice in Sanctuary serves as example; Faulkner is com-
     pared with Capote and Styron.

87 PFEIFFER, ANDREW. "'No Wiser Spot on Earth': Community and
     the Country Store in Faulkner's The Hamlet," NMW, VI
     (Fall), 45-52.
         Extracting material about Varner's store from The Ham-
     let, the author briefly discusses its typicality to the
     Southern country store as chronicled in Thomas D. Clark's
     Pills, Petticoats and Plows (Bobbs-Merrill, 1944).

1973

88 PHILLIPS, REV. GENE D., S. J. "Faulkner and the Film: The
Two Versions of Sanctuary," L/FQ, I (July), 263-73.
The 1932 and 1961 film versions of Faulkner's novel,
Sanctuary, are compared.

89 PINEDA, RAFAEL. "William Faulkner: Pais de Magnolias y
Sangre," and "Yoknapatawpha, El Condado de William Faulkner," Hierbas, Purpura y Magnolias. Caracas: Monte Avila
Editores, pp. 85-120.
A survey of Faulkner's work, his themes and characters,
and some discussion of his humanism, combine with a consideration of his geography and his myth-making. Faulkner's remarks upon receiving the Order of Andrés Bello in
Caracas in 1962 are reproduced in Spanish. Absalom, Absalom! and "The Bear" receive substantial attention.

90 POLK, NOEL. "'Hong Li' and Royal Street: The New Orleans
Sketches in Manuscript," MissQ, XXVI (Summer), 394-402.
Royal Street is a bound, hand-written booklet containing
slightly revised versions of ten of the eleven short
pieces Faulkner had published as "New Orleans" in the New
Orleans Double Dealer issue of January-February 1925. It
omits "The Tourist," but includes "Hong Li," a new sketch,
printed with this essay for the first time.

91 _____. "William Faulkner's Marionettes," MissQ, XXVI (Summer), 247-80.
The one-act play which Faulkner wrote in 1920 and prepared in several hand-lettered and -illustrated texts,
Marionettes, is ambitious, serious work, a complete product of his youthful imagination. It draws on the moods
and words of the Symbolist and decadent poets such as
Mallarmé and Wilde, and on Eliot's "Prufrock," but it
seems to offer an early example of Faulkner's own thinking about man's fate--the "marionettes" are not figures
manipulated by some remote puppet-master, but characters
whose "gutful compulsions," basically narcissistic, have
created the lassitude, misfortune, and sterility of their
lives; a clear moral emerges from the play.

92 POWNALL, DAVID E. "William Faulkner," Articles on Twentieth
Century Literature: An Annotated Bibliography, 1954 to
1970, Vol. 2. New York: Kraus-Thomson Organization Limited, pp. 885-1025.
Six hundred ninety-nine items on Faulkner and his work,
arranged alphabetically by title of work and annotated,
are included; the section is an expanded version of the
"Current Bibliography" appearing in TCL, I-XVI (1955-1970).
Includes some foreign criticism.

93   PUTZEL, MAX. "Evolution of Two Characters in Faulkner's Early
      and Unpublished Fiction," SLJ, V (Spring), 47-63.
         Faulkner's early fiction, particularly unpublished and
      MSS pieces at the University of Virginia, is surveyed,
      with emphasis upon the development of an autobiographical
      male character and an idealized, innocent female figure
      who would both be transmuted into fuller figures in Faulk-
      ner's more mature fiction, especially Quentin and Caddy.

94   RAISOR, PHILIP. "Up from Adversity: William Faulkner's A
      Fable," SDR, XI (No. 3), 3-15.
         Man's ability to define his adversity in broad terms and
      to seek meaningful solace in timeless values, as defined
      by Kenneth Burke's "circumferential logic" (A Grammar of
      Motives) is demonstrated in A Fable, which is "affirmative
      and soberly optimistic." Rebellion and self-transcendence,
      the ability to do good in a bad situation, is what Faulk-
      ner celebrates, opposing it to the fearful view of man as
      one who seeks only control and order.

95   ROSENMAN, JOHN B. "A Note on William Faulkner's As I Lay Dy-
      ing," SAF, I (Spring), 104-05.
         The author argues for parallels between the character of
      Macbeth and Dewey Dell Bundren.

96   ROUBEROL, JEAN. "Les Indiens dans l'oeuvre de Faulkner," EA,
      XXVI (January-March), 54-58.
         The rather limited physical appearance of Indians in
      terms of Faulkner's whole work does not suggest their
      historical or thematic importance there. Noble savages,
      they represent a lost time. Unlike the blacks, they do
      not endure into a corrupted modern age.

97   RUIZ RUIZ, JOSÉ M. "El sentido de la vida y de la muerte en
      "The Sound and the Fury" de W. Faulkner," FMod, XIII,
      117-38.
         The attempt to keep the knowledge of death away is the
      subject of The Sound and the Fury. The author points out
      biblical parallels (the Fall) in Caddy's act in the tree
      and Christian parallels elsewhere in the novel. Dilsey
      sees the meaning of life and death.

98   RUOTOLO, LUCIO P. "Isaac McCaslin," Six Existential Heroes:
      The Politics of Faith. Cambridge, Mass.: Harvard Uni-
      versity Press, 57-78.
         A study of six modern fictional heroes--from the work
      of Woolf, Greene, Faulkner, Ralph Ellison, Golding, and
      Malamud--who survive the absurdity of contemporary exist-

1973

(RUOTOLO, LUCIO P.)
ence includes Ike McCaslin. Created for Go Down, Moses,
he answers objections to Faulkner's devotion to the past
by dramatizing a "scriptural intention" in terms of the
hunt ritual. Faulkner affirms Being and declares that it
is beyond rational understanding. Ike learns to face his
family past and personal future through Sam Fathers and
by facing the "nothingness" of the wilderness. Though
Ike suffers final failure, he passes the hunting horn,
symbol of life's fullness, to "his children."

99   SACHS, VIOLA. "Absalom, Absalom!" The Myth of America: Es-
      says in the Structures of Literary Imagination. The
      Hague: Mouton, pp. 103-24.
         Discoveries of word-play and allusion in Absalom, Absa-
      lom! are coupled with a discussion of the book as a dram-
      atization of the collapse of a New World cosmogony.

100   _____. "The Bear," The Myth of America: Essays in the Struc-
      tures of Literary Imagination. The Hague: Mouton,
      pp. 125-42.
         In "The Bear," the "primeval mythical past of America"
      is shown in contrast to the missed second chance of the
      profane New Canaan.

101   SCHLEPPER, WOLFGANG. "Knowledge and Experience in Faulkner's
      Light in August," JA, XVIII, 182-94.
         The first paragraph of chapter six of Light in August,
      which sets up memory, knowing, and believing as key terms,
      is the basis for a syntactic analysis of how Faulkner uses
      verbal forms of these words to create a version of percep-
      tion that may be very important to an understanding of the
      novel. Joe Christmas is not a free agent when he meets
      Joanna Burden. Is he one when he ends his life?

102   SCHROETER, JAMES. "Technology and the Sexual Revolution,"
      YR, LXII (Spring), 392-405.
         Caddy, Jason and Benjy Compson are mentioned briefly,
      along with other modern literary characters, as depicting
      the "central myth of the twentieth century."

103   SHEPHERD, ALLEN. "Code and Comedy in Faulkner's The Reivers,"
      LWU, VI (March), 43-51.
         The Reivers may be usefully compared with Sherwood An-
      derson's story "I Want to Know Why." Faulkner uses an
      adult narrator and portrays a boy who is more firmly a
      part of family and the "code" of the gentleman at the end
      of his adventure than he was at the beginning of his jour-
      ney. The happy ending defines the novel's comic nature.

104   SMITH, GERALD J.   "A Note on the Origin of Flem Snopes," NMW,
      VI (Fall), 56-57.
         The "opes" sound in the name of Flem Snopes was probably
      inspired by the famous trial of John Scopes in Dayton,
      Tennessee, in July 1925.   It suggests the progressivist,
      atheistic, tradition-hating forces of the New South.

105   SPIVEY, HERMAN E.   "Faulkner and the Adamic Myth: Faulkner's
      Moral Vision," MFS, XIX (Winter), 497-505.
         A careful reading of Faulkner distinguishes "no sharp
      shift from despair to affirmation."   Faulkner has always
      believed in man's innate propensity to sin or err and his
      need for acknowledging his guilt and bearing his deserved
      punishment, and he has always believed that "life has
      meaning and significance."   A survey of the criticism
      which discusses Faulkner's morality is included.

106   STARK, JOHN.   "The Implications for Stylistics of Strawson's
      'On Referring,' with Absalom, Absalom! as an Example,"
      Language and Style, VI (Fall), 273-80.
         A stylistic approach to Absalom, Absalom! based on dis-
      tinctions between expressions as references or as descrip-
      tions points out that the "utterances" of an expression
      may be quite a different thing from its use in different
      forms.   P. F. Strawson's "On Referring" is the critical
      tool, and the first paragraph of Faulkner's novel is ex-
      amined to demonstrate how his style involves the reader.

107   STEWART, DAVID H.   "Faulkner, Sholokhov, and Regional Dissent
      in Modern Literature," William Faulkner: Prevailing Veri-
      ties and Modern Literature, edited by W. T. Zyla and Wen-
      dell M. Aycock.   Lubbock, Texas: Interdepartmental Com-
      mittee on Comparative Literature, Texas Tech University
      Press, pp. 135-50.
         The lives, as well as the writings, of the Russian
      Sholokhov and Faulkner are similar.   Their work is used to
      illustrate a "new regionalism" emergent after World War I
      that opposed itself to the concept of the "superstate."
      Faulkner's first novel after returning from New Orleans is
      full of vernacular, folk material, hymns to the earth like
      the paean to the mule.

108   STONE, WILLIAM B.   "Ike McCaslin and the Grecian Urn," SSF, X
      (Winter), 93-94.
         In the Go Down, Moses version of "The Bear," Keats'
      poem, "Ode on a Grecian Urn," is paralleled in ways that
      underscore the incompleteness and failure of Ike's ideal-
      ism.   This is not apparent in the Saturday Evening Post
      version of the story.

1973

109   TOBIN, PATRICIA. "The Time of Myth and History in Absalom,
         Absalom!" AL, XLV (May), 252-70.
             Using the approaches and terms of the structuralist and
         semiological schools of criticism, Tobin investigates the
         roles of myth and history in Absalom, Absalom! She ques-
         tions the view that the fall of the house of Sutpen is a
         tragedy of human fate and a paradigm for the fall of a
         social order and a culture too. To the reader of the nov-
         el, however, this movement in time is less obvious than
         are the impediments to understanding deliberately employed
         by Faulkner: multiple point of view and Joycean language.
         Sutpen does not qualify as tragic because he ignores re-
         sponsibility and feels no shame, doubt or guilt, only puz-
         zlement; his static gigantism makes him mythic instead.
         His children become a part of history and tradition, dis-
         play loyalty and love, and "subvert the implacable inhu-
         manity of the father's master plan." The root of the mat-
         ter is Sutpen's fighting back against racial insult in
         like manner. Quentin is destroyed by what he puzzles out
         because of his deep mythological involvement.

110   TRAVIS, MILDRED K. "Echoes of Pierre in The Reivers," NConL,
         III (September), 11-13.
             Allusions to common expressions like "crossing the Rubi-
         con" and "mess of pottage" which occur in Melville's
         Pierre are taken as evidence of Faulkner's borrowing in
         The Reivers.

111   TUCKER, EDWARD L. "Faulkner's Drusilla and Ibsen's Hedda,"
         MD, XVI (September), 157-61.
             The scene in "An Odor of Verbena," the final tale of The
         Unvanquished, where Drusilla presents Bayard the pistols,
         is compared to a similar scene in Hedda Gabler. The women
         characters are compared on several grounds.

112   UTTERBACK, SYLVIA W. Essay-Review of Bedell's Kierkegaard and
         Faulkner: Modalities of Existence [1972.A3], MissQ, XXVI
         (Summer), 421-35.
             Bedell's "confused understanding" and inappropriate ap-
         plication of the concepts of Kierkegaard tend to defeat
         his project and vitiate the book's claim to be a notable
         contribution to either literary or religious scholarship.

113   VARE, ROBERT. "Oxford, Miss., Which Faulkner Transcended, Is
         As He Left It," NYT (14 January), Section X, pp. 3, 11.
             An anecdotal account of a visit to Faulkner's home town.
         Photographs.

114   WALKER, RONALD G.   "Death in the Sound of Their Name: Charac-
            ter Motivation in Sartoris," SHR, VII (Summer), 271-78.
               The reality of loss is what the Sartorises have fled,
            generation after generation, with increasing desperation.
            For Young Bayard the force of the Sartoris legend, which
            goes against his nature at the same time that it causes
            his acts, makes his life a series of empty gestures.   Nar-
            cissa, who was drawn to Johnny because he embodied the
            Sartoris legend, takes Bayard when he begins to manifest
            similar violence and recklessness.

115   WATSON, JAMES GRAY.   "'The Germ of My Apocrypha':   Sartoris
            and the Search for Form," Mosaic, VII (Fall), 15-33.
               In Sartoris, Faulkner discovers not only his material
            but also a new vision of 20th-century man and new tech-
            niques in the modernist vein.   Though Bayard, and others,
            perish in devotion to a false ideal, life goes on in sev-
            eral forms; Buddy McCallum, Loosh Peabody, and young Ben-
            bow Sartoris are free of the Civil War legend.   Sartoris
            is Faulkner's first modern book.

116   WELTY, EUDORA.   "Some Notes on Time in Fiction," MissQ, XXVI
            (Fall), 483-92.
               In the course of observations about the crucial impor-
            tance of time to the form of the novel--which is "time's
            child"--the Mississippi author discusses Faulkner's use of
            time in The Sound and the Fury and his belief that there
            is no such thing as the past, only its effects upon the
            present.

117   WHEELER, SALLY PADGETT.   "Chronology in Light in August," SLJ,
            VI (Fall), 20-42.
               A chronology of Light in August, with a few paragraphs
            of discussion of Faulkner's thematic use of time in the
            novel; the author concludes that Joe is 35 or 36 when he
            dies.   See 1973.B17.

A Note on the Index

   In addition to authors, titles, the titles of Faulkner's works, and the names of people and places, this index includes a number of subject entries; as in the case of the Faulkner titles, only substantial treatments have been indexed, and the reader should not presume that subjects are exhaustively surveyed. The following are the subjects which have been indexed:

Author/Title Index

"A. E. Housman and Faulkner's Nobel Prize Speech," 1971.B64

"A propos d'Absalon, Absalon!," 1953.B35

"A propos de 'Le Bruit et la Fureur': la temporalité chez Faulkner," 1939.B28; 1947.B7

"A própósito de la ultima novela publicada por William Faulkner," 1935.B8

Abel, Darrel, 1957.B3

"Aborted Sacrament in Absalom, Absalom!," 1964.B48

"About the Sketches," 1958.B15

"Absalom, Absalom!" (Sewall), 1959.B59; (Sachs) 1973.B99

Absalom, Absalom!, 1936.B1, B6–B9, B12, B14–B18; 1937.B1, B4, B7, B9–B11, B14–B17; 1938.B11, B15; 1940.B6; 1945.B2; 1947.B9; 1948.B6; 1950.B2, B27; 1951.A1–A2, B7, B10, B32, B46, B61; 1953.A1, B5–B6, B17, B20, B22, B27, B35, B37, B42; 1954.A2, B17, B19, B69; 1955.B35–B36, B49–B50; 1957.B42, B50; 1958.B17; 1959.A4–A5, B6, B10, B27, B59, B81; 1960.A1–A2, B45, B57, B62, B64; 1961.B55, B62; 1962.A5, B26, B58, B74, B95, B111; 1963.A1, A4, A6, B5, B13–B15, B18–B19, B21, B25, B39, B48, B73–B74, B86; 1964.A8, A10–A11, B11, B33, B44, B47, B48, B77; 1965.A2,

(Absalom, Absalom!)
B5, B35, B44, B68; 1966.B1, B17, B24, B36, B68, B71; 1967.A3, B17, B20, B36, B39, B59–B61, B64, B67, B75, B85, B88, B90, B100, B101; 1968.A1–A2, A8, B2, B4, B6, B43, B72; 1969.B2, B7, B11; 1970.B11, B13, B21, B43, B47, B66–B67, B79, B82; 1971.A2, A4, B30, B41–B42, B48, B83, B85–B86, B96, B103; 1972.A1, A3, A7, B1, B13, B35, B39, B40, B45, B55, B78, B83, B93, B99, B107, B109, B111; 1973.A4–A5, A7, A9, B16, B23, B44, B46, B49, B99, B106, B109

Absalom, Absalom!: manuscript, 1955.B49; 1971.A4; 1972.B93

"Absalom, Absalom! and the Meaning of History," 1957.B42

"Absalom, Absalom! and the Negro Question," 1973.B49

"Absalom, Absalom! as Gothic Myth," 1950.B27

"Absalom, Absalom! as a Portrait of the Artist," 1972.B40

"Absalom, Absalom!: The Definition of Innocence," 1951.B10

"Absalom, Absalom! The Edge of Infinity," 1958.B17

"Absalom, Absalom!: The Extended Simile," 1967.B36

"Absalom, Absalom! The Historian as Detective," 1971.B42

"As I Lay Dying: A Strange Come-
dy," 1967.B77
"As I Lay Dying and The Waste
Land: Some Relationships,"
1964.B18
"As I Lay Dying as a Study of
Time," 1972.B86
"As I Lay Dying as an Existential
Novel," 1963.B77
"As I Lay Dying as Ironic Quest,"
1962.B78
"As I Lay Dying, by William
Faulkner," 1930.B14
"As I Lay Dying: Christian Lore
and Irony," 1957.B6
"As I Lay Dying: Christian Sym-
bols and Thematic Impli-
cations," 1969.B70
"As I Lay Dying: Distortion in
the Slow Eddy of Current
Opinion," 1959.B73
"As I Lay Dying: Faulkner's Inner
Reporter," 1959.B30
"As I Lay Dying: The Insane
World," 1962.B102
As I Lay Dying: manuscript,
1956.B44
"As Much Truth as One Can Bear,"
1962.B11
"As Whirlwinds in the South: An
Analysis of Light in
August," 1949.B14
Asals, Frederick, 1968.B3
Ashraf, S. A., 1960.B6
"Aspects of American Fiction: A
Whale, a Bear, and a Mar-
lin," 1966.B77
"Aspects of Space: John Marin
and William Faulkner,"
1964.B79
"Aspekte der Faulkner-Kritik in
Frankreich," 1961.B73
"'Assalonne, Assalonne!': Il
demone della memoria,"
1963.B19
Asselineau, Roger, 1959.B7
Astre, George Albert, 1951.B6
Aswell, Duncan, 1968.B4-B5
Atkins, Anselm, 1969.B2
Atkinson, Brooks, 1962.B8;
1963.B3
"Atlantic Bookshelf," 1933.B22;
1935.B35

"Atmosphere and Theme in Faulk-
ner's 'A Rose for
Emily,'" 1949.B38;
1951.A2
"Au-dela du déchirement:
L'héritage méridional
dans l'oeuvre de William
Faulkner et d'Albert
Camus," 1963.B52
"Auntee Owned Two," 1972.B36
Aury, Dominique, 1953.B5;
1962.B9
Die Aussage der Form: Zur
Textur und Struktur des
Bewusstseinsromans.
Dargestellt an W.
Faulkners The Sound and
the Fury, 1969.A7
"Autant n'en emportera pas le
vent," 1952.B5
"Authoritarianism in William
Faulkner's Light in
August and Alberto
Moravia's Il
Conformista," 1973.B20
"Autumn Books--That Time in the
Wilderness," 1962.B98
"'Avant-Propos,' Requiem pour
une Nonne," 1957.B8
"L'avénir du roman," 1943.B4
Aycock, Wendell M., 1972.B65;
1973.B3, B6, B14, B18,
B23, B25, B27, B61, B107
"The Aydt and the Maze: Ten
Years of Faulkner Studies
in America," 1961.B30
Aymé, Marcel, 1950.B1; 1954.B7
Aytür, Necla, 1973.B6

B., E., 1948.B2
Bache, William B., 1954.B8
Bachelard, Gaston, 1952.B11;
1959.A3; 1967.B6
"The Background of Snopesism in
Mississippi Politics,"
1964.B26
Backman, Melvin A., 1954.B9;
1956.B4; 1957.B14;
1959.B8; 1961.B5-B6;
1962.B10; 1965.B5;
1966.A1

Backus, Joseph, 1958.B7
"Bad Conscience," 1955.B13
Baird, Helen, 1972.B66
Baiwir, Albert, 1943.B1
Baker, Carlos, 1954.B10; 1959.B9
Baker, James R. 1952.B3-B4
Baker, Julia K.W., 1930.B4-B5;
    1931.B9
Baldanza, Frank, 1959.B10;
    1961.B7; 1967.B1
Baldwin, James, 1956.B5; 1962.B11;
    1966.B7
Baldwin, Joseph Glover, 1959.B23
Balzac, Honoré de, 1934.B25;
    1944.B2; 1948.B20; 1954.B4,
    B55; 1972.B3; 1973.B4
    Les Chouans, 1967.B70
    "Un Coeur Simple," 1948.B15
Banašević, Nikola, 1969.B10
"Bankruptcy in Time: A Reading
    of William Faulkner's
    Pylon," 1958.B43
Banning, Margaret Culkin, 1939.B5
"'Baptism in the Forest': Wisdom
    and Initiation in William
    Faulkner," 1967.B71;
    1968.B45
Barber, Marion, 1973.B7
Barbusse, Henri, Le Feu, 1973.B73
Barjon, Louis, 1953.B6
Barksdale, Richard, 1961.B8
"Barn Burning," 1959.B35; 1960.B28;
    1961.B65; 1965.B54;
    1967.B97; 1968.B25, B50;
    1971.B9, B106
Barnes, Daniel R., 1972.B4
Barnett, Suzanne B., 1967.B2
Barretto, Larry, 1926.B3
"The Barrier of Language: The
    Irony of Language in
    Faulkner," 1967.B59
Barth, J. Robert, 1954.B11;
    1960.B7; 1964.B5; 1972.A1,
    B5-B6, B14, B34, B55-B56,
    B58, B87, B100, B112
Bashiruddin, Zeba, 1968.B6
Bass, Eben, 1961.B9
Bassan, Maurice, 1964.B6
Bassett, John E., 1971.B5;
    1972.A2
Basso, Hamilton, 1935.B4;
    1962.B12

Bates, Ophelia, 1962.B13
Baum, Catherine B., 1967.B3
Baumgarten, Murray, 1961.B10
"Bayard Sartoris et Quentin
    Compson, héros malades de
    William Faulkner,"
    1957.B14
"Bayard Sartoris: Mourning and
    Melancholia," 1973.B2
Beach, Joseph Warren, 1932.B5;
    1941.B1; 1942.B2
Beale, Betty, 1954.B12; 1957.B5
"The Bear." See under Go Down,
    Moses
"'The Bear': An Unromantic
    Reading," 1972.B87
"'The Bear' and Faulkner's Moral
    Vision," 1961.B74
"'The Bear' and Huckleberry Finn:
    Heroic Quest for Moral
    Liberation," 1963.B1
"A Bear Hunt," 1963.A6;
    1970.B50
Bear, Man, and God: Seven
    Approaches to William
    Faulkner's "The Bear,"
    1964.A9
Bear, Man and God: Eight
    Approaches to William
    Faulkner's "The Bear,"
    1971.A11
Beardsley, Aubrey, 1967.B14
Beatty, Jerome, 1959.B29
Beauchamp, Gorman, 1970.B5;
    1972.B7
"'The Beautiful One': Caddy
    Compson as Heroine of The
    Sound and the Fury,"
    1967.B3
Beauvoir, Simone de, 1962.B14
Beck, Warren, 1941.B2-B4;
    1942.B3; 1951.A2; 1955.B4;
    1959.B11-B12; 1960.A1, B8;
    1961.A1; 1962.B15-B16;
    1966.A8; 1973.A9
Bedell, George C., 1972.A3;
    1973.B112
Bedient, Calvin, 1968.B7
"A Bedroom Scene in Faulkner,"
    1956.B23
Beebe, Maurice, 1956.B6;
    1957.B14; 1967.B4

469

Beer Broadside, 1951.B60
Beidler, Peter G., 1968.B8;
 1973.B8
"'Being Pulled Two Ways': The
 Nature of Sarty's Choice in
 'Barn Burning,'" 1971.B106
Beja, Morris, 1964.B7; 1971.B6
Bell, Haney H., Jr., 1962.B17;
 1965.B6; 1973.B9-B10
Bellah, James Warner, 1973.B38
Bellman, Samuel I., 1968.B9
Ben Hur (play), 1955.B8
"Bench for Two" see "Pennsylvania
 Station"
"Beneath the Dust of 'Dry Septem-
 ber,'" 1964.B78
"Beneath the Hammer of Truth,"
 1959.B58
Benét, Stephen Vincent, 1934.B2;
 1940.B2
 John Brown's Body
 1965.B24
Benét, William Rose, 1927.B3;
 1929.B1; 1931.B6-B8;
 1933.B3; 1935.B5
"Benjamin Compson--Flower Child,"
 1969.B48
"Benjy at the Monument," 1964.B6
"Benjy's Branch: Symbolic Method
 in Part I of The Sound and
 the Fury," 1972.B41
"Benjy's Names in the Compson
 Household," 1968.B55
Bennett, Arnold, 1963.B46
Benson, Carl, 1954.B13
Benson, Jackson J., 1971.B7;
 1972.B8
Benson, Warren R., 1966.B3
Bentley, Phyllis, 1939.B6
Bergel, Lienhard, 1947.B1
Berger, Yves, 1960.B9
Bergson, Henri, 1954.B14;
 1955.B58; 1957.B3;
 1960.A2, B11; 1962.B44;
 1963.B22, B39; 1964.B79;
 1966.B25; 1967.B33;
 1968.B36, B62; 1970.B43;
 1973.B66, B79
 Laughter, 1966.B60
Beringause, A. F., 1963.B4
Berland, Alwyn, 1962.B18

Berman, Louis, 1971.B28
Bernberg, Raymond E., 1958.B8
Bertin, Celia, 1959.B13
"Beside Addie's Coffin," 1930.B8
"Best Novel Still Unwritten,
 Faulkner Admits at
 Oxford," 1937.B2
Bettis, Valerie, 1949.B6
"'Between Grief and Nothing':
 Hemingway and Faulkner,"
 1971.B70
Bevington, Helen, 1967.B104
Bewusstseinseinlagen des Erzählens
 und Erzählte
 Wirklichkeiten
 dargestellt an Amerikani-
 schen Romanen des 19. und
 20. Jahrhunderts
 insbesondere am Werk
 William Faulkners, 1966.A7
Bianchi, Ruggero, 1962.B19
Bible, 1954.B4; 1958.B32;
 1959.B57; 1962.B75;
 1965.B73; 1966.A3;
 1967.B68; 1972.B30
"The Biblical Rhythm of Go Down,
 Moses," 1967.B68
Bibliography, 1973.B40
 Collecting: 1931.B8; 1952.B1-
  B2; 1955.B49; 1956.B3;
  1965.B85
 Collections: Dust jackets,
  1971.B21; George Lazarus
  Library, 1955.B49; U. S.
  Military Academy,
  1966.B10; University of
  North Carolina, 1972.B43;
  University of Texas,
  1955.B49; 1959.B48;
  1973.B61; University of
  Virginia, 1968.A4
 Criticism. See Criticism,
  Bibliographies and Check-
  lists
 Descriptive: British editions,
  1961.A4; 1965.B57; 1971.A5
  Manuscripts and Type-
  scripts, 1955.B49;
  1959.B48; 1960.B47;
  1961.A4; 1968.A4; 1971.A5;
  1973.B22

(Bibliography),
  Movie Writing: 1961.A4, B60;
    1968.A4; 1971.A5
  Non-fiction prose: 1954.B66;
    1957.B48; 1961.A4;
    1964.A7; 1968.A4: 1971.A5
  Non-print materials: 1956.B3
  Novels: 1934.B25; 1942.A1;
    1957.B48; 1960.B47;
    1961.A4; 1964.A7; 1968.A4
    1970.A5; 1971.A5
  Poetry: 1954.B67; 1957.B48;
    1960.B47; 1961.A4;
    1964.A7; 1968.A4; 1971.A5
  Stories and Sketches:
    1957.B48; 1960.B47;
    1961.A4; 1964.A7; 1968.A4;
    1971.A5, B66-B67
  Translations: 1955.B45, B54;
    1961.A4, B61; 1968.A4;
    1969.A4; 1971.A5, B18;
    1972.A8
"Bibliography of William Faulk-
    ner in Japan," 1960.B29
Bickerstaff, Thomas Alton, 1965.A5
Bier, Jesse, 1970.B6
Bierce, Ambrose, 1931.B21
"The Big Bear of Arkansas," See
    Thorpe, T. B.
"Big Chip Off the Old Block,"
    1961.B41
"The Big Shot," 1973.B59
Big Woods, 1955.B3-B4, B6, B14,
    B48; 1956.B51; 1959.B78;
    1961.B67
Bigelow, Gordon E., 1960.B10
"The Bill Faulkner I Knew,"
    1965.B43
"Bill's Friend Phil," 1970.B26
Biography, 1929.B4; 1930.B1, B3;
    1932.B7, B10, B12;
    1934.B25-B26; 1938.B4,
    B16; 1940.B11; 1942.B16;
    1945.B2; 1947.B10;
    1948.B4; 1950.B23;
    1951.B2, B8; 1952.A2, B8;
    1953.B8-B9, B14; 1954.A1,
    B12; 1957.B9, B49;
    1958.B30; 1959.B19, B61,
    B64; 1960.B71; 1961.A2,
    A5, B35, B61; 1962.B6,
    B7, B12, B30, B35, B41,

(Biography)
    B46, B89, B117; 1963.A2,
    A7-A8, B23, B40, B55,
    B84; 1964.A4, A8, B40,
    B58; 1965.A5, B16, B.21
    B31, B38, B50, B51, B65,
    B71-72, B79; 1966.A2, A6,
    B13, B52, B57, B59, B69,
    B76; 1967.A1, B7, B25,
    B76, B86, B89, B93;
    1968.A6, B23, B32, B37,
    B47; 1969.B5, B6, B15,
    B27, B46, B53, B79, B85;
    1970.B1, B27; 1971.B8, B25
    B94; 1972.B53, B66, B67,
    B84, B88
Birney, Earle, 1938.B2
Bishop, John Peale, 1939.B7
Björk, Lennart, 1963.B5
"Black Music," 1934.B2, B11
Black Portraiture in American
    Fiction: Stock Charac-
    ters, Archetypes, and
    Individuals, 1971.B91
Black, White and Gray: Twenty-
    one Points of View on the
    Race Question, 1964.B17
Blackwell, Louise, 1967.B5
Blair, John G., 1969.B3
Blair, Walter, 1972.B116
Blake, Nelson M., 1969.B4
Blanchard, Margaret, 1970.B7
Bleikasten, André, 1966.B4;
    1967.B6; 1970.A7; 1973.A1
Blöcker, Günter, 1958.B9
Blonski, Jan, 1961.B11
Bloom, Lynn Z., 1971.A11
Blotner, Joseph, 1957.B6, B26;
    1959.A1, 1963.B6;
    1964.A2; 1965.A1; 1966.B5,
    B10; 1967.B7; 1969.B5-B6;
    1971.B8; 1973.B11
"The Blues as a Literary Theme,"
    1967.B8
Bluestein, Gene, 1967.B8
Blum, Irving D., 1958.B10
Blumenberg, Hans von, 1958.B11
Bode, Carl, 1959.B9
Bongartz, Roy, 1956.B7
"Book Note," 1973.B5
"Book Notes: Many Souths,"
    1957.B53

Brown, Deming, 1956.B10;
    1962.B29
Brown, James, 1958.B15
Brown, Maggie, 1965.A5
Brown, Maud Morrow (Mrs. Calvin,
    Sr.), 1956.B11; 1965.A5
Brown, Ray B., and Donald Pizer
    1969.B6, B51
Brown, Ruth, 1962.B30
Brown, Sterling, 1931.B10;
    1937.B3
Brown University, 1955.B5
Brown, William R., 1967.B15
Bruccoli, Matthew J., 1967.B16
"'Le bruit et le tumulte' de
    William Faulkner,"
    1939.B11
Brumm, Anne-Marie, 1973.B20
Brumm, Ursula, 1950.B2; 1955.B10;
    1957.B7; 1960.A1;
    1963.B15; 1967.B17;
    1969.B11; 1970.B14;
    1972.B18
Bryer, Jackson R., 1969.B59
Brylowski, Walter, 1968.A2
Buckley, G. T., 1961.B14
    1962.B28
"Building Blocks of a Gentle-
    man," 1962.B62
Bungert, Hans, 1963.B16-B17;
    1971.A1
Bunker, Robert, 1949.B5
Burger, Nash K., 1964.B12
Burgum, Edwin Berry, 1947.B2
Burke, Kenneth, A Grammar of
    Motives, 1973.B94
Burnham, James, 1931.B11
Burroughs, Franklin G., Jr.,
    1973.B21
Burrows, Robert N., 1961.B15
Burson, Harold, 1965.A5
Burton, Thomas G., 1969.B21
Butcher, Fanny, 1963.B17
Butler, Francelia, and R. H. W.
    Dillard, 1967.B18
Butor, Michel, 1960.B15;
    1962.B31; 1972.B68
Butterworth, Keen, 1973.B22
Buttita, Anthony, 1938.B4
Byam, Milton S., 1951.B12
"Byron Bunch," 1952.B30

Byron, Don Juan, 1963.B83;
    1966.B54
Byronism, 1965.B80

Cabaniss, Allen, 1965.B12;
    1970.B15
Cable, George Washington, "Jean-
    Ah Poquelin," 1960.B65;
    1970.A1
"Caddy Compson's World,"
    1970.B34
"Calculation Raised to Mystery:
    The Dialectics of Light
    in August," 1963.B68
Caldwell, Erskine, 1939.B20
"Caliban as Prospero: Benjy and
    The Sound and the Fury,"
    1970.B52
"Call Me Ishmael: The Hagio-
    graphy of Issac McCaslin,"
    1961.B68
Callen, Shirley, 1963.B18
Calverton, V. F., 1938.B5;
    1939.B8
Calvinism: See Puritanism
"The Calvinistic Burden of Light
    in August," 1957.B35
Cambon, Glauco, 1954.B17;
    1961.B16; 1963.B19;
    1965.B13; 1973.B23
Camerino, Aldo, 1934.B4;
    1968.B19
Cameron, May, 1936.B4
Campbell, Harry M., 1943.B3;
    1948.B6; 1950.B3;
    1951.A1; 1952.B7;
    1954.B18; 1970.B16
Campbell, Harry M., and Ruel E.
    Foster, 1951.A1
Campbell, Harry M., and J. P.
    Pilkington, 1946.B1
Campbell, Jeff H., 1972.B19
Camus, Albert, 1951.B13;
    1956.B2; 1957.B8;
    1960.B16, B22; 1963.B52;
    1965.B28; 1967.B71, B95;
    1969.B3, B12, B51
"Camus and Faulkner: The Search
    for the Language of Modern
    Tragedy," 1960.B22

"Camus' Faulkner: Requiem for a Nun," 1969.B3
"Camus' Illuminating Answers to Searching Questions," 1960.B16
Canby, Henry Seidel, 1931.B12; 1932.B8; 1934.B5; 1935.B6; 1936.B5
Cantrell, Frank, 1971.B14; 1973.B24
Cantwell, Robert, 1931.B13; 1952.B8; 1953.B8-B9; 1958.B16; 1960.A1; 1964.B13
Cape, Jonathan, 1965.B51
Capote, Truman, 1949.B6; 1954.B4; 1973.B86
Capps, Jack L., 1966.B10
"Caravan to Faulkner Country and Beyond," 1973.B68
"Carcassonne," 1933.B2
Carey, Glenn O. 1964.B14; 1965.B14; 1971.B15-B16; 1972.B20-21
Cargill, Oscar, 1941.B6
Carlock, Mary Sue, 1973.B25
Carpenter, Frederic J., 1959.B15
Carpenter, Richard C., 1956.B12
Carpenter, Robert Allen, 1965.B15
Carpenter, Thomas P., 1967.B19
Carr, John, 1972.B22
Carrouges, Michel, 1954.B19
Carter, Everett, 1952.B9
Carter, Hodding, 1953.B10; 1957.B9; 1962.B32; 1963.B20; 1965.B16
Carter, Thomas H., 1955.B11
Cash, W. J., The Mind of the South, 1940.B4; 1941.B7; 1963.B18; 1964.B38; 1965.B5
Cassill, R. V., 1968.B20
A Catalogue of the Writings of William Faulkner, 1942.A1
Catastrophe and Imagination: A Reinterpretation of the Recent English and American Novel, 1957.B43
Cate, Hollis L., 1970.B17

Catullus, 1965.B56
Cavalcade of the American Novel, 1952.B54
Cecchi, Emilio, 1934.B6; 1957.A1; 1959.B16
Cecil, L. Moffit, 1970.B18
"A Census of Manuscripts and Typescripts of William Faulkner's Poetry," 1973.B22
"The Centaur and the Pear Tree," 1952.B44
Center for Editions of American Authors, 1972.B73
"Certain Ladies of Quality: Faulkner's View of Women and the Evidence of 'There Was a Queen,'" 1968.B13
A Certain Morbidness: A View of American Literature, 1969.B78
Cervantes, Miguel de, Don Quixote, 1954.B4; 1967.B77
Cestre, Charles, 1933.B5
Chamberlain, John, 1931.B14; 1939.B9
"Changing Moral Standards in Fiction," 1939.B5
Chapman, Arnold, 1959.B17; 1966.B11
Chapman, Maristan, 1935.B7
Chapsal, Madeleine, 1955.B12
The Chapter in Fiction: Theories of Narrative Division, 1970.B77
Character indexes, 1963.A1, A3, A5; 1964.A7-A8; Absalom, Absalom!, 1963.B25
Character studies:
  Ab Snopes, 1961.B65
  Addie Bundren, 1970.B10
  Anse Bundren, 1965.B45
  Autobiographical male and idealized female, 1973.B93
  Bayard Sartoris, 1956.B4; 1971.B19; 1972.B65; 1973.B2, B114
  Benjy Compson, 1964.B6; 1969.B48, B62; 1970.B18, B52
  Byron Bunch, 1952.B30; 1961.B45

"The Civil War of 1936: Gone
    With the Wind and Absalom,
    Absalom!," 1967.B67
Clark, Charles C., 1968.B21
Clark, Eulalyn W., 1972.B24
Clark, Thomas D., 1965.A5; Pills,
    Petticoats and Plows,
    1973.B87
Clark, William G., 1967.B20;
    1968.B22
Clark, William J., 1969.B13
The Classic Vision: The Retreat
    from Extremity in Modern
    Literature, 1971.B49
Classics and Commercials,
    1948.B28
"Claude Simon and William Faulk-
    ner," 1973.B39
Claxton, Simon, 1962.B33
"Clearer Road Signs in His
    Country," 1964.B57
"The Clearing House," 1934.B20
Clemens, Samuel L.: See Twain,
    Mark
Clements, Arthur L., 1962.B34
Clerc, Charles, 1965.B17
"A Closer Look at 'As I Lay
    Dying,'" 1954.B41
Coanda, Richard, 1958.B17
Coates, Robert M., 1930.B6;
    1931.B15; 1932.B9, B13
Cobau, William W., 1969.B14
Cobb, Irving S., 1973.B15
Cobb, Humphrey, Paths of Glory,
    1968.B65
Cochran, Louis, 1932.B10;
    1964.B51; 1965.A5
"Code and Comedy in Faulkner's
    The Reivers," 1973.B103
Coffee, Jessie A., 1965.B18;
    1967.B21
Cofield, J. R., 1965.A5
Cohen, B. Bernard, 1959.B18
Cohen, Hennig, 1969.B39
"Coincidence in the Novel: A
    Necessary Technique,"
    1968.B43
Coindreau, Maurice E., 1931.B16;
    1934.B16; 1935.B8-B10;
    1936.B6; 1937.B4-B6;
    1938.B6-B7; 1950.B4-B5;
    1952.B11-B12; 1954.B22;

(Coindreau, Maurice E.)
    1956.B13; 1957.B11;
    1960.B17; 1963.B23-B24;
    1965.B19; 1966.B12, B31;
    1971.B18, B32;
    1972.B42; 1973.B4
Cole, Douglas, 1960.B18
Coleridge, Samuel Taylor,
    1953.B2
Collected Stories of William
    Faulkner, 1950.B8, B11,
    B17, B28; 1951.B38, B55,
    B57; 1960.B27; 1961.B41;
    1962.B77, B101
Collecting Faulkner: See
    Bibliography, Collecting
"Collecting Faulkner Today,"
    1952.B2
"A Collection of Studies,"
    1931.B17
Collins, Carvel, 1951.B16;
    1953.B11-B13; 1954.B23-
    B27; 1957.B12-B13;
    1958.B18-B19; 1959.B19;
    1960.B19; 1962.B35;
    1965.B20; 1968.B23-B24
Collins, R. G., 1970.B19;
    1973.B26
"Collisions and Confrontations,"
    1960.B35
Collmer, Robert G., 1973.B27
"Col. Falkner Killed 75 Years
    Ago Today; Old Papers
    Turned Up In Frisco Depot
    Tell Story," 1964.B2
"Colonel Falkner's Preface to
    The Siege of Monterey,"
    1970.B4
"Col. Sartoris and Mr. Snopes,"
    1963.B34, B40, B57
"Colonel Sartoris Snopes and
    Faulkner's Aristocrats,"
    1959.B35; 1968.B25
"Colonel Sartoris Snopes and
    Gabriel Marcel: Alle-
    giance and Commitment,"
    1971.B9
"Colonel Thomas Sutpen as Exis-
    tentialist Hero,"
    1962.B111
Colum, May, 1937.B7

"The Crisis in Literature,"
    1939.B18
"Critical Misconceptions of
    Southern Thought,"
    1957.B29
Criticism:
  Anthologies and collections of
    articles: Absalom,
    Absalom!, 1971.A2; "The
    Bear," 1964.A9; 1971.A11;
    Faulkner and Religion,
    1972.A2; General, 1951.A2;
    1957.A1, B14; 1959.B20;
    1960.A1; 1966.A8; 1973.A8-
    A9; Light in August,
    1969.A5; 1971.A3, A12;
    "A Rose for Emily,"
    1970.A1; The Sound and the
    Fury, 1968.A3; 1970.A6
  Bibliographies and checklists:
    As I Lay Dying, 1973.A1;
    British criticism,
    1965.B57; General,
    1950.B15; 1951.A2, B6;
    1952.B50, 1953.B34;
    1955.A1; 1956.B6; 1960.A1,
    B70; 1961.B50; 1962.B109;
    1965.B33; 1967.B4;
    1968.A4; 1970.A5, B29;
    1971.B53; 1972.A2;
    1973.B92; French criti-
    cism, 1955.B54; 1957.B72;
    1959.A6; German criticism,
    1955.B45; 1972.A8;
    Japanese criticism,
    1960.B29; Light in August,
    1971.B44; 1973.A6; Novels,
    1961.B26; 1970.B29; See
    also General; Polish
    criticism, 1969.A4; The
    Sound and the Fury,
    1971.B5
  Survey reviews: 1954.B73;
    1955.B22; 1957.B71;
    1959.B3; 1960.A1;
    1961.B30, B48; 1965.B2-
    B3, B57; 1966.B1;
    1967.B102; 1968.B81;
    1969.B59, B86; 1970.B80;
    1971.B68; 1972.A8, B75;
    1973.B72; See also Faulk-
    ner's Reception and Faulk-
    ner's Reputation

"Criticism of William Faulkner:
    A Selected Checklist,"
    1967.B4
"Criticism of William Faulkner:
    A Selected Checklist with
    an Index to Studies of
    Separate Works," 1956.B6
"The Critics and Faulkner's
    'Little Postage Stamp of
    Native Soil'," 1970.B64
"Critique Faulknerienne,"
    1957.B14
"La critique Faulknerienne en
    France: Essai de
    synthese," 1957.B14, B71
Critiques and Essays on Modern
    Fiction, 1920-1951,
    1952.B50
Cronache letterarie anglosassoni,
    1931.B25
Cronin, Mary A., 1964.B16
Cross, Barbara M., 1960.B23;
    1961.B20
Cross, Richard K., 1967.B24
Crowell's Handbook of Faulkner
    1964.A8
Crunden, Robert M., 1972.B27
"Cry Enough," 1954.B10
"A Cryptogram: As I Lay Dying,"
    1961.B64
Cullen, John B., 1961.A2
Cult of Cruelty criticism,
    1931.B12; 1932.B23;
    1934.B5, B13-B15;
    1935.B22; 1936.B5;
    1939.B18; 1952.B42
    1970.B25
"Cultural Primitivism in Faulk-
    ner's 'The Bear,'"
    1950.B13
Cummings, E. E., 1933.B3
Cunliffe, Marcus, 1954.B29
The Curious Death of the Novel:
    Essays in American Litera-
    ture, 1967.B83, B84
Curley, Thomas F., 1962.B37
"Current Literature," 1933.B8
Curtains, 1959.B68; 1961.B70
Cushing, Edward, 1931.B17
The Cycle of American Literature
    1955.B55
Cypher, James R., 1962.B38

Dabit, Eugene, 1934.B7-B8;
    1952.B12
Dabney, Lewis M., 1972.B28;
    1973.A2
D'Agostino, Nemi, 1955.B15
Dahl, James, 1973.B29
Dain, Martin, 1964.A4
Dallas (Texas) Morning News
    {subject}, 1932.B19;
    1953.B38;
A Dangerous Crossing: French
    Literary Existentialism
    and the Modern American
    Novel, 1973.B62
Daniel, Bradford, 1964.B17
Daniel, Frank, 1931.B18
    1948.B9
Daniel, Robert W., 1942.A1;
    1950.B6,B15; 1972.B34
Dante, 1943.B6; The Inferno,
    1962.B61; 1964.B29
"Dark Laughter in the Towers,"
    1960.B60
Darmon, Martine, 1951.A2
Darnell, Donald G., 1969.B18
"Die Darstellung des Kampfes bei
    Stephen Crane, Hemingway,
    Faulkner, und Britting,"
    1968.B38
Darwin, Charles, 1973.B8
"A Darwinian Source for Faulk-
    ner's Indians in 'Red
    Leaves,'" 1973.B8
Dashiell, Alfred, 1973.B69
Davenport, Basil, 1929.B2;
    1930.B7
Davenport, F. Garvin, Jr.,
    1970.B21
Davidson, Donald, 1926.B5;
    1927.B4; 1929.B3;
    1957.B15; 1966.B42
Davidson, Marshall B., et al.,
    1973.B30
Davis, Scottie, 1972.B29
Davis, William V., 1972.B30;
    1973.B31
Dawson, Margaret Cheney, 1930.B8;
    1932.B11
Day, Douglas, 1961.B21; 1973.B32
"The Day the Balloon Came to
    Town," 1965.B21

Deakin, Motley, and Peter Lisca,
    1972.B40
"Death Drag," 1973.B67
"Death in the Sound of Their
    Name: Character Motiva-
    tion in Sartoris,"
    1973.B114
"The Death of the Old Men,"
    1964.B24
"The Decadence in Faulkner's
    First Novel: The Faun,
    the Worm, and the Tower,"
    1968.B61
"The Decay of Yoknapatawpha
    County," 1969.B4
Le déclin de l'individualisme
    chez les romanciers
    américains contemporains,
    1943.B1
"The Decline of Regionalism in
    Southern Fiction,"
    1964.B69
"A Deer Hunt in the Faulkner
    Country," 1970.B50
"A Defense of Difficulties in
    William Faulkner's Art,"
    1963.B86
"A Defense of Faulkner's Sanc-
    tuary," 1967.B65
Defoe, Daniel, Moll Flanders,
    1963.B17
Degenfelder, E. Pauline,
    1973.B33-34
"Deja Vu and the Effect of Time-
    lessness in Faulkner's
    Absalom, Absalom!,"
    1963.B39
de Labriolle, Jacqueline,
    1973.B35
Delay, Florence, and Jacqueline
    de Labriolle, 1973.B35
Delgado, F., 1959.B22
Dell, Floyd, 1967.B18
"Delta Autumn": See Go Down,
    Moses
"'Delta Autumn': William Faulk-
    ner's Answer for David H.
    Stewart," 1964.B46
"Delta Cycle: A Study of William
    Faulkner," 1946.B5
"Delta Hunt," 1960.B71

"Faulkner," <u>American Literary
Scholarship: An Annual</u>
See <u>American Literary
Scholarship</u>
"Faulkner Among the Puritans,"
1964.B9
"Faulkner: An Experiment in
Drama," 1951.B33
"Faulkner and American Sophisti-
cation," 1964.B71
"Faulkner and Balzac: The Poetic
Web," 1972.B3
"Faulkner and Bennett," 1963.B46
"Faulkner and Camus," 1965.B28
"Faulkner and Certain Earlier
Southern Fiction,"
1954.B23
"Faulkner and Child, Faulkner
and Negro," 1967.B105
"Faulkner and Children," 1970.B30
"Faulkner and Christ's Crucifix-
ion," 1956.B36
"Faulkner and Comedy," 1963.B3
"Faulkner and Contemporaries,"
1951.B55
"Faulkner and Desegregation,"
1956.B5
"Faulkner and Existentialism:
A Note on the Generalis-
simo," 1963.B80
"Faulkner and Hardy," 1970.B42
"Faulkner and 'Helen'--a Further
Note," 1968.B66
"Faulkner and Hemingway: Image
of Man's Desolation,"
1957.B70
"Faulkner and Hemingway: Impli-
cations for School Pro-
grams," 1965.B74
"Faulkner and Hemingway--Their
Thought," 1957.B52
"Faulkner and Hemingway: Values
in a Modern World,"
1962.B25
"Faulkner and His Bibliogra-
phers," 1973.B40
"Faulkner and His Critics,"
1968.B77
"Faulkner and His Folk," 1957.B9;
1963.B20
"Faulkner and His Friend: An
Interview with Emily W.
Stone," 1971.B25

"Faulkner and His Snopes Family
Reach the End of Their
Trilogy," 1959.B41
"Faulkner and His Sources,"
1970.B63
"Faulkner and History," 1972.B13
"Faulkner & Hollywood,"
1959.B70
"Faulkner and Human Freedom,"
1960.B54
"Faulkner and Keats: The
Ideality of Art in 'The
Bear,'" 1969.B32
"Faulkner and Lanier: A Note on
the Name Jason," 1972.B76
"Faulkner and <u>Mosquitoes</u>:
Writing Himself and His
Age," 1971.B15
"Faulkner and Sartre: Metamor-
phosis and the Obscene,"
1963.B75
"Faulkner and Scott," 1967.B40
"Faulkner and Scott: Addendum,"
1969.B71
"Faulkner and Scott and the
Legacy of the Lost Cause,"
1972.B52
"Faulkner and Stein: A Study in
Stylistic Intransigence,"
1959.B10
"Faulkner and the Adamic Myth:
Faulkner's Moral Vision,"
1973.B105
"Faulkner and the Air: The
Background of <u>Pylon</u>,"
1964.B53
"Faulkner and the Black Shadow,"
1953.B15
"Faulkner and the Calvinist
Tradition," 1964.B5;
1972.B6
"Faulkner and the Civil War,
Myth and Reality,"
1963.B64
"Faulkner and the Colossus of
Maroussi," 1972.B84
"Faulkner and the Contours of
Time," 1958.B60;
1959.A4
"Faulkner and the Critics,"
1955.B22

Faulkner in the University:
    Class Conferences at the
    University of Virginia
    1957-1958, 1959.A1;
    1960.B67; 1965.A1
"Faulkner in the University: A
    Classroom Conference,"
    1957.B26
"Faulkner in Toronto: A Further
    Note." 1968.B47
"Faulkner in Turkish," 1973.B6
"A Faulkner Item in a Limited
    Edition," 1932.B3
"Faulkner, James Baldwin, and the
    South," 1966.B7
"Faulkner Land and Steinbeck
    Country," 1971.B23
"Faulkner le tragique," 1951.B28
"Faulkner l'universel," 1962.B1,
    B31, B41, B56, B75
"Faulkner le voyant," 1954.B19
"Faulkner: Light in August:
    The Inwardness of the
    Understanding," 1965.B77
"Faulkner, Mailer, and Yogi
    Bear," 1971.B61
"Faulkner, moraliste puritain,"
    1959.B7
Faulkner: Myth and Motion,
    1968.A1
"Faulkner of Mississippi,"
    1931.B30
"Faulkner on Broadway," 1959.B53
"Faulkner on Man's Struggle with
    Communication," 1964.B36
"Faulkner on the Literature of
    the First World War,"
    1973.B73
Faulkner on Truth and Freedom,
    1956.A1; 1968.A6
"Faulkner, or Theological In-
    version," 1972.B69
"Faulkner, ou le sens tragique,"
    1952.B34
"Faulkner ou l'inversion theo-
    logique," 1948.B20;
    1949.B31; 1972.B69
Faulkner par lui-meme, 1963.A7,
    B37
"Faulkner Parle," 1955.B8
"The Faulkner Place," 1965.B26
"Faulkner Publication," 1959.B61

The Faulkner Reader, 1954.B45
"Faulkner Returns to Yoknapataw-
    pha," 1957.B44
"Faulkner, Sanctuary," 1946.B3
"Faulkner, Sartre, and the New
    Novel," 1966.B2
"Faulkner: Saying No to Death,"
    1970.B56
"Faulkner Scholarship and the
    CEA," 1963.B44
"Faulkner Sensed Impending
    Crisis," 1962.B69
"Faulkner, Sholokhov, and
    Regional Dissent in
    Modern Literature,"
    1973.B107
"Faulkner Smiles," 1962.B37
"Faulkner: Social Commitment
    and the Artistic Tempera-
    ment," 1970.B78
"Faulkner, Soldati, and America,"
    1936.B13
"Faulkner: Sorcerer or Slave?,"
    1952.B19; 1959.B29
"Faulkner Speaking," 1954.B2
"Faulkner tel que je l'ai connu,"
    1963.B23
"Faulkner--the Great Years,"
    1957.B10
"Faulkner: The Image of the
    Child in The Mansion,"
    1962.B103
Faulkner: The Major Years,
    1966.A1
"Faulkner, the Man and His
    Masks: A Biographical
    Note," 1964.B40
"Faulkner, the Mule, and the
    South," 1969.B25
"Faulkner, The Rhetoric and the
    Agony," 1942.B9
"Faulkner: The South and the
    Negro," 1965.B78
"Faulkner: The Theme of Pride
    in The Sound and the
    Fury," 1965.B7
"Faulkner: The Triumph of
    Rhetoric," 1963.B36
"Faulkner: The Word as Principle
    and Power," 1958.B40;
    1960.A1

(Faulkner's reception–America)
    B36–B37; 1963.B24, B61;
    1964.B71; 1967.B67;
    1968.B77
  Brazil, 1953.B21
  Britain, 1938.B5; 1952.B55;
    1959.B4; 1962.B87;
    1963.B46; 1965.B57;
    1973.B14
  Europe, 1949.B25
  France, 1931.B1; 1934.B12,
    B17; 1937.B5; 1946.B12–
    B13; 1947.B6; 1950.B1,
    B5, B20; 1952.B12;
    1953.B17; 1954.B7;
    1955.B54; 1957.B71–B72;
    1959.A6, B13; 1960.B1;
    1961.B73; 1963.B37;
    1971.B18, B32; 1973.B3
  Germany, 1938.B15; 1955.B45;
    1959.B42; 1960.B61;
    1966.B66; 1972.A8
  Iceland, 1959.B44
  Italy, 1959.B16; 1965.B70;
    1971.B60; 1973.B23
  Japan, 1959.B51; 1960.B29
  Latin America, 1966.B11;
    1973.B27
  New York Critics, 1936.B1;
    1940.B14
  Poland, 1961.B11; 1969.A4
  Russia, 1956.B10; 1959.B24;
    1962.B29; 1968.B42;
    1972.B61
  Southern Reviewers, 1959.B75;
    1964.B23; 1966.B42
  Spain, 1971.B43
  Turkey, 1973.B6
"The Faulkners: Recollections
    of a Gifted Family,"
    1952.B8; 1960.A1
"Faulkner's Relation to the
    Humor of the Old South-
    west," 1967.B2
"Faulkner's Relationship to
    Gavin Stevens in Intruder
    in the Dust," 1972.B79
Faulkner's reputation (See also
    Faulkner's Influence and
    Faulkner's Reception):
  America, 1954.B24; 1955.B27;
    1960.B36–B37; 1963.B24;

(Faulkner's reputation–America)
    1972.B54; Mississippi,
    1959.B75; 1963.B20;
  Brazil, 1953.B21;
  Britain, 1959.B1; 1963.B46;
    1965.B57;
  France, 1950.B20; 1959.B13;
    1960.B1;
  Germany, 1959.B42; 1960.B61;
    1972.A8;
  Japan, 1959.B51;
  Latin America, 1961.B56;
    1966.B11;
  Russia, 1956.B10; 1959.B24;
  Spain, 1971.B43
"Faulkner's Reputation and the
    Contemporary Novel,"
    1954.B24
"Faulkner's Reputation in
    Brazil," 1953.B21
"Faulkner's Revisions: A
    Stylist at Work,"
    1969.B87
Faulkner's Revision of Absalom,
    Absalom!: A Collation
    of the Manuscript and the
    Published Book, 1971.A4
Faulkner's Revision of Sanctu-
    ary: A Collation of the
    Unrevised Galleys and the
    Published Book,"
    1972.A5
"Faulkner's Road to Realism,"
    1972.B85
"Faulkner's Sanctuary,"
    (Bergel), 1947.B1,
    (Slabey), 1963.B78
"Faulkner's Sanctuary and the
    Southern Myth," 1968.B70
"Faulkner's Sanctuary: Retreat
    from Responsibility,"
    1960.B18
"Faulkner's Sanctuary: The
    Discovery of Evil,"
    1963.B11
"Faulkner's Sartoris," (Carpen-
    ter), 1956.B12; (Howell),
    1959.B36
"Faulkner's Sartoris and the
    Mississippi Country
    People," 1961.B37

George, Henry, 1958.B14
Gérard, Albert, 1954.B39;
    1969.B33; See also
    Guerard, Albert
"The Germ of My Apocrypha,"
    1973.B115
Gerstenberger, Donna, 1961.B25
Gerstenberger, Donna, and
    George Hendrick,
    1961.B26; 1970.B29
"Geschichte als Geschehen und
    Erfahrung: Eine Analyse
    von William Faulkner's
    Absalom, Absalom!,"
    1967.B17
Giannitrapani, Angela, 1959.B27;
    1960.B32; 1963.A4
Gibbons, Kathryn G., 1962.B50
Gibson, William M., 1964.B29
Gidley, Mick, 1967.B33;
    1970.B30-B32; 1971.B28
    1973.B44
Giermanski, James R., 1969.B34
Giles, Barbara, 1948.B13;
    1950.B9
Gill, Brendan, 1954.B15, B40
Gilley, Leonard, 1965.B27
Gilman, Richard, 1962.B51
Gilman, William H., 1950.B25
Giordano, Frank R., Jr.,
    1972.B40
Giorgini, J., 1965.B28
"Give Them Time: Reflections
    on Faulkner," 1956.B7
"Giving Racism the Sanctity of
    Law," 1956.B35
Glasgow, Ellen, 1935.B4;
    1966.B36
Glicksberg, Charles I.,
    1949.B10-B12; 1966.B26;
    1971.B29
Gloster, Hugh M., 1948.B14;
    1949.B13
Go Down, Moses, 1942.B1, B5, B8,
    B10-B13, B15, B17-B18;
    1949.B28-B29; 1950.B10;
    1952.B26-B27; 1954.B36;
    1955.B10, B14; 1956.B27;
    1959.B43, B66; 1960.B4;
    1961.B6, B68; 1962.B120,
    B124; 1963.A1, A4, A6,
    B30, B43, B63, B81, B86;

(Go Down, Moses)
    1964.A10, B39, B46, B52;
    1965.B46, B55; 1966.A1,
    A5-A6, B35; 1967.B68,
    B71, B96; 1968.B15, B45;
    1969.B24; 1970.B2, B45,
    B50, B81; 1971.B34;
    1972.A4, B107-B108;
    1973.A2, B3, B28, B36-
    B37, B81, B98;
"Was," 1961.B68; 1963.B88;
    1966.B9, B73; 1967.B10;
    1971.B59; 1972.B28;
"The Fire and the Hearth,"
    1964.B52; 1967.B91;
"Pantaloon in Black,"
    1965.B13; 1971.B92;
    1972.B108;
"The Old People," 1961.B16;
    1965.B13; 1969.B23, B89;
    1970.B6, B45;
"The Bear", 1949.B37;
    1950.B13; 1951.B40;
    1952.B29, B56; 1953.B11,
    B26, B31, B39; 1954.B26,
    B36, B52; 1956.B23, B30;
    1958.B10, B36; 1959.B15,
    B43; 1960.B4, B15, B53;
    1961.B6, B10, B32, B66-
    B68, B74; 1962.B17, B25-
    B26, B40; 1963.A10, B1,
    B14, B47, B49-B50, B71;
    1964.A9, B15, B42, B46;
    1965.A2, B27, B42, B49,
    B67, B72; 1966.B6, B32,
    B47, B58, B64, B77;
    1967.A3, B11, B19, B62;
    1968.B40, B49, B76;
    1969.B18, B23, B32, B39,
    B61, B66, B89; 1970.B2,
    B39, B45, B75; 1971.A9,
    A11, B61, B74, B99;
    1972.B7, B12, B64;
    1973.B9-B10, B37, B81,
    B89, B100, B108;
"Delta Autumn," 1961.B68;
    1964.B46; 1969.B23;
    1970.B1, B6, B17;
    1971.B36; 1973.B37;
"Go Down, Moses," 1964.B54;
    1971.B99

Go Down, Moses typescript,
    1949.B28
"Go Down to Faulkner's Land,"
    1942.B5
Go Slow Now: Faulkner and the
    Race Question, 1971.A8
"God the Father and Motherless
    Children: Light in
    August," 1973.B21
Goellner, Jack Gordon, 1954.B41
"Götterdämmerung in Yoknapataw-
    pha," 1963.B48
Goforth, David, 1962.B52
Going, William T., 1958.B27
"Gold is Not Always," 1964.B52
Gold, Joseph, 1960.B33-B34;
    1961.B27-B28; 1962.B53-
    B54; 1963.B32; 1966.A3,
    B27; 1969.B35-B36,
    1973.B45
"Golden Book of Yoknapatawpha,"
    1962.B90; 1965.B53;
    1967.B57; 1969.B83;
    1970.B54
The Golden Bough, See Frazer,
    Sir James G.
"Golden Land," 1965.B8;
    1969.B74
Golding, William, Lord of the
    Flies, 1960.B45
Goldman, Arnold, 1971.A2, B30-
    B31
Goldsborough, Murray Lloyd,
    1965.A5
Goldstein, Melvin, 1963.B33
Golub, Lester S., 1970.B33
"The Good Earth in Light in
    August," 1964.B45
Gordon, Caroline, 1946.B4;
    1948.B15
Gorman, Thomas R., 1966.B28
Gosset, Louise Y., 1965.B29
"Gothic as Vortex: The Form of
    Horror in Capote, Faulk-
    ner, and Styron,"
    1973.B86
"Gothic Versus Romantic: A Re-
    valuation of the Gothic
    Novel," 1969.B42
Gothicism, 1932.B21; 1934.B1;
    1945.B5; 1950.B22, B27;
    1952.B46; 1956.B18;

(Gothicism)
    1960.B65; 1969.B42;
    1970.B47; 1971.B83;
    1973.B86
"Gothicism in Sanctuary,"
    1957.B14
"Gothicism in Sanctuary: The
    Black Pall and the Crap
    Table," 1956.B18
Gottesman, Ronald, and Scott
    Bennett, 1970.B55
Graham, Mary Washington,
    1963.B34
Graham, Philip, 1963.B35
"The Grain of Life," 1932.B8
Grand Guignol horror, 1931.B24;
    1934.B10; 1937.B14
Grant, Douglas, 1965.B30
Grant, William E., 1972.B41
Graves, John Temple, II,
    1942.B8
Graves, Robert, The White
    Goddess, 1967.B54
Gray, Richard, 1973.B46
Great Locomotive Chase,
    1965.B41
The Great Tradition: An Inter-
    pretation of American
    Literature Since the War,
    1933.B9
"A Great-hearted Writer Belongs
    to the Ages," 1962.B3
Greek tragedy, See Tragedy
Green, A. Wigfall, 1932.B12;
    1951.A2; 1965.A5, B31
A Green Bough, 1933.B3, B18;
    1954.B67; 1957.B27.5;
    1958.B27; 1968.B16; See
    also Poetry and The
    Marble Faun and A Green
    Bough
Green, Martin, 1963.B36
Greenberg, Alvin, 1965.B32
Greenburg, Al, 1949.B3
Greene, Graham, 1937.B9
Greene, Theodore M., 1961.B29
Greer, Dorothy D., 1962.B55
Greer, Scott, 1958.B28
Greet, Tom Y., 1950.B10;
    1957.B23
Gregory, Eileen, 1970.B34;
    1973.B47

Gregory, Horace, 1950.B11
Greiner, Donald J., 1968.B27
Grenier, Cynthia, 1956.B19;
    1957.B24
Grenier, Roger, 1962.B56
Gresham, Jewell H., 1966.B29
Gresset, Michel, 1963.B37;
    1964.B30, B31; 1966.B30-
    B31; 1967.B34; 1968.B28;
    1969.B37; 1970.A7, A16;
    1971.B18, B32; 1972.B42;
    1973.B48
Gribbin, Daniel V., 1972.B43
Griffin, Robert J., 1963.B38
Griffin, William J., 1954.B24;
    1956.B20
Griffith, Benjamin W., 1971.B33
Groseclose, Frank, 1951.B25
Gross, Beverly, 1968.B29
Grotesque, 1959.B52; 1965.B48;
    1972.B104
The Grotesque: An American
    Genre, 1962.B92
"The Grotesque-Comic in the
    Snopes Trilogy," 1965.B48
"The Grotesque in Modern Ameri-
    can Fiction," 1959.B52
Gruen, John, 1967.B35
Guérard, Albert, 1951.B27;
    1952.B18; 1956.B21
Guérard, Albert, Jr., 1951.B26;
    See also Gérard, Albert
Guereschi, Edward, 1962.B57
"La guerra civil y la novela
    norteamericana,"
    1938.B6
Guetti, James, 1967.B36
"Guides to Yoknapatawpha
    County," 1959.B2
Guilloux, Louis and Renée,
    1932.B16
Guiraldes, Ricardo, Don Segundo
    Sombra, 1959.B17
"The Gum Tree Scene: Observa-
    tions on the Structure of
    'The Bear,'" 1967.B11
"A Gun for Faulkner's Old Ben,"
    1967.B19
Gunter, James, 1957.B25
Gunter, Richard, 1969.B38
Guttmann, Allen, 1960.B35;
    1967.B37

Guyard, Marius Françoise,
    1951.B28
Gwynn, Frederick L., 1953.B19;
    1957.A1, B26; 1958.B29;
    1965.A1
Gwynn, Frederick L., and Joseph
    L. Blotner, 1957.A1;
    1965.A1

Hafley, James, 1956.B22
Hagan, John, 1962.B58; 1963.B39
Hagopian, John V., 1959.B28;
    1961.B30; 1967.B38;
    1973.B49
Hagopian, John V., and Martin
    Dolch, 1964.B32
Hahn, Otto, 1962.B59
Hale, Nancy, 1963.B34, B40, B57
Hale, William Harlan, 1957.B27
Hall, James, 1968.B30
Hall, Susan Corwin, 1965.B33
Halpenny, Francess G., 1972.B73
Halsband, Robert, 1955.B22
Hamblen, Abigail Ann, 1965.B34
Hamilton, Edith, 1952.B17, B19;
    1959.B29
Hamilton, Gary D., 1971.B34
The Hamlet, 1940.B1-B2, B5, B7-
    B10, B14-B18; 1941.B11-
    B12; 1952.B7, B44, B48;
    1955.B26, B33, B58;
    1957.B23; 1958.B5, B22,
    B31, B56; 1959.B23, B45,
    B67; 1960.A1-A2, B2, B9,
    B44, B51, B74; 1961.B34,
    B44, B58; 1962.B39, B42,
    B53, B59, B72; 1963.A1,
    A6, B12, B58; 1964.B26;
    1966.A1, B23; 1967.B23-
    24; 1968.B25-B27, B30,
    B64, B75; 1969.B1, B8,
    B68; 1970.B20; 1971.B3,
    B10, B79; 1972.B31, B51;
    1973.B55-B56, B77, B83,
    B87; See also Snopes
    Trilogy
"The Hamlet: Genesis and Re-
    visions," 1954.B48
"The Hamlet, The Town and The
    Mansion: A Psychological
    Reading of The Snopes
    Trilogy," 1973.B83

Hammond, Donald, 1967.B39
Hand, Barbara, 1972.B44
"Hand Upon the Water," 1973.B44
Handy, William J., 1959.B30;
    1971.B35
Hanoteau, Guillaume, 1958.B30
Happel, Nikolaus, 1962.B60
Harakawa, Kyoichi, 1973.B50
Harder, Kelsie B., 1958.B31;
    1959.B31
Harding, D. W., 1961.B31
"Hardly Worth While," 1930.B9
Hardwick, Elizabeth, 1948.B16;
    1951.A2
Hardy, John Edward, 1964.B33
"Hardy, Faulkner, and the
    Prosaics of Tragedy,"
    1961.B55; 1971.A2
Hardy, Thomas, 1938.B5; 1958.B1;
    1970.B42; The Mayor of
    Casterbridge, 1961.B55;
    1971.A2; Return of the
    Native, 1973.B56
Harkness, Bruce, 1967.B40
Harmon, J. W., 1965.A5
Harnack-Fisch, Mildred,
    1935.B16
Harrington, Evans B., 1952.B20
Harris, George Washington,
    Sut Lovingood's Yarns,
    1962.B72; 1967.B2;
    1972.B51
Harris, Wendell V., 1963.B41;
    1968.B31
Harrison, Jane, Themis,
    1962.B121
Harrison, Robert, 1966.B32
Hart, John A., 1961.B32
Hartt, Julian N., 1955.B23;
    1963.B42
Harter, Carol C., 1971.B36
Hartwick, Harry, 1934.B13
Harzic, Jean, 1973.A3
Hastings, John, 1954.B42
Hatcher, Harlan, 1934.B14;
    1935.B17
Hathaway, Baxter, 1964.B34
Hauck, Richard B., 1970.B35;
    1971.B37
Haugh, Robert F., 1961.B33
Haury, Beth B., 1972.B45

Hawkins, Desmond, 1940.B8
Hawkins, E. O. 1965.B35-B36
Hawthorne, Nathaniel, 1945.B1;
    1956.B46; 1957.B51;
    1959.B7; 1961.B62;
    1962.B92; The House of
    the Seven Gables,
    1970.B67; "My Kinsman,
    Major Molineux,"
    1968.B21; The Scarlet
    Letter, 1956.B46;
    1957.B16; 1964.B29;
    1965.B11; 1967.B81;
    1972.B50; "The White Old
    Maid," 1972.B4; "Young
    Goodman Brown," 1968.B21
"Hawthorne and Faulkner,"
    1956.B46
"Hawthorne and Faulkner and the
    Pearl of Great Price,"
    1967.B81
"Hawthorne and Faulkner: Some
    Common Ground,"
    1957.B51; 1962.B92
"A Hawthorne Echo in Faulkner's
    Nobel Prize Acceptance
    Speech," 1971.B24
Hawthorne to Hemingway: An
    Annotated Bibliography of
    Books from 1945 to 1963
    about nine American
    Writers, 1965.B33
Hays, Ann L., 1961.B34
Hays, Peter L., 1971.B38
"He Created Life in Fictional
    County," 1962.B123
Heald, William F., 1962.B61
Healy, George W., Jr.,
    1965.A5
"'The Heart's Driving Complex-
    ity': An Unromantic
    Reading of Faulkner's
    'The Bear'," 1960.B53
Heidegger, Martin, 1961.B18
Heilman, Robert B., 1952.B21-B22
Heimer, Jackson W., 1973.B51
Heiney, Donald W., 1955.B24
"Hell Creek Bottom Is: A
    Reminiscence," 1968.B80
Heller, Terry, 1972.B46
Hellman, Lilian F., 1927.B5

506

Hellström, Gustaf, 1971.B39
Hemenway, Robert, 1970.B36
"The 'Hemingwaves' in Faulkner's
    Wild Palms," 1959.B56
Hemingway, Ernest, 1930.B1, B5;
    1932.B13-B14, B16, B18-
    B19; 1935.B11, B18;
    1936.B4; 1939.B23;
    1952.B56; 1954.B22;
    1955.B6, B44; 1956.B4,
    B9, B29, B39; 1957.B52,
    B70; 1959.B28, B47;
    1961.B11; 1962.B25, B91;
    1964.B25; 1965.B3;
    1966.B41; 1971.B70;
    1972.B23, B66; Death in
    the Afternoon, 1932.B13;
    A Farewell to Arms,
    1959.B49, B56; 1960.B57;
    1962.B91; 1966.B55, 59;
    1972.B66; For Whom the
    Bell Tolls, 1971.B70;
    "My Old Man," 1968.B50;
    The Old Man and the Sea,
    1962.B25; 1967.B12; The
    Sun Also Rises, 1966.B41
    The Torrents of Spring,
    1934.B18-B19; 1972.B66
"Hemingway and Fitzgerald in
    Sound and Fury,"
    1966.B41
"Hemingway and Faulkner: The
    Pattern of their
    Thought," 1956.B39
◆Hemingway and Faulkner: Two
    Masters of the Modern
    Short Story," 1952.B56
"Hemingway, Faulkner, and Wolfe
    . . . and the Common
    Reader," 1968.B9
"Hemingways 'My Old Man' und
    Faulkners 'Barn Burning':
    Ein Vergleich," 1968.B50
Henderson, Philip, 1936.B10
Hendrick, George, 1970.B29
Hennecke, Hans, 1957.B27.5
Hergesheimer, Joseph, 1969.B30
Hermann, John, 1970.B37
Hepburn, Kenneth W., 1971.B40

"Heritage of a Generation of
    Novelists: Anderson and
    Dreiser, Hemingway,
    Faulkner, Farrell and
    Steinbeck," 1949.B22
"Hero in As I Lay Dying,"
    1954.B68
"The Hero in the New World:
    William Faulkner's 'The
    Bear,'" 1951.B40
The Hero with the Private Parts,
    1966.B48
"Ein Herr aus den Sudstaaten:
    Besuch bei William Faulk-
    ner," 1957.B34
Herron, Ima Honaker, 1939.B15
Heseltine, H. P., 1972.B47
Hettich, Blaise, 1956.B23
Hewes, Henry, 1959.B32
Hickerson, Thomas Felix, 1964.A6
Hicks, Granville, 1931.B21;
    1932.B14; 1933.B9;
    1951.B29-B30; 1959.B33;
    1962.B62
The Hidden God: Studies in
    Hemingway, Faulkner,
    Yeats, Eliot, and Warren,
    1963.B14
Hierbas, Purpura y Magnolias,
    1973.B89
Hieronymus, Clara, 1970.A2
Highet, Gilbert, 1954.B43
Hill, Archibald, 1964.B35
"The Hill," 1973.B70
"The Hill-Billies," 1951.B48
Hines, Tom S., Jr., 1965.A5
Hirano, Nabuyuki, 1967.B41
Hirschleifer, Phyllis, 1949.B14
Histoire littéraire des États-
    Unis, 1953.B4
Historia de la Literatura Uni-
    versal, 1959.B69
History, 1958.B6; 1960.B21;
    1962.A1; 1967.B17, B60;
    1968.B54; 1969.B11, B52;
    1970.B41, B82; 1971.B49;
    1972.B13, B18, B49, B72,
    B77; 1973.B46, B52, B57,
    B109
"History and Legend in William
    Faulkner's 'Red Leaves,'"
    1973.B60

"History, Tragedy and the Imagi-
nation in Absalom,
Absalom!," 1963.B13
"The Historical Novel and the
Southern Past: The Case
of Absalom, Absalom!,"
1970.B82
Hoadley, Frank M., 1957.B28
Hoar, Jere R., 1961.B35
Hodgson, John A., 1971.B41
Hoffman, Daniel, 1969.B39
Hoffman, Frederick J., 1951.A2,
B31; 1955.B25; 1960.B36-
B37; 1961.A3; 1966.A4;
1967.B42; 1968.B32
Hoffman, Frederick J., and Olga
W. Vickery, 1950.A1;
1957.A1; 1960.A1
Hoffmann, A. C., 1951.B31;
1953.B20
Hoffmann, E. T. A., 1933.B13
Hogan, Patrick G., Jr.,
1957.B29; 1963.B43-B44;
1966.B33-B35; 1971.A8
Hogan, Patrick G., Jr., Dale A.
Myers, and John E.
Turner, 1966.B35
Holland, Norman N., 1972.B48
Holley, John Reed, 1965.A5
Holly Springs, Miss., 1961.B14
Hollywood, California, 1939.B24;
1959.B70; 1961.B61;
1964.B28; 1965.B50;
1967.B7; 1968.A6;
1969.B74
Hollywood in Fiction: Some
Versions of the American
Myth, 1969.B74
"Hollywooden Hero," 1939.B23
Holman, C. Hugh, 1958.B32;
1966.B36; 1969.B16;
1971.B42; 1972.B49
Holmes, Edward M., 1966.A5;
1972.B50
"Honest But Slap-Dash," 1926.B4
"Hong Li," 1973.B90
"'Hong Li' and Royal Street:
The New Orleans Sketches
in Manuscript," 1973.B90
"Honor," 1973.B67
Hooper, Johnson Jones, 1959.B23
Hooper, Vincent, 1947.B4

Hopkins, Viola, 1955.B26
Hornback, Vernon T., Jr.
1965.B37
Hornberger, Theodore, 1953.B21
"'The Horns of Dawn,'" Faulkner
and Metaphor," 1973.B75
"The Horrible South," 1935.B19
"Horrors, Charm, Fun,"
1940.B7
Horsch, Janice, 1964.B36
Houghton, Donald E., 1970.B38
"The Hound," 1934.B11; 1957.B31
The House of Fiction, 1948.B15
"The House of the Seven Gables
and Absalom, Absalom!:
Time, Tradition and
Guilt," 1970.B67
The Houses That James Built and
Other Literary Studies,
1961.B64
Housman, A. E., 1933.B3;
1954.B67; 1968.B16;
1971.B64; 1972.B11
"A Housman Source in The Sound
and the Fury," 1972.B11
Hovde, Carl F., 1964.B37
"How a Writer Finds His
Material," 1965.B72
"How Colonel Falkner Built His
Railroad," 1967.B86
"How Do You Read Faulkner?,"
1957.B30
"How Faulkner Went His Way and I
Went Mine," 1967.B76
"'How Much It Takes to Compound
a Man,' A Neglected Scene
in Go Down, Moses,"
1973.B37
"How to Misread Faulkner: A
Powerful Plea for Inno-
cence," 1956.B20
"How to Read The Sound and the
Fury," 1962.B43
Howard, Alan B., 1972.B51
Howard, Brian, 1938.B10
Howard, Edwin, 1965.B38-B39
Howard, Leon, 1960.B38
Howe, Irving, 1948.B17;
1949.B15-B16; 1951.B33-
B35; 1952.A1, B17;
1954.B44-B45; 1959.B34;
1962.A2, B63-B64;
1963.B45

Howe, Russell Warren, 1956.B16,
    B24-B26; 1967.B80
Howell, Elmo, 1958.B33;
    1959.B35-B37; 1960.B39;
    1961.B36-B37; 1962.B65-
    B68; 1964.B38; 1965.B40-
    B42; 1966.B37-B41;
    1967.B43-B51; 1968.B33-
    B35; 1969.B40-B41;
    1970.B39-B41; 1972.B52-
    B53; 1973.B52
Howorth, Lucy Somerville,
    1965.B43
Hubbell, Jay Broadus, 1955.B27;
    1972.B54
"Huck Finn and The Bear: The
    Wilderness and Moral
    Freedom," 1969.B61
"Huck Finn in the House of
    Usher: The Comic and
    Grotesque Worlds of The
    Hamlet," 1972.B51
Hudson, Tommy, 1950.B12
Hughes, Richard, 1930.B10;
    1931.B1, B22, B33;
    1963.B46; 1964.B1, B4
Hull, Cecil, 1965.A5
Hulme, T. E., 1962.B26
Humanism, 1954.A2, B1; 1955.B23,
    B31-B32; 1957.B52;
    1958.B12; 1959.A2;
    1960.B33; 1961.B27, B63,
    B74; 1962.B15, B54, B98;
    1963.B2, B51, B67;
    1966.A3, B72; 1967.B42,
    B79; 1968.B62; 1969.B51;
    1970.B16; 1972.B25;
    1973.B62, B89
"The Humanism of William Faulk-
    ner," 1960.B33
"The Humanities: Something
    More: On Camera: Welty
    on Faulkner," 1965.B82
Hume, Robert D., 1969.B42
"Humor as Structure and Theme in
    Faulkner's Trilogy,"
    1964.B3
"The Humor of The Hamlet,"
    1967.B24
Humphrey, Robert, 1952.B23;
    1954.B46

Huneker, James G., 1963.B53
Hunt, Joel A., 1967.B52;
    1969.B43; 1970.B63
Hunt, John W., 1965.A2;
    1972.B55-B56
Hunt, Wallace, 1952.B24
Hunter, Edwin R., 1973.A4
Hunter, Marjorie, 1962.B69
Hunting, 1960.B71; 1961.A2;
    1968.B49; 1969.B39;
    1970.B50
Hurt, Lester E., 1964.B39
Hutchens, John K., 1948.B18
Hutcherson, Dudley R., 1959.B38
Hutchinson, D., 1973.B53
Hutchinson, E. R., 1963.B47
Hutchinson, James D., 1968.B36
Hutten, Robert W., 1973.B54
Huxley, Aldous, 1964.B4
Huxley, Julian Sorell, 1935.B18
Hyman, Stanley Edgar, 1958.B34;
    1962.B70

I Hear America. . . Literature
    in the United States
    Since 1900, 1937.B12
"I Look at American Fiction,"
    1939.B6
I Wanted to Write, 1949.B27
"Ichabod Crane in Yoknapataw-
    pha," 1962.B42
The Idea of an American Novel,
    1961.B2, B4, B71
The Idea of the South, 1964.B63
"Ideas and Queries," 1952.B45
"Identity Diffusion: Joe
    Christmas and Quentin
    Compson," 1967.B88
"The Idiot Boy in Mississippi:
    Faulkner's The Sound and
    the Fury," 1955.B59
Idyll in the Desert, 1931.B8;
    1972.B90
"'If I Just Had a Mother':
    Faulkner's Quentin Comp-
    son," 1973.B85
Igoe, W. J., 1962.B71
"Ike McCaslin and Chick Mallison:
    Faulkner's Emerging
    Southern Hero," 1963.B71

Isaacs, Neil D., 1961.B38;
   1963.B48
Israel, Calvin, 1968.B37
"It is a Nightmare World,
   Wearing a Mask of
   Reality," 1961.B2
Izard, Barbara, and Clara
   Hieronymus, 1970.A2
Izsak, Emily K., 1967.B53

Jack, Peter Munro, 1939.B14
Jackson, Charles, The Lost Week-
   end, 1968.B28
Jackson, Esther Merle, 1962.B73
Jackson, James Turner, 1946.B5
Jackson, Naomi, 1967.B54
Jacobs, Robert D., 1953.B15,
   B22, B32, B40; 1957.B30;
   1961.B39; 1973.B55
Jacobson, Dan, The Evidence of
   Love, 1960.B5
Jaffard, Paul, 1953.B23
Jäger, Dietrich, 1968.B38-B39
James, Henry, 1961.B64; The
   American, 1964.B11
James, Stuart, 1971.B46
James, William, 1968.B36
"Jane Cook and Cecilia Farmer,"
   1965.B36
Jankovic, Mira, 1964.B41
"The Janus Symbol in As I Lay
   Dying," 1955.B30
Jarlot, Gerard, 1946.B6
Jarrett, David, 1973.B56
Jarrett-Kerr, Martin, 1970.A3
"Jason Compson and the Costs of
   Speculation," 1969.B14
"Jason Compson: Humor, Hostil-
   ity, and the Rhetoric of
   Aggression," 1969.B58
"Jason Compson: The Demands of
   Honor," 1971.B98
"Jason Compson's Paranoid
   Pseudocommunity,"
   1970.B61
Jeffers, Robinson, 1931.B21;
   1932.B23; 1933.B9, B12;
   1934.B14; "Roan Stal-
   lion," 1965.B24; "Tamar,"
   1969.B56; 1971.B57;
   1972.B45

"Jeffers' 'Tamar' and Faulkner's
   The Wild Palms," 1971.B57
"The Jefferson Courthouse: An
   Axis Exsecrabilis Mundi,"
   1969.B17
Jelliffe, Robert A., 1956.A2;
   1968.A6
Jennings, Elizabeth, 1967.B55
Jensen, Eric G., 1964.B42
"Jeunesse de Faulkner,"
   1964.B55
Jewkes, W. T., 1961.B40
Jobe, Phyllis, 1958.B36
"Joe Christmas and the 'Social
   Self,'" 1958.B28
"Joe Christmas, Faulkner's
   Marginal Man," 1960.B58
"Joe Christmas: The Hero in
   the Modern World,"
   1957.B38; 1960.A1
"Joe Christmas: The Tyranny of
   Childhood," 1971.B1
"John Dos Passos," 1932.B14
"John Faulkner: An Annotated
   Checklist of His Pub-
   lished Works and His
   Papers," 1970.B84
"John Faulkner's Vanishing
   South," 1971.B94
"John Sartoris, Friend or Foe?,"
   1967.B78
Johnson, C. W. M., 1948.B19
Johnson, Gerald W., 1935.B19
Jones, Howard Mumford, 1935.B20;
   1949.B17
Jones, Lionidas M. 1957.B31
Jones, Madison, The Buried Land,
   1963.B73
Jordan, Robert M., 1960.B40
"Joseph Conrad, William Faulk-
   ner, and the Nobel Prize
   Speech," 1967.B92
Josephson, Matthew, 1933.B10
Josephus, Antiquities of the
   Jews, 1969.B81
"Journey South," 1955.B7
Joyce, James, 1926.B4; 1929.B8;
   1930.B4; 1931.B20;
   1935.B2, B22; 1937.B10;
   1948.B28; 1953.B4;
   1955.B58; 1957.B13, B19,
   B26; 1959.B6; 1961.B24;
   1963.A9; Portrait of the

"Knowledge and Experience in
      Faulkner's Light in
      August," 1973.B101
Kobler, J. F., 1972.B60
Köhler, Mathilda, 1957.B34
Kohler, Dayton, 1949.B18-B19;
      1955.B31-B32
Korn, Karl, 1938.B11
Kowalczyk, Richard L., 1966.B44
Krause, Sydney J., 1964.B15
Kreuz, Hieronymo, 1963.B53
Kreymborg, Alfred, 1969.B47
Krieger, Murray, 1971.B49
Krim, Seymour, 1951.B38
Kronenberger, Louis, 1926.B7;
      1938.B12; 1940.B9
Krutch, Joseph Wood, 1956.B29
Kubie, Lawrence, 1934.B3, B15,
      B24; 1935.B6
Kulin, Katalin, 1971.B50
Kulseth, Leonard I., 1969.B50
Kunkel, Francis L., 1965.B47

Labor, Earle, 1959.B39
LaBudde, Kenneth, 1950.B13
"The Lady of The Dakota,"
      1965.B63
LaFrance, Marston, 1967.B74
Lamar, L. Q. C., 1969.B71
Lambert, J. W., 1962.B80
Lamont, William H. F., 1958.B39
Lanati, Barbara, 1968.B41
Lancess, Harold, 1958.B22
Landmarks of American Writing,
      1969.B39
Landor, Mikhail, 1968.B42;
      1972.B61
"The Landscape in Light in
      August," 1970.B62
Lang, Beatrice, 1973.B59
Langford, Beverly Young, 1973.B60
Langford, Gerald, 1931.B23;
      1971.A4; 1972.A5, B62,
      B93; 1973.B61
Langford, Richard E., 1963.B38
Langford, Richard E., and
      William E. Taylor,
      1966.B59
Langston, Albert Douglas Beach,
      1961.B42

"Language of Irony: Quiet Words
      and Violent Acts in
      Light in August,"
      1971.B102
"The Language of Faulkner's 'The
      Bear,'" 1961.B10
Lanier, Sidney, "Corn," 1972.B76
Lanzinger, Klaus, 1966.B77
Larbaud, Valéry, 1934.B16;
      1936.B11; 1950.B15;
      1966.B31
"Les larrons," 1964.B30
Larsen, Eric E., 1967.B59
"The Last Gentleman," 1968.B37
"The Last of the Snopeses,"
      1959.B33
"The Last of William Faulkner,"
      1962.B4; 1965.B30
"The Last Scene of Sanctuary,"
      1972.B81
"Latter-Day Christ Story,"
      1954.B38
Latorre, Mariano, The Old Woman
      of Peralillo, 1954.B61
Lauras, Antoine, 1962.B81
Lawrence, D. H., 1949.B37;
      St. Mawr, 1965.B24
Laws, Frederick, 1937.B10
Lawson, Lewis A., 1965.B48;
      1971.B51
Lawton, Mary, 1936.B12
LeBreton, Maurice, 1937.B11;
      1939.B17; 1951.B39;
      1959.B40
Leach, Macedward, 1966.B45
Leaf, Mark, 1970.B46
Lear, Edward, 1960.B39
Leary, Lewis, 1964.A8; 1965.B4;
      1971.B52; 1973.A5
Leaver, Florence, 1955.B33;
      1958.B40; 1960.A1
Leavis, F. R., 1933.B11
Lebende Antike: Symposium für
      Rudolph Suhnel 1967.B103
Lee, Edwy B., 1954.B47
Lee, Jim, 1961.B43
"Leg," 1934.B1
Legend of the South, 1945.B2;
      1949.B22; 1950.B10, B18;
      1951.B34, B55; 1952.A1,
      B14, B29; 1953.B27;
      1956.B33, B41; 1960.B62;

McCole, Camille, 1935.B22;
 1937.B13
McCormick, John, 1957.B43;
 1971.B55
McCullers, Carson, 1941.B9;
 1971.B56
McDonald, Walter R., 1967.B62;
 1968.B43; 1972.B64-B65
McDonald, W. U., Jr., 1963.B58
McElderry, B. R., Jr., 1958.B41-
 B42
McGill, Ralph, 1935.B23; 1954.B51
McGinnis, John H., 1932.B19;
 1953.B38
McGlynn, Paul D., 1969.B55
McGrew, Julia, 1959.B44
McHaney, Thomas L., 1966.B49-B50;
 1969.B56; 1970.B50;
 1971.B57-B58; 1972.B66-
 B67; 1973.B66
McIlwaine, Shields, 1939.B20;
 1940.B10
McKean, Keith F., 1960.B43
MacLachlan, John M., 1945.B4;
 1953.B25; 1960.B44
Maclaren-Ross, Julian, 1955.B38;
 1965.B51
McLaughlin, Richard, 1951.B41
Maclean, Hugh N., 1954.B52
MacLeish, Archibald, 1951.B42;
 1967.B63
McLuhan, Herbert Marshall,
 1947.B5; 1969.B57
MacLure, Millar, 1956.B33;
 1960.B45-B46;1964.B49
MacMillan, Duane, 1973.B67
McNeir, Waldo, and Leo B. Levy,
 1960.B55
McWilliams, Dean, 1972.B68
Madden, Charles F., 1968.B24
Madden, David, 1970.B1
Madeya, Ulrike, 1970.B51
Madge, Charles, 1935.B24
"The Magic of William Faulkner,"
 1942.B13
"The Magic World Within the
 Mind," 1961.B24
Magny, Claude-Edmonde, 1948.B20;
 1949.B31; 1954.B53;
 1972.B69
Mair, John, 1939.B21

"A Major Revision in Faulkner's
 A Fable," 1973.B54
"Make-Beliefs," 1930.B12
Makers of the Modern World,
 1955.B60
The Making of Go Down, Moses,
 1972.A4
"The Making of a Myth: Sartoris,"
 1958.B62; 1959.A4
Malbone, Raymond G., 1971.B59
Malcolm, Donald, 1957.B44
Malherbe, Henry, 1943.B4
Malin, Irving, 1957.A2
Malraux, André, 1933.B13;
 1952.B31; 1957.B1
Man and Literature, 1943.B5
Man and the Movies, 1967.B7
"The Man Behind the Faulkner
 Myth," 1953.B14
Man in Motion: Faulkner's Tri-
 logy, 1961.A1
"Man in Recent Literature,"
 1959.B58
Man in the Modern Novel,
 1964.B33
Manglaviti, Leo M. J., 1972.B70
Mailer, Norman, Why Are We in
 Vietnam?, 1971.B61
Manila, Philippines, 1956.A1
Mann, Thomas, 1951.B43; 1952.B42;
 1959.B52; "Mario und die
 Zauberer," 1967.B52
"'A Man's Voice, Speaking':
 A Continuum of American
 Humor," 1972.B116
Mansions of the Spirit: Essays
 in Literature and Reli-
 gion, 1967.B71
The Mansion, 1959.B33-B34, B41,
 B46, B54-B55, B77;
 1960.B8, B25, B50, B52;
 1961.B1, B29, B31, B44,
 B58; 1962.B39, B90, B103,
 B125; 1964.A10, B38, B69;
 1969.B1, B19, B49;
 1970.B46; 1972.B25;
 1973.B83; See also Snopes
 Trilogy
Manuscripts and typescripts,
 See Faulkner's Manuscripts
 and Typescripts

"Memory-Narrative in Absalom,
Absalom!," 1953.B42
"Memphis in Fiction: Rural
Values in an Urban Set-
ting," 1972.B98
Memphis, Tenn., 1972.B98
Men Without Art, 1934.B19
"Men Without Faces," 1926.B3
Mencken, H. L., 1971.B76;
1972.B70
"Mencken, Faulkner, and Southern
Moralism," 1971.B76
Mercer, Caroline, and Susan J.
Turner, 1959.B45
Mercier, Vivian, 1954.B54
Meriwether, James B., 1957.B47-
B48; 1959.B46-B48;
1960.B47; 1961.A4, B47-
B49; 1962.B85-B86;
1963.B61-B62; 1964.B51;
1965.B53; 1967.B70;
1969.B59; 1970.A5-A6,
B54-B55; 1971.A5, B64-
B67; 1972.B72-B74;
1973.B69-B70
Meriwether, James B., and
Michael Millgate,
1968.A6, B44
The Merrill Studies in Light in
August, 1971.A3
The Merrill Studies in The Sound
and the Fury, 1970.A6,
B34
Merton, Thomas, 1967.B71;
1968.B45; 1973.B71
Merwin, W. S., 1957.B49
Michel, Laurence, 1970.B56
The Middle Distance: A Compara-
tive History of American
Imaginative Literature,
1971.B55
Milano, Paolo, 1948.B22
Miles, George, 1949.B21
Millay, Edna St.Vincent,
1969.B47
Milledge, Luetta Upshur,
1963.B63
Miller, David, 1967.B72
Miller, Douglas T., 1963.B64
Miller, James E., Jr., 1967.B73
Miller, Wayne Charles, 1970.B57
Millett, Fred B., 1940.B11

Millgate, Jane, 1964.B52;
1968.B46
Millgate, Michael, 1961.A5, B50;
1962.B87; 1963.B65;
1964.B53; 1966.A6, B52;
1967.B74; 1968.A6, B44,
B47; 1971.A6, B68-B69;
1972.B75-B77; 1973.B72-
B74
Mills, Ralph J., Jr., 1961.B51
Milne, A. A., When We Were Very
Young, 1963.B17
Milton, John, Paradise Lost,
1964.B3
Milum, Richard A., 1973.B75
"The Mind of Vardaman Bundren,"
1960.B73
Miner, Ward L., 1952.A2;
1956.B36; 1959.B2;
1966.B53
"Mink Agonistes," 1960.b50
"Mink Snopes and Faulkner's
Moral Conclusions,"
1968.B33
"Minor Faulkner," 1949.B15
Minority Report, 1940.B6
Minter, David L., 1969.A5
"Mirror Analogues in The Sound
and the Fury,"
1952.B53; 1954.B75;
1960.A1
"Mirror Imagery in The Sound and
the Fury," 1969.B31
Mirrors of Chartres Street,
1954.B1
"Mirrors of Chartres Street,"
1965.A4; 1966.B34
Misanthropy, 1933.B9; 1934.B20;
See also Misogyny
"Miscegenation and its Meaning
in Go Down, Moses,"
1970.B81
Misogyny, 1942.B7; 1957.B18;
1961.B76; 1966.B67;
1973.B51
"Miss Hale's Faulkner Caricature
Explained," 1963.B34,
B40, B57
"Miss Havisham and Miss Grier-
son," 1958.B54
"Miss Quentin's Paternity
Again," 1960.B19

Moose, Roy C., 1948.B23

"Moral and Temporal Order in The Sound and the Fury," 1953.B41

"Moral Awareness in 'Dry September,'" 1954.B8

"A Moral Play," 1952.B43

"The Moral World of Faulkner," 1966.B18

"A Moralist with a Corn-Cob: A Study of William Faulkner," 1934.B18-B19

"Morality and Act: A Study of Faulkner's As I Lay Dying," 1973.B79

"Morality in 'Spotted Horses,'" 1962.B61

Moravia, Alberto, Il Conformista, 1973.B20

"More Gold Medals," 1951.B57

"More Light Needed," 1932.B26

Morell, Giliane, 1972.B81

Morgan, Frederick, 1952.B36

Morillo, Marvin, 1966.B54

Morley, Christopher, 1933.B15

Morris, Lawrence S., 1926.B9; 1929.B6

Morris, Lloyd, 1949.B22

Morris, Wright, 1952.B37; 1958.B45

Morrison, Sister Kristin, 1961.B52

The Mortgaged Heart, 1971.B56

Moseley, Edwin M., 1963.B66

Moses, Edwin, 1973.B77

Moses, W. R., 1953.B26; 1956.B37; 1957.B14; 1959.B49; 1962.B90; 1966.B55

Mosquitoes, 1926.B1; 1927.B1-B7; 1953.B19; 1958.B2, B61; 1961.B3; 1962.B86, B99, B108; 1963.A4, B46, B69; 1964.B1, B4, B27, B75; 1965.A4; 1966.B42, B74; 1969.A6, B22, B30; 1970.B20; 1971.B15, B40, B100

Motion pictures, 1959.B70; 1973.B33, B88

Mottram, Eric, 1971.A7

Mottram, R. N., The Spanish Farm, 1973.B73

Motyleva, Tamara L., 1966.B56

"Mountain Victory," 1934.B2; 1962.B68; 1972.B59

Muehl, Lois, 1967.B75; 1968.B48; 1972.B82

Mueller, William R., 1959.B50; 1963.B67

Muhlenfeld, Elisabeth, 1972.B83; 1973.B78

Muir, Edward H., 1971.B71

Mullen, Phillip E., 1965.A5; 1966.B57

Muller, Herbert Joseph, 1937.B14

Mulqueen, James E., 1968.B49

"El mundo complejo de William Faulkner," 1959.B22

"El mundo novelesco y real de William Faulkner," 1958.B38

Munson, Gorham Bert, 1931.B24; 1932.B16

Murphy, Frank, 1961.B53

Music, 1931.B34; 1938.B7; 1939.B3; 1943.B4; 1954.B60; 1962.B44; 1963.A9; 1967.B1, B8; 1968.B12

Muste, John M., 1965.B55; 1966.B35

"Muste's 'Failure of Love in Faulkner's Go Down, Moses,'" 1966.B35

My Brother Bill: An Affectionate Reminiscence, 1963.A2

"My Faulkner: The Untranslatable Demon," 1973.B23

"My Friend, William Faulkner," 1965.B50

"My Grandmother Millard, General Nathan Bedford Forrest, and the Battle of Harrykin Creek," 1963.A6; 1970.B41

Myers, Dale A., 1966.B35

Myers, Walter L., 1930.B12

Myres, W. V., 1969.B60

"The Myriad Perspectives of Absalom, Absalom!," 1954.B69

"Mysticism in 'Go Down, Moses,'"
1964.B39
"Mystique et tragique de Faulk-
ner," 1949.B30
Myth and Literature: Contempo-
rary Theory and Practice,
1966.B47
"Myth and Manners in Sartoris,"
1962.B106
"Myth and Modern Literature,"
1939.B7
"Myth and Ritual in Light in
August," 1960.B59
Myth and Symbol: Critical
Approaches and Applica-
tions, 1963.B50
"Myth and Symbol in Criticism of
Faulkner's 'The Bear,'"
1963.B50
"Myth and Truth About America's
South," 1958.B47
Myth criticism
  Absalom, Absalom!, 1963.B5;
    1964.B44; 1972.B78;
    1973.B109
  As I Lay Dying, 1934.B16;
    1961.B20; 1962.B78;
    1966.B16
  "The Bear," 1953.B26;
    1963.B50; 1966.B47;
    1969.B39; 1972.B7
  "Dry September," 1962.B121;
    1965.B24
  General, 1959.A3; 1968.A1-A2;
    1969.B17
  Light in August, 1961.B42;
    1963.B66
  "Pantaloon in Black," 1971.B92
  Sanctuary, 1963.B78;
    1971.B58
  The Sound and the Fury,
    1957.B13; 1961.B7
The Myth of America: Essays in
the Structures of
Literary Imagination,
1973.B99-B100
The Myth of Southern History:
Historical Consciousness
in Twentieth-Century
Southern Literature,
1970.B21

Myth of the South; See Legend
of the South and Saga
Theory
"The Mythic Background of Faulk-
ner's Horse Imagery,"
1965.B24
"Mythical Elements of 'Pantaloon
in Black,'" 1971.B92
Mythical method, 1963.A9;
1967.B103; 1968.A1-A2;
1971.B58
"Myth-Makers and the South's
Dilemma," 1945.B5
"La mythologie faulknérienne
dans Pylon," 1945.B3
"Mythos und Ethos Amerikas im
Werk William Faulkner,"
1958.B11
Myths and Realities: Conflicting
Values in America,
1972.B98

Nadeau, Robert L., 1973.B79
Nagel, James, 1969.B61
"A Name for Faulkner's City,"
1968.B34
Name studies:
  "Barn Burning," 1971.B106
  General, 1959.B31; 1963.B4;
    1970.B9
  Go Down, Moses ("Callina"
    McCaslin), 1963.B43
  Light in August, 1970.B19
  Snopes Trilogy (Suratt,
    Ratliff), 1971.B47;
    (Snopes), 1973.B104
  The Sound and the Fury (Benjy),
    1968.B55 and 1972.B30;
    (Jason), 1958.B7;
    1961.B7; 1969.B81;
    1972.B76;
  "Wash," 1968.B72
"Names of Characters in Faulk-
ner's The Sound and the
Fury," 1958.B7
"Narrative Management in As I
Lay Dying," 1967.B29
Narrative Situations in the
Novel, 1971.B90
"The Narrative Structure of Light
in August," 1958.B41-B42

Notes on a Horsethief, 1951.B1;
    1953.B10; 1956.B3;
    1960.B20; 1973.B23, B54
"Notes on a Rear-Guard Action,"
    1964.B63; 1967.B84
"Notes on Faulkner and Flaubert,"
    1948.B15
"Notes on Faulkner's 'Light in
    August'," 1951.B11
"Notes on Mr. Faulkner,"
    1947.B10
"Notes on Recent Novels,"
    1937.B17
"Notes on the Surnames of Faulk-
    ner's Characters,"
    1970.B9
"Notes on the Textual History
    of The Sound and the
    Fury," 1962.B85; 1970.B55
"Notes on the Unrevised Galleys
    of Faulkner's Sanctuary,"
    1956.B34
"The Not-So-Mythical Town of
    Jefferson, Miss.,"
    1962.B122
Novas Calvo, Lino, 1933.B16
The Novel and the World's
    Dilemma, 1947.B2
"The Novel Faulkner Never Wrote:
    His Golden Book or
    Doomsday Book,"
    1970.B54
"The Novel in the South,"
    1943.B7; 1972.B49
"Novel of the Twenties,"
    1964.B27
The Novel of Violence in America,
    1957.B20
The Novel Today (Henderson),
    1936.B10; (Allen),
    1960.B3
The Novelist and the Passion
    Story, 1960.B24
"Novelist Gives Forth on Work,
    Food, Football,"
    1951.B37
"The Novelist in the American
    South," 1959.B65
Novelists' America: Fiction as
    History, 1910-1940,
    1969.B4

The Novels of William Faulkner,
    1959.A4; 1964.A10
"Novila de William Faulkner,"
    1934.B4; 1968.B19
"Nympholepsy," 1973.B70

Obituaries, 1962.B1-B5, B9, B32,
    B46, B114; 1963.B27
Obituary summaries, 1962.B115,
    B119, B122-B123, B127
La Obra de William Faulkner,
    1953.A1
O'Brien, Edward J., 1935.B26
O'Brien, Frances Blazer,
    1961.B54
O'Brien, Kate, 1939.B25;
    1942.B10
O'Brien, Matthew C., 1968.B52;
    1973.B84
Occasions and Protests, 1964.B19
O'Connor, William Van, 1952.B38-
    B39; 1953.B27-B31;
    1954.A2; 1955.B41;
    1957.B51; 1958.B46;
    1959.A2, B52-B53;
    1960.A1, B52; 1962.B91-
    B92; 1966.B59; 1968.A7
O'Dea, Richard J., 1968.B53
Odets, Clifford, Awake and Sing!,
    1971.B77
O'Donnell, George Marion,
    1932.B17; 1939.B26;
    1943.B6; 1951.A2;
    1959.B33; 1960.A1;
    1971.B79
"An Odor of Verbena," See The
    Unvanquished
Odum, Howard W., 1953.B32
"Of Mules and Men: Faulkner and
    Silone," 1963.B82
"Of Time and Character in The
    Sound and the Fury,"
    1966.B25
"Of Time and the Novel"
    (Harris), 1968.B31;
    (Fetz), 1969.B28
O'Faolain, Sean, 1935.B27;
    1956.B38
"The Old Frenchman Place: Sym-
    bol of a Lost Civiliza-
    tion," 1968.B26

527

(Oxford, Miss.)
    1952.A2, B48; 1954.A1;
    1961.A2, B14, B35;
    1962.B28; 1963.A2;
    1964.A4, B61; 1965.A5,
    B58-B59; 1967.A1;
    1969.B64; 1970.B15;
    1971.B13; 1972.B2, B53,
    B67, B88; 1973.B68, B84,
    B113
"Oxford, Miss., Which Faulkner
    Transcended, Is As He
    Left It," 1973.B113
"Oxford, Mississippi," 1929.B4;
    1961.B35; 1965.B59;
    1969.B64

P., J., 1949.B24
Page, Ralph, 1967.B78
Page, Sally R., 1972.A6;
    1973.B78
Page, Thomas Nelson, 1935.B31:
    1965.B40; Two Little
    Confederates, 1962.B113
Painting, 1962.B1; 1964.B79;
    1971.B97; 1973.B66
"The Pairing of The Sound and
    the Fury and As I Lay
    Dying," 1957.B13
Palievsky, Pyotr V., 1972.B85
Palmer, William J., 1967.B79
"Les palmiers sauvages:
    Structure et unité du
    roman," 1957.B14
"Pampas and Big Woods: Heroic
    Initiation in Guiraldes
    and Faulkner," 1959.B17
Panichas, George, 1967.B71;
    1971.B51
"Panorama de la actual literatura
    joven norteamericana,"
    1937.B6
"Pantaloon in Black," See Go
    Down, Moses
"Paradox in Faulkner's Intruder
    in the Dust," 1973.B58
"Paradoxal Faulkner," 1962.B81
"The Parallel Philosophy of
    Emerson's Nature and
    Faulkner's The Bear,"
    1958.B10

"Parnassus in the 1920's: Floyd
    Dell Contemplates His Own
    Period," 1967.B18
"Parentheses in Faulkner's
    Absalom, Absalom!,"
    1971.B85
Parkes, H. B., 1940.B12
Parks, Edd Winfield, 1937.B15;
    1956.B39; 1957.B52
"Parmi les livres," 1934.B27
Parsons, Thornton, 1969.B63
Partlow, Robert, 1969.B29
"Party of One," 1955.B17
Party of One, 1955.B18
Paschal, Walter, 1936.B14
The Passive Voice: An Approach
    to Modern Fiction,
    1966.B43
"The Past and Future of William
    Faulkner," 1931.B21
"The Past in the Present: A
    Reading of Go Down,
    Moses," 1971.B34
Pate, Willard, 1968.B55;
    1969.B64
Paterson, Isabel, 1936.B15
Paterson, John, 1961.B55
Patten, Mercury, 1933.B17
"The Pattern and Devices in
    Light in August,"
    1968.B73
"The Pattern of Nightmare in
    Sanctuary; or Miss Reba's
    Dogs," 1970.B68
"The Pattern of Thought in Light
    in August," 1970.B86
Patterns of Commitment in
    American Literature,
    1967.B74
"Pattern in Faulkner's Sanctuary
    and Requiem for a Nun,"
    1963.B35
Patty, James S., 1965.B19
Paulding, Gouverneur, 1954.B56;
    1957.B53; 1959.B54;
    1962.B93
Pavese, Cesare, 1934.B21;
    1953.B33; 1962.B94;
    1970.B59
Payne, Ladell, 1969.B65
Pearce, Richard, 1966.B60;
    1970.B60; 1971.B77

Pearson, Norman Holmes, 1952.B40;
1954.B57; 1962.B95
Peavy, Charles D., 1966.B61, B63;
1967.B80; 1968.B56-B57;
1970.B61; 1971.A8;
1973.B85
"Le péché des origines,"
1953.B5
Peden, William, 1959.B17
Peeples, Edwin, 1942.B11
Peery, James R., 1942.B12
Penick, Edwin A., Jr., 1955.B43
People-to-People Program,
1956.B8; 1957.B27;
1966.B5
Peper, Jürgen, 1966.A7
"The Perceptive Few and the
Lost Generation,"
1955.B64
Percy, Walker, 1968.B60
Perlis, Alan D., 1972.B86
Perluck, Herbert A., 1960.B53;
1972.B87
Perry, Bradley T., 1951.B44.5;
1952.B50; 1953.B34
Perry, J. Douglas, Jr., 1973.B86
"Personae at Law and Equity:
The Unity of Faulkner's
Absalom, Absalom!"
1967.B90
Perspective und Erzählstruktur
in William Faulkners
Romanen von "The Sound
and the Fury" bis
"Intruder in the Dust,"
1972.A7
Peterson, Richard F., 1971.B78
Peyre, Henri, 1947.B6
Pfaff, William, 1951.B45
Pfeiffer, A. H., 1972.B88
Pfeiffer, Andrew, 1973.B87
Phillips, Gene D., 1973.B88
Phillips, William L., 1955.B44
"The Philosophy of Life Implicit
in Faulkner's The
Mansion," 1961.B29
"Phoenix Nest," 1927.B3;
1929.B1; 1931.B6-B8;
1935.B5
Photographs, 1931.B30; 1948.B10,
B25; 1952.B48; 1953.B14;

(Photographs)
1954.A1, B2; 1956.B42;
1958.B30; 1961.B17;
1962.B3, B116; 1963.A7;
1964.A4-A5; 1966.B57;
1969.B64; 1973.B30; See
also Portraits
The Picaresque Saint: Represen-
tative Figures in Contem-
porary Fiction, 1959.B43
Pick, Robert, 1949.B25
Picon, Gaëtan, 1940.B13
"The Picture of John and
Brother Will," 1970.B27
"Picturesque Faulknerisms,"
1968.B11
Pierle, Robert C., 1971.B79
"The Pilgrim and the Picaro: A
Study of The Bear and
The Reivers," 1969.B66
"Pilgrimage to Yoknapatawpha,"
1969.B64
Pineda, Rafael, 1961.B56;
1973.B89
Piper, Henry Dan, 1960.B11
Pitavy, François, 1970.A7, B62;
1972.B89-B90; 1973.A6
Pitts, Stella, 1972.B91
Pizer, Donald, and Ray B. Brown,
1969.B6, B50
"Place and Time: The Southern
Writer's Inheritance,"
1954.B5
Place in fiction, 1932.B28;
1954.B5; 1955.B63;
1957.B49, B68; 1970.B62
"Place in Fiction," 1955.B63
Place in Fiction, 1957.B68
"Planter and Poor White in
Absalom, Absalom!,
'Wash,' and The Mind of
the South," 1963.B18
"The Play Element in Faulkner's
'The Bear,'" 1964.B42
"Play, The Fractured Self, and
American Angry Comedy:
From Faulkner to Salin-
ger," 1968.B30
Plimpton, George, 1962.B96
Plomer, William, 1937.B16
"Plot as Discovery," 1960.B21

Ripley, Mississippi, 1948.B1;
    1955.B9; 1961.B14;
    1962.B57, B121; 1964.A4,
    A6; 1970.B50; 1972.B7,
    B67; 1973.B68
"The Rite of Initiation in Faulk-
    ner's The Bear," 1972.B7
Ritual, 1948.B1; 1951.A2;
    1960.B59; 1961.B20;
    1962.B57, B121; 1968.B59;
    1972.B7; See also Myth
    Criticism
"Ritual and Humor in the Writing
    of William Faulkner,"
    1948.B1, 1951.A2
"Ritual and Myth in William
    Faulkner's Pylon,"
    1962.B57
"Ritual and Theme in Faulkner's
    Dry September," 1962.B121
Rivallan, Jean, 1946.B12
"The River of Faulkner and
    Twain," 1963.B85
"The Roaring Twenties and William
    Faulkner's Sanctuary,"
    1968.B10
Robb, Mary Cooper, 1957.A3
Robbe-Grillet, Alain, 1966.B4
Robbins, Frances Lamont,
    1931.B26
Roberts, Bramlett, 1965.A5
Roberts, Ernest F., 1954.B63
Roberts, James L., 1960.B55-B56;
    1961.B58; 1963.B70
Roberts, Kenneth L., 1949.B27
Robinson, Cecil, 1968.B63
Robinson, Clayton, 1972.B98
Robinson, James Harvey, 1971.B28
Robinson, W. R., 1967.B7
"Robinson Jeffers and William
    Faulkner," 1933.B12
"Robinson Jeffers' 'Tamar' and
    The Sound and the Fury,"
    1969.B56
Robson, W. W., 1958.B49
Rodnon, Stewart, 1970.B67
Rodrigues, Eusebio L., 1965.B60
Rogers, Katharine M., 1966.B67
Rogers, Thomas M., 1957.B57
Rogers, W. G., 1951.B54

"The Role of Lion in Faulkner's
    'The Bear': Key to a
    Better Understanding,"
    1968.B76
The Role of Mind in Hugo, Faulk-
    ner, Beckett, and Grass,
    1969.B62
"The Role of Myth in Absalom,
    Absalom!," 1964.B44
Rolle, Andrew F., 1958.B50
Rollins, Ronald G., 1963.B71
Rolo, Charles J., 1954.B64
Le roman américain au XXe siècle,
    1950.B20
"Le roman d'après guerre aux
    états-unis," 1932.B16
"Un roman de William Faulkner,"
    1950.B14
"Un roman de William Faulkner.
    Tandis que j'agonise,"
    1934.B16; 1936.B11
Roman noir, 1952.B15
Roman nouveau, 1962.B49;
    1966.B2, B4; 1967.B32
"Les romanciers américains de-
    vant le public et la
    critique des États-Unis,"
    1946.B15
Romanova, Elena, 1955.B47
"Les romans horribles de M.
    William Faulkner,"
    1931.B3
"The Romantic Coordinates of
    American Literature,"
    1970.B6
"Romantic Openess and the Un-
    conscious," 1958.B3
Romanticism, 1952.B19; 1963.B79;
    1964.B70; 1970.B6;
    1972.B15
"The 'Romanticism' of The Sound
    and the Fury," 1963.B79
The Roots of Southern Writing:
    Essays on the Literature
    of the American South,
    1972.B49
"A Rose for Emily," 1934.B4;
    1937.B8; 1943.B2;
    1948.B19, B27; 1949.B38;
    1952.B56; 1954.B79;
    1958.B27, B54; 1959.B14;

(Source studies - "The Bear")
1965.B72; ("Metaphysics of
Bear-Hunting"), 1968.B49;
(Keats' "Ode on a Grecian
Urn"), 1969.B32,
1973.B108; (Leonid meteor
shower of 1833), 1971.B74;
1973.B80; ("Diary of a
Mississippi Planter"),
1972.B12
"An Error in Chemistry"
(Mann's "Mario and the
Magician"), 1967.B52
A Fable (Cobb's Paths of Glory)
1968.B65; (Taldoth Jesu),
1965.B12
General, (Balzac), 1934.B25;
(Frontier humor) 1954.B23;
(apprentice work and
reading), 1962.B1;
(Sherwood Anderson),
1964.B60; (poems about
horses), 1965.B24; (Boy
Scout work), 1966.B9;
(detective fiction),
1967.B31; (music)
1968.B12; (Dickens),
1969.B35; (Provincetown
drama), 1969.B47;
(reading), 1957.B10,
1970.B31-B32; 1971.B28;
(Freud), 1971.B28;
(French literature)
1973.B4; (Civil War lore),
1973.B84
Go Down, Moses (Thoreau)
1970.B6; (See also "The
Bear," above.)
The Hamlet (Sir Walter Scott),
1967.B40; (L.Q.C. Lamar),
1969.B71; (The Golden
Bough and Catullus),
1970.B87; (Faulkner's
"The Flowers That Died"),
1973.B75; (John Scopes),
1973.B104; (Keats' "Ode
on a Grecian Urn"),
1973.B108
Intruder in the Dust (history),
1965.B36
Knight's Gambit (Peabody Hotel,
Memphis), 1971.B89

Light in August (Second Shep-
herd's Play), 1971.B33;
(Keats' "Ode on a Grecian
Urn"), 1972.B60
The Mansion (Rabelais),
1969.B43, 1970.B63;
(Balzac's Gobseck),
1973.B4
Marionettes (Symbolist poets)
1973.B91
"Mr. Arcarius" (Jackson's The
Lost Weekend), 1968.B28
Mosquitoes (Hergesheimer's
novels), 1969.B30
Nobel Prize Acceptance Speech
(Dylan Thomas), 1963.B33;
(Conrad), 1967.B92;
(Hawthorne), 1971.B24;
(A. E. Housman) 1971.B64
Poetry (Housman and Swinburne),
1968.B16
The Reivers (Mississippi
bottom), 1968.B80;
(Mississippi landmarks),
1971.B13; (Second
Shepherd's Play),
1971.B33; (Melville's
Pierre), 1973.B110
"Red Leaves" (Darwin), 1973.B8;
(history), 1973.B60
Requiem for a Nun (history),
1965.B36; (WPA Mississippi
Guide), 1966.B49
"A Rose for Emily" (Poe's "To
Helen"), 1968.B66 and
1968.B69; (Ransom's
"Emily Hardcastle,
Spinster"), 1973.B7, B63
Sanctuary ("Popeye" Pumphrey),
1958.B16; (myth),
1963.B78; (The Golden
Bough), 1971.B58;
(Comic strips), 1973.B41
Sartoris (Dolly and Polly
Sartoris), 1967.B16;
(Bible), 1967.B78;
(Hamlet), 1969.B77;
(1920's airplane),
1971.B71; (Harris Dick-
son's House of Luck),
1972.B17

"Technology and the Sexual Revo-
lution," 1973.B102
The Teller in the Tale, 1967.B85
"The Telltale Hair: A Critical
Study of William Faulk-
ner's 'A Rose for Emily,'"
1972.B46
"Temps et destin chez Faulkner,"
1964.B31
"Temps et destinée chez Faulk-
ner," 1946.B9
"Le temps et la destinée chez
William Faulkner,"
1948.B21
"Temps et personne chez William
Faulkner," 1951.B39
Temps et Roman, 1946.B9
"Tendencies of the Modern Novel
III. America," 1933.B21
"Le ténébreuse malédiction
faulknérienne," 1962.B56
Tennessee, 1962.B68
"Tennie's Jim and Lucas Beau-
champ," 1969.B84
Terrey, John, 1965.B74
The Territory Ahead, 1958.B45
TeSelle, Sallie McFague,
1966.B71
"The Testimony of William Faulk-
ner," 1955.B43
"Textbook Uses of Hemingway and
Faulkner," 1972.B23
"The Text of Faulkner's Books:
An Introduction and Some
Notes," 1963.B62
Textual studies:
  Absalom, Absalom!, 1971.A4;
    1972.B93
  As I Lay Dying, 1958.B25
  A Fable, 1973.B54
  "Delta Autumn," 1971.B36
  Faulkner edition, 1972.B73
  General, 1961.B47; 1963.B62;
    1966.A5; 1969.B87
  Go Down, Moses, 1971.B36;
    1972.A4; 1973.B28
  Light in August, 1972.B37
  The Mansion, 1961.B47
  Sanctuary, 1956.B34; 1961.B49;
    1963.B65; 1972.A5
  The Sound and the Fury,
    1962.B85; 1967.B53

(Textual studies)
  "That Evening Sun," 1972.B70
  The Town, 1973.B47
"That Evening Sun," 1935.B26;
    1952.B20, B56; 1953.B18;
    1954.B57, B82; 1960.B28;
    1961.B43; 1963.B87;
    1964.B66; 1966.B8, B20,
    B33; 1967.B87; 1969.B37;
    1970.B37; 1971.B11;
    1972.B29, B70
"That Evening Sun Go Down,"
    1931.B10; 1935.B26;
    1954.B57; 1962.B43;
    See also "That Evening
    Sun"
"That Not Impossible He: Faulk-
ner's Third-Person
Narrator," 1961.B32
"Thematic Design in Light in
August," 1954.B13
"The Thematic Unity of Knight's
Gambit," 1969.B49
"The Theme and Structure of
Faulkner's The Hamlet,"
1957.B23; 1960.A1;
1973.A9
"Theme and Symbol in Faulkner's
Old Man," 1958.B48
"La theme de la vie et de la
mort dans As I Lay Dying,"
1959.B40
"Theme, Imagery, and Structure
in The Hamlet," 1969.B68
"The Theme of Endurance in As I
Lay Dying," 1970.B85
"The Theme of Suffering: William
Faulkner's The Sound and
the Fury," 1959.B50
Theme studies
  Alienation, 1966.B18
  American Dream, 1970.B1
  Collisions, 1960.B35
  Community, 1954.B13, B16;
    1962.B27, B95; 1963.A1,
    B10; 1969.B49; 1972.B112
  Dynasty, 1972.B33
  Empty Steeples, 1967.B21
  Endurance, 1946.B11, B16;
    1970.B85; 1972.B92
  Eternal Verities, 1962.B40;
    1970.A8

Wad, Soren, 1972.B109
Waddle, Mary Betsy, 1965.A5
Wade, John Donald, 1931.B37
Wagenknecht, Edward, 1952.B54
Waggoner, Hyatt H., 1957.B66;
    1958.B63; 1959.A5;
    1970.B82; 1972.B110
Wagner, Geoffrey, 1952.B55;
    1954.B77
Wagner, Linda Welshimer,
    1971.B97-B98; 1973.A9
Wait Without Idols, 1964.B72
Waiting for the End, 1964.B24
"The Wake in Faulkner's
    Sanctuary," 1960.B63
Wald, Jerry, 1959.B70
Waldman, Milton, 1933.B21
"A Walk with Faulkner," 1955.B6;
    1956.B9
Walker, Ronald G., 1973.B114
Walker, William E., 1964.B74
Walker, William E., and Robert
    L. Welker, 1964.B20, B23,
    B74
Wall, Carey, 1968.B75; 1970.B83
Walter, James, 1971.B99
Walters, Thomas N., 1966.B73
Walters, Paul S., 1967.B99
Walton, Gerald W., 1969.B84
"War: A Faulknerian Commentary,"
    1970.B69
"War and Peace and Mr. Faulkner,"
    1954.B27
War Birds: The Diary of an Un-
    known Aviator, See
    Springs, Elliott W.
"War in Tennessee," 1938.B1
"The War Stories of William
    Faulkner," 1961.B21
Wardle, Irving, 1964.B75
Warren, Joyce W., 1966.B74;
    1968.B76
Warren, Robert Penn, 1932.B28;
    1934.B28; 1941.B12;
    1943.B2; 1946.B16;
    1949.B34; 1951.A2, B62;
    1958.B64; 1959.B71;
    1960.A1; 1961.B71;
    1965.B76, B78; 1966.A8,
    B75
"War's Aftermath," 1926.B2

Warwick, Ray, 1935.B34
"Was," See Go Down, Moses
"'Was': Faulkner's Classic
    Comedy of the Frontier,"
    1972.B28
"Wash," 1963.B18, B48; 1967.B43;
    1968.B67, B72
Wasiolek, Edward, 1959.B72-B73
Wasser, Henry, 1954.B78
Wasson, Ben, 1965.B63
"Water, Water Everywhere: Old
    Man and A Farewell to
    Arms," 1959.B49
Watkins, Floyd C., 1954.B79;
    1959.B74-B75; 1960.B71-
    B72; 1961.A2; 1967.B100;
    1968.B77; 1971.B100-B105
Watkins, Floyd C., and William
    B. Dillingham, 1960.B73
Watkins, Floyd C., and Thomas
    Daniel Young, 1960.B74
Watson, James Gray, 1970.A8;
    1973.B115
Watt, David, 1957.B67
Waugh, Evelyn, A Handful of Dust,
    1968.B40
Way, Brian, 1961.B72
"The Ways That Faulkner Walked:
    A Pilgrimage,"
    1964.B61; 1965.B58
Weatherby, H. L., 1967.B101
Weatherby, W. J., 1962.B122
Webb, Clifton Bondurant, 1965.A5
Webb, James W., 1965.A5, B79;
    1966.B76
Webb, James W., and A. Wigfall
    Green, 1965.A5
Weber, Robert, 1961.B73;
    1965.B80
Weber, Robert Wilhelm, 1969.A7
"Weekend, Lost and Revisited,"
    1968.B28
Weeks, Edward, 1933.B22;
    1935.B35
Weigel, John A., 1959.B76
Weisgerber, Jean, 1965.B81;
    1968.B78-B79
Weiss, Daniel, 1963.B88
Weiss, Miriam, 1968.B80